The White Pine Industry in Minnesota

THE FESLER–LAMPERT MINNESOTA HERITAGE BOOK SERIES

This series reprints significant books that enhance our understanding and appreciation of Minnesota and the Upper Midwest. It is supported by the generous assistance of the John K. and Elsie Lampert Fesler Fund and the interest and contribution of Elizabeth P. Fesler and the late David R. Fesler.

Other Fesler–Lampert Minnesota Heritage Books of Interest

Lob Trees in the Wilderness by Clifford Ahlgren and Isabel Ahlgren

The Long-Shadowed Forest by Helen Hoover

Canoe Country and Snowshoe Country by Florence Page Jaques

Minnesota Logging Railroads by Frank A. King

North Star Country by Meridel Le Sueur

Lake Superior by Grace Lee Nute

Listening Point by Sigurd F. Olson

Reflections from the North Country by Sigurd F. Olson

The Singing Wilderness by Sigurd F. Olson

A-Rafting on the Mississip' by Charles Edward Russell

THE WHITE PINE INDUSTRY IN MINNESOTA

A HISTORY

Agnes M. Larson

FOREWORD BY BRADLEY J. GILLS

University of Minnesota Press

Minneapolis

London

Publisher's Note

Our knowledge and appreciation of the culture and history of Minnesota have advanced considerably since this book was first published, and the attitudes and opinions expressed in it may strike the contemporary reader as inappropriate. This classic has been reprinted in its original form as a contribution to the state's heritage.

Copyright 1949, 2007 by the Regents of the University of Minnesota

ALL RIGHTS RESERVED. No part of this publication may be reproduced, stored in a retrieval system, or transmitted, in any form or by any means, electronic, mechanical, photocopying, recording, or otherwise, without the prior written permission of the publisher.

Published by the University of Minnesota Press
111 Third Avenue South, Suite 290
Minneapolis, MN 55401-2520
http://www.upress.umn.edu

LIBRARY OF CONGRESS CATALOGING-IN-PUBLICATION DATA
Larson, Agnes M. (Agnes Mathilda), 1892–1967.
[History of the white pine industry in Minnesota.]
The white pine industry in Minnesota : a history / Agnes M. Larson ; foreword by Bradley J. Gills.
p. cm. — (The Fesler-Lampert Minnesota heritage book series)
Includes index.
Originally published under title:
History of the white pine industry in Minnesota. c1949.
ISBN-13: 978-0-8166-5149-8 (pb : alk. paper)
ISBN-10: 0-8166-5149-3 (pb : alk. paper)
1. White pine industry—Minnesota—History. 2. Lumbering—Minnesota—History. 3. Lumber trade—Minnesota—History. I. Title.
SD397.P65L3 2007
338.4'767409776—dc22

2007017411

Printed in the United States of America on acid-free paper

The University of Minnesota is an equal-opportunity educator and employer.

12 11 10 09 08 07   10 9 8 7 6 5 4 3 2 1

TO MY MOTHER AND FATHER
Born on the frontier, they as children saw the Indian and the deer roaming past their doors. From childhood to old age they shared in the building of a great state.

Contents

List of Illustrations

* Unless otherwise indicated these illustrations are reproduced courtesy of the Minnesota
Historical Society.

In a later period, cables pulled by steam brought logs to the skidway.

The caterpillar tractor speeded the movement of logs in the woods.

The logging railroad was the most signficant factor in the evolution of the logging industry after 1890.

This load, hauled a distance of one mile by four horses on February 13, 1892, was 21 feet high, 20 feet wide, and contained 31,480 feet of logs. It was the ice road that made such a load possible (courtesy of Mrs. Maud Burnett, Anoka, Minnesota).

Bark-marked logs, ready by the rollway for the spring drive

At the landing every log was given a bark mark and a stamp mark to denote its ownership. This page of stamp marks is recorded in the office of the Surveyor General of Logs, Minnesota.

Log jam on the St. Croix

On the drive

A jam breaker hunts the key log (courtesy of C. L. Brundage, Virginia, Minnesota).

In the rear of the drive always followed the wanigan, serving as a cook-shanty and, if large enough, as a bunkhouse.

A meal out-of-doors held no appeal for the wet and shivering river-driver.

A log raft moving down the Mississippi

Rafted logs at their downriver destination

The capital invested in the Northwestern Mills of Hersey, Bean & Brown, Stillwater, came largely from the white pine in Maine.

The H. C. Akeley Mill startled Minneapolis with a 50,500,000 foot cut in 1890.

Moving out from the mill, a lumber raft carried laths and shingles on top of the lumber. The runners and grub pins are visible here.

The H. O. Larson farm home in Bloomfield Township, Fillmore County, Minnesota, was built of white pine. The denuding of the forest had as a direct result the more rapid settlement of the region and the better housing of its people.

Foreword

BRADLEY J. GILLS

FOR as long as hearty souls have ventured into the woods to clear the way for civilization, Americans have enjoyed reading about life in the lumber camps and the larger-than-life lumberjacks who called them home. Scholars have likewise been long interested in the men who made their fortunes in lumber, as well as in the larger economic importance of the industry. Yet, from colonial harvests in New England to the development of modern lumbering in the Pacific Northwest, the history of lumbering is far more than a simple tale of technological advancement, economic fluctuations, or hardscrabble characters enduring endless hardships. The reality of lumbering in America is remarkably complex, and, perhaps more than any other economic enterprise of the Industrial Age, it intersected social, cultural, economic, and political landscapes wherever it took root. This was particularly the case in the Upper Midwest, where the vast pineries of Michigan, Wisconsin, and Minnesota collectively made the region the "king" of American lumber production during the last half of the nineteenth century. Agnes Larson understood this, and it is her appreciation for this socioeconomic complexity that makes this volume such a valuable study.

Considering that the lumber industry of the late-nineteenth and early-twentieth centuries was one of the greatest social and economic influences on the development of the Great Lakes states, there is a surprising dearth of scholarship on the subject. Larson's history of the industry in Minnesota remains unparalleled. She explores the national and global contexts of the economics involved, while providing meticulous detail about the wide array of individuals who made up the multiethnic classes of laborers. Anyone who has researched the history of lumbering in the Upper Midwest is faced with one considerable hurdle: sorting out the often-labyrinthine network of businessmen and corporate interests that controlled the industry. *The White Pine Industry in Minnesota: A History* tackles this challenge head-on, and succeeds in spades. Scholars looking to build on her work (which she graciously acknowledged should occur—but sadly it has not) will find a wealth of information here. But general readers should find this aspect of her writing rewarding as well. The sum total of Larson's exhaustive portrait is in many respects an anthology of local histories woven together into a grand tapestry of Minnesota's past.

Any book on the timber industry worth its salt must also examine everyday life in the camps that pervaded the North Woods. This includes describing the roles of everyone from the mill foreman to the camp cooks—all are represented here. Whether you are interested in camp song lyrics, what was on the breakfast table (flapjacks, of course!), or the definition of a Swedish snowstorm, you will find the answers in this book. The chapters on life in the camps are rich in detail and remind us that the great range of diversity among men who went to work in the woods transformed the Midwest into a landscape as cosmopolitan as any urban center in America. Across the Upper Midwest, Finns, Swedes, Italians, French-Canadians, and Germans joined Yankee lumberjacks from New England to create a patchwork of ethnic enclaves across the region. The culture of lumbering was truly born from a melting pot of ethnicities, and we are treated here to numerous examples of how these groups coalesced yet also maintained strong ties to their respective cultural traditions.

The timber industry of nineteenth-century America was highly susceptible to the vagaries of local social, economic, and political influences. Larson's attention to the different markets and developments in Minneapolis, Duluth, and the St. Croix and Chippewa River Valleys illustrates how these local conditions influenced the progress and profitability of various lumber enterprises as well as Minnesota's growth from a territory to America's thirty-second state. Her chapter on the Winona and St. Anthony mills shows that these mills were vital cogs in the local economy, and as the population of Minnesota rapidly grew in the late 1850s and 1860s, employment in the mills and the lumber camps that fed them was a crucial draw for emigrants, while their products helped build the towns that sprouted across southern Minnesota. Larson offers a compelling portrait of the companies and men behind them that competed in both locales.

We are also treated to an excellent overview of how the spread of railroads in the Midwest was inextricably linked to the fortunes of lumber companies. As competition increased among the timber barons, so too did the push to build railroads that could reach more distant markets. You simply cannot tell the history of lumbering in the Great Lakes without also detailing the history of railroads in the region. Larson's appreciation for this important distinction rounds out her discussions of Winona, St. Anthony, and dozens of other settlements across the state.

The importance of railroads is especially evident in her nuanced examination of Minneapolis's place in the regional and national economy—a position that was dependent on the expansion of railroads that could transport its products to distant markets.

Before such growth could even begin, however, Minnesotans first had to acquire title to the lands within the state's boundaries. Treaties of cession with the Sioux and Ojibwe were critical to opening up Minnesota's pinelands to industry. These treaties also created reservations like those at White Earth and Red Lake—reserves that removed more than four million acres and hundreds of millions of board feet of timber from market. The establishment of these reservations occurred before the value of the pine they contained was fully appreciated. Indian lands and the timber on them became prime targets for less-than-scrupulous businessmen, speculators, and government officials in the late-nineteenth century. The schemes that were devised to profit from Indian timber in the region have been well documented in recent years, but Larson's discussion of Indian pinelands is remarkable in its frankness. Larson was perhaps the first scholar to fairly judge the now infamous swindles that took place on Indian lands. Her conclusion that "it was quite clear that the . . . Indians had been robbed" (314) distinguishes her as a uniquely judicious scholar in this respect. Furthermore, by detailing the federal and state legislation that governed the sale and scale of lumbering on public, private, and Indian lands in Minnesota, she sheds light on the varying degrees of fraud that occurred elsewhere as well.

Nonetheless, readers may be struck by the language Larson employs in her assessment of Indians and their place in Minnesota's history. Anachronisms such as "Red Men" appear periodically, but even though these terms may seem dated or even racist, we must not judge too harshly. Larson wrote at a time when such ethnocentricities were commonplace. Just as "Negro" was the accepted term for African Americans in 1950, so too was Red Men a typical appellation for American Indians. Are they racist terms? From today's perspective the answer is, of course, yes. In the context of mid-twentieth-century America, however, these references are no more derogatory than Larson's calling Scandinavian immigrants "Vikings" or commenting on the hairy chests of French-Canadian log drivers. These examples are standard flourishes of the more folksy style of writing that often characterizes stories of loggers and their various ethnic backgrounds and fabled strengths. These reputations were certainly based in reality, as certain groups were drawn to specific roles within lumber operations. American Indians were often praised for their work as guides and drivers in the North Woods, where they preferred to work and where they were ethnocentrically assumed to have an inherent advantage. In the end, Larson's use of this language adds an important layer to this volume: we can read it today as a part of the history it is telling.

The evaluation of any work of history for republication requires comparisons to its contemporary and modern counterparts. In the former category, surprisingly few books compare to Larson's. Those covering lumbering in Wisconsin and Michigan are Robert Fries's *Empire in Pine: The Story of Lumbering in Wisconsin, 1830–1900* (1951) and Rolland Maybee's "Michigan's White Pine Era, 1840–1900," an article that appeared in volume 34 of *Michigan History* in 1959. Fries's work compares well to Larson's, and his book remains in print—testimony to the relevance of such work today. Maybee's article can be found only in academic libraries that house *Michigan History* dating back to the 1950s. Its brevity alone renders it inferior to Larson, but it also resorts too much to the casual style that tends to characterize books published on nineteenth-century lumbering. Maybee's work joins books like Stewart Holbrook's *Holy Old Mackinaw* (1938; now out of print) in the tendency to pursue folklore and emphasize the fantastic types of tales that gave birth to legendary characters like Paul Bunyan.

Far more prevalent in Larson's day were popular reminiscences published by descendants of pioneer loggers and their families. These are the volumes that often dominate library shelves, and, while they are always fascinating, the writing is often colloquial and hardly up to the standards of academic presses. Instead, they are better classified as historical documents that focus on the experiences of individuals, providing an almost mythical portrait of logging's heyday. Some examples in this vein include Harry Palm's *Lumberjack Days in the St. Croix Valley* (1969) and Joseph A. DeLaittre's *A Story of Early Lumbering in Minnesota* (1959), a family history centered on the author's father's experiences as a lumberman. As a work of scholarship, Larson's book does not belong in this class, though she used many firsthand accounts in shaping her explorations of life in the camps (and many more can be found in her notes).

In terms of how her work measures up to today's standards of scholarship, Larson also passes with flying colors. No book matches Michael Williams's magisterial *Americans and Their Forests* (1989), but it is noteworthy that *The White Pine Industry in Minnesota* is among the sources Williams mentions in his overview of the industry in the Great Lakes states. As for studies particular to the Great Lakes region, there simply are none that parallel the breadth of Larson's treatment. Jeremy Kilar's *Michigan's Lumbertowns: Lumbermen and Laborers in Saginaw, Bay City, and Muskegon, 1870–1905* is solid, but as its title suggests, it is much more specific in both temporal and geographic coverage. *Deep Woods Frontier: A History of Logging in Northern Michigan* (1989) by Theodore Karamanski casts a wider net in its focus on lumbering across Michigan's Upper Peninsula and its border with Wisconsin, but it cannot be considered an equal to Larson. A collection edited by Susan Flader, *The Great Lakes Forest: An Environmental and Social History* (1983), attempts to cover the entire region, but the nature of the essays speaks only to specific locations, themes, and time frames, and too often resorts to postmodern jargon. Finally, John Vogel's *Great Lakes Lumber on the Great Plains: The Laird, Norton Lumber Company in South Dakota* (1992) offers an interesting look at economics of railroads and more distant markets for Great Lakes lumber products, but it is a perfect example of how focused many scholarly studies have become. Note as well that all of the works referenced here are at least ten years old. I believe this also testifies to the importance and timeliness of this paperback edition of Larson's book. Both scholars and laymen interested in lumber industry's past are continually frustrated by the lack of gratifying books in print. This new edition of *The White Pine Industry in Minnesota* is a welcome contribution to the available offerings.

Ultimately, Agnes Larson's book is a landmark study that explores its complex subject with uncommon diligence and attention to detail. The writing is clear and accessible, free of academic jargon that too often alienates general readers. What distinguishes Larson's work is its expansive appeal: it will prove valuable to students and academics interested in labor, immigration, social organization, and the history of the lumber industry, and it will be an eminently rewarding read for anyone interested in Minnesota's history.

Preface

THIS study was undertaken with the utilitarian purpose of providing a doctoral thesis; but early in my research I saw that here was an opportunity to break new ground in the study of the history of a region. As I worked, I came to realize more fully the breadth and the significance of such a study.

Fur, lumber, wheat and flour, and the "contented" cow have in successive stages been basic to the economy of Minnesota. All, drawn from the resources of nature, have contributed to the development and support of the state. The fur industry was a fleeting one, and when it was gone it left few traces in the trackless forests or the early settlements. The lumber industry was different. It converted the pine reaches of Minnesota to the uses of man, providing homes and barns, churches and schools, commercial buildings, and the ties on which rested the rails that bound the state together and gave it easy access to neighboring states and distant regions. Moreover, the lumber industry gave a livelihood to many, and to others it brought the business experience and riches which went into the building of other industries important in the state.

The white pine and the voracious appetite for lumber of a fast growing country provided the opportunity for the building of the lumber industry; but the opportunity became fact through the driving cooperation of the promoters and managers of little and big business units and the sturdy lumberjacks and other workers in lumber who, with the help of tools and machines and rivers and lakes, felled the trees, manufactured the lumber, and sent it where it was needed, to home markets or distant plains and cities. It is the story of this work that I have tried to tell in this book.

For all this a price was paid. One cannot with impunity rob Mother Nature of her treasures, for truly the sins of the fathers are avenged unto the third or fourth generation. The price we must pay for the rapid use of our forests is a vast area of wasteland for generations, or else a wise and vigorous policy of reforestation.

Nature's resources are no respecters of man-made boundaries. Though this study pertains chiefly to the white pine industry of Minnesota, there are occasional references to the industry in Wisconsin — because from that state some firms extended their business into Minnesota and in it several Minnesota lumber mill operators sought the white pine of the Chippewa and its tributaries.

It is my hope that the study I have begun will be followed by further research by others. The history of the different phases of the lumber industry could be expanded into several volumes. Until the history of the companies that were long active in the industry has been written, we shall not know the full story. Social historians, morevoer, have here an opportunity to study the influence of this industry on the social development of Minnesota and the country as a whole.

Now remains the pleasant task of acknowledging the assistance of the many institutions and persons who have helped make this book possible. I cannot make as complete an acknowledgment as I should like. The list would be too long.

I must acknowledge my appreciation to the American Association of University Women, which through granting me the Dorothy Bridgman Atkinson scholarship made my first year of research possible. The Social Science Research Council gave me a grant-in-aid; the University of Minnesota assisted me financially by awarding me a fellowship in regional writing.

My work in the Minnesota Historical Society Library was made easy and pleasant because of the help and the interest of the staff. Particularly do I wish to express appreciation to Gertrude Krausnick, then librarian of the institution, to Lois Fawcett, reference librarian, and to Arthur Larsen, at that time in charge of the newspaper department. In the Land Office of the Department of the Interior in Washington, D.C., in the State Historical Library in Madison, Wisconsin, in the Baker Library and the Widener Library at Harvard University, and at the Library of the University of Minnesota, I was given considerate and efficient service.

Laird Bell of Chicago arranged for me to use the business records and the private papers of the Laird, Norton Lumber Company of Winona, one of the oldest lumber firms in Minnesota. Original research on most aspects of an industry can be done only with the help of such records and is an essential in such a study as this. To Mr. Bell and to the staff of the company in Winona I am deeply obligated, as I am also to Karl De Laittre of Minneapolis, who directed me to the records of the firm of which his father had been a member, an old lumber company in Minnesota.

I have drawn heavily on the memory of men sometime active in the industry. My interviews took me into various walks of life, and I always met courtesy and consideration. The late Captain Fred Bill and ex-Governor Samuel Van Sant gave me fine assistance in the study of the rafting of logs and lumber on the Misssissippi River. Their experience reached back to pioneer days in Minnesota, and their interest and information gave me an understanding of an important phase of the industry of which there is little record. Long conversations with many who had worked in the woods, in the mills, and on the rivers gave me an insight into the men who worked with muscle and daring and into the way they lived and labored. Hearing Mike McAlpine sing lumberjack ballads was one of the rare experiences I had. Most of these men are now gone.

Professor Frederick Merk of Harvard University guided this study during the early difficult period when the way seemed obscure and the goal remote. Professor N. S. B. Gras of Harvard University gave generously of his unusual critical acumen. Dean Theodore C. Blegen of the University of Minnesota encouraged me with his interest in the study and in various ways contributed from his store of information about Minnesota history.

I shall always appreciate the generous help of the late Minna Voelker of Rochester, Minnesota, who typed much of the early copy. Florence Glynn typed the final copy, and Mrs. Elsie Hight Bishop, also of Harvard University, edited the manuscript with her usual care. To the staff of the University of Minnesota Press, who have guided the manuscript into print, I express my appreciation.

To my sister, Henrietta M. Larson, I owe more than I can say. Without her steady encouragement this study would probably never have been completed. Another sister, Lela Larson Ronken, has been most diligent and patient in the reading of proof. My niece, Emilie Larson, assisted me with research in Washington. To my whole family I owe much.

To all these and many more not named, I give my warm thanks for their help and their encouragement. Truly, a book is not the work of one person alone.

AGNES M. LARSON

The White Pine Industry in Minnesota

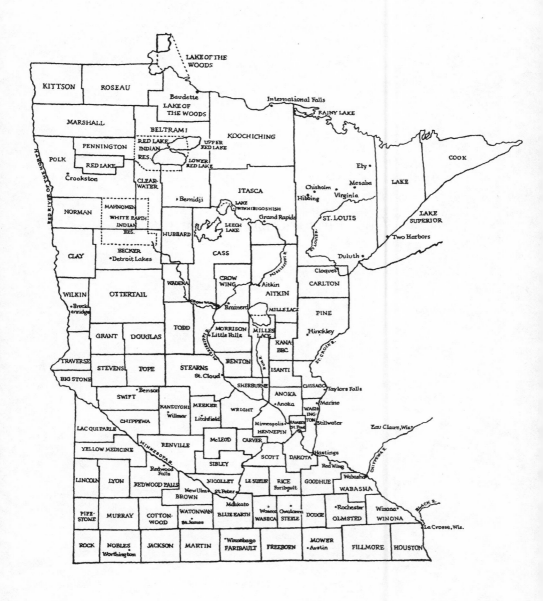

CHAPTER I

Minnesota's Forest Treasure

ONE summer day in 1634, fourteen years after the coming of the *May-flower,* a dramatic figure clad in damask stepped from a canoe, manned by red men, onto the white sands of the shores of that water which we today call Green Bay, on the western reaches of Lake Michigan. He was Jean Nicolet from Cherbourg in France, who had been sent by his king to find another route to Cathay.[1] His king wanted gold; he wanted silver; he wanted precious jewels; he wanted spices. Cathay, it was supposed, had all these.

Jean Nicolet never found the northwest route to Cathay, but he marched in the vanguard of that quick, imaginative, inquisitive race, the French, who were to be first in the possession of the Mississippi Valley. Nicolet had sought Cathay; he found the valley which as a dwelling place for civilized man ranks first upon our globe, a region which in extent is the second valley of the world.[2]

The valley Nicolet looked out upon was rich — but not in actual gold or in actual silver. Neither silks nor spices were there. But there was wealth. Generations of men were to come and go in this great valley, and in passing they were to snatch from it different treasures in turn.

The first great treasure was fur. About the middle of the seventeenth century Radisson and Groseilliers took the first fur from the Upper Mississippi to Montreal, already a great fur market, and thus placed the western region in commercial relationship with the civilized world.[3] Thereupon developed a great trade. The voyageur, swinging his light canoe from one lake to another in the "land of lakes," collected the fur, which was carried by boats from the swift rushing streams of the upper reaches of the Mississippi to the Great Lakes and, finally, to

---

[1] Louise Phelps Kellogg, editor, *Early Narratives of the Northwest, 1634–1699* (New York, 1917), pp. 4, 12, 16.

[2] James K. Hosmer, *A Short History of the Mississippi Valley* (Cambridge, 1901), p. 4. The area drained by the Mississippi and its tributaries is 1,020,050 square miles, or 41 per cent of the mainland of the United States exclusive of Alaska. The Amazon drains a larger valley, 2,500,000 square miles.

[3] Louise Phelps Kellogg, *The French Régime in Wisconsin and the Northwest* (Madison, 1925), pp. 104, 111; Henry Cohn Campbell, "Radisson and Groseilliers," *Partman Club Publications,* vol. ii (Milwaukee, 1896), pp. 17–35.

Montreal.[4] The first fur traders were French, but soon the British came to play an important part. After the War of 1812 the British largely gave way to American fur traders, and the Upper Mississippi became the special preserve of the American Fur Company and its associates under John Jacob Astor.[5] They developed a trade of vast proportions. The chief market for these traders came to be St. Louis, the great trading place on the Middle Mississippi.

But eventually the fur trade gave way to the lumber industry. About 1837 the fur business began to decline noticeably, and by 1850 fur no longer held first place. The Lake region was then yielding the second great resource to be taken from its forests. Lumber had become the dominant industry both in Minnesota and in other parts of the Upper Valley.[6] Lumber had replaced the fur trade in towns, on merchants' books, and in the forest; and in that day lumber was white pine on the Upper Mississippi. A new, swaggering, fearless man of destiny in hobnailed boots appeared, and he was to further a second great industry in Minnesota.

Someday lumber, too, was to find a mighty rival in a third great treasure: wheat. The time was to come in Minnesota when in pre-harvest weeks the fields of grain were to look like a vast sea as the soft breeze made the golden wheat sway in regular waves. The ploughboy, turning the rich, tillable soil and laying it bare to the heavens in preparation for the sowing, was to become as important in the building of Minnesota as the lumberjack had been when he spent lonely months in the pine forest hewing down trees in order to furnish homes on the prairie.

But in the meantime, lumber was to make great changes in that region. It was going to people the region thickly. Large cities were to spring up where lumber was made. Lumber was to produce capital, so basic in the building of a new country. Lumber was to go in advance of wheat, to prepare the way as it were. Eventually these two treasures would fall into step to march forward together, the one indispensable to the other. It is this successor of fur and precursor of wheat with which we are concerned. And the chief factor in the production of lumber in this region was the white pine, the *Pinus Strobus*.

[4] At one time furs were carried down the Mississippi to Prairie du Chien, whence they were carried northward and eastward on the perilous Wisconsin and then on to the Fox. In the high-water season portages were unnecessary and furs were transported by a complete water route from Minnesota to Montreal.

[5] For further details on the fur trade see Zebulon Montgomery Pike, *Expeditions to Head-waters of the Mississippi River*, vol. i (New York, 1895), p. ix; Kenneth Wiggins Porter, *John Jacob Astor, Business Man*, vol. ii (Cambridge, 1931), p. 694; *United States Statutes at Large*, vol. iii (1813–23), 14th Cong., 1st Sess., chap. clxv.

[6] Edward Van Dyke Robinson, *Early Economic Conditions and the Development of Agriculture in Minnesota* (Minneapolis, 1915), p. 39; Porter, *op. cit.*, p. 693.

The white pine of the Upper Mississippi was a magnificent tree. Sometimes it stood in the forest 200 feet high with a diameter of 5 feet; 160 feet was a more usual height, while many trees reached only 120 feet with a diameter of 30 inches.[7]

The white pine grew in a variety of soils, but wherever it grew moisture was necessary. It grew luxuriously in heavy clay and loam soils, where it intermingled with the hardwoods. The white pine grew best in a soil that had a mixture of sand. Far north on the steep rocky slopes of Lake Superior it grew with the spruce and the tamarack.[8] The white pine grew in river bottoms where there was good drainage, or where the rainfall was heavy, averaging between 26 and 35 inches. It stopped abruptly within about forty miles of the prairie country where the rainfall was less.[9]

No other soft wood had so many desirable qualities.[10] It was strong, slow to decay, light in weight, odorless, and easy to cut, thus yielding readily to pattern work. It seasoned well and it had strong resistance to weather and time.[11]

No wood has served more usefully in America than has the white pine.[12] Its abundance, cheapness, and varied usefulness made it an important factor in the westward movement. It furnished the early settler with shelter. The logs for the cabin, the shakes for the roof, and the puncheons for the floor all came from the white pine. It also provided the incoming settler with implements, furniture, fences — all of them necessities in a new country.

Before 1855–90 the term *lumbering* as used in Michigan, Wisconsin, and Minnesota applied almost exclusively to work in white pine.[13] Even the red pine, incorrectly called the Norway, was little esteemed until the white pine was growing scarce. Hemlock, spruce, tamarack, birch, elm, ash, and basswood were unsought timber until white pine was nearing its end.

The white pine has played an important part in the settlement of the northern part of the United States. The Pilgrim Fathers used it for shelter. In New England, New York, northern Pennsylvania, Michigan, Wisconsin, and Minnesota it not only provided shelter but also served for decades

[7] V. M. Spalding (revised by B. E. Fernow), *The White Pine*, U.S. Department of Agriculture, Division of Forestry, Bulletin No. 22 (1899), p. 26.

[8] Christopher C. Andrews, *Report of the Forestry Commissioner of Minnesota*, 1906, pp. 27–28.

[9] Christopher C. Andrews, *Report of the Chief Fire Warden of Minnesota*, 1895, p. 175.

[10] United States Bureau of Corporations, *The Lumber Industry*, vol. iv (Washington, 1914), p. 491.

[11] Nelson C. Brown, *American Lumber Industry* (New York, 1923), p. 170.

[12] George W. Hotchkiss, *History of the Lumber and Forest Industry of the Northwest* (Chicago, 1898), p. 752.

[13] *Ibid.*, p. 727.

as a most important commercial product. In Minnesota, where at last the prairie stopped the pine — longitude 95° 30′ marked the western limit of white pine, the *Pinus Strobus*, in the United States — the white pine made its last great contribution to advancing settlement.[14]

The forests in Minnesota were to play a major role in the development of the state and the surrounding region. It is hard to realize that a century ago a magnificent forest covered 38,000,000 acres, 70 per cent, of the total land area of Minnesota. The remainder of the state was prairie land where trees grew occasionally — usually the cottonwood or the willow. The forests of Minnesota covered more than 300 of the 375 miles east and west and extended over a distance of 364 of the 400 miles north and south.[15]

This great forest was of two general types: the hardwood forests, known generally in Minnesota as the "Big Woods," and the "pineries," sometimes called the "North Woods." The hardwood forests lay in rich soil in the region to the west of the Mississippi, chiefly between the Crow Wing and Minnesota rivers, immediately south of the Minnesota River, and extending to the southeastern and eastern boundaries of the state and south and west to the prairies.[16] The Big Woods comprised 5000 square miles, 4000 of which lay north of the Minnesota River. The southern base of this body of timber lay in Rice, Blue Earth, Scott, and Le Sueur counties; the western line crossed the counties of McLeod and Meeker diagonally; all of it lay on the western side of the Mississippi.

The Big Woods consisted of hardwoods, with no coniferous trees except those within the transition zone.[17] This hardwood forest, largely of oak, formed the northwestern extremity of the forests characteristic of the states to the southeast.[18] There were large stands of maple, basswood, elm, ash, butternut, black walnut, and other broad-leafed species mixed with the prevailing oak. In the development of Minnesota these hard forests counted for little. It was the rich soil in which they grew that was attractive to the settler. So the strong oaks, the stately butternuts, and the

[14] George R. Shaw, *The Genus Pinus* (Cambridge, 1914), p. 36; J. E. Defebaugh, *History of the Lumber Industry*, vol. i (Chicago, 1906), p. 311. The white pine of Idaho, sometimes called Western White Pine, whose botanical name is *Pinus monticola,* is spoken of as the western representative of the *Pinus Strobus*. It differs, however, from the *Pinus Strobus* in several ways. See L. H. Bailey, *The Cultivated Conifers in North America* (New York, 1933), pp. 76–77; J. E. Rogers, *The Tree Book,* vol. i (New York, 1923), pp. 23–27.

[15] William T. Cox, *Report of the State Forester of Minnesota,* 1911, p. 9; Defebaugh, *op. cit.,* p. 286.

[16] Warren Upham, *The Geology of Central and Western Minnesota* (St. Paul, 1880), pp. 26–27.

[17] Oscar B. Jesness and Reynolds I. Nowell, *A Program for Land Use in Northern Minnesota* (Minneapolis, 1935), p. 17.

[18] *Land Utilization in Minnesota* (Minneapolis, 1934), p. 112. This study, made by a committee appointed by Governor Olson in 1932, has valuable information on forest lands in that state.

queenly maples were felled merely to be cast into the fire so that wheat could grow where once they had stood.

Not so with the forest which lay on the east side of the river. There was coniferous forest reaching from the east banks of the Mississippi to the boundary line of Canada. The tree that gave character and distinction to this whole region, which was larger than all of the state of Maine, was the white pine. This tree for at least five decades dominated the lumber industry in Minnesota. The section which lay nearest the Mississippi and in the region of the St. Croix and its tributaries was most prominently the home of the white pine and its relative the red (Norway) pine and a more remote relative, the jack pine. The soil in this region was less rich than on the west side of the Mississippi where the hardwoods grew, but the white pine is the most discriminating of the conifers in selection of soil, and this was by no means Minnesota's poorest soil. Several species of hardwood were found in the region but the white pine was master there. That region was generally thought of as the real "pineries."

Farther to the north lay a vast forest of many varieties of conifers, making really a third division in the forests of Minnesota, which reached to the Canadian border and to the west of Red Lake. The white pine, red pine, and jack pine were all to be found in this region, but white spruce in the highlands, black spruce in the swamps, cedar, tamarack, balsam, and other varieties freely intermingled with the pine. This section had a greater variety of conifers, but its forest was not so valuable on the whole as the pineries of the St. Croix and the region nearest the Mississippi.

The white pine was found in every county in Minnesota east of the Mississippi from Minneapolis to Canada. It reached its general southern limit in the north edge of Isanti and Chisago counties. Itasca, St. Louis, Mille Lacs, Kanabec, Pine, Aitkin, Beltrami, Cass, and Carlton counties had especially fine stands, but Carlton County was its favored abode. That county was originally more heavily timbered with white pine than any other county in the state. There is authentic evidence of one acre of white pine in Carlton County which yielded, by actual measurement, 94,000 feet of lumber.[19] That was a record. A yield of 25,000 feet on an acre was considered satisfactory,[20] and in parts of Minnesota, 10,000 feet to the acre was not at all uncommon. Carlton County, therefore, was accorded a high place by lumbermen, and it was not strange that Cloquet, the lumber center of that county, should be called "The Home of White Pine."

Cass County is said to have been the home of the largest white pine

[19] Andrews, *Report of Fire Warden*, 1895, pp. 118–19; Samuel B. Green, *Forestry in Minnesota* (St. Paul, 1902), p. 124.

[20] Hotchkiss, *op. cit.*, p. 727.

tree that was made into lumber in Minnesota. To be sure, one treads on dangerous ground in making such claims — several places have claimed to have had the largest tree and the largest stand. Even cruisers and scalers, the wise men in the timber world, will disagree heatedly on such issues. There is authentic evidence to support the reputation of the Cass Lake tree, but whether or not it was the largest tree, it gives an idea of the age of some of this white pine forest and of the size of a large white pine tree.

The famous white pine at Cass Lake was 425 years old. When it was cut it yielded 6300 board feet of lumber.[21] Such a yield was enormous, for even on the Jump River, a branch of the Chippewa in Wisconsin which was famous for its huge white pine, a tree made a record when it scaled 7000 feet of lumber.[22] The spot where this great Minnesota pine stood was in section 35, township 145, range 30 west, in Cass County.[23]

Good as it was, Minnesota's white pine did not rank with that of Michigan, though the original forest area of Minnesota was 10 per cent larger than that of Michigan and almost 30 per cent larger than that of Wisconsin.[24] Michigan's white pine was the best in the Lake states, owing no doubt to the sandy loam soil. The white pine in Michigan had a taproot that dug itself into the earth and met no obstruction in seeking its sustenance, whereas in northern Minnesota the root found opposition in its search for food — the rocky soil was difficult to penetrate — and the trees therefore grew less vigorously.[25] Though Minnesota boasted splendid white pine in parts where the soil was not rocky, Michigan undoubtedly had the heavier yield per acre.[26]

Minnesota had valuable resources, but resources in themselves can be of little value. Resources must be in demand; there must be a market. Markets must be made accessible, and they can become so only by means of transportation. Before the days of railroads men were dependent upon natural routes, and rivers were an important factor in the development of a region. Lands untouched by waterways and with resources remote from market were regarded as undesirable for settlement. Not so Minnesota! Her strategic location played no small part in the development of that great resource which formed the basis of the lumber industry.

Minnesota lay within easy reach of large areas whose forests had no

[21] Andrews, *Report of Forestry Commissioner*, 1908, p. 27.

[22] Mary Dopp, "Geographical Influences in the Development of Wisconsin," *Bulletin of the American Geographical Society*, vol. xlv (Oct. 1913), p. 742.

[23] Andrews, *Report of Forestry Commissioner*, 1908, p. 42.

[24] Edward G. Cheney, "Development of the Lumber Industry in Minnesota," *Journal of Geography*, vol. xiv (Feb. 16, 1916), p. 195.

[25] Interview of the author with J. W. Bayly, assistant to the vice-president of Alger, Smith and Company, Duluth, Minnesota, Aug. 14, 1932, at Duluth.

[26] Spalding, *op. cit.*, p. 19.

commercial value.[27] Its neighbors to the south and west were largely prairie. Immediately west of Minnesota — in what is now North and South Dakota — lay fertile prairie regions ready to yield to the pioneer's plow, and beyond was a treeless expanse of great plains reaching westward into Montana and Wyoming. To the southwest stretched Nebraska and Kansas, where arable lands offered splendid wheat farms for settlement when the strife between slaveholder and free farmer should be laid aside. Beyond the grassy prairie within these states lay immense reaches of treeless plains which sometime would be forced to yield to the persistence of the pioneer. To the immediate south of Minnesota lay Iowa, only in small part forested and known to have less wasteland than any other state in the United States. It was in these prairie and plains sections that large-scale farming with extensive machine equipment came to prevail. The products of the forest would facilitate the settlement of these areas, and Minnesota's white pine lay most accessibly adjacent to this vast region, amazingly fertile but comparatively woodless.[28] Someday those prairies were to provide a great market for Minnesota's white pine.

Nature had also endowed Minnesota with a magnificent system of waterways which provided highways for carrying her resources to market. From her midst issued the headwaters of three great river systems; east, north, and south these poured their waters. In the period of history when navigable streams were the only means of transportation, the movement of population was facilitated or retarded according to the convenience of waterways. The ease with which raw materials could be assembled at a convenient point was important also in determining the precedence of settlement in one region over another. Therefore, Minnesota, richly blessed with three river systems, had much in her favor.

One of these waterways is the Red River of the North. This river, its source close neighbor to the source of the Mississippi, flows northward. Its water finds its way into Hudson Bay, but on its way thither it makes a fertile and broad valley through northwestern Minnesota, eastern North Dakota, and on into Manitoba. This Red River Valley, 300 miles long, was once the glacial Lake Agassiz.[29] Out of its rich soil were to come great measures of wheat to be exchanged for lumber. The Red River Valley was to furnish a quick market for Minnesota's white pine, and the river of that valley was to offer a mode of transportation for lumber and then for wheat.

[27] B. E. Fernow, *Report upon the Forestry Investigations of the United States Department of Agriculture*, 55th Cong., 3rd Sess., *House Doc.*, no. 181, p. 48.

[28] Jenks Cameron, *The Development of Government Forest Control in the United States* (Baltimore, 1928), p. 135.

[29] Warren Upham, "The Settlement and Development of the Red River Valley," *Minnesota Historical Society Collections*, vol. viii (St. Paul, 1898), pp. 12–24.

In northeastern Minnesota the St. Louis River and its tributaries form a part of an immense water system which extends to the Atlantic Ocean. This river with its tributaries has a drainage area of about 8725 square miles covered with forest. Such a river would naturally become important in the lumber industry. The St. Louis and its larger tributaries, the Cloquet, the Embarass, and the Whiteface, were easy log-driving streams, while at several points the St. Louis itself had water power that made sawmills possible. The product which this stream was to carry would find markets eastward through the immense water route of the Great Lakes and the St. Lawrence.

But no outlet from Minnesota was so important as the great Father of Waters. From the highlands of the watershed came this river, sometimes flowing leisurely, sometimes bursting forth in rapid and broken descent, cutting its way through immense forests of pine. It alone afforded Minnesota's products a highway of more than 2000 miles from St. Anthony Falls to its mouth. Its source lies in Minnesota in the land of deep snow and white pine, but it empties its waters into the Gulf of Mexico in the land of subtropical growth. On its way to the sea it forms the boundary line, total or partial, of ten states.

The Mississippi is joined by countless tributaries, fifty-four of which create a navigable system of 13,912 miles reaching east to Olean, New York, on the Allegheny, and west to Great Falls, Montana, on the Missouri.[30] Some of these rivers, majestic in size, gave rich tribute; and some, like lesser subjects, offered what little they had. The St. Croix River had much to offer. Born in the midst of millions of mighty trees, the St. Croix was to become second only to the Mississippi as a carrier of logs. Its energy, also, would help make logs into lumber. It was on this stream that the first commercial lumber was made from Minnesota's white pine; it was on this stream that logging began in Minnesota.

It is evident, then, that in Minnesota nature had supplied the elements of growth and wealth. As an abundant resource, there was merchantable pine of the finest type. To turn these logs into lumber, Minnesota was richly endowed with water power. An industry governed as much by the convenience of transportation as by the presence of merchantable timber found Minnesota highly desirable, for navigable streams, touching vital spots that would consume great quantities of the white pine which Minnesota had to offer, had their sources in Minnesota. Singly these elements meant little, but under guiding hands shrewdly able to combine them, they were to be converted into an industry basic in the building of the state. It is this phase of the economic development of the Upper Mississippi, with special emphasis on Minnesota, which this book will try to describe.

[30] Harold U. Faulkner, *Economic History of America* (New York, 1931), p. 610.

CHAPTER II

The Lumber Industry Comes to the
Upper Mississippi Valley

AT A convention of delegates from the then West and Southwest of the United States meeting at Memphis, Tennessee, in 1845 to consider internal improvements, there was much agitation for improving the river for lumber shipments from the St. Croix and other headwaters of the Mississippi.[1] The states of the Lower and Middle Mississippi had entered statehood considerably earlier than Minnesota and were well populated at an early date. Some of these states with a relative scarcity of timber were demanding lumber from the immense pineries of the Upper Mississippi[2] — lumber for the building of homes. Therefore, there was agitation at Memphis for the improvement of waterways from the forest regions whence lumber came.

Of the cities along the Mississippi, none was then more eager to garner the lumber from the Upper River than St. Louis. Nor was any other place in the early years of lumbering on the Upper Mississippi to figure so prominently as a lumber market for the white pine of that distant north. St. Louis was a terminal point for commerce in the newer West. It brought together the trade of the Missouri, the Upper and the Lower Mississippi, and the Ohio; it served as a point of exchange between East and West, North and South.[3]

As early as 1819 Pittsburgh and its surrounding country had supplied the white pine market at St. Louis. But as the white pine of the Lake region entered the market, Pittsburgh gave way; in 1860 the Lake and Upper Mississippi region — comprising Michigan, Wisconsin, and Minnesota — took precedence the country over, and from that period until 1890 it furnished most of the nation's lumber.[4]

By 1856 one third of all the receipts at St. Louis came from the region

---

[1] Orin G. Libby, "Significance of the Lead and Shot Trade in Early Wisconsin History," *Wisconsin Historical Collections*, vol. xiii (Madison, 1895), p. 297.
[2] Tom O. Edwards, "The Progress, Condition, and Prospects of Wisconsin," *Wis. Hist. Coll.*, vol. ii (Madison, 1856), p. 498.
[3] Spalding, *The White Pine*, pp. 17–18.
[4] Harold S. Betts, *Timber, its Strength, Seasoning, and Grading* (New York, 1919), p. 8.

lying above the Des Moines Rapids of the Mississippi,[5] which included Iowa, Minnesota, Wisconsin, and a part of Illinois, all bordering on the river. Minnesota was then no contributor of wheat;[6] lumber was her commercial product at that time. Wisconsin's chief contribution also was lumber from the Chippewa, the Black, and the Wisconsin. No doubt a large proportion of the northern products came in the form of lumber and logs. That the river trade was important to St. Louis is shown by the city's concern as to what the Rock Island Railroad bridge would do to the lumber rafts coming from the north.[7] In 1862, 2,200,000 feet of lumber were received at St. Louis by way of the Upper River in one week.[8]

The importance of the Upper River to St. Louis is illustrated by the lean years when water was low. A St. Louis *Prices Current* never failed to give the condition of the Upper River — it was as essential as the weather report of the present time. Business in lumber suffered at St. Louis if there were "fleets of lumber" aground on the Lower Rapids in the slow process of "working off."[9] The river was low in 1863: the first week in August only 350,000 feet came from the Upper River;[10] the following week only 220,000 feet came.[11] The low waters of the Mississippi made lumber scarce and the market bare. Prices stiffened — telling evidence that the Upper Mississippi was an important log and lumber source.[12] A St. Louis newspaper expressed the fear that there would be no more logs "until our friends in the icy North will have more rain."[13] On August 31 the good news came — the spell was broken; rain had come; the rivers were rising and rafts were on the way from the tributaries of the Upper Mississippi.[14]

From early days St. Louis sought pine from the Upper Mississippi. In 1845, Field, West and Van Deventer, of St. Louis, were ordering pine from the Upper River.[15] Clark and Child was another St. Louis firm which sought its supply from the pine forests of the North. Borup and

[5] St. Louis *Prices Current*, July 10, 1856. (This was a sheet giving market prices and information, not a newspaper.)

[6] Henrietta M. Larson, *The Wheat Market and the Farmer in Minnesota, 1858–1900* (New York, 1926), p. 16.

[7] St. Louis *Prices Current*, July 10, 1856; *St. Paul Dispatch*, Dec. 16, 1921, p. 8. "Hurd vs. the Rock Island Rail Bridge Company" was a case that marked the height of the struggle between river captains and the rising railroad interests. Hurd was captain of the *Effie Afton*, which had collided with the bridge. St. Louis backed the river interests, while the railroad was backed by Chicago. Abraham Lincoln defended the bridge company (*St. Paul Dispatch*, Dec. 16, 1921). Rivermen referred to this bridge as "that invention of satan and the Rock Island Railroad" (Charles E. Russell, *A-rafting on the Mississipp'* [New York, 1928], p. 73).

[8] *Daily Missouri Democrat* (St. Louis), Oct. 20, 1862.

[9] *Tri-Weekly Missouri Democrat* (St. Louis), July 20, 1863.

[10] *Ibid.*, Aug. 3, 1863.   [11] *Ibid.*, Aug. 10, 1863.

[12] *Ibid.*, June 29, July 20, Aug. 3, 31, Sept. 21, 1863.

[13] *Ibid.*, Aug. 10, 1863.

[14] *Ibid.*, Aug. 31, 1863.

[15] L. H. Bunnell, *Winona and its Environs on the Mississippi in Ancient and Modern Days* (Winona, 1897), p. 287.

Oakes, a merchandise firm of St. Paul which was a branch of the firm of Pierre Chouteau of St. Louis, took logs in payment for goods.[16] In 1850 Borup received from Franklin Steele, a lumber pioneer in Minnesota, 333 logs, scaling 106,007 feet.[17] Whether this was all in payment for goods purchased we do not know, but Borup and Oakes sent their logs to St. Louis.[18] Both John Prince and Daniel Stanchfield of St. Paul took logs for merchandise; the logs became money at the lower market, though sometimes it required all of one year to make the exchange.[19]

Men from downriver moved northward up the St. Croix, up the Chippewa, wherever there was white pine to be had. These men were to become manufacturers, wholesalers, and retailers and were to supply the already established and growing downriver market. It was this busy market of the Middle and Lower Mississippi — established before the forest empire of the northland had been touched — which gave the initial commercial impulse to the establishment of the white pine industry in the region that was to become Minnesota.

As early as March 13, 1837, Henry H. Sibley, Lyman M. Warren, and William A. Aitkin had contracted with the Chippewa bands along the St. Croix and the Snake River to be allowed to cut timber and erect mills on certain of their lands. Forty-nine chiefs and headmen, designating their names by an X, had given these white men written permission to cut the white pine on the Chippewa land.[20] The timber so to be cut reached one mile to the east of the St. Croix River and three miles to the west.

At that time all the white pine of the area which is Minnesota today was still in the hands of red men — that is, all but the military reservation of Fort Snelling. And whenever the white man wished to lay his ax to the tree, only the Indian could give him permission. Men were eager, however, for the government of the United States to buy the land; then the arrangement for taking the timber could be made more readily, for timber, the people thought, belonged to them "as citizens inheriting an interest in the government." [21]

[16] Daniel Stanchfield, "The History of Pioneer Lumbering on the Upper Mississippi and its Tributaries with Biographic Sketches," *Minn. Hist. Soc. Coll.*, vol. ix (St. Paul, 1901), pp. 340–41.

[17] Steele Papers, Borup to Steele, Sept. 27, 1850; Sibley Papers, Rice to Sibley, Dec. 1847. The Franklin Steele Papers and the Henry Hastings Sibley Papers are in the possession of the Minnesota Historical Society.

[18] Walter A. Blair, *A Raft Pilot's Log* (Cleveland, 1930), p. 37.

[19] Stanchfield, *op. cit.*, p. 341.

[20] Copy of contract in Sibley Papers, Mar. 13, 1837. The original contract, with the crosses of the Indians and the signatures of the white men, is in the possession of the Minnesota Historical Society. (See Wilson P. Shortridge, *Transition of a Typical Frontier* [Menasha, Wisconsin, 1922], p. 28.)

[21] Robinson, *Early Economic Conditions*, p. 39; William H. C. Folsom, "History of Lumbering in the St. Croix Valley with Biographic Sketches," *Minn. Hist. Soc. Coll.*, vol. ix (St. Paul, 1901), p. 207.

Lyman M. Warren, writing to Henry H. Sibley on June 22, 1837, urged the speeding-up of the purchase of the pineland in the St. Croix region.[22] This effort bore fruit, for later in the summer of 1837 Governor Dodge of Wisconsin Territory, by treaty with the Indians, secured this valuable pineland in the St. Croix Valley for the United States government.[23] The treaty was ratified in 1838.

The land thus purchased from the Indians was the most remote part of the old Northwest Territory. It was triangular in shape. On the east it was bounded by the swift waters of the St. Croix and on the west by the Mississippi; it reached northwest to the junction of the Crow Wing and the Mississippi rivers. The purchase by the United States government of the land in 1838 was the first step toward the establishment of lumbering as a commercial enterprise in the last outpost of the white pine which had extended from Maine to Minnesota.[24] How ownership of that land was acquired by men seeking timber will be told in Chapter IV.

Hardly was the ink dry on the St. Croix treaty when men with an interest in lumber came up the St. Croix River. The United States government had not even had time to survey the new region when Dr. Fitch of Muscatine, Iowa, Washington Libby of Alton, Illinois, W. S. Hungerford and James Livingstone of St. Louis, and one Hill and W. Holcombe of Quincy, Illinois, chartered the steamer *Palmyra,* loaded it with sawmill machinery, and set out for the pine regions of the St. Croix. In July 1838 their boat, very likely the first steamboat ever to ply the St. Croix, anchored at a place now known as St. Croix Falls on the Wisconsin side of the river.[25] With Franklin Steele, who had arrived in Minnesota a bit earlier and who had studied the resources of this region carefully, they formed the St. Croix Lumber Company.[26] They were all downriver men, with the exception of Franklin Steele, who was a sutler at Fort Snelling, and it was their plan to supply Iowa, Illinois, Wisconsin, and Missouri with lumber made from the white pine of the St. Croix Valley.

Men from St. Louis knew the upper country well, for St. Louis had been the entrepôt for the fur trade.[27] They knew something about the

[22] Sibley Papers.

[23] J. Fletcher Williams, "History of the City of Saint Paul and of the County of Ramsey, Minnesota," *Minn. Hist. Soc. Coll.,* vol. iv (St. Paul, 1876), p. 58; Charles J. Kappler, editor, *Indian Affairs,* vol. ii (Washington, 1904), pp. 491–93.

[24] Shortridge, *op. cit.,* p. 27.

[25] Folsom, *op. cit.,* p. 293.

[26] Capt. Fred A. Bill, "Navigation on the Chippewa River in Wisconsin," *Burlington Post* (Burlington, Iowa), Mar. 29, 1930, p. 2; Capt. Edward W. Durant, "Lumbering and Steamboating on the St. Croix River," *Minn. Hist. Soc. Coll.,* vol. x, pt. 2 (St. Paul, 1905), pp. 468–69; Return I. Holcombe, *Minnesota in Three Centuries,* vol. ii (New York, 1908), p. 138.

[27] William J. Peterson, "Steamboating in the Fur Trade," *Minnesota History,* vol. xiii (Sept. 1932), p. 225.

uncharted virgin forests of the North. The location which these first
comers shrewdly selected was an important one, for it marked the head of
navigation on the St. Croix about fifty miles from the junction of that
river and the Mississippi. The water power at this spot was thought
inexhaustible,[28] since there were violent rapids, with a descent of forty
feet within a mile.[29] And the place had the decided advantage of being
a natural point of business for the vast pineries reaching out toward
Lake Superior. That the site of the first sawmill on the St. Croix was a
place of promise is evident from the fact that nineteen years later, in 1857,
a company of eastern men, of whom Caleb Cushing of Boston was a
director, with a capital of $300,000, established itself at this place in the
business of sawing lumber.[30] Cushing must have had his eye on these
falls for some time, for as early as 1847 he had purchased some property
there.[31]

The first commercial sawmill on Minnesota soil was built in 1839 by
another group[32] — also men who came from downriver. Their choice of
location was likewise on the St. Croix. Early in 1839 they established,
twenty miles below the Falls of the St. Croix, the first white settlement in
Minnesota and gave it the name Marine.[33] L. S. Judd and David Hone
chose the site in 1838. They were followed by Orange Walker, who became clerk and manager, and George B. Judd, both of whom came from
Marine, Illinois. Hiram Berkey and Asa Parker followed the next year;
together with a few others, they formed the Marine Lumber Company.[34]
These enterprising men had no capital, but they had an untiring interest
in their venture, and in 1849 their properties at Marine were said to be
valued at $50,000.[35] The *Fayette,* probably the third steamboat to come
up the St. Croix, brought supplies and sawmill machinery, and on August
24, 1839, the first commercial sawmill in Minnesota cut its first lumber.[36]

This first commercial sawmill in Minnesota was very crude. It was propelled by a small stream falling upon an overshot wheel, while a slow
muley saw cut deliberately through the logs. A muley saw could cut only
five thousand feet a day at the most. Nevertheless it was an improvement

[28] *Act of Incorporation and By-laws of the St. Croix Manufacturing and Improvement Company* (Washington, 1857), pp. 23–24.
[29] Charles M. Foote and George F. Warner, editors, *History of Washington County and the
St. Croix Valley* (Minneapolis, 1881), p. 181.
[30] *Act of Incorporation and By-laws,* 1857.
[31] Steele Papers, George to Steele, Boston, Nov. 28, 1848.
[32] William W. Folwell, *A History of Minnesota,* vol. i (St. Paul, 1921), p. 227.
[33] A. E. Jenks, "The People of Minnesota," *Proceedings, Minnesota Academy of Social
Science,* vol. ii (Northfield, Minnesota, 1909), p. 201.
[34] *Stillwater Lumberman,* Mar. 16, 1877.
[35] *Minnesota Pioneer* (St. Paul), Aug. 16, 1849.
[36] Durant, *op. cit.,* p. 667; Cheney, "Development of Lumber Industry in Minnesota," *Journal of Geography,* vol. xiv, p. 190; Folsom, *op. cit.,* p. 298. Dr. Lucas Green, William Dibble,
Joseph Cattrell, and Albert Judd were other members of this company.

over the old up-and-down saw, for it cut a bit thinner, with only a fourth of an inch kerf; it was constructed so that it had a quicker reciprocating action but the muley was slow in contrast with later mill-saws.[37] Settlement of the prairie would have been slow indeed if the lumber necessary had been furnished entirely by the muley.

The town of Marine on the St. Croix in 1839 placed the first lumber on the market from the region that was to become Minnesota.[38] Its market was largely at St. Louis, where George B. Judd spent much of his time disposing of lumber. The Marine mills grew. A traveler in Minnesota in 1848 spoke of the "Marine Mills" as doing good business,[39] and in 1850 they were said to be doing "a jam up business."[40] In that year the company was reorganized as Judd, Walker and Company, which in 1852 built a new mill, 60 by 80 feet in size; in 1863 it became Walker, Judd and Veazie.[41] In 1855 the lumber production of this firm at Marine was 2,000,000 feet. For fifty years this mill remained in operation. From time to time the equipment changed, but Walker and Judd were a part of the concern through the entire half century. In the course of its history a total of 197,000,000 feet of lumber was produced.[42]

Orange Walker was a New Englander. He was born at St. Albans, Vermont, the year of the Louisiana Purchase. He had come west to Marine, Illinois, and now he had followed the line of the frontier to a newer outpost. He became manager of the company — at a salary, in 1845 and for three years following, of three hundred dollars a year, not exorbitant for the responsibility that was his in developing business in a virgin country. He was a leader in his community: for twenty-five years he was Marine's postmaster, and he served in the state legislature in 1859–60. From 1839 until he died in 1887 he directed affairs at Marine. He lived to see the industry in which he had pioneered in Minnesota become big business.

Orange Walker and his company entered other fields of business in Marine as well. In so new a country there was no near place where supplies could be purchased by the people who came to work for this concern. Therefore, to meet this demand, the new sawmill company established itself as a storekeeper at Marine. As such it was the first, except the fur traders, to sell goods in the St. Croix Delta.[43] The company catered to the general needs of the people; in their charge accounts are

[37] *Minnesota Pioneer*, Aug. 16, 1849; Henry Disston and Sons, *The Saw in History* (Philadelphia, 1916), p. 28. The kerf is the slit which the saw makes when it cuts through the log.
[38] Robinson, *op. cit.*, p. 39.
[39] John Rollins, Diary, Nov. 6, 1848. This diary is in the Minnesota Historical Society.
[40] *Minnesota Pioneer*, Feb. 13, 1850.
[41] *Stillwater Lumberman*, Mar. 16, 1877.
[42] Cheney, *op. cit.*, p. 190.
[43] Foote and Warner, *op. cit.*, p. 471.

found items ranging from beans, tea, butter, coal, oil, soap — the essentials of life — to choicer things, such as hoop skirts, canary bird seed, and a "first reader." Even postage stamps were listed in these accounts.[44]

In 1856 this same firm went into the business of making flour. This, too, was done in order to supply the growing demand. As the lumber industry grew, the number of workmen engaged in it increased, and flour, whether it came from Pembina, from below on the Mississippi, or from other sources, became an item of much importance. The significance of all this is that the lumber industry was a factor in the development of other lines of business; in its path settlement and commerce took hold where previously the red man had roamed alone, except as now and then a trader in fur had chanced to come.

Lumbering, however, was the chief industry at Marine. The Reverend George Spaulding, writing to the American Home Missionary Society in 1857, stated that most of the people of the village were engaged in lumbering. But, said he, their interests were as unfavorable to religion as those of the gold-hunting Californians.[45]

The fame of the white pine of the Upper Mississippi was spreading far, and soon the first comers on the St. Croix were followed by men from Maine. The woodsman from Maine, reputed "to know logging," shouldered his ax and began his march toward the setting sun when the white pine of his own state was giving out; it was necessary to seek new forests to supply homes for the ever-growing and westward-moving population. From the Atlantic to the Mississippi, north of the fortieth parallel from Maine to Minnesota, men from Maine moved westward with the lumber industry. Many eventually set themselves down in the St. Croix country.

In 1840 one John McKusick, from Stillwater in Maine, visited the pinelands of the St. Croix country.[46] He had journeyed to Illinois during the previous year; then he had gone on to Iowa, and finally northward to an even newer country. In the fall of 1840 he began work for the St. Croix Lumber Company at St. Croix Falls.[47] The pinelands of the St. Croix evidently pleased him, for on October 10, 1843, he selected the spot which was to bear the name of his old home town in Maine.[48] Later generations of Stillwater dwellers evidently thought well of John McKusick, for on one occasion a visitor in the schools of that city asked the children who

[44] Judd, Walker, Veazie Papers (1855–1904), Day Book, Apr. 5 to July 30, 1870. These papers are in the possession of the Minnesota Historical Society.

[45] George Spaulding to American Home Missionary Society, Mar. 24, 1857. Film copies of the American Home Missionary Society Papers are in the possession of the Minnesota Historical Society.

[46] Folsom, op. cit., p. 302.

[47] Foote and Warner, op. cit., p. 512.

[48] St. Croix Union (Stillwater), Apr. 3, 1855; Holcombe, op. cit., p. 108.

discovered America. "'John McKusick,' cried a curly-headed little girl whose countenance lit up with rapture at the sudden inspiration." [49]

The site McKusick selected lay on the west bank of the St. Croix about thirty-five miles above its junction with the Mississippi. Stillwater on the St. Croix had all the possibilities of a second Bangor. In the lumber world Bangor in Maine was a name to conjure with. Stillwater on the St. Croix, like Bangor on the Penobscot, stood at the edge of a black forest. Thoreau said of Bangor that it was like a star on the edge of the night; the same could be said of Stillwater. Bangor sent its lumber to Spain, England, and the West Indies; Stillwater on the St. Croix was to furnish the lumber that would build farmsteads, towns, and cities on the American prairies.

The first sawmill in Stillwater began its steady hum in 1844, when the Stillwater Lumber Company, under the management of John Mc-Kusick, established itself there. [50] Elam Greeley of New Hampshire, Elias McKean of Pennsylvania, and one Calvin F. Leach were in the company with John McKusick; they had agreed at St. Louis on October 26, 1843, to build a sawmill at Stillwater. [51] The construction of the mill had been started in November 1843 and in April of the next year the mill began to make logs into lumber. This mill, the first frame building in Stillwater, was run by water power. It had a water wheel 36 feet in diameter. The size of the mill was 40 by 65 feet. [52] One of the first well-known buildings for which it furnished lumber was the old American House at St. Paul, historically interesting because it served as a terminal point for stagecoach lines. [53] This pioneer Stillwater firm also had St. Louis as its chief lumber market. It must have prospered, for in 1855 it was said that $50,000 could probably not buy its properties. [54]

Stillwater grew notably; it was a salient point of lumbering operations on the St. Croix. A visitor in 1849 spoke of it as a robust town, "which after seeing, no traveler would think of leaving Minnesota." [55] In 1853 it was said to have "more substantial, reliable business, for the extent of it, and more capital . . . than any other town in Minnesota." [56] Two years later this lumber town had a population of twelve hundred people, most of whom were connected with the chief industry — lumber. The population was chiefly from Maine, and it is an interesting fact that when the

[49] *Stillwater Messenger* (supplement), Dec. 15, 1871.
[50] Cheney, *op. cit.*, p. 190.
[51] E. D. Neill, "The Beginning of Organized Society in the St. Croix Valley, Minnesota," *Macalester College Contributions*, no. 33, p. 55.
[52] *Stillwater Messenger*, June 30, 1871.
[53] *Ibid.*; Henry A. Castle, *History of St. Paul and Vicinity*, vol. i (New York, 1912), p. 416.
[54] *St. Croix Union*, June 9, 1855.
[55] *Minnesota Pioneer*, Mar. 5, 1849.
[56] J. W. Bond, *Minnesota and its Resources* (Chicago, 1856), pp. 35–36.

Maine Law, a prohibition law, was submitted to the people of the territory, Stillwater gave it the largest majority of any town in Minnesota.[57] Stillwater was confident of its future. Its papers boasted freely of "our immense pine forests, our water power, our rich agricultural lands, and our position on the longest navigable stream in the world, together with our geographical relation to the great railroad enterprises, which will eventually connect the waters of the Mississippi and Lake Superior."[58]

Within the ten years that followed the establishment of the first sawmill in Stillwater, five more mills were added.[59] The first of these was the famous Hersey and Staples mill. To Stillwater in 1853 came Isaac Staples, another Maineite, from Old Town. Like John McKusick, he was seeking the virgin pine. He saw the possibilities of Stillwater, with pines to the back of it, water power at its feet, and a navigable river stretching two thousand miles ahead. After careful investigation of the new pine country he returned to Maine. There he evidently gave his salesman's talk with conviction, for upon his return to Stillwater the Herseys, old lumbermen in Maine, began their investment in this Eldorado of the West.[60] Staples became the resident partner in Stillwater, while Samuel Freeman Hersey, who had made his fortune in pinelands in his own state, headed the new firm of Hersey, Staples and Company, which began operations in the St. Croix area on the first day of June 1854.[61]

The sawmill erected by Hersey, Staples and Company at Stillwater made history in the lumber industry in Minnesota. It was said to be the finest sawmill in the West. "It is, in all its departments, as near perfection as machinery can be brought by human skill," was a statement made at that time.[62] But what characterized a first-class sawmill in 1854? asks the student of today, accustomed to the speed and efficiency of a twentieth-century sawmill.

A careful analysis of the machinery of the Hersey mill makes it clear that no longer was lumbering the industry where men "loaded on a big log, turned on the water to its primitive water wheel, greased the journals of the shafting, and then went off to hunt squirrels, when there were no crafty Indians in sight, having ample time for the diversions of the hunt before the saw completed its cut."[63] Steam was beginning to come into its own. It could be economically used because slabs and saw-

[57] *St. Croix Union*, Apr. 3, 1855.   [58] *Stillwater Messenger*, Feb. 1, 1859.
[59] Cheney, *op. cit.*, p. 190.
[60] Augustus B. Easton, editor, *History of the St. Croix Valley*, vol. i (Chicago, 1909), pp. 62–63.
[61] *Kanabec County Times* (Mora), June 28, 1934 (75th anniversary edition), p. 1.
[62] Hotchkiss, *History of Lumber and Forest Industry of Northwest*, p. 525.
[63] This is the description of the government mill in Minnesota which, in 1822, located at St. Anthony Falls, cut the logs into lumber to be used in the construction of Fort Snelling. (Hotchkiss, *op. cit.*, p. 539.)

dust, castoffs in the lumber industry of that day, supplied the fuel. A steam sawmill would bring an increase in production, and steam power was used in the Hersey and Staples mill.

The first-class Hersey mill had another improvement over the other mills: it was equipped with a gang saw. Gang saws were parallel sash saws, with many in one frame. This mill had one frame which could hold twenty saws.[64] It also had a circular saw which could cut 16,000 feet of lumber in eleven hours. The circular saw, sometimes called a rotary or rip saw, was used almost exclusively in Michigan by the time of the Civil War. The Hersey, Staples mill was the first to use it in Stillwater. In 1854 a circular saw was usually 5 to 5½ feet in diameter. The minimum cut of a good circular was 1000 feet per hour in 1850, though its speed was increased to an output of 4000 feet per hour even before 1870.

Thus, equipped with a gang saw and a circular saw, as well as with three of the usual upright saws, the Hersey, Staples mill could produce 125,000 feet in twenty-four hours.[65] With saws producing so rapidly, the handling of lumber and the removal of slabs must also be done with greater speed. And so it was. "Everything about the mill is done by machinery, even to the filing of the saws, the handling and shifting of the lumber, and the removal of slabs," reads a report of the mill at that time.[66] This mill, spoken of as the "mammoth" steam sawmill of Hersey, Staples and Company, was said to have cost $80,000.[67]

But whence came capital for such construction? From the East, and particularly from New England. New England was feeling more and more the strength of old England on the high seas and was therefore turning from the sea to the rapidly growing West. New England, gradually becoming more industrial, also needed a market for its goods; the new West was such a market. The new West in turn furnished the growing industrial East with food. Thus the interests of the East and West became complementary and eastern capital found western investment promising. Caleb Cushing turned with confidence to white pine logs in the Lake states. He had carefully investigated the St. Croix region in 1846, shortly after he returned from China, where as American commissioner he had negotiated a successful treaty. At St. Croix Falls and St. Anthony Falls his money was a factor in the building of sawmills. Other eastern capitalists, too, became interested.

The famous firm of Hersey, Staples and Company was backed entirely by eastern money. The four stockholders in this company were Samuel

[64] *St. Croix Union,* June 23, 1855.
[65] Hotchkiss, *op. cit.,* p. 524.
[66] *Ibid.*
[67] *Stillwater Messenger,* May 1, 1860.

Freeman Hersey of Bangor, Maine, who held one fourth of the capital; Dudley C. Hall of Medford, Massachusetts, who held another fourth; James A. Whitney and John Brooks Fenno, who, under the firm name of Whitney and Fenno of Boston, held one fourth; and Isaac Staples, once from Maine and later from Minnesota, who held the last fourth. So it was out of Maine and Massachusetts that money for this venture came.

This company continued in lumber at Stillwater as long as the industry lasted there. In 1860 Whitney died, and Hersey, Staples, and Hall each took a one-third share. The concern was known as Hershey, Staples and Hall until 1866, when Hall was no longer a member of the company and the name became Hersey, Staples and Bean. Charles and Jacob Bean, who had logged for Hersey in Maine, had come to log for him in Minnesota and Hersey furnished the money for them when they purchased Hall's share of the stock. In 1875 Samuel Freeman Hersey died. Isaac Staples had withdrawn from the company. Therefore, the four sons of Samuel Freeman Hersey — Roscoe F., Edward L., Dudley H., and Eugene M.— took one half the stock of the concern and the two Bean brothers held the other half. The firm continued business under the name of Hersey and Bean. In 1900 all the timber property of this firm was deeded in trust to William H. Bean, a son of one of the early loggers.[68]

Hersey, Staples and Company in the early days became owners of standing timber; they were loggers; they were manufacturers of lumber; they were wholesale distributors; and they were retailers as well. Apparently they carried on all the branches of the lumber industry, a highly integrated business.[69]

In addition they became active promoters in various fields of business that had to be developed to support their lumbering operations — such fields as supplying food, providing transportation, and banking. By 1859 they were well along in the business of merchandising, for "Hersey, Staples and Company on the Levee, Stillwater, Minnesota" advertised dry goods, clothing, provisions, hardware, boots, shoes, and other things. Three years later they advertised that they had the largest stock of goods "ever brought here," listing groceries, fish, cordage, cutlery, queensware, Britannia plated silverware, mat rugs, port, alpacas, challis, shawls, sun umbrellas, and fanning mills.[70]

In 1859 Hersey and Staples announced that they had 1,000,000 feet of fencing and common lumber which they would exchange for grain and

[68] The article from which this material has come was written by William H. Bean on the occasion of the 75th anniversary of the *Kanabec County Times* (Mora), June 28, 1934, and was printed in the newspaper on that occasion.

[69] Wilson Compton, *The Organization of the Lumber Industry* (Chicago, 1916), p. 48.

[70] *Stillwater Messenger,* June 1, 1862.

flour.[71] Money was scarce in the new country so recently after the Panic of 1857, and barter was not uncommon. Moreover, in a day when flour was somewhat at a premium in Minnesota, grain and flour were important to the continued life of the company, the largest working out of Stillwater. So Isaac Staples soon built a flour mill at Stillwater that was considered "mammoth" at that time.[72]

In 1871 Hersey and Staples were active in the Lumberman's National Bank, which had a capital of half a million dollars.[73] Staples also helped to organize the Second National Bank of St. Paul.[74] When the day of railroads came, Hersey actively interested himself in two enterprises. He was on the board of directors of the St. Paul and Sioux City Railroad, known today as the Chicago, Saint Paul, Minneapolis and Omaha Railway, during the trying years of its beginning,[75] and he took an active interest in the short line that connected Stillwater with the St. Paul and Sioux City at St. Paul. That line was the St. Paul, Stillwater and Taylor's Falls, which was built to carry lumber from Stillwater to St. Paul, a distributing center.[76]

Though Hersey himself never moved to the West, his interest in this new country in which he had chosen to make his investments was important to the western lumber town. Stillwater thought well of him; when he visited there in 1868 the *Stillwater Messenger* said, "Samuel Freeman Hersey smiled upon us yesterday. Neither Maine nor Minnesota could prosper without him." He died in 1875.[77]

It grew, this business of lumber in the St. Croix Valley. In 1855 John McKusick found it necessary to add two circular saws to his establishment in order to meet the demand. Such saws required more power than the earlier ones, and therefore an immense overshot wheel 93 feet in circumference replaced the first mill wheel in the McKusick mill.[78] In 1857 Stillwater and its hinterland was leading in lumber exportation in Minnesota. The St. Croix Valley, with Stillwater as the chief depot, exported 30,000,000 feet of lumber and 40,000,000 feet of logs in that year. St. Anthony, on the Mississippi proper, exported only 3,000,000 feet of sawed lumber and 31,000,000 feet of logs.[79]

In 1855 F. Schulenburg and A. Boeckeler and Company built a mill at

[71] *Ibid.*, Oct. 25, 1859.
[72] Hotchkiss, *op. cit.*, p. 531.
[73] Foote and Warner, *op. cit.*, p. 525.
[74] Hotchkiss, *op. cit.*, p. 531.
[75] Warren Upham, "Minnesota Geographic Names," *Minn. Hist. Soc. Coll.*, vol. xvii (St. Paul, 1920), pp. 377–78.
[76] *Stillwater Messenger*, Feb. 5, 1875.
[77] *Ibid.*
[78] Hotchkiss, *op. cit.*, p. 649; *St. Croix Union*, June 9, 1855.
[79] Joseph A. Wheelock, *Minnesota: Its Place among the States* (Minnesota Bureau of Statistics, First Annual Report, 1860), p. 155.

Stillwater. Unlike McKusick, Staples, and Hersey, they were downriver men from St. Louis, where they operated a sawmill and had a large yard. Their mill in Stillwater sawed exclusively for the St. Louis market; [80] every board they cut was sent to their lumberyard there. Boeckeler came to manage operations in Stillwater; Schulenburg controlled further movements of lumber in the market from St. Louis.[81] They were interested in lumbering on a large scale and for many years were the biggest cutters in Stillwater.

In 1860 this firm built a new mill at Stillwater, a huge steam mill with two gang saws, one with eighteen saws and the other with twenty-four.[82] Five years later this mill was cutting 57,248 feet in an average day, and its largest cut was 71,360 feet in a day. It beat any mill in the rival town of St. Anthony.[83] Schulenburg and Boeckeler were setting the pace in the state with their output; in 1866 the firm cut 15,000,000 feet in 197 working days. A Stillwater newspaper ventured, "Can any mill in this state beat this? If so, we'd like to hear from its proprietors." [84]

But where was Stillwater's market generally? Certainly not in and around Stillwater. The population — only 609 in 1849 — was too limited in the early years. St. Paul's quick growth had not yet begun, and 804 was the extent of her population in 1849. Little Canada and St. Anthony together totaled 571 persons. The other three settlements within Minnesota Territory had even fewer. Altogether, there were in Minnesota only 4680 persons in 1849.[85] Minnesota's original market lay not at home, but there was some occasional demand for lumber. In the summer of 1845, Stephen B. Riggs of Traverse des Sioux, a missionary to the Sioux Indians, wrote Franklin Steele to send him a few hundred feet of inch boards when Sibley came up on his next trip.[86] Two years later an order for lumber was sent to H. H. Sibley for John McKusick of Stillwater.[87] In the spring of 1849 one William H. Nobles, appointed by the United States government to lay a wagon road to the Pacific, advertised in the *Pioneer* for timber, saying he would pay the highest price in cash.[88] Such orders were few and small, however, and Minnesota's early lumber industry was not developed by a home demand.

[80] *Stillwater Lumberman*, Apr. 23, 1875.
[81] *Ibid.*
[82] *Stillwater Messenger*, Mar. 27, 1860.
[83] *Ibid.*, Dec. 12, 1865.
[84] *Ibid.*, Dec. 12, 1866.
[85] Census of Minnesota Territory, June 11, 1849, in Documents accompanying the Governor's Message. It is bound with the Governor's Message, pp. xxiii–xxiv, Sept. 4, 1849, in the Minnesota Historical Society.
[86] Sibley Papers, Riggs to Steele, July 1, 1845.
[87] Sibley Papers, L. H. Laroche to McKusick, July 16, 1847.
[88] *Minnesota Pioneer*, Apr. 28, 1849; *United States Census, 1900*, vol. viii: *Manufactures*, pt. 2, p. 441.

From 1844 to 1871 — that is, until the competition of the railroads in 1871 entered into the life of the river traffic — Stillwater's market, like that of St. Croix Falls and Marine, was all "down stream." The states of Iowa, Illinois, and Missouri, with St. Louis as their entrepôt for the country lying westward, provided the original market for Stillwater lumber.

Stillwater, however, was not important only for its lumber; it became the mecca for men who needed log stock for mills which were to be established farther down the river. The business of buying and selling logs at Stillwater was no small matter, for Stillwater stood guard, as it were, over the logs from the hinterland, collected in the giant's mouth which was the St. Croix Boom.

A boom was an institution in logging. It was an important part of the system, for it was the terminal point of the log drive. Here the many millions of logs were sorted, and here their ownership was determined. The scalers and the tally boys attended strictly to business, for at a moment's notice they must judge quickly and correctly the number of board feet in a log. Every man who sent logs down the St. Croix or its tributaries must send them through the gateway known as the St. Croix Boom. Here, after the logs had been sorted, "fitting-up" crews plied busily day in and day out, arranging rafts for movement down the river. No idler, no dreamer could get on here!

The boom at St. Croix was chartered in 1851 with a capital of $10,000. The original incorporators of the boom company were Orange Walker and George B. Judd of Marine, John McKusick, Socrates Nelson, and Levi Churchill of Stillwater, Daniel Mears and William Kent of Osceola, and William H. C. Folsom of Taylor's Falls.[89] The first boom was located opposite Osceola. Later it was moved nearer Stillwater, to a point three miles above that city. There it took on immense proportions — at one time extending over a distance of nine miles. In 1857 the company was reorganized, with a capital stock of $25,000. All the original incorporators were still active in it. So well-known did this institution come to be in the St. Croix Valley that men referred to it as "The Boom." In time the stockholders were not limited to the St. Croix area. As the mills on the Mississippi grew in number and the demands for log stock increased, large companies such as Laird, Norton and Company of Winona purchased stock in the St. Croix Boom. No fewer than 2000 log marks have been recorded at the boom during the course of its history.[90]

[89] Trade News (Stillwater and Bayport), July 4, 1930, p. 1.

[90] Folsom, op. cit., p. 312; Samuel McClure, Stillwater, Minnesota, to Laird, Norton Company, Dec. 22, 26, 1892, among the "Letters concerning St. Croix Lands" in the Laird, Norton Papers, Box 284. These papers are still in the possession of the Laird, Norton Company of Winona, Minnesota.

Out of that boom came logs, logs without end! Some of them were made into lumber at Stillwater; others traveled as logs until they reached the mills farther down on the Mississippi. In the period from 1840 to 1874, 3,504,000,000 feet of logs passed through the St. Croix Boom.[91] From 1840 to 1862 there was a steady increase in the number of logs sent through the boom. Then in 1862 the river was low and it remained low in 1863 and 1864. Logs, at any price, could not be rafted downriver. The demand was there; it was wartime; prices were high. But neither lumber nor logs could reach market with the low water. In 1861, 140,000,000 feet of logs passed the St. Croix Boom; in the next year only 20,000,000 feet were

TABLE 1. LOGS SCALED AT THE ST. CROIX BOOM, 1840 TO 1874

Year	No. of Feet (in millions)	Year	No. of Feet (in millions)
1840	5	1858	142
1841	8	1859	145
1842	9	1860	150
1843	10	1861	140
1844	15	1862	20
1845	20	1863	20
1846	40	1864	40
1847	60	1865	130
1848	62	1866	145
1849	75	1867	128
1850	90	1868	145
1851	100	1869	150
1852	110	1870	165
1853	120	1871	170
1854	125	1872	180
1855	130	1873	160
1856	135	1874	120
1857	140		

SOURCE: This record was compiled by A. D. Cooke, Surveyor General's Office in St. Paul.

sent through, one seventh the amount of the previous year; 1863 saw no increase, for again only 20,000,000 feet passed the boom. In 1864 the total reached 40,000,000 feet, but it was not until the following year that the boom regained its steady pace. After a slight decline in 1867, its volume rose steadily again, reaching in 1872 the largest output the boom had ever known — only to be retarded slightly again in the panic years of 1873 and 1874. Table 1 shows the number of feet of logs scaled each year at the St. Croix Boom, with Stillwater as the lumber and log mart.

The logs from the St. Croix competed in the market with the white pine of the Chippewa Valley, which was opened at almost the same time by men who also had come from the more settled parts of the Mississippi

[91] Logs were scaled even before the boom was organized, so there are complete records of the amount of logs sent down as far back as 1840.

Valley. The Chippewa River is not in Minnesota, but its lumber industry was so closely associated with Minnesota that no study of the industry in the latter region can be made without reference to the Chippewa.

The Chippewa River, like the St. Croix, empties its waters into the Mississippi. With its tributaries, it touches 7,000,000 acres of land, of which 6,000,000 were once covered with dense forest, principally with white pine.[92] This valley was an excellent source of white pine, no doubt the best white pine of the entire Mississippi region.

As early as 1829 Jefferson Davis, stationed as lieutenant at Fort Crawford (Prairie du Chien), sought out the white pine on the Chippewa River. It is likely that he cut white pine where Menomonie now stands.[93] The Chippewa pine did not become important commercially, however, until about 1836.[94]

One of the early comers seeking pine in the Chippewa Valley was John H. Knapp. As early as 1846 he and his associates were making lumber there. In 1832 he had come to Iowa, where in 1835 he helped to lay out the town of Fort Madison on the Mississippi.[95] Rising above it to the west was splendid farm land awaiting the immigrant. Iowa was not yet a state when Fort Madison was platted, but in 1846, when John H. Knapp's mill was sawing lumber in the Chippewa country, Iowa boasted enough settlers to enable it to enter the Union. This immense hinterland, reaching westward from the Mississippi, offered a great market, and John H. Knapp knew it. He was a pathbreaker. In 1849 he piloted the first steamboat up the Chippewa River. It was in April and the ice was not yet out of Lake Pepin when, with the steamboat *Dr. Franklin No. 2* laden with goods for his business, he ventured on this maiden trip.[96] John H. Knapp, keen businessman that he was, knew the value of steam navigation in the rapid transport of such products as his customers would demand, for he meant to serve the settlements developing along the Mississippi and inland to the west.

In 1853, Henry L. Stout, a wealthy lumber dealer at Dubuque, Iowa, joined the Knapp company and its name became Knapp, Stout and Company, with headquarters at Menomonie, Wisconsin.[97] Dubuque, located on the Mississippi, was an admirable market place, and it was good busi-

[92] Hotchkiss, *op. cit.,* p. 474.

[93] *Chippewa Herald* (Wisconsin), Oct. 31, 1873.

[94] John M. Holley, "Waterways and Lumber Interests of Western Wisconsin," *Proceedings, Wis. Hist. Soc.,* 1906, p. 212.

[95] Henry E. Knapp Papers, Notebook. The papers are in the possession of the Wisconsin Historical Society.

[96] *Ibid.*; *Read's Landing in the Pioneer Days,* a pamphlet compiled through the cooperation of the Womans Progressive Club of Reads and published by the *Wabasha County Herald Standard,* Wabasha, Minnesota, June 1933.

[97] *Rice Lake Chronotype* (Wisconsin), Sept. 21, 1927.

ness on the part of John H. Knapp to take Stout into his concern. More capital and bigger and better markets made the firm grow, and in time it became the largest single lumber firm operating in the Chippewa Valley. In their early years 250,000 feet was the annual output; but in their top years they produced 100,000,000 feet in a year.[98]

This firm distributed its wares at Dubuque, Fort Madison (the original Knapp home), and St. Louis.[99] Their markets were, therefore, along the Mississippi, the only road to market which Knapp, Stout and Company knew until 1871.[1]

Close neighbor to Menomonie, but safely placed on the Chippewa River, was Eau Claire. This site was chosen as a strategic one by Dole, Ingram and Kennedy for their lumber operations among the millions of fine white pine. With this company, also, it was a downriver market which spurred them on. As early as 1858 they were delivering lumber to the John Whitehill Company at St. Louis.[2] In that city Dole, Ingram and Kennedy had wholesale yards which supplied the territory roundabout.[3] The Mussers of Muscatine, Iowa, bought lumber from the Ingram firm before they began to operate their own mills.[4] Dole, Ingram and Kennedy sold shingles to a Chicago firm in 1860, even when Michigan pine was in its heyday. These shingles were evidently taken down the river to Galena or Rock Island, and thence by rail to Chicago. Rock Island (Illinois), Hannibal (Missouri), Keokuk and Clinton (Iowa), all were markets to which this concern sent its lumber.[5] Though railroads were eventually to carry the lumber of this firm far and wide, the markets which sought its product in the 1850s continued to receive lumber by way of the Mississippi until there was no more to be had in the Chippewa Valley.

Daniel Shaw was another name to conjure with in the lumber world. He came from Maine. Shawtown, on the edge of Eau Claire, was his mill town, and he operated one of the most substantial lumber concerns of the Chippewa Valley. He plied his business on the Mississippi until the very end, for his was the last raft of lumber ever to leave Eau Claire. This was on June 28, 1901, and the passing of this last raft from Eau Claire meant the passing of the white pine industry in the Chippewa Valley.[6]

The Chippewa sent flotillas of logs, as well as lumber, to the towns

[98] Hotchkiss, op. cit., p. 476.

[99] Mississippi Valley Lumberman, vol. xxix, Jan. 21, 1898, p. 11.

[1] John H. Knapp Diary, 1869–70. This is in the possession of the Wisconsin Historical Society.

[2] Orrin H. Ingram Papers, receipt for the lumber sent to John Whitehill Company at St. Louis, Sept. 16, 1858. These papers are in the possession of the Wisconsin Historical Society.

[3] Ibid., Kennedy to Ingram, Jan. 9, 1860.

[4] Ibid., Rogers to Ingram, Sept. 29, 1860.

[5] Ibid., Dole to Ingram and Kennedy, Sept. 20, 1858; Rogers to Ingram, 1859–60.

[6] Bill, "Navigation on the Chippewa," Burlington Post (Iowa), Sept. 27, 1930, p. 2.

and their hinterlands downriver. It yielded thousands, even millions, of feet of logs every season, to be cut by the mills all along the way to St. Louis in order to furnish lumber for the expanding West.

Thus the lumber industry had come to the Upper Mississippi and its branches, the St. Croix and the Chippewa. From the humble beginnings on those streams in the 1830s and 1840s had grown busy mill towns and log booms and an increasing flow of logs and lumber downriver. This center of activity, however, did not long remain alone; as the migration of settlers into the Minnesota country began, other centers of lumbering sprang up along the Mississippi, and among these the earliest and most important were at the Falls of St. Anthony and Winona.

CHAPTER III

The Home Market Stimulates the Mills at St. Anthony and Winona, 1850–1870

IT IS axiomatic to say there is no single cause that shapes development in history; rather, many things act on each other and from the interaction arise new situations, new developments, and new events. So it was with the lumber industry on the Upper Mississippi during the 1850s and 1860s. World developments were helping to set the stage for the growth of that industry.

The eyes of Europe were turned toward the great midland empire of the United States. English free trade and the Industrial Revolution had created a great and growing market for the food that could be produced in the good soil of this great region. The Crimean War had opened another market for the foodstuffs of the West. Gold in California had made money more plentiful in the United States, and prices had risen throughout the whole country. The new West stood out as a land of promise to the English farmer who had felt the competition created by free trade, to the Irish on whom the clammy hand of starvation had fallen, to the German worn out with his struggle for freedom in the Revolution of 1848, and to other Europeans eager to improve their lot. Hopefully they set forth, many of them making the long trek into the region beyond the Mississippi River. Marching westward with them were large numbers of native Americans from the East, attracted by what the new region had to offer.

The new Minnesota Territory, farthest to the north of the states and territories adjoining the Mississippi, was eager to draw onto its lands a goodly share of this immense population moving into the West. In 1851 large sections of good farm land had been obtained in the Treaty of Traverse des Sioux, by which the Sisseton and Wahpeton bands of the Sioux had sold to the United States all their lands lying east of the Red River and Lake Traverse, with the exception of a ten-mile strip on each side of the Minnesota River from New Ulm to Big Stone Lake.

Altogether the Indians had sold to the United States 24,000,000 acres, of which 19,000,000 lay in Minnesota.[1]

The territorial officials were sure these new lands would attract settlers if they could only be made known to the people entering the West. Governor Gorman of Minnesota Territory urged that some system be devised to draw immigration to Minnesota, and on March 2, 1855, the territorial legislature enacted his suggestion into law when it provided for an agency to encourage settlement.[2] The newspapers of Minnesota suffered no modesty in extolling the virtues of the region in order to attract settlers. "We wish all the world were here in Minnesota to enjoy the magnificent weather which now comes off daily," read an item in the St. Anthony Express of June 14, 1851. "Skies are blue and air as balmy as Italy can boast, and an atmosphere so pure as to defy the approach of disease — of such marvelous virtue indeed as might create a soul under the ribs of death." Health as well as wealth lay in the pine forests, they declared . . .

> For health comes sparkling in the streams from Namekagan stealing;
> There's iron in our northern winds, our pines are trees of healing.[3]

The strategic factor in bringing the westward migration to Minnesota was the new railroad to the Mississippi River. Minnesota had the good fortune of splendid river transportation to the South, but more rapid and cheap connections with the East were necessary for bringing settlers to Minnesota and for carrying products eastward to market. In 1853 New York and Chicago were connected by rail. On February 22, 1854, with the completion of the Chicago and Rock Island to Rock Island, Illinois, the railroad reached the Mississippi.[4] This made the first continuous railroad from Chicago to the Mississippi. It was a great occasion — the Mississippi and the Tidewater were united, the East and West were joined.

To celebrate the completion of this first railroad to the Mississippi, a great excursion was planned. Invitations were extended to "the wise men of the East" to travel by rail to the Mississippi River and then by boat up the Father of Waters to St. Paul.[5] The invitations brought twelve hundred sight-seers to St. Paul. They were distinguished guests. Former President Fillmore was the leading spokesman of the visitors, and George Bancroft, the well-known historian, was one of the party; but perhaps the most influential guests were thirty-eight prominent editors of eastern

[1] 32d Cong., 1st Sess., *Senate Exec. Docs.*, no. 1, pp. 279–82; Thomas Hughes, "Treaty of Traverse des Sioux in 1851," *Minn. Hist. Soc. Coll.*, vol. x, pt. 1 (St. Paul, 1905), pp. 101–29.
[2] Livia Appel and Theodore C. Blegen, "Official Encouragement of Immigration during the Territorial Period," *Minnesota History Bulletin*, vol. v (Aug. 1923), p. 170.
[3] Easton, *History of the St. Croix Valley*, vol. i, p. 357.
[4] Folwell, *History of Minnesota*, vol. i, p. 358; Arthur C. Cole, *The Era of the Civil War, 1848–1870*, vol. iii (Illinois Centennial Publication, Springfield, Illinois, 1919), p. 41.
[5] Edward D. Neill, *The History of Minnesota* (Minneapolis, 1882), p. 595.

newspapers, whose comments were of greater value in advertising Minnesota than any plans for publicity the new region could possibly have devised.[6] On their return downstream the group drew up resolutions which made good advertising for a territory as eager for settlers as Minnesota then was. In these resolutions they spoke of the boundless physical resources and potentialities of the new country, as well as of the lavish hospitality they had enjoyed "from the pioneers of the advancing millions with which this region is to teem." [7]

Other railroads drew nearer to Minnesota. In 1856 the Milwaukee and Mississippi Railroad reached the river at Prairie du Chien. In 1858 the Milwaukee and La Crosse completed its track to La Crosse, Wisconsin, a point farther north on the Mississippi. Though Minnesota herself did not yet have one mile of railroad, she felt the touch of an outside world as she had never felt it before.

Navigation on the Mississippi increased as railroads were built to the river, and in the season when the boats were operating there was a daily mail and Chicago could be reached within thirty hours. But most important was the fact that the journey westward became shorter and easier. These were factors that caused the immigrant to turn his steps toward the newer Northwest. In 1849 only 95 boats had docked at St. Paul; in 1856 there were 857 boats registered there; in 1858 the number reached the astonishing total of 1068.[8] "Old Man River" had become much busier, and the railroads at Rock Island, Prairie du Chien, and La Crosse had helped to make it so.

Minnesota counted all this for gain. In 1850 the territory had a population of about 6000 people; in 1855 the figure had risen to 40,000; in 1856 the population numbered 100,000, an increase of 60,000 people in one year; and in 1857, when the census necessary for the Enabling Act was taken, 150,037 people claimed Minnesota as their place of residence.[9] Even before the government was ready to offer the lands for sale in "Suland," the area acquired from the Sioux Indians, people began to swarm into the valleys of the Minnesota River, the Root, the Zumbro, and the Cannon; settlement came to vary inversely with the distance from these streams.[10] People came to St. Paul in such numbers that they could not be housed. Many of them had to camp in the streets until they could make proper

[6] *Daily Minnesotian* (St. Paul), June 10, 1854.

[7] Neill, *History of Minnesota*, p. 597; *Weekly Minnesotian* (St. Paul), June 17, 1854; *Minnesota Democrat* (St. Paul), June 14, 1854; *Minnesota Pioneer,* June 15, 1854; Thomas M. Newson, *Pen Pictures*, vol. i (St. Paul, 1886), p. 428.

[8] *Minnesota Executive Documents,* vol. i, no. 10 (1874), p. 98. This is based on the report of the Deputy Collector of Customs at St. Paul.

[9] Wheelock, *Minnesota: Its Place among the States*, pp. 123, 125–26, 144.

[10] *Minnesota Democrat,* Nov. 16 and Dec. 7, 1853; *Report of the Commissioner of the General Land Office,* 1855, 34th Cong., 1st Sess., *House Exec. Docs.,* no. 1, p. 155.

arrangements.[11] The "advancing millions" were fast taking possession of the new territory.

To the lumber industry this movement of population was of double consequence. Minnesota was beginning to produce its own foodstuffs — a fact that enabled the lumbermen to venture on a bigger scale in Minnesota because they were assured of food for their men in the woods at a more reasonable price than the almost prohibitive cost of products brought the long distances from downriver or from Pembina. But even more important, the increasing population within the state opened a new market for the white pine of Minnesota.

Towns in Minnesota whose life depended on lumber increased in size as the new demand developed. One of these, which was to outgrow the others, is known today as Minneapolis. The first settlement of what is the present Minneapolis, however, was made on the east side of the Mississippi and remained a separate town known as St. Anthony until 1872 when it was incorporated with Minneapolis. Father Pierre Louis Hennepin, coming upon this site in 1680, had named the Falls for his patron saint, St. Anthony of Padua, who had guided him well in his long journey from Montreal to the Mississippi in the day when red men ruled the whole great valley of that river.

A ledge of limestone rock lying across the bed of the Mississippi determined the site of present-day Minneapolis. This ledge produced a waterfall whose force, once harnessed, would make this spot a manufacturing center. The hinterland to the west and northwest would someday be a market belonging exclusively to the town above the Falls. Stillwater, Red Wing, Winona, and other towns down the river might have the markets bordering along that stream, but the trade of the great Northwest was to be the prize of the town developing at the Falls. A traveler from Pennsylvania in 1855 said of St. Anthony that it was "one of the most romantick places on the Mississippi; nature has done for this place what she has not done for many others viz the river here falls over the rock some 20 feet and on both sides for 1½ miles leaves a butiful plain for building a city." [12]

It was Franklin Steele who first sensed the possibility of bringing together the forests of pine, which lay only about forty miles away on the Rum River, and the great water power of the Falls.[13] On the day after the receipt of the official notice of the ratification of the Treaty of 1837, by which the United States government purchased the lands of the Delta

[11] Williams, "History of the City of Saint Paul and of the County of Ramsey, Minnesota," *Minn. Hist. Soc. Coll.*, vol. iv, pp. 357–58.
[12] William K. McFarlane, "Minnesota as seen by the Travelers," *Minnesota History*, vol. vii (Dec. 1926), p. 337.
[13] *Minneapolis Tribune*, Aug. 31, 1873.

from the Indians, Steele located a claim on the east bank of the Mississippi at the Falls.[14] In 1848, when the government survey of this region was complete and the land was offered for sale at St. Croix Falls, Franklin Steele became the rightful proprietor of the lands on the east side of St. Anthony Falls by paying the sum of $1.25 an acre.[15] His claim reached from above Nicollet Island to a point below the Falls,[16] giving him control of the water power east of the middle of the main channel of the Mississippi. He was about to lay the foundation of the parent industry of Minneapolis, that of lumber.[17] Virtually he was the founder of Minneapolis.[18]

The hinterland was still in the hands of red men in 1848 when Steele began the erection of the first commercial sawmill at St. Anthony Falls,[19] but he must have foreseen that Minneapolis would become a great market. Credit is due him for his stamina in holding on under difficulties that at times would have made a less resolute man give up.

Franklin Steele had come to the Minnesota wilderness from Pennsylvania in 1837. President Van Buren had appointed him, presumably at the suggestion of Van Buren's predecessor, Andrew Jackson, to come to Fort Snelling as post sutler.[20] Steele accepted the appointment and in a short time established himself as a leading citizen of the territory.[21]

In 1847, while casting about for help in the venture of building a sawmill, Steele met Daniel Stanchfield, who had come from the pine woods in Maine. Stanchfield's background was lumber. He was born in the pine woods and for years had been cutting and driving logs down the Penobscot. On his way west in 1845 Stanchfield had stopped in the Wisconsin pineries. In 1847 he journeyed on to Minnesota, and on September 1 of that year he set out for the Rum River to cruise for white pine, having been engaged to do so by Steele. Stanchfield reported a tremendous range of pine. He had explored the Rum River to its source, Lake Mille Lacs,

[14] John H. Stevens, *Personal Recollections of Minnesota and Its People* (Minneapolis, 1890), p. 14; Folwell, *op. cit.*, vol. i, p. 452; Horace B. Hudson, editor, *A Half Century of Minneapolis* (Minneapolis, 1908), p. 27.

[15] Folwell, *op. cit.*, vol. i, pp. 183–84.

[16] Return I. Holcombe and William H. Bingham, historical editors, *Compendium of History and Biography of Minneapolis and Hennepin County, Minnesota* (Chicago, 1914), p. 152.

[17] Stanchfield, "History of Pioneer Lumbering on the Upper Mississippi," *Minn. Hist. Soc. Coll.*, vol. ix, pp. 340–41.

[18] Holcombe, *Minnesota in Three Centuries*, vol. ii, pp. 95–96.

[19] Cheney, "Development of Lumber Industry in Minnesota," *Journal of Geography*, vol. xiv, p. 190; N. S. B. Gras, "Significance of the Twin Cities," *Minnesota History*, vol. vii (1926), p. 9.

[20] Holcombe and Bingham, *op. cit.*, pp. 52–53.

[21] The *St. Anthony Express*, Jan. 24, 1852, notes a complimentary supper given by the people of St. Anthony in honor of Franklin Steele; on this occasion men came all the way from St. Louis to pay him honor. Daniel Stanchfield, another lumberman, speaks of this occasion in his article, "History of Pioneer Lumbering on the Upper Mississippi," *loc. cit.*, pp. 354–55.

and had found pine enough to furnish log stock for at least one genera-tion.[22] Steele accepted Stanchfield's report with enthusiasm.

On Stepember 1, 1848, exactly one year after Daniel Stanchfield set out to cruise the Rum River pineries, the first commercial sawmill in St. Anthony began its long grind. The machinery for the mill came from Bangor, Maine. An experienced millwright, Ard Godfrey, was brought from Orono in Maine to superintend the erection of the mill, and with him worked Calvin Tuttle, Caleb D. Dorr, and other Maineites who had come to seek their fortune at St. Anthony Falls. A Vermonter, R. P. Russell, who established himself at the Falls to furnish food supplies for the men at the mill, became the first merchant at St. Anthony.[23]

The mill was equipped with two up-and-down saws and a lath saw. Its maximum production was 15,000 feet a day. For two years Daniel Stanchfield was to furnish the raw material in the form of logs from the Rum River white pine.[24] From 500,000 to 700,000 feet of lumber was its output the first year.[25] The *Minnesota Pioneer* on August 9, 1849, stated that "the saws went into operation last autumn, and have had no rest since, night or day, except Sundays, and the demand for lumber at the Falls and at St. Paul, has not nearly been supplied. There will not be a sufficient supply for years, however many mills may be built, to keep pace with the growth of Minnesota and our wants for building and fencing materials."

The lumber industry was to become the greatest factor in the develop-ment of Minneapolis, even exceeding that of wheat and flour.[26] Indeed, the first known evidence of civilization at St. Anthony was a sawmill which the government had completed in 1822 to saw the lumber neces-sary for Fort Snelling.[27] The first commercial lumber mill, as we have noted, was built in 1848. There was no sign of any other private industry there until a grist mill put in its appearance in 1849.[28]

Capital was scarce in the new country, and it required skillful maneu-vering on the part of Franklin Steele to interest eastern investors in this

[22] Stanchfield, *op. cit.*, pp. 325–27, 333.

[23] Holcombe and Bingham, *op. cit.*, p. 152; Rodney C. Loehr, "Caleb D. Dorr and the Early Minnesota Lumber Industry," *Minnesota History*, vol. xxiv (1943), pp. 125–41.

[24] Stanchfield, *op. cit.*, pp. 341–43.

[25] Fred H. Gilman, "History of Minneapolis as a Lumber Manufacturing Point," *Mississippi Valley Lumberman*, vol. xxvi, Feb. 1, 1895, p. 72.

[26] Thomas B. Walker, "Minneapolis and her Lumber Industry," *Mississippi Valley Lumber-man*, vol. xxvi, Jan. 4, 1895, p. 8.

[27] Gilman, *op. cit.*, p. 71; Philander Prescott, "Autobiography and Reminiscences of Phi-lander Prescott," *Minn. Hist. Soc. Coll.*, vol. vi (St. Paul, 1894), p. 479; Edward A. Bromley, "The Old Government Mills at the Falls of St. Anthony," *Minn. Hist. Soc. Coll.*, vol. x, pt. 2 (St. Paul, 1905), p. 637; Folwell, *op. cit.*, vol. i, p. 140. A grist mill is also said to have been built there at that time.

[28] N. S. B. Gras, *An Introduction to Economic History* (New York, 1922), p. 300.

place on the edge of the frontier. It was said in 1840 that Steele was the wealthiest man in the Minnesota country, and he could command a capital of only $15,000 [29] — quite a sum of money for a pioneer of that day, but not a large capital with which to develop a new industry in a new country.

Casting about for assistance, Steele met William A. Cheever, who in 1847 made a claim on land near the present location of the University of Minnesota, and through Cheever and his brother Benjamin, who knew a number of wealthy Boston men, Steele was able to negotiate for money. Caleb Cushing, foremost citizen of Newburyport, Massachusetts, and Robert Rantoul of Boston were induced to invest $12,000 in Steele's mill. The agreement was signed on July 10, 1847, making these men from the East owners with Steele of the water power and the mill at St. Anthony. The property later reverted to Steele, however, since neither Rantoul nor Cushing was able to keep the agreement; drafts on Rantoul came back protested, and Cushing had become too heavily involved in the Mexican War.[30] Steele then associated Ard Godfrey with himself in the St. Anthony mill company. They did not incorporate, but Godfrey held a one-twentieth interest in the whole property.

On November 28, 1848, P. R. George, Steele's agent, wrote Steele from Boston that A. W. Taylor had made him a written proposition offering "fifteen thousand dollars for one undivided half of Mr. Steele's property at the falls of St. Anthony including the Island to which the dam is attached." Taylor stated further, "I will pay in a mortgage of a note of Ten Thousand dollars in my House in Somerset St. Ashburton place and the note of five thousand dollars, on other Real Estate making the note secure on Real Estate said notes to run three years int annually. The papers to be executed on the acceptance of Mr. Steele in writing to you at such time and place and in form as Mr. George may elect in the city of Boston or New York with three months of answer to this proposition."

George went on to say that this was the best arrangement he could make with the money market as it then was, and he urged Steele to accept the arrangement.[31] Steele accepted, and Arnold W. Taylor, "Esq.," of Boston became the principal owner with Steele and Godfrey in the mill property.[32] Not for long, however. In January 1852, Taylor sold his interest at the Falls back to Steele. In 1855 Steele sold one half of his interest

[29] Holcombe and Bingham, *op. cit.*, p. 67.
[30] Brackett Papers, 1855–1864, "History and Business of St. Anthony and Minneapolis," in Minnesota Historical Society.
[31] Steele Papers, George to Steele, Boston, Nov. 28, 1848.
[32] *St. Anthony Express*, Oct. 18, 1852.

to Davis, Sanford and Gebhardt of New York City, and John S. Prince and Richard Chute purchased one eighth.[33]

In the meantime lumber as a business was taking hold at St. Anthony. In 1849 two additional mills were built. The following year Caleb D. Dorr from Penobscot County in Maine brought the first shingle machine to Minnesota.[34] That same year Sumner W. Farnham from Maine took charge of the Steele mill and operated it for several years, cutting annually 1,200,000 feet.[35] In 1851 the Mississippi Boom Company was organized by Steele, Stanchfield, and Joseph R. Brown, and the St. Anthony Boom Company was formed by Steele, Godfrey, Farnham, and several others, in order to take care of the logs coming in ever-increasing numbers down the Mississippi to the mills just above the Falls.[36] In 1853 Minnesota newspapers freely ventured the opinion that the forests of the territory were more valuable to it than gold was to California.[37] White pine was gold in another form.

In 1854, the year in which the railroad reached the river at Rock Island, the demand for lumber became urgent and St. Anthony felt a pressing need for more mills.[38] That year Dorilus Morrison, a Maine lumberman, and J. A. Lovejoy, also from Maine, put in the first gang saw at St. Anthony Falls. The following spring a flood of immigrants poured into Minnesota and the steadily increasing home demand left little lumber to be exported.[39] But in 1856 the number of mills at the Falls again increased. That year Joel Bassett built a mill with a circular saw, the first such saw to operate at St. Anthony Falls. Its power was steam. The machinery for this mill came from Northampton, Massachusetts, and was brought by team from Dubuque, Iowa.

By this time eight mills were making logs into lumber at the Falls to the amount of 12,000,000 feet a year.[40] Yet it appeared that the home market would demand all that the mills could produce. Dorilus Morrison said no lumber was accumulating on his hands although his eight sash saws were making 40,000 feet every twenty-four hours.[41] His gang saw cut 15,000 feet per day. His equipment also included two circular saws. Morrison's mill, the best-equipped mill at the Falls of St. Anthony, had a capacity of 20,000,000 feet a year. This, at a time when lumber was selling for $16 to $25 per 1000 feet, meant substantial earnings for Morrison.

[33] Isaac Atwater, editor, *History of Minneapolis* (New York, 1893), p. 529.
[34] Stanchfield, *op. cit.,* pp. 355–56.
[35] *Minneapolis Tribune,* Jan. 1, 1887, p. 1.
[36] Atwater, *op. cit.,* p. 537.
[37] *St. Anthony Express,* June 10, 1853.
[38] *Ibid.,* Jan. 28, 1854.
[39] Folwell, *op. cit.,* vol. i, p. 359.
[40] Hotchkiss, *History of Lumber and Forest Industry of Northwest,* pp. 525, 539.
[41] *St. Anthony Express,* Apr. 5 and May 31, 1856.

An important factor making for increased building in St. Anthony itself in the late 1850s was the relation of rents to the cost of money for construction. Rents were high; the current rate of interest was low. There was consequently a remarkable increase in building, and a great improvement in the character of the buildings constructed.[42] The resulting demand for lumber pushed production. Fortunately, the necessary raw materials had been made even more easily accessible by the Chippewa Treaty of 1855 which opened up great pine forests around the headwaters of the Mississippi.

In 1858 one mill in St. Anthony was selling 50,000 feet of long lumber a day in season, plus 20,000 shingles and 25,000 laths a day.[43] At that time the mills at the Falls had a capacity of about 60,000,000 feet a year, but the home market — that is, the market within Minnesota — was eating voraciously of this production.[44]

The lumbermen who established themselves at St. Anthony came largely from Maine. The coming of Daniel Stanchfield marked the beginning of a migration of woodsmen from that state to the Falls of St. Anthony which in the 1850s became continuous. From Maine and other New England states on the very eastern border of the white pine came armies of lumbermen, carrying the ax into the unexploited regions of the same kind of forest in the West. They came as though drawn by a magnet. Maine and Minnesota had much in common. The climate, much of the topography, and the natural resources of Minnesota were like those of Maine. The men who had learned lumbering firsthand on the banks of the Penobscot, or the Androscoggin, or the turbulent St. Croix, easily transplanted themselves to the business of rolling logs on the Mississippi, the Rum, or the St. Croix in Minnesota. "I'm from Maine" was all the reference necessary to secure a job in and around St. Anthony in the lumber days.[45]

Prominent in this group of Maine lumbermen were Ard Godfrey, Caleb Dorr, S. W. Farnham, C. C. Washburn, W. D. Washburn, Dorilus Morrison, Clinton Morrison, and Leonard Day and his three sons. From the same "White Pine" state came John De Laittre, Howard De Laittre, J. M. Robinson, J. A. Lovejoy, O. A. Pray, and Charles A. Bovey.

New Hampshire followed Maine's example, sending equally able men such as John S. Pillsbury, George A. Pillsbury, and their nephews, Charles A. and E. C. Pillsbury, together with old Joel B. Bassett, William W. Eastman, and John W. Eastman. Captain John Martin and Roscoe

[42] Wheelock, *Minnesota: Its Place among the States,* p. 150.
[43] *Minneapolis Gazette,* Apr. 20, 1858.
[44] *Minneapolis Tribune,* Jan. 1, 1883, p. 8.
[45] *Mississippi Valley Lumberman,* vol. xxvi, Feb. 1, 1895, p. 71.

P. Russell came from Vermont. Massachusetts sent A. W. Taylor, and Connecticut, Henry Titus Welles.[46] These men were to change trees into hard dollars and make the "wilderness bud and blossom as the rose." [47] There is hardly one of them whose career would not cover important pages in the history of Minneapolis, and the descendants of many of them are still active in that city and in the Northwest today.

One of the early lumbermen who left a strong impress on the state was John S. Pillsbury, who established the leading hardware house in the Northwest at St. Anthony with the chief purpose of supplying lumbermen. He soon read the signs of the time and invested in pinelands. Pillsbury was always associated more or less with lumber after 1857, and in 1878 he was the principal in the formation of C. A. Smith and Company, one of the few concerns to survive when lumbering became "big business." He was a lumberman before he became a flour manufacturer. Indeed, there is evidence that "Pillsbury's Best" owes something to Minnesota's white pine. It was in 1872 that Pillsbury joined his nephew, C. A. Pillsbury, in the manufacture of flour. In the development of industry in Minnesota John S. Pillsbury holds a key place — and in government too, for Minnesota elected him governor three successive times.[48]

William D. Washburn stood shoulder-high with John S. Pillsbury. From Androscoggin County in Maine he came to practice law at St. Anthony. He hung out his shingle, but in 1867 he advertised that he carried "every variety of pine lumber" [49] and he came in time to be regarded as one of the most intelligent lumbermen in the Northwest.[50] He, too, turned eventually from lumbering to flour milling, and like Pillsbury he served his state; he became United States senator from Minnesota.

Another lumberman who became a public figure in Minneapolis was Dorilus Morrison, the veteran from Bangor, Maine, who, as we have seen, came to St. Anthony Falls in 1853 and who chose to grow old there sawing lumber. In 1867, when Minneapolis received its first charter, he was chosen its mayor.[51] So might continue the list of lumbermen who pioneered in the development of an industry which was powerful enough to build a city and to forge a strong link in the making of a state.

[46] Atwater, *op. cit.*, p. 527; Hotchkiss, *op. cit.*, pp. 539–63; Stanchfield, *op. cit.*, pp. 348–61.

[47] *St. Anthony Express*, Nov. 11, 1854; *Minneapolis Tribune*, Jan. 26, 1868, pp. 1–2, and Mar. 1, 1885, p. 16.

[48] Stanchfield, *op. cit.*, pp. 359–60; *Minneapolis Tribune*, Mar. 1, 1885, p. 16; Atwater, *op. cit.*, pp. 566, 592.

[49] *Minneapolis Tribune*, June 5, 1867.

[50] Hotchkiss, *op. cit.*, pp. 547–48.

[51] *Minneapolis Tribune*, Jan. 26, 1868; *Report of the Minneapolis Board of Trade*, 1876, p. 70. (After 1883 this was called *Annual Report of the Minneapolis Chamber of Commerce*.)

The sawing of rough lumber was not the only work which these men developed in the new country. Subsidiary industries in which lumber was used as a material developed almost as fast as the sawmills. Such industries served as a market for lumber in the rough. The incoming settlers needed doors, window sashes, plows, carriages, chairs, churns, and other things essential even to the crude life of the frontier. To make such supplies men set themselves up in business near the sawmills. Every saw-town had sash and door industries, but St. Anthony and Minneapolis quickly acquired more than their competitors. In 1854 at least three firms in Minneapolis were making doors and sashes.[52] When the first Nicollet House opened its doors in Minneapolis all the furniture from "the most magnificent fauteuil to the commonest chair," with the exception of the mirrors, was made in George F. Warner's shop in Minneapolis.[53] Carriages and chairs were made by one James F. Bradley in Lower Town, Minneapolis.[54] Several plowmakers had also settled at the Falls.[55] In 1856 fanning mills too were made there.[56]

An even newer industry found its way to Minnesota, since no wood ranks above the white pine in the making of boxes and crates;[57] it is tasteless and odorless as well as inexpensive. Boxes and crates were being made in St. Anthony in 1856, but it was Joel Bassett who entered that business in an extensive way a few years later. Bassett made pails, tubs, bushel measures, churns, sap buckets, and other similar utensils which found markets in St. Louis, Cincinnati, Chicago, and Pittsburgh in an annual volume aggregating thousands of dollars.[58] By 1861 a million feet of logs were being used annually in the manufacture of pails, tubs, and the like in Minnesota.[59]

Rapid and extensive as the growth of lumbering at St. Anthony was, it was not the sole center of the industry to develop in this period. In the southern part of Minnesota Territory was located the county of Wabashaw, so named for the great Sioux chief who was active in the negotiation of the Indian Treaty of 1851. Wabashaw County was not the size of an ordinary county in Minnesota today; it was bounded on the south by Iowa, on the east by the Mississippi, on the west by the Missouri, and on the north by a line drawn westward from the junction of the St. Croix and the Mississippi. This section had no extensive forest of white pine

[52] *Northwestern Democrat* (St. Anthony), Oct. 7 and Jan. 21, 1854.
[53] *Minneapolis Gazette*, June 22, 1855.
[54] *Northwestern Democrat*, Nov. 25, 1854.
[55] *St. Anthony Express*, Jan. 21, 1854.
[56] *Minnesota Democrat*, Sept. 6, 1856, and Mar. 14, 1867.
[57] H. W. Maxwell, "The Story of the White Pine," *American Forestry*, vol. xxi, pp. 34–36.
[58] *State Atlas* (St. Anthony), July 27, 1864.
[59] Joseph A. Wheelock, *Minnesota: Its Progress and Capabilities*, 1862, pp. 82–83.

as did much of Minnesota Territory, but it did have the finest farming land in the region. A substantial market for white pine would develop in the process of settlement in the region.

In the southeastern portion of Wabashaw County the first installment of lands surveyed by the United States in this newly acquired "Suland" was offered for sale in 1855. Then began settlement, which as usual followed the river valleys branching off from the Mississippi. The rich farm lands of the Whitewater, the Rollingstone, and the Zumbro valleys, all reaching westward from the Mississippi, were settled first. A point on the Mississippi where a number of these small valleys converged became the center of trade for that region. The place was first called Wabasha Prairie, but shortly people of a romantic mind gave it the name of Winona in memory of the comely Indian maid whose loyalty had become a legend in Minnesota.

Winona, on flat land on the west bank of the Mississippi, was snugly protected by hills at her back, and beyond those hills lay some of Minnesota's richest farm land. The pioneers on that farm land had to have shelter, which meant lumber. Winona became a point of lumber manufacture. There was no commercial white pine in the vicinity of Winona, but logs came from the St. Croix or the Chippewa in the form of rafts, and at Winona those logs were changed into lumber with which to build farm homes.

The history of this lumber town dates from 1852. It was in that year that John Chamberlain Laird came to Winona (still called Wabasha Prairie) to assist his sister, who had recently lost her husband. The sister had come from the Susquehanna Valley in Pennsylvania as the bride of a Goddard who had moved to Wabasha Prairie to serve as its first postmaster. Shortly after their arrival the husband died from malaria. Winona's possibilities must have appealed strongly to John C. Laird, for in 1855 his two brothers, Matthew J. and William H., came to join him. On November 20, 1855, the *Winona Republican* presented "Laird and Brothers as Wholesale and Retail Dealers in Lumber, Shingles and Lath, Winona, M. T.," although their first lumber had been sold in June 1855.

At first the Lairds, having no sawmill, purchased all their lumber ready-made from mills in Chippewa and St. Croix valleys and brought it to Winona in rafts handled by sweeps and poles. In 1856 they were joined by their cousins, James L. and Matthew G. Norton, the firm name becoming "Laird, Norton & Company." John C. Laird and Matthew J. Laird retired shortly from the business to enter other fields, but William H. Laird and the two Norton brothers continued as co-partners in the firm.[60] In 1883 they reorganized and took the name by which the firm is known today: the Laird, Norton Company.[61]

Meanwhile, in 1855, the very year in which the Lairds began to market lumber, was built the first of the ten sawmills of Winona's lumber history. This mill was owned by James Highland and James Wycoff. It was a steam mill equipped with a muley and a circular saw, and it could produce from 25,000 to 30,000 feet a day, a quantity hitherto unheard of in the new frontier country.[62] The muley had formerly held the ground as the best saw, but the muley was cutting at breakneck speed when it was producing 5000 feet a day. So, with markets growing steadily, all new mills in Minnesota were adding the circular saw as an essential improvement. This first Winona mill had also purchased Kendall's double-acting shingle river and shaver, which was warranted to rive and shave 3000 shingles per hour from the block. The machine-made shingle was said to be superior to handmade ones.[63]

The Highland-Wycoff mill was soon sold to L. C. Porter and William Garlock, who in 1858 advertised that they would take farmer's produce — wheat, flour, corn, oats, beans, pork, and butter — in exchange for lumber.[64] They offered credit, too, with a part payment down and security for the remaining principal and interest. Winona rapidly became the market to which the farmers brought their grain to exchange for what they needed.[65] Porter's and Garlock's property passed through several hands until in 1866 it was owned by Charles Horton and Andrew Hamilton, who came to be lumbermen of long standing in Winona.

In 1857 Laird, Norton and Company built their own mill, the second in Winona. It had the usual muley saw used for slabbing and cutting logs, and also a circular saw used for cutting cants into lumber. In ten hours this mill could produce 25,000 feet of lumber.[66]

The Lairds and the Nortons were followed soon by Earle S. and Addison B. Youmans, who came from New York to establish themselves

[60] This information was given the writer in a personal interview with Orrin F. Smith, a nephew of the Lairds, on May 4, 1934; George W. Hotchkiss to Laird, Norton Company, April 20, 1898, private letter books of W. H. Laird, vol. v, Laird, Norton Papers, Laird, Norton Company, Winona, Minnesota.

[61] Paul Thompson, "Lumber Barons Guided Community through Early History," *Winona Republican Herald*, Feb. 22, 1934, p. 9.

[62] Hotchkiss, *op. cit.*, p. 564.

[63] *Winona Republican Herald*, Jan. 6, 1856.

[64] *Ibid.*, Sept. 1, 1858.

[65] In 1860 Winona shipped 1,000,000 bushels of wheat, while Red Wing and Hastings, her competitors on the river in Minnesota, shipped 600,000 and 350,000 bushels, respectively (Wheelock, *Minnesota: Its Place among the States*, p. 92).

[66] Franklyn Curtiss-Wedge, editor, *The History of Winona County* (Chicago, 1913), pp. 178, 180; Laird, Norton Papers, George W. Hotchkiss to Laird, Norton Company, Apr. 20, 1898.

in the new West.[67] They established their mill at Winona in October 1857 and figured largely in the development of the vast hinterland that lay on the plateau above them.[68] Their mill began modestly with one muley saw. Two years later, however, they added a circular saw and thereafter steadily improved their mill to meet the demands of the market. In 1865 their mill boasted two circular saws, an edger, a slab saw, and a shingle and lath mill. In 1871 this firm employed a hundred hands and cut 9,000,000 feet of lumber.[69] Youmans Brothers secured their log stock largely from the St. Croix country in the early period of operations from 1858 to 1870.[70]

Four firms figure prominently in Winona's lumber life: the Laird, Norton Company; Youmans Brothers, who were later joined by A. L. Hodgins; the Empire Lumber Company, which entered the field in 1886 with Charles Horton as a member of the firm; and the Winona Lumber Company, headed by Andrew Hamilton.[71] These companies turned to their profit the wealth of raw lumber, the ready Mississippi, and the market of Winona's hinterland; and in so doing they made Winona a leading lumber center.

It is interesting to observe that Maine men played no part in the development of the lumber industry in Winona. In Stillwater and Minneapolis the industry drew its leadership as well as its labor from Maine or some other New England state, but the leadership in Winona came from New York and Pennsylvania. Both these states were prominent in the production of white pine, but the men who set themselves up in the lumber industry in Winona had not had the immediate experience in lumber that the Maine men had had.

The two Youmans brothers came from New York state, where their forebears were "honest farmers."[72] Like other young men of the time, the two brothers set out to find their fortune in the West, staked partly by money which their father had made in the California gold rush. One brother had already visited Wisconsin, so they decided to settle there, choosing La Crosse on the Mississippi as a desirable place. They planned to become bankers but were advised that lumbering would be a less precarious business in the panic year of 1857. Wabasha Prairie on the Mississippi, they were told, was an excellent place for a sawmill. There the formation of the river was such that log booms could easily be made to

[67] Interview of the writer with C. M. Youmans, Winona, May 2, 1934.

[68] Thompson, *op. cit.*, p. 9.

[69] Hotchkiss, *op. cit.*, p. 564.

[70] Folsom, "History of Lumbering in the St. Croix Valley," *Minn. Hist. Soc. Coll.*, vol. ix, pp. 320–21.

[71] *Mississippi Valley Lumberman*, vol. xx, Nov. 27, 1891, p. 4; interview of the writer with Roscoe Horton, Winona, May 2, 1934.

[72] Interview of the writer with C. M. Youmans, Winona, May 2, 1934.

which logs could be sent from the St. Croix and the Chippewa. Now three generations of Youmans have sold lumber at Winona.

John Chamberlain Laird and his brothers came from Lewisburg, located on the west branch of the Susquehanna in Pennsylvania not far from Williamsport, a great white pine center. John had taught school and had worked on his father's farm but seems never to have made any close acquaintance with the ax. He, also, had come west to La Crosse, Wisconsin, where he had secured a position as deputy register of deeds. In 1852 he went a little farther up the Mississippi to Wabasha Prairie — to help his sister, as we have seen — and there he stayed. Of his two brothers, Matthew J. had worked on the farm while his father held the position of judge of probate in their home county in Pennsylvania, and William H. had clerked in a store owned and operated by his brother-in-law. William was only twenty-two when he sold his first lumber in Winona.

James and Matthew Norton also came from Lewisburg, Pennsylvania. James, the older, was thirty-one when he came to Winona. His business career had begun at the age of twelve when he rode a mule on the tow-path of the Pennsylvania Canal for six dollars a month. At sixteen he was apprenticed to a carpenter and he continued in carpentry until he was twenty-seven — excellent training, no doubt, for a future lumberman. Then he and his brother Matthew, who had had the advantage of graduating from Lewisburg Academy, a Baptist school which later became Bucknell University, had gone to work for an uncle who was building a railroad from Portland, Maine, to Montreal. Lumber was used in large quantities in railroad construction in those days, and the Norton boys came to know the quality as well as the price of lumber. They learned where the sources of labor were, and, even more important, they saved some money with which they could begin operations in the West. James and Matthew Norton and William H. Laird remained lumbermen in Winona until the end of their days.[73]

From 1858 to 1868 Winona produced 160,000,000 feet of lumber. A small portion of this was marketed downriver, but the larger share was sold to the incoming settlers on the uplands above. Winona in the sixties could hardly keep pace with the demand for lumber.[74]

Three counties in Minnesota had mills producing commercial lumber by 1860 — Hennepin, Winona, and Washington, all of which were located on navigable streams. Winona County, with its chief mills at Winona, in the census year produced lumber valued at $97,050; Hennepin County,

[73] Letter to the writer from Orrin F. Smith, July 21, 1937; Laird, Norton Papers, George Hotchkiss to Laird, Norton Company, Apr. 20, 1898.
[74] *Minneapolis Tribune*, July 3, 1869.

whose mills were at St. Anthony Falls, valued its lumber production at $212,400; while Washington County, with mills at Marine and Stillwater, established a bit earlier than those of Hennepin and Winona, set the value of its lumber output at $419,650.[75] That year Governor Ramsey estimated that the exportable surplus of lumber produced in those counties was worth $629,000.[76]

The growth of sawmills in Minnesota at this time was largely dependent on the expansion of settlement. In spite of the Panic of 1857, which halted somewhat the march into the West, Minnesota's population in 1860 reached 172,023.[77] The areas known as Maine Prairie and Sauk Valley were fast filling with people from New England and Germany. In the fall of 1858 eighty-seven immigrant wagons were reported to have passed into Stearns County at Fowlers Ferry.[78] Those wagons brought to Minnesota hard-fisted farmers with families, cattle, and farm implements. Thrifty Swedes were already claiming Chisago County as their own even as early as 1858.[79]

The Homestead Act of 1862 added greater strength to the movement. Where unoccupied land still remained, 160 acres were given on certain conditions without any charge to any citizen or anyone who had declared his intention of becoming a citizen. Three years after the passing of the Homestead Act, the population of Minnesota totaled 250,099 — an increase of 78,077, or 43 per cent, since 1860.[80]

Settlement was moving inland and away from the Mississippi. The hardwood zone was sought first. Its soil was unusually productive and it had fuel and water, which were important to the settler in a new country. In 1865 Minnesota's well-populated counties were in the southeast corner, the hardwood zone of the state. Fillmore County — lying in the second tier of counties west of the Mississippi — had, with its 17,524 inhabitants, the largest population in the state. Fillmore was distinctly an agricultural county — it boasted not a single town with a population of 2000; it had rich soil, largely covered by hardwood, with its western edge on the fringe of the prairie.

Hennepin County was second in population, and Winona was third, followed in turn by Olmsted, Ramsey, Goodhue, Dakota, Wabasha, and Rice. These nine counties each had a population of more than 10,000

---

[75] *U.S. Census, 1860*, vol. iii: *Manufactures*, pp. 278–79.

[76] Message of Governor Ramsey, Jan. 9, 1861, *Minn. Exec. Docs.*, 1860, no. 1, p. 4.

[77] Jenks, "The People of Minnesota," *Proceedings, Minnesota Academy of Social Science*, vol. ii, p. 202; Wheelock, *Minnesota: Its Place among the States*, pp. 109–12.

[78] *St. Cloud Democrat*, Oct. 21 and Dec. 9, 1858.

[79] *Stillwater Messenger*, Sept. 7, 1858.

[80] *Census of the State of Minnesota*, 1865, extracted from the *Annual Report of the Secretary of State of Minnesota*, p. 112.

in 1865.[81] Six of them lay along the Mississippi, and three were in the second tier of counties back from the river.

All these counties lay in southeastern Minnesota, where settlement was now pushing farther inland. Fillmore, Olmsted, and Rice counties were not located on navigable streams. Fillmore had the Root River as the main stem of its waterway; Olmsted had the Zumbro, joined by a number of lesser streams; Rice County had the Cannon. But none of these was large enough for navigation and the settlers along them could get to market only by ox team. A committee in the state legislature reported even as early as 1861 that the mean distance for the farmers of the state to the nearest navigable river was eighty miles.[82] Those who lived within a distance of three days of the market by ox team were considered fortunate. The markets to which they carried the wheat and where they purchased lumber at this time were Mankato and St. Peter on the Minnesota; Stillwater on the St. Croix; and St. Anthony, St. Paul, Hastings, Red Wing, Wabasha, and Winona on the Mississippi.

Farmers came to Winona all the way from Owatonna, Clinton Falls, and Blooming Prairie to buy their lumber; all these towns were located in Steele County, in the fourth tier of counties west of the Mississippi. The length of the smoothly paved state highway from Owatonna to Winona at the present time is ninety miles, a distance comfortably covered in two hours by automobile. But in the late 1850s and early 1860s it was a long and hard trip.

Farmers would travel in groups with four, six, or eight teams of oxen. These grizzled men of the new West were accustomed to the cold, so they could sleep out in the open under the winter sky. They carried their food because inns were few and far between. A round trip from Blooming Prairie to Winona required at least six days. Stockton, located on the western edge of the Winona hills, marked the gateway from the plateau to the valley below. To reach the river town from the uplands was a rough, winding drive of eleven miles. Before beginning the descent into the valley the farmers from the back country spent the night at Stockton's well-known inn. After a long day's trip from Stockton to Winona and back, they again spent the night at the inn before they started on their tedious journey homeward. They usually carried wheat to Winona and brought back lumber and groceries.

Winona lumbermen considered the region westward, including Owatonna and its environs, their market in the days of oxen.[83] They sensed

[81] *Ibid.*, pp. 110–11.
[82] *Minn. Exec. Docs.*, 1861, p. 2; *Winona Daily Republican*, May 21, 1863.
[83] Interviews of the writer with the following: C. M. Youmans, Winona, Minn., May 2, 1934; Orrin F. Smith, Winona, Minn., May 4, 1934; Mrs. E. E. Hauge, Northfield, Minn., Feb. 14, 1935, whose grandfather, a pioneer settler at Clinton Falls, hauled lumber from Winona.

early the need for better roads, and on August 13, 1857, a meeting was called in Winona to plan the building of a road up the Stockton Hill.[84] These men of business in Winona were always mindful of the market in the interior. In 1857 Laird, Norton and Company urged their "interior friends" to note that they could "supply all our inland towns" with lumber "of qualities to satisfy the most particular."[85] Lumber advertisements stating that "grain will be taken in part pay at cash prices" were not unusual.[86] Steele County, Olmsted, and Fillmore were all a part of the back country whose market belonged to Winona, although farmers in southern Fillmore County sometimes hauled their lumber from Mc-Gregor, farther south on the Mississippi in Iowa.[87] But that lumber, too, was white pine from the Upper Mississippi which had been rafted down-river.

The long haul to the river town was fraught with difficulty and danger. The roads were little better than prairie trails and forest paths. The present generation speeding up Stockton Hill on a beautifully constructed piece of road, which cost the state of Minnesota about $700,000, can hardly imagine the unfordable streams of the spring and the heavy, almost impassable roads where the pioneer made his way when the winter thaw was passing.[88] Much hauling was done in the winter, but the snow drifts, the pitch holes, and the sharp, cold wind made the trip to market one the farmers dreaded. There were the Indians, too, and at times there were robbers.[89] The trip to market was no small incident in pioneer life.

Farmers also drove long distances to St. Anthony.[90] In the spring of 1862 teams carried loads 150 miles into the interior; some of them went as far as 50 miles southwest of Mankato. Although lumber was costly at this period because of war demands and a generally high price level, scores of teams early made their way to Carver County heavily laden with lumber for building. Carver was being settled by immigrants from Germany, ambitious folk who were planting permanent homes in a new land. They provided a market for the mills at the Falls.[91]

[84] Interview of the writer with Orrin F. Smith, May 4, 1934.

[85] *Winona Republican*, Oct. 6, 1857.

[86] *Ibid.*, Mar. 24, 1858.

[87] The writer's mother, Mrs. H. O. Larson, said that her father built a new home in 1858 in western Fillmore County and that the siding and the shingles were hauled by oxen from McGregor, a distance of over a hundred miles.

[88] C. C. Colwell, Office Engineer, Department of Highways, Minnesota, at St. Paul, stated in a letter to the writer, Aug. 28, 1935, that the Stockton Hill road of about 4.16 miles cost the state as follows: construction, $491,271.93; right of way, $27,819.90; engineering, $27,686.08; total $546,777.91. It was estimated that the cost of paving which was under way then would be about $125,000.

[89] H. M. Larson, *Wheat Market and Farmer in Minnesota*, pp. 23–24.

[90] *Minneapolis Gazette*, Apr. 13, 1862.

[91] *State Atlas*, Oct. 21, 1863.

Even as late as 1869 farmers drove their teams a distance of 140 miles from Fort Dodge, Iowa, to Mankato in order to obtain lumber which had come from St. Anthony Falls.[92] Eastman, Bovey and Company, who established themselves in the lumber business in Minneapolis in the late sixties, made their first sale to William Van Elps from Big Sioux Falls, Dakota Territory, 225 miles from Minneapolis. That lumber was carried by railroad to St. James, a railroad terminus in Minnesota, whence it was hauled by teams 120 miles to Big Sioux Falls.[93]

There was, however, a limit to the distance over which horse or ox team could be used economically in hauling heavy loads. Only the railroad could extend the market on the prairie, for only the railroad could provide sufficiently cheap transportation for long-distance hauling. Minnesota early had played with the idea of railroad building within its own boundaries — the territorial legislature granted a total of twenty-seven railroad charters — but even in 1857 there was not a single mile of railroad within the territory.[94] Railroads chartered in Minnesota had ambitious names — for instance, the "Great New Orleans & Minnesota Railroad" and the "Lake Superior, Puget Sound & Pacific"; the latter, with an authorized capital of $50,000,000, had the most ambitious plan of all the roads chartered in the state.[95] The territorial government in 1857 granted a $5,000,000 loan for the purpose of aiding railroad construction, but 1857 was no time in which to issue bonds and the project failed.[96]

Lumbermen early foresaw how railroads would affect their industry. "What an enormous extent of country will buy lumber of us as soon as there are railroads to carry it!" was the cry of newspapers at the lumber centers.[97] Not one fiftieth as much lumber was manufactured in Minnesota as would be if railroads were established, said a paper from the Falls in 1858. When the $5,000,000 railroad loan was being considered, the same newspaper from the Falls, in an article on the lumbermen and the railroads, stated: "They will not vote against it. This class we are satisfied will present a solid phalanx in favor of it when they go to the polls on the 15th of April. . . . The lumbermen are too well acquainted with their interests to oppose it. They know what their market now is,

---

[92] *Minneapolis Tribune*, July 7, 1869.

[93] *Minneapolis Daily Tribune*, June 9, 1871.

[94] Rasmus S. Saby, "Railroad Legislation in Minnesota, 1849–1875," *Minn. Hist. Soc. Coll.*, vol. xv (St. Paul, 1915), p. 11.

[95] *Report of the Minnesota Railroad Commission*, 1871, pp. 6, 27–32, 35–50, 52. Folwell, *op. cit.*, vol. i, pp. 327, 329. The title of the reports of the railroad commission changed with the years. From 1871 to 1874 and from 1876 to 1884 it was *Report of Railroad Commissioner*; in 1875 it was *Report of Railroad Commission*; from 1885 on, it was *Report of Railroad and Warehouse Commission*.

[96] Folwell, *op. cit.*, vol. ii, pp. 37–58.

[97] *State Atlas* (Minneapolis), Mar. 5, 1862.

and they also know what it would be, were these roads in operation." [98]
In the official canvass Winona cast 1182 votes, of which all but one were
in favor of the loan! [99]

Even towns depending on the river urgently felt the need of railroads,
for the river was not reliable. In the winter it was frozen; in the summer
it was often too low for navigation. This was the experience of Mankato,
lumber emporium on the Minnesota River. It received its lumber by a
water route from St. Anthony and distributed it to a wide hinterland.
The price as well as the supply of its lumber was in some measure determined by the condition of the river.

"There is a large country to be supplied from this town," S. Randall
of Mankato stated in a letter to Franklin Steele in 1859.[1] Later in the
same year the Mankatoan addressed a letter to the sawmill operator at
St. Anthony saying, "My sales are increasing and the greatest trouble
is going to be that I will not have enough lumber to last me until Spring
so I want you to improve the Boating while it lasts and send me all the
lumber the Boat will put on." On one occasion, when an order for lumber
came from Fort Ridgeley, Randall wrote Steele that the water was so
low he could not send the lumber up by boats but "they will probably
send after it with Teams." [2] A single order sent by Randall to Steele
gives evidence that the lumber used in the back country was of no small
account to the manufacturer: [3]

23 to 40 m. feet clear inch Bds.	
20 to 30 m. feet clear 1½ inch Bds.	
10 to 15 m. feet clear 1¼ inch Bds.	
10 to 15 m. feet clear 2 inch Bds.	
25 to 40 m. feet	Siding
60 to 80 m. feet	Good Common Bds.
15 to 20 m. feet	Flooring
5 m. feet	Dim. 4x4
5 m. feet	Battings.
5 m. feet	Dim. 6x6 and 6x8
15 m. feet	Pickets, 1x3–4 feet long.
5 m. feet	Do light 1½
150 to 200 m.	Laths
100 to 150 m.	Sawed Shingles

On April 9, 1860, clear boards to the amount of 12,335 feet were shipped
from Mendota to Randall at Mankato on the *Little Dorrit*. Along with

---

[98] *Minneapolis Gazette*, Apr. 13, 1858.
[99] Folwell, *op. cit.*, vol. ii, p. 49.
[1] Steele Papers, S. Randall to Steele, Mankato, Minn., July 20, 1859.
[2] *Ibid.*, Aug. 12 and Sept. 1, 1859.
[3] *Ibid.*, Jan. 26, 1860.

the shipment were sent twelve bunches of window sash and 5250 shingles.[4] But there was the usual complaint: "The water is very low this spring, and unless we have a considerable rise soon . . . lumber will be higher."[5]

Finally in 1862 the railroads made a modest beginning in Minnesota. The St. Paul and Pacific was the pioneer road which, in a ten-mile stretch, united St. Paul and St. Anthony. In less than a decade that road crossed the state in a northwesterly direction, reaching the rich Red River Valley and the Minnesota boundary at Breckenridge. The promoters of the road soon built another line to Sauk Rapids, where a large agricultural hinterland was in the making.[6] The St. Paul and Pacific opened up the richest wheat land of Minnesota to settlement.[7] St. Anthony had lumber and the Red River Valley had wheat, and railroads were to carry wheat to the Falls and lumber back again.

Winona, meanwhile, was well aware that, if it intended to extend its industry, it must not allow St. Anthony or any other lumber town to seize its market.[8] It had another competitor in La Crosse, a town to the south on the Wisconsin side of the Mississippi whose life was also lumber. La Crosse was eager to extend its market westward and capital was advanced to aid in building a railroad from Grand Crossing, opposite La Crosse on the Minnesota side of the Mississippi, into the western country. This road, called the Southern Minnesota, was built through the southernmost tier of counties in Minnesota, a rich agricultural region where the population was filling in more rapidly than in any other part of the state. The road reached Winnebago in the fateful panic year.

Winona had no choice; in order to preserve its market in the hinterland, it, too, must build railroads. So in 1862 the rails of the Winona and St. Peter (sometimes called the Transit Railroad) began to climb Stockton Hill and head straight west to tap the newer settlements developing in Winona's hinterland. Five years later the *Daily Republican* reported that "every day the freight trains going west take large quantities [of lumber] to the interior,"[9] and soon the Winona papers were boasting that "the shortest and most direct route from Puget Sound to Chicago is by way of . . . Yellowstone, Breckenridge and Winona."[10] In 1872 the Winona and St. Peter reached Dakota Territory.[11]

Even so, Winona's one railroad could not long compete with the many

[4] Steele Papers, bill for lumber shipped to S. Randall, Mankato, Apr. 9, 1860, from Mendota.
[5] Steele Papers, Henry Reynolds to Steele, Fort Snelling, Mar. 31, 1860.
[6] *Report of the Minnesota Railroad Commissioner,* 1872, pp. 7–8.
[7] *Report of the Minneapolis Board of Trade,* 1876, pp. 34–37.
[8] *Winona Republican Herald,* Nov. 20, 1930, p. 8.
[9] *Winona Daily Republican,* July 17, 1867.
[10] *Winona Republican,* Jan. 5, 1870.
[11] *Ibid.,* Feb. 14, 1872.

taking their start from St. Anthony and St. Paul. Those towns were well on the way to becoming metropolitan centers, and promoters seemed to sense in them possibilities not offered by the others. In 1867 through traffic began from St. Paul to Chicago via the Minnesota Central, which traveled southward from St. Paul through Northfield, Faribault, Owatonna, and Austin; in Iowa it connected with the McGregor and Western, which joined the Milwaukee and St. Paul at Prairie du Chien.[12] The region penetrated by these roads was good farming country and for some time had been regarded by lumbermen as an important outlet for lumber.[13]

In 1869 St. Paul became the starting point of another railroad when the River Road was constructed along the winding course of the Mississippi on its west side. This road reached Winona two years later and was completed to La Crescent, opposite La Crosse, the following year.[14] The river at La Crosse was bridged in 1871, and the two Minnesota roads running to La Crescent were joined to the Milwaukee Road on the Wisconsin side of the river. Minnesota was feeling more intensely the busy throb of a larger commercial world.

In 1870 the Lake Superior and Mississippi struck northward, eventually uniting St. Paul and Duluth. That was a great occasion because it brought St. Paul nearer, so to speak, to the Atlantic coast; but even more important, it gave St. Paul a way east which was independent of Chicago. Yet another railroad was to find its way out from St. Paul, through the hardwood zone into the prairie to the southwest: the St. Paul and Sioux City, once called the Minnesota Valley. This road followed the Minnesota River as far as Mankato; then striking off to the southwest, it reached St. James, where it was joined to the Sioux City and St. Paul in 1872. Hitherto this southwestern prairie region had had no practicable means of transportation.[15]

By 1870, then, the railroads of Minnesota totaled 1550 miles, and they had begun to influence the great industry in the white pine country. In 1867 the two saw-towns on opposite sides of the Falls of St. Anthony cut 77,419,548 feet, a distinct increase since 1856. In 1868 the mills at the Falls were shipping daily from fifty to seventy-five cars of lumber by way of the Milwaukee and Minneapolis Railroad and the Minnesota Valley Railroad. Alongside the tracks of the Milwaukee in Minneapolis, piles and piles of assorted lumber awaited shipment.

In the winter and spring of 1869 the demand at the Falls was so heavy

[12] Report of the Minnesota Railroad Commissioner, 1872, p. 7.
[13] State Atlas (Minneapolis), July 27, 1864.
[14] Report of the Minnesota Railroad Commissioner, 1872, p. 9.
[15] Ibid., 1871, p. 39; 1872, pp. 13–14.

that mills were nearly cleaned out of shingles and flooring, and men talked about the "magnitude" of the Minneapolis lumber industry. Mankato, a market for Minneapolis lumber, on some days during that summer sold 40,000 feet of lumber. The yardmaster of the Milwaukee Railroad, John Jarvis, reported that on July 27 of that year eighty-one cars of lumber were loaded in their yard in Minneapolis.

In an opposite direction the St. Paul and Pacific was forging its way into a region as yet quite unsettled, but as the railroad gradually made conquest of the Northwest possible the demand for lumber from that section became immense. In the summer of 1869 railroads were taxed to capacity to transport lumber, and dealers could hardly keep lumber in the yards long enough to season it well.[16]

In that year the Falls lumbermen gave evidence of the growing importance of their industry when they formed the Lumbermen's Association of Minneapolis and St. Anthony; manufacturers and dealers came together "to encourage conformity of prices and the general encouragement of the lumber interest."[17] The following prominent lumbermen and firms at the Falls were listed in the group:[18]

W. E. Jones & Company	Leonard Day & Sons
W. H. Eldred	B. S. Bull & Company
Harris & Putnam	Farnham & Lovejoy
J. Dean & Company	John Martin
W. D. Washburn & Company	J. B. Bassett
Ankeny, Robinson & Pettit	Todd & Squires
Morrison Brothers	

A great change had come over the lumber industry in twenty years. The total capital investment of $3,311,140 in 1870 was a marked increase over the capital of $1,134,100 ten years earlier.[19] The lumber produced in 1870 was valued at $4,299,162, while the production of 1860 has been estimated at $1,234,203,[20] and that of 1850 at a humble $57,800.[21] The lumber industry of 1870 gave employment to 2952 men earning $880,028, in contrast to the 1146 men who earned $363,612 in that industry in 1860.[22]

[16] *Minneapolis Tribune*, May 20, Mar. 13, May 3, and Dec. 23, 1868, and Mar. 4, July 29, Sept. 10, and June 4, 1869.

[17] *Ibid.*, Apr. 13, 1869.

[18] *Mississippi Valley Lumberman*, vol. xxvi, Feb. 1, 1895, p. 76.

[19] *U.S. Census, 1870*, vol. iii: *Wealth and Industry*, pp. 10, 612; *U.S. Census, 1860*, vol. ii: *Manufactures*, p. 284.

[20] *U.S. Census, 1870*, vol. iii: *Wealth and Industry*, pp. 612–13; *U.S. Census, 1900*, vol. ix: *Manufactures*, pt. 3, p. 843; Lester B. Shippee, "Effects of the Civil War," *Minnesota History Bulletin*, vol. ii (May 1918), p. 399.

[21] *U.S. Census, 1860*, vol. ii: *Manufactures*, p. 284; *U.S. Census, 1900*, vol. ix: *Manufactures*, pt. 3, p. 843.

[22] *U.S. Census, 1870*, vol. iii: *Wealth and Industry*, pp. 535–36.

The bigger and more efficient industry developed by lumbermen as the years passed had been spurred on by a constantly increasing market, both home and remote, ever since 1854. Stillwater still sent her product down the St. Croix and on into the Mississippi, but from the mills at the Falls of St. Anthony and at Winona the flow of lumber was westward to supply a local market.

Behind all this development of the lumber industry lay the work in the forest. That, too, had its small beginnings. In 1837, as we have seen, timber had been purchased from the Indians, and logs were sometimes obtained by ways known only to millmen. But no considerable industry could develop until the sawmill owners had some certainty that logs could be obtained — that is, until lumbermen became owners of the forest lands. In the summer of 1837 the United States government had bought the great forest region west of the St. Croix from the Indians by treaty. The transfer of that public domain into private hands is an important chapter in the history of Minnesota's white pine industry.

CHAPTER IV

The Pinelands of the St. Croix Delta Become the Property of Lumbermen

IN 1845 the Commissioner of the General Land Office of the United States recommended in his annual report that lands near St. Anthony Falls and the mouths of the St. Croix, Chippewa, and Black rivers should be surveyed. These lands, his report stated, were rapidly being stripped of timber and would soon become unsalable and comparatively valueless.[1] His recommendation was adopted, and in 1847 the General Land Office ordered the survey of the land lying west of the St. Croix and around the Falls of St. Anthony.[2] That very year surveyors came into the St. Croix Delta and began their work, dragging their chains through forest and swamp and over streams, packing their supplies on their backs, risking their lives when they dashed through "white water" with loaded canoes, or in the biting frost of a Minnesota winter penetrated the deep forest behind a dog team, sleeping in the open, and eating by campfire day in and day out. In July 1848 their work had progressed far enough that lands could be offered for sale in the Delta. This region, a portion of which was rich in pine, was the first of Minnesota's land to be offered;[3] no lands had as yet been surveyed in the territory outside the Delta.

Because there was no land office on the Minnesota side of the St. Croix, the first sales of Minnesota's land were made at St. Croix Falls, on the Wisconsin side.[4] The opening day was July 24, 1848, and the first purchase was made by one James Purinton, who became the owner of 137.70 acres of Minnesota's soil, paying for it at the rate of $1.25 an acre, the minimum but usual price for land. To him was granted the first certificate issued by Sam Leech, Receiver, and C. P. Whitney, Register.

---

[1] 29th Cong., 1st Sess. (1845–46), *Senate Exec. Docs.*, no. 2, pt. 2, p. 54.
[2] Folwell, *History of Minnesota*, vol. i, p. 225.
[3] 31st Cong., 2d Sess. (1850–51), *Senate Exec. Docs.*, no. 2, p. 26.
[4] The land office was moved to Stillwater in 1849, to Cambridge in 1858, to Sunrise in 1860, and to Taylor's Falls in 1868 (all in the St. Croix Delta).

The second certificate was given to Samuel Burkleo, Orange Walker, and Hiram Berkey, who bought 108.35 acres. This land, says the record, lay to the west of the river — that is, the St. Croix. As early as 1839, as we have already noted, these men had established the first sawmill in Minnesota on the banks of the St. Croix at Marine,[5] and in ways known only to the frontier they had obtained timber for their mill for almost a decade without being owners of pineland; at that time settlers could not legally preëmpt unsurveyed lands.

These men who bought pineland in the Delta in 1848 were not investing to hold the lands for a higher value. They bought land to furnish logs for their sawmill. They had come to stay in Minnesota, and in the development of the St. Croix region they played an important part.

John McKusick, who had built a mill at Stillwater in 1844, was an early buyer of land in the Delta, as his receipts numbering 24, 25, 27, 28, and 29 indicate.[6] On August 14, 1848, he became the owner of more than 360 acres, most of which were in and near Stillwater.[7]

Albert H. Judd, a partner in the sawmill at Marine on the St. Croix, was an active land buyer in the month of August. He bought 320 acres for his concern; this tract later furnished some fine logs for the company's mill, which in time produced 197,000,000 feet of lumber. Judd and his firm knew good timber, and they continued to buy regularly in the St. Croix region. Levi Churchill and Socrates Nelson, two more who were converting logs into lumber at Stillwater, also strengthened their position with timberlands in the summer of 1848.[8]

During this land sale, which continued into the month of September, the basis for the present city of Minneapolis was laid when Franklin Steele became the proprietor of land bordering on the east side of St. Anthony Falls. He had had his eye on this place for some time, and when it was offered he immediately purchased, among other plots, eighty acres in section 23, township 29 north, range 24 west. He paid the usual price of $1.25 an acre — one hundred dollars for eighty acres in the heart of what is Minneapolis today![9] This land gave him control over important water power.[10] He had carefully explored the pine in the Delta not

[5] See above, p. 15.

[6] See above, p. 17.

[7] General Land Office, Land Tract Books, Minnesota, vol. 82, Township 30 North, Range 20 West, p. 123. Hereafter the General Land Office will be abbreviated G.L.O. The records of the General Land Office used by the author in the Department of Interior in Washington have since been moved to the National Archives. The references to those records throughout this book, unless otherwise stated, are in accordance with the way in which they were kept by the Department of Interior.

[8] G.L.O., Records of Receiver and Register, Cash Books, Stillwater, Minn., July 1848 to Dec. 18, 1852, and St. Croix Falls, Wis., July 24, 1848, to Jan. 1849.

[9] Ibid.

[10] See above, pp. 32–33.

far from the Falls at St. Anthony, and he knew the value of the 332 acres which became his property in this sale.

The men who invested in Minnesota lands in 1848 were largely associated with lumber production, and most of them were already established as useful citizens on the frontier. Their purchases, however, were neither numerous nor large. Franklin Steele's first receipt was number 92, an indication that a relatively small number of men had bought land in the Delta from the first day of the sale, July 24, 1848, through September of that year. Nor were sales large: only 9098 acres had become private property. The importance of the sales lay rather in the strategic locations which the buyers acquired. Among those acres was some of the land on which St. Paul stands at the head of navigation on the Mississippi River; likewise, lands were selected at St. Anthony, Stillwater, and Marine because of the valuable water power, the nearness of white pine, and the splendid waterway to market.

No land sales of record size were made in 1849. The month of November had larger cash sales than any other month of the year, but, even so, only 873 acres were sold. Land was passing into private hands by means other than cash, however, for in that year began the acquisition of land through military bounty land warrants. Over 10,000 acres became private property through warrants in 1849.[11]

Military bounty land warrants were not new in the United States. In the American Revolution and in the War of 1812 soldiers were paid in promises of land. Men who fought the Indians were also rewarded in this way. But it was during the Mexican War and the years immediately following that Congress began to use very freely this type of payment for soldiers.

From 1847 to 1855 bills providing for the payment of soldiers from public lands were presented to every Congress. Four of these bills — the Acts of 1847, 1850, 1852, and 1855 — became law. All of these made provision for the payment of soldiers who had fought the Indians or foreign foes — even those who had fought in the American Revolution — by giving them a share of the great public domain. The Act of 1855 was the most liberal, giving 160 acres of America's soil to any soldier who had served not less than fourteen days from the time he was inducted until he was discharged.[12]

Like most of the frontier regions, Minnesota was fearful of the military bounty land warrants. It had no vote on the matter in Washington, however, for it was not even organized as a territory in 1847 when the

[11] G.L.O., Records of Receiver and Register, Military Bounty Land Warrants, Stillwater, Cambridge, and Taylor's Falls, Minn., Act of 1847, vol. 44, Oct., Nov., and Dec. 1849.
[12] 33rd Cong., 2d Sess., *U.S. Statutes at Large*, vol. x, p. 701 (May 3, 1855).

first bill became law.[13] In fact, most of the public domain which was to be subject to the warrants had no representation in Washington when these bills were being considered. The *Minnesota Pioneer,* expressing the general attitude of frontiersmen, said in 1851, "As for speculators and non-residents, we desire them to understand that Minnesota is a poor sterile, frozen up, God-forsaken territory. A man who doesn't want to live here had better throw his land-warrant into the fire."[14] The law of 1852 made the military warrants even more objectionable to the frontier, because it made them all assignable.[15] The *St. Anthony Express* said that this measure concerned Minnesota more than any other bill except the Sioux Treaty. If it passed, it would be disastrous to the true interests of Minnesota.[16] One Minnesota paper called the men with warrants "obscene Harpies." [17]

The frontier held that land warrants favored the man with capital, placing him in a position to buy warrants from soldiers who had no interest in a faraway piece of public domain or who upon discharge needed money more than land. In this way the man with ready capital could possess himself of large holdings of desirable land at even less than the regular government minimum of $1.25 an acre. Horace Greeley contended that many warrants were sold for prices as low as $16 for 160 acres.[18] It was said that only one in five hundred of the recipients of warrants located his land, and it is thought that the soldier received in cash probably an average of 75 per cent of the minimum price of the land.[19]

Congressmen from the eastern states, on the other hand, favored the military bounty land warrants as against homesteads and railroad grants. Homesteads would draw labor from the industrial East, they believed, while railroads would people the West more rapidly and would develop competitive sections. Since land warrants would pass chiefly into the hands of those who had capital, the bulk of the people would not be affected.

The military land warrants were important in Minnesota's early history. They came into being, were legalized, and were in reality a form of currency just at the time when the pinelands of the Lake states were

[13] 29th Cong., 2d Sess., *Congressional Globe,* p. 272 (Jan. 27, 1847) and p. 273 (Jan. 30, 1847).
[14] *Minnesota Pioneer,* Sept. 18, 1851.
[15] 32d Cong., 1st Sess., *U.S. Statutes at Large,* vol. x, p. 2 (Mar. 22, 1852).
[16] *St. Anthony Express,* Feb. 28, 1852.
[17] *Minnesota Pioneer,* Mar. 4, 1852.
[18] *New York Weekly Tribune,* Nov. 13, 1852.
[19] 40th Cong., 1st Sess., *House Exec. Docs.,* pt. 2, p. 106; 31st Cong., 2d Sess., *Senate Docs.,* no. 2, pt. 2, p. 6; F. H. White, "The Administration of the Land Office, 1812–1911," manuscript thesis, Widener Library, Harvard University, p. 331.

being sought by lumbermen from the older states where pine was becoming scarce. In 1850 the warrants were replacing sales for cash in the St. Croix Delta. More land became private property in 1850 than in 1849, and the method most generally used to make the transfer was the land warrant of 1847. The record, month by month, is shown in Table 2.

TABLE 2. AMOUNT OF LAND WHICH BECAME PRIVATE PROPERTY IN THE
ST. CROIX DELTA IN 1850

	By Warrants (in acres)	By Cash (in acres)
January	1,120.00	244.05
February	1,612.44	138.69
March	1,761.07	193.50
April	2,118.05	333.30
May	4,667.22	1,120.18
June	2,802.38	705.26
July	1,593.78	146.76
August	2,352.51	60.80
September	2,857.66	183.99
October	5,054.72	17.37
November	4,632.01	355.33
December	1,449.13	315.03
	32,020.97	3,814.26*

* At $1.25 an acre, the total cash paid was $4,767.83.
SOURCE: G.L.O., Records of Receiver and Register, Cash Entries, Stillwater, Minn., July 24, 1848, to Dec. 18, 1852, and St. Croix Falls, Wis., July 24, 1848, to Jan. 1849; G.L.O., Military Bounty Lands Act of 1847, vol. 44, Stillwater, Cambridge, Taylor's Falls, 1850.

Among those locating lands in 1850 with warrants under the Act of 1847 were such well-known men as James Goodhue, editor of the *St. Paul Pioneer*; Alexander Ramsey, territorial governor; Ard Godfrey, the millwright from Maine who had moved to St. Anthony to assist Franklin Steele in his lumber mill; Charles Borup, a St. Paul merchant; and Stephen and Rufus Farnham, lumbermen from the East who had established themselves at St. Anthony Falls.[20]

Land warrants continued to lead in the fifties. In 1851 about 6000 more acres were located by warrants than were sold for cash. In 1852 almost all the land which became private property was located by warrant — perhaps in part because in March of that year land warrants had become assignable. In June 1852, only three months after warrants had become assignable, 4999 acres were located with land warrants of the Act of 1850. The cash sales in that same month of June were meager — only 151 acres.

[20] G.L.O., Military Bounty Lands Act of 1847, vol. 44, Stillwater, Cambridge, and Taylor's Falls, Minn., 1850.

The sale of pinelands in the Stillwater land office increased sharply in 1853, when approximately 77,000 acres passed from public to private possession. Land warrants and cash ran nip and tuck, cash being paid for 35,506 acres, while land warrants were presented for 38,592. This year definitely marks the beginning of buying on a large scale by individuals.

The men who bought Minnesota's pineland that year were to become important in the world of lumber. In August 1853 the name of Dorilus Morrison of Bangor, Maine, appeared for the first time in the records of the register and receiver of the Stillwater land office. He was to settle at St. Anthony Falls as a lumberman in 1854.[21] The certificates he received at the land office in August 1853 were numbered 674, 675, 676, and 677, indicating that he was an early buyer in that area. In September he visited the Stillwater land office again to pay for more land which he had selected; and in October, when 10,454 acres of the St. Croix Delta became private property, Dorilus Morrison bought 3165 acres. Before 1853 had run its course, he had purchased 5300 acres of land with cash.

Morrison was equally well provided with land warrants. Though land warrants had become assignable only a year before, he brought large amounts of warrants of the issue of the Acts of 1850 and 1852, with which he located 5678 acres in the fall of 1853. It was said that Morrison located about $12,000 worth of land warrants in the forest lands along the Rum River alone.[22] In less than six months he had established himself as the owner of approximately 11,000 acres of Minnesota's valuable white pine.

In selecting his pinelands Morrison made Mille Lacs County his base of operations in Minnesota. That northernmost county of the Delta, sixty miles above St. Anthony Falls, was a wilderness where the white man was almost unknown when Morrison and his men found it. He knew good timber and chose his stands of pine wisely. Quickly and correctly he could reckon the number of feet of timber in a forty. He could tell which forties could be logged most easily and most reasonably. With a keen eye he looked for a logging stream, which was marked as especially valuable if in the spring freshet it could carry logs to a river that would deliver them into the jaws of a sawmill.

Mille Lacs County was the source of the Rum River, a stream famous in Minnesota's logging history. The Rum was joined by many lesser streams in carrying the logs into the Mississippi River, the main waterway to the mills at St. Anthony. Dorilus Morrison had followed the Rum and had explored its subsidiary streams as well as its pinelands. Page Township, rich with pine, was opened for sale in 1852, and Morrison's

---

[21] See above, p. 36.
[22] Hotchkiss, *History of Lumber and Forest Industry of Northwest*, p. 531.

first choice of land in Mille Lacs County lay where the Rum River cut through the center of Page Township from north to south.

In 1853 Morrison acquired land in practically every section in Page Township except sections 16 and 36, which were reserved as school lands. This township was literally plastered with land warrants, and Dorilus Morrison was the heaviest buyer. The men who owned most of the township by the end of that year were Morrison; Cyrus Woodman of Mineral Point, Wisconsin; Henry T. Welles, a lumberman and later a banker at St. Anthony who came to Minnesota from Connecticut in 1853; and William J. Larned, another lumberman at the Falls.[23]

To the east of the Rum River in Mille Lacs County lay South Hayland Township, well watered by streams that flowed into the Rum and the St. Croix, which afforded excellent means of bringing logs to Marine and Stillwater on the St. Croix as well as to St. Anthony on the Mississippi. Lumbermen became the owners of this township, too. Dorilus Morrison bought land there in October 1853; Cyrus Woodman in the same year; Isaac Staples in the following year; and in 1855 Caleb Woodbury of St. Cloud. Practically the whole township was disposed of by military bounty land warrants issued under the Acts of 1850, 1852, and 1855.[24]

North Hayland and Milaca townships in Mille Lacs County had been opened for sale in 1852. North Hayland became private property in the years between 1854 and 1857, largely through land warrants of the Act of 1855, with the exception of five sections set aside for railroad and swamp land and the usual two for education.[25] In Milaca Township, well watered by Chase Brook and Story Brook and the Rum River itself, Dorilus Morrison located land by warrants in 1853. But 1856 and 1857 were the most active years, for then section after section in this township became private property in exchange for land warrants of the 1855 issue.[26]

By 1857 Dorilus Morrison was well established in the pine forests of the Delta. He had acquired in a few years enough timber to run his contemplated mill at St. Anthony for many years. And his holdings were not limited to the purchases made at the office at Stillwater; his name was often listed on the records of the land office established in 1853 at Sauk Rapids on the Mississippi above St. Anthony. Here, too, Morrison purchased pinelands with cash or with warrants.

No history of the pinelands of the Delta would be complete without

[23] G.L.O., Tract Books, Minn., vol. 88, T. 39 N., R. 27 W., pp. 56–64.
[24] Ibid., vol. 87, T. 39 N., R. 26 W., pp. 172–79.
[25] Ibid., T. 40 N., R. 26 W., pp. 180–88.
[26] Ibid., vol. 88, T. 38 N., R. 27 W., pp. 47–55.

the story of Samuel Freeman Hersey and Isaac Staples, sawmill men from Maine.[27] They had been trained in lumber, and armed with experience and capital they came to buy pinelands and to establish Hersey, Staples and Company in the business of sawing lumber in Stillwater. Isaac Staples had visited the region in order to examine the pine in 1853; the following year he returned to buy; and within ten years he had secured, in exchange for military land warrants at the Stillwater office, title to approximately 40,000 acres of pineland in the St. Croix Delta. Of these about 35,000 acres were located by warrants of the Act of 1855 and the remainder by those of the Acts of 1847, 1850, and 1852.[28] In January 1854 Samuel F. Hersey, president of the firm, bought 11,397 acres of pineland in the Delta, paying $14,246 in cash.[29] In all the St. Croix Delta no one owned more land than the firm of Hersey, Staples and Company. They located large portions by warrant, but they also made large investments directly in cash.

As Mille Lacs had been Dorilus Morrison's choice, so Kanabec County passed largely into the ownership of Hersey and Staples and another partner named Hall. The county was well watered by the Snake, Knife, and Ann rivers, and by lesser streams emptying their waters into the St. Croix, which carried logs directly to the mills at Stillwater and Marine.

The township of South Forks in Kanabec County became almost entirely the property of Staples and Hersey. They owned land in fifteen consecutive sections of this township, section one through section fifteen, and all of it was purchased in January and February of 1854. In sections 12 and 13 Hersey bought 1240 acres out of a possible 1280 in one day, paying the usual price of $1.25 an acre. In Arthur Township in the same county, a township excellently watered by the Snake and Ann rivers, Isaac Staples became the owner of land in twenty sections, located almost entirely with the warrants of the Act of 1855. The rest of the township was reserved for railroad lands, swamp lands, and school lands. Staples alone controlled the holdings in that township.[30]

North Peace Township in the same county was offered in November 1852. The Snake River, a good logging stream and the chief highway

[27] See above, p. 19.

[28] G.L.O., Records of Receiver and Register, Military Bounty Lands, Act of 1855: vol. 245, Stillwater, Minn., July 1855 to Dec. 1857; vol. 244, Cambridge, Minn., Jan. 1858 to Dec. 1859; vol. 247, Taylor's Falls, Minn., Jan. 1861 to Dec. 1864. *Ibid.*, Act of 1850: vol. 131, Stillwater, Sunrise City, Taylor's Falls, Minn., June 1851 to May 1870. *Ibid.*, Act of 1852: vol. 182, Stillwater, Sunrise City, Taylor's Falls, Minn., Dec. 1852 to Dec. 1868. *Ibid.*, Act of 1847: vol. 44, Stillwater, Cambridge, and Taylor's Falls, Minn., Oct. 1849 to Feb. 1860.

[29] *Ibid.*, Cash Entries, Stillwater, Minn., Jan. 1853 to Dec. 1855.

[30] G.L.O., Tract Books, Minn.: vol. 86, T. 40 N., R. 24 W., pp. 133–41; vol. 86, T. 39 N., R. 24 W., pp. 124–31; vol. 86, T. 41 N., R. 24 W., pp. 142–46; vol. 87, T. 38 N., R. 25 W., pp. 19–23.

of the township, empties into the St. Croix. Isaac Staples and Samuel Hersey became the chief proprietors of land in North Peace in the years 1854–57. In January and February 1854 they bought 4000 acres for cash. Other lumbermen who shared the land in this township were the millmen at Marine: Orange Walker, Asa Parker, A. H. Judd, G. B. Judd, and Hiram Berkey. They bought 3000 acres in North Peace in 1854.[31] Their names occur often on the records of buyers of timberlands in the Delta, and they became owners of large portions of pineland; but they did not rank with Staples and Hersey in the amount of acreage acquired, nor did they locate by land warrants on so large a scale as did Isaac Staples and Dorilus Morrison. This whole township definitely became the property of men who were manufacturing lumber along the St. Croix. The men from St. Anthony did not buy in the Kanabec area because its waterways entered the St. Croix and not the Rum and the Mississippi.

Whited was another township surveyed and opened for sale in Kanabec County in 1852. There, too, Isaac Staples was a substantial buyer, locating land by warrants, again of the 1855 issue. This township passed into private ownership largely in 1855 and 1856, section after section of it through the exchange of land warrants of the Act of 1855. Two lumbermen from Stillwater shared in the ownership of land here: Elam Greeley, one of the founders of Stillwater who had arrived before Isaac Staples, and his associate John D. Ludden, who had come to the St. Croix in 1845. In those early days Ludden's business was that of a lumberman, but he was active in other ways. He was a representative in the territorial legislature in the early fifties, serving one year as speaker. He became a member of the Minnesota Historical Society in 1866, and for the next three years he served on the executive council of that organization. At his death in 1907 he willed his library to the State Historical Society and a large portion of his estate to the Minnesota School of Agriculture.[32]

Greeley and Ludden bought holdings in South Peace Township, too, but here again Isaac Staples became the largest landowner. Land warrants of the Act of 1855 were given in exchange for almost the whole township, which became private property in the boom years 1854–57.[33]

Other lumbermen active in buying in the Delta were Henry and Leonard Day, who had come from Maine to buy pinelands and to establish themselves at St. Anthony in 1853. Caleb Dorr, another Maineite, made substantial purchases with one William Garland in the early fifties. Sumner W. Farnham and William H. C. Folsom, both from the white

[31] *Ibid.*, vol. 85, T. 42 N., R. 23 W., pp. 198–207.
[32] *Minn. Hist. Soc. Coll.*, vol. xii, 1908, p. 782.
[33] G.L.O., Tract Books, Minn., vol. 85, T. 41 N., R. 23 W., pp. 186–96.

pine regions of the East, became owners of pineland in Pine and Chisago counties in the booming years of this decade.

In those counties, as elsewhere, lumbermen were the most active buyers. Of the 14,438 acres sold at the land office in Stillwater in January 1854, 11,603 acres were purchased by men whose interest was in lumber and who expected to turn their timber into log stock.[34] These men all settled either at St. Anthony Falls or on the St. Croix River, and all stayed on to help develop the region. Of the group, William H. C. Folsom probably became the best known; he was a member of the convention that drew up the constitution of Minnesota, was state senator for five sessions, and wrote a valuable record of the period, *Fifty Years in the Northwest.*[35]

While Yankees from the East, particularly from Maine, were buying pinelands by the hundreds and thousands of acres in Minnesota in the middle fifties, a small group of immigrants from Sweden were buying modest plots in that area, hopeful that there they might establish homes. Since no other land was open for sale or settlement in Minnesota west of the Mississippi in 1853 when this immigration began, the Delta was their only recourse. There was wood; there was water; and to eke out the bare living on the frontier, there was a chance to labor in the forests in winter, changing the tall pine into logs ready for the sawmill.

Daniel Nelson and Sven Anderson left their homes in Sweden and came to the St. Croix land in October 1853. Nelson bought 34 acres and Anderson bought 40 acres in the present New Scandia Township not far from Marine. The following year Mons Lund and John Magnusson followed the first comers, each buying 70 acres. That same year John Okerson and John Petter Sjöstrand purchased 120 and 155 acres, respectively, in May Township, not far from Marine, and Sven Rosenquist bought 80 acres near Stillwater. In 1855 another group arrived from Sweden, settling in New Scandia Township in the neighborhood of their fellow countrymen. They were Jonas Granstrand, who purchased 80 acres; Charles Ekdahl, who selected 120 acres; Nels Bengtson and Peter Peterson, each of whom bought 160 acres. In 1856 Magnus Hokanson, Jonas Gabrilson, and Gustav Petterson came to New Scandia Township, where they bought 120, 80, and 159 acres, respectively.[36]

These Swedish immigrants and others who followed them became the loggers who toiled in the deep forest, harvesting the logs that were to be converted into lumber. When the timber was gone, however, they

[34] G.L.O., Records of Receiver and Register, Cash Entries, Stillwater, Minn., Jan. 1853 to Dec. 1854.

[35] "Minesota Biographies, 1655–1912," *Minn. Hist. Soc. Coll.,* vol. xiv, 1912, p. 231.

[36] G.L.O., Tract Books, Minn., vol. 82, T. 28, 30, 31, 32 N., R. 20 W., pp. 103, 126, 131, 138, 142.

stayed on. The lumbermen who bought the hundreds and thousands of acres are but memories in those townships today, but those Swedish names are still on the active records of the register of deeds. When the pine forests had been exhausted, those immigrants found other ways of making the land useful and they contributed to the development of permanent agricultural communities. Their descendants live there today.

The year 1854 was important in the history of the St. Croix lands. As we have seen, that year brought Isaac Staples and Samuel Freeman Hersey, lumbermen with experience and capital, into the region. Not in any year in the whole decade was so much land sold for cash. The land office at Stillwater did a "land-office" business that year when it turned over to the United States government the sum of $217,801.

The boom continued in 1855, and the next year the record for the decade was made when approximately 425,000 acres became private property by warrants and cash at Stillwater. Warrants quite held the edge that year, when 361,819 acres became private property in exchange for warrants of the Act of 1855. These many acres were covered with majestic pine.

To be sure, this expansion had its parallel in all the western states, but it may be doubted "whether its violence and rate were elsewhere quite equaled. Fortunes seemed to be dropping from the skies, and those who would not reach and gather them were but stupids and sluggards." [37] Minnesota had shared in the great upswing of trade which came to a peak in 1856 and which had been most striking in the West.[38] In 1848 St. Paul, at the head of navigation on the Mississippi, was a collection of rude cabins where lived mostly half-breeds; in 1857 a writer told of its "tall spires and elegant buildings, it commodious warehouses and busy levees; its fleet of barges and steamboats." [39] St. Anthony, the chief business of which was the sawmill, had equipment which could produce 60,000,000 feet of lumber a year in the late fifties; while the St. Croix Valley, with Stillwater and Marine as the sawmill towns, exported 30,000,000 feet of lumber and 40,000,000 feet of logs in 1857.[40] The chief industry in Minnesota in the 1850s was lumbering, which had led the way in opening up the territory.

In 1857, however, Minnesota shared in the distress that fell upon the newly expanded West. In fact, the panic struck Minnesota with extreme violence; many men who were in debt to eastern bankers and creditors were pushed to the wall. Investment in the public domain, the chief

[37] Folwell, *op. cit.*, vol. i, p. 363.
[38] Arthur H. Cole, "Statistical Background of the Crisis of 1857," *Review of Economic Statistics*, vol. xii, 1930, pp. 170–80.
[39] "Minnesota: The Growth and Progress of the Northwest," *Hunt's Merchants' Magazine*, vol. 37, 1857, p. 51.
[40] See above, p. 19.

investment in Minnesota, stopped almost completely.[41] In 1858 only 500 acres, and in 1859 only 600 acres, of the Delta pinelands were sold for cash. Isaac Staples, alone, continued his usual acquisition of pineland. He had cash, and in 1859, when the buying of pinelands was still at low ebb, he located about 13,000 acres with warrants of the Act of 1855. When Knife Lake Township in Kanabec County was offered for sale in 1859, Isaac Staples became the owner of pineland in 21 of its 36 sections; whole sections of it became his property.[42]

Staples of course was an exception. The sale of lands definitely reflected the panic, but not even a period of financial depression could destroy the well-founded lumber industry in Minnesota.

In the pinelands of the Delta lay the real basis for this industry. From 1850 through 1859 over 1,000,000 acres had become private property in this region. More land had been transferred through the military bounty land warrants than for cash, but altogether a huge domain had passed into private ownership, as is shown in Table 3.

TABLE 3. PUBLIC LAND WHICH BECAME PRIVATE PROPERTY IN THE ST. CROIX DELTA BY MILITARY BOUNTY LAND WARRANTS AND BY CASH, 1850–1859

Year	By Warrants (in acres)	By Cash (in acres)	Cash Received
1850	33,870.97	3,814.26	$ 4,769.07
1851	20,798.22	14,774.97	18,468.65
1852	28,953.15	3,740.79	4,675.99
1853	38,591.96	35,505.60	43,610.51
1854	17,313.71	174,621.15	217,801.25
1855	54,294.12	122,124.67	152,155.83
1856	361,812.71	54,048.86	67,536.07
1857	101,505.88	5,418.13	6,701.19
1858	6,518.26	500.73	626.30
1859	28,883.61	597.47	747.02
Total	692,542.59	415,146.63	$517,091.88

SOURCE: G.L.O., Records of Register and Receiver, Cash Entries, Stillwater, Minnesota Territory, July 1848 to Dec. 1852; St. Croix Falls, Wisconsin Territory, July 24, 1848, to Jan. 1849; Stillwater, Minnesota Territory, 1853–58; Cambridge, Minnesota, 1858–60. Military Bounty Land Warrants: Act of 1855, vols. 244 and 245, Stillwater, July 1855 to Dec. 1860; Act of 1847, vol. 44; Act of 1850, vol. 131; Act of 1852, vol. 182.

In the 1850s much of the capital which flowed into the Delta was brought directly by easterners who came to establish themselves in the lumber industry. They brought either their own capital or the funds of some eastern acquaintance or relative invested in joint enterprise or as a loan. Some of them were well supplied with money and were able to

[41] Folwell, *op. cit.*, vol. i, p. 363.
[42] G.L.O., Tract Books, Minn., vol. 87, T. 38 N., R. 25 W., pp. 19–23; G.L.O., Military Bounty Land Warrants, Act of 1855, Stillwater and Cambridge, Minn., vol. 244, Jan. 1858 to Dec. 1859.

establish a substantial enterprise in the frontier country. Some of them had been successful lumbermen in the East, especially in Maine, and in transplanting themselves to a new region rich with virgin white pine, they provided the capital and industrial leadership necessary to its prosperous development. Some had only small amounts and worked modestly, reinvesting as their earnings grew.

As we have seen, most of the men who bought large portions of the Delta pinelands in the fifties established themselves in the lumber industry — men like Dorilus Morrison, Isaac Staples, Samuel F. Hersey, and Orange Walker and his associates at Marine — but a few large buyers did not become lumbermen in Minnesota. Among these were Erastus Edgerton, Weston Merrit, and Cyrus Woodman.

Having succeeded to the management of an estate of some size upon the death of his father, Erastus Edgerton had at his command a considerable amount of capital. In 1854 he established himself as a banker in St. Paul, and in 1865 he organized the Second National Bank, of which he was the principal stockholder and president. He later became a director of the Commercial National Bank of Chicago.[43] Weston Merrit gave his address as Hudson on the Wisconsin side of the St. Croix; he had come there from Suffolk County in Massachusetts. Cyrus Woodman had come into the West early. He lived in Mineral Point, Wisconsin, where he was associated with C. C. Washburn of lumber fame in that state. Woodman was three generations removed from those who began life in the pine forests of Maine, where his forefathers were lumbermen on the Saco, a famous log and lumber stream. Woodman never lived in Minnesota; in his home state of Wisconsin he was active in lumbering, banking, mining, railroad promotion, and politics, as well as in supporting early cultural efforts.[44]

In the 1860s, as in the depression years following the Panic of 1857, the sale of public lands in Minnesota was slow compared with the boom years of the fifties. Capital entered channels necessary for the success of the war effort, and this fact was reflected in the reduced sale of public lands. All the lands sold for cash at the land office of the Delta from January 1, 1861, to December 31, 1869, totaled only 32,771 acres, a fraction of the 174,621 acres sold for cash in the one year of 1854.

New pineland areas had been opened in Minnesota on the upper reaches of the Mississippi in 1855 and in the region north of Lake Superior in 1854, and the buying in those areas probably made some difference in the sale of the Delta lands. The latter, however, were still the most conveniently

[43] Newson, *Pen Pictures*, vol. i, p. 400.
[44] Ellis P. Usher, "Cyrus Woodman, A Character Sketch," *Wisconsin Magazine of History*, vol. ii (June 1919), pp. 393–412.

TABLE 4. CASH LAND SALES IN THE ST. CROIX DELTA
JANUARY 1861 TO DECEMBER 31, 1869

Year	Acres Sold	Amount Paid
1861	489.97	$ 612.43
1862	371.07	363.82
1863	3,947.79	3,561.83
1864	2,485.07	3,267.49
1865	1,608.64	2,010.83
1866	2,365.85	2,960.72
1867	3,305.10	4,170.19
1868	12,921.69	17,222.13
1869	5,276.16	7,243.50
	32,771.34	$41,412.94

SOURCE: G.L.O., Records of Receiver and Register, Cash Entry, Taylor's Falls, Minn.: Jan. 1, 1860, to Dec. 31, 1864; Jan. 1865 to Dec. 13, 1868; Jan. 1869 to Dec. 31, 1870.

located for the mills at St. Anthony and particularly for those at Marine and Stillwater.

The lands that were sold in the sixties, as in the decade immediately preceding, became the property largely of men who were living in Minnesota and who were engaged in business of some kind, usually in the manufacture of lumber at St. Anthony, Stillwater, or Marine. Samuel F. Hersey and Isaac Staples from Stillwater bought steadily throughout the 1860s. Other men from Stillwater who were to figure strongly in the lumber life of that region and whose names now began to appear prominently on the records of the receiver and register were David Tozer, Louis Hospes, Lewis E. Torinus, Frederick Schulenburg, and Edward W. Durant.

Levi Butler, a physician who had moved to St. Anthony in 1855, became active in the lumber life of Minneapolis and in the sixties was a prominent buyer of pinelands in the Delta. John Martin, a Vermonter who had come to St. Anthony to manufacture lumber, was also acquiring pinelands in the sixties, buying substantially in West Onamia Township in Mille Lacs County on streams tributary to the Mississippi. In that same township Joseph Dean, who was associated with the Pacific Mill and was a cashier of the Security Bank of St. Anthony, was also buying land. In October 1868 he bought 2735 acres, most of which were located in West Onamia Township.[45] Other lumbermen from St. Anthony who were buying at that time on a smaller scale were Oren B. Sturtevant, William P. Ankeny, and Sumner W. Farnham.

The military bounty land warrants continued to be popular, though they did not equal the number or the volume of warrants used in the Delta in

[45] G.L.O., Tract Books, Minn., vol. 88, T. 41 N., R. 27 W., p. 76; Records of Receiver and Register, Cash Entries, Taylor's Falls, Minn., Jan. 1865 to Dec. 31, 1868.

the fifties. From January 1861 to December 31, 1869, approximately 60,000 acres were located by land warrants of the Acts of 1850, 1852, and 1855, according to the land office records of this area. The warrants of the Act of 1855 were used for almost 59,000 of the 60,000 acres.[46] Isaac Staples became the owner of at least 17,000 acres through military bounty land warrants during the sixties, and his partners, Samuel F. Hersey and Dudley C. Hall, were also active in locating land through the use of warrants. In July 1861 Hall took 2600 of the 4271 acres located that month. Frederick Schulenburg, Louis Hospes, and David Tozer, all from Stillwater, became holders of good pineland through warrants in those years.

One of the largest buyers by means of warrants was John Martin of St. Anthony, whose preferred location was West Onamia Township of Mille Lacs County. This township was well watered by North Bradbury Brook and by the south branch of the Rum River, which could carry logs to the Mississippi River and thence to Martin's mill in Minneapolis. Martin located six quarters of land in sections 5 and 6 of this township, 960 acres of good pineland; in section 7 he located 480 acres; in section 8 he became the owner of all its 640 acres; in sections 9 and 10 he located 320 acres, the rest being swamp; in section 11 he located 160 acres; in section 17 he became the owner of 480 acres; and in section 18 he located 160 acres. Most of his land was acquired in 1862; in one month of that year he located 2080 acres with thirteen military bounty land warrants. He also made some locations in 1863 and again in 1865.[47]

Levi Butler, also, acquired much of his land through the use of warrants. In April 1864 he located no fewer than 1600 acres of pinelands with the military bounty land warrants of the Act of 1855.[48] His selections, too, were in the pine forests of Mille Lacs County, largely in Milo Township, which had been opened in May 1859.[49]

Other St. Anthony lumbermen active in locating land with warrants were William P. Ankeny, Oren B. Sturtevant, and James A. Lovejoy. Smaller buyers from St. Anthony were George Warren, a surveyor and real-estate dealer; John B. Gilfillan, a lawyer from Vermont who had come to Minnesota in 1855 and lived at St. Anthony; William Stevens, who had come to St. Anthony in 1852 and was interested in the buying and selling of land; and one Stephen Emerson from Calais, Maine.

[46] G.L.O., Military Bounty Land Warrants, Taylor's Falls, Minn., Act of 1855: vol. 247, Jan. 1, 1861, to Dec. 31, 1864; vol. 248, Jan. 1, 1865, to June 31, 1868; vol. 252, July 1868 to Dec. 31, 1876. *Ibid.*, Act of 1850, vol. 131, June 1851 to Mar. 1870. *Ibid.*, Act of 1852, vol. 182, Dec. 1852 to June 1868.
[47] G.L.O., Tract Books, vol. 88, T. 41 N., R. 27 W., pp. 74–81.
[48] G.L.O., Record of Receiver and Register, Military Bounty Land Warrants, Act of 1855, Taylor's Falls, Minn., vol. 247, Jan. 1, 1861, to Dec. 31, 1864.
[49] G.L.O., Tract Books, Minn., T. 37 N., R. 27 W., pp. 38–43.

In the sixties the United States adopted a new policy in the disposal of its public domain. In July 1862 the Morrill Land Grant Bill was enacted, granting to each state, for establishing and supporting agricultural and mechanical colleges, thirty thousand acres for each of that state's representatives and senators in Congress. The states which still had public domain within their boundaries subject to sale were entitled to land "in place," which meant that such states should take their allotment out of the public domain within their boundaries. This land would become the property of the state, to use as it wished for the purpose of securing funds to establish the type of school for which the Morrill Act made provision. The states which had no public domain were to be given their allotment "in scrip" — redeemable, assignable land scrip which might be sold and located by its assignees on any public land in states or territories according to stipulations in the act.[50]

Some of this scrip found its way into Minnesota, where much of the forest land was still public domain. In 1865 land was being located in East Onamia Township in Mille Lacs County by Weston Merrit of Suffolk County in Massachusetts with scrip granted to the states of New Jersey and Kentucky.[51] In May 1867 a rising lumberman of Stillwater, Edward W. Durant, located 480 acres with Kentucky scrip in the St. Croix area.[52] In June of the same year he located 160 acres with Indiana scrip, and Isaac B. Tozer, also of Stillwater, located 1800 acres of pineland with Ohio scrip.[53] Sumner Farnham, Oren B. Sturtevant, John Martin, and Isaac Staples, all lumbermen, located lands with agricultural scrip from Ohio, Maine, Pennsylvania, and Tennessee.[54] John B. Gilfillan, who was acquiring much timberland, located 960 acres with Pennsylvania and Tennessee scrip in July 1868.

A newcomer who used agricultural college scrip in considerable amounts in the St. Croix Delta was Calvin F. Howe of Kings County, New York, who had moved to Illinois in 1857 and later moved to Minnesota. In a year's time, from June 1869 to June 1870, he located 6877 acres, using scrip from Tennessee, Delaware, North Carolina, Pennsylvania, and New York. He selected land in Comfort and Brunswick townships in Kanabec County, a region covered with white pine.[55]

In the short period from December 1865 to July 1872 agricultural college

[50] Thomas Donaldson, *Public Domain* (Washington, 1884), pp. 223, 229.
[51] G.L.O., Land Tract Books, Minn., vol. 87, T. 41 N., R. 26 W., pp. 189–94.
[52] G.L.O., Record of Receiver and Register, Agricultural College Scrip, Taylor's Falls, Minn., 1865–72, nos. 1–179.
[53] *Ibid.*
[54] *Ibid.*
[55] G.L.O., Land Tract Books, Minn.: vol. 85, T. 39 N., R. 23 W., pp. 162–73; vol. 86, T. 38 N., R. 24 W., pp. 115–23. Daniel W. Howe, *Howe Genealogies* (New England Historic Genealogical Society, Boston, 1929), p. 245.

scrip was exchanged for approximately 26,000 acres of good pineland in the St. Croix Delta, according to the records of the land office of the district. From December 1865 to December 31, 1869, about 17,000 acres passed into private hands through the use of agricultural college scrip in the region.[56] Military bounty land warrants and agricultural college scrip, however, had almost run their course in the St. Croix area by the early seventies. A more liberal land law, the Homestead Act, signed by President Lincoln on May 20, 1862, had become operative by that time.[57]

The Homestead Act was designed to give an advantage to the sturdy man of lesser means who wished to make a home on the frontier. It was enacted for the benefit of the average man rather than the man of capital. The West had opposed the military bounty land warrants and the agricultural college scrip, but free homesteads had long been its hue and cry. Under the Homestead Act the applicant was allowed 160 acres of land, which would become his free of charge when he had lived on it for five years, provided that during that time he had made certain improvements. If, however, the applicant wished to make himself complete owner before the expiration of five years, he could do so by paying the minimum price with cash, military bounty land warrants, or agricultural college scrip, after giving proof of settlement and cultivation for a period of not less than six months from the date of entry to the time of payment.[58]

The new law applied to all the forest lands as well as to the great plains and prairies of the United States. Nineteen applicants filed for homesteads in the St. Croix Delta in the very month in which the law became operative, January 1863. That year a hundred applications for homesteads were made in the area. In 1868 and 1869 a total of 13,858 acres were "proved up" and passed into private ownership, according to the final homestead records.[59]

The transfer of land by homesteading became more common in the St. Croix Delta in the seventies, but it is a curious question why men should have wished to homestead this pine-covered land, which required such arduous labor to make it productive for agricultural purposes, when great sections of prairie lands in Minnesota were available. An examination of the advertising of the Delta lands may help to explain why the immigrant from Europe thought them a satisfactory place for a home. In 1871 Hans Mattson — a well-known Minnesotan of Swedish origin who had served as immigration commissioner and was in that year secretary of state in

[56] G.L.O., Records of Receiver and Register, Agricultural College Scrip, Taylor's Falls, Minn., Dec. 1865 to July 1872, nos. 1–179.
[57] U.S. Statutes at Large, vol. xii, pp. 392–94.
[58] Donaldson, op. cit., p. 1027.
[59] G.L.O., Records of Receiver and Register, Final Homesteads, Taylor's Falls, Minn., Jan. 1868 to Dec. 1873, nos. 1–512.

Minnesota — wrote a pamphlet to advertise Minnesota's lands. It was directed particularly to the Scandinavian people and was written in their language. This quotation, translated, indicates the nature of his appeal:

For the poor emigrant who has nothing on which to depend for the care of himself and his family except his willingness to work and the work of his hands, it is most important to find employment near his place of abode. The great forests will for hundreds of years furnish work for loggers at the same time that sawmills and other factories using lumber will need large numbers of workers. . . . There will be an opportunity to make greater progress financially in a shorter time than in any other western state.[60]

Such advertisements no doubt attracted settlers who had little money. Whether they really brought large numbers of settlers into the Delta, it is hard to say; but in any case, during the seventies more land became private property through homesteading than through cash purchase. From January 1, 1870, to December 31, 1879, only 47,270 acres were sold for cash, whereas 176,733 acres were turned over to private interests in the final homestead entries during that period.[61] Location of land by military land warrants and agricultural college scrip had become negligible in the Delta of the St. Croix.[62]

The men who were using cash in purchasing land in the St. Croix region in the period of the sixties, seventies, and early eighties were engaged in the sawing of lumber along the St. Croix River. The names generally found in groups making purchases were David Tozer, Isaac Staples, Louis E. Torinus, W. H. Bronson, Charles N. Nelson, Edward W. Durant, Charles Bean, Roscoe Hersey, Frederick Schulenburg, Orange Walker, Samuel Judd, W. H. Veazie, William O'Brien, Mark C. Scanlon, Thomas Brennan, and Dwight Sabine. Some of these men had been in the group of early purchasers when the Delta lands first were opened. Many of them arrived with small capital; they remained to become industrial capitalists. They built industries around which grew towns with stores and banks and railroads. They were not speculators. They had purchased land largely with the idea that the resources on that land would furnish them with raw materials for their lumbering. Many of them had purchased large holdings, for they sensed that in years to come a huge lumber market would develop in this region. They were right.

[60] Hans Mattson, *Land for Emigranter ved Lake Superior og Mississippi Jernveien mellem St. Paul og Duluth* (Minneapolis, 1871), p. 5.

[61] G.L.O., Final Homesteads, Taylor's Falls, Minn., nos. 1–512, Jan. 1868 to Dec. 1873; nos. 513–1120, Jan. 1874 to Dec. 1876; nos. 1121–1749, Jan. 1877 to Dec. 1879. Cash Records of the Receiver and Register, Taylor's Falls, Jan. 1, 1869, to Dec. 31, 1870; Jan. 1, 1871, to Dec. 31, 1873; Jan. 1, 1874, to Dec. 31, 1876; Jan. 1, 1877, to Dec. 31, 1879.

[62] G.L.O., Military Bounty Land Warrant Act of 1855, vol. 252, Taylor's Falls, Minn., July 1868 to Feb. 1877; Agricultural College Scrip, Taylor's Falls, Dec. 1865 to July 1872.

CHAPTER V

Logging in the St. Croix Forests

THE first crew of loggers in the St. Croix Delta of which there is any record operated at the junction of the Snake and St. Croix rivers in the winter of 1837, even before Minnesota had become a territory. John Boyce, who had come from St. Louis in a Mackinaw boat, carried on his logging there with eleven men and six oxen.[1] Franklin Steele had as his crew an ox with a cart and six half-breeds when he first "fleshed his axe" in the wilderness of the St. Croix that same year.[2]

When lands began to pass into private ownership, logging camps rapidly increased in number.[3] In 1852 there were twenty-two crews of loggers operating on the Rum River in the western part of the Delta. In the usual outfit of these loggers there were from twelve to fourteen men and from six to eight oxen.[4] The regular crew, called a team by the Maineites, by 1852 consisted of two choppers, two or three swampers, two sled tenders, two barkers, two sawyers, one teamster, and one cook.[5] A crew of such size was expected to cut about one million feet in a winter.[6]

In the fall of 1854 a vast army of workers left Stillwater for winter in the woods. Eastern capital was at this time entering the lumber industry in the Stillwater region, giving a great impetus to the logging industry.[7] Eighty-two teams, or crews, operated late that fall on the St. Croix and its tributaries. Of these, twenty-eight teams were on the Snake River, where stood the choicest of white pine.[8] That same autumn the streets of St. Anthony were said to have a "bustling appearance"; ox-drawn wagons bound for the pineries of the Rum River and its tributaries were going northward in great numbers, loaded with cooking utensils, bales of goods, groceries, whole sides of beef — supplies to last the winter through. These

[1] Wilson P. Shortridge, "Henry Hastings Sibley and the Minnesota Frontier," *Minnesota History Bulletin*, vol. iii (Aug. 1919), p. 120; Durant, "Lumbering and Steamboating on the St. Croix River," *Minn. Hist. Soc. Coll.*, vol. x, pt. 2, p. 648.
[2] *St. Anthony Express*, Jan. 21, 1854.
[3] See above, p. 52.
[4] *St. Anthony Express*, Jan. 31 and Apr. 10, 1852, and Jan. 21, 1853.
[5] Hotchkiss, *History of Lumber and Forest Industry of Northwest*, p. 530.
[6] *Minnesota Pioneer*, Feb. 13, 1850.
[7] *St. Croix Union*, Nov. 3, 1854. See above, Chapter IV.
[8] *St. Croix Union*, Dec. 2, 1854.

71

teams of oxen were traveling to remote points, sometimes as far as two hundred miles north of St. Anthony. The newspapers stated that merchants sent immense quantities of grain and provisions into the woods, and the preparations for that particular winter in the pineries exceeded those of any earlier winter.[9] Logging furnished employment to a greater number of men in Minnesota at that time than any other industry, including agriculture. In the winter of 1855 about a thousand men were laboring in the forests of the St. Croix.[10]

The logging industry was handicapped by the scarcity of food in the new country. In the winter of 1853 logging teams on the Rum River were reduced in number because of the scarcity and high prices of food.[11] Even as late as 1856 agriculture had no place in Minnesota Territory, according to James J. Hill.[12] Horace Greeley, editor of the powerful *New York Tribune,* remarked scornfully that Minnesota "imported not only loafers in great abundance, but the bread they ate as well as the whiskey they drank." [13]

Loggers were dependent upon outside sources for foodstuffs. Flour was brought up the Mississippi from the neighboring states of Iowa, Wisconsin, and Illinois, or hauled down the Red River Trail in ox carts from the Pembina district.[14] In 1846 Stephen B. Hanks bought at St. Louis for John McKusick, the lumber magnate of Stillwater, several tons of food, including eggs, beans, hominy, and dried apples. At Bellevue, above St. Louis, he bought fifty barrels of flour and several barrels of whiskey. Nearly all the pork consumed in Minnesota — and pork was a very necessary article for woodsmen — was brought in from "below." [15] Even horses and oxen were purchased outside the territory.[16]

Food prices were high because the source of supply was so far away and because transportation, whether against the current of the Mississippi or by slow-moving ox cart from Pembina, was expensive. In 1837 Franklin Steele paid four dollars a barrel for beans, two dollars a gallon for molasses,

[9] *St. Anthony Express,* Nov. 11, 1854; *St. Croix Union,* Dec. 2, 1854, and May 19, 1855.

[10] *Ibid.,* June 9, 1855.

[11] *St. Anthony Express,* Jan. 21, 1853; S. B. Hanks, *Memoir of Capt. S. B. Hanks,* vol. iii. These recollections, in six volumes, of an early Minnesota woodsman, later a river pilot and captain, were written from his dictation by C. B. Paddock in 1907 and 1908. The manuscript is now in the possession of the Minnesota Historical Society.

[12] E. S. Seymour, *Sketches of Minnesota* (New York, 1850), p. 157; *Minnesota Chronicle* (St. Paul), Sept. 29, 1849; *Minnesota Pioneer,* Dec. 12, 1859.

[13] John W. McClung, *Minnesota As It Is in 1870* (St. Paul, 1870), pp. 92–93.

[14] H. M. Larson, *Wheat Market and Farmer in Minnesota,* p. 17; W. C. LeDuc, *Minnesota Year Book* (St. Paul, 1853), pp. 82–83; *Seventh Census of the U.S.,* pp. 1007–8; *Minnesota Pioneer,* Mar. 6, 1850; Shortridge, "Henry Hastings Sibley and the Minnesota Frontier," p. 120.

[15] *Stillwater Messenger,* Apr. 2, 1861.

[16] Hanks, *Memoir,* vol. iii; *St. Anthony Express,* Jan. 21, 1853.

eleven dollars a barrel for flour, and forty dollars a barrel for pork.[17] In 1855 loggers in the St. Croix country were offering a dollar a bushel for corn, but they complained that even at that price none was to be had; corn, flour, oats, and pork must be purchased from "below." [18] Even in the late 1850s wheat cost four dollars a bushel and flour ten dollars a barrel.[19]

Walker and Judd, who were engaged in both the logging and the sawmill phases of lumbering, had their own supply store at Marine to furnish supplies to loggers. They carried regular accounts for the "Snow Shoe Logging Camp" and the "Mud Creek Camp," both belonging to Hersey and Staples. In 1857 Walker and Judd were selling butter at forty-five cents a pound. Flour was selling at nine dollars and a half a barrel, potatoes at one dollar and twenty-five cents a bushel, pork at thirty dollars a barrel, and corn at two dollars a bushel. Coffee and plug tobacco, choice bits for the woodsman, were priced at twenty cents a pound. Hip boots and calf boots were priced at five dollars; pants were selling for four dollars and a half, and overalls for seventy-five cents.[20] Altogether, living in the St. Croix country was not cheap, and since it was the high cost of supplies which made logging expensive, lumbermen became strong agitators for the development of agriculture in Minnesota.

The influx of population into Minnesota's farm area gradually increased agricultural production, and by 1860 Minnesota had become an exporting rather than importing state in farm products. This, said Stillwater newspapers, was attended with visible and happy effects.[21] They had in mind the possibility of increasing the size of crews when food could be purchased more conveniently and at a better price.

In the fall of 1863 woodsmen poured into the pineries. The coming spring would see such drives of logs as the "Father of Waters had been a stranger to," predicted the *St. Cloud Democrat*.[22] In 1867 Albert Stimpson of Stillwater, who had logged on the St. Croix for seventeen winters, was in charge of a crew of twenty-nine men with twelve horses; they spent three months and ten days in the woods, and during this time they cut 14,247 logs, measuring 4,029,839 feet — an unusual cut for one winter.[23] With the

[17] *Ibid.*, Jan. 21, 1854.

[18] *St. Croix Union*, Apr. 24, 1855.

[19] Holcombe and Bingham, *Compendium*, p. 67; interview with O. D. Dahlin of Port Wing, Wisconsin, June 5, 1932. Dahlin's father was one of the early Swedes who logged in the St. Croix country, and the son, when only a young boy, went to work in the woods.

[20] These prices are listed in the charge accounts in the Day Book of the store of Walker and Judd at Marine for 1857. This book is in the Walker, Judd and Veazie Papers in the Minnesota Historical Society.

[21] *Stillwater Messenger*, May 24, 1859, and Apr. 2, 1861.

[22] *St. Cloud Democrat*, Nov. 6, 1863.

[23] *Stillwater Messenger*, May 1, 1867.

increase in local food production, larger crews could be hired to fell more trees for a rapidly growing lumber market.

In the pioneer period in Minnesota crews operated in a simple way. There was no complex organization of the work and the loggers' equipment was in keeping with the slow-moving saw at the mill. Individual loggers, with several helpers, worked in the forest, selling their winter's yield wherever there was a market. Working on a larger scale were trained woodsmen from Maine, such as Daniel Stanchfield and Sumner W. Farnham, foremen of crews, who cut logs for the mills at St. Anthony. Hersey and Staples of Stillwater brought from Maine skilled loggers who worked on lands belonging to their firm, and the sawmill men from Marine likewise had their own logging crews.

Maine men were the pioneer loggers in Minnesota. As early as 1841 Stephen Hanks, a cousin of Abraham Lincoln, in logging on the Snake River, found that most of his co-workers were old loggers from Maine and other eastern logging states.[24] Men from Maine were numerous.[25] A congressman from Maine complained in the House on March 30, 1852, of "the stalwart sons of Maine marching away by scores and hundreds to the piny woods of the Northwest." But proudly he continued, "All I can say is, most fortunate that State or Territory which shall receive the largest accession of them." [26]

Maine newspapers carried advertisements placed by men in the West who wanted sawyers, teamsters, choppers, and other workers. One such advertisement appeared in the *Daily Whig and Courier* of Bangor, located in the heart of lumbering in the old White Pine State.[27] Maine newspapers also carried news and descriptions of the work done in the region of the St. Croix and Chippewa, and wages in the new country were discussed in them.[28] Altogether, there was keen interest among Maine people in what was happening on the St. Croix and other waters of the Upper Mississippi.

Faithful loggers followed their masters into the new country — for example, Charles and Jacob Bean, who followed Hersey and Staples to the St. Croix Delta in order to furnish logs for the Hersey and Staples mill at Stillwater. Maine men were said to have such a hold on logging that men unfortunate enough to hail from other parts had difficulty in getting

[24] Hanks, *Memoir*, vol. ii.

[25] George H. Warren, *The Pioneer Woodsman As He Is Related to Lumbering in the Northwest* (Minneapolis, 1914), p. 78; *Mississippi Valley Lumberman*, vol. xiv, Sept. 14, 1888, p. 2; Stanchfield, "History of Pioneer Lumbering on the Upper Mississippi," *Minn. Hist. Soc. Coll.*, vol. ix, p. 346.

[26] 32d Cong., 1st Sess., *Congressional Globe*, Appendix, p. 389.

[27] Richard G. Wood, *A History of Lumbering in Maine, 1820–1861* (Orono, Maine, 1935), p. 234.

[28] *Maine Farmer* (Augusta), Dec. 29, 1853. This reference was generously sent to me by Dr. Richard G. Wood.

jobs.[29] In 1847 Daniel Stanchfield, who had learned logging on the Penobscot, placed the first logging camp on the Rum River, and in 1848 Sumner W. Farnham, son of the surveyor of logs on the St. Croix River in Maine, established the second.[30]

It is said that the best loggers in Minnesota were those who came first, for only the best could have endured and survived the strenuous life which the pathbreakers in the mighty forests had to face. A few of these loggers became captains of industry; but the great majority remained just plain woodsmen.[31] They were reputed to be a class by themselves, who as ax-men or top-loaders have not been equaled since. They were a loyal crew, laboring not only for what they could earn but also for the honor of their camp. "Those were the days when men were men and knew how to work," said one old-time lumberman in recalling the early days.[32]

Maineites were proud of their work in the new country, and they boasted not a little to their friends back home. In the *Bangor Daily Journal* of May 5, 1855, one Roberts from Maine, foreman of a crew of loggers operating on the Ground House River, a tributary of the St. Croix in Minnesota, challenged his friends in the Penobscot country to do better than his crew had done. He said that in 117 days they had cut and hauled into the river eight thousand logs which would scale between two and three million feet.[33] Roberts no doubt had followed Hersey and Staples from Maine to Minnesota; their chief operations were on the Ground House River. In 1867 Albert Stimpson, logging in the St. Croix region with a crew of twenty-nine men, cut 4,029,839 feet. He, too, challenged loggers in Maine or Canada to beat that winter's job.[34]

The early loggers did not come in big gangs, here when the season was on and gone when it was over. They brought their families and settled in the woods to carry on logging as their chosen lifework. If they had little farms, those farms were but incidental to their chief business. The first loggers in the pine forests of Minnesota were pioneers who ventured into the new country for the purpose of cutting timber for a livelihood, and not to speculate in lands.[35]

Though the early woodsmen came largely from Maine, or from other New England states, there were in the crews some from New York state,

[29] *Mississippi Valley Lumberman*, vol. xxvi, Feb. 1, 1895, p. 71.

[30] Stanchfield, *op. cit.*, p. 357.

[31] *Mississippi Valley Lumberman*, vol. xiv, Sept. 14, 1888, p. 2.

[32] A letter in the possession of the writer, written by George M. Mashek, Escanaba National Bank Building, Escanaba, Michigan, Jan. 6, 1933; Warren, *op. cit.*, p. 78.

[33] Wood, *op. cit.*, p. 234.

[34] *Stillwater Messenger*, May 1, 1867.

[35] Folsom, "History of Lumbering in the St. Croix Valley," *Minn. Hist. Soc. Coll.*, vol. ix, p. 296; interview of the writer with J. H. Ames, President of the Teachers College at River Falls, Wisconsin, on May 18, 1932. Ames' father was an early Maine logger on the Wolf River in Wisconsin.

some French, some Scotch, some Irish (who often became foremen), occasionally a German or a Norwegian. The Swedes increased in number as the years passed.

The Scotsmen who came to Minnesota usually came from Canada — from the Glengarry district below Ottawa. MacDonald, MacIntosh, Mac-Lain, and MacLaughlin are names still heard in Minnesota, particularly in the St. Croix region. The Scotch loggers were men of good repute who often developed sufficient skill to be advanced to the position of cruiser; others became foremen of camps, and some went into the business of logging for themselves.[36]

Important in felling the white pine in Minnesota was also the hardy, rawboned French Canadian, proud of his hairy chest which showed through the unbuttoned collar of his black and red flannel shirt. He came to Minnesota in the pioneer days of the industry and was known for his speed and general efficiency. He was at home in no place but the pine forest, and when the pine was gone, he, too, was gone.[37] The Canadian, whether Scotch or French, played no humble part in the development of the lumber industry of Minnesota; he well deserves a place among the best of woodsmen. But the man who surged to the top and became a master in lumber was usually the shrewd Yankee from New England.

In 1865 the first Scandinavian logging firm, under the direction of J. G. Nelson and Alexander Johnson, established itself in the St. Croix country.[38] Swedes had been known for at least a decade on the St. Croix. As early as 1855 such unmistakably Swedish names as Nils Welender, Rosengren, Oleson, Erickson, Ole Hanson, and Magneson began to appear on the charge accounts of the store of Judd, Walker and Company at Marine.[39] It must have been logging and lumber that brought these men, for Marine had no other attraction.[40]

The industry seems to have continued to draw the Swedish, for in 1858 three hundred families of that nationality established a settlement at Swede Lake in Chisago County, already a prominent logging region. They bought

---

[36] Warren, *op. cit.*, p. 78; interview of the writer with Robert ApRoberts of the office staff of the surveyor general of logs, St. Paul, June 17, 1932; W. W. Bartlett, "Old Lumberman Looks Back on Struggles for Riches in Vast Pine Forests," *Daily Telegram* (Eau Claire, Wis.), Jan. 21, 1923 (a clipping in the William W. Bartlett Collection, Minnesota Historical Society).

[37] *Mississippi Valley Lumberman*, vol. xxi, Jan. 22, 1892, p. 6; interview of the writer with J. W. Bayly of Duluth, Aug. 13, 1932, a member of the one-time lumber firm of Alger, Smith and Company.

[38] Hotchkiss, *op. cit.*, p. 533.

[39] Walker, Judd and Veazie Papers, Journal, 1855–58, of Judd, Walker and Company's Marine Mills.

[40] A letter written by George Spaulding to the American Home Missionary Society, Mar. 24, 1857, at Marine. This is taken from film copies of the papers of that organization in the Minnesota Historical Society.

lands which they cleared and worked in the summer, while in the winter they added cash to their scant resources by working in the logging camps.[41] They were industrious and frugal and were reputed to be good workers in the woods. Scandinavians rarely became leaders in Minnesota's lumber industry, but they were steady workmen, thoroughly dependable, who served their employers as though they were partners in the work. Many of the farmers in the St. Croix region today are descendants of those early loggers.

The wages paid to the loggers varied with the type of work they did. It has been customary throughout the history of the lumber industry for the man in the woods to receive his board and keep. In the pioneer period his board was simple; pork and beans and blackstrap molasses constituted the main fare, substantial but plain. Living was generally plain on the frontier, and the worker in the woods was quite accustomed to the kind of food served in the lumber camp. Whatever he earned was clear gain, except the sum subtracted at the wanigan (the camp store) for "Spearhead" or "Peerless" or for an extra woolen shirt or some other necessary article. There was little occasion for spending money in the woods; the small wage was usually the woodsman's when the winter chore was over.

In 1848, when Daniel Stanchfield was foreman of logging operations for Franklin Steele on the Rum River, his wages were $50 a month. A memorandum on wages of the crew stated definitely that Stanchfield was not to go on the drive. His crew members each received about half the wage of the foreman. W. H. Sked, Henry Augell, James Dougherty, John Wilcox, and one Buckman were engaged to "do anything" and to go on the drive, their wages being $26 a month. S. H. Bliss and one Howard were paid $22 a month, Stephen Augell was to be paid $19, and "French John" $16. E. Knowles was paid $30 a month — the memorandum stated that he was a "teamster and a good one." [42]

In 1850 the usual wage for the average woodsman in the St. Croix area was $26 a month, while the inexperienced received $20 and sometimes a little less.[43] But there were master choppers who were paid $75 a month.[44]

The period of logging in Minnesota when Maine men and therefore Maine methods predominated can well be called the hand-tool period. It was a period characterized by heavy lifting and plain brute strength. It was a period of slow motion, when power was made by the deliberate movement of the oxen — called cattle by the Maineites — and by the hand

[41] *Stillwater Messenger*, Sept. 7, 1858.
[42] A memorandum of men who were logging and driving for Franklin Steele under the direction of Daniel Stanchfield in 1848 (Steele Papers).
[43] Hotchkiss, *op. cit.*, p. 530.
[44] Martin Page, "The Camp in the 50's," *Daily Telegram* (Eau Claire, Wis.), Feb. 24, 1916 (a clipping in the Bartlett Collection, Minn. Hist. Soc.).

of man. The Maine men brought to Minnesota forests the ax and the go-devil, and a little later that instrument so necessary in the drive, the peavey.[45]

The ax was the chief weapon of the men from Maine in their attack on the Minnesota forests. To swing the ax and strike right every time was the mark of an expert, and the chopper was an artist in the opinion of the woodsman of that day. Therefore he could command wages above those of other woodsmen. The men from Maine did not know the crosscut saw,[46] which would later replace the ax and take from the chopper his jealously guarded position.[47]

There was no need to hew out roads during the early period of logging in Minnesota, for the pine stood thick on the banks of streams. A go-devil, a wishbone-shaped affair with a crossbar — only the crotch of a hardwood tree — was at first the chief aid to transportation in the woods. This simple vehicle was also called a *travoy,* mostly by the Scotch loggers from Canada; the French Canadians called it the *mogie. Go-devil* was the name applied by the loggers from Maine. It was a crude bit of equipment made on the spot where it was to be used. With this rough sled one ox dragged the felled trees to the landing, whence they floated downstream when the spring freshet came. Later the dray came to take its place alongside the go-devil. The dray had runners like a sled and could carry larger loads than its predecessor; a good-sized dray could take three thousand feet at one time from the stump to the landing.

The hand-spike, a predecessor of the peavey, was a dependable instrument for many operations in logging, but the peavey, having a sharp point and a clasp, combined the hand-spike and the cant-dog. This tool was made by Joseph Peavey, a blacksmith of Stillwater, Maine, in 1858, and it became a valued instrument in the moving of the log.

Changing the standing tree to a floating log involved several processes. When the chopper had finished his work — having aimed to fell his tree in the best position relative to the stream — and the tree was prostrate on the ground, the swamper came to cut the branches. Then came the barker, who ripped the bark from the underneath side so that the tree would slide more easily.[48] The chainer followed to fasten it to the go-devil, and, when

[45] Wood, *op. cit.,* p. 170.

[46] In an interview on May 18, 1932, Jesse H. Ames, whose father was an early Maine logger in the Northwest, told the writer that the first loggers in this region did not use crosscut saws. Also, William McDonald, "Logging Equipment and Methods of Early Days," *Daily Telegram* (Eau Claire, Wis.), Oct. 7, 1916 (a clipping in the Bartlett Collection, Minn. Hist. Soc.).

[47] William Tibbetts, a logger who came from Maine to Minnesota, said in an interview with the writer, Aug. 15, 1932, at Ball Club, Minnesota, that the first crosscut saw he ever saw was on the Prairie River in Minnesota in 1874.

[48] Hotchkiss, *op. cit.,* p. 530.

the ox had pulled it through the brush and snow to the landing, the sawyer made it into logs ready for the spring drive.

No great amount of capital was necessary for a logger's outfit in those days, because the simple equipment was made largely by the men themselves. The go-devil, the peavey handles, and the hand-spike were generally homemade in the pioneer period of logging,[49] and the axes were often made by the camp blacksmith. The most expensive part of the logging equipment was the oxen or horses, which had to be purchased. Using the primitive equipment of his time as a measuring stick, Daniel Stanchfield stated that seventy mills in seventy years couldn't exhaust the white pine he had seen on the Rum River; he failed to reckon with the ingenuity of man, whose inventions would level the forest within one generation.

The woodsman's way of living in the pineries was as meager and as simple as his tools. A one-room shanty, low and dark — for windows were very rare — served as his living quarters. It was built of logs, with sides never more than four feet high, and a roof so steep it sometimes ran almost to the ground. "One had to learn to stoop in those days," according to a tall, lanky Irishman of eighty-one years, who had lived most of his life in the logging camps. The shanty, often called a State-of-Maine camp, varied in size according to the number in the crew. One shanty on the banks of the Snake River in 1841 was 25 by 40 feet.[50] Swamp moss and clay filled the openings between the logs to keep the warmth in. The shanty had but one big room, where often as many as twenty men lived during the coldest days of the year. Another loggers' shanty, located in Wisconsin on the Chippewa River, was described as being 24 by 36 feet in size, with walls three feet high.[51]

Not a nail was used in any part of these structures. The roof of a shanty was made of poles covered with marsh hay, over which a layer of earth was placed.[52] The poles were cut to form either a shake roof or a scoop roof. A shake roof was made of thin flat pieces of split pine logs; the scoop roof was made by splitting hollow basswood logs in half and laying one course with the hollow side up and another with the hollow side down. The floor was commonly made of puncheons, known in the woodsmen's vernacular as "punchings." These were logs that were split straight with the top surface adzed off so as to make a smooth floor.[53] A camp in the region of Marine in 1855 was 25 feet square with a roof running almost

[49] Hanks, *Memoir*, vol. ii.

[50] *St. Croix Union*, Mar. 6, 1855; Hanks, *Memoir*, vol. i.

[51] William W. Bartlett, "Lumbering in the Chippewa Valley," *Daily Telegram* (Eau Claire, Wis.), Feb. 24, 1923 (a clipping in the Bartlett Collection, Minn. Hist. Soc.).

[52] Wright T. Orcutt, "The Minnesota Lumberjacks," *Minnesota History*, vol. vi (Mar. 1925), pp. 5–7.

[53] *Ibid*. In the Public Library at Eau Claire, Wis., is a model of the State-of-Maine camp.

to the ground; the gables had no windows but were built up with logs.[54] One kind of log never used in the construction of camps was the balm of Gilead. Legend has it that the Saviour's cross was made from that tree, and woodsmen regarded it as ill-omened to set foot inside a camp in which it had been used.

The life of the shanty centered about a big open fire which baked the bread, dried the many woolen socks that hung below the roof at night, gave cheer and warmth, and lighted many a squaw dance.[55] The early camps knew no chimney of the modern type. Their chimney was a hole in the roof above the fire, or a boxlike chimney that extended somewhat above the roof. Daniel Stanchfield spoke of a chimney 4 by 6 feet in one of his camps, built in the middle of the roof and formed of round poles. But the smoke wasn't always minded to go up such a chimney, and sometimes it became quite a nuisance.[56] The open fire, which the woodsmen called a caboose, would sometimes burn throughout an entire "campaign."

The men's quarters were on one side of the fire. Their furnishings were quite in keeping with the surrounding meagerness. Balsam boughs usually a foot deep constituted the bed. Each man arranged his own boughs, and the more sensitive woodsmen removed the projecting twigs. Sometimes the men slept on hay or straw strewn on the floor; all in a row, they lay with their heads to the wall, their feet to the fire, covered by blankets so large that one served for many men.[57] The woodsman slept with his tussock, or turkey, under his head, or with a sack of straw or hay to serve as a pillow. The turkey, or tussock, forerunner of the modern knapsack, was a seamless sack holding about two bushels. A piece of small rope was tied from one of its lower corners to the upper end of the sack, making it more convenient to carry. The tussock held all the worldly possessions of a shanty-man; a satchel or suitcase was unthought-of as a part of his outfit.

Strange it must have been at night to see, by the glow of the fire, the whiskered faces of the woodsmen peering out above the blankets. A grindstone, a wash sink, and a barrel of water completed the usual equipment in the men's quarters of the shanty.[58]

At the farther end of the shanty on the other side of the fire was the

[54] St. Croix Union, Mar. 6, 1855.
[55] Minneapolis Tribune, Dec. 13, 1873. There were few white women living near the lumber camps, and the Indian women came to the lumberjacks' dances. Woodsmen tell that the endurance of the squaws when dancing surpassed even that of the lumberjacks.
[56] St. Cloud Democrat, Feb. 13, 1862.
[57] An interview of the writer with Michael McAlpine of Grand Rapids, Minn., on Aug. 14, 1932. He recalled that on the drive he had slept with eleven other men under one blanket. St. Croix Union, Mar. 6, 1855.
[58] Bartlett, "Lumbering in the Chippewa Valley," Daily Telegram (Eau Claire, Wis.), Feb. 24, 1923, p. 7.

kitchen, where the simple but substantial food was prepared for the rowdy appetites created by hard work out-of-doors in a Minnesota winter. The food was prepared over the open fire or in the bean hole. The cook had a wooden crane by which he moved the red-hot kettles over the burning logs. Bread was baked in a reflector, which was nothing more than a big tin box shoved against the fire. The heat reflected against the open cover and thus baked the bread.[59]

Beans were put into a Dutch oven and buried in the bean hole, the original fireless cooker, a mere hole in the ground about two feet in diameter and about eighteen inches deep. To make the bean hole all roots were cut away and the soil was loosened; a good fire in the hole heated the soil, and when a bed of coals had been formed, an iron kettle with a tight cover was set in the hole.[60] Coals were placed around and over it. The bean hole was then covered, and safe from man and animals the beans cooked mysteriously all night long. They were ready for serving in the morning, with boiled salt pork. Both dishes appeared again at noon and at night, and for a change on Sundays the cook fried the salt pork!

Bread (sometimes in the form of hot biscuits), salt pork, blackstrap molasses, and bean-hole beans, eulogized by the early woodsmen, provided the woodsman's regular diet.[61] Once in a while mince or apple pie appeared. Venison, fish, and fowl were sometimes a welcome change, and one woodsman speaks of being served with a "fine mess of red squirrels in a delicious stew." [62] Another one writes, in 1852, of catching in Lake Mille Lacs pickerel which weighed between thirty and forty-three pounds.[63] Some of the Swedes in camp complained of the cooks from Maine whose skill was limited to the cooking of codfish. Rolled oats or rice pudding was the choice dessert and was always a part of the Christmas dinner.[64] Tea was the national drink of the woodsmen from Maine, and it was standard in the camps until the Swedes introduced coffee.

The men engaged in logging during a Minnesota winter needed much food. Orders were placed in great quantities; the regular outfit of twelve to fourteen men with six to eight oxen consumed in one season 300 bushels

[59] O. D. Dahlin of Port Wing, Wis., whose father was employed by Walker, Judd and Veazie at Marine, Minn., said that the bread baked in the reflector was often baked only on top.

[60] "The Bean Hole," *North Woods*, vol. iv, Mar. 1915, p. 27; Orcutt, *op. cit.*, pp. 8–9.

[61] Page, *op. cit.*

[62] *St. Anthony Express*, Jan. 31, 1852; *St. Croix Union*, Mar. 6, 1855; Hanks, *Memoir*, vol. ii.

[63] Jonas Fairweather, a logger in a camp on the Rum River, nine miles south of Mille Lacs, wrote the editor of the *St. Anthony Express* a letter which was published in that paper on Jan. 31, 1852.

[64] *Mississippi Valley Lumberman*, vol. xx, June 13, 1891, p. 2.

of corn, 200 bushels of oats, 20 barrels of flour, 6 barrels of pork, 250 pounds of butter, 150 pounds of lard, 10 bushels of beans, 600 pounds of beef, and 15 tons of hay.[65] The loggers on the Rum River alone, in the winter of 1853, needed 5400 bushels of corn, 3600 bushels of oats, 360 barrels of flour, 108 barrels of pork, 4500 pounds of butter, 2700 pounds of lard, 180 bushels of beans, 10,800 pounds of beef, and 270 tons of hay.[66]

A shanty-man worked no eight-hour day; the industrious woodsman plied his ax from daylight to dusk. The end of a day in the woods was at dark, though as the days lengthened in the spring the men were allowed to leave work at sundown. Once home, they "dressed for dinner," a process that consisted chiefly of removing several layers of stockings and heavy mackinaws and replacing the heavy working shoes with stags (old boots whose tops were cut off) or old discarded shoes without laces.

After their evening meal the woodsmen competed in the telling of tall stories. Those old-timers did not know Paul Bunyan; they did not call upon the imagination for their characters — all around were real men of the forest, just as interesting as Paul Bunyan, or in many ways more so. These early loggers were interesting in themselves, a strong lot of men who had lived hard, though picturesque, lives. Every man was expected to furnish his mite to make up the social program. Should he be short a story, he was fined a contribution to the tobacco box.

Life was made gay by a fiddler, who was as necessary in camp as a teamster. The mouth organ and the accordion were not unusual instruments in a State-of-Maine camp in Minnesota's St. Croix country. These instruments furnished music for the dances, in which a number of the men, designated by grain sacks tied around their waists, represented the gentler sex. "Hot Bottom," "Shuffle the Brogue," and "Buy My Sheep" were favorite games. Sometimes the men played cards, but cards and whiskey were not allowed in all camps.[67]

Singing, too, was a favored amusement, and the loggers' songs bespoke the prowess of their own kind, for woodsmen had pride in their accomplishments. "The Shanty-Man's Life" was one of the oldest of the ballads sung in the camps, and probably one of the most widely known. It is likely that it came from New England or eastern Canada.[68]

[65] *St. Anthony Express,* Jan. 21, 1853.
[66] *Ibid.*
[67] Some woodsmen expected a "gill of rum" as a part of their rations. But J. H. Knapp, in 1846, in making the order for supplies, arranged that the gin order was not placed and, when the gin didn't arrive, the woodsmen were told that the order had been forgotten (miscellaneous papers of Henry E. Knapp, Wis. Hist. Soc.); Page, *op. cit.*
[68] This version of "The Shanty-Man's Life" was sung by A. C. Hannah at Bemidji, Minnesota. He had learned it forty years before in Ontario, Canada. Edith Granger, *Granger's Index to Poetry and Recitations* (Chicago, 1940), p. 458; Carl Sandburg, *The American Songbag* (New York, 1927), p. 390.

1. Oh, a shanty-man's life is a wearisome life,
   Although some think it void of care,
   Swinging an ax from morning till night
   In the midst of the forest so drear,
   Lying in the shanty bleak and cold
   While the cold stormy winter winds blow,
   And as soon as the daylight doth appear
   To the wild woods we must go.

2. Oh, the cook rises up in the middle of the night
   Saying, "Hurrah, brave boys, it's day!"
   Broken slumbers ofttimes are passed
   As the cold winter night whiles away.
   Had we rum, wine, or beer, our spirits for to cheer,
   As the days so lonely do dwine,
   Or a glass of any shone, while in the woods alone,
   For to cheer up our troubled minds.

3. But transported from our lass and our sparkling glass
   These comforts which we here leave behind
   Not a friend to us so near as to wipe the falling tear,
   When sorrow fills our troubled mind.

4. But when spring it does set in, double hardships then begin,
   When the waters are piercing cold,
   And our clothes are dripping wet and fingers benumbed,
   And our pike-poles we can scarcely hold.
   Betwixt rocks, shoals, and sands gives employment to all hands
   Our well banded raft for to steer,
   And the rapids that we run, Oh, they seem to us but fun,
   For we're void of all slavish fear.

5. Oh, a shanty lad is the only lad I love,
   And I never will deny the same;
   My heart doth scorn those conceited farmer boys
   Who think it a disgraceful name.
   They may boast about their farms, but my shanty boy has charms
   So far, far surpassing them all,
   Until death it doth us part, he shall enjoy my heart,
   Let his riches be great or small.

The woodsman thought of himself as a conqueror. His weapon of conquest was his ax, with which "with a sweep and a blow, you strike your foe." This was a line in the "Song of the Western Pioneer": [69]

> Hurray for the axe, the brave, sharp axe,
> Hurrah for its notes that ring,

[69] Dillon O'Brien, "Song of the Western Pioneer," *Stillwater Messenger,* June 5, 1867.

Through the valley wide, up the mountain side,
When it sweeps like a falcon's wing.
And down crashes the pine, with its lordly crest,
For the axe hath cleaved through its knotted breast.
Let others sing of the sword and flash
Of a forest of dancing spears;
But their path is red with the blood of the dead,
Whilst behind them a sea of tears.
And the maiden shall wait for her lover in vain,
For he sleeps where the moon-beams glance cold on the stain.
Not such thy triumph, my brave sharp axe,
On your blade are no stains of sin,
With a sweep and a blow, you strike your foe,
And up from his grave doth spring
The yellow grain, the broad leaved corn,
And my children bless you at early morn.

Thus the early pioneers in the logging industry ate and slept and spent their free time in the one-room Maine shanty or hovel. Here they patched their clothes; here they vied with each other in telling tall tales characteristic of strong men in the woods. They lived together like one family.[70] The crews were small in number. The crudeness of the shanty, the primitiveness of the tools, and the plainness of the food were quite in keeping with the scale of work. The thousands of loggers of a later day in Minnesota could not have been accommodated in the pioneer period.

The Sabbath was desecrated in camp, wrote the Reverend E. Newton, who represented the American Home Missionary Society; it was given over to idleness, dissipation, and card playing, he wrote home to his Board. From November to April, he stated, these men were in the woods where there were no hallowed associations, where men were without the restraint of female society and a Christian community. He wrote despairingly of liquor, which he said was "doing awful work." [71] But the woodsman could hardly sit with his hands folded on Sunday; it was "boil up day" for him. In the big outdoors he scrubbed his clothes, using half of a barrel as his tub and doing his boiling in a big lard can over a roaring fire. Then he mended his clothes and sewed on buttons. He had his hair cut and a shave. He also changed his bed of balsam boughs. If cleanliness is next to godliness, he was not too far wrong in his use of the day.[72]

[70] *Duluth News Tribune,* Feb. 22, 1925.

[71] The Reverend E. Newton, Belle Prairie, to the American Home Missionary Society, Jan. 4, 1856. Film copies of the Society's papers are in the possession of the Minnesota Historical Society.

[72] F. E. Cummings, "Lumbering in the Chippewa Valley," *Daily Telegram* (Eau Claire, Wis.), Apr. 21, 1916 (a clipping in the Bartlett Collection, Minn. Hist. Soc.).

Occasionally ministers traveled to the camps, and prayer and praise were not uncommon in the remote woods on Sunday.[73] A special committee of the Young Men's Christian Association sent reading matter to the pineries,[74] and the American Home Missionary Society was persuaded to furnish religious tracts for the men in the woods. Such reading matter and the visits of the ministers did something to relieve the monotony of camp life.

Crude though the beginnings of the logging industry were in the St. Croix forests, the early loggers produced logs to meet the rapidly growing demands of sawmills in the Upper Mississippi region. Five million feet were scaled in the St. Croix Boom in 1840, ninety million feet in 1850, and a hundred and fifty million feet in 1860.[75] "Centuries will hardly exhaust the pineries above us," James M. Goodhue, editor of the *Minnesota Pioneer,* wrote in 1852, referring to the St. Croix Delta. He did not foresee how rapidly the increasing cut of each decade would destroy the forests. As early as 1870 the loggers of the St. Croix were moving out of the Delta, seeking other forests northward. Contributing to this rapid development was the ease with which the product of forest and mill could be rafted to downriver markets.

[73] *Anoka Star,* Feb. 25, 1865.
[74] *Minneapolis Tribune,* Jan. 26, 1868.
[75] See Table 1, p. 25.

CHAPTER VI

Rafting and Selling Downriver

IN THE early years of the lumber industry on the Upper Mississippi the product found its market chiefly downriver, and even after the coming of the railroad the Mississippi carried logs and lumber to market. The river way to market was long and uncertain and the market widely scattered. But the Mississippi was available without any expense of construction; it offered the most rapid form of transportation before railroads came to the region; and it was the most convenient method of transportation for heavy products at the time.

The cutting of the white pine on the upper reaches of the Mississippi brought a new industry to the river, that of rafting. Earlier, the river had carried rich bundles of fur, which could be transported in small craft, but heavy craft were needed for carrying lumber, and as a result the rafting industry developed. For seventy years rafting gave an atmosphere of activity and liveliness to the mighty river.[1] At first only lumber went down this great trunk line, but shortly, by a peculiar circumstance, it was discovered that logs could ride the river as well.

No attempt had ever been made before 1843 to take logs down the Mississippi. Then occurred an accident, unfortunate at the time but with far-reaching consequences. In 1843, because of the rising of the St. Croix, the log boom broke at St. Croix Falls, scattering logs in every direction and sending the whole winter's cut of 400,000 feet down St. Croix Lake. It was a loss of considerable importance for the mills at St. Croix because all their raw material for that season's lumber was instantly swept away. But one John B. Page had the foresight to gather the scattered logs and attempt to raft them down the Mississippi. It worked. The logs reached St. Louis, where they were sold to Thomas West.[2] Thus was made the discovery that logs could be rafted on the Mississippi. Mills sprang up at strategic points along the water route, and log-rafting came to vie with lumber-rafting.[3]

[1] Russell, *A-rafting on the Mississipp'*, pp. 95, 326.
[2] Folsom, "History of Lumbering in the St. Croix Valley," *Minn. Hist. Soc. Coll.*, vol. ix, p. 317.
[3] Cheney, "Development of Lumber Industry in Minnesota," *Journal of Geography*, vol. xiv, p. 190.

The business of rafting grew with the lumber industry. From small beginnings in the 1840s it developed into a large and well-organized industry in the 1870s. Able leadership steadily improved methods during those years and, strangely, neither the railroad nor the new market to the west could destroy the business on the river. Only when there were no more trees to be cut did the rafting industry finally come to an end.

Two battalions of workmen were outstanding in lumbering. In the first was that unusual lot of men who hewed down the pine during the savage winter; equally strange were the men of the second battalion who directed the rafts of logs and lumber on the river in summer, whether the humor of the Father of Waters was good or bad. (Not a few men were members of both groups, logging in the winter and rafting in the summer.) Adventure was in the very blood of these men. The journey to market was not a pleasure trip. Sometimes the rafts were lashed by summer storms; sometimes low water caught them; sometimes they were hurled to pieces on fierce rapids.

Indeed, rafting was never easy; it involved many problems and difficulties with the river and the men. In the late summer of 1850 one Spencer H. White wrote from Moline, Illinois, to Steele and Godfrey of Minnesota about a trip downriver with logs he had purchased from the Minnesotans: "I have at last got down with my logs being thirty one days since I started, with all sorts of luck coming, high waters, bad weather, bad Pilot &c." [4] The fate of another lot of logs sent downriver by Steele in the fall of 1850 has been recorded by one familiar with the case: [5]

With regard to two rafts of whitepine logs belonging to Franklin Steele Esq. and by him placed in charge of Herrall & Jackson for safe running to St. Louis or a market. That said Herrall & Jackson were pilots — ordered to send to St. Paul 4 men to couple up a quantity of Pine Logs in St. Pauls. To form 2 rafts to consist of 6 strings each. Done Oct. 8, 1850. Herrall came to Pigs Eye & on Oct 10, 1850. Herrall left with 2 strings from Pigs Eye. On way down he picked up 4 other strings left by Mr. Steeles rafting crew at a convenient point and intended for a descending raft. Franklin no 2 took them thro Lake Pepin — bill sent to Mr. Steele for that. After leaving Lake Pepin raft was formed in three divisions and after considerable difficulty because of low water we finally arrived at Holmes, a trading post. Then formed into 2 rafts. Herrall had charge of one and one Wm Ganly of other. Below Holmes Herrall struck a bow head and carried away about 200 logs. At Prairie LaCrosse Herrall struck his raft on a sandbar. Ganly tried to push Herrall off but thus Ganly injured his raft & spent 3 days in refitting. Then Herrall's raft went to pieces. Herrall then decided to leave logs there until spring. Herrall was so disgusted that he said "God Damn

---

[4] Steele Papers, White to Steele, Aug. 30, 1850.
[5] *Ibid.*, Oct. 1850, quoting Thomas Kerling. Pig's Eye was an early name for the river landing settlement that became St. Paul.

the Logs and God damn Steele that he had done with the logs for ever, and for all time. They might go to Hell."

Low water tried men's souls and exhausted their purses as well. One always had to reckon on extra expense in rafting down. A bill sent to Franklin F. Steele with orders to pay one Timothy Burns shows the extra cost involved in removing a "sticker": [6]

La Crosse 26 May 1851

Mr. F. Steele
   To Timothy Burns Dr.
1850

Oct	25	For provisions of Sundries furnished to your pine Log Raft in charge of P Herrall Pilot	$38.89
	"	Labor of self & 5 Hands 2 days each in removing Logs from Sand Bars at $2 p. day each	24.
	"	Labor 4 hands 1 day @ $2	8.00
	"	" 2 " 2 " @ $2	8.00
		4 Bed Cords @ 37½¢ ea	1.50
		Work done in securing rafting	5.00
	21st	Securing Logs at Wild Cat	1.50
	27	Labor on Logs	4.50
			$91.39

At best the Mississippi was a difficult river on which to drive a raft. It was a long way — 800 miles, according to old records, from St. Paul to St. Louis and 450 miles from St. Paul to Rock Island [7] — to bring rafts carrying thousands of feet of logs and lumber. And the great stream twisted and turned continuously with never a straight mile. But there were long, monotonous stretches, too. There were moments of sharp danger — moments when "the Old Mississippi is showing her teeth," when the strongest raft seemed a frail craft that might in an instant be smashed by furious wind or torn assunder on a sharp reef.

The place in the Mississippi where the river widens into island-studded Lake Pepin was the raftsman's dread; the devil spent both his summers and his winters there, according to rivermen. Lake Pepin was twenty-seven miles in length, twenty-seven miles of water "walled as it were by rocky ramparts." Lake St. Croix and Lake Pepin were often very "ornery"; either there was too much breeze or there was too little. Stephen Hanks tells us that he once spent two weeks passing through the two, which together total fifty-seven miles.

[6] The bill is from the Steele Papers, May 26, 1851, Burns to Steele.
[7] George Byron Merrick, *Old Times on the Mississippi* (Cleveland, 1909), p. 85. The discrepancies in reported distances may be due partly to inaccuracies in estimates and partly to the fact that the river's course actually changed.

Farther downstream another terror awaited the pilot and his crew. This was the Upper and Lower Rapids; no pilot ever breathed easily until he had passed them. The Upper Rapids, beginning at Le Claire, Iowa, were fourteen miles in length with a fall of twenty-two feet. At the very bottom lay the big and bare Rock Island, which capped the fears of raftsmen coming that way. At that time there was no channel cut by the government in the rock as there now is, and the raftsmen felt no security except that which lay in having the best of pilots and right wind and right water. One hundred and thirty miles below the Upper Rapids, where the Des Moines flows into the Mississippi, lay the Des Moines Rapids, or Lower Rapids, reaching from Montrose to Keokuk. From Muscatine to Keokuk, a distance of twelve miles, the river fell twenty-four feet. The Mississippi had an average current of two and a half miles an hour; the floating raft had the same speed if there was no wind.[8]

The men who ran rafts on the Mississippi had no definite working hours — not even from sun to sun. As long as the raft was traveling downstream they were on the job, in the dead of night as well as in the middle of day. Competition was in their blood; to pass other rafts going downstream was much to their credit. A letter to Dole, Ingram and Kennedy of Eau Claire, Wisconsin, by a man responsible for their products makes clear some of the life and interests of men who brought lumber and logs to market:[9]

On The Raft
Thursday 21st Sep/60

Messrs Dole Ingram & Kennedy
Gent[a]

We left Reeds [Landing] yesty morning at half past 4 and have not tied up since. during the 3 or 4 days prior to our starting from 10 to 12 rafts left the foot of the Lake [Pepin] — we have already past four of them including 2 belonging to Chapman and Thorpe and are in hopes of showing our heels to the others

I write this within an hours run of La Crosse where it will be posted and will drop you a note from McGregor's

The River is about a foot higher than it was at its lowest stage

Do not forget to let me know whether it is imperative that a part of the raft should go to St. Louis.

The black River has risen but not sufficient to let lumber out I have not heard how the Wisconsin is

Yours Respt
James Robert

[8] Hanks, *Memoir of Capt. S[tephen] B. Hanks*, vol. ii.
[9] Orrin H. Ingram Papers, Robert to Dole, Ingram and Kennedy, Sept. 21, 1860. These papers are in the Wisconsin Historical Society.

The most important person in this business of rafting was without question the pilot. Alert, sober, intelligent pilots were much in demand. There were no government engineers to sound the river then, and skilled pilots who knew the drafts of water at different stages never lacked a job. The pilot of that day had to "know the river" — every bend and every range of bluffs and hills. Nor were there beacons to light the way. Raft pilots then groped in darkness up and down the river from St. Louis to St. Anthony.

The pilot, attired in French calf boots, in black cashmere trousers, finely knitted red flannel shirt, a large black silk necktie tied in a square knot with flowing ends, and a soft, wide-brimmed black or white hat, was master of all he surveyed.[10] The responsibility for the raft was his. Every man on the river wanted to ship with a good pilot who would not jeopardize his crew by a jam. Any lumber concern would pay a pilot well who knew how to steer clear of a sharp reef, for what the Mississippi took it never willingly gave back. Lumbermen knew that thousands of dollars could be lost if the pilot did not know his business. A good pilot was a severe taskmaster — he ruled with an iron hand; but it was no small task to rule a crowd of surly and sometimes unwilling raft hands. A raftsman lived by orders; the pilot was the one who hired out his brains. Such a pilot received from $300 to $500 a month in the years from 1852 to 1857;[11] pilots were paid $1600 and $1800 for the season in 1886, and in 1888 about $1400.[12]

Sandy McPhail was one of the great pilots in early rafting on the Upper Mississippi. Not only was he a model raftsman; he was a raft-running teacher and a great handler of men.[13] It was under Sandy Mc-Phail's direction that Stephen Hanks became one of the best pilots ever to see service on the Upper River.[14]

Stephen Hanks, like his cousin, Abraham Lincoln, was born in Kentucky. In 1836, when he was fifteen years old, he went to Albany, Illinois, long the home of rivermen and the place from which all good pilots were said to come.[15] Hanks first rafted logs from the pineries to the mill at St. Croix Falls; then he ran rafts of lumber with Sandy McPhail to St. Louis. In 1844 he piloted his first raft of logs to St. Louis and, in spite of the fact that he could not run it at night, his raft was second into St. Louis in the

[10] Durant, "Lumbering and Steamboating on the St. Croix River," *Minn. Hist. Soc. Coll.*, vol. x, pt. 2, pp. 663–65; Blair, *A Raft Pilot's Log*, p. 73; Russell, *op. cit.*, p. 282.

[11] Durant, *op. cit.*, pp. 664–65.

[12] *Mississippi Valley Lumberman*, vol. xiv, July 6, 1888, p. 2.

[13] Merrick, *Old Times on the Mississippi*, p. 115. His name was James McPhail, but he was always called Sandy by his men.

[14] Capt. Fred A. Bill, "Career of Captain Jerome E. Short," *Clinton Herald* (Iowa), Apr. 1, 1933, p. 3; George Byron Merrick, "Steamboats and Steamboating of the Upper Mississippi," *Saturday Evening Post* (Burlington, Iowa), Jan. 23, 1915, p. 7.

[15] *Clinton Herald*, Mar. 11, 1933, p. 5.

flotilla of rafts with which he traveled.[16] The men who shipped with him on this trip came mostly from Albany, Illinois, too. They were William Ewing, Jim Hugunin, Jim McMahan, Matt Thompson, Flack, Laird, Witherau, and two Robinsons. His "colleagues" were back in the St. Croix country exactly thirty days from the time they started, and Stephen Hanks had become a full-fledged pilot.

In the summer of 1846 Hanks made three trips with rafts to St. Louis; the distance from Stillwater to St. Louis was said to be more than 700 miles. The lumber which Hanks carried in the early part of his career was rafted from the McKusick mill in Stillwater and delivered to Robert Holmes of St. Louis.[17] Hanks piloted in the very beginning of the lumber industry, and he saw its close. He died in 1917, at the age of ninety-six.

Rafting gave employment to large numbers of men. Scandinavians who had just come from Europe generally found ready employment in the woods in winter and appeared as red-shirted raftsmen on the river in summer. On the St. Croix and the Chippewa they were almost as numerous as the Canadians, whether in the woods or on the river.[18] Even as early as 1860 the booming and rafting business of Stillwater, alone, gave employment to twenty-five hundred men.[19] In 1864 ten rafts of logs, manned by two hundred men, were sent south from Stillwater in ten successive days. The raftsmen received thirty-five dollars each for the trip down, and fare was given them for the return trip. When we think of the toiling, comfortless life, this may seem a meager wage, but for unskilled labor — and representing probably about one month from the time the men left until they returned — it was not exceptionally low. Even in 1888 raft hands were receiving no better wage, though their work may have been a bit easier.[20]

Accurate and careful construction was necessary in preparing a raft for its journey. A raft of lumber was made up of eight to ten strings, a string being a row of lumber in cribs not uncommonly five hundred feet in length.[21] The number of cribs would vary according to the size of the stream which carried them. A Chippewa raft usually had from 24 to 28 cribs, while a Mississippi raft would have from 120 to 200 cribs.[22]

A crib was a frame, or heavy crate, designed to hold the lumber tightly

---

[16] Hanks, *Memoir*, vol. ii.

[17] *Ibid.*, vol. iii.

[18] Blair, *op. cit.*, p. 40.

[19] Wheelock, *Minnesota: Its Place among the States*, p. 119; *Stillwater Messenger*, May 15, 1860; Hanks, *Memoir*, vol. iii.

[20] *Mississippi Valley Lumberman*, vol. xiv, July 6, 1888, p. 2.

[21] Durant, *op. cit.*, pp. 663–65.

[22] Interview of the writer with Capt. Fred A. Bill, July 29, 1933. A crib 32 feet by 16 feet by 16 courses equals 8000 feet (*Eau Claire Leader*, Sept. 12, 1930, a clipping in the Bartlett Collection, Minn. Hist. Soc.).

in place. It had to be built well, to hold the lumber firmly whatever the whims of the river might be. A crib was built on a slanting platform or on rollers resting on the shore of some stream where it could be readily slid into the water. It was 32 feet in length and 16 feet in width. Two pieces, 8 inches by 10 inches by 16 feet, were laid end to end on each side of what was to be the crib. Two similar pieces were placed in the center, which lay parallel to the planks on either side. These boards were called runners. At right angles to the runners were laid planks 2 inches by 8 inches by 16 feet, which were known as binders. Three sets of binders were placed in parallel arrangement just as there were three parallel runners.

Next, near the end of the runners, about eight feet from the end of the crib, holes were bored — with augurs so big it usually took two men to handle them. In these holes were placed grub pins, so-called since the days long ago when in Pennsylvania the crown of a tree root grubbed out of the earth formed the head of the pin.[23] The grub pin was sturdy, usually of hickory or oak and always of some hard wood. It was 42 inches in length and was pushed into the hole by means of a lever with a clamp on each end. This instrument, the sole business of which was to push the grub pin into place, was called a witch. The head of the grub pin was at the bottom and the point projected. The grub pin must fit tightly, so a wedge was often pushed in alongside. When the bottom framework of the crib had been formed in this way, boards were placed to make a floor. Such boards were brought to the level of the binders and were placed crosswise. When these were in position, the piling of lumber began.

Lumber was arranged in the cribs in courses. A course was one thickness of one-inch lumber; a two-inch plank would count as two courses.[24] The number of courses varied according to the "height of the freshet and the judgment of the pilot." [25] In 1858 Dole, Ingram and Kennedy of Eau Claire, Wisconsin, sent to Read's Landing 91 cribs of lumber; 29 of these were eleven courses deep, 61 were twelve deep, and one crib was thirteen courses deep. These were much smaller than the Mississippi rafts.[26]

When the courses had been laid in the crib, a framework was placed on top similar to that on the bottom: runners and binders were again put in place, ropes were stretched crisscross and otherwise, and the witch did

[23] *Burlington Post* (Iowa), Nov. 8, 1930, p. 2.

[24] Note by William W. Bartlett, Oct. 1931, Daniel Shaw Lumber Company Papers, 1861–1911, Minnesota Historical Society; Hanks, *Memoir,* vol. iii.

[25] William A. Fox, *A History of the Lumber Industry in the State of New York,* U.S. Department of Agriculture, Bureau of Forestry, Bulletin 34 (Washington, 1902), p. 19.

[26] Ingram Papers, receipt for lumber sent to John Whitehill and Company, St. Louis, dated Sept. 16, 1858.

duty by driving in the grub pins. With these pins tightly in place in the corners and on the sides, a crib of lumber was ready. It was attached to other cribs to form a string.[27]

A log raft was not prepared with all the detail of a lumber raft. Like that of lumber, however, it was arranged in strings sixteen feet wide. The length of a string was about four hundred feet. The logs were placed in rows, close together, side by side, butt to butt. They were held together by sixteen-foot poles laid across the string. In the earlier period of rafting these poles were fastened to each log by hickory, elm, or birch branches bent over the pole like a staple with the ends stuck into holes bored in the log. This arrangement was called a lockdown. Plugs were driven in the holes in the logs in order to hold the lockdown in place. Changes occurred in the rafting of logs, however, as will be observed later in this study.

Manpower ran the raft in the early days. Each raft carried its oarsmen. The oars were heavy, for sometimes they were forty-five feet long.[28] There were usually twelve oarsmen on each raft, besides a cook, a helper, and the pilot. There were oars at the bow and oars at the stern — that is, there was an oar at each end of each string.[29] The stem of each oar was made of a pine tree about 8 inches thick at the butt and 30 feet long. The blade of the oar was a plank 16 feet long, 14 inches wide, 3 inches thick where it was spliced to the stem, and three fourths of an inch thick at the extreme end.[30] In quiet water one man could handle an oar alone, but elsewhere it often took the strength of two men.[31]

The first rafts were taken through Lake St. Croix and Lake Pepin by means of sails. Such sails as they were — shanty boards standing on end, with blankets tied to them to catch the breeze! When the weather was calm — and too calm weather was an annoyance — cordelling was not uncommon. In this method of propulsion the raft was pulled along by men walking on shore with a hand line. Sixteen hours of such work would cover two or three miles and constitute a day's progress.[32] When the wind was from the south, there was nothing to do but lie idle near the bank.[33]

In 1851 came the first great change that was to revolutionize rafting.

[27] Bill, "Career of Captain Jerome E. Short," *Clinton Herald* (Iowa), Mar. 18, 1933, p. 3; Blair, *op. cit.,* p. 34; K. K. Boyd, "Up and Down the Chippewa River," *Wisconsin Magazine of History,* vol. xiv, Mar. 1931, p. 247; interview of the writer with Charles Skrief, Nelson, Wisconsin, Apr. 22, 1934.

[28] Durant, *op. cit.,* p. 664.

[29] Bill, "Navigation on the Chippewa," *Burlington Post* (Iowa), Feb. 7, 1931, p. 3.

[30] Bill, "Career of Captain Jerome E. Short," *Clinton Herald* (Iowa), Mar. 18, 1933, p. 3.

[31] *Winthrop News* (Winthrop, Minn.), Sept. 16, 1926, p. 1.

[32] Durant, *op. cit.,* p. 663.

[33] Hanks, *Memoir,* vol. iii.

The shanty boards standing on end were discarded, and the towboat was introduced. The *Cabel Cape,* a towboat pushing the raft from behind, began its work in that year.[34] In 1855 Captain W. H. Carbut advertised in the *St. Anthony Express* that he with his steamboat, the *Dubuque,* would tow rafts the coming season through Lake St. Croix and Lake Pepin.[35] But "towing through" the whole distance to downriver markets was not tried at first. In the streams proper, rafts still continued to float by current and to be propelled by manpower.

The change in this process began in 1863, when George Winans attempted to run a raft with a steamboat in the Mississippi proper. The raft ran like magic from Read's Landing to Winona; there it was released from the steamboat and continued under manpower to Dubuque, where the lumber was delivered to Knapp, Stout and Company.[36]

Winans' boat, the *Union,* was a small, side-wheel, geared boat of 28.56 tons built at Durand, Wisconsin, in 1863. The Chippewa River was her place of duty. Water in the Chippewa was low then and the *Union* was lying idle at Read's Landing. Water was also low in the Mississippi and it looked as though no rafts would get downriver for a month or more. Early in the morning of September 12, 1863, the *Union* slid up to a raft on the shore opposite Read's Landing. The steamer took the place of the oars at the stern, and the first raft to be towed below Lake Pepin started downstream. Rafting history was made that day. George Winans was the pilot, Seth Scott the engineer, and Louis Webber the cook. A double crew had been put on the bow.[37]

George Winans was no novice on the river and no doubt he had actively studied the possibilities. In 1857 he had piloted lumber rafts from Read's Landing to Knapp, Stout and Company at Dubuque.[38] He made his last trip in 1916 when he took a raft from St. Paul to Prescott; with the exception of two or three years he had followed the river for sixty years.[39]

Others now became interested in rafting boats. In 1866 Jonathan Zebley of Le Claire, Iowa, built a raft-towing boat for Thomas Daughty. This boat did not work successfully; it was probably not large enough. Then the master builders on the river, J. W. Van Sant and his son, of Le Claire, built a raft boat. It was a stern-wheeler, 100 feet long with

[34] Durant, *op. cit.,* pp. 664–65.

[35] *St. Anthony Express,* Mar. 31, 1855, p. 3.

[36] Blair, *op. cit.,* p. 192; Bill, "Navigation on the Chippewa," *Burlington Post* (Iowa), May 3, 1930, p. 3.

[37] *Ibid.,* Jan. 18, 1919. Edward W. Durant gives the credit of towing the first raft with a steamboat to C. G. Bradly (Durant, *op. cit.*), but Captain Fred A. Bill gives the honor to George Winans (*Burlington Post,* May 30, 1930), as does Walter A. Blair (*op. cit.,* p. 191).

[38] Blair, *op. cit.,* p. 221.

[39] *Ibid.*

4 foot draft and a 20-foot beam, and it had powerful engines. It began its work in 1870, and the first raft it pushed downriver was owned by Frederick Weyerhaeuser and Frederick C. D. Denkmann of Rock Island, Illinois. Weyerhaeuser was on the raft as it was towed down.[40]

Twenty years later at least a hundred stern-wheel boats were engaged in the rafting business.[41] This business became for its time one of the largest and most profitable in the Mississippi Valley, though the season of navigation for rafting was seldom longer than seven months.

The rafting of lumber illustrates the remarkably varied organization of the lumber industry. Many mill owners owned their own boats,[42] but even in the pioneer days lumber was carried by contract. Stephen B. Hanks, who in the late 1840s and early 1850s had carried lumber to St. Louis for John McKusick of Stillwater, was the first of whom we have any record to carry lumber by contract.[43]

As the industry developed, the specialized rafting company rose to prominence. The leading enterprise of this kind was the Van Sant Company, with headquarters at one time at Le Claire, Iowa. Shipbuilding was in the Van Sant blood, for the family had originally come from Holland and had established themselves on the Delaware as shipbuilders. The great-grandfather of Samuel R. Van Sant had fitted boats for the American Revolution. His grandson, J. W. Van Sant, had gone west to St. Louis; later he went up the river to Rock Island, and later still north to Le Claire. There he and his son, Samuel R. Van Sant, built the first real raft boat.[44] Le Claire, at the head of the Upper Rapids, was a fitting place for boat-building and towboat men.

In 1884 the Van Sants moved to Winona, Minnesota, near the source of rafting. Samuel Van Sant was subsequently governor of Minnesota for two terms, after serving in the state legislature as Speaker of the House.[45] Though he became the wealthiest man of the rafting group, his first money had been modestly earned while working for Frederick Weyerhaeuser at fifty cents a day before the American Civil War.[46] In 1892 Captain Samuel R. Van Sant and his company ran more logs and lumber to market than anyone else connected with transportation on the Mississippi River.[47]

The principal towboat man of Stillwater was Edward W. Durant. He had come from Roxbury, Massachusetts, where he was born in 1829. His

[40] Interview of the author with Samuel R. Van Sant, Feb. 21, 1933; Blair, op. cit., p. 200.
[41] Ibid.
[42] Interview with Samuel R. Van Sant, Feb. 21, 1933.
[43] Hanks, Memoir, vol. iii.
[44] Interview with Samuel R. Van Sant, Feb. 21, 1933.
[45] Blair, op. cit., p. 253.
[46] Interview with Samuel R. Van Sant, Feb. 21, 1933.
[47] Mississippi Valley Lumberman, vol. xxiii, Jan. 13, 1893, p. 3.

family had moved to Albany, Illinois, the same town in which Stephen
Hanks's family had settled. With Hanks, Durant had early gone north
into the pine country. In 1852 he was towing logs and lumber from
Stillwater, and he ran logs over the Falls of St. Anthony for the Northwest
Fur Company of St. Louis, in which market those logs were bought by
Tom West.[48]

Durant had been trained as a raft pilot, and his skill at keeping the
towboat away from the shore was without equal. He was known to wait
less for a wind than anyone who ever "coiled a line in a skiff." [49] His
boats were reputed always to look like June brides.[50] He had an interest
in the Stillwater Lumber Company and in the Lumberman's National
Bank,[51] and in 1883 he was president of the Lumber Manufacturers'
Association of the Northwest.[52] Stillwater thought well of him and in
1878 made him its mayor.[53] It is said that he made men in all walks of
life feel at ease with him — he could yell "two beer" as naturally as a
Dutch barkeeper; on the other hand, he was at home in the most delicate
drawing-room atmosphere.[54] He was a member of the firm of Durant,
Wheeler and Company of Stillwater, the chief towing concern of that
saw-town.

We have some records of charges for rafting in the early days. Stephen
B. Hanks charged $3.00 for each thousand feet of lumber and $3.50 for
each thousand feet of logs rafted, and he carried a thousand laths for
twenty-five cents and shingles at the same rate.[55] These rates were higher
than those of later days, but not greatly so.

In 1862 the Daniel Shaw Lumber Company of Eau Claire, Wisconsin,
contracted with J. Turner, later Captain Turner, to carry lumber from
Shawtown, near Eau Claire, for marketing at various places along the
Mississippi.[56] The rates agreed upon are shown in Table 5.[57]

A little later, when Beef Slough, near the mouth of the Chippewa,
was developed as a boom for collecting, sorting, and rafting logs, the Beef
Slough Logging Company was established. It began work in the early
1870s and provided an immense traffic in log-rafting. In 1876 about two
hundred million feet of logs were driven out through Beef Slough south-

[48] Ibid., vol. xviii, July 11, 1890, p. 4.
[49] Stillwater Messenger, Mar. 1, 1879.
[50] Blair, op. cit., p. 230.
[51] Ibid., p. 229.
[52] Hotchkiss, History of Lumber and Forest Industry of Northwest, p. 534.
[53] Stillwater Messenger, Mar. 29, 1879.
[54] Ibid., Mar. 1, 1879.
[55] Hanks, Memoir, vol. iii. These rates applied to St. Louis.
[56] Bill, "Navigation on the Chippewa," Burlington Post (Iowa), Oct. 25, 1930, p. 3.
[57] The mileage figures were sent to the author by Capt. Fred A. Bill of St. Paul in a letter
dated Mar. 8, 1934. Shingles were carried to St. Louis by Turner at five cents a thousand, and
laths and pickets at ten cents a thousand.

ward on the river.[58] The rafting charges of the Beef Slough Logging Company are shown in Table 6.[59]

Though logs were rafted down the Chippewa at seventy-five cents for each thousand feet, $1.10 was the usual charge for towing them in rafts from Beef Slough or West Newton to Davenport or Rock Island.[60] This was regarded as cheap transportation.

TABLE 5. COST OF SHIPPING LUMBER ON THE MISSISSIPPI, 1862

From Shawtown to:	Distance (in miles)	Freight Rate (per thousand feet)
Read's Landing	54	$0.80
Wabasha	57	0.80
Winona	95	1.00
McGregor, Iowa	160	1.30
Hannibal, Missouri	411	2.10
St. Louis	699	2.30

TABLE 6. RAFTING CHARGES FOR LUMBER ON THE MISSISSIPPI, 1870–1880

From Beef Slough to:	Distance (in miles)	Freight Rate (per thousand feet)
Clinton, Iowa	231	$0.90–$1.00
Rock Island, Illinois	301	1.00– 1.15
Muscatine, Iowa	330	2.00
St. Louis, Missouri	633	2.25

Samuel R. Van Sant stated that his company's best rate for 1000 feet of lumber was $2.25.[61] Nonetheless, Pound, Halbert and Company of Chippewa Falls paid Captain George Winans $2.40 for each thousand feet of lumber from Read's Landing to Hannibal and St. Louis, and this was regarded as one of the best contracts on the river.[62] The lowest towing rate ever known on the Mississippi was twenty-five cents for each 1000 feet, which was once paid to Samuel R. Van Sant.[63]

Towing, or rafting, was a lucrative business! In 1878 A. L. Gillespie of Stillwater, owner of two boats, did a towing business of $15,000, while Durant, Wheeler and Company, the owner of six boats, did a towing business of $90,000, in spite of low water.[64] The Van Sants of Winona

[58] *Stillwater Lumberman*, Sept. 29, 1876.
[59] Bill, "Navigation on the Chippewa," *Burlington Post*, Feb. 7, 1931, p. 3. Capt. Bill supplied the information on "distance in miles" in a letter to the author dated Mar. 8, 1934. The distance is given as from Alma, Wisconsin; Beef Slough lay about two miles above Alma.
[60] Blair, *op. cit.*, p. 130.
[61] Interview with Samuel R. Van Sant, Feb. 21, 1933.
[62] Bill, "Navigation on the Chippewa," *Burlington Post* (Iowa), Feb. 7, 1931, p. 3. In measuring lumber, in order to determine the amount carried, the solid contents of the crib were figured — for instance, 16 feet by 32 feet by number of courses, less 10 per cent.
[63] This information was given the writer by Orrin F. Smith, Winona, Minn., May 4, 1934.
[64] *Stillwater Lumberman*, Dec. 20, 1878.

were financially the most successful in the business of towing. They had a contract as carrier for the Musser Lumber Company of Muscatine, Iowa. This contract lasted for about thirty-five years, and during that time the Mussers paid the Van Sants $1,000,000 for towing.[65] The Mussers were, of course, only one of the companies for which Captain Van Sant and his company towed.

Rafting by steamboat speeded up the lumbering process just when lumber was in such great demand for building the new settlements on the prairie lands in Iowa, Illinois, and Missouri. In 1871 the *Molly Whitmore,* captained by Bob Dodd, took a lumber raft of 2,000,000 feet for Schulenburg, Boeckeler and Company from Stillwater to St. Louis, returning in sixteen and a half days. At that time this was the quickest trip that had ever been made.[66] In 1873 the towboat *Chauncy Lamb,* captained by young Jerome E. Short, ran a raft of logs from La Crosse, Wisconsin, to Clinton, Iowa, a distance of 221 miles. The logs were rafted, made into lumber, and delivered in a city in Kansas, 400 miles away, in ten days.[67]

The final process in the lumber industry of the Upper Mississippi was that of marketing the product. The methods of selling varied greatly, especially at first, but the marketing came to be organized more systematically as the industry grew.

The earliest information we have about downriver marketing is for the year 1850 and concerns the logs of Steele and Godfrey of St. Anthony. There is not sufficient other information against which to check these instances to test how representative they are, but they do reveal something about marketing. In the summer of 1850 a sawmiller of Moline, Illinois, named White made a trip to the upper waters of the Mississippi to buy logs. On his return he wrote as follows to Steele and Godfrey, from whom he had apparently purchased logs: [68]

I have at last got down with my logs being thirty one days since I started, with all sorts of Luck coming, high waters, bad weather, bad Pilot &c having the consolation of its being the last of my running logs myself as my time is worth to[o] much at home find everything going on well at home my mill is doing good business although the water is high I am putting in a Rotary saw hope to have it running in three or four weeks or soon as the water falls sufficient to get a wheel in. I have not heard from you since I saw you, if you have not sent down the notes yet you can send them to whom you think proper I think Bailey & Boyd, Rock Island would be as suitable persons as you could send them to as they are perfectly responsible and would do the business cor-

[65] This statement was made by Samuel R. Van Sant in an interview, Feb. 21, 1933. The figure was later verified in a letter written by Van Sant, Feb. 28, 1933.

[66] *Stillwater Messenger,* June 2, 1871.

[67] *Clinton Herald,* Apr. 29, 1933, p. 3.

[68] Steele Papers, Spencer H. White to Steele and Godfrey, Aug. 30, 1850.

rect and I will pay them prompt as Possible my being so long on the way down puts me back considerable in my calculations but my mill is doing well and will soon cut them up. I find the demand for lumber was never better than at the present time if you have another raft to run you ought to get it run to molin [Moline] for one Dollar and fifty cents pr thousand and I think you can [afford] to higher [hire] hands by the day with a good Pilot it will not cost half of that to run them but do not get the Pilot I had a man by the name of Wright If [you] think propper to run them to me I think I can do as well by you as you can do in this part of the country there has been considerable many St Croix logs offerd for sale here before I got home for seven Dollars and fifty cents pr thousand and the Payments on as good or better terms than I offerd you but it was before I got home if you think propper to run your logs to me I will pay you as I was speaking when I saw you viz 7.50 pr M soon as I can saw and sell the lumber which I am certain will all be before the river closed. I have contracted for and expect to get ten or twelve hundred thousand from St Croix but the payment for them will not interfere with the sawing and paying you for yours

This letter is full of interesting points. It shows that the sawmiller considered it a waste of time to go north to purchase and then to raft logs down when he could be spending his time more profitably on his main business, sawing, since the demand was so brisk. It also shows how payments were made — that is, through notes which were to be sent for collection to what was presumably a private banking and commission firm in Moline. Evidently payment had to wait upon the sawing of the logs and the sale of the lumber. This sawmiller suggests that logs be sent to him; he would pay as well as anyone in the region.

In the autumn of the same year Steele sent a raft of logs to Moline, consigned to the same Bailey and Boyd referred to in the above letter. We have already quoted the letter reporting the disaster that overtook this raft.[69] The deserted logs somehow got attached to another raft and were sold to the same White of Moline whose letter was quoted above. Godfrey and Steele's agents in Rock Island, Bailey and Boyd, in February wrote to Steele about what had happened to the logs and, incidentally, pointed to one problem of marketing in those days of slow communication: "The distance between us is too great and mail facilities too slow for your good, when we rec'd your documents pertaining to your logs, White had sawed the most of them." Bailey and Boyd had, in the meantime, engaged lawyers to look after the matter for Godfrey and Steele.[70]

That orders were received by Minnesota loggers from downriver is indicated by another letter in the Steele Papers. A sawmiller from Caron-

[69] See above, p. 87.
[70] Steele Papers, Bailey and Boyd to Steele, Feb. 5, 1851.

delet, five miles below St. Louis, in December 1850 ordered logs to be delivered at the end of the following May. An excerpt from his letter follows: [71]

I want an average lot of logs, say, from 12.40 to 50 feet long: the long logs to be straight and sound, so that I could saw them the whole length but it is understood, that all these must be good and sound logs. Now if you will take the above contract, I will pay the highest market price & it will be the means of enabling you to liquidate your claim & any balance that may remain over, I will pay you in cash.

There must be no disappointment in this business, as having made a contract with the county to supply it with timber for plank roads: if I am disappointed it may prove ruinous to us both. — If you could not undertake the whole I would wish you to inform me immediately what part you could furnish. — Perhaps you are not aware that raftsmen prefer landing at this point above mentioned from the mouth of the Missouri down, as being more easily gained, arising from the eddies at points above.

Sometimes the producer and owner of the logs sold them downriver himself, soliciting purchases as the log raft moved downstream.[72] The towboat stopped to drop off a brail of logs, "now here, now there," as it went downstream.[73] Edward W. Durant, the log king of Stillwater, traveled regularly with log rafts downstream to dispose of them along the way.[74]

In the 1860s, however, there is evidence that men from "below" began to come more often to log- and lumber-producing centers to make purchases. Newspapers of the lumber region noted this as an encouraging development.[75] As mills along the Mississippi increased in number, their owners went north to buy log stocks in large lots. Those mills took no less than one half of all the logs cut in the St. Croix country.[76] It is evident, however, that this was not done regularly or on any large scale before 1870.

The papers of a number of firms reveal interesting changes in methods of marketing over a long period as the industry grew. Knapp, Stout and Company of Menomonie, which was by the 1880s considered one of the largest lumber firms in the world, in the forties sold its first lumber by rafting it from place to place.[77] It was the particular job of John H. Knapp, the founder of the firm, to manage the sale of its product down-

[71] *Ibid.*, K. Mackenzie to Steele, Dec. 21, 1850.
[72] *Stillwater Messenger*, Apr. 7, 1863.
[73] Hotchkiss, *op. cit.*, p. 584.
[74] *Stillwater Messenger*, Mar. 8, 1864.
[75] *Ibid.*, Apr. 7, 1863.
[76] Hotchkiss, *op. cit.*, p. 531.
[77] *Rice Lake Chronotype* (Wis.), Sept. 2, 1927; Bill, "Navigation on the Chippewa," *Burlington Post* (Iowa), Feb. 7, 1931, p. 3.

river. He was only twenty-five years old when he undertook this responsibility.[78] He traveled with his rafts in the days when rafts moved under manpower. It must have been a tedious job, but it probably gave him much time to plan his selling methods. Knapp was a serious young man and, when he was not engaged in selling lumber on those trips, he spent his time reading such books as the Bible and *Paradise Lost*. Occasionally, he said, he made a "cursory perusal" of the book entitled *Fowler on Matrimony*.[79]

As the years passed, Knapp's firm established wholesale yards at Fort Madison (the original Knapp home), at Dubuque, and at St. Louis. In St. Louis they advertised themselves as "Manufacturers and Dealers in Pine Lumber, Laths, Shingles, Pickets and so on, with office and yards at Bremen Avenue near the river." [80]

Dole, Ingram and Kennedy of Eau Claire also pioneered by selling its lumber from door to door along the Mississippi. Farmers would come to make purchases of two or three thousand feet at a time. General country stores took the lumber of this firm to sell. One of the three members of the firm usually traveled with the raft, which was not entrusted to an agent. The partners were constantly on the watch for promising places where they might establish yards. A letter of the time, sent by the traveling partner to another at home, illustrates their sales methods and problems in the early period: [81]

Mr. O. H. Ingram   St. Louis, Oct. 24th, 1859
Eau Claire,

Dear Sir: I arrived in St. Louis yesterday morning from Hannibal and Louisiana Mo. I think that we will be able to dispose of the balance of Playter's raft in Louisiana. I could have disposed of it very readily if there was a part of it narrow lumber, for it was a very great blunder in him to sell off all the fencing and flooring but of course he did what he thought was best about it; I don't know but that he has done as well as Mr Dole did after all. He has at least sold more lumber and received as much cash; I enclose to you New York exchange for five hundred dollars (500) which I received from Playter. . . . We are selling all the time, to the farmers 2,000 to 3,000 at a time. I can see that Mr Dole missed it considerably by being too precise with people; if he had stayed here much longer he would have got the lumber scattered all over the State of Illinois. He has got a yard commenced at the Ohio and Miss.

[78] The Diary of John H. Knapp, 1848, 1851. This is in the Henry E. Knapp Papers in the possession of the Wisconsin Historical Society.

[79] *Ibid.*, 1848.

[80] Henry E. Knapp Papers, Mar. 14, 1889. This quotation is from the letterhead used by the firm in their St. Louis office.

[81] Written by Donald Kennedy to Orrin H. Ingram, Oct. 24, 1859, and printed in the *Eau Claire Leader*, Oct. 24, 1920. The item from the *Leader* is a clipping in the Bartlett Collection, Minn. Hist. Soc.

R. R. depot, and an agency at Venice. . . . the parties at Venice are doing very well. They have disposed of nearly all of their stock and paid over the cash. . . . They have a general country store and the lumber helps to make up an assortment for them. . . . We can sell a great deal to country people at Illinois — town and also supply yards at Belleville and points on the O. & M. R. R. . . . I have not had much chance to see it but it looks to me as if Louisiana would be a good place for a yard. There is a great deal of lumber sold to the farmers from there, and the lumber dealers there say that they expect to sell a large amount of fencing next season. The farmers are just beginning to throw aside their rail fences and build board fence. It looks to me like a good place for retailing and we can wholesale anywhere that we get a chance. . . .

I am yours,

D. Kennedy

In 1858 A. M. Dole of the same firm, on a trip down the river, checked likely markets for lumber. Clinton, Iowa, he listed as the best possibility, while Hannibal City in Missouri and Keokuk and Muscatine in Iowa were also listed.[82] It was disheartening at times to try to market lumber when prices were low and lumber was plentiful, as it was after the Panic of 1857. "There is an enormous quantity of lumber here at present. . . . I was in to See Mr. Patrick this morning. He says that he will come and look at our next raft when it comes and that is about all that any of them will say," wrote Donald Kennedy from St. Louis in 1859.[83]

But as the years passed, Dole, Ingram and Kennedy — later known as Ingram and Kennedy — established wholesale yards along the Mississippi. They had such a yard early at St. Louis.[84] In 1874 they were wholesaling at Dubuque, where W. H. Day, then a member of the firm, directed their sawmill and sales. In 1881 this firm, under the name of the Empire Lumber Company, built a yard at Hannibal City, one of the best market places on the Mississippi at that time. Their interests at that place were directed by Dulaney and McVeigh. Later Ingram and Kennedy joined the Hortons at Winona, where a good market was available.

Other firms worked in the same way. Schulenburg and Boeckeler, who in the 1850s came to Stillwater to saw lumber, divided their work. They had large yards at St. Louis, and Schulenburg managed the business there; every board they cut was sent to St. Louis. Walker and Judd of Marine divided their work likewise; while Walker sawed lumber at Marine, Judd directed its sale in St. Louis, which was their main market.

No series of price figures can be given for the Upper Mississippi logs

<hr />

[82] Ingram Papers, Dole to Ingram and Kennedy, Fulton City, Illinois, Sept. 20, 1858.

[83] This is part of a letter written by Donald Kennedy to Orrin H. Ingram from St. Louis, Oct. 26, 1859. It was printed in the *Eau Claire Leader,* Oct. 24, 1920. The letter is a clipping from the *Leader* in the Bartlett Collection, Minn. Hist. Soc.

[84] Ingram Papers, Kennedy to Ingram, St. Louis, Jan. 9, 1860.

and lumber in the early period, but a few scattered figures may have some meaning. It is significant that in those early years even the simple grading used in Chicago and eastern markets was not followed in the Upper Mississippi trade. Only the best trees in the forest became lumber in that pioneer period. There was so much of the best, why bother about the rest? Even culls were not culls as we think of them today, and they were seldom, if ever, sent downriver.[85] Price quotations of that period seemed little concerned with grade; lumber was not classified in the many divisions of a later period, but it is fairly certain that both logs and lumber were of good stock.

In 1850 lumber was retailed in Minnesota at $10 to $12 per thousand feet; in 1856 $20 a thousand feet was not an unusual price; in 1857 the price ranged from $20 to $30 per thousand feet. To be sure, these prices were high, but it was a boom period. With the panic coming in the wake of the boom, prices went down; good lumber could be had for $12 a thousand feet, though the very best still rated $22.[86] Even in the panic period of 1857, however, the prices stayed fairly high in Minnesota's home market. The population was increasing and high rents impelled people to build their homes. The demand for lumber kept the price fairly good.[87]

But the panic soon brought lower prices in the wholesale markets downriver. In 1858 John Whitehill and his company of St. Louis bought 307,000 feet of lumber from Dole, Ingram and Kennedy. According to the receipt, $12 per thousand was paid for lumber washed clean and delivered on the bank of the river at St. Louis. One third of the sum was to be paid in cash while the balance was to run six months. This was a wholesale price.[88] The usual price of Wisconsin lumber at St. Louis ranged from $11 to $12 per thousand feet wholesale at that time. Such lumber was taken directly from the boats on arrival. Lumber at such a price was considered a cash article, but usually it sold for part cash, the rest payable in sixty or ninety days.[89] Dole, dismayed by falling prices resulting from the panic, wrote his associates that times were hard and that expenses must be in keeping with returns. "If we could afford it, we would pile every board in yard and keep until better prices," he commented.[90]

Money was scarce in 1858. Dole, Ingram and Kennedy received from a firm in Dixon, Illinois, a letter stating that it wanted lumber but could

[85] One of the largest firms on the Chippewa — Ingram and Kennedy — is said to have sent no culls but only the best boards to market below (*Eau Claire Press*, Oct. 28, 1874).
[86] Wheelock, *op. cit.*, p. 150.
[87] *Ibid.*
[88] Ingram Papers, John Whitehill and Company to Dole, Ingram and Kennedy, St. Louis, Sept. 16, 1858.
[89] *Ibid.*, Apr. 29, 1858.
[90] *Ibid.*, Dole to Ingram and Kennedy, Ottawa, Canada, July 19, 1858.

place an order only if butter and cheese could be taken in exchange.[91] In 1859 Delano, McKusick and Company of Stillwater offered to exchange common lumber for corn and oats at a price of $10 per thousand feet.[92] In 1860 lumber reached an amazingly low price.[93]

War brought back higher prices. By 1864 lumber prices were up considerably, resulting in an advance in log prices. Edward W. Durant sold 675,000 feet of his logs from the St. Croix at Dubuque at $16 a thousand, receiving cash. This was a pronounced increase over the years immediately preceding, when $6.50 to $8.00 per thousand feet had been the price.[94] But that summer lumbermen and logmen could only sit with folded hands, watching prices soar without benefit to them, for the gods had decreed that no rains should fall and that the Mississippi with its low water should be unable to carry the rafts.[95] The high prices were the result to some extent of the low water's creating a scarcity of goods, but in the long run war demands and inflation of the currency were most effective in raising prices.

In 1865, with peace, came a slump in the market, but in 1866 prices reached the peak of postwar inflation, a height that was not to be touched again until 1902.[96] In January 1866 common lumber was retailing at $22 per thousand feet at Winona and also in Stillwater. Dressed flooring was ranging in price from $35 to $40 per thousand feet.[97] In June of that year common lumber was retailing at $28 per thousand feet and dressed flooring was selling at $40 per thousand feet.[98] This lumber was not red pine, or spruce, or fir; it was white pine, the finest of the soft woods.

It would be both interesting and useful to know what profits these pioneer log and lumber concerns made. Even the highest prices they received are not so high as those of recent decades. Costs were, on the other hand, relatively low. Timber could be had for a mere pittance, and transportation by water was cheap. The harvesting of logs and the sawing of them into lumber were the heaviest items of cost. Because throughout most of the period the demand grew rapidly and log and lumber prices on the whole tended upward, it was a profitable time for the log and lumber concerns.

[91] *Ibid.*, McKay to Dole, Ingram and Kennedy, Dixon, Illinois, Sept. 17, 1858.
[92] *Stillwater Messenger*, Mar. 15, 1859.
[93] Compton, *Organization of the Lumber Industry*, p. 77.
[94] *Stillwater Messenger*, Apr. 7, 1863, and Mar. 8, 1864.
[95] Shippee, "Effects of the Civil War," *Minnesota History Bulletin*, vol. ii, p. 399.
[96] Compton, *op. cit.*, p. 77.
[97] *Winona Daily Republican*, Jan. 17, 1866; *Stillwater Messenger*, Jan. 23, 1867.
[98] *Winona Daily Republican*, June 11, 1866.

CHAPTER VII

Railroads Broaden the Market for the White Pine of the Upper Mississippi, 1870–1890

IN AN earlier chapter we have seen how the railroad reached the Mississippi, crossed it, and moved into the vast stretches of fat land beyond. The trans-Mississippi railroad came first to the states south of Minnesota. Immediately after the Panic of 1857 two railroads made important progress there. The Hannibal and St. Joseph was completed in 1859, connecting the Mississippi at Hannibal with the Missouri River at St. Joseph north of St. Louis; Hannibal, the railhead on the river, was to become a prominent river market for lumber from the St. Croix and the Chippewa rivers. The Missouri Pacific from St. Louis to Kansas City, completed in 1865, was to carry westward lumber coming from the Upper Mississippi.

In the 1860s Iowa towns on the Mississippi also became initial points for very important roads moving westward. Iowa was the only state in the first tier west of the Mississippi not to grant substantial aid to railroads, but her fortunate location made most railroads building west from Chicago lay their tracks her way. The Chicago and Northwestern crossed the Mississippi at Clinton in 1865 and was finished to Council Bluffs two years later. Clinton had a sawmill before 1865, and in the period between 1870 and 1890 that city at times produced more lumber than any city on the river except Minneapolis. Its log stock came from the Upper Mississippi, and millmen from Clinton were very active in the log life of that river. The Chicago, Burlington and Quincy crossed the river at Burlington, and from there went on to Council Bluffs in 1869. The Illinois Central made Dubuque its stopping place on its way to Sioux City on the western boundary of Iowa, which it reached in 1870. Dubuque, already prominent as a distributing point for lumber as well as a manufacturing center, drew men from the Upper River to establish mills and markets there. All these Iowa towns with railroads reaching westward became important markets for log and lumber from above.

What the railroads did for the lumber industry of the Upper River may be seen from a closer investigation of developments in Minnesota. With the coming of railroads began a rapid settlement of the state. The desire of people in the East and in Europe for rich land was encouraged in the 1870s and 1880s by the state itself and by railroads having lands to sell. Minnesota organized a consistent system for advertising her virtues and encouraging settlement: she hired and sent men to Germany and the Scandinavian countries to secure settlers.[1] The land-grant railroads in Minnesota were active in urging immigration; the Northern Pacific no doubt had the most thorough organization for such work.[2] The railroads offered their lands on generous, long-time terms, and they offered rebates for the breaking and cropping of land. Some of the roads built "immigrant houses" where new settlers might be taken care of for a short time. In 1872 the towns of Litchfield, Benson, Morris, Willmar, and Breckenridge, all in rich agricultural areas, had such accommodations, as did Duluth, Brainerd, and Glyndon.[3]

The region was settled rapidly. In the years between 1860 and 1880 the population of Minnesota more than quadrupled, increasing from 172,000 persons to 780,000.[4]

In the year 1877, 1,006,520 acres of land were entered in Minnesota and in the neighborhood of Fargo in Dakota Territory. The largest entries were made at Benson, in Swift County, which lay out of the hardwood zone and on Minnesota's prairie. Worthington, in Nobles County in the prairie region of southwestern Minnesota, had the second largest number of entries, and Redwood Falls, in Redwood County, also on the prairie, ranked third in the number of entries. It was estimated that ten thousand new farms would be opened in the Northwest in 1878.[5] Not only Minnesota, but the Dakotas, Montana, and lands farther westward were being settled. By the close of the eighties virtually all the lands of the Northern Pacific had been settled as far west as the Missouri River.[6]

In this process of settlement a new regional market was added to the downriver market for the white pine of the Upper Mississippi. This second great market for Minnesota's lumber came to be the state itself

[1] John Schroeder, clerk of the Minnesota State Board of Immigration, "How to secure with the least expense the Homogeneous Immigration," Governor's Archives, 1871, File 608, Minnesota Historical Society; Albert Wolff, Commissioner of Immigration, to State Board of Immigration, Sept. 7, 1870, Governor's Archives, File 608; Hans Mattson, *Reminiscences: the Story of an Emigrant* (St. Paul, 1891), p. 121.

[2] James B. Hedges, "The Colonization Work of the Northern Pacific Railroad," *Mississippi Valley Historical Review*, vol. xiii (Dec. 1926), pp. 314–19.

[3] Harold F. Peterson, "Early Minnesota Railroads and the Quest for Settlers," *Minnesota History*, vol. xiii (Mar. 1932), pp. 31–35.

[4] *Ibid.*, p. 43.

[5] *Report of the Minneapolis Board of Trade*, 1877, pp. 70–71.

[6] Hedges, *op. cit.*, pp. 340–41.

and its neighboring prairie and plains country. How the lumber market was extended westward is seen from the work of various railroads in the 1870s.

In 1874 the St. Paul and Sioux City Railroad, which made connections touching Yankton in Dakota Territory, Omaha, and Kansas City, reported 37 per cent of its entire tonnage as lumber, and in the next year 44 per cent was lumber. That year, though it penetrated a distinctly agricultural area, the road carried more lumber than wheat and other grain.[7] In 1876 33,453,000 feet of lumber were sent westward from St. Paul on the St. Paul and Sioux City Road.[8] The next year St. James in Minnesota, the connecting link between the St. Paul and Sioux City and the Sioux City and St. Paul, forwarded westward 37,850,000 feet of lumber, comprising about five sevenths of its entire tonnage.[9] That year the lumber tonnage of the St. Paul and Sioux City, excluding other forest products, was 28 per cent of its entire tonnage, while wheat constituted 25 per cent.

On October 1, 1876, the Worthington and Sioux Falls Railroad, a 44-mile branch of the St. Paul and Sioux City, was completed; this line, though short, penetrated a rich agricultural section of southeastern Dakota. In 1878 it carried 8,316,000 feet of lumber from Worthington into the prairie hinterland.[10] Not only were farmsteads and villages built of white pine dotting the prairies of Minnesota, Iowa, and Dakota, but the prairies of Kansas and Nebraska were likewise made habitable with the help of the white pine from the upper reaches of the Mississippi River.[11]

The St. Paul and Sioux City distributed large amounts of the lumber produced at Stillwater; sawmill men from that city had been active in building the railroad.[12] On January 12, 1872, Stillwater sent its first rail shipment from the pine forests of the St. Croix into the interior of Iowa, directed to Marshalltown. By December 27 of that year Stillwater had shipped 7,000,000 feet of lumber into the interior of Iowa and Minnesota.[13]

The business by rail from Stillwater was then still in its infancy; by 1875, however, it was maturing rapidly. In the week of June 25 of that year 141 carloads of lumber were shipped from Stillwater to points in Minnesota, Iowa, Missouri, Nebraska, and Dakota. This was the largest

[7] *Report of the Minnesota Railroad Commission*, 1875, p. 23.
[8] *Report of the Minnesota Railroad Commissioner*, 1876, p. 87.
[9] *Ibid.*, 1878, p. 48.
[10] *Ibid.*, p. 53.
[11] *Report of the Minneapolis Board of Trade*, 1878, p. 50.
[12] *Stillwater Messenger*, Dec. 27, 1879. Samuel F. Hersey of Bangor, Maine, whose capital was invested in Stillwater lumber, was a director of the St. Paul and Sioux City Railroad.
[13] *Stillwater Messenger*, Dec. 27, 1872.

shipment by rail within one week so far recorded in Stillwater.[14] Lumber was billed to Omaha and Council Bluffs during that year; Columbus in Nebraska, in the fourth tier of counties west of the Missouri, was ordering its lumber from Stillwater; and when, on April 23, the *Stillwater Lumberman* reported that John M. Keller was sending lumber as far west as Colorado, the news was as exciting to that saw-town as though its lumber were reaching Mars.

The importance to Stillwater of the inland market is further illustrated by shipments of several lumber manufacturers in one week in 1875. Hersey, Bean and Brown shipped five carloads to Sioux City, Iowa; three each to St. Paul and Le Sueur, Minnesota; two each to St. Joseph, Missouri, and Mountain Lake, Minnesota; and one each to Sheldon, Sibley, and East Orange in Iowa, Vermillion, Dakota Territory, and St. Peter and Shakopee in Minnesota.[15] Hersey, Bean and Brown owned yards at various places in Minnesota and retailed a large portion of their mill products.[16]

Isaac Staples at the same time sent six carloads to LeMars, Iowa; three to Yankton, Dakota Territory; three to Charles City, Iowa; two to Greene, Iowa; and four to Faribault, five to Mankato, twelve to St. Paul, and two to White Bear in Minnesota. Seymour, Sabin and Company shipped three carloads to Cedar Rapids, where they owned their own yards, seven to Sioux City, and three to St. Paul.[17] The St. Croix Lumber Company of Stillwater shipped to points on the St. Paul and Sioux City Railroad, while McKusick, Anderson and Company retailed at St. James.[18]

Thus, although Stillwater had a continuous water route to the Gulf, its lumber was finding its way in great quantities to the prairie by way of railroads. The railroads had made new markets which increased the stature of this lumber town, and in 1876 Stillwater had its own Lumberman's Board of Trade, with Edward W. Durant as president.[19]

Winona coveted her portion of the hinterland, newly opened by the railroad. With one hand she plucked the tall white pine from the Chippewa and St. Croix valleys, brought it to Winona, and changed it into lumber; with the other she furrowed her way into the western country and established lumberyards. Winona's railroad followed the trail of the oxen from the uplands. Rochester, Dodge Center, Owatonna, and Waseca were fast-growing farm communities that had used Winona as their mar-

[14] *Ibid.*, June 25, 1875.
[15] *Ibid.*, May 21, 1875.
[16] *Ibid.*, Jan. 21, 1876.
[17] *Ibid.*, May 21, 1875.
[18] *Ibid.*, Jan. 21, 1876.
[19] *Stillwater Lumberman*, Sept. 1, 1876.

ket in the days before railroads. "Winona's Opportunity" was the subject of an address given by A. F. Hodgins to the Winona Board of Trade in 1880, in which he impressed upon the men the opportunities along the line of the railroad. He urged that a committee be chosen to study the "resources, capabilities, and wants of the country along the Winona and St. Peter Railway." [20]

Hodgins at that time was of the lumber firm of Youmans and Hodgins at Winona,[21] which then had branch yards at St. Charles, Dover, Chester, Rochester, Zumbrota, Byron, Kasson, Dodge Center, Marshall, Minneota, Canby, Gary, Plainview, and Chatfield, all in Minnesota. The firm had also extended its business into Dakota Territory, with branch yards at Watertown, Brookings, and Volga, and it supplied independent yards at New Ulm, Sleepy Eye, and Redwood Falls, towns located on Winona's railroad.[22] Youmans and Hodgins found that their plant in Winona had to be enlarged to meet the demand of their increasing business [23] — they were growing with the new West.

As early as 1870 Laird, Norton and Company, who had the largest capital investment in lumber in Winona, had branch yards at Rochester and St. Charles and were moving westward with the railroad.[24] They early preëmpted certain regions as their own markets, and they were among the leaders who saw the value of branch yards along the railroad westward.

In 1871 the Winona and St. Peter Railroad carried westward 12,793,931 feet of lumber, of which 12,377,587 feet were billed from Winona. The market along that road was Winona's monopoly.[25]

La Crosse, Wisconsin, like the other lumber towns, preëmpted markets on the railroad it controlled. It sought its markets across the river along the Southern Minnesota running from Grand Crossing to Winnebago. In 1872 there were 6,189,000 feet of lumber sent westward from Grand Crossing; [26] in 1873, 8,324,000 feet; and in 1874, 10,350,078 feet.[27] In the next two years the increase was pronounced, but the invasion of the grasshoppers in the territory of the La Crosse markets caused a reduction in lumber sales in 1877.[28] The following year, however, the market was good again and 34,789,000 feet went westward. Practically no freight but lumber was taken into the prairie country on that road, and wheat

[20] *Winona Weekly Republican*, Jan. 21, 1880.
[21] See above, p. 42.
[22] *Winona Weekly Republican*, Sept. 8, 1880.
[23] *Ibid.*
[24] *Ibid.*, Oct. 5, 1870. These yards will be discussed in Chapter XIX.
[25] *Report of the Minnesota Railroad Commissioner*, 1871, p. 171.
[26] *Ibid.*, 1872, p. 106.
[27] *Ibid.*, 1873, p. 70; 1874, p. 203.
[28] *Ibid.*, 1875, p. 109; 1876, p. 119; 1877, p. 53.

was carried on the return trip. This road's lumber market belonged exclusively to La Crosse, and in response to the increasing demand La Crosse rose to prominence in the lumber world.

Thus three emporia — as they were then ambitiously called — developed on the river: Stillwater, Winona, and La Crosse. But grow as each of these towns did, none of them could keep pace with Minneapolis; she had the choicest location.[29] Minneapolis, though in competition with other centers for the control of the prairie area, was assuming the earmarks of a metropolitan center more decidedly than any other town in Minnesota. She controlled more railroads than any competitor; with the exception of the roads controlled by La Crosse, Winona, and Hastings and the Northern Pacific with Duluth as a pivot, every railroad in Minnesota touched the Minneapolis and St. Paul area. An article in the *Minneapolis Tribune* spoke of the five gates to the city. One was the Mississippi River; the others were railroads. Minneapolis, "acknowledged as the railroad center of the Upper Mississippi Valley, and of the State," dreamed dreams and saw visions of the roaring metropolis she was to become:[30]

Thus in time to come, New England will not exchange her cotton fabrics for our flour. . . . Here will be the cotton mills of the Mississippi Valley, and from hence will go our flour in exchange for this great raw material — the South supplying us and we them. . . . For teas and raw silks and the productions of that ancient still dreaming Asiatic world, we will exchange our cotton fabrics, our yarns and woolens, while here at our very doors, the song of the shuttle, and saw, and millstone, will mingle with the rush and roar of the travel of the nations of the earth.

As we have seen earlier, the initial manufacturing industry of Minneapolis was sawmilling, and lumber was her first export and the basis of her early growth. It was like "Adam to his descendants," said A. T. Ankeny in response to a toast on "Our Manufacturing Interests" at the Merchant's Banquet in Minneapolis in the winter of 1877.[31]

The Milwaukee and Minneapolis Railroad, which came later to be called the Chicago, Milwaukee and St. Paul, headed the list as the chief lumber carrier out of Minneapolis in the 1870s. The division of that road known as the Iowa and Minnesota penetrated the productive wheat region of southern Minnesota, the section of the state in which settlers were concentrating at that time. In 1874 that branch of the Milwaukee

[29] After 1870 the region around St. Anthony Falls was called Minneapolis. The town of St. Anthony became a part of Minneapolis through incorporation in 1872 and the Minneapolis name took precedence.
[30] *Minneapolis Tribune*, Jan. 7, 1868.
[31] *Ibid.*, Jan. 16, 1877.

Road carried 25,414,000 feet of lumber from Minneapolis, the next year 49,481,000 feet, and in 1876, 54,272,000 feet.[32] What a block of forest that railroad moved!

Another railroad, distinctly a Minneapolis road, was the Minneapolis and St. Louis. It was financed by Minneapolis capital and directed by Minneapolis men. This road crossed the Winona and St. Peter at Waseca and the Southern Minnesota, a branch of the Milwaukee, at Albert Lea. In 1877 it reached the Iowa line and met the Burlington, Cedar Rapids and Northern.[33] In 1876 the Minneapolis and St. Louis carried southward 27,083,000 feet, of which 23,432,000 came from Minneapolis.[34] In 1878 it carried southward 48,951,000 feet of Minneapolis lumber.[35] Wheat and lumber were freight of first importance on this road, with wheat in the lead but lumber not far behind.

In 1877 the country through which the St. Paul and Pacific cut its way was receiving as large a share of immigration as any section of the state. That railroad covered northwestern Minnesota like a network. In 1874 its main line struck through the rich soil of old Lake Agassiz northwestward to Dakota Territory, and it sent another line to Sauk Rapids from St. Paul. It reached in every direction by means of branch lines — from Glyndon one line north to Crookston was later extended to the Canadian border, where it was linked with the Canadian Pacific, while another line dug itself into the white pine region of Brainerd. In 1879 this same St. Paul and Pacific sent a line into southwestern Minnesota, to Tracy and Jackson.[36] Settlements in these prairie regions made accessible by railroads were all to demand much lumber.

The St. Paul and Pacific, known after 1879 as the St. Paul, Minneapolis and Manitoba, early became James J. Hill's road. Hill sensed the possibilities of the region; the Northwest, as he saw it, had in it the "potentialities of greatness." To help develop better commercial agriculture was always an object of his efforts. The Northwest was a "hawking wilderness" when he first saw it; at the close of his day it was an important part of America.

This railroad in the 1870s drew its lumber from Minneapolis; as early as 1869, when the road was advancing westward beyond the hardwood country, immense demands for lumber came from the regions it was penetrating.[37] It carried wheat to Minneapolis to be made into flour at

[32] Report of the Minnesota Railroad Commissioner, 1874, p. 153; 1875, p. 152; 1876, p. 41.
[33] Ibid., 1878, p. 81; Report of the Minneapolis Board of Trade, 1878, p. 44; Minneapolis Tribune, Nov. 13, 1877, p. 4.
[34] Report of the Minnesota Railroad Commissioner, 1876, p. 69.
[35] Ibid., 1878, p. 81.
[36] Report of the Minnesota Railroad Commissioner, 1876, p. 14; 1879, pp. 3–4; Report of the Minneapolis Board of Trade, 1878, p. 36.
[37] Minneapolis Tribune, Sept. 10, 1869.

the Falls; it carried lumber back again. The main line of the St. Paul and Pacific, passing through the heart of the Minnesota prairie country, in 1872 carried away from the Falls a total of 8,998,000 feet of lumber, of which Willmar, a new prairie town, alone got 2,041,000 feet.[38] Two years later Minneapolis sent 14,334,000 feet west by that road.[39]

Towns along the St. Paul and Pacific were all in the making, and Minneapolis lumber was in demand: in 1875 Breckenridge received 1,602,000 feet, Benson 1,105,000, Litchfield 1,272,000, and Willmar 1,773,000.[40] These towns were representative of a large number of small towns springing up all over the prairie. The individual orders were small, but in the aggregate the towns provided a sturdy market. In 1876 this same road carried 18,257,000 feet westward from Minneapolis.[41] As the road advanced, the market widened, and the producing centers increased their cut. Government and railroad lands were being taken at an unprecedented rate, and immigrants were coming in ever-increasing numbers.[42]

A city that controlled as much territory by means of railroads as Minneapolis did was almost certain to outdistance its rivals in lumber production. In 1876 Minneapolis distributed 137,373,000 feet of lumber to markets in Minnesota, Iowa, Missouri, Kansas, Nebraska, and Dakota Territory.[43] Minneapolis mills cut a total of 200,371,277 feet that year, enough to make 28,800 houses of average size; if laid lengthwise in boards one foot wide, the cut would have reached 36,960 miles, or almost one and a half times around the globe. The lumber, laths, and shingles of that year's cut in Minneapolis would have filled 24,000 cars.[44] In 1879, 139,450,000 feet of lumber were shipped from Minneapolis.[45] Thus every year the amount shipped from Minneapolis increased, while in Minneapolis itself there was a growing demand for lumber; in 1879 the city experienced such a demand for stores and residences as never before.[46] In 1876 the lumber industry of Minneapolis paid freight bills to the amount of more than half a million dollars.[47]

The greatest expansion of the Minneapolis lumber market came

[38] *Report of the Minnesota Railroad Commissioner*, 1872, p. 70.
[39] *Ibid.*, 1874, p. 73.
[40] *Ibid.*, 1875, pp. 186–87.
[41] *Report of the Minneapolis Board of Trade*, 1876, p. 104.
[42] *Ibid.*, 1878, p. 36. There is an error in the date of the *Report of the Minneapolis Board of Trade* for this year which is corrected in these footnotes. In the *Report*, "1879" is used, whereas it should be "1878."
[43] *Report of the Minneapolis Board of Trade*, 1876, p. 50.
[44] *Ibid.*, p. 47; *Minneapolis Tribune*, Nov. 28, 1876. The freight car then was smaller than it is now; in the 1860s the normal capacity was 15,000 pounds; in 1900 cars usually carried 100,000 pounds (Edward C. Kirkland, *A History of American Economic Life* [New York, 1934], p. 384).
[45] *Report of the Minneapolis Board of Trade*, 1879, p. 44.
[46] *Ibid.*, p. 61.
[47] *Minneapolis Tribune*, Nov. 28, 1876.

with the settlement of northwestern Minnesota, which was favored by two developments in the late 1870s: one was the lifting of the depression that had followed the Panic of 1873; the other was the boom in spring-wheat farming which came with improved milling methods. By 1880 it was widely recognized that the Northwest's spring-wheat flour could compete with flour made from the winter wheat of other regions.[48]

This discovery led to the development of a vast new market for white pine. Large portions of Minnesota and the Dakotas had rich virgin soil well suited to the growing of spring wheat. Population began to shift into the area, and the acreage under cultivation mounted. The treeless region of the Red River Valley rapidly rose to first place in both the amount and the quality of wheat raised, causing the older counties to yield their position as the leading growers of wheat.

In 1870 eight counties, each producing more than a million bushels of wheat, were all in a section bounded by the Minnesota and Mississippi rivers and Iowa. By 1884 the shift to the western prairie was well under way; of thirteen counties producing more than a million bushels each, ten lay in the southern half of Minnesota, one (Stearns County) lay northwest of Minneapolis just below the center of the state, while two (Ottertail and Polk) were in the Red River district. Polk, far to the north, was deep in the heart of the Red River Valley, and next to Goodhue, which had long been settled, it had that year the largest wheat acreage in Minnesota. By 1885 the change was even more striking; of the five leading wheat counties, one was Goodhue, in the southeastern part, another was Stearns, and the rest were Polk, Norman, and Ottertail in the Red River district. Though Polk County was second in wheat acreage in the state, it led all the counties in wheat production — Polk was on the prairie.[49]

From 1875 to 1890 the Red River Valley filled rapidly with people, who became owners of land either by homesteading or preëmption or by purchase of lands from railroad corporations. Another Viking movement was on the way! These Vikings were settling not only western Minnesota but Dakota as well; there they dislodged the trappers of the Hudson's Bay Company who were making their last stand in what promised to be good wheat country. In 1887 Scandinavians comprised 33 per cent of the farmers of Minnesota and Dakota.[50] In the ten years from 1880 to 1890 the population of Minnesota grew from 780,773 to

[48] *Northwest Miller,* vol. xvi, Sept. 7, 1883, p. 222, and vol. xvi, Oct. 5, 1883, p. 319; Charles B. Kuhlmann, *The Development of the Flour Milling Industry in the United States* (New York, 1929), p. 120.

[49] *Annual Report, Minnesota Commissioner of Statistics,* 1885, p. 19, and 1886, p. 18.

[50] *Mississippi Valley Lumberman,* vol. xi, June 10, 1887, p. 2.

1,301,826, an increase of 67 per cent.[51] At that time almost every train through St. Paul and Minneapolis carried large numbers of foreigners to Dakota and northwestern Minnesota. Six Minnesota counties lying mainly within the Red River Valley had a total of 21,123 inhabitants in 1880 and 71,190 ten years later. Polk County, with Crookston as its county seat, had gained the most, with an increase of 13,759. Likewise six North Dakota counties lying largely within the same valley had gained 62,031 inhabitants. Manitoba in Canada, also a market for Minnesota lumber, had gained 84,046 inhabitants.[52]

White pine provided lumber for these immigrants, whose resources were meager and who, without the aid of cheap lumber, could not have set themselves up on the prairie. For the lumber manufacturer of the Upper Mississippi the northwest market was more profitable than the southwest market at that time.[53]

With the settlement of the state came great changes in its railroad system. It was no longer necessary for the farmers of Minnesota to sleep under the steel-cold winter sky alongside their oxen when bringing their produce to market. By 1881 there was hardly a cultivated farm in the state from which the farmer could not drive to a railroad station and return in a day.[54] Also, railroads were now in a position to give more efficient service than earlier railroads had offered. Whereas before 1873 at least twenty companies had controlled Minnesota's railroads, by the beginning of the next decade they had been amalgamated into six major systems. The Chicago, Milwaukee and St. Paul, the Chicago and Northwestern, and the Chicago, St. Paul, Minneapolis and Omaha (once the St. Paul and Sioux City and the Sioux City and St. Paul) served the southern part of the state; the Minneapolis and St. Louis Railway served the central part of the state; and the Northern Pacific and the St. Paul, Minneapolis and Manitoba served the north and northwest.[55]

In the 1880s the railroad system of the region continued its rapid growth. By 1886 more than twenty-five thousand miles of railroad centered in Minneapolis. These roads cut through the wheat belt and the agricultural districts of Minnesota, Iowa, Nebraska, and Dakota Territory; some lines reached Chicago; four went to St. Louis; some joined transcontinental lines at Kansas City, St. Joseph, and Omaha; four lines connected with ports on Lake Superior.[56] Altogether, Minnesota and

[51] *Census of Minnesota, 1890*, p. 2.
[52] Upham, "Settlement and Development of the Red River Valley," *Minn. Hist. Soc. Coll.*, vol. viii, pp. 11–24.
[53] *Mississippi Valley Lumberman*, vol. xi, June 10, 1887, p. 2.
[54] *Report of the Minnesota Railroad Commissioner*, 1881, p. 5.
[55] *Ibid.*, p. 4.
[56] *Report of the Minneapolis Chamber of Commerce*, 1886, p. 107.

particularly Minneapolis had ready access to markets both near and far. The extension of settlement and the growth of the railroad system in the eighties favored Minneapolis, inasmuch as the greatest growth came in territory closely dependent on that city.

An important new railroad system reaching out from Minneapolis had its beginning in this decade. In 1886 a prominent businessman proposed the building of a line to the Atlantic, by-passing Chicago. His plan was for a road going straight east through Wisconsin, passing the northern end of Lake Michigan at Sault Ste. Marie, continuing eastward through northern Michigan, uniting finally with the Canadian Pacific and the Vanderbilt lines, and thence reaching to the Atlantic. He planned also to run a line westward into that part of the prairie still untouched by railroads.

This railroad promoter was W. D. Washburn, whose first love was lumber but who later became enamored of wheat; he sensed that railroads were necessary if either was to live. In the 1880s he foresaw the passing of the Michigan forests, and he realized that Minnesota would be an heir to their eastern market. But to reach that market Washburn held that it was necessary to avoid Chicago, which was then influencing freight rates in her own interests, against the interests of Minnesota wheat and lumber.

Washburn's Minneapolis, St. Paul and Sault Ste. Marie Railway was an important addition to Minnesota's marketing facilities; it was the first railway in the whole Upper Mississippi country to reach the ports of the Atlantic without going through Chicago, and it provided the most direct route to the seaboard for Minnesota wheat, flour, and lumber.

Westward, too, Washburn's dream became a reality. He projected the other railroad across the prairie; with the hope that it would eventually reach the western ocean, he named it the Minneapolis and Pacific. In 1887 this line extended seventy miles into the Dakota prairie, passing over the lake bed of what was once glacial Lake Agassiz, fertile alluvial soil in which spring wheat was to grow like a weed. The part of Minnesota through which it passed would yield readily to cultivation and was then in the process of being settled.

The home of this road was Minneapolis, and lumbermen there were to control the sale of lumber along its tracks by means of branch yards — to the exclusion of other lumber retailers. In 1888 Washburn's two railroads reaching eastward and westward were consolidated and became known to the railroad world as the Minneapolis, St. Paul and Sault Ste. Marie.[57]

[57] *Ibid.*, 1888, p. 157.

In the 1880s Minnesota's railroads carried increasing amounts of lumber to market. One of the older railroads, the Minneapolis and St. Louis, a faithful Minneapolis road, was for a time the city's greatest carrier of lumber. It had joined itself to the well-established Chicago, Rock Island and Pacific Railway, acquiring a right-of-way from Minneapolis to St. Louis through thickly settled portions of Illinois, Iowa, and Minnesota. In 1885 this road carried 85,000,000 feet of lumber away from Minneapolis, more than was carried by any other road from that city.[58]

The St. Paul, Minneapolis and Manitoba Railway, though crossing territory much younger in settlement than the territory served by the Minneapolis and St. Louis, held second place in 1885 as a lumber-carrying railroad from Minneapolis. Through the decade of the eighties the Manitoba increased its lumber tonnage every year. From June 30, 1880, to June 30, 1881, it carried 48,814,000 feet of lumber into the treeless West; of this total Minneapolis sent 32,957,000 feet while Anoka contributed 12,623,000.[59] In 1882 this road almost doubled its carriage, transporting westward from Minnesota stations 107,908,000 feet of lumber;[60] Minneapolis furnished more than any other place, a total of 46,580,000 feet, again a considerable increase over the amount sent the previous year. St. Paul sent 25,501,000 feet, presumably brought there from Stillwater and the sawmills along the Duluth and Lake Superior Road. In 1883 the St. Paul, Minneapolis and Manitoba again increased its carriage when it carried 154,879,000 feet to the prairies.[61] In 1885 the wheat carried to market by that road made up 58 per cent of its entire tonnage, while lumber, brought in to build towns and farmsteads, ranked next, providing 21 per cent.[62]

The Chicago, Milwaukee and St. Paul Railway, moving through the hardwood region into the prairie farm lands of southern Minnesota and northern Iowa, placed third in lumber carriage from Minneapolis in the 1880s. The new Minneapolis and Northwestern, later called the Chicago, St. Paul and Kansas City Railway, also took a heavy load of Minneapolis lumber to distribute on its way through growing farm regions to Kansas City and Chicago; the major portion of this road's mileage lay in Iowa, which lumbermen considered their richest market during the eighties and nineties.[63] No less important was the Chicago,

[58] *Report of the Minneapolis Board of Trade*, 1886, p. 117.

[59] *Report of the Minnesota Railroad Commissioner*, 1881, pp. 76, 79.

[60] *Ibid.*, 1882, p. 222.

[61] *Ibid.*, 1883, p. 273.

[62] *Report of the Minnesota Railroad and Warehouse Commission*, 1885, p. 321.

[63] Interview of the writer with the late E. L. Carpenter, formerly president of the Shevlin-Carpenter Lumber Company of Minneapolis, May 31. 1935.

Burlington and Northern, reaching out to Cheyenne in Wyoming in the days when fences became the style in the so-called cow country, because the farmer, replacing the cowboy, needed fences, stock sheds, and barns.[64]

The growing demand was becoming too much for the Minneapolis mills to handle. The year 1882—a banner year in which 186,739,000 feet were shipped out from Minneapolis—found that city unable to produce sufficiently to meet the needs of the hinterland, for she herself was consuming nearly 200,000,000 feet. Minneapolis sawmills put forth a supreme effort and cut 314,363,000 feet in one year—a record cut for Minneapolis sawmills at that time.[65]

But this was not enough. From this time on, lumber had to be shipped into Minneapolis in increasing amounts and another record was made when in one year 49,680,000 feet came there from other places. Minneapolis came more and more to be looked upon as a distributing center and long after the whir of sawmills had ceased in Minneapolis, that city served as a distributing center for lumber. The railroads made Minneapolis a great terminal point, giving it an advantage possessed by no other city handling lumber in the West, except Chicago. In 1880, 20,400,000 feet of lumber were shipped into Minneapolis, and 117,510,000 feet were received there in 1890. Railroads entering Minneapolis by way of the white pine forests were fortunate, for those forests gave them important additional tonnage.

The Chicago, St. Paul, Minneapolis and Omaha, known generally as the Omaha Road, was the largest carrier into Minneapolis in the period of the eighties. With one arm it reached into the white pine in the region of Superior, Bayfield, Washburn, and Ashland, Wisconsin, where still stood mighty forests of virgin pine. Today, traveling on that railroad into the very same country, one sees here and there a single white pine tree—lonely, like a mourner for the vanished past. Along this railroad sprang up Cumberland, Barronett, Shell Lake, Hayward, Drummond, Mason, Rice Lake—almost forgotten towns today. They arose only because the sawmills were there, and the Omaha, supplied by their mills, carried their lumber far and wide. In 1885 that road took 23,820,000 feet into Minneapolis; in 1887, 26,550,000 feet.[66]

With its other arm the Omaha reached south and west into the wheat fields of Dakota and the rich corn belts of Iowa and Nebraska, even out into the oil fields of Wyoming. In 1887 the demand for lumber in these areas was so great that the railroad was hardly able to supply

[64] *Mississippi Valley Lumberman*, vol. xii, Aug. 26, 1887, p. 2.
[65] *Report of the Minneapolis Chamber of Commerce*, 1900, p. 133.
[66] *Ibid.*, 1885, p. 53; 1887, p. 42.

rolling stock to meet it — which was true of other lines as well.[67] At times Minneapolis looked apprehensively at the Omaha Road and its mills, for it made competition, but that city alone could not meet the demands of a growing West.

The St. Paul and Duluth Railway, successor to the Lake Superior and Mississippi, was another road that served Minneapolis. In 1885 it brought in 18,570,000 feet of lumber. But this road's supply dwindled as the decade passed, for its region was attacked so drastically by the levelers of the forest that it could withstand the onslaught for only a short period.[68]

In the late 1880s the Minneapolis, St. Paul and Sault Ste. Marie also became a regular contributor of lumber to Minneapolis. This road ran directly east into the white pine of the Chippewa, and then farther on into Wisconsin, continuously through pine forest.

TABLE 7. FIELD AND FOREST PRODUCTS CARRIED BY MINNESOTA RAILROADS, YEAR ENDING JUNE 30, 1886

Railroads	Grain (in tons)	Flour and Meal (in tons)	Lumber and Other Forest Products (in tons)
Chicago, Milwaukee & St. Paul	412,000	383,320	334,500
St. Paul, Minneapolis & Manitoba	587,562	45,560	219,656
Chicago & Northwestern	136,562	24,433	127,242
Northern Pacific	319,016	36,598	212,815
St. Paul & Duluth	287,916	135,968	308,742
Minneapolis & St. Louis	123,434	189,767	216,815
Chicago, St. Paul, Minneapolis & Omaha	146,478	144,753	275,533
Burlington, Cedar Rapids & Northern	76,207	125,059	37,733
Minneapolis Eastern	108,738	155,848	49,768
Duluth & Iron Range	321	281	9,899
Wisconsin, Minnesota & Pacific	51,422	23,396	40,212
Minnesota, St. Croix & Wisconsin	24,610	97,560	26,677
Minnesota & Northwestern	23,211	24,475	60,432
Total	2,297,477	1,387,018	1,920,024

SOURCE: *Report of the Minnesota Railroad and Warehouse Commission,* 1886, p. 112. Estimated on basis of percentage of earnings in Minnesota.

The study of individual railroads in any given year demonstrates that railroads and lumber were under deep obligation to each other. (See Table 7.) For example, the tonnage of the St. Paul and Duluth Railway was predominantly in lumber as long as the industry flourished along its way. In 1886 lumber and forest products provided 29 per cent of its total tonnage, while grain made up 27 per cent.[69] In 1887 its lumber

[67] *Mississippi Valley Lumberman,* vol. xi, Mar. 25, 1887.
[68] *Report of the Minneapolis Chamber of Commerce,* 1885, p. 53; 1886, p. 127; 1887, p. 42; 1889, p. 40.
[69] *Report of the Minnesota Railroad and Warehouse Commission,* 1887, pt. 2, p. 291.

tonnage was 30 per cent of the total, and grain was next, with a tonnage of 29 per cent. In 1890 it had a lumber tonnage of 34 per cent, with a grain tonnage of 5 per cent.[70] In 1899 the figures signaled the passing of a great industry, for that year the lumber tonnage of the St. Paul and Duluth was a mere 15.36 per cent, while grain (presumably wheat seeking transportation eastward at Duluth on Lake Superior) had finally taken the lead with a percentage of 20.[71]

The St. Paul, Minneapolis and Manitoba, which served a wheat region, was a heavy lumber carrier. In 1885 the entire line, with a mileage of 1509 of which 998 lay in Minnesota, headed its freight list with grain, which made up 58 per cent of its tonnage, while lumber and forest products came second with 21 per cent. The following year the grain carried was 54 per cent of the total, while lumber constituted 20 per cent; and the next year, 58 and 18 per cent.[72] These two products provided three fourths of the freight on this road, which carried wheat to Minneapolis or Duluth and lumber back to the places from which the wheat came.

There were on the Manitoba no empty rumbling cars to be carried back at a dead loss; its cars both ways were filled with substantial freight that yielded good money. "Jim" Hill, then at the head of the Manitoba — soon thereafter to become the Great Northern — said that an "empty" was a thief.

The lumber carried on the Manitoba was used to build farm homesteads in the 1880s and 1890s. But a new country needed more than houses and barns; it needed railroad ties, railroad bridges, depots, elevators almost without number, and warehouses. Today men talk of steel, but then white pine was the preferred material for a structure expected to outlast man. Builders of railroads selected it as their choice lumber for bridges, especially for horizontal timbers because, of all available woods, it checked the least.[73] In 1890 a trestle at Cutbank, Montana, 180 feet high, required 800,000 feet of lumber, while at Two Medicine Pass in that same state a trestle 214 feet high was expected to take close to 2,000,000 feet of lumber.[74] Clough Brothers of Minneapolis sold 40,000,000 feet of ties in 1889 to be used by the St. Paul, Minneapolis and Manitoba Railway in its development westward.[75] Railroad building offered only a temporary market for lumber; nevertheless it gave a strong stimulus to the white pine industry.

Lines of elevators, favored by the railroads and backed by the re-

[70] *Ibid.*, 1890, p. 461.
[71] *Ibid.*, 1899, p. 659.
[72] *Ibid.*, 1886, p. 422, and 1887, p. 315.
[73] *Mississippi Valley Lumberman*, vol. xvi, Sept. 13, 1889, p. 4.
[74] *Ibid.*, vol. xviii, Oct. 10, 1890, pp. 12–13.
[75] *Minneapolis Tribune*, Jan. 1, 1889, p. 3.

sources of the flour millers, reached out into the country to the south-west, west, and northwest of Minneapolis. And it took large amounts of lumber to build elevators and warehouses — especially terminal elevators. In the summer of 1893 Bovey-De Laittre of Minneapolis was busy getting out lumber for a new elevator for the Peaveys, who owned terminal elevators in Minneapolis and Duluth. That order called for 2,500,000 feet of lumber, one of the largest contracts among the lumber companies of Minneapolis that summer.[76] Previously, in the spring of 1891, the H. C. Akeley Company of Minneapolis had filled an order of 1,250,000 feet to be used for one elevator.[77]

Numerous towns — just small towns, but towns nevertheless — were dotting the prairie. They served the farmers who came to exhange their produce for other necessities; they also served the farmer as a place for the repair of parts of his machinery that might have failed him in the midst of a harvest. It must be remembered that Henry Ford tested his first automobile in 1893 and that it was not until 1895 that a motor car was driven through the streets of Chicago. The farmer's mode of travel in the eighties and nineties was by horse, which made it necessary that he live not too far away from a town. Such towns were a strong factor in the lumber industry of Minnesota and western Wisconsin.

Some of these small towns grew into cities in this prairie and plains country: Omaha, Kansas City, Des Moines, St. Joseph, Wichita, Topeka, and others, beginning as mere hamlets, became emporia of meat or of wheat. And in the process they consumed vast quantities of lumber. In 1892 E. W. Backus and Company had an order for 8,000,000 feet of lumber for the construction of the Armour packing plant at Kansas City, Missouri. It was a gala day when that order came in, for it was one of the largest single orders ever received in Minneapolis.[78]

St. Paul and Minneapolis were themselves great consumers of lumber. Houses in which to live, places in which to work, were necessary for the incoming population. In 1880 Minneapolis had 46,887 people; ten years later, 164,738. St. Paul had grown, too, though not so much. In 1880 that city had 41,473 people; by the beginning of the next decade it had a population of 133,156. These cities at the gateway to the prairie had during those ten years a combined increase of 256,421 people.[79]

Minneapolis became her own greatest customer in lumber, consuming in 1882 (a banner year) almost 200,000,000 feet.[80] In that year permits

---

[76] *Mississippi Valley Lumberman*, vol. xxiii, Aug. 25, 1893, p. 7.

[77] *Ibid.*, vol. xix, Apr. 10, 1891, p. 6.

[78] *Mississippi Valley Lumberman*, vol. xxi, June 10, 1892, p. 1.

[79] *Census of Minnesota, 1890*, pp. 2–3.

[80] *Joint Annual Report of the Chamber of Commerce and Board of Trade of Minneapolis*, 1882, p. 25.

of a total value of $4,623,925 were granted for residences in Minneapolis.[81]
The West Hotel, the Chamber of Commerce building, the new Post
Office building, and the Union Depot, all were constructed in that year.
These four buildings were of stone, to be sure, but they were large structures requiring lumber for floors and woodwork.[82] Altogether, thirteen
continuous and solid miles of new buildings were erected in that one year
in Minneapolis.[83]

One considerable item in lumber consumption in a growing city
before the era of concrete was sidewalks. In 1887 Minneapolis laid sixty-
seven miles of boardwalk, consuming 6,000,000 feet of lumber.[84] In 1892
Carpenter and Flourney, newcomers in Minneapolis sawmilling, received
the bid for furnishing 4,000,000 feet of sidewalk lumber in St. Paul.[85]

Minneapolis and St. Paul together, in several years during the decade
of the eighties, consumed 300,000,000 feet of lumber annually, while
Minneapolis at no time during that period cut more than 337,663,000.[86]
Minneapolis, therefore, was producing not much more than the two
cities themselves could use. She could supply her own needs and those
of her hinterland only by means of the lumber she received by railway
from Minnesota and Wisconsin.

It might appear that lumber was so much in demand that the industry
in Minnesota needed no direction. But this was not so, for competitors
beset the industry on several sides. White pine from other regions —
aided by railroads — sought the market Minnesota claimed as hers, and at
times the rivalry was intense. The keenest competitor was Michigan white
pine, which came west by way of Chicago. Michigan had excellent
white pine lying in the path of lumbermen moving westward from Maine
and New York, and it was the first of the Lake States' white pine regions
to feel the hand of man; its white pine therefore had such a hold on the
market that its competition was devastating.

Chicago was the outlet for Michigan's production, for it lay at the
foot of Lake Michigan. After railroads had been built into its hinterland,
Chicago left St. Louis behind in a bitter race for commercial dominance.
In 1861, before a foot of rails had been laid in Minnesota, Chicago lumber
was traveling into the prairie country by way of the Illinois Canal; the
Galena and Chicago, the Illinois Central, and the Chicago, Burlington

[81] *Minneapolis Tribune*, Jan. 1, 1883, p. 2.
[82] *Joint Annual Report of the Chamber of Commerce and Board of Trade of Minneapolis*, 1882, p. 20.
[83] *Minneapolis Tribune*, Jan. 1, 1883, p. 9.
[84] *Mississippi Valley Lumberman*, vol. xi, Mar. 4, 1887, p. 6.
[85] *Ibid.*, vol. xxi, June 10, 1892, p. 6.
[86] *Ibid.*, vol. xii, Oct. 28, 1887, p. 1; *Report of the Minneapolis Chamber of Commerce*, 1888, p. 135, and 1900, p. 133.

and Quincy were heavy carriers westward from Chicago.[87] By 1869 the Chicago, Burlington and Quincy had reached across Iowa to Council Bluffs. It was the second heaviest lumber-carrying railroad out of Chicago; that year its lumber carriage was 117,453,000 feet. The Burlington struck right into the prairie country which Minnesota's railroads were struggling to reach. The third lumber-carrying railroad in 1869 out of Chicago was the Chicago and Northwestern with its load of 99,508,000 feet,[88] and that, too, penetrated the territory which Minnesota's lumber aimed to reach.

Chicago's railroads carried increasing loads of lumber into the trans-Mississippi country. In 1875 the Chicago, Burlington and Quincy carried from Chicago 176,469,000 feet, which was more than the total output of Minneapolis for that year. The Chicago, Rock Island and Pacific, stretching westward across the Iowa prairie, carried 57,456,000 feet that year, which was more than any Minnesota railroad had carried up to that time.[89] To be sure, Chicago had the advantage of a location where rails and water meet; too, it received its lumber from forests along the shores of Lake Michigan at a trifling advance above the cost of production. Chicago had the advantage also of numerous competing rail lines, and these roads on their way west penetrated country already well settled where there was certain to be more paying freight. They could afford to offer cheaper freight rates.

Chicago became the leading wheat market in America because of its position as a railroad center.[90] Wheat from the area south and southwest of Minneapolis was under the trade influence of Chicago and Milwaukee; the millers in Minneapolis, according to an investigation in 1874, got most of their wheat from the St. Paul and Pacific, which ran west and northwest of Minneapolis.[91] Freight rates depended on the amount of freight carried, and Minnesota's railroads could not easily meet the competition of Chicago's roads. Less wheat carried by the railroads meant higher rates for lumber; higher freight rates for lumber meant higher lumber prices; and higher lumber prices meant smaller sales. So it was a matter of concern to the producer of lumber whether wheat was carried by roads centering in Minneapolis or in Chicago.[92]

[87] *Chicago Board of Trade, Annual Report*, 1862, p. 39.

[88] *Ibid.*, 1869, p. 77.

[89] *Ibid.*, 1876, pp. 102–3.

[90] H. M. Larson, *Wheat Market and Farmer in Minnesota*, p. 67; *St. Paul Pioneer Press*, Oct. 1, 1878, p. 10.

[91] *Minnesota House Journal*, 1874, pp. 234–36.

[92] In the early 1870s there were Chicago roads that supported six well-loaded freight trains a day with uniform return freight. This was quite in contrast with the situation at St. Paul, where on some lines one freight train a day was sufficient and where more than half the time it was loaded only one way. Report of the Special Joint Railroad Investigating Committee, *Report of the Minnesota Railroad Commissioner*, 1871, p. 88.

Chicago and Milwaukee capital largely controlled the Minnesota railroads lying to the south of Minneapolis and St. Paul. It was to the advantage of these roads to arrange freight rates favorable to themselves, which in turn would be profitable for Chicago and Milwaukee. In 1878 the Chicago market was decidedly favored when the Minneapolis rate for lumber to Omaha was sixty-five dollars a car and the Chicago rate was only thirty dollars a car.[93] Minneapolis merchants complained at that time that the market in Nebraska, Kansas, Missouri, and Iowa was practically closed to Minneapolis because Chicago controlled it.

The lumber industry of Minnesota was influenced by another factor of even greater importance than Chicago's heavy hand: the uncertain financial status of the farmer. The Northwest farmer lived by wheat in the sixties, seventies, and eighties — the Holstein cow had not then been heard of even in the Holstein-famous Cannon Valley of today. Wheat was king, and it enslaved the farmer of the North as cotton had the farmer of the South. Wheat determined his financial condition. Lumbermen followed closely the rise or fall of wheat prices, for it was sure to be reflected in lumber sales. When grasshoppers, too much rain, or too little rain played havoc with the farmer's income, the market for lumber suffered too. A shortage of wheat in Europe meant better prices in America, and that promised a busy season for lumber. The years 1870, 1871, and 1874 were not satisfactory crop years, and this reduced lumber production in the Upper Mississippi Valley. The Chicago fire in 1871, however, tended to offset this development; Chicago was prevented from supplying lumber, which was then furnished by the Upper Mississippi Valley mills.

The panic, an evil which no decade seemed to escape, also pressed hard in the seventies. As a result, one of Minnesota's most aggressive lumbermen, W. D. Washburn, made assignments to his creditors in 1874. His mills were running in both Minneapolis and Anoka, and he was the owner of large pine tracts. Perhaps because he was one of the most daring of Minneapolis promoters, he was caught worse by the depression following the panic than any other prominent lumberman in the Upper Valley.[94]

In 1875 the Minneapolis lumber cut showed the influence of the panic, but in the following year it rose to the highest cut the city had known so far — only to be retarded by the grasshopper plague in 1877 and the rust, blight, and chinch bug in 1878. The sale of lumber almost stopped in the district ravaged by grasshoppers.[95] In 1878 this plague caused an

[93] *Minneapolis Tribune*, Apr. 25, 1878; *Stillwater Messenger*, Nov. 22, 1878.
[94] *Anoka Republican*, Oct. 29, 1874.
[95] *Minneapolis Tribune*, July 2, 1877, p. 4.

almost complete failure of the wheat crop in the agricultural lumber market of Minneapolis.[96]

In the spring of 1877 another evil fell upon the lumber market: low rainfall caused low water in the streams. The Washburn mill at Anoka feared that it could not operate until after the Fourth of July because the logs could not come down.[97] There was an almost unprecedented want of water.[98] Lack of logs made idle mills, which in turn made idle labor. Logs, in which capital was locked up, could not move from where they had been wintered.[99] This interfered, too, with lumber stocks and strengthened Chicago's hold: Chicago's transportation of raw lumber, via Lake Michigan, was not dependent on rainfall. It was in this year that the Chicago, Burlington and Quincy hauled an immense load from Chicago to the prairie, the largest it had ever carried. No doubt one factor in the making of that load was the falling-off of the cut in Minnesota because of lack of rainfall.

Surely few industries are more dependent on the elements than was lumbering in Minnesota. On the one hand, rainfall affected transportation, especially the carrying of logs from the forest to the mills. And on the other hand, the prairie demand that determined production was subject to the risks of grasshopper, chinch bug, blight, hail, and lack of rain. If all went well with the prairie, all went well with lumber.[1]

Though competition from other regions, panics, crop failures, and low waters sometimes took a heavy toll in the market, the lumber industry of the Upper River was on the whole in a favorable position so far as the sale of its product was concerned. In spite of its difficulties, that industry served an expanding market; the winning of the West would have been difficult without it.

Indeed, wheat and lumber were the warp and the woof in the weaving of the pattern that is the Northwest. And the railroad was the shuttle. One without the others could not have made this Midland Empire. It is a significant fact that in the period in which Minnesota reached the high point in its handling of wheat and making of flour, it also came to rank third among the states in its output of lumber.[2]

[96] *Report of the Minneapolis Board of Trade,* 1878, pp. 15–16.
[97] *Anoka County Union,* June 30, 1877.
[98] *Stillwater Messenger,* Apr. 27, 1877, and May 11, 1877.
[99] *Minneapolis Tribune,* May 16, 1877.
[1] *Stillwater Messenger,* Aug. 6, 1875, and July 23, 1875.
[2] *Forest Products of the United States,* U.S. Department of Agriculture, Forest Service Bulletin 74, 1907.

CHAPTER VIII

Lumber and Logs on the Mississippi
after 1870

MINNEAPOLIS, Stillwater, and Winona, as we have seen, increased their lumber production and expanded their market as railroads developed and opened up new regions to the westward. Activity on the Mississippi River increased, too, as railroads struck out from that artery. When railroads first entered American life they were planned primarily as adjuncts to water transportation: the widening market made possible by railroads would increase traffic on the river. This proved to be quite correct in regard to the Mississippi, for railroads did speed up the log and lumber industry of that river between 1870 and 1890.

Between 1840 and 1915 about seventy-five mills of varying sizes were operating along the route from Stillwater to St. Louis to furnish lumber to meet the demand from the growing West.[1] Some of the mill towns below the junction of the St. Croix and the Mississippi became very prominent markets.

Winona was one of these, and since it still obtained its log stock from the pine forests farther up on the Mississippi and its tributaries, the rafting of logs and lumber to Winona became a big business. Samuel R. Van Sant, the head of the chief rafting firm on the river, established himself there in 1883.[2] In 1886 Ingram and Kennedy of Eau Claire joined Charles Horton, an early lumberman of Winona, in organizing the Empire Lumber Company, thus adding another able firm to the Winona group. In 1887 Winona ranked second in the state in the manufacturing of lumber, and as a market she ranked third.[3] Between 1868 and 1878 her mills cut 325,000,000 feet of lumber; in the next decade their cut increased to a total of 1,150,000,000 feet.[4]

La Crosse, thirty-one miles south of Winona, on the Wisconsin side

[1] Blair, *A Raft Pilot's Log*, p. 257.
[2] Interview of the writer with Samuel R. Van Sant, Minneapolis, Feb. 21, 1933.
[3] *Mississippi Valley Lumberman*, vol. xi, Apr. 29, 1887.
[4] Folsom, "History of Lumbering in the St. Croix Valley," *Minn. Hist. Soc. Coll.*, vol. ix, pp. 320–21.

where the Black River joins the Mississippi, kept pace with her Minnesota rival. The Black River had early been important in lumber; in 1842 the Mormons had sought logs there for their home at Nauvoo in Illinois.[5] In 1844 logs were sent from the Black River to St. Louis, and the same river furnished pine for the lead mines at Galena and Dubuque.[6] As early as 1839 a sawmill was chugging away at Black River Falls.[7]

La Crosse commanded quite a hinterland on the Wisconsin side of the river, but it also, as we have seen, sought and got markets in southern Minnesota. The rafting of logs to markets farther down was also a part of the business at La Crosse, just as it was at Stillwater and at Read's Landing.

C. C. Washburn, one-time governor of Wisconsin, was prominent in the lumber life of La Crosse. He had come from Maine, and the white pine on the Black River plus the favorable location of La Crosse caught his eye. In 1871 he organized the La Crosse Lumber Company.[8] John Paul, who had come from Scotland in 1857, C. L. Coleman, who had come from New York state in 1854, and Sawyer and Austin, who had begun operations in 1872, were other men with foresight who directed the expansion of the lumber business at La Crosse. In 1893 La Crosse had twelve sawmills and six plants manufacturing sash, doors, blinds, and other planing-mill products. That year the value of the city's output of timber products reached $3,950,109.[9] It is estimated that in the period from 1853 to 1897 more than six billion feet of lumber were cut at La Crosse from Black River logs only.[10]

The advantages of Dubuque as a distributing point for upper Iowa were early recognized by the Chippewa lumbermen. Thither went John H. Knapp of Menomonie to interest Henry L. Stout in sawmilling, and these men successfully established themselves there as early as 1853. In 1856 two mills were operating there, and in 1874 four mills were at work to meet the still growing demand. Ingram and Kennedy of Eau Claire went to Dubuque to join with W. H. Day in forming the Standard Lumber Company. This concern in 1880 cut 12,000,000 feet of the 29,000,000 cut in that city.[11] All these mills purchased their logs from the regions of the St. Croix or the Chippewa.

Clinton, Iowa, still farther down the Mississippi, was no small lumber city. In fact its only close competitors on the river below Minneapolis

[5] Blair, *op. cit.*, p. 35.
[6] Folwell, *History of Minnesota*, vol. i, p. 159.
[7] Holley, "Waterways and Lumber Interests of Western Wisconsin," *Proceedings, Wis. Hist. Soc.*, 1906, p. 211.
[8] Blair, *op. cit.*, p. 35.
[9] *Mississippi Valley Lumberman*, vol. xxiii, Mar. 24, 1893, p. 6.
[10] Hotchkiss, *History of Lumber and Forest Industry of Northwest*, p. 501.
[11] *Ibid.*, p. 584.

were Winona and La Crosse. Even in 1866 it was said to have the "largest sawmill in the world."[12] The mill, which belonged to W. J. Young of Clinton, boasted an engine of 1000 horsepower and an annual sawing capacity of 80,000,000 feet of lumber. It was Young of this famous mill who introduced the brail system of rafting logs, which will be considered later.[13]

Another Clinton firm well known in the lumber world consisted of members of the Lamb family. When the first Lamb came west to Clinton, his credit was such that nothing but ready cash would buy even an ax.[14] He was poor, but he was a man of vision and energy. In 1877 he owned a sawmill which could cut 250,000 feet of lumber per 24-hour day.[15] His firm had its own towboats on the river; the *Chauncy Artemus* and *Lady Grace* of C. Lamb and Sons were handsome rafters that graced the Mississippi.[16]

David Joyce and his son, W. T. Joyce, were other sawmill men of prominence in Clinton and its near neighbor, Lyons. Clinton's market was the prairie land of Iowa; there was no rafting of lumber down the Mississippi by the mills below La Crosse.[17]

Close by Clinton was Rock Island, the home of the future leader of western lumbermen, Frederick Weyerhaeuser. In 1856 Weyerhaeuser and his brother-in-law, F. C. A. Denkmann, made their initial investment in a sawmill at the spot where the Rock River meets the Mississippi. The mill was on the Illinois side at the foot of the Upper Rapids.[18] A railroad had already been built there from Chicago, and Rock Island promised well as a point of distribution. Five hundred dollars was their down payment on a humble business for which they were to pay $3000; it grew so rapidly that by 1887 Weyerhaeuser was known as the outstanding lumberman in the United States.[19] In the early 1860s the two brothers-in-law purchased their first timberland.[20] Then their growth in lumbering began to gather momentum.

At Muscatine, Iowa, the chief lumberman was Peter Musser. Like the Lairds and the Nortons at Winona, Musser had come from Pennsyl-

[12] *Ibid.*, pp. 588–89; Bill, "Career of Captain Jerome E. Short," *Clinton Herald*, Mar. 25, 1933, p. 3.

[13] Durant, "Lumbering and Steamboating on the St. Croix River," *Minn. Hist. Soc. Coll.*, vol. x, pt. 2, pp. 663–65; Hotchkiss, *op. cit.*, p. 588.

[14] Bill, "Career of Captain Jerome E. Short," *Clinton Herald*, Apr. 15, 1933, p. 3.

[15] *Stillwater Lumberman*, Feb. 23, 1877.

[16] *Mississippi Valley Lumberman*, vol. xxiv, Mar. 16, 1894, p. 4.

[17] Interview of the writer with Capt. Fred A. Bill, July 29, 1933.

[18] *Mississippi Valley Lumberman*, vol. xi, Apr. 22, 1887.

[19] *Ibid.*, Nov. 18, 1887, p. 8; vol. xxiv, Mar. 23, 1894, p. 5.

[20] "Letters from Early Lumbering Days on the Chippewa River," with notes by William W. Bartlett, *Daily Telegram* (Eau Claire, Wisconsin), Feb. 12, 1931 (a clipping in the Bartlett Collection, Minn. Hist. Soc.); *American Lumberman*, Apr. 11, 1914, pp. 30–31.

vania. Like the Lairds and Nortons, also, he at first manufactured no lumber but bought his ready stock from the mills above, on the St. Croix or the Chippewa or at Winona or La Crosse. But in 1871 he built his own mill at Muscatine and in that year his mill cut 10,000,000 feet of lumber. In 1880, 45,000,000 feet was the season's output of his mill.[21] For fifty-five years Musser furnished lumber to the farmers of Iowa, and he came to be recognized as one of the authorities on lumber in the Middle West.

No history of the market for lumber on the Mississippi would be complete without some reference to Hannibal, Missouri. Hannibal could make no boast about its milling — that was not its chief business; but it served as a market place to which men came to buy lumber in quantity. It had yards, big yards, which disposed of their goods through wholesaling, retailing, or branch yards. In 1852 a Hannibal newspaper advertised lumber from the best mills in the pinery.[22] The same paper in a later issue carried this advertisement for a lumber concern: "We will lumber out more lumber for less money lumbered in than any other lumber men will lumber out for the same amount in all this lumber country. One of the partners resides in Pinery which gives us advantage. F. Bull & Co." [23]

Lumbermen powerful in the business established yards at Hannibal. It was an attractive market, for early it came to have railroads which reached out to Missouri, Kansas, Colorado, Arkansas, Indian Territory, Texas, and New Mexico.[24] The Northwestern Lumber Company of Eau Claire, Wisconsin, of which Samuel T. McKnight (later of Minneapolis) was a prominent member, maintained one of the leading yards at Hannibal. J. T. Barber of Hannibal handled the distribution business of this company. Ingram and Kennedy of Eau Claire also established a yard at Hannibal in 1881; it was managed by Dulaney and McVeigh. These large Eau Claire firms sent rafts of lumber to Hannibal to be distributed to the prairie land west of the Mississippi. Even as early as 1882 a total of 230,890,664 feet of lumber was handled in this emporium — enough to have filled 22,491 railroad cars. Hannibal was a market to reckon with in the River Age.

St. Louis continued to be the most distant and the greatest market downriver for the pine of the Upper Mississippi — both as a wholesale market and as a consuming market. In 1874 St. Louis received 84,439,000

[21] *Little Falls Daily Transcript,* Jan. 21, 1905.

[22] *Missouri Courier* (Hannibal), June 27, 1852.

[23] *Ibid.,* Aug. 19, 1852. The term *pineries* was used because pine was the only timber considered worth cutting; Patrick Gunn, "Lumbering in Chippewa Valley," *Eau Claire Leader* (Wisconsin), Apr. 12, 1916 (a clipping in the Bartlett Collection, Minn. Hist. Soc.).

[24] Capt. Fred A. Bill, compiler and editor, "A Tourist's Manual and Guide to the Scenes, Legends, Cities of the Upper Mississippi River," *Saturday Evening Post* (Burlington, Iowa), May 15, 1920, p. 10.

feet of white pine by raft from the Upper River.[25] In addition, the railroads that year carried 6,056,000 feet of white pine to St. Louis from the north country. Clearly, the river had no need to fear rail competition as yet.

St. Louis' demands for white pine increased steadily. In 1875 it sold 30,000,000 feet more of white pine than in 1874. The explanation of this lies partly in the fact that "St. Louis was more particularly favored in the extent of her building operations, which were certainly large and on a scale that marks the year as an exceptional one, and the city as especially prosperous." [26] In 1875 the Upper Mississippi rafted to St. Louis 89,217,880 feet of white pine, while the railroad carried 9,464,000 feet. Yellow pine gave no heavy competition as yet, for only 21,326,850 feet of yellow pine were received in St. Louis in 1875. In 1878 a total of 193,831,404 feet of lumber was sold, of which 129,806,733 was white pine and 18,286,421 yellow. Of the lumber sold in St. Louis, a little more than half went to the hinterland market.[27]

St. Louis was growing; its population increased from 77,860 in 1850 to 350,187 in 1880. It was developing as a manufacturing center.[28] Homes were constantly in demand in order to house the growing population. Factories, elevators, warehouses, and stores were continuously in the building.[29] Building materials in those days meant lumber and the prevailing lumber on the market was still white pine.

St. Louis was also developing as a distributing center. Railroads spreading out like a fan from St. Louis were opening up far-reaching markets. In 1881 the Missouri Pacific, reaching southward to the Rio Grande, had a mileage of 5944, and it carried in that year 60,719,000 feet of lumber, ranking first as a lumber carrier out of St. Louis. Next in importance was the St. Louis, Wabash and Pacific, which ran from St. Louis out into Missouri and the farming regions of Iowa; in 1881 it distributed along its path 83,801,000 feet of lumber.[30] Third was the St. Louis and San Francisco Railroad, which directed its way into Arkansas, Oklahoma, and Colorado; it carried 47,850,000 feet.[31] To be sure, these railroads carried other lumber besides white pine, but white pine was still master in the St. Louis market.

The heaviest river traffic in the shipment of lumber to St. Louis occurred in the decade of the eighties. It held steady from 1880 to 1888,

[25] *St. Louis Trade and Commerce*, 1874, p. 72.
[26] *Ibid.*, 1875, p. 109.
[27] *Ibid.*, 1875, p. 110, and 1878, p. 86.
[28] *U.S. Census, 1850: Statistical View of the United States*, p. 380; *St. Louis Trade and Commerce*, 1880, pp. 98 and 246; *Stillwater Messenger*, Jan. 8, 1875.
[29] *St. Louis Trade and Commerce*, 1894, p. 241.
[30] *Ibid.*, 1881, p. 123.
[31] *Ibid.*, 1882, pp. 43–46.

but after this the decrease became quite pronounced. From 1870 to 1890 lumber shipment by way of the Mississippi reached its highest point in 1882, when 162,682,630 feet of white pine reached St. Louis; the lowest point of the two decades came in 1889, when 71,935,820 feet of white pine were rafted to that city. Table 8 illustrates the interesting course of the white pine market at St. Louis.

TABLE 8. WHITE PINE RECEIVED AT ST. LOUIS BY WAY OF THE UPPER MISSISSIPPI, 1880–1899

Year	Lumber (in millions of feet)	Logs	Shingles (in millions of pieces)	Laths
1880	142	4	56	35
1881	100	10	35	18
1882	163	4*	57	35
1883	129	5	60	30
1884	135	5	75	41
1885	132	7	67	51
1886	124	7	48	37
1887	131	6	70	43
1888	79	8	26	15
1889	72	10	43	11
1890	72	10	45	26
1891	80	5	41	10
1892	89	8	39	22
1893	83	7	37	28
1894	87	10	36	31
1895	74	9	25	18
1896	65	9	16	13
1897	46	3	17	10
1898	40	7	15	10
1899	42	2	21	11

* After this they spoke only of logs, not white pine; there were a few cottonwoods and walnuts that came, but very few, so it is safe to think of them as white pine.

SOURCE: *St. Louis Trade and Commerce*, 1880, pp. 15, 98; 1882, p. 55; 1883, pp. 135, 149; 1884, p. 36; 1885, p. 150; 1886, p. 62; 1887, p. 200; 1888, pp. 169, 197; 1894, p. 242; 1896, p. 73; 1897, p. 60; 1899, p. 142. Logs are in superficial feet.

As we have seen, the coming of the towboat made a great change in the mode of traffic on the Mississippi. Stillwater on the St. Croix illustrates this development. There the St. Croix teemed with towboats which, current or no current, pushed huge rafts of logs downriver. The size of the rafts became steadily larger. In 1864 ten rafts of logs left Stillwater in as many successive days, carrying altogether 4,000,000 feet of logs.[32] This would average 400,000 feet of logs to a raft, which was a small raft even at that time. One May day in 1866 seven rafts left Stillwater holding 3,000,000 feet of logs and 1,000,000 feet of sawed lumber billed for St. Louis, Albany (Illinois), and Muscatine (Iowa).[33] But in 1874 a single raft descending the St. Croix into the Mississippi carried

[32] *Stillwater Messenger*, June 7, 1864.
[33] *Ibid.*, May 23, 1866.

TABLE 9. LOADS FROM STILLWATER DELIVERED DOWNRIVER, MAY 14–28, 1875

Boat	Load	Destination
MAY 14–21, 1875		
Penn Wright	Raft No. 3	W. J. Young and Company, Clinton
Helen Mar	14 Strings logs	Downstream for sale*
James Means	4 Strings lumber	Berry and Company, Burlington
James Means	4 Strings	Berry and Company, Burlington
James Means	400,000 feet	Red Wing Mills
James Means	100,000 feet	Hastings Mills
Minnie Will	400,000 feet	R. C. Libby, Hastings
Minnesota	16 Strings	J. J. Dickie, Burlington
Minnesota	4 Strings	La Crosse
Minnesota	1 String	Daniels & Company, Red Wing
Hudson	14 Strings	Boeckeler, St. Louis
Henderson	Raft No. 4	W. J. Young and Company, Clinton
McDonald	12 Strings	P. Musser, Muscatine
McDonald	3 Strings	Seymour, Sabin and Company, Cedar Rapids, Iowa
James Means	Raft	Berry and Company, Burlington
MAY 21–28, 1875		
Wyman X	1,500,000 feet lumber	Downriver for sale
	600,000 lath	Downriver for sale
Penn Wright	7 Strings	Dimock Gould and Company, Moline
Penn Wright	8 Strings	J. L. Davis and Son, Davenport
Helene Schulenburg	2,000,000 feet lumber	
	600,000 lath	Schulenburg and Boeckeler, St. Louis
	5,000,000 shingles	
James Means	22 Strings	Berry and Company, Burlington
James Means	4 Strings	Downstream for sale
Minnie Will	400,000 feet	Red Wing
Louisville	6 Strings	Culvertson Smith and Company, Fulton
Louisville	8 Strings	Downstream for sale
Henderson	15 Strings	W. J. Young and Company, Clinton
Wild Boy	15 Strings	W. J. Young and Company, Clinton
Hudson	3 Strings	John Paul, La Crosse
Hudson	8 Strings	Pelan and Zimmerman, Guttenberg
Hudson	2 Strings	Carr and Austin, Dubuque
Hudson	2 Strings	Dorchester and Company, Bellevue
Mark Bradley	15 Strings	W. J. Young and Company, Clinton
Minnie Will	3 Strings	Clinton Lumber Company, Clinton
Minnie Will	1 String	Ira Stockwell, Lyons
Minnie Will	7 Strings	D. Joyce, Lyons
James Means	16 Strings	Berry and Company, Burlington
Louisville	5 Strings	Dorchester and Company, Bellevue
Louisville	10 Strings	Wadleigh Wells and Company, Lyons
Henderson	15 Strings	W. J. Young and Company, Clinton
Jonathan	15 Strings	Berry and Company, Burlington
Wild Boy	15 Strings	W. J. Young and Company, Clinton

* *For sale* means that they were sold en route; otherwise they were sold before they left Stillwater.

SOURCE: *Stillwater Messenger,* May 21 and 28, 1875.

1,242,092 feet of Totogatic and Chippenaga logs![34] This was the largest raft yet to leave the sparkling St. Croix for the Mississippi markets.

[34] *Ibid.,* July 3, 1874. Totogatic logs were so called because of the stream they bordered. They were the largest logs in the St. Croix region, and *Totogatic* came to serve as a synonym for large. Logs were usually given the name of the stream on whose banks they were cut.

Stillwater grew busier every year. From spring until fall towboats were busy steering large numbers of unwieldy rafts into the great stream. In one week in May 1875 eight towboats, making fifteen trips, left Stillwater pushing lumber rafts to be delivered to at least thirteen different concerns down the river, located all the way from Hastings to Burlington, Iowa. The following week eleven towboats, making twenty-five trips, pushed rafts from Stillwater to be delivered to twenty-four firms along the river all the way to St. Louis. In the first seven weeks of the season of 1875 Edward W. Durant sold 9,000,000 feet of logs downriver by taking orders for his wares as his rafts moved downstream.[35] By the eleventh day of June that year Durant's concern had towed 27,201,528 feet of logs down the Mississippi.[36]

The number of logs scaled through the boom at Stillwater increased. In 1878 more than 200,000,000 feet of logs were sent through the boom, and in 1890 the number of feet passed the 400,000,000 mark. The increase was steady, with rarely a setback until the white pine was gone. In the twenty-eight years from 1875 to 1903 the log output through the St. Croix Boom measured 7,781,835,650 feet.

Logs were to Stillwater what pork once was to Cincinnati and wheat to Chicago, and Stillwater newspapers, from the beginning to the end of each season, reported the sales and deliveries of logs.[37] These reports are interesting because they give information as to both prices and returns for the Stillwater producers.

The price of logs varied considerably in the decade of the seventies. In 1871 Totogatic logs were sold by Durant and his partner, Hanford, for $18 per thousand feet. These logs were sent to Moline, Illinois. They were an unusual lot of logs, for the 1940 logs in the group totaled 827,145 feet.[38] Totogatic logs were always given the highest rating, but $18 was a high price for even the best of logs. That year 71,510,964 feet of logs were exported from the St. Croix to mills along the Mississippi; the sale of these logs brought $718,685 to dealers of the St. Croix area.[39]

In the spring of 1873 Totogatic logs were rafted at $13.25.[40] This lower price may have been set because the grade was a bit inferior, or possibly the panic had already begun to lay its deadly hands on business. But $13.25 was not a low price for logs. In 1873 Durant and his partner, Wheeler, rafted long pine at $9.75 per thousand feet.[41]

[35] *Ibid.*, May 14, 1875. Edward W. Durant was in the business of rafting, sawing, and logging.
[36] *Ibid.*, June 11, 1875.
[37] *Ibid.*, June 4, 11, 18, 25, July 2, 7, 16, 23, 30, Aug. 6, 12, 20, 1875.
[38] *Ibid.*, Dec. 22, 1871.
[39] *Ibid.*, Jan. 12, 1872.
[40] *Ibid.*, May 30, 1873.
[41] *Ibid.*, May 30, 1873.

TABLE 10. LOGS PASSING THE ST. CROIX BOOM, 1875–1903

Year	Logs	Measurement (in feet)
1875	782,685	121,389,720
1876	898,340	153,252,000
1877	765,004	130,540,890
1878	810,320	132,735,870
1879	1,146,850	201,763,500
1880	1,178,940	201,440,800
1881	1,528,250	231,000,500
1882	1,652,890	273,810,400
1883	1,672,350	271,272,800
1884	1,723,450	274,350,600
1885	1,590,860	225,540,800
1886	1,556,820	191,454,500
1887	1,726,800	270,060,100
1888	2,256,570	365,480,300
1889	1,987,689	262,385,980
1890	3,468,320	452,360,890
1891	2,520,380	315,180,700
1892	3,361,799	436,899,700
1893	3,030,844	359,468,720
1894	2,496,262	281,470,400
1895	3,441,991	373,062,850
1896	3,258,622	321,764,530
1897	3,082,456	311,084,290
1898	3,213,537	336,479,950
1899	3,676,958	391,083,770
1900	2,397,940	239,227,730
1901	3,130,448	251,448,220
1902	1,761,015	160,149,910
1903	3,010,750	245,675,230
Total	63,129,140	7,781,835,650

SOURCE: These figures are recorded in the Surveyor General's office in St. Paul.

In 1874 Totogatic logs were selling at $12.50 per thousand feet for cash, but this did not include fitting for the pilot or rafting; 1,000,000 feet were sent to Bellevue, Iowa, at that price. That same summer Durant and Wheeler sent 2,000,000 feet to Muscatine, Iowa, at $13.50, but these logs were fitted for the pilot and rafted to their destination as a part of the price. That lot brought Durant and Wheeler $27,000. In two days in the month of June that concern had total sales of more than $35,000. A fair price for logs that year ranged from $9 to $10, but long white pine was usually in the market for $12 per thousand.[42]

In spite of low prices in 1875 sales were large. In early May W. J. Young of Clinton, Iowa, purchased 14,500,000 feet of logs from Hersey, Staples and Bean of Stillwater on a cash basis, paying $6.75 per thousand feet for logs loose in the boom.[43] And in the last week of June Isaac

[42] *Ibid.*, June 26, 1874.
[43] *Stillwater Lumberman*, May 7, 1875.

Staples returned from a trip to St. Louis and other towns on the Mississippi having sold logs and lumber in the amount of $87,000.[44] In 1875 Walker, Judd and Veazie at Marine, selling all their Totogatic logs to Schulenburg and Boeckeler at Stillwater for $12.37 per thousand feet, received $65,000 in cash for their product. From Stillwater in the spring of this same year went also 9,000,000 feet of logs to Berry and Company of Burlington, Iowa, who paid $100,000 for the lot.[45] The general price for white pine logs in 1875 was about $8.25.

In 1876 Totogatics were selling at $12.37 per thousand feet, the highest price for logs that season. The lowest-priced log in the market then was selling at $5.50 per thousand feet. The average price that year was $10.50 for logs fitted for the pilot and rafted downriver to their destination.[46] That year 112,036,649 feet of logs were rafted to mills below Stillwater. If the average price of those logs was $10.50, they brought to the valley $1,288,421. In the summer of 1880 Durant, Wheeler and Company sold 72,000,000 feet of logs, which brought them more than $650,000.[47]

Stillwater was also increasing its cut of lumber. In 1874 that city had nine mills with a combined capacity of 82,000,000 feet a year.[48] In 1875 Schulenburg and Boeckeler cut 25,086,386 feet in Stillwater, only a portion of the 40,000,000 feet which they sold annually at St. Louis.[49] They were at that time the biggest lumber firm in Stillwater. But the St. Croix Lumber Mills also kept quite a steady pace; in the season of 1875 they rafted about 50,000 feet of lumber a day downriver.[50] McKusick, Anderson and Company, too, were shipping mostly by water. In 1871 the St. Croix River mills made 61,466,680 feet of lumber and the value of the lumber exported was $922,000; in 1876, when lumber totaling 88,669,639 feet was made and sold, largely at $13.50 per thousand, it brought the sawmill men over a million dollars.[51]

The Chippewa River also sent to market a mighty stream of logs and lumber. The Chippewa Valley in its heyday was the home of at least twelve great lumber companies, and the name of each was familiar to the world of lumber: (1) Knapp, Stout and Company, Company, (2) Ingram, Kennedy and Company, (3) Daniel Shaw Lumber Company, (4) Union Lumber Company, (5) Eau Claire Lumber Company, (6) LaFayette Lumber Company, (7) Badger Lumber Company, (8) Chippewa Lum-

[44] *Stillwater Messenger,* July 2, 1875.
[45] *Ibid.,* May 28, 1875.
[46] *Stillwater Lumberman,* Jan. 21, 1876.
[47] *Stillwater Messenger,* Dec. 11, 1880.
[48] Hotchkiss, *op. cit.,* p. 530.
[49] *Stillwater Messenger,* Jan. 21, 1876.
[50] *Stillwater Lumberman,* Apr. 23, 1875
[51] *Stillwater Messenger,* Jan. 12, 1872.

ber and Boom Company, (9) Valley Lumber Company, (10) Dells Lumber Company, (11) Sherman Lumber Company, and (12) Northwestern Lumber Company. There were lesser firms, too, that played a part in the making of the fourteen billion feet of lumber cut in the Chippewa Valley from 1830 to 1901.[52]

Knapp, Stout and Company, Company, with a capital of $2,000,000 in the seventies, had a mill at Menomonie that produced an annual cut of 50,000,000 feet,[53] an unusual cut for those days. Knapp, Stout increased their capital to $4,000,000 in the eighties, evidence that they were successful men of business.[54] This firm disposed of its lumber at important points on the Mississippi.

Ingram, Kennedy and Company became almost a legend on the Mississippi. The Mussers of Muscatine, Iowa, at one time purchased lumber stock from this firm. Their boats went regularly to St. Louis, to Hannibal, Missouri, and to Keokuk and Clinton, Iowa. In 1889 this firm became the Empire Lumber Company, with mills and yards at Eau Claire (Wisconsin), Winona (Minnesota), Dubuque (Iowa), and Hannibal (Missouri).[55] It operated on the Mississippi until there was no more white pine in the Chippewa Valley.

At the head of navigation on the Chippewa was the town named for the river itself, Chippewa Falls. As early as 1836 there was a mill at the Falls, but its life was a bit unsteady until in 1869 a group of men from Pennsylvania purchased it and formed the Union Lumber Company, of which Thaddeus Pound became the president. The Panic of 1873 dealt harshly with this concern, which had hardly had time to establish itself before the panic came, and the company was not revived until the steady hand of Frederick Weyerhaeuser and his associates came to control it in 1881. They commanded the mill until it cut its last log on August 2, 1911.[56]

Not merely lumber but logs by the billions of feet poured forth from the Chippewa. Every season flotillas of logs — hundreds, thousands, even millions of logs — set forth to be cut by the mills all along the way to St. Louis. From 1867 to 1905 the Chippewa sent 11,365,875,930 feet of logs to the mills of the Mississippi.[57] Possibly as many as 600,000,000 logs passed the great boom.

This boom, five miles below Wabasha on the Mississippi, is the

[52] Blair, *op. cit.*, pp. 33–34.
[53] *Stillwater Messenger*, Feb. 27, 1874.
[54] *Rice Lake Chronotype*, Sept. 2, 1927; Bill, "Navigation on the Chippewa," *Burlington Post* (Iowa), Feb. 21, 1931, p. 3.
[55] Knapp Papers, letterhead in letter sent by Ingram to Knapp, Sept. 19, 1889.
[56] Bill, "Navigation on the Chippewa," *Burlington Post* (Iowa), Sept. 27, 1930, p. 2.
[57] Blair, *op. cit.*, p. 289.

celebrated sand bar known to boatmen as Beef Slough. The Beef River of Wisconsin, a timid little stream, pours its waters into the Mississippi alongside those of the Chippewa River; it is sometimes even called one of the mouths of the Chippewa. At its very outlet this stream has deposited sand, forming a sluggish place — a fine base for a boom.[58] Today the appearance of Beef Slough is unassuming; no one would ever know that once it teemed with life. In the great River Age of lumbering Beef Slough meant Chippewa logs, for in that boom were sorted, scaled, and rafted all the logs that rode the Chippewa.[59] It was a busy mart which was to lumbermen what the exchange was to the merchants of a big city. There the logs were sorted according to their log marks and stamp marks, and there they were formed into rafts to be towed downriver to the firm whose marks they bore.

Among the earliest downriver mills to seek logs on the Chippewa were the Schricker and Mueller mill at Davenport and the Weyerhaeuser establishment at Rock Island. Gradually men all the way from St. Louis northward sought logs on the Chippewa with which to stock their growing mills; downriver men early sensed the value of Beef Slough as a place for rafting.

The men owning mills on the Chippewa River objected to the purchases by the downriver men; they wanted to reserve the forests for their own mills. They were alarmed at the loss of wealth which Wisconsin was suffering in the form of vast log export. The great white pine of the Chippewa, they said, was not to be made into lumber at "foreign points."[60] Their position was not disinterested; the Mississippi millmen were competitors of the Chippewa millmen, and the logs and the dams used to float them to market were obstructions in the way of lumber rafts and steamboats. They were said to be both a menace and a nuisance.[61]

These were a few of the circumstances that brought on the so-called Beef Slough War, a war of lumber against logs. Able lumbermen were found on each side. In the group of Chippewa millmen were Daniel Shaw and Orrin H. Ingram of Eau Claire and the Knapps of Menomonie. These men commanded some of the largest mills on the Upper Mississippi; they would tolerate no interference. On the other side were the downriver men, who must have logs for their mills: Frederick Weyerhaeuser of Rock Island, W. H. Laird and the Nortons of Winona, Young and Lamb of Clinton. Such men were not easily stopped when so much was at stake.

[58] *Minnesota Railroad and River Guide,* 1857–1868 (St. Paul, 1867), p. 375.
[59] Matthew G. Norton, *The Mississippi River Logging Company* (n.p., 1912), p. 13.
[60] *Mississippi Valley Lumberman,* vol. xiv, Aug. 10, 1888, p. 4.
[61] Norton, *op. cit.,* p. 15.

The battle was a long one. The mill owners of the Chippewa obtained control of the land surrounding Beef Slough. They did not plan to use it; their object was to keep it from being used.[62] Their fears increased when in 1867 the Beef Slough Manufacturing, Booming, Log Driving and Transportation Company was formed, with a capital of $100,000. Its stock was held by men from Michigan and from Chippewa Falls, Oshkosh, and Fond du Lac in Wisconsin.[63] Francis Palms of Detroit was prominent in this group. He dealt in Wisconsin pineland and had substantial holdings on the Jump River, famous for the best white pine. He was interested in a competitive market for his product which he knew the downriver men would help to create.

The new company applied for a charter, but under pressure from the Chippewa millmen the Wisconsin Assembly was loath to grant it. Fortunately for the projected company, the two sawmill towns of Eau Claire and Chippewa Falls found themselves in conflict over the proposed Dells Dam in the Chippewa River which would impede navigation for the Chippewa Falls interests. As a result the Chippewa Falls men turned against those from Eau Claire and came to the support of the group asking for the charter. One of the Chippewa millmen who had secured control of the land at Beef Slough granted the right of franchise to the Beef Slough Manufacturing, Booming, Log Driving and Transportation Company. This was legal, according to a bill passed previously by the Wisconsin Assembly for the Portage City Gas Light Company, since one person might accept and exercise a franchise alone though it had been granted to a number of persons.[64] The new company was ready to operate in 1870.

However, the battle was not fought out only in the Wisconsin Assembly: rafters and millmen, representing producers on the Chippewa, and log drivers, representing the Beef Slough group, took it upon themselves to settle it. Axes, pike poles, peavies, and cant hooks became instruments of warfare. T. B. Wilson, resident manager of the Knapp and Stout interests at Menomonie, was once thrown into the river by log drivers; there was evidence that he had cut ropes at Beef Slough.[65]

When the issue was finally settled, the so-called Beef Slough Company faced a difficult situation. The construction of piers, dams, and booms at Beef Slough would require a good deal of capital, and the company, after its long battle with the legislature, found its resources nearly exhausted; an almost bankrupt company was in no position to carry on.

[62] Frederick Merk, *Economic History of Wisconsin during the Civil War Decade* (Madison, 1916), p. 92.
[63] C. H. Cooke, "Diary," *Daily Telegram* (Eau Claire, Wisconsin), Apr. 22, 1918.
[64] Merk, *op. cit.,* pp. 91–92; Norton, *op. cit.,* p. 11.
[65] Bill, "Navigation on the Chippewa," *Burlington Post* (Iowa), Nov. 8, 1930, p. 3.

The situation was serious; logs were the breath of life to the millmen on the Mississippi. To protect themselves, Weyerhaeuser and Denkmann of Rock Island, and Schricker and Mueller of Davenport leased the boom at Beef Slough for two years. Nearly all the millmen on the Mississippi joined them in the venture.[66] At all odds they must have logs! A group of these men had met at the Briggs House in Chicago on December 28, 1870, to discuss their problems. Out of this meeting grew the Mississippi River Logging Company, which was chartered under Iowa laws on January 12, 1871, with the home office at Clinton, Iowa. The capital stock was $1,000,000 divided into forty-three shares.[67]

The appearance of this concern marks the beginning of the pooling of interests by the Mississippi River lumbermen. The real object of the newly formed company was to secure for the mills of the Mississippi River a readier supply of logs at cheaper rates, to cooperate in their operations on the Chippewa River, and to speed the delivery of log stock to the mills on the Mississippi. Such an organization could buy hundreds of thousands of acres of timber; individual enterprise could not make such an investment. This concern was one of the greatest industrial combinations of that time in the Northwest.[68] Prominent lumbermen all along the Mississippi became stockholders in the Mississippi River Logging Company. The members of the first board of directors were the following: [69]

L. Schricker, Davenport, President	H. H. Hemenway, Lansing
W. J. Young, Clinton, Vice-President	B. Hersey, Muscatine
W. H. Laird, Winona, Secretary	C. Lamb, Clinton
C. R. Ainsworth, Moline	P. B. Paul, La Crosse
W. G. Clark, St. Louis	F. Schulenburg, St. Louis
John L. Davies, Davenport	F. Weyerhaeuser, Rock Island
L. S. Davies, Davenport	J. H. Wilson, Rock Island
John Fleming, McGregor	E. S. Youmans, Winona

The amount of stock to which each member subscribed was based on the amount of logs his mill could use.[70] Each stockholder was allowed about 6,000,000 feet for each share of stock he held. The larger firms, of course, invested heavily in stock in order to assure themselves of raw material.

The newly formed company turned immediately to Beef Slough in order to make that place secure for the rafting of their logs. In 1872

[66] Norton, *op. cit.*, p. 14.

[67] *Ibid.*, p. 34.

[68] *Winona Republican Herald*, Feb. 22, 1934, p. 9.

[69] *Chippewa Falls Democrat* (Wisconsin), Feb. 2, 1871; Hotchkiss, *op. cit.*, p. 635; Bill, "Navigation on the Chippewa," *Burlington Post* (Iowa), Nov. 15, 1930, p. 3.

[70] Bernhardt J. Kleven, "The Mississippi River Logging Company," *Minnesota History*, vol. xxvii (Sept. 1946), p. 195; Paul W. Gates, *The Wisconsin Pine Lands of Cornell University* (Ithaca, New York, 1943), p. 13.

they purchased 502 of the 1000 shares of the Beef Slough Manufacturing, Booming, Log Driving and Transportation Company; ten years later they purchased the entire stock. The company set to work at once to secure a constant supply of log stock. In 1871 President Schricker purchased for the company 34,625,765 feet of logs at $4.97 per thousand on the riverbank. This involved an investment of $170,847, all of which was paid at once.

The company also had in its plan the purchase of timberland. It had been the usual thing in the past for the millmen on the Mississippi to purchase their logs from independent loggers.[71] Weyerhaeuser and Denkmann were an exception, since early in the sixties they had started to purchase pinelands in the Chippewa country. Now the members of the Mississippi River Logging Company began to realize that the life of a mill depended upon its log supply and that security lay in assembling large pine holdings. The purchase of such timberlands came to be a very important phase of the company's work. In October 1875 the Mississippi River Logging Company purchased 50,000 acres of selected pine formerly belonging to the Ezra Cornell interests but offered by McGraw and Dwight in Wisconsin. For this they paid what was then considered a good price, ten dollars an acre.[72] From then on the Mississippi River Logging Company came to control more and more of Wisconsin's white pine and eventually to reach out beyond the boundaries of that state to other virgin regions.

The Mississippi River Logging Company did not begin its operations without opposition, for the Chippewa millmen were still determined to remove the competition of the Mississippi group. During the first year of its existence, the Mississippi company experienced a log shortage. Of the 35,000,000 feet logged for them only 10,000,000 passed through Beef Slough.[73] This happened partly because when the Chippewa millmen closed the booms in order to ferret out their own logs, they stopped the movement of all logs. This retarded the driving of logs, and the men far down on the Mississippi, the last to be served, naturally accused the Chippewa millmen of trying to monopolize the Chippewa.[74] Some of the millmen on the Mississippi had grown so weary of the struggle that they were ready to close out their interests on the Chippewa. But Frederick Weyerhaeuser urged them to be patient and to try it for another year.

The Chippewa millmen pressed their case in Washington, with a

[71] Norton, *op. cit.*, pp. 35, 38, 48.
[72] *Ibid.*, pp. 42, 43; Gates, *op. cit.*, pp. 216–17.
[73] Norton, *op. cit.*, p. 15.
[74] Kleven, *op. cit.*, p. 194.

resulting suit against the Mississippi River Logging Company brought by the United States Attorney General. The Chippewa millmen were in high hopes that they could win, but the final decision was in favor of the Mississippi millmen. On December 11, 1879, Laird, Norton and Company of Winona, in a letter to the editor of the *Chicago Tribune,* said they were enclosing a copy of the decision "in the famous Beef Slough and Chippewa case which virtually settles the right to run loose logs in all waters of the United States navigable or otherwise." [75] Letters containing a copy of the decision were sent also to the editor of the *Mississippi Valley Lumberman* at Minneapolis, to the *Pioneer Press* of St. Paul, and to officers of the Mississippi River Logging Company. It was an announcement of great importance to the men on the Mississippi River.

Gradually the two groups realized that they had interests in common and that cooperation would bring more satisfactory results than conflict. Frederick Weyerhaeuser deserves much of the credit for the development of this spirit — one of his associates in the Mississippi River Logging Company said that Weyerhaeuser showed great ability in co-operating with the group which had opposed him. "Whatever he thought best to be done they fully concurred in, and all through the life of the enterprise his genius for controlling men and making them feel that they were safe in trusting him and following him, made operations on the river easy and successful." [76] Credit must also be given to Orrin H. Ingram of the Chippewa millmen, whose clear-sighted leadership and keen ability were factors in shaping an intelligent understanding between the two groups. [77]

In 1876 was formed the Chippewa River Improvement and Log Driving Company, in which the Mississippi River Logging Company was prominent. The purpose of this organization was to improve the Chippewa River for driving, to take charge of the logs on the banks, and to drive them down the Chippewa to Beef Slough. [78]

In 1881 the Mississippi River Logging Company, together with the millmen on the Chippewa, purchased the mill, saw logs, river improvement, and 100,000 acres of pine from the Chippewa Lumber and Boom Company. This concern had stood as an obstacle to the millmen on the

[75] Laird, Norton and Company to editor, *Chicago Tribune,* Dec. 11, 1879, Letter Book, Nov. 1879 to Jan. 1880, records of the Laird, Norton Company, Winona, Minnesota. The business records of this company are remarkably complete from the opening day of business in 1855 until the end of its operations. They are preserved in the firm's office at Winona.
[76] Norton, *op. cit.,* p. 18.
[77] Bill, "Navigation on the Chippewa," *Burlington Post* (Iowa), Dec. 6, 1930, p. 3; Hotchkiss, *op. cit.,* p. 494.
[78] *Mississippi Valley Lumberman and Manufacturer,* vol. iv, Feb. 26, 1879, p. 2; *Northwestern Lumberman,* June 7, 1884, pp. 3–6.

Mississippi, and Weyerhaeuser had been anxious to secure control of it. A sizable fortune of $1,250,000 was paid for all this. The company was organized as the Chippewa Lumber and Boom Company, in which three fifths of the stock was held by the Mississippi River Logging Company and the remainder by millmen on the Chippewa.[79]

The next step in cooperation and concentration was the organization of the Chippewa Logging Company in 1881, to make more secure the supply of logs. It purchased timberlands, bought logs from others, logged its own lands, and drove the logs on the river to their destination. Such cooperative arrangements were not accomplished by a flip of the hand. It took arduous work and convincing arguments on the part of some to show others that long-range planning would bring results. Even Frederick Weyerhaeuser at times almost despaired of continuing the Chippewa Logging Company. After a meeting of the company at Beef Slough in 1882, W. H. Laird of Winona wrote to Matthew G. Norton, his cousin and associate in lumber, "It is certainly a case where some have got to sacrifice personal interests for the success of the whole." [80]

Men of foresight won, however, for the Mississippi River Logging Company and its affiliates, such as the Chippewa Lumber and Boom Company and the Chippewa Logging Company, eventually came into control in the Chippewa Valley, where they owned more pine than any other group and no one surpassed them in capacity production. In 1887 the Mississippi River Logging Company purchased all the properties of the Eau Claire Lumber Company — pinelands, logs, farms, mill dams, and mills — at a price of $1,025,000.[81] The only concern in the Chippewa area that never came under the control of this group was Knapp, Stout and Company, Company at Menomonie.

Though it purchased immense holdings, the Mississippi River Logging Company never entered land at government price and never acquired land at that low figure in any other way.[82] But such speculators in Wisconsin pinelands as Ezra Cornell, Francis Palms, Henry Sage, and Dwight and McGraw profited greatly because of the foresight of Frederick Weyerhaeuser and his associates in organizing an industry that could utilize the millions of feet of white pine growing on their holdings. In 1875 the millmen paid $10 an acre for pinelands; in 1882 they paid $16.80 an acre for some and $23.59 for others. In the late eighties and early nineties one lumberman on the Mississippi was known to

[79] Roujet D. Marshall, *Autobiography,* vol. i (Madison, Wisconsin, 1923), pp. 277, 282–83; Norton, *op. cit.,* pp. 50–56; Hotchkiss, *op. cit.,* p. 635.

[80] W. H. Laird to M. G. Norton, Winona, Minn., July 29, 1882, personal letters of W. H. Laird, Letter Book No. I.

[81] Norton, *op. cit.,* p. 68.

[82] *Ibid.,* p. 92.

have paid $82 an acre for a quarter section of land owned by Cornell University.[83]

Even though the Mississippi River Logging Company paid high prices for its pineland, it prospered under the direction of Frederick Weyerhaeuser as president and Thomas Irvine as secretary. As early as 1884 its stock was valued at $100,000 a share.[84] Matthew G. Norton, a stockholder, praised highly the excellent management and fine spirit that existed in the group.[85] There was never adverse criticism, he said. Surely Weyerhaeuser's leadership must have satisfied them — for forty years he was their only president. This well-grounded organization expanded its operations westward with the white pine; Weyerhaeuser and his associates became extensive operators in Minnesota.

To return now to Beef Slough. In 1873, 91,000,000 feet of logs passed its boom,[86] and in a busy season from 1200 to 1500 men found employment there. This lively exchange of the log world teemed with activity from five to seven months in the year. The spring breakup in the river was the signal that the quiet hamlet would soon begin to stir from its winter's sleep. There were piles to be driven into the bottom of the Mississippi to replace those which the huge ice floes had torn away and other repairs had to be made before the logs began to appear.

The workers came from Canada; they came from the South; they came from parts in between. Hobo Shorty migrated every winter to sunnier climes but summer found him back at Beef Slough — back to work with Douglas, McKenzie, and MacLeod. The Scotch Canadians were so numerous at Beef Slough that one could scarcely toss a boom plug without striking one. As the years went by, Scandinavians replaced them, and in time two thirds of the help at these rafting works were of that nationality. Much of the labor at Beef Slough worked in the pineries in the winter, but the first signs of spring found them back at the Slough again. Crews at this place shifted little, for men returned regularly year after year.

Seven camps, huddling against the side of the bluff, housed the labor at Beef Slough. Each man was assigned to a camp; each man was assigned to a bunk; each man was assigned to his definite place at the table; each man had his own peg on which to hang his hat. There was a two-story office building for the secretary and his force, well equipped for the transaction of business.

[83] Gates, *op. cit.*, contains an excellent chapter entitled "Sales of Pine Land" discussing the prices of pinelands at various periods.
[84] *Northwestern Lumberman*, June 7, 1884, pp. 3–6.
[85] Norton, *op. cit.*, p. 45.
[86] *Chippewa Herald*, Nov. 21, 1873.

The workday at Beef Slough was long; ten hours was a real man's day. When the sun shot its early rays around the bluffs, the men knew it was time to roll out of their three-decker bunks. Breakfast followed in quick train, and at seven o'clock, when the bell at the boom rang out over the valley, every man was in his place, ready for another day with the logs at the Slough.

The catchmarker with his four-foot ax and his caulked shoes was on the job among the logs which had been sheered into the upper boom, known as the log-jam or pool. The catchmarker made his way among the logs with such easy assurance that one would have thought he knew the tricks of the water beetle. The log-jam was sometimes as much as two and a half miles in length, depending on the number of logs which had come down from the Chippewa. One hundred catchmarkers spent their day at the jam, swinging the long-handled ax to make the mark in the end of each log. The log had been given a bark mark and a stamp mark before it left the banks of the Chippewa. Such marks denoted the firm to which the log belonged, and they were as effective in determining ownership as a real-estate deed. Logs with such marks were subject to mortgage, lien, and labor claims. The catchmarker agilely swung his ax to reproduce the mark in a place where it could be seen more readily as it moved swiftly down the race and to indicate that it had been received in the boom.

After the log had felt the ax of the catchmarker, it was sent down the race — a long, narrow avenue of water, bordered on the sides by boom sticks to keep the logs in place. At intervals boards resting on the piling were placed across the race; there were five such boards at Beef Slough. On these stood the sorters, who with eagle eyes sorted the logs and sent them their various ways. Logs bearing certain marks were stopped at each bridge and there sent down a street of water running at right angles to the race. Bordering these streets of water were pockets into which the logs were directed.

Each pocket was surrounded by a boom, and in each pocket logs of the same mark were housed. Boards were placed on pilings in front of the pockets, and on these the sorter stood as he guided the log to its proper resting place. Each mill whose logs passed through Beef Slough had its own pocket or pockets, depending on the volume of its business. Big concerns such as the Weyerhaeusers, the Lambs, and the Youngs had a number of pockets. Pockets were square booms; they were called brailing pockets, for there the brail was made.

The brail system was introduced by an able lumberman, W. J. Young of Clinton, Iowa. It made possible a great saving of lumber, for the old system of boring and lashing damaged the logs and threw them into lower grades. Usually a deduction of 10 per cent had been made for logs damaged by augur holes. By the new method of brailing, logs were saved from such blemishes.[87] The logs were swung straight as they came into the pocket. They lay close together in tiers; when about 150,000 feet of logs had been packed side by side, the pocket was considered full. Then it was ready for the brailing crew, whose job it was to put the brail in shape to float down the river.

Ten brailing crews were busily engaged at Beef Slough. The crews moved from pocket to pocket, fitting up brails as they went. Each crew numbered from sixteen to eighteen men, including scalers and tally men; each crew had its own boss. This crew arranged boom sticks around the loose logs. The framework was made of stout logs placed so that they overlapped at the ends. Near the end of each log a big hole was bored, a hole from eight inches to a foot deep. Plugs were put into those holes, one in each log, and over the head of each plug was slipped the link of a chain. This famous three-link iron boom chain, each link measuring about a foot, was invented by a French Canadian named Charley Prue, a blacksmith at Beef Slough. It was a great improvement over the old rope booming, and, since there was no wearing it out, it was much cheaper.

In this way logs were fastened together, ends overlapping, holding the loose logs in place. The end links of the chain fell over the two plugs in adjoining logs and the middle link allowed the necessary play. The logs at the bow and the stern were usually 24 or 26 feet long and were always two in number. Except at the corners, where the double plugs and double chains were used, they were all fastened the same way as the side logs. St. Paul, Beef Slough, and West Newton brails when complete were usually 600 feet long and 55 feet wide, but the Stillwater brail was about 550 feet long and 60 feet wide.[88] At every 50 feet inside the brail, wire a quarter-inch in width was stretched from side to side to hold each tier of logs in place. This tight wire was fastened into the brail, which held the wire firm.

The scalers and the tally men were an important part of the brailing crew. There were four scalers and two tally men in every crew, and it was their business to compute the contents in board feet of every log. Their implement was the scale rule with its long hook, which enabled

[87] Durant, op. cit., pp. 664–65.
[88] Bill, "Career of Captain Jerome E. Short," Clinton Herald (Iowa), Mar. 11, 1933, p. 5; "Log Rafting on the St. Croix River," information communicated to Charles E. Brown by Harry Dwyer of Madison, Wisconsin, Aug. 1912, Charles E. Brown Papers in the possession of the Wisconsin Historical Society.

the scaler to lift the log out of water as he measured its diameter. This multiplied by the length of the log gave its contents in board feet. It was no game to lift these logs, for many a log contained 1000 feet of lumber. It was strenuously exacting and no scaler could work more than an hour at a time. The scaler's right hand was his tally man, who entered the size of every log on his sheet as the scaler called it out. When a log not bearing the proper mark was found, the scaler called "scrabble" and a man was on the job immediately to sink the log under the brail and put it in its right place. If the mark could not be determined, the log was placed in a scrabble brail and the boom company took these logs as its own.

The scaler received the best wages at the Slough, for he had reached the top in the rafting world. But his apprenticeship was long. His first job, which he might begin as a twelve-year-old, was to scratch. In this job he followed the scaler and with a four-foot stick ending in a pointed iron he scratched the log when the scaler had determined its footage. Then he became a tally boy, still following the scaler. When this art had been mastered he advanced to the position of scaler and, if fortune smiled, he might even become a head scaler. Then he would be master of his game, earning $3.00 a day. As a regular scaler $2.50 was his wage; the tally boy was paid $1.35 a day; the scratcher started at 50 cents a day. Common laborers at Beef Slough worked sometimes for 90 cents a day, while the highest possible wage was $3.00.

When the brailing crew with scalers and tally boys had finished their job, the brail was ready to be "lined up." With forty-foot pike poles the line men steered the brail out of the pocket and tied it up until two other brails for the same company were ready. Three brails made the usual size of a raft going downstream from Beef Slough. The three brails were fastened together with plugs and chains, the towboat was attached, and the logs moved downriver to become lumber.

Men at Beef Slough worked from seven to six with an hour at noon when they went to their assigned camps, hung their hats on a peg, and ate their dinner — in silence, for there the cook was master. Since peace and order in camp depended on satisfied stomachs, the cook was important. He ranked with the head scaler, his wage being $3.00 a day. The bean-hole beans and proverbial salt pork of the lumber camps were little known at Beef Slough. The farming community roundabout supplied fresh meat, bread was baked at the camp, and pies and cookies were a part of the regular menu. Oleomargarine was still in good repute — the dairy farmer of the land o' lakes had not yet made it a pariah.

Beef Slough had its own church — a Union church for all — and its own pastor. Thither went the men in large numbers on Sundays, whether because so inclined spiritually or simply for diversion. The church had an organ, quite a library, and writing materials, and it filled the place of a Young Men's Christian Association or a community hall.

Such was life at Beef Slough for the 1500 men who prepared logs for the whirring saws downriver.[89] It was a busy life while it lasted, but it did not last long. In 1889, 542,000,000 feet of logs passed that boom, but this was the last year of action there.[90] The river mouth was clogging with sand and new quarters had to be found.

West Newton Slough on the Minnesota side of the river was selected for the new boom. This lay about eight miles below Beef Slough and about twelve miles below Wabasha at Buffalo City. West Newton was so named for a steamer which once had come to grief there; after it had sunk to the bottom the only part above water was the pilot house with this name.[91] From 1889 to 1905 West Newton served as the loggers' boom. In 1892, 600,000,000 feet of logs passed through on the way to become lumber below.[92] It was the largest amount ever to pass in one year.

Here, too, from 1300 to 1500 men found jobs in season. Irish and Scandinavians vied with each other; Ole Severson and Pat Murphy raced neck and neck the whole day through, all for the sake of a bit of praise from Edward Douglas, superintendent of the boom.[93] Forty scalers and twenty-five tally men worked steadily, recognizing the log marks and stamp marks.

In 1892 West Newton reached its peak year. There was an end to Chippewa logs, too, and in June 1905 the Mississippi River Logging Company made its last drive; Weyerhaeuser and Denkmann took the last raft down.[94] West Newton became an ordinary slough again. But it had seen real activity, for in the period from 1889 to 1896, 3,064,856,760 feet of logs had passed through its boom. From 1897 to 1905, 3,000,000,000 feet had come through.[95] Many a monarch of the forest had passed West Newton on its way to the mill to become lumber.

[89] Interview with Charles Skrief, Apr. 22, 1934; interview with M. J. Thornton, Surveyor General of Logs and Lumber, St. Paul, Minn., Jan. 23, 1934.

[90] Blair, op. cit., p. 53.

[91] History of Winona and Wabasha Counties (Chicago, 1884), p. 932.

[92] Blair, op. cit., p. 34.

[93] Interview with M. J. Thornton, Surveyor General of Logs and Lumber, St. Paul, Minn., Jan. 23, 1934.

[94] Bill, "Navigation on the Chippewa," Burlington Post (Iowa), Jan. 24, 1931, p. 3.

[95] Blair, op. cit., p. 289.

CHAPTER IX

Growth of Sawmills in Minnesota, 1870–1890

IN 1839 only one mill was cutting lumber in Minnesota. By 1870 the industry of sawmilling had come of age; there were 207 mills operating in Minnesota, the capital invested equaled $3,311,140, and 2952 people were earning their daily bread in those mills.[1]

In that thirty-one year period great changes had come over the industry. New methods had been developed, and mills had increased not only in number but in amount of production per mill as well. The pit saw, the up-and-down saw, and the old muley, all of which had once seen service in Minnesota, were replaced by newer saws of greater speed, such as the circular saw and the gang saw. The circular saw, invented by men from Maine and patented in 1820, could cut 4000 feet in an hour while a muley saw did well to cut 5000 feet in a day. The gang saw was equally important in expanding output.

Such saws taxed the ability of the other equipment. Because the old edging tools could not take care of the fast sawing, unedged boards accumulated in piles; the new edging machine, which could edge both sides at once, remedied this. The log carriage also had to work faster; logs had to be brought in from the boom in shorter order; and logs had to be turned more easily. In response to the last need came the terrifying steam nigger, introduced in 1868–69, which in the blink of a second turned logs of 1000 feet as though they were mere saplings.[2] As a result of the speed-up in sawing the lumber, the men known as off-bearers, who removed the piles of lumber, were nearly exhausted. This situation was shortly remedied when human hands were replaced by power-driven machinery which automatically carried the lumber away from the saw. These were the live rolls. The water wheel was superseded by steam power. Water power did not lose its place completely, but steam came into wide use when it was discovered that the abundance of shavings

[1] *U.S. Census, 1890: Manufacturing Industries*, pt. iii, p. 610.
[2] Hotchkiss, *History of Lumber and Forest Industry of Northwest*, p. 649.

147

and sawdust as well as slabs could be fed directly from the saws into the furnaces.[3]

Logs were handled rapidly once they had entered the storage booms of those mills. Log slips extended into the river, and the endless chains running down the center of these slips, with the help of a jacket, could carry four logs at a time. Logs passed through the gangs where they became boards; then they passed as boards on to the patent edgers; then through the trimmer. As ready lumber they passed on to the sorting sections; then they were piled, hauled to the yards, and stacked.

Of all the saw-towns of the Upper Mississippi, Minneapolis had the largest number of mills by 1870. In 1871 thirteen mills were cutting lumber at St. Anthony Falls, giving employment to 831 people. Of those thirteen mills, eight were run by water power and five by steam turbine. The largest production in Minneapolis in 1870 was in the steam mill of J. Dean and Company, known generally as the Pacific Mill; it cut 13,000,000 feet of lumber and shingles, laths, and pickets. W. D. Washburn's mill, run by water power, cut 10,170,388 feet, next to the largest production in that year. Several mills could cut 7,000,000 feet a year. The mills of Minneapolis cut a total of 118,233,113 feet of lumber in 1870.[4]

A review of the equipment of some of the Minneapolis mills in the 1870s will give an idea of the changes that had come to the industry. The Pacific Mill of J. Dean and Company had two double circular saws, one gang, and two gang edgers. It was a steam mill with a capacity of 100,000 feet of lumber a day. Farnham and Lovejoy were reputed to have one of the largest mills on the Mississippi. It was equipped with one double gang, two large double circulars, double edgers, double trimmers, and Frazer's patent double lath machine. This mill also had a daily capacity of 100,000 feet. Todd and Company's mill had one double gang (Barlow's oscillating gang), two double circulars, and two patent edgers; it, too, could produce 100,000 feet a day. It had a double block shingle machine which could produce 60,000 shingles a day. L. Butler and Company had one double Barlow gang, two double circulars, and two patent edgers — with the same potential output of 100,000 feet a day.

Morrison Brothers had a mill with two live gangs, one double circular, and one patent edger. Their production was 75,000 feet a day. Leonard Day and Sons had one mill with a gang of twenty-four saws and one double circular, which produced 50,000 feet in a day. Another

[3] *Minneapolis Tribune*, Apr. 25, 1874, p. 2.
[4] *Ibid.*, Apr. 17, 1870, p. 2. and Mar. 16, 1871, p. 3.

mill under their management had a double Barlow gang, a double circular, and a patent edger. Their output was 60,000 feet a day.

Old Joel Bassett had a double pony gang in his mill, a double circular saw, and a patent edger. These cut for him 60,000 feet per day. W. W. Eastman, Charles A. Bovey, and John De Laittre, all from New England, had formed a copartnership under the firm name of Eastman, Bovey and Company in Minneapolis, and in 1869 they had purchased the Pioneer Mill for the sum of $19,000, each partner paying one third.[5] Their mill had a gang of twenty-four saws, one double circular, and two patent edgers, with an output of 60,000 feet per day.

As a result of these well-equipped mills, in 1873 Minneapolis had the largest cut of its history up to that time: 189,909,782 feet. It contended that it could cut "a right smart heap" of lumber.[6] But its lumber output continued to grow. In 1875 one of its mills could change logs into lumber

TABLE 11. PRODUCTION OF LUMBER IN MINNEAPOLIS, 1870–1879

Year	Lumber (in feet)	Shingles (in pieces)	Laths (in pieces)
1870	118,233,113	57,718,250	16,128,000
1871	117,157,024	79,798,825	17,880,330
1872	167,918,814	99,235,750	30,563,100
1873	189,909,782	114,554,260	32,843,150
1874	191,305,679	167,757,000	36,907,950
1875	156,665,000	109,066,000	24,420,000
1876	200,371,277	90,004,250	25,193,350
1877	129,676,000	50,997,000	21,907,000
1878	130,274,076	47,289,750	19,612,200
1879	149,754,547	......	......

SOURCE: *Annual Report of the Minneapolis Board of Trade*, 1877, p. 66; 1878, p. 56; 1879, p. 53.

at the rate of 130,000 feet in a day; this mill was equipped with two double circular saws, two gang edgers, one gang saw with forty saws, six trimming saws, two edging saws, one slab saw, and one saw for cutting shingles. The capital investment of this mill was $375,000.[7] In 1877 eighteen gang saws and twenty-five circulars were operating in Minneapolis. The sale of the lumber they produced brought to the city $3,560,000, and 1500 men found employment in the mills and yards there in that year.[8] The high point of Minneapolis' production in the 1870s was in 1876, when 200,371,277 feet were cut. Table 11 gives the annual cut for the decade.

[5] Bovey-De Laittre Papers, Feb. 15, 1870, in Journal A, p. 2. These papers are in the office of the De Laittre, Dixon Lumber Company, 1301 West Broadway, Minneapolis.
[6] The information on the equipment of the mills was given in an article entitled "Lumber," *Minneapolis Tribune*, Mar. 28, 1873, p. 4.
[7] *Ibid.*, Nov. 14, 1875, p. 5.
[8] *Statistics of Minnesota, 1877* (St. Paul, 1878), p. 170.

By 1878 there were seventeen mills in Minneapolis. Many of the owners of these mills had been active in Minneapolis since lumbering began there. Among the more recent arrivals was T. B. Walker, who had purchased the Pacific Mill for $44,000 from J. Dean and Company in 1877. Walker's entry into the sawmill life of Minneapolis was significant, since he became a leading American lumberman. Even in 1878 his mill ranked well up among the others in production.

TABLE 12. FIRMS IN MINNEAPOLIS AND THEIR CUT IN 1878 *

Firm	Lumber Cut (in feet)
J. F. Bassett & Company	7,000,000
Leavitt Chase & Company	9,574,579
McMullen and Company	2,500,000
F. G. Mayo	3,400,000
Eastman, Bovey & Company	7,343,658
Farnham & Lovejoy	16,744,661
Clark & McClure	10,576,708
Merriman, Barrows & Company	8,508,383
Camp and Walker	9,442,900
L. Butler (Estate)	6,250,261
W. C. Baker	5,705,532
Cole & Hammond	2,000,000
Minneapolis Mill Company	6,179,265
Minneapolis Lumber Company	2,000,000
Morrison Brothers	9,326,132
L. Day & Sons	8,471,996
J. H. Thompson	750,000

* W. D. Washburn's Anoka mill is reported in the original count with the Minneapolis cut, but the Anoka cut is not listed here.

SOURCE: *Annual Report of the Minneapolis Board of Trade, 1878*, p. 55. This report is wrongly marked "1879."

To Minneapolis were also attracted other types of manufacturing using lumber as a base. In the seventies everything from railroad cars to lucifer matches was made there. The other lumber towns of Minnesota also attracted such industries, but none so much as Minneapolis. In 1870 Hennepin County, in which Minneapolis was the chief town, made planing products valued at $116,000; Winona County with Winona as its leading town was second with a product valued at $79,000.[9] In 1876 there were seventeen establishments in Minneapolis for dressing rough lumber — that is, making doors, sashes, and blinds — exclusive of those attached to the mills.[10] Three years later Wheaton Reynolds and Company, makers of such products, stated that their business had increased 50 per cent over other years.[11]

[9] *U.S. Census, 1870*, vol. iii: *Wealth and Industry*, pp. 683–84.
[10] *Report of the Minneapolis Board of Trade*, 1878, p. 51.
[11] *Minneapolis Tribune*, Oct. 30, 1879, p. 4.

Lounges, bedsteads, wagons and carriages, barrels for flour and pork, boats, clothes bars, and other things dependent upon the white pine were manufactured in Minneapolis.[12] In 1874 there were eight barrel factories in the city, where in the previous year 350,000 barrels had been made.[13] In 1870 Hennepin County had sixteen establishments making furniture valued at $148,300. Ramsey County, with St. Paul as its center, was the only county that approached Hennepin in the making of furniture; its product in 1870 was valued at $64,300. In 1871, when the "New Nicollet Hotel" swung open its doors, every piece of furniture had been made in Minneapolis by the firm of Barnard and Shuey.[14] Dorilus Morrison was one of the promoters of the Harvester Works of Minneapolis,[15] and he found that industry a ready consumer of his dimension lumber.

Stillwater did not have so many sawmills as Minneapolis, but it had mills which in production surpassed any one Minneapolis mill in the 1870s. In 1871 Schulenburg, Boeckeler and Company cut 26,340,680 feet, by far the largest cut in Stillwater at that time.[16] In 1874 this firm in a season of seven months, running night and day except Saturday night and Sunday, made 30,000,000 feet of lumber.[17] At that time the nine mills at Stillwater were equipped to cut 82,000,000 feet per year. These mills contained seven gangs, nine circulars, and one old muley; five hundred men found employment in them.[18] In 1876 Isaac Staples cut 17,256,000 feet, while Hersey, Bean and Brown cut 15,300,000 feet.[19] These were good-sized cuts for the seventies. Singly, Stillwater mills had the edge on Minneapolis mills, but in the aggregate Minneapolis led.

Hersey, Bean and Brown had two gangs and one circular in their equipment, as well as one old muley. Their well-known Northwestern sawmill could, in 1875, produce 150,000 feet in eleven hours; when it had begun operations in 1854, it established a record in the new West by sawing 125,000 feet in twenty-four hours.[20] This is typical of the increase in production which the use of the new machinery made possible.

The St. Croix Mills, under the direction of Isaac Staples, had one gang containing thirty-eight saws which could cut 1000 feet "at a lick." Two circular saws operated in Staples' mill, which was also equipped with a speedy edger and had an output of 100,000 feet in a day of eleven hours; as a subsidiary industry, the firm carried on door, sash, and scroll work.

[12] Ibid., Mar. 16, 1871, p. 3.
[13] Ibid., May 24, 1874, p. 6.
[14] Ibid., July 25, 1871, p. 14.
[15] Ibid., Nov. 1, 1876, p. 4.
[16] Stillwater Messenger, Jan. 12, 1872.
[17] Stillwater Lumberman, Apr. 23, 1875.
[18] Hotchkiss, op. cit., p. 530.
[19] Stillwater Messenger, Jan. 21, 1876.
[20] Stillwater Lumberman, Apr. 23, 1875; Hotchkiss, op. cit., p. 524.

John McKusick, the first to introduce sawing in Stillwater, had a single rotary, a pony gang, a gang edger, and shingle apparatus in his mill; 30,000 feet was the daily cut of McKusick, Anderson and Company.

The famous firm of Schulenburg, Boeckeler and Company were not only the largest producers of lumber in Stillwater but had also branched out into other lines. They were building an integrated business. They were loggers; they ran their own towboats, of which the *Helene Schulenburg* was well known on the Mississippi; they established themselves as merchants; they built boardinghouses and residences for their employees; and they had their own farms.

In Stillwater, as in Minneapolis, subsidiary industries using lumber as a base, developed. Of these the most important was Seymour, Sabin and Company, which annually manufactured agricultural implements valued at $650,000. They were also engaged in the cooperage business, producing an annual product worth $75,000; and their sash, door, and blinds factory brought them $60,000 a year.[21] This company manufactured coal and box cars, receiving orders more rapidly than they could fill them. Seymour, Sabin and Company employed prison labor from the state institution located at Stillwater.

Both Minneapolis and Stillwater found a heavy competitor in Winona. Laird, Norton and Company employed a hundred men in 1870.[22] In 1874 they were cutting 12,000,000 feet of lumber, a very unusual amount. In 1879 they built a new mill, the capacity of which was 200,000 feet in ten hours; this mill served the company until it burned in 1887. A new one was built immediately, with all the modern equipment. There were gangs, two of them; but, more than that, there were two bands, saws new to Minnesota. This new mill produced a total of 250,000 feet of lumber daily. Laird, Norton and Company, which as early as 1868 had a planing mill and a sash, door, and blind factory, was particularly famed for its interior house finish.[23]

Youmans Brothers and Hodgins rebuilt their mill in 1870. Their new mill had two circular saws, one gang edger, a slab saw, and a shingle and lath machine; in 1876 a gang saw was added. Besides its mill this concern had a sash shop and branch yards. When the firm was incorporated in 1887, an elegant new mill was built. This mill had a gang saw, two band saws, one rotary (which was shortly exchanged for a third band), a steam feed, double edgers, trimmers, and live rolls. What more did a modern mill want? It produced 25,000 feet an hour, 250,000 in ten hours; its annual

[21] *Stillwater Lumberman*, Dec. 20, 1878.
[22] *Winona Republican*, Oct. 5, 1870.
[23] Curtiss-Wedge, *History of Winona County*, p. 180.

cut was about 40,000,000 feet. Youmans' was the best-equipped mill in Winona.[24]

The Winona Lumber Company came into existence in 1880 as a joint-stock company with paid-up capital of $250,000; Andrew Hamilton was its president, William H. Laird its vice-president, and William Hayes its secretary and treasurer. Its first mill was equipped with two gangs and two rotaries which cut 200,000 feet a day.[25] It added a planing mill in 1882, and a sash, door, and blind factory in 1883.

In 1886 the last prominent lumber concern of Winona was established; Ingram and Kennedy, well-known lumbermen of Eau Claire, joined Charles Horton, a pioneer in Winona's lumber life, to make and market lumber at Winona. Their mill, with its brand new equipment, had two Allis band saws and two Wicker gangs which cut 175,000 feet a day.[26]

Winona prospered with her improved lumber mills. The great change in their equipment came in the period between 1878 and 1888; during that ten-year period she produced 1,150,000,000 feet, which was 825,000,000 feet more than in any previous ten-year period.[27]

With the completion of the Lake Superior and Mississippi Railroad from St. Paul to Duluth in 1870 a new lumber source was opened and another group of saw-towns entered Minnesota's lumber industry.[28] This railroad penetrated the famous St. Croix Valley, and its influence on the lumber business was so immediate that no region in the state, in proportion to its supply, was stripped of its white pine as fast as the forests of the St. Croix.[29] Scores of sawmills were established in haste along the railroad. Two years after the completion of the railroad, Hinckley sent 5,855,840 feet of lumber southward; Pine City, 3,733,720 feet; and North Branch, which the present generation remembers chiefly for its potatoes, 1,379,480 feet. Just two years after its completion, then, the Lake Superior and Mississippi carried 21,869,920 feet of lumber southward.[30] The output of each town was small, but in the aggregate the production was large.

Today little towns along what was the Lake Superior and Mississippi remind us that at one time the region was a place of great activity. Present-day lumberjacks raise their heads at the mention of Hinckley, Kettle River,

[24] Ibid., p. 183; interview of the writer with C. M. Youmans, Winona, May 2, 1934; Thompson, "Lumber Barons Guided Community through Early History," Winona Republican Herald, Feb. 22, 1934, p. 9.

[25] Curtiss-Wedge, op. cit., p. 184.

[26] Mississippi Valley Lumberman, vol. xx, Nov. 27, 1891, p. 4; vol. xxiii, Aug. 4, 1893, p. 5; interview of the writer with Roscoe Horton, Winona, May 2, 1934.

[27] Folsom, "History of Lumbering in the St. Croix Valley," Minn. Hist. Soc. Coll., vol. ix, pp. 320–21.

[28] Report of the Minnesota Railroad Commissioner, 1872, pp. 14–15.

[29] Mississippi Valley Lumberman, vol. xi, Mar. 25, 1887, p. 1.

[30] Report of the Minnesota Railroad Commissioner, 1873, p. 126.

Moose Lake, and Pine City, but the lumberjacks no longer work in that country — they left it when the timber was gone, with the decade of the eighties.

The Lake Superior and Mississippi was not alone in the penetration of untouched forests in the 1870s. The Watab Branch of the St. Paul and Pacific cut into another white pine region. At Anoka, eighteen miles above Minneapolis, it touched a vital spot which, though busy in the days of river transportation, seemed to gain new life with the coming of railroads. Anoka lay at the confluence of the Rum and the Mississippi. The banks of the Rum, reaching back to Lake Mille Lacs, were the source of the first white pine cut for market at St. Anthony Falls; it was princely pine, and Anoka, with water power, lay closest to it.

In 1870, when the venturesome W. D. Washburn purchased the McCaan mill, sawmilling became bigger business at Anoka. That mill under Washburn's direction made from 90,000 to 100,000 feet of lumber a day in 1873 and employed from 175 to 200 men; the model mill of Anoka, it equaled the best Minneapolis mills at the time. It made building and bridge timber, dimension lumber, dressed lumber, moldings, laths, shingles, and pickets. It had a Barlow double gang of thirty-five saws, two double circulars with patent edgers; cut-off, crosscut, and trimming saws; shingle machinery, lath machinery, and a planing mill.

Another mill which cut 100,000 feet in ten hours was that of the so-called St. Paul Lumber Company at Anoka; this mill, which gave employment to 130 men the year around, had a double gang of thirty-six saws, two double circulars, two patent edgers, one shingle machine, one lath machine, and a planing mill. The Anoka Lumber Company, owned by Warren, Day, and Flint, had a single gang of twenty-five saws, one double circular, one patent edger, and three trimmers; it employed seventy-five men and could cut 50,000 feet in ten hours.[31] In 1873 these Anoka mills shipped on the Watab branch line 23,523,000 feet of lumber billed for Fargo and Yankton in Dakota Territory and for central and western Iowa.[32]

Early in the 1870s Anoka spoke of itself as "the largest lumbering town in Minnesota" and vigorously advertised that it was as near to the leading markets by rail as was any point on the Mississippi.[33] Anoka was no negligible factor in lumber production, but she did not approach Minneapolis and was not the largest lumbering town in Minnesota. Of the logs which passed the Mississippi River Boom in 1873, a total of 31,100,400

[31] *Minneapolis Tribune,* Oct. 25, 1874, p. 6.
[32] *Report of the Minnesota Railroad Commissioner,* 1873, p. 53; *Minneapolis Tribune,* May 8, 1873, p. 2.
[33] *Anoka County Press,* Sept. 2, 1871.

feet out of 161,757,770 were scaled for Anoka; the remainder continued on to the mills at Minneapolis.

In 1875 Reed and Sherwood entered the sawmill business at Anoka with a steam mill on the bank of Rum River. Equipped with two circular saws and one double gang of thirty-five saws, this mill could saw 90,000 feet in ten hours. Reed and Sherwood had a planing mill as well.[34] Since Sherwood was a railroad contractor and a bridge and elevator builder in the Northwest, he could bring at once to his new establishment a nice bit of business. The firm took good root in Anoka and became a real institution in the town. Even before their business had entered its fourth year, they distributed a pay envelope of $2500 every two weeks.

In 1882 W. D. Washburn and Company, of Anoka, became a stock company with a capital of $500,000. With Washburn were associated W. D. Hale, Joseph E. Stevens, Jr., and Willard G. Hollis, all of Minneapolis, and Caleb C. Crane of Anoka. This company dealt in logs, lumber, timberland, grain, flour, feed, and real estate.[35] Washburn and Hale had heavy holdings of pine on the Rum River and its tributaries; as long as this pine lasted, Anoka figured in lumber production.

St. Cloud, on the same Watab Branch of the St. Paul and Pacific running from Minneapolis to Fargo, was another town rising to prominence. The white pine lay on one side of it, the prairie on the other; it grew to be the largest town on the railroad line. It was located seventy-five miles from St. Paul on the Mississippi River. As early as 1855 St. Cloud was making lumber, and in 1859 it boasted a lumber mill and a sash, door, and blind factory.[36]

The first men to establish a lumber industry at St. Cloud were N. P. Clark and T. C. McClure. In the 1860s these men were active in buying land in the white pine region over which the St. Cloud land office had jurisdiction. In 1863 N. P. Clark located nine quarters and an eighty of pineland with the military bounty land warrants of the Act of 1855. In 1864 he located lands again, and the land records at St. Cloud show him to have located 14,400 acres of pineland in June 1870, all in quarter sections, with the warrants of the Act of 1855. His associate, T. C. McClure, located 7243 acres with agricultural college scrip from New Jersey, Rhode Island, Maine, West Virginia, Connecticut, and Pennsylvania at the land office at St. Cloud in the summer and fall of 1866. This was only a portion of the pineland these two owned in the vicinity of St. Cloud; it furnished them raw material for an expanding business.[37]

[34] *Anoka County Union,* Aug. 28, 1879.
[35] *Ibid.,* Oct. 19, 1882.   [36] *St. Cloud Democrat,* July 28, 1859.
[37] G.L.O., Records of Receiver and Register, Military Bounty Land Warrants, St. Cloud, Minn., Act of 1855, vol. 252, July 1868 to December 1876; Agricultural College Scrip, St. Cloud, Minn., 1864–1873.

In 1873 Clark and McClure were selling lumber as far away as Winnipeg. Flooring, siding, common boards, shingles, and dimension lumber shipped to that Canadian prairie town went by rail to Moorhead, whence it was carried by Kittson's Red River Transportation Line on the Red River to Winnipeg.[38] Clark and McClure also established a mill at Perham on the Northern Pacific Railroad, nearer the Red River, and opened retail yards at Melrose, Moorhead, St. Joseph, Winnipeg, Minneapolis, and Alexandria.[39]

Brainerd lay north of Anoka and St. Cloud on the Mississippi. In 1880 the Pillsburys, who owned beautiful virgin forest near Gull Lake shortly west of Brainerd, made preparations to establish mills there. In this group were John S. and Charles A. Pillsbury, Jonathan Chase, W. Leavitt, and G. Horr, all of whom had been actively associated with lumber in Minneapolis. These men were owners of much standing timber, and they were attracted by the market developing in the Red River Valley and westward. With the Northern Pacific passing near on its way from Duluth westward, Gull Lake offered a promising place for a mill. The mill was established, an up-to-date steam sawmill in the wilderness. It had a gang of thirty-six saws, two edgers, two trimmers, a slab and a bolt saw, and a shingle machine. It employed 125 men. Since the mill was so far from any settlement, the company had to establish a general store to furnish the laborers with necessities.[40] Brainerd at this time was like Marine and Stillwater in their pioneer period.

In 1880 T. B. Walker moved from his strategic position at the Falls of St. Anthony into a pine region known as the Northwest Slope, the waters of which flowed northward, eventually into Hudson Bay. Walker's was the initial undertaking of any size along the Clearwater and Red Lake rivers. These rivers, with arms reaching into the large and useful body of white pine in northwestern Minnesota, were the only outlets or practicable exits to the channels of trade.[41] In 1883 Walker and his son Gilbert began active logging in these parts when they established sawmills at Crookston [42] in Polk County. That town became the entrepôt between pineries and prairies, for it was the first contact that logs from the Clearwater or Red Lake made with railroads; more than that, it was the "Queen City of the Red River Valley."

[38] James W. Taylor Papers, June 26 and 27, 1873. These papers are in the possession of the Minnesota Historical Society.

[39] T. C. McClure to William Houlton, Apr. 16, 1880, William Houlton Papers, Minnesota Historical Society.

[40] *Brainerd Tribune,* Sept. 11, 1880, and Jan. 21, 1882.

[41] *Northern Tier* (Crookston), Oct. 25, 1879.

[42] Atwater, *History of the City of Minneapolis,* p. 536.

In 1889 Crookston was called the center of the greatest wheat-producing region in the world and at the same time "Saw-Dust City"—properly so, for in that year the Red River Lumber Company, Walker's concern, cut 45,000,000 feet and had a monthly payroll of $18,000.[43] The Walkers had access here to the whole Red River Valley, on past the Missouri River, and into the more remote West, wherever the Manitoba Railroad wound its way.

Walker with wise foresight saw the rich possibilities of the untouched Northwest Slope and soon had mills sawing lumber at Grand Forks as well as at Crookston. Grand Forks, utterly treeless, was a good market for lumber. Walker sensed that in the very near future the pine conveniently located for the Mississippi would be gone; he would move his mills nearer the stump and nearer the market before the evil day came, while he could still operate in timberlands to the northwest without heavy competition.

Minnesota sawmills were thus rapidly increasing in number and in output. They were also growing in capital investment. In 1870 a total of 207 mills operating in Minnesota had a capital investment of $3,311,140; in 1880, mills numbering 234 had a capital investment of $6,771,145.[44] In the space of ten years only twenty-seven mills had been added, but the capital investment had doubled. By 1890 the number of mills had grown to 317, but the capital invested had quadrupled the amount of 1880, reaching a total of $28,321,062.[45]

Many mills which began their operations on the capital of one or two men had now become stock companies in order to secure more capital for operating on the scale necessary to success. Not all of the increased capital had gone into the new equipment, but that much had done so appears from the unusual increase in cut. Where the mills of the 1870s had cut 100,000 feet of lumber in a day, the mills of 1880 were cutting 200,000 and 250,000 feet in a day; a big mill in the late eighties was cutting not less than 40,000,000 feet in a year. No such production was possible without the right equipment.

Important in the equipment of a first-class mill in the 1880s was the band saw, which was replacing the circular saw as the circular in the 1850s had replaced the up-and-down saw and the muley. In the production of lumber it was no longer merely a question of speed but of economy as well. The legend of the inexhaustibility of our forests was wearing thin. Michigan's white pine was growing distressingly scarce and lumbermen were beginning to realize that heavy inroads were being

[43] Crookston Times, Dec. 7, 1889.
[44] U.S. Census, 1890: Manufacturing Industries, pt. iii, p. 610.
[45] Ibid.

made on the supply in Wisconsin and Minnesota. Therefore stumpage was going up in price, and the circular saw fell into disrepute because of its wastefulness. Men far down the river, whose logs sometimes had to come as far as eight hundred miles, were looking for saws that cut economically; the band saw did so. The circular saw cut a kerf of at least one-fourth inch, which meant that one one-inch board in every four was wasted; a band saw cut a one-eighth-inch kerf, thus wasting only one board in eight. It was estimated that even a small mill with a daily cut of only 40,000 feet could save $40 per day with a band saw when lumber was $10 per 1000 feet.[46]

James J. McCormick of Bay City, Michigan, was the first to experiment with a device which had the principle of the band saw, in 1858. He had had it made to order in France and when it broke after having produced only one board he abandoned his experiment. In 1876 J. C. Hoffman of Fort Wayne, Indiana, exhibited a mill in which a band saw was operating at the Philadelphia Exposition. He used it in the sawing of hardwood timber. Lumber manufacturers became interested. By 1884 it had been perfected and was accepted as a necessary part of the equipment of a good mill.

On the Mississippi the downriver mills adopted the band saw before the Minnesota mills took to it. Those downriver mills were farther from the source of supply; transporting logs to their mills cost money, and therefore every log must produce to the limit. In 1888 W. J. Young of Clinton, Iowa, had seven band saws in his "Great Mill." [47] It was the general belief that downriver sawmen usually got more out of their logs by cutting them close.[48]

Winona was the first place in Minnesota where band saws replaced the circular. Winona, like Clinton, imported all its log stock, and as stumpage advanced in price the level-headed Winona lumbermen considered such economy nothing more than good business. By the end of the eighties, all four lumber companies of Winona had adopted the band saw. The Empire Lumber Company, the last comer into the sawmill life of that city, had two Allis bands. The Laird, Norton Company had the same.[49] Youmans Brothers and Hodgins' mill had three Allis bands and so remained the best-equipped mill in Winona.[50]

[46] *Mississippi Valley Lumberman*, vol. xiii, Jan. 13, 1888, p. 5; Hotchkiss, *op. cit.*, pp. 655–56.
[47] *Mississippi Valley Lumberman*, vol. xiv, July 18, 1888, p. 3; Hotchkiss, *op. cit.*, pp. 655–56; Henry Disston and Sons, *The Saw in History*, pp. 45–49.
[48] *Mississippi Valley Lumberman*, vol. xiii, May 18, 1888, p. 2.
[49] Laird, Norton and Company was reorganized in 1883 under the name of the Laird, Norton Company.
[50] Allis and Company of Milwaukee specialized in band saws and were especially known for their make of saws. Filer and Stowell of Milwaukee made the Wilkin band, though they were more generally known as makers of the Wilkin gang. The McDonough Manufacturing

Minneapolis was slow to adopt band saws. The lumbermen of that city were at this time accused of being "content to stay home and use old methods." They were not ambitious to find out what others were doing, it was said. Such was not the case with Norton and Weyerhaeuser and others downriver.[51] There can be no doubt that the downriver men were more aggressive than the Minneapolis men. Probably the fact that Minneapolis lay so near the source of material made her less concerned with economy in production. Minneapolis had a few band saws in the eighties, but not until the following decade did they become general there. New sawmill men who located in Minneapolis brought them; the old-timers in Minneapolis had to be shown.[52]

Lumber was seldom shipped green because its moisture content raised shipping costs. The dry kiln was introduced to save time in the drying process, which had previously consisted of stacking the lumber in yards for air drying. The live rolls, the nigger, the planing mill, the tramway for carrying lumber to the yards, automatic firing of engines with sawdust and other lumber refuse, and smoke consumers were some of the other additions to sawmills in the eighties that required more capital but made for an enormous increase in production.

But what of the men who ran the engines, who set the saws, who piled the lumber? What of their wages, their hours, their risks and hazards of employment? Such concepts as economic security, protective legislation, and status for labor in the courts had not become a part of the language or the thinking of the American people, for the 1870s and 1880s were dominated by rugged individualism, the keynote of which was laissez-faire. Labor organization had not yet even appeared in the lumber industry.

In Minnesota in the early period there was a strong demand for workmen, and, as we have seen, the first millmen in Minnesota imported labor from their native states. This explains the presence of so many workmen from Maine, in the sawmills as well as in the timber. As the industry grew and showed promise, labor was attracted to the saw-towns, and immigrants from Europe began to replace labor from the eastern states in the sawmill industry. Winona, as an example, had almost fifteen hundred Polish workmen in its mills at one time; their living quarters were designated as the Polish section. Minneapolis was the mecca of the Swedish and the Norwegian immigrants, who supplied workmen for the mills.

Company of Eau Claire made bands as did the Diamond Iron Works of Minneapolis. Interview of the writer with Roscoe Horton and C. M. Youmans, Winona, May 2, 1934; *Mississippi Valley Lumberman*, vol. xxiii, Aug. 4, 1893, p. 5.

[51] *Ibid.*, vol. xi, June 3, 1887, p. 14.

[52] *Minneapolis Tribune*, Aug. 1, 1887, p. 5.

The number of workmen employed varied with the size of the mill. The average mill in Minnesota had a superintendent who was the general overseer. Immediately under him were the men who supervised the various sections: the boom master, or log foreman; the yard master, who supervised the lumber as it was piled and made ready for sale by his assistants; and the mill foreman, who had charge of activities within the mill proper. Very important were the chief engineer and his assistants. There were also the men who operated the saws, such as the circular sawyers, the gang sawyers, the lath sawyers, and the shingle sawyers. In the hierarchy of the sawmill these men ranked high, for they were skilled workmen on whose judgment would depend the number of feet to be secured from a log. On the platform, checking the lumber, were the surveyor and his assistants. Every mill had also a filer, whose job it was to keep the saw teeth sharp; a scaler, whose business it was to know exactly the number of feet of lumber sawed; and a shipping clerk.

There might be many or few in each division of the work, according to the output. In Anoka, in 1873, a mill producing 50,000 feet a day employed 70 men.[53] The following year a mill in the same city, producing 100,000 feet in ten hours, employed 130 men.[54] At about the same time a Minneapolis mill with 200 men was producing 130,000 feet a day.[55] In 1888 the Laird, Norton Company of Winona produced 250,000 feet of lumber daily with a crew of 400 men.[56] That same year Youmans Brothers and Hodgins produced 250,000 feet a day with 300 men.[57] (The Laird, Norton Company employed one hundred more men than Youmans Brothers and Hodgins for the same cut, but they were a more diversified firm and it is likely that their men were engaged in a greater variety of work.)

Eleven hours seems to have been a normal workday in the mills in the seventies, though references are made to a ten-hour day. Stillwater mills in 1875 referred to the cut produced in an eleven-hour day as though that was the regular thing,[58] but a Minneapolis mill at the same time referred to a 130,000-foot cut in a ten-hour day.[59] In 1887 Youmans Brothers and Hodgins spoke of their production in a ten-hour day.[60] Minneapolis, complaining that cutting lumber there was more expensive than in other places, said one reason for this was the prevailing ten-hour

[53] Ibid., May 8, 1873, p. 2.
[54] Ibid., Oct. 25, 1874, p. 6.
[55] Ibid., Nov. 14, 1875, p. 5.
[56] Curtiss-Wedge, op. cit., p. 180; Mississippi Valley Lumberman, vol. xiii, Jan. 6, 1888, p. 5.
[57] Ibid.
[58] Stillwater Lumberman, Apr. 23, 1875.
[59] Minneapolis Tribune, Nov. 14, 1875, p. 5.
[60] Curtiss-Wedge, op. cit., p. 183.

day, while an eleven-hour day was general elsewhere.[61] In 1887 the workers in the sawmills of R. A. Gray and of Hubbard and Vincent, both of Duluth, struck for a ten-hour day, refusing to begin work until seven o'clock in the morning, six being their usual hour.[62] So even in the eighties there were mills where the ten-hour day had not been won.

In 1870 the 207 sawmills in Minnesota employed 2952 men. The wages paid these men totaled $880,028, making the average wage about $295 a year.[63] In the sawmill the season was usually six months, seven at the most. With a season of 180 working days, a wage of $295 would bring about $1.60 a day. But this wage was not paid to every man; even in the sawmill industry there was a difference between skilled and unskilled labor. The men who piled lumber in the yard needed brawn. The sawyer, who in the flash of a moment had to determine how the log was to be cut, needed quick brains. In 1873 one mill at Anoka paid $1.50, $1.75, and $2.00 per day for labor, according to the work done. Payday in this mill came the fifteenth day of the month, and a bonus of 25 cents per day was paid to men who worked through the whole season.[64] In 1875 Anoka spoke of a monthly payroll of about $20,000 for its mill labor, of which a newspaper said, "This money will make business lively." [65]

In 1880, 2854 employees in Minnesota sawmills had a total wage of $924,473, averaging about $325 for the year.[66] With a season of 180 working days, the daily wage would be about $1.80. This was not a high wage, and men often eked out their living by working in the woods in winter. In 1888 Youmans and Hodgins of Winona were paying 300 men $10,000 a month; the Empire Lumber Company of that city paid 250 men $10,000 a month; the Winona Lumber Company was paying 350 men $13,000 a month; the Laird, Norton Company was paying 400 men $15,000 a month.[67] These figures show that the Winona mills varied somewhat in their wages, paying from $33.33 a month to $37.50.

In 1889 wages in Minnesota's sawmills ranged from $1.00 to $8.00 a day, only two workers receiving the latter amount. The majority were paid wages ranging between $1.25 and $2.50, the average rate per day being $1.83.[68] There was little security in such a wage, and evidently labor was not satisfied with it, for occasionally there were strikes for higher wages. In 1889 men in T. B. Walker's mill in Crookston struck

[61] *Mississippi Valley Lumberman*, vol. xiii, Apr. 6, 1888, p. 2.
[62] *Ibid.*, vol. xi, June 3, 1887, p. 11.
[63] *U.S. Census, 1890: Manufacturing Industries*, pt. iii, p. 610.
[64] *Minneapolis Tribune*, May 8, 1873, p. 2.
[65] *Anoka Union*, May 18, 1875, p. 3.
[66] *U.S. Census, 1890: Manufacturing Industries*, pt. iii, p. 610.
[67] *Mississippi Valley Lumberman*, vol. xiii, Jan. 6, 1888, p. 5.
[68] *Report of the Minnesota Bureau of Labor Statistics*, 1889–1890, p. 336.

for an increase in wages. They asked for an increase of 25 cents a day to make a wage of $1.75. But they were apparently not successful, for a trade journal of that day said that the strikers' places were filled and the mill went on.[69]

The mills sometimes claimed the lives of men, for neither life nor limb was safe with swiftly moving saws, live rolls, and the lightning-quick steam nigger. A common accident was that in which a man's jacket was caught by the shaft supporting the rotating machinery, entangling him with fatal results. A slasher-saw quickly took a man's leg, and the ripsaw was a demon for killing men who got in its way. Amputation of arms or fingers torn by the circular saw or ripped by the siding-saw took much space in the reports of sawmill accidents.[70]

TABLE 13. LUMBER CUT IN MINNEAPOLIS, 1880–1888

Year	Lumber Cut (in feet)
1880	195,452,182
1881	234,245,071
1882	312,239,800
1883	280,195,271
1884	300,724,373
1885	313,998,166
1886	267,196,519
1887*	220,822,974
1888	337,663,301

* In 1887 the cut was lowered considerably, owing to a fire which destroyed five sawmills that year (*Mississippi Valley Lumberman*, vol. xii, Sept. 16, 1887, p. 6).

SOURCE: *Report of the Minneapolis Chamber of Commerce*, 1883, p. 76; 1884, p. 92; 1887, p. 118; 1888, p. 134.

During the 1880s Minneapolis maintained its leadership in lumber production in Minnesota. Neither Stillwater nor Winona could keep pace with the city at St. Anthony Falls in output. There the mills were increasing in size as well as in number; from Fourth Avenue North to Thirty-eighth Avenue North, almost unbroken for two and a half miles, were lines of sawmills with piles of lumber.[71]

In the eighties the Minneapolis cut increased greatly, reaching a high point in 1888 (Table 13). In that year the mills of the city at the Falls cut 137,292,024 more feet than in any previous single year. At that time thirteen concerns were sawing lumber in Minneapolis. A comparison of the cuts of the six largest mills in 1882 and 1888 is given in Table 14. Winona

[69] *Mississippi Valley Lumberman*, vol. xv, Aug. 30, 1889, p. 7.
[70] *Bureau of Labor Statistics*, Minnesota, 1891–1892, pp. 108–9, 116.
[71] *Minneapolis Tribune*, Jan. 1, 1889, p. 3.

ranked second to Minneapolis in both production and selling;[72] in 1888 the downriver city made the largest cut in its history,[73] and its lumber was selling far into the West — at Atchison and at Denver.[74]

TABLE 14. LUMBER CUT OF LARGEST MINNEAPOLIS MILLS

1882		1888	
Company	Lumber Cut (in feet)	Company	Lumber Cut (in feet)
Farnham & Lovejoy.......	29,500,000	Hall and Dusey..........	43,500,000
McMullen & Son..........	26,550,000	Diamond Mill Company...	41,224,117
Cole & Weeks.............	24,000,000	McMullen and Company...	34,222,210
Merriman, Barrows & Company	23,194,000	Plymouth Mill Company....	33,570,702
Eastman, Bovey & Company	19,509,228	DeSoto Lumber Company...	32,998,572
John Martin & Company...	18,070,074	J. W. Day and Company....	21,000,000

SOURCE: *Joint Annual Report of the Minneapolis Chamber of Commerce and Board of Trade*, 1882, pp. 25–26; *Report of the Minneapolis Chamber of Commerce*, 1888, p. 132.

In 1889 there was a reduction in the cut of sawmills. This was not due to any lessening in the local market, for the year was an exceptional one in the lumber trade. December 1888 and January and February 1889 were record months; a mild winter made building possible and trade was brisk as a result.[75] But the light snowfall and consequent low water made logs fewer and harder to drive, and the cut of the Upper Mississippi in 1889 decreased 756,404,777 feet.[76] The largest decrease was experienced in the region above Minneapolis; Anoka, in particular, was unable to secure logs. Minneapolis, also dependent on the Mississippi for log supply, was second in the decrease of cut. The demand was there, however, and a strong comeback was the response in 1890.

In the eighties Minnesota's industries using lumber as a material also increased greatly. In 1880 concerns making agricultural implements in Minnesota had a capital of $2,315,222; ten years later they had a capital of $5,136,542.[77] Six such firms were operating in Minneapolis in 1890.[78] In addition there were thirty-eight makers of wagons and carriages; in such a growing hinterland as Minneapolis served farm wagons were much in demand. In 1890 twenty-two establishments in Minneapolis were specializing in millwork and almost every sawmill had such a division; this industry had grown up in the preceding decade.

[72] *Mississippi Valley Lumberman*, vol. xi, Apr. 29, 1887 (issue unpaged).
[73] *Minneapolis Tribune*, Nov. 23, 1888, p. 8.
[74] *Mississippi Valley Lumberman*, vol. xi, June 3, 1887, p. 9.
[75] *Report of the Minneapolis Chamber of Commerce*, 1889, p. 155.
[76] *Ibid.*, p. 160.
[77] *U.S. Census, 1890: Manufacturing Industries*, pt. i, p. 643.
[78] *Ibid.*, pt. ii, pp. 342–46.

In 1891 the *Northwest Miller* estimated that the product of the cooper shops in Minneapolis was valued at $1,007,000.[79]

Henry Hastings Sibley had once said of Minnesota that agriculture and lumber were "to be the great levers in raising us in our career of prosperity." [80] Time confirmed Sibley's statement. In the 1880s Minnesota's largest city had become the world's primary wheat market; in the next decade it was to achieve national leadership in the production of white pine.

[79] *Mississippi Valley Lumberman*, vol. xxii, Sept. 23, 1892, p. 6.
[80] Henry H. Sibley, "Annual Address," *Minn. Hist. Soc. Coll.*, vol. i (St. Paul, 1902), p. 391.

CHAPTER X

Logging and Driving, 1870–1890

IN THE business of estimating timber as to quality and quantity — of determining which areas and which trees should be cut by the logger — confidence was placed in one man. On his decision depended tens of thousands of dollars; if he made an error in his estimate, his employer was a loser in cold coin. This important individual who marched in the vanguard of the army of lumbermen was called the cruiser. The typical cruiser was a successor to the *coureur de bois,* the ranger of the woods. The *coureur* looked for furs, for peltries; the cruiser looked for valuable timber, and he came to be called the "land looker." The cruisers were often men with rough exteriors, living just on the borderline between savagery and civilization; strange it seems that they contributed so much toward making their employers men of fortune.

The early cruisers were not trained in a school of forestry; they learned their craft largely through observation. How does one determine where he is in the dense forest away from all roads and trails and many miles from human habitation? How can he tell one tract of land from another? How can he tell what land belongs to the United States, what to the state, and what to his employer? These and many more things the cruiser had to know. He had to know a sound tree, and a defective one. A tree that appeared healthy might have an infection concealed, and no good cruiser could afford to make a mistake in such an instance. He had to reckon almost without error the number of feet of timber in each acre of the "forty" — forty acres of land, which was the basic unit for his calculations. He had to see the possibilities of the lay of the land. Were there logging streams? What were their connections? How could timber best be taken out of the forest? How much would it cost to log the section? All this information he had to have formulated in definite plans ready to present to his company when his cruising was done.

The cruiser was a secretive man; only his employer must know his findings. Often no one but the employer knew that the cruiser and his companion had been sent to estimate lands which, if satisfactory, would become the employer's property. The cruiser had to be a man of his word, honest, industrious, and courageous. He also had to know how to live in the deep woods in winter, hundreds of miles from the nearest outpost. He must have loved or learned to love the solitude of the great forest.

The methods used by cruisers varied from time to time. In the early days in Minnesota cruising was referred to as "the great guessing game from Maine." It is quite likely that at first it was a matter of merely estimating the amount as one looked at the forest. But, as the white pine grew more scarce and competition for timber increased, more scientific methods came to be necessary and cruisers had to become more accurate. One cruiser whose method seems to have worked well explained the method he used: he selected a forty-acre piece of timberland; on that forty he measured off four rods square, one tenth of an acre, and within this portion he counted every tree; he then measured the diameter of each of these trees, and, computing by the United States volume table, he calculated the exact feet of timber in each tree and the total for the trees measured; then he multiplied the figure by ten to find the number of feet per acre. He worked in this way, acre by acre, until he had the total for the whole forty. Then he proceeded to the next forty.[1]

The speed with which a cruiser worked depended upon the condition of the land; swamps, lakes, rivers, and heavy underbrush made labor slow. One cruiser said that the computing of one section, or sixteen forties, was a three-day job under usual conditions.[2] One of the best cruisers in recent years in Minnesota estimated a million-dollar timber tract in a little less than forty days. That was record speed. When this timber was logged, his computation was found to have been just 1.7 per cent less than the exact log scale of the tract. With pride this cruiser said that the timber was not logged until a year after he had cruised it and that this lapse of time was enough for that much growth. It was a remarkable piece of work, and it is not surprising that the International Lumber Company in Minnesota has employed this man as its expert cruiser for more than twenty-two years.

When cruisers lived in the woods for long months at a time, a certain minimum of equipment was absolutely necessary to them. They had to be clothed to withstand the many zeros-below of winter weather. They generally wore mackinaws. A knit cape, which the Indians call a *chuke,* was not uncommon among the earlier cruisers.[3] The parka, an Eskimo

---

[1] Interview of the writer with Mark Hessey (cruiser for E. W. Backus of Minneapolis), June 5, 1932, at Iron River, Wisconsin. Hessey then had a large farm; farming was his avocation.

[2] Interview of the writer with John C. Daly, a former cruiser, eighty years of age, Port Wing, Wisconsin, June 6, 1932.

[3] Interview of the writer with T. H. Merritt, Lenox Hotel, Duluth, June 13, 1932.

hood attached to a jacket which later had a zipper arrangement closing it tight, became a popular wrap.[4] The parka protected the wearer
from cold winds that without it blew in around the neck. The men
wore spiked shoes, but they usually carried moccasins to wear with snowshoes. They generally carried only one change of clothing, resorting to
streams to do their washing when the weather permitted.

Their necessities were usually transported in packsacks, though dog
teams often carried their heavier equipment and supplies. A tent, heavy
blankets, one tin plate, one cup, one spoon, one fork apiece, one knife
for the crew, a kit of pails, a sheet-iron stove, a gun, a cruiser's ax,
candles, matches, and a compass were a part of the regular equipment.
Only such foodstuffs were carried as had high food value: flour, salt
pork or bacon, beans, rice, raisins, dried fruits, sugar, and extras like
pepper, salt, soda, and tea.

The cruiser and his men depended to a great extent on wild berries,
game, and fish for food. One cruiser smacked his lips as he told of
shooting a two-and-a-half-month moose calf, which became delicious
stew served with dumplings.[5] Hot biscuit was a popular item in their
fare. One cruiser explained that in preparing the biscuit he poured a
bit of water right into the flour which he had scooped together a bit in
the sack; it was mixed right there, in the top of the sack, and then
baked in the reflector by the fire. The reflector was a part of the equipment of all men in the woods; it was a boxlike utensil of copper so
constructed as to catch the heat when placed near a fire. Biscuit and
bread were commonly baked in this way unless they were placed in
the bean hole; and that a "right good biscuit" was made was the verdict
of all woodsmen, whether the biscuit was baked in the reflector or in
the bean hole.

When the men prepared their beds at night in winter, they put on
their snowshoes and brushed the snow away; on this cleared spot they
then laid a bed of boughs, preferably balsam; on top of the boughs
they placed a fur robe and on this they slept, with two Hudson's Bay
Company blankets over them. Some cruisers carried arctic sleeping bags
lined with blankets and eider down, which protected them from cold
while they rested on a bed of boughs, night after night, sometimes for
six months in succession. The sheet-iron stove, filled full of wood and
then closed, gave heat for a portion of the night.

It took stamina for the cruisers to withstand the intense cold, deep
snow, and biting wind of the northland, trudging day after day through
the snow with no prospect of the comforts of home at nightfall. Mis-

[4] Interview of the writer with Mark Hessey, June 5, 1932.
[5] Interview of the writer with William Quinn, a cruiser, Duluth, June 16, 1932.

haps were not uncommon in the woods: broken legs and accidents with
the ax were the most common; illness might overtake the men anywhere. Such accidents and illness, hundreds of miles from where aid
could be obtained, made the life of the cruiser and his companions
perilous.[6]

The size of a cruiser's crew varied. Sometimes he went to his work
alone; sometimes he was accompanied by one man. A large crew consisted of the cruiser, two compassmen, and a cook.

The woodsman was always taking the measurement of men. Who
was the best foreman? Who was the best cook? Who was the strongest
man in camp? Who was best on the drive? So we ask, not who was
Minnesota's best cruiser? — such a choice would be too difficult — but who
were some of the outstanding men who cruised her forests?

Daniel Stanchfield was without question one of the earliest men, if
not the earliest, sent to make a proper estimate of timber in a Minnesota
region where the purchase of timberland was being considered.[7] In 1847
he explored the Rum River pinery for Franklin Steele, Caleb Cushing
and his partners, Rantoul and Company, and other eastern capitalists
interested in western investments.[8] On an autumn day, September 1,
1847, Stanchfield and his companions set out on their perilous journey
into the wilderness where the Indian still roamed and the white man
had hardly trod. Stanchfield's route led up the Mississippi to the confluence of that stream with the Rum, at the point where Anoka stands
today.

It was a lonely country that these men penetrated, broken only by
the swish of the water as they paddled their canoes up the river. Stanchfield had two companions. One was Severre Bottineau, a brother of the
famous guide, Pierre Bottineau. Severre knew four languages: French,
English, Ojibway, and the Dakota. His other companion was Charles
Manock, who went as cook and guide.[9] Both Bottineau and Manock
were mixed-bloods. At the confluence of the Mississippi and the Rum,
the men guided their canoe into the Rum, where they became "land-
lookers" for white pine. The third night they camped three miles northwest of what is now Cambridge, Minnesota. There Stanchfield and his
companions complained of the mosquito, the gnat, and the moose-fly
which they said was the worst of the pests.[10]

At first they found only deciduous trees, but at the place on the Rum

[6] *Mississippi Valley Lumberman,* vol. xxii, Dec. 2, 1892, p. 3.
[7] See above, p. 33.
[8] Stanchfield, "History of Pioneer Lumbering on the Upper Mississippi," *Minn. Hist. Soc. Coll.,* vol. ix, p. 329.
[9] *Ibid.*
[10] *Ibid.,* p. 330.

where Princeton stands today they came upon the white pine they were seeking.[11] They explored some of the tributaries of the Rum on which stood magnificent trees. One of these was the West Branch and the other was Bradbury Brook, both well known to loggers of a later day. They followed the Rum River to its source, the beautiful Lake Mille Lacs.

Stanchfield was greatly impressed with his discovery. "Seventy mills in seventy years couldn't exhaust the white pine I have seen on the Rum River," was his reply to the men whose investments depended on his word. He could not fail to see that the country he had explored was not only rich in timber; it had remarkable streams for driving as well. The delta through which the Rum River flowed was crisscrossed by many streams that would make good highways to carry logs to the sawmill.

Daniel Stanchfield made Minnesota his home. As long as he lived he was an authority on timber, though he became a merchant at St. Anthony Falls, where he furnished supplies largely to loggers. In 1852, according to his advertisement in the *St. Anthony Express*, he dealt in a variety of things, including cashmeres and broadcloth, butter, cove oysters, and grindstones.[12] But he will always live in the history of Minnesota as one of its great woodsmen.

Probably no man in the whole forest history of America has cruised more timber than did Lyman W. Ayer.[13] He was a native of Minnesota's soil. His parents were New England missionaries to the Indians and, when Lyman was born, they lived in the vicinity of what is Pine City today. That region was the most remote part of the old Northwest Territory and was in 1832, the year of Ayer's birth, a part of Crawford County, Michigan.[14]

Ayer's life was characteristic of the frontier. He grew up with the redskins; the Indians of the Rainy Lake country said that he could speak better "Indian" than they themselves. He had never worn a white man's shoe until he enlisted for the Civil War. He was by turn a pioneer schoolteacher, a buffalo hunter, a carrier of dispatches from Fort Snelling to Fort Garry (Winnipeg), a fur trader in the Red River country, and a cruiser. Ayer was self-educated: he was a prolific reader and a keen observer. One of his greatest assets was his uncommon good sense. He knew the forest like a book and seemed to have no fear of wrapping himself in a blanket and sleeping in the open wherever the end of day might find him.

Ayer was the first of the "old-timers" in cruising to substitute systematic methods for the prevailing custom of guessing, which consisted

[11] *Ibid.*
[12] *St. Anthony Express*, Mar. 6, 1852.
[13] "Lyman Warren Ayer," *North Woods*, vol. vii, Apr. 1920, p. 7.
[14] *Ibid.*

largely in comparing tracts that the cruiser had seen logged. His system consisted in "Averages taken at *regular* intervals along compass lines that *crossed* the *'formation'* at right angles." Modern forestry practice has, to be sure, improved somewhat upon Ayer's way, but the principle on which he based his system is still considered fundamental.[15] This method was recognized as being far more scientific than that used earlier, and it produced higher totals than the "guessers" cared to vouch for. So at first Ayer's judgment on timber stands was questioned, but since no timber tract which he cruised was ever reported as overestimated after it had been cut and scaled, it is likely that his system was safe.[16]

Lyman W. Ayer cruised for the Northern Pacific in 1878 when it was trying to select and appraise indemnity lands. He worked for the Merritt brothers, the famous iron men on the Mesabi Range, in the 1880s. About 1900 he began cruising for Backus and Brooks of Minneapolis, whose holdings were in the most remote and unexplored regions of northern Minnesota.

Ayer did not use liquor, tobacco, or profanity. That was enough to set him apart from the "ordinary man of the woods," and perhaps it accounts for his remarkable physical endurance; even at the age of seventy-four "he could follow his compassman all day long, through the hardest walking the northwoods offers."[17] He would endure without a murmur the long physical discomfort and privation which was so much a part of the cruiser's life. He looked like a patriarch with his long white beard and stately gait, quite in keeping with his manner and habits.

Lyman Ayer died in 1919 at the age of eighty-seven. He had seen the white pine timber of Minnesota advance in price from 25 cents a thousand feet, when only the cream of the timber was touched, to $14 a thousand feet, when men were almost grateful for the husks.[18] Ayer was born seven years before the establishment of the first commercial sawmill on Minnesota soil; he died after the industry had passed its zenith. Within the lifetime of this man had come and gone an era vital in the history of the state. Where he had seen the moose stalk fearlessly, where the carefree deer had romped with her young, where the bear had prowled oblivious to the white man and his gun, there Ayer lived to see the plowman turn the sod, to hear the low of the cow and the ring of the school bell.

[15] A letter from Murdo Gibson, Dalmore Hotel, Kenora, Ontario, Canada, to the writer on July 15, 1932. Murdo Gibson was at one time Camping Editor of the Izaak Walton League of America. He cruised at various times with Lyman W. Ayer in the region adjacent to Rainy, Kabetogama, and Namakan lakes in Minnesota.
[16] *Ibid.*
[17] *Ibid.*
[18] Ralph Clement Bryant, *Logging* (New York, 1914), p. 539.

In front of the capitol building in St. Paul, Minnesota, is a statue of a cruiser with his tussock on his back; he stands alongside another statue, of a tiller of the soil. It is fitting that the timber cruiser should occupy so prominent a place among Minnesota's monuments. It is fitting, too, that the model for this statue was Leonidas Merritt, one of those who cruised the "Great Mesabi" — "without trail or blaze but only a compass to guide them on their way."

Leonidas Merritt and his brother Alfred, both cruisers, explored a great stretch of land to the north of Duluth.[19] In 1882 they cruised the land in the heart of the Mesabi range.[20] As young boys they had moved in 1855 with their parents to Oneota, where their father had established a sawmill; so the forest was their playground in childhood and in maturity it became their workshop. But though they cruised for timber, they dreamed of finding iron. And they found it in rich and abundant measure. But others were to profit from their discovery. In the Panic of 1893 the Merritts — less wise in finance than in cruising — lost their holdings on the iron range to the Rockefellers, from whom they had borrowed money. When Leonidas died in 1926 his fortune was valued at $1500 in household goods, $800 in miscellaneous, and $150 in cash.[21] It was a meager fortune to be left by the man who had started the development of the great iron treasure of the Mesabi. Honor is his, even though fortune was not.

But the "Great Mesabi" did make one rich cruiser: Marshall H. Alworth, who came to cruise for a Michigan firm. When his work was done, his firm paid him in timberland on the Mesabi, and underneath the roots of his pines, concealed from the eye of man, lay iron ore. When Hibbing was platted, a portion of the land belonging to Alworth lay within the village, and as the mines were developed, his land became almost priceless.[22] He was one of Duluth's early millionaires.

Those, in brief, were a few of Minnesota's famous cruisers. Today things are different for the cruiser. He no longer has to trudge in the swamp and forest, over windfall, and through brush; today he can, on occasion, travel by airplane.[23] So the old-time cruiser, like the forest in which he worked, belongs to the past.

The passing of the pioneer stage of logging cannot be precisely dated,

[19] *Duluth Herald*, July 23, 1925.

[20] Walter Van Brunt, editor, *History of Duluth and St. Louis County*, vol. i (Chicago, 1921), p. 396.

[21] *Duluth Herald*, July 23, 1925.

[22] Van Brunt, *op. cit.*, vol. ii, p. 539.

[23] The writer interviewed Mark Hessey, cruiser for E. W. Backus of Minneapolis, on June 5, 1932. The following day this seventy-four-year-old cruiser was leaving by airplane for the Canadian forests to cruise for his employers.

for the change depended to a considerable extent on whether a given logging establishment belonged to a small owner, a jobber, or a firm of big business. It was in the 1870s that the more primitive methods of logging began to disappear, however. The heavier market demands were speeding up the mills, and the increased capacity of the mills called for more speed in the woods. In the seventies every phase of the lumber industry was in a state of flux.

The early loggers cut the timber where it was largest and best, and where it was easiest to handle. Naturally, they followed the Mississippi River and its tributaries upstream. Far north the Mississippi had tributaries where the white pine was almost equal to that of the Rum River. Among these streams were the Swan River and the Prairie River, along whose banks hundreds of millions of feet of logs waited to be cut; for nearly a generation these streams were to carry to market an annual springtime load of pine. It was along these streams that men began to cut logs in the early 1870s. In 1874 men were hewing down the tall pine north of Grand Rapids in Itasca County.[24] Other loggers were at the same time chopping their way into more remote parts of the St. Croix Valley; they had reached the Kettle River, whose saw-town, Pine City, grew up during the seventies.

Among the loggers who again stepped into the vanguard and moved northward was Leonard Day, known as "Len Day" to his associates. Already a leader in the business life of Minneapolis, he was not young when he came to the Grand Rapids country, but he was a vigorous character, extremely popular with his men. Day had cut his first white pine on the Rum River, but high water carried away the logs in which he had invested the money he had brought from Maine. A man named Hurlbut financed him in another venture, and from then on Leonard Day became prosperous, getting possession of good pineland in the region of Lake Pokegama, where later he also found iron ore. Day, something of a dandy, always wore a plug hat around town, and he always drove a good horse.[25] He had three sons, Wesley, Lorenzo, and Harrison, who became as well known in the later logging history of Minnesota as their father had been in the earlier.[26]

Another early comer to the white pine of the Pokegama, along with Leonard Day, was Al Nason, reputed to be the strongest man ever to

[24] McClung, *Minnesota as It Is in 1870*, p. 149; Warren, *Pioneer Woodsman*, p. 78.

[25] Interview of the writer with John E. Gilmore of Minneapolis (who had married Nellie Day, a daughter of Leonard Day, in 1877), Aug. 15, 1932. Gilmore was eighty years old at the time of this interview. He was one of the few men then living who had any knowledge of the early logging on Pokegama Lake or in the whole Grand Rapids country.

[26] *Grand Rapids Herald-Review*, Oct. 24, 1934. This paper carries a section on early history, entitled "Up in This Neck of the Woods."

Isaac Staples   *Dorilus Morrison*

TITANS OF THE LUMBER INDUSTRY

William H. Laird   *Frederick Weyerhaeuser*

E. W. McQUEEN.

MINNEAPOLIS LABOR AGENCY.
JOHNSON & COMPANY.
105 ~~~~ Nicollet Avenue.

No .... Minneapolis, Minn. *Dec 1st* 189 7

LABOR TICKET to.. *Simon Rowe*

Hired f *At. Johnson*

Kind of Labor.. *Swamper*

Wages $ *18.00* per Mo. Board $ _____ per week

Destination.. *47 miles from Amery Wis*

Report at office *8:15* ___ M. *Dec 2* 189 7

Labor agencies hired men for the logging crews.

The foreman's office and its staff

Typical loggers and river-drivers

An early logging camp, showing a one-room shanty

In the roomier camp of a later day, the crew posed on the deacon's seat and the bunks.

The bull-cook presided over the men's living quarters.

Jacks at Christmas dinner in the cook's domain

Night life in camp

Oxen skidding logs in the woods

The horse replaced the ox, but the go-devil retained its usefulness.

When manpower loaded the logs, the top-loader had a dangerous job.

The crosscut saw replaced the ax.

After 1870 logs were carried in bobsleds over log roads to the river-bank. The "hayman on the hill" kept the roads in condition.

In a later period, cables pulled by steam brought logs to the skidway.

The caterpillar tractor speeded the movement of logs in the woods.

The logging railroad was the most significant factor in the evolution of the logging industry after 1890.

This load, hauled a distance of one mile by four horses on February 13, 1892, was 21 feet high, 20 feet wide, and contained 31,480 feet of logs. It was the ice road that made such a load possible.

Bark-marked logs, ready by the rollway for the spring drive

MARKS	EXPLANATION	DATE OF RECORD
M E L / Diamond	Called M E L / " Diamond M E (End Mark) / Cut and owned by / Mullgren and Olson Co	Nov 5. 1900
M A 4 4	Called M A two S" / Cut and owned by / Geo. H. Atwood	Nov 5. 1900
4 A W X / 4 A Y Y X	Called S A W Cross / " S A two Y Cross / Cut and owned by / Atwood Lumber Co	Nov 5. 1900
N . N X / M I	Called N notch N Cross / " M S / Cut and owned by John Sinclair	Nov 7. 1900
G	Called Block G (End Mark) / Cut and owned by / George Moores	Nov 7. 1900
X Y X .	Called Cross Y Cross Notch / Cut and owned by / Mike McAleer	Nov 7. 1900
: X M : / V X M V	Called two Notches Cross M two Notches / " V Cross M V / Cut and owned by / Geo A Dulan	Nov 7. 1900
M A 4 . / M A 4 4 .	Called M A S Notch / " M A two S" Notch / Cut and owned by / Geo. H. Atwood	Nov 7. 1900

At the landing every log was given a bark mark and a stamp mark to denote its ownership. This page of stamp marks is recorded in the office of the Surveyor General of Logs, Minnesota.

Log jam on the St. Croix

On the drive   *A jam breaker hunts the key log.*

In the rear of the drive always followed the wanigan, serving as a cook-shanty and, if large enough, as a bunkhouse.

A meal out-of-doors held no appeal for the wet and shivering river-driver.

A log raft moving down the Mississippi

Rafted logs at their downriver destination

The capital invested in the Northwestern Mills of Hersey, Bean & Brown, Stillwater, came largely from the white pine in Maine.

The H. C. Akeley Mill startled Minneapolis with a 50,500,000 foot cut in 1890.

Moving out from the mill, a lumber raft carried laths and shingles on top of the lumber. The runners and grub pins are visible here.

The H. O. Larson farm home in Bloomfield Township, Fillmore County, Minnesota, was built of white pine. The denuding of the forest had as a direct result the more rapid settlement of the region and the better housing of its people.

come to Itasca. He, it was said, could shoulder a barrel of salt pork weighing 330 pounds and walk off without any effort.

One W. W. Hale from Pennsylvania came into the Grand Rapids country to cut pine in 1872.[27] He acquired a reputation among loggers as the man who would not allow the washing of clothes in his camps on Sunday. For Hale's men Saturday was wash day and Sunday was a real Sabbath.[28]

Into this same region about 1870 came Nathaniel Tibbets, whose father, also Nathaniel Tibbets, had come from Maine to log on the St. Croix at an earlier date. As the pine gave way in the lower logging regions, the younger Tibbets moved farther north. His son, William Tibbets, cruised for the Northern Pacific Railroad in the 1870s. William continued to work in that north country until the white pine was gone. Thus three generations of Tibbets spent their lives logging the great forests of white pine reaching from the St. Croix to the region shortly above Grand Rapids on the Mississippi.[29]

Dorilus Morrison, Joel Bassett, Ankeny and Company, and Eastman, Bovey and Company, as well as others prominent in lumbering in Minneapolis, had logging interests at the bend of the Mississippi in the early seventies.[30] The Mississippi region north from Minneapolis was logged in the seventies by men whose interests centered in Minneapolis, Anoka, and St. Cloud, or at other sawmill points north along the river.

As the demand for lumber mounted, the number of men, oxen, and horses in the woods increased. From Stillwater in the fall of 1871, 500 teams of horses and oxen and 2000 men went into the woods for the winter's logging.[31] That year 146,536,000 feet of logs were harvested on the St. Croix and its tributaries.[32] In 1878–79 the Mississippi and its tributaries had 2093 men and 1920 horses and oxen in their woods; these, it was estimated, would cut 159,444,000 feet.[33] Itasca County, just being opened for logging, had about 600 loggers in the early 1870s.[34]

Crews were increasing in size. The small crew of the State-of-Maine camp of the pioneer decades could not provide enough logs to produce

[27] With him came John E. Gilmore of Minneapolis (referred to in note 25) to work as a logger.

[28] *Grand Rapids Herald-Review*, Oct. 17, 1934.

[29] The writer interviewed William Tibbets on Aug. 16, 1932, at Ball Club, Minnesota. He had all the appearance of a gracious patriarch with his white hair and white whiskers; he was eighty years old. His speech was that of Maine. His wife was a Chippewa, and his six sons were sturdy-looking Indians with a Maine accent. His only daughter's son was named Ole. Thus races and nationalities were mixed in the north country.

[30] *Minneapolis Tribune*, Feb. 26, 1870.

[31] *Stillwater Messenger*, Nov. 24, 1871.

[32] *Stillwater Lumberman*, Jan. 21, 1876.

[33] *Minneapolis Tribune*, Dec. 13, 1878, p. 4.

[34] Interview of the writer with Michael McAlpine, Grand Rapids, Minnesota, Aug. 15, 1932. McAlpine had come there from Canada to log in 1873.

the lumber demanded. In 1875 Isaac Staples had two crews working on the Groundhouse River, located two miles apart; the two crews together had 75 men, 10 spans of horses, and 14 oxen. These crews, working 115 days, delivered on the riverbank more than 12,000,000 feet during the season — altogether 60,000 logs. The timber yielded about 10,000 feet to the acre. The hauling distance was one to one and a half miles on level ground.[35]

In 1879 Page Brothers on the East Branch of Rum River had one camp of 25 men and 20 horses and oxen; in January of that winter it was estimated that their cut would be 2,500,000 feet. Another firm on the same river, with 35 men and 30 horses and oxen, estimated their cut at about 3,500,000 for the season. Still another concern on Tibbets Brook, also a tributary of the Rum, with a camp of 80 men and 80 horses and oxen, estimated that 8,000,000 feet would be cut.[36] W. D. Washburn, who operated four camps on tributaries of the Rum River, with 76 men working and 64 horses and oxen, had an output of 7,500,000 feet in a season.[37] From 35 to 40 was not an unusual number of men in one camp in the 1870s.[38] Thirty-five camps produced a total of 55,348,000 feet on the Upper Snake in 1877, while five camps on the Totogatic produced 10,840,000 feet.[39]

The log cut became enormous in those years. In the fall of 1876 it was estimated that 150,000,000 feet of logs would be cut in the St. Croix Valley. Of this, Isaac Staples was expected to cut 15,000,000 feet, which was the largest amount cut by any single producer in the state of Minnesota that year.[40] The largest cut on the Mississippi and its tributaries in 1876 was made by Gould and Carrich, who logged 6,000,000 feet for the Minneapolis Lumber Company. Leonard Day and Sons were a close second, with 5,500,000 feet, while Farnham and Lovejoy logged 5,000,000 feet, also on the Mississippi. Howard M. De Laittre was at Lake Pokegama getting out 3,000,000 feet of logs for Eastman and Bovey of Minneapolis in that same year. The names of the logging outfits and buyers of logs produced on the Mississippi sound like a roll call of Minneapolis sawmill men.[41]

In 1877 the log cut above Brainerd, in a region then recently opened, was 61,300,000 feet.[42] This, however, was not so large a cut as had been anticipated; the winter had been mild and there had been thirty con-

[35] *Stillwater Lumberman*, Apr. 29, 1875.
[36] *Anoka Union*, Jan. 11, 1879.
[37] *Ibid.*
[38] Interview of the writer with Michael McAlpine, Aug. 14, 1932.
[39] *Stillwater Lumberman*, Apr. 13, 1877.
[40] *Ibid.*, Dec. 15, 1876; *Minneapolis Tribune*, Nov. 27, 1876, p. 4.
[41] *Ibid.*
[42] *Ibid.*, Apr. 28, 1877, p. 4.

secutive snowless and nonfreezing days in January and February, which caused a general suspension of labor and a reduction in log output.[43] In the winter of 1878–79 it was estimated that the Mississippi and its tributaries would yield about 236,000,000 feet of logs according to the number of men in the woods — there were 2096 of them.[44] That winter 13,000,000 feet of logs came from the region of the Willow River, a Mississippi tributary which joins the big river at Aitkin. The Prairie River, one of the important logging streams near Grand Rapids, sent more than 11,500,000 feet into the Mississippi that winter.[45] In the winter of 1879–80 the Willow River sent 23,000,000 feet into the Mississippi, while the Prairie River sent 20,000,000.[46] In 1880, 247,000,000 feet of logs were hewn along the Mississippi and its tributaries.[47]

Roads were a part of the new equipment which the logger after 1870 found necessary in his work. It was unschooled engineers of the lumber industry who laid out and built the first roads into the pine regions of Minnesota. The roads they built were of two kinds, the log road and the tote road.

Until 1870 the go-devil served for dragging the tree from where it fell to the riverbank. The Maine men did not saw the tree into logs until it lay beside the river. But as logging operations pushed farther back from the streams — half a mile, a mile, or two, even twenty miles — the go-devil proved too slow. So the log road came into being, to get more logs to the stream in at least the same length of time. The trees were now cut into logs in the woods where they fell — a practice called the "Canadian Way." The logs were then carried in bobsleds over the log roads to the riverbank. The log road became an important part of logging in Minnesota and it steadily improved as bigger and bigger loads had to be transported. Eventually it became an iced road of glassy smoothness.

The tote road, over which provisions were brought in for the men in the woods, was in use even before 1870. But after 1870 the tote road covered great distances and became well worn with heavy loads, increasingly numerous as the logging years grew busier. The tote road usually started at some river point where navigation was possible, or later, when railroads came, from some railhead. Such a railhead was Aitkin; it was also an important stopping point for boats going up the Mississippi. From there tote roads radiated into the deep forest. A road out from Aitkin was at times known to have forty teams, one after another,

[43] *Stillwater Messenger*, Apr. 27, 1877.
[44] *Minneapolis Tribune*, Dec. 13, 1878, p. 4.
[45] *Brainerd Tribune*, Mar 15, 1879.
[46] *Minneapolis Tribune*, Mar. 18, 1881, p. 6.
[47] *Ibid.*

carrying pork, feed, sugar, and many other provisions back to the camps.[48]

Another feature of logging prominent after 1870 was the use of the crosscut saw instead of the ax for felling the trees. The chopper had been the expert in the woods, but he had gradually to yield to the sawyer, for the new saw was both rapid and economical. Men who handled the crosscut saw, since skilled labor was not required, were paid less than the choppers; a good chopper received at times $40 a month, while a crosscut sawyer got only $25 a month. The crosscut saw was not well received in the forest at first, for the sawdust would clog and choke it. But the well-known makers of saws, the Disston Company, worked out improvements, arranging the teeth of the saw so that there were alternating rakers and cutters; the rakers cleared out the sawdust and kept the saw from choking. The saw could strike the tree much nearer the base than could the ax; therefore it was more economical, for it left a much shorter stump. It saved the best part of the tree. The crosscut saw was managed by two men, a right-handed and a left-handed man in each pair.

It was Canadian loggers who contributed the skidway to logging in Minnesota. This device was not used by Maine men.[49] The skidway was located alongside the log road, and to it the logs were snaked or skidded from the stump on a go-devil, or later by means of skidding tongs. When the logs reached the spot selected to be a skidway, they were piled in a space bordered on each side by logs about ten feet apart and arranged perpendicularly to the log road. Here the logs were piled, butt end close to the road, almost sky-high, ready to be placed on the sleds of the log road.

The go-devil still played a part in the forest, but it was increasingly less important; the dray and later the bobsled were the new log carriers that replaced it. The dray had long runners set parallel; chains held the logs in place. The sled, however, became the most useful carrier in the moving of logs in the woods. As the log roads improved, sleds grew bigger and immense loads were carried. In the early seventies sleds six and eight feet wide were used in hauling logs, but they eventually gave way to immense bunks, for an eight-foot sled could carry only 3000 feet.[50]

Horses replaced oxen to a considerable extent as log roads and sleds

[48] Interview of the writer with O. D. Dahlin of Port Wing, Wisconsin, June 5, 1932. Dahlin was an old Swedish logger on the St. Croix whose father had logged there as early as the 1850s.

[49] Interview of the writer with Michael McAlpine, Aug. 15, 1932.

[50] Interview of the writer with George Galbreath, Grand Rapids, Minnesota, Aug. 16, 1932; also, interviews of the writer with Arthur Sjoberg of Mora, an old lumberjack, on several occasions during the winter of 1932. A bunk consisted of long timbers placed on the sled runners; on these timbers the logs rested as they were piled.

came into use, because with those facilities the horses' speed could be used to better advantage. The oxen, steady and dependable, kept their place on the skidway. They cost less than horses, and, being slow and deliberate, they were less likely to be injured. They were also easy to keep. In the spring they were let loose, with a man to care for them; if they were lost, they would usually turn up at the salt lick. No expensive harness was required for them, only a yoke and chain. The ox teamster used a good pointed stick about six feet long to direct his oxen as he called "Gee" (to the right) or "Haw" (to the left). When the ox grew old, he could be slaughtered and fed to the men as good, fresh beef. However, on the iced road the ox had no place; the four- and six-horse team took the oxen's place as the tempo of logging quickened.

Preparations for the winter's logging began in the summer when men went into the area of the next winter's camp to gather whatever hay there might be; this was cut and stacked, ready for winter use.[51] In September, October, and November tote teams carried supplies in for the winter. It was a slow process to carry provisions either by horse or by ox; wagons were drawn by two, four, or six horses, or by four, six, or eight oxen.[52]

In November the crews began moving in. They arrived at their destination in various ways, as ox freight or "by the foot and walker route," by canoe, by poled scow, or by steamboat. The earlier lumber companies paid the way of the men to the camps, for once the men were brought out they could be trusted to stay. Other companies sometimes advanced the money for their tickets, taking it later from their wages. Minneapolis, St. Paul, and Duluth had employment agencies which supplied men for the camps. After railroads had been developed, the men were sent to camp in a car which carried only those bound for the woods; they were accompanied by a "man catcher" whose job it was to see that they all reached their destination. The swampers, the sawyers, and the skidders came in the month of November. Teamsters often came later, for the sawyers had to have a good start before the teamsters could begin their work, which was often not until Christmastime. Each man had his job, and in the average crew were teamsters, chainmen, swampers, loaders, a road monkey, a scaler, a landing man, a cook, a cookee, a shanty boss, and always a foreman.

The first step in logging operations was to prepare for the work. It was the business of the swampers to clear and make roads. Roads were

[51] In the fall of 1881 Isaac Staples cut about six hundred tons of hay on his own woodland and stacked it ready for winter use at his camp. Such hay cost him about $6.00 a ton, while hay in the market was selling at $20.00 a ton and up, according to the *Stillwater Messenger*, Oct. 22, 1881.

[52] McClung, *op. cit.*, p. 144.

carefully laid, for hills had to be avoided—a hill reduced the size of the load, thus increasing the cost of hauling. The road was cleared of all roots and any other obstructions that might make the driving of heavy loads difficult or dangerous. The swampers also cleared the underbrush and trimmed away branches in the forest where trees were to be dragged to the skidway. They built the camp and prepared the banking grounds, where the logs were stored until the spring drive. A letter written to the editor of the *Minneapolis Tribune* by a logger in the winter of 1875 told of these preliminaries: "On the 13th of November 12 men left Minneapolis for this point to work for parties who are hauling logs for D. Morrison. We had to build our camps, cut our roads, and did not get to hauling until about 15 of December, when we commenced with six four horse teams." [53] With the completion of the preliminaries, the real winter's job began.

The most important job of the foreman was to lead, direct, and help, for on his leadership depended much of the success of a winter's work. A good foreman said little; he led by example. When he had finished his breakfast, he took his jacket from the wall and stepped into the woods as the last threads of night were giving way to day. The others followed and every man was in his place at daylight. "The sharp ring of well plied axes, the crash of falling trees, and the seesaw clang of crosscut saws . . . the rattling of chains and the crunching of snow" announced to the silent forest that the foreman's crew was in place for another day.

In the smaller crews the foreman was the "under cutter." He picked out the sound trees and cut a notch into them about elbow high. The notch determined for the sawyer or chopper in which direction the tree should fall. This was important, for the direction in which the tree fell determined the ease with which the logs could be hauled away. When the tree was notched, it was ready for the chopper or the sawyer. Two sawyers, one at each end of the crosscut saw, attacked the huge pine. When the tree was cut through, the sawyers yelled "Timber!" and "with a swishing crescendo culminating in a crash the great pine falls to earth." When the tree lay prone, the work of dissection began. The swamper removed the branches and cleared them away. The tree was then "laid off" to best advantage in standard lengths and sawed into logs.

The tree in the form of logs was then ready to be removed. The chainer fastened the logs to the go-devil and the logs were snaked to the skidway. There the decker or the rigging gang put them in place

[53] A letter from Jannison's Camp on Whiting Brook, *Minneapolis Tribune*, Feb. 16, 1875.

beside the log road. The men who laid logs in place on the skidway or loaded the sleds had one of the most precarious jobs in the forest; mind and muscle had to act promptly in that work, for judgment, strength, skill, and a correct eye were all necessary in the makeup of a good top-loader. To pile logs safely ten or twelve feet high was quite a performance. The top-loader was on top whether he was piling logs on the skidway or on the sled. Two men sent the logs up to the loader. If logs were being placed on the sled, one man was busy "tailing down" logs from the skidway. The old top-loader was an expert, and he hated the instrument called the jammer which came to replace him and lessen his importance in the forest. This instrument, which came into use in the eighties, was like a derrick pulled by horses.

The life of the teamster was difficult, and it was as dangerous as that of the loader. The teamster was out at four o'clock in the morning to feed, curry, and harness his horses for the day. His breakfast was the earliest in camp, and often his meal was the last at night; ten o'clock was not rarely the end of his day. The teamsters drove thousands of feet of logs in a single load with two, four, or six horses. In the 1870s a 3000-foot load was usual, and one of 5000 feet was good.[54] But with the advent of iced roads, which came into prominence about 1884, loads of 10,000, 15,000, and 20,000 feet became practicable.[55] The teamster had a daredevil's job; one accident, and he was gone forever from the list of able teamsters. Teamsters in Minnesota were almost always Americans; foreigners were not interested in the handling of horses and seemed to lack that understanding of the horse which only a long and close acquaintance can give.

Important to the work of the teamster was the "road-monkey" or "hayman on the hill," whose business it was to keep the road in order. If there was a bare spot, he had to see that it was covered with snow; he placed hay or sand on steep hillsides in order to hold the sled back. Later he was responsible for the icing of the roads. His job required no great skill, but if he was careless or unreliable, the results might be very serious.[56]

When the logs were safe at the landing, the stamp-marker and the scaler took charge. Every log was given a bark mark and a stamp mark to denote its ownership. These marks were registered with the state surveyor of logs and lumber; they determined property rights and were

[54] *Stillwater Lumberman,* Feb. 8, 1877.

[55] Interview of the writer with William Tibbets, Aug. 16, 1932; with George Galbreath, Aug. 16, 1932.

[56] *Mississippi Valley Lumberman,* vol. xvii, Feb. 28, 1890, p. 3; Cheney, "Development of Lumber Industry in Minnesota," *Journal of Geography,* vol. xiv, p. 194; *Stillwater Messenger,* Feb. 28, 1880.

subject to mortgage, lien, and labor claims.[57] Thousands of such marks are registered in Minnesota, many of them dating back to 1864. The stamp mark was pounded into the end of the log with a huge stamper that looked like a mallet; as it was applied, it drove the end of the grain back into the log. The bark marks made by the swampers with their axes were placed in the bark at a number of places so that they could be seen readily when the log rolled over in the water. The marks were important, for there were both written and unwritten laws in regard to lost, stolen, or unmarked logs.[58]

The bark marks and stamp marks were as difficult for the amateur to decipher as the hieroglyphics of ancient times. But scalers, river-drivers, and boom-workers recognized them as readily as though they were plain writing. The marks did, for the greater part, consist of the alphabet in various combinations, but signs, figures, and characters permitted an almost limitless variety.[59] These marks indicated the owner's name, on what piece of property the tree was cut, and the season in which it was cut. Thus one logging firm might have many marks. In 1887 Eastman, Bovey and Company of Minneapolis recorded forty-five different marks in their books.[60]

Scaling, as applied to the lumber industry, meant the measurement of round logs to determine their contents in board feet. At the riverbank the logs received their first measurement by the scaler, who recorded every log with its size in board feet. This measurement was recognized in the logging industry as the bank-scale. Lumbermen who purchased logs wished to know exactly the number of feet they were buying; loggers wished to know how many feet of logs they cut from various pieces of land; river-drivers were paid according to the number of feet of logs they drove. Therefore the work of scaling was important. One of Minnesota's veteran scalers was Albert Stimson of Anoka. In the winter of 1884, when he was sixty-seven years of age, he scaled 26,800,000 feet of logs. From the first of January until he finished scaling that winter, he never missed an hour of work.[61]

Beside the river logs were piled high, close to the water's edge. Usually they were placed in regular tiers, but some loggers simply put

[57] Interview of the writer with M. J. Thornton, Surveyor General of Logs and Lumber, Minnesota, Apr. 10, 1931.

[58] Elizabeth M. Bachmann, "Minnesota Log Marks," *Minnesota History*, vol. xxvi (June 1945), pp. 126–37.

[59] *Stillwater Lumberman*, Jan. 12, 1877; *La Crosse County Historical Sketches*, series I (La Crosse, 1931), p. 67.

[60] Log Record, 1887, p. 1, Eastman, Bovey and Company, Minneapolis. These papers are in the possession of the De Laittre, Dixon Company, 1301 West Broadway, Minneapolis.

[61] *Anoka Union*, Apr. 3, 1884; *Mora Times*, Mar. 6, 1886.

them in a jumbled heap. There they were, ready by the rollway, await-ing the waters to be let loose by the warmth of spring.

Opinion varies as to the quality of the woodsmen in the pineries. The best are said to have been those in Minnesota in the pioneer period.[62] Obviously, the type changed as the industry grew larger. In the years from 1870 to 1890 there were loggers not of first rank; crude and un-disciplined, they gave to their craft a bad reputation. They were not all so, however. There were many who were sober and industrious and took pride in their work.[63] Competition was in their blood, and at the end of the day each man or group was credited on the bulletin board, a hewn block of wood, with the work accomplished during that day. The top-loaders, often called the "sky-men," competed to see who could put the best peak on the load; sawyers were ambitious to put the best and most logs on the skidway; teamsters tried to haul the big-gest load to the landing. Even the "road-monkey" liked to be told that his was the best piece of road. For the winner or winners "Peerless" tobacco or "snoose" was forthcoming; the gift was not much but the glory was great.

Those were the days when men stayed "upriver" from November until the logging season was over. But what did it net the workmen? Capital was at times so difficult to get that the worker in the woods was often not paid in cash but in checks payable the following autumn when the logs had arrived downriver. This meant a great loss to the lumberjacks, for they needed money the moment they were out of the woods and their checks could be cashed early only at a discount. Speculators bought the checks at a considerable discount and the lumber-jacks were the losers. Some lumbermen bought the checks and held them until fall. According to law the men's wages constituted a first lien on the logs, but the lien had to be filed before the first of May. This created a difficult situation, for logs were rarely down before the last of May and oftentimes much later. It would be of little advantage to a lumber-jack to file a lien on logs that were still in the woods or on the way down, for it would cost him more than the loss of his wages to bring the logs to market himself. In cases where checks could not be cashed until fall, no one could know whether such checks would be honored or not. But it was too late then to place a lien on the logs, for the first of May was long since past.[64]

Some logging companies issued their own money to lumberjacks —

[62] That is, Maine loggers, the first to come to Minnesota, were said to be the best.
[63] Orcutt, "The Minnesota Lumberjacks," *Minnesota History*, vol. vi, p. 3.
[64] Bartlett, "Lumbering in the Chippewa Valley," *Daily Telegram*, July 16, 1917 (a clip-ping in the Bartlett Collection, Minn. Hist. Soc.).

for example, Neil and Eustis, who logged at La Prairie, later called Neilsville, in the Grand Rapids region. Their money was called Neil scrip. It looked like the old shinplasters and was worth less and less to the lumberjack as he got farther away from his place of labor.[65] Some firms had definite arrangements for cashing their checks sixty days after the log was in the boom;[66] ten per cent was the discount if the checks were cashed earlier.[67] Most lumberjacks had to cash checks immediately, and the one place which charged them no discount was the saloon. There checks were accepted at face value.[68] Bovey and De Laittre, formerly Eastman, Bovey and Company, of Minneapolis, was one of a number of firms that used cash paper and paid promptly.[69] But there are instances on record where checks were cashed at a very heavy discount.[70]

Every lumberjack was given his board and shelter in camp. His board was usually of substantial quality and if its cost had been added into his wage his cash income would have been considerably higher. His living was a part of his pay, though it was not figured in the actual amount he received.

The foreman was, of course, the best-paid man in camp because he had the greatest responsibility. His was often an eighteen-hour day. Usually foremen were men of ability, and often they became lumbermen of considerable wealth. They were generally hired by the year; in 1870 their wages ranged from $70 to $100 a month.[71] Sometimes a foreman was responsible for several camps and was called a "walking boss." His wages varied with his responsibility. In the eighties, foremen's wages ran from $1200 to $1800 a year.[72]

Cooks and teamsters were in the upper hierarchy of the logging world and were paid accordingly. In 1870 cooks were getting $45 a month, while teamsters ranged from $40 to $70 a month.[73] In 1875 a teamster hauling with four horses was getting $55 to $60 a month.[74] In 1870 choppers were receiving $35 to $40 a month, while swampers and sawyers were working at $30; ordinary hands were getting $20 to $25.[75] Altogether, wages were unusually high in the woods at that

---

[65] Interview of the writer with George Galbreath, Aug. 16, 1932.
[66] Interview of the writer with O. D. Dahlin, June 5, 1932.
[67] *Ibid.*
[68] *Ibid.*
[69] Interview of the writer with George Galbreath, Aug. 16, 1932.
[70] Interview of the writer with William Tibbets, Aug. 16, 1932.
[71] McClung, *op. cit.*, p. 149.
[72] Interview of the writer with John E. Gilmore and William Tibbets, Ball Club, Minnesota, Aug. 16, 1932.
[73] McClung, *op. cit.*, p. 149.
[74] Interview of the writer with George Galbreath, Aug. 16, 1932.
[75] McClung, *op. cit.*, p. 149.

time. In 1873, when the pressure of the panic was felt in the log world, plenty of men offered to do the hard labor of the woods for $16 and $18 a month.[76]

Records were kept of the number of days a man worked, his wage, and his charge accounts at the camp store, which were subtracted from his wage when the season was over. A highly trained accountant would be aghast at the methods of bookkeeping, but a wielder of the cant-hook might also serve as the clerk, and his way of doing things was sometimes primitive, as the records reveal. Bergman and Company, who logged in the St. Croix country, had such accounts as the following:[77]

Emil Elmstrom
    Comins Workin the 23th day of Nov. 1881 at $15 a month

Alfred Benson
    Komens Worken Nov. 15, 1881. $19 per month.

14 days in Nov.	½ Pound Sm. tobacco	.25
27 days in Dec.	1 over shirt	1.50
26 days in January	1 lb. tobacco plug	.80
23-½ days in February	½ lb. smoking tobacco	.25
	1 Pair Overalls	.80
	1 Bottle Linnement	.35
	1 Papper envelopes	.08
	1 lb. Sm. tobacco	.50

Edving Johnson
    Commens Worken Nov. 15, 1881. $22 per month.

14 days in Nov.	½ lb. Sm. tobacco	.25
27 days in Dec.	1 shirt	1.40
26 days in January	1 lb. Sm. tobacco	.50
23 days in February	1 plug tobacco	.50
	1 pair overalls	.75
	½ pound Sm. tobacco	.40
	1 pound Plug tobacco	.80
	½ pound smoke tobacco	.25
	Postage Stamps	.06
	1 Bottle Yohn Linement	.35
	1 Plug tobacco	.50
	1 Bt. Y. Linement	.35
	1 Plug Tobacco	.50
	½ lb. Sm. tobacco	.25

Men left camp after a hard winter of work with little to show for it. One Andrew Olson, working in a camp belonging to Bergman and

[76] *Minneapolis Tribune*, Nov. 12, 1873, p. 4.
[77] Bergman and Company, Camp Book, Winter 1881–82, pp. 52–53, in Walker, Judd and Veazie Papers, Minn. Hist. Soc.

Company, worked 104 days; he earned $112, but his camp bill was $18.45, netting him $93.55. Another man, C. H. Peterson by name, worked 98½ days; his camp bill was $10.38, which, subtracted from the $90.02 he had earned, left him $79.44. Still another man worked 95½ days, earning $66.11; after the deduction of his camp bill of $12.36 he had $53.75 when he left the woods.[78] In the winter of 1887–88 one Tom Anthony worked for Abraham Johnson, a logger on the St. Croix, from November 16 to March 31. For his services he received $124.90 and his camp bill was $32.95 — among other things, he had purchased homemade socks at $1.20 and a blanket jacket at $3.50; he was given his net wage of $91.85 in what lumberjacks called "a bill of time," payable August 15, 1888.[79] Abraham Johnson paid his cook, one A. Nelson, $35 per month during the winter of 1887–88; his teamster, John Dalin, received $40 a month; Peter Eger, who did common labor in the camp, earned $12 a month. Johnson's scale of wages ranged from $12 to $40, between $20 and $26 being the most common sum.[80]

To eke out his living the lumberjack worked in the sawmills in summer, and his total average earnings, both in mill and in camp, for 9.9 months in 1889 were $474.43. This sum included the cost of board furnished in the lumber camp in the winter and, as an average wage payment, did not represent the actual money paid the worker.[81] In the winter of 1889–90 the average wage for the logger in Minnesota's forests was $1.86 a day. The foreman received the highest wage, $2.40 a day; the cook was paid $2.00 a day; while the swamper, as usual, received the lowest wage of $1.25 a day.[82]

Sam Simpson of the logging firm of Simpson and Dwyer, one of the largest in Minnesota, operating in the Grand Rapids country, knew lumberjacks at their best and at their worst. He said the lumberjack was "the best man and the damnedest fool who ever worked for wages." [83]

Logging companies, however, had to meet rising costs. Stumpage in the 1880s was growing increasingly expensive, cattle and horses were higher in price, foodstuffs generally were higher, and labor was growing more expensive. Even in 1875 Isaac Staples, an efficient logger in Minnesota, found that it cost him $1.50 per thousand feet to "bank" timber, and that winter his crews banked over twelve million feet.[84] Since

[78] *Ibid.*, pp. 10, 14, 16.
[79] Abraham Johnson Papers, 1863–1900, vol. 13. These papers are in the possession of the Minnesota Historical Society.
[80] *Ibid.*
[81] *Report of the Minnesota Bureau of Labor Statistics*, 1889–90, p. 303.
[82] *Ibid.*, p. 336.
[83] *Grand Rapids Herald Review*, Sept. 19, 1934 (anniversary edition), p. 4.
[84] *Stillwater Lumberman*, Apr. 29, 1875.

Staples' timber had been banked for 85 cents per thousand feet the previous year, the $1.50 represented a considerable increase.[85] In 1880 loggers found that it cost $2.00 more per thousand feet to deliver logs in the boom than it had cost the previous season.[86] So with millions of feet of logs finding their way out of the forest at an additional cost of $2.00 per thousand feet, it is clear that a greatly increased capital was needed in the operation of the industry.

When the last log had been placed on the landing, when the snow had melted and the ice had broken up, the lumberjack vanished until the next season. Equipped with spike-shod shoes (caulked boots), mackinaw, and peavey pole, he became a "river pig," ready to convey "vast flotillas" of logs to the saws downstream. On the banks of all the rivers, as well as on the shores of many lakes, the logs lay piled high waiting to ride the spring waters to the mills.

Careful planning and preparation were necessary before the spring drive began. Crews labored to clean the river of obstreperous rocks; brush along the riverbanks was cut and windfalls were removed; grading along the streams and the building up of dirt walls were necessary to keep the water in line. The smaller streams needed more attention, for the larger streams naturally had more water.

Water was stored to be let loose in a rush in order to give the logs a push. On the small rivers water was stored in swamps, sometimes only five miles apart. A wall built up with logs piled against it constituted the simple method of damming used at first. Without dams river-driving could not be done in many shallow streams except during floodtime. As the logging industry grew in size, dams were constructed in a more scientific way.

The method of driving logs on the lakes was somewhat different from that used in river-driving. The logs were placed on the frozen ice in the winter. A boom framework was placed around them, and when the ice melted the logs lay on the water. The boom of logs was then towed across the lake to whatever stream the logs were to be turned into. Horse headworks provided the power which pushed the logs. This was a raft fitted with a windlass and a stall for two horses and a workroom for the men. Around the windlass was wound a heavy rope up to one thousand feet in length, and to this was attached a deep-sea anchor. A batteau carried the anchor out as far as the rope would go, and there the anchor was cast into the lake. Then the team hitched to the windlass was started, the rope dragged in, and the raft began to move. As the rope came in, a man sitting at the front of the raft coiled

[85] Ibid.
[86] Stillwater Messenger, Oct. 22, 1881.

it neatly for another "shot." This method of towing logs through the lakes is still in use in Rainy Lake, the only difference being in the power. Horses have been replaced by steam power, and today the headworks is called the "alligator."[87]

At first every company drove its own logs, but eventually driving companies were formed to handle all the logs on a river; this development made for efficiency and economy. Each firm paid according to the number of feet of its logs there were in the drive. Among the companies that became prominent in the business of driving were the Chippewa Log and Lumber Company, operating on the Chippewa River in Wisconsin, where Frederick Weyerhaeuser was the directing spirit; the St. Louis Drive and Improvement Company, which operated on the St. Louis River and its tributaries; and the Mississippi River Lumber Company, which drove logs from the regions north of Minneapolis through the Falls of St. Anthony, to be distributed to mills along the Mississippi south of Minneapolis.

When all was ready for the spring drive, the rollway was broken. This was a dangerous and difficult operation — broken arms and legs were sometimes the result of breaking up the immense piles of logs.[88] The logs were rolled into the water and then guided into the main channel. That was at times the work of several days, depending upon the strength of the current. Men did not, however, break rollways until there was plenty of water. Sometimes this was in April, sometimes in May, even in August; there are instances where logs were "hung up" a whole year waiting for a "spring" freshet.[89]

The river-drivers who guided logs to their destination included every kind of human nature and every condition of man. Indians were often in the river crews; the thrills appealed to them. And the French Canadian was an expert on the river, for more than any other he could bear what the work entailed.

In no other phase of lumbering did men endure such hardships as in river-driving. An experienced lumberman remarked, "A man that can stand the log drive and not get sick need have no fears of death by sickness or exposure. Some accident must happen to him, or I think he will live on through ceaseless ages of eternity."[90] The drivers were

[87] The writer observed the method used on the lakes at Rainy Lake when one of the last booms of white pine logs was towed from the Minnesota side of the lake. The writer, a guest of the International Lumber Company, was invited to ride on the "alligator" and spent most of the day on the wanigan, observing the towing of logs.

[88] *Stillwater Messenger*, Apr. 19, 1878.

[89] Bovey-De Laittre of Minneapolis had this experience in 1889, when many of their logs never left the landing where they had been piled the previous winter. (Log Record, 1889, Bovey-De Laittre. These records are in the office of the De Laittre, Dixon Company, 1301 West Broadway, Minneapolis.)

[90] Notebook, p. 15, Henry E. Knapp Papers, Wisconsin Historical Society.

soaked to the skin most of the time; there was no chance to change into dry clothes, and the wet clothes dried on the body. One river pig had ten duckings the first day on the drive, in a stream with ice chunks all around. But he was still living long years afterward; river-driving seems to have had no ill effect on him.[91] Five dollars a day seems small compensation for men who had to plunge into ice-cold water at daylight and "sack" logs until dark.[92] This hard life explains the river pig's appearance — sunburned, with beard and long hair, slouch hat, red shirt, coarse trousers, and an ungainly gait. But he was "catty on his caulks"! If they were driving through treacherous parts or breaking a jam, drivers were on twenty-four-hour duty.[93] This may partly explain why they felt the need of plenty of good hot whiskey when they struck town.

Their work was a constant gamble with death. Little wonder that Joe Brault, one of the best drivers on the Upper Mississippi, crossed himself three times before he went through certain dams with logs.[94] Casualties among rivermen in the springtime of the year were of regular report in the newspapers. On April 24, 1870, the *Chippewa Falls Democrat* stated that three men were drowned and a number were seriously injured in a log jam where 50,000,000 feet were to be loosened. The same paper reported on April 13, 1871, that during the preceding week no fewer than five men had drowned on the drive. On April 15, 1871, the *Chippewa Herald* reported that five men on the drive had drowned that week and one had suffered a broken leg. Life was cheap, and many rode to death in "white water" while on the drive.

Three crews usually guided the logs on their way. One crew was in the vanguard; they were known as the driving crew and were spread along the streams for ten or fifteen miles. Everywhere they were urging the logs along, keeping them out of shoal water, steering them away from blind inlets, and keeping them in mainstream.[95]

Next in line came the jam crew, whose business it was to see that the river did not jam full of logs, to see that channels were kept open so the logs could float down. Miles of logs sometimes filled a river from bank to bank, and at rapids or cascades these would sometimes form terrific jams. Log jams were dangerous. They meant backed-up water, floods of destructive force when the jam was broken and the waters went rushing down. Or, if the waters escaped, mountains of logs were left

---

[91] Interview of the writer with Richard Swanson, Port Wing, Wisconsin, June 5, 1932. Swanson was a river-driver on the Big Fork River, a well-known logging stream in Minnesota which flows into the Rainy River.

[92] *Morrison County Democrat* (Little Falls), May 4, 1893.

[93] *American Lumberman*, Sept. 2, 1911, p. 25.

[94] Joe Brault, a French Canadian in the Grand Rapids country, was a very popular logger and driver, but life on the river did hold certain terrors for him.

[95] *American Lumberman*, Sept. 19, 1908, p. 87.

high and dry, sometimes stranded until another summer came around. In spring the St. Louis River has been known to be filled from bank to bank for five or six miles, with logs twenty or thirty feet deep.[96] Just such piles of logs caused log jams and made the life of the jam crew precarious.

In the history of logging in Minnesota, apparently no jam was more defiant than the one two miles above St. Croix Falls in 1886,[97] in which 150,000,000 feet of logs were tied in a knot. Two hundred men worked for six weeks to break it, but finally the key log was touched and the jam gave way. A jam was always an expensive affair, and one of such long duration greatly increased the cost of the drive. Since mills dependent on logs were forced to lie idle, it caused a tie-up in the whole industry.

Every jam crew had at least one man who knew how to break a jam; his job was to find the key log. The moment the peavey yanked at the vital spot, the whole mass began to tumble, and men moved with speed, for life was in the balance then. To move the key log was a daredevil job, and the man who did it was the hero of the crew. It is not strange that one old-timer in the woods, Otis W. Terpening, paid tribute to the jam breaker in verse: [98]

> Straight up from the edge of the river
> Where the tall whispering Hemlock still waves,
> In a cool shady nook of the forest
> I first saw the river Jacks grave
> In the shade of a Hemlock they laid him
> Where the sweet fern and maden hair bends.
>
> Just a circle of pebbles to mark it
> Placed there by the hands of friends,
> He died on the drive, so they told me
> Went under with peavy in hand,
> Still holding it tight when they found him
> Halfburied in water and sand.
>
> All day he'd worked like a madman
> On a wing jam that formed at the bend,
> All day unafraid he had faced it
> And was faceing it still at the end,
> No chance to escape when it started
> 'Twas swift as the thrush of a knife.

---

[96] *Ibid.,* Sept. 2, 1911, p. 25.

[97] Ruth T. Woodsworth, *Old Man of the Dalles* (Stillwater, Minnesota, 1924), p. 30; *Minneapolis Tribune,* June 20, 1886, p. 4.

[98] Otis W. Terpening, "The River Driver's Grave," Charles E. Brown Papers, Wisconsin Historical Society.

He had gambled, with death as the forfeit
And was paying the debt with his life,
Not for fame nor fortun he struggled
'Twas simple the part of the game,
But friends, if he wasent a hero
Then no one is worthy the name.

The monotonous work on the drive was that of the rear crew. Theirs was the task of finding every log which might have become lodged in the inlets, swamps, and sloughs along the way. It was their business to see that every stray log was put afloat, for none must be left behind. The rear crew, also called the sacking crew, worked in the water, and it was an inevitable part of their job to be soaked all the time. They were scattered at various places, sometimes thirty or forty miles behind the vanguard, the men often working alone. Rear crews had a batteau, a boat about thirty-five feet long, to carry them back and forth across the river when hunting logs.

There was always a boss driver, often called the "head push," who was in charge of the drive. His was a job of heavy responsibility. The extent of his authority depended upon the force of his personality — and at times of his fists. To be chosen boss was a commentary on both the character and the ability of the man selected.[99] Many a boss driver on the Mississippi or the St. Croix was an able man, but Sam Hunter, a driver on the Mississippi from the Grand Rapids country, seems to have been a favorite. He was considered "the best man on the river." It was said that on the first day out he pitched all his "green hands" into the river; then he ordered them to get busy and warm up. He was exacting of his men, and he himself was "strength incarnate." But an appreciative friend commented that "he never drowned anyone."[1]

Men on the drive were better paid than men in the woods. Two to five dollars a day plus board seems to have been a regular wage for rivermen throughout Minnesota's lumber history.[2] This totaled a fair amount of money for good-sized driving crews. In 1875, 12,000,000 feet of logs were guided by 50 men on the St. Croix.[3] In 1903, 150 men drove 60,000,000 feet of logs on the Mississippi.[4] Even in 1913, when lumbering had passed its prime in Minnesota, about 25,000 men were engaged in the work of driving logs to the mills.[5] The number of working days varied according to the weather. If there was sufficient rain, logs would

[99] Clifford F. Butcher, "One in Every Thousand Is a Millionaire in Merrill," *Milwaukee Journal*, Feb. 24, 1935, p. 11.
[1] *Grand Rapids Herald Review*, Feb. 8, 1934.
[2] McClung, *op. cit.*, p. 148; *Morrison County Democrat*, May 4, 1893.
[3] *Stillwater Lumberman*, Apr. 30, 1875.
[4] *Little Falls Daily Transcript*, Aug. 13, 1903.
[5] *North Woods*, vol. ii, Apr. 1913, p. 30.

drive easily; but if the river was low, driving was a slow job. The trip from Grand Rapids to Minneapolis, about 320 miles, took forty days in good weather.[6] In the summer of 1877 logs in the Mississippi which had been on the way for seventy-five days were not yet in the boom.[7] The St. Croix in 1877 had a drive of 35,000,000 feet of logs which were traveling at the rate of a mile a day.[8] That was slow movement and, therefore, an expensive process for the company that owned the logs or the firm that had contracted to drive them down; but it did mean more days of work for the crews.

A letter addressed to E. W. Durant of Stillwater by a man on the drive, who was keeping Durant informed of the movement of the logs, was published in the *Mississippi Valley Lumberman and Manufacturer* on April 26, 1878. It gives an interesting picture of the immense volume of logs to be moved and of some of the problems associated with the undertaking.

Alex Johnson commenced driving on Mud Creek today, with a full head on dam. He will come right along with 2,000,000. John Dudley is below, on Sand Creek, with 1,500,000 feet. One of Johnson's men broke an arm today, breaking landings. The Groundhouse drive is all in the flowage of the big dam, and they will sluice tomorrow and reach this point next Sunday. It consists of 2,000,000 feet for Hersey, Bean & Brown and 7,500,000 feet for C. N. Nelson; also less than a million feet for Isaac Staples.

Isaac Staples crew on Ann hoisted their gates today and sluiced what few they had above the dam commenced driving. They have everything in good order, with plenty of men and water, and expect to reach Snake in eight days. He has over 4,000,000 feet together with some of Wm. Elliott's last year's logs.

Everything on Knife is sluiced except the Mackey and Cates logs, on Upper Knife, which will hang up unless there is lots of rain. The Knife drive consists of 3,000,000 feet for H., B. & B., 700,000 feet of old logs for Fred Bean, 260,000 for Tuttle and some for Elliott.

On Snake, above Knife, we have Sinclair & Co., D. Tozer, Isaac Staples, Jordan & Matthews, and McCarty Bros., representing about 15,000,000 feet, with their rear at Hell Gate today. The O'Briens are driving today with fair water.

In my opinion everything below the mouth of Knife is dead sure — from 20,000,000 to 25,000,000 including a part of last year's hung up drive. I consider everything below Snake Dam reasonably sure without rain, while a very little rain would make it certain.

The class of logs cut this year is inferior to those of former years. Still there are some very fine logs in the drive.

[6] *Minneapolis Tribune*, May 5, 1889, p. 1.
[7] *Anoka Union*, June 30, 1877, p. 3.
[8] *Stillwater Messenger*, July 28, 1877.

The way of living on the drive was hard, too. In the rear of the drive always followed the wanigan, a sort of houseboat serving as a cook-shanty. If it was large enough, it served also as a bunkhouse; otherwise the men slept on the ground — not so pleasant in the springtime when the winter's frost was just leaving the ground. The wanigan was the domain of the cook, who had the responsible job of keeping the men well fed, because well-fed men were necessary for a successful drive. The cook was a busy man; he fed his men four times a day. Breakfast came at four-thirty in the morning; another meal was served at nine in the morning; two o'clock was lunchtime; and at seven in the evening came a substantial supper. Food was eaten in the open air unless the crew was small or the wanigan large.[9] Quite often the cook built a fire along the shore; the fire was a welcome sign to the river-driver because he knew then that food was being prepared. For the amateur a meal out-of-doors may have a romantic appeal, but for the river-driver, who day after day was wet and shivering when he ate, it had no charms.

To provide one meal for twenty-five men the lunch packer would carry fifty or more pounds of food and tinware. Beans, salt pork, ham, bread, oleomargarine, potatoes, beef stew, baking-powder biscuits, and always tea were the foodstuffs. As drivers became more demanding, cake, cookies, cornstarch pudding, and stewed raisins were added to their diet.[10] River pigs needed immense quantities of food. A crew of forty men consumed one hundred pounds of flour a day.[11] In 1873 one Philip Beal, when preparing for a spring drive on the St. Croix, ordered three barrels of pork, two barrels of beef, two kegs of butter, two kegs of lard, fifty pounds of tea, two hundred pounds of codfish, one barrel of sugar, and one-half barrel of dried apples.[12]

The fast rapids, the swirling waters, the log jams called for men of courage, prowess, and endurance. It was a "clear year" when all drives came down with neatness and dispatch.[13] The drive was the climax of the logging industry, and the climax of the drive was the arrival of the log in the boom. Then the river pigs were free — all too often to pursue hilariously their own ruin.

[9] The writer ate on a wanigan where the crew ate in relays because of lack of space. It was a hot summer day and the heat from the cook's stove made the wanigan an uncomfortable place.

[10] The sacker who worked alone carried his "nosebag" — so-called from the nosebag used in feeding horses — and ate his lunch alone.

[11] *American Lumberman*, Aug. 3, 1907, p. 59.

[12] Walker, Judd and Veazie Papers, Order Book, Feb. 24, 1873, Minnesota Historical Society.

[13] *Minneapolis Tribune*, July 20, 1872, p. 2.

CHAPTER XI

Life in the Woods

THE logger who worked in the heavy timber has been almost forgotten in Minnesota. He represents a phase of frontier life which can never return. This industrial pioneer lived in the deep forest where his life was simple, even elemental; his clothes were rough, often a strange combination of store clothes and fringed buckskins. His manner was rough too, though most often there was a "heart in him." Logging called for strong, daredevil men; there was no place in it for either invalids or shirkers — they were "shown the tote road." The man in the woods was usually strong and clear-eyed, with the vigorous, masculine charm characteristic of men who live "free lives" in the energizing air of a northern winter. This woodsman had respect for physical prowess; he was skillful; he was trustworthy and generous. He was not an angel, but the rip-roaring lumberjack we read about is not representative of the majority; most of the woodsmen are said to have been as sober and steady-going men as one would find in any occupation.[1]

Men in more civilized places have heaped derogatory criticism upon the man of the forest. They have pictured him as a mean tramp whom they could smell from a considerable distance. They may not have known that the woodsman had spent a season in the woods where his accommodations were exceedingly crude, where his clothes were rough, where his boss was hard. Sometimes this man, returning to civilization with a little money in his pocket, found that society, other than the saloon, offered him no place. Only the dance house of the lowest sort gave him a welcome.[2] The whole group ought not to be judged by the worst of its members, but all woodsmen, good or bad, have been placed in one class by those who did not know the problems of men living in such isolation. The man of the woods, moreover, lived in a world which did not accept the usual conventions; his world came to have a culture distinctly unique, which rose out of the environment in which he found himself.

[1] Cummings, "Lumbering in the Chippewa Valley," *Daily Telegram* (Eau Claire, Wis.), Apr. 21, 1916 (a clipping in the Bartlett Collection, Minn. Hist. Soc.).
[2] Thomas D. Whittles, *The Lumberjack Sky Pilot* (Chicago, 1908), p. 16.

With the changes that came to the lumber industry in the 1870s the workers in the woods increased in number. The shanty-boy from Maine or other New England states was joined in ever-increasing numbers by "Ole" from Norway or "Hans" from Sweden, and by the Canadians, French, and Scotch also. The crews were bigger; the shanty gave way to a camp; the whole organization became more complex. Then it was that the term *lumberjack* succeeded shanty-boy, pinery-boy, woodsman, and lumberman. The term was used more or less in the seventies; in the eighties it was used frequently; in the nineties it was the only term used.[3] Like the cowboy, the lumberjack is distinctly an American product — a product of the logging world that came into being in the great white pine forests of Michigan, Wisconsin, and Minnesota.

The lumberjack needed more room than the shanty-boy had in his day, so the one-room shanty, with its hovel for the oxen and horses, gave way to a good-sized camp. No longer was there merely a combined shelter and eating-room. Now, besides the men's living quarters, there was the office where "his Nibs," the foreman, had his headquarters. Since the office was also the wanigan, where men could buy the necessary supplies of mittens, socks, mackinaws, rubbers, tobacco, and painkiller, it was there the clerk, known as "commissary Jimmie," "pencil pusher," or "Johnny Inkslinger," held forth. The clerk not only sold supplies but also kept the record of the crew and the count of logs. He also sent any necessary reports to headquarters. His wanigan was often called the "first graft of the lumberjack." In the office lived also the scaler, who was in the upper caste of loggers; in the woods his implement was nicknamed the "robber stick." The hovel had given way to good-sized stables, and there was a granary, a shed where baled hay was kept. There were the blacksmith shop, the root houses, and the saw-filer's shack. Altogether the camp had taken on the appearance of a village in the wilderness.

The living quarters of the men no longer consisted of one room where men ate, slept, and lived the whole winter through. In its place was a good-sized camp of logs or lumber with perpendicular sides, warmly built and lighted with windows. The windows, however, were small in size, their usual size being two by two feet; a building generally had one such window in each end. Some camps had skylights which served the double purpose of better light and better ventilation. These new camps of the seventies housed from fifty to eighty men. They had a special room where the cooking and eating were done. Another part

[3] The *Stillwater Messenger* referred to the lumberman rather than to the lumberjack as late as Oct. 15, 1881. But the term *lumberjack* replaced all other terms applied to the worker in the woods as logging became a large industry employing all types of men.

of the same building served as the bunkhouse for the workmen. Between these two sections was a storeroom called the "dingle room."

The men's bunkhouse was the center of life during the long winter months. Men no longer slept on the floor, on boughs, or on a thin spreading of hay or straw. Bunks were built along the wall. Some camps had only a row of single bunks; some had one tier above the other; others had three tiers.[4] The number of bunks depended upon the size of the crew. Bunks were of two kinds, the "muzzle-loader" and the "side-loader," called "breech-loader" by the lumberjacks. The muzzle-loader was built from the side wall out into the center of the room; the side-loader was built along the side and in an arrangement not unlike the berths in a pullman car. The bunks were built of cedar if it could be had, because that was insurance against vermin. "Grey backs" or "crumbs" were almost constant companions of the men in the woods if no cedar could be procured.[5]

When the men arrived at camp, they filled their bunks with a bale of hay or straw. Later straw ticks came into use. A blanket was placed over the hay and straw, and another blanket covered the lumberjacks — two men always slept in one bunk. This bed certainly did not grow softer as the season passed. Neither sheets nor pillow cases were used. His turkey or tussock under his head was the only pillow the lumberjack had.

The other furnishings of the bunkhouse were few. In the center of the room a box stove had replaced the open fire of the shanty period. Long sticks of cordwood served as the fuel for such a stove. This room also had a water barrel, a wash-sink, and a table for writing, were the lumberjacks so inclined. Every bunkhouse had the famous deacon's bench, a thick-hewn slab placed in front of the bunks. Here the men sat, particularly on Saturday evening, stringing out long tales of prowess. Here they sat in the early morning, dressing their feet in preparation for a cold day. Here they sat in the evening and spat into the fire as they thought of the folks back in the settlement. The deacon's seat, because of court cases in which it was involved, had been recognized by the Supreme Court of Minnesota as a definite and legal term designating a distinct and exact location in camp.[6]

The bunkhouse was lighted by a small kerosene lamp. It gave scant light, but since the only reading done by most of the men was the letter from home or from the "best girl," this mattered little. A few feet below the roof were strung wires on which the men hung wet socks, mittens,

[4] *Minneapolis Tribune*, Apr. 29, 1876, p. 4.
[5] *Mississippi Valley Lumberman*, vol. xiv, Oct. 5, 1888, p. 4.
[6] *Trade News* (Stillwater and Bayport), June 27, 1930.

or clothing of any kind. The lumberjack often wore three or four pairs of woolen socks at a time; when at night each of the fifty men hung his stockings — wet from honest sweat or from the slush of the day — over the wire, the aroma can be imagined. Each lumberjack was assigned a definite place for his clothes on the wire. If his socks were hung in the wrong place once, it was all right, but if it happened again, the socks were gently placed on top of the stove.

The bull-cook presided over the men's quarters, replacing the shanty-boy of an earlier day. His job was to supply the wood and the water; he washed the roller towel; he washed the lamp chimney and filled the lamp with kerosene; he swept the floor and blew out the lights at night.[7] He was up and about early in the morning; it was his job to build the fires in the bunkhouse and in the office in time to heat those places properly before the men got up. He did not make the "beds," however; each lumberjack took care of his own.

On all nights except Saturday, lights were out at nine o'clock. "Morning always came about three o'clock," said one lumberjack with a groan,[8] and a loader wrote that for three weeks one winter he never saw the camp in daylight; he was deep in the woods before daylight and returned to camp after dark.[9] Four o'clock was the most common hour for the morning call. When the cookee put his lips to the five-foot tin horn, the sound on a still day could be heard for two miles.[10] That awful din was followed by another, the call of "Daylight and the swamp boys — roll out!" Sometimes the call was a mere "Roooooll out." Perhaps the most original of calls was the one used on the St. Croix: "Roll out, tumble out, any way to get out. This is the day to make the fortune."[11] It caused the sleeper "to tremble and start from the land of dreams to the land of pork and beans," wrote a would-be poet in 1875.[12]

As the lumberjacks assembled for breakfast, they were a quaint group in "costumes of many hues and patterns."[13] The scarlet, bright blue, or gay plaid mackinaw with white or red stockings reaching to the knees was the jack's gayest attire. Some, however, wore buckskins. The chief concern of any lumberjack was to be warmly dressed. He wore the heaviest of two-piece woolen underwear. The undershirts were like little

[7] F. E. Cummings, "Confession of a Camp Cook," *Daily Telegram* (Eau Claire, Wis.), Mar. 17, 1916 (a clipping in the Bartlett Collection, Minn. Hist. Soc.).
[8] Charles E. Brown Papers, Terpening to Brown, Mar. 1, 1931, Wis. Hist. Soc. Terpening had worked as a lumberjack in Michigan and in northern Wisconsin on the shores of Lake Superior.
[9] *Ibid.*
[10] *Minneapolis Tribune*, Feb. 20, 1875, p. 4.
[11] This call was used on the St. Croix in the 1880s according to O. D. Dahlin of Port Wing, Wisconsin, in an interview with the writer on June 5, 1932.
[12] *Minneapolis Tribune*, Feb. 20, 1875, p. 4.
[13] *Ibid.*, Mar. 12, 1873, p. 4.

coats. He wore a heavy outside shirt, usually gray, and heavy mackinaw pants. He wore three or four pairs of socks pulled up over his pants. Over all this he wore size forty-four overalls, "stagged" at the knees. The larrigan or boot pack, a kind of moccasin, was the usual shoe of the woodsman. With his heavy mackinaw, mittens, and a warm cap — often a Canadian muskrat cap with a tail or two at the back — he was ready to tackle a cold day. Thus clad, he stepped out of the bunkhouse and into the cook's domain for his breakfast.

The cook was second only to the foreman of the camp; his precinct no one dared to invade.[14] It was good business, too, to stand in well with the cook, for quite likely he had a bit of toddy stored somewhere. Changes had come also in the cook's domain. The bean hole and the open fire had gone and a big cookstove had replaced them. The kitchen was usually supplied with two long tables bordered with benches where the men sat and ate. There were also the cook's work table and a few shelves. The kitchen sink was hewn out of a pine log and had a drain running out the side of the building. A water barrel, camp kettles holding about four gallons each, bread pans ten by sixteen inches, and tin dishes completed the kitchen equipment.[15]

Every meal was a hearty one in the woods, and breakfast was no exception. Buckwheat pancakes, the traditional flapjack, were important in the lumberman's diet. A big griddle that covered the whole top of an eight-lid range was busy long before dawn to supply the demands of forty, fifty, or sixty woodsmen. There was always the traditional hash of potatoes and salt pork, and never did beans with blackstrap molasses fail to appear at breakfast. A tin full of fried cakes with black coffee sweetened with brown sugar was the final touch that put a woodsman right for a brisk forenoon in the woods. The fried cakes, similar to the present-day doughnut with a hole, were old stand-bys; "cold shuts" was the lumberjack's term for them, taken from an emergency link for mending a chain without welding. It was perhaps not entirely a complimentary name but a friendly one bestowed by one who dunked them three times a day. After breakfast the woodsman took a short pull at his pipe while waiting for the first glimmer of daylight.

Despite the husky breakfast, a long morning of tugging and pulling in the woods made him eager for the bull-cook's horn at noon. "Flaggins," or dinner in the woods, was usual if the men were a mile or more from camp. The "junk wagon," manned by the bull-cook and the cookee, commanded operations for this outdoor meal. At the "works"

[14] Ibid., Apr. 29, 1876, p. 4.
[15] McDonald, "Logging Equipment and Methods," Daily Telegram (Eau Claire, Wis.), Oct. 7, 1916 (a clipping in the Bartlett Collection, Minn. Hist. Soc.).

they built the fire and heated the tea. On bitter winter days eating in the open was unpleasant, for the beans froze on the tin plates. The lumberjacks' whiskers sometimes froze, too, though the men ate around a big open fire.

The day's work was considered done when the moon, called the "jobbers' sun," came up; [16] then the men rushed back to camp to be ready for their evening meal. In the cook's domain the long oilcloth-covered table was set with tin plates, tin basins, and iron-handled knives and forks. Each man had his regular place: a new lumberjack stood aside until the cook placed him. "If you were a new man and got in a hurry and went in and sat down in some Jack's place he would tap you on the shoulder, and say 'Pard, I guess you are in the wrong stall. Move out.' If you did it again look out for a hit on your ear. For a man was looked upon as a coward that would be driven from his place at the table." [17] Even company officials waited their turn when they visited camps. [18]

When the lumberjack was partaking of food, there was no talking; the room was still except for the "champing of jaws." The cook quelled any conversation, and it was an orderly place. The evening meal consisted of the usual strong fare of pork, salted beef, beans, potatoes, bread made in camp, tea, dried apple sauce, rice pudding, cookies, doughnuts, and black molasses cake. The cook was assisted in camp by the cookee, who washed the dishes, dried the "silver" by shaking it in a grain sack, kept the floor clean, and assisted the bull-cook with the "flaggins." The cookee was the butt of many a joke in camp and gave much fun to the lumberjacks.

A tremendous amount of food was consumed. In 1887 the Staples' camps in Minnesota had a food order for 18,000 pounds of beef, 104 barrels of pork, 200 barrels of flour, 9000 pounds of sugar, 1100 pounds of tea, 1700 pounds of dried apples, 1500 pounds of currants, 1400 pounds of prunes, 1000 pounds of raisins, 1900 pounds of tobacco, and 1000 turkeys and chickens. [19] Isaac Staples had his own farms, famous for model equipment, which furnished a large proportion of the supplies for his camps. [20] In 1876, 500 porkers were slaughtered on one of his farms near Stillwater. He also raised cattle in large numbers. In 1874 Knapp, Stout and Company of Menomonie ground 60,000 bushels of wheat, which was consumed in their camp; this was raised largely on

---

[16] The small jobbers were often not so systematic in their work as those who worked on a bigger scale. Lack of organization caused them to keep irregular hours, and their day was not ended until the moon was high — therefore, the "jobbers' sun."

[17] Charles E. Brown Papers, Terpening to Brown, Mar. 1, 1931.

[18] John Hynan, "Lumber Jack Lore," *Daily Telegram* (Eau Claire, Wis.), Jan. 25, 1918 (a clipping in the Bartlett Collection, Minn. Hist. Soc.).

[19] *Kanabec County Times*, Mar. 12, 1887.

[20] *Stillwater Lumberman*, Sept. 1, 1876.

six farms of almost 7000 acres of improved land belonging to them in Dunn County and Barron County, Wisconsin.[21]

A satisfactory cook made a satisfied crew. Men were not slow in "walking the cook" when there was occasion. In 1883 a logging crew struck because of food. On the day of the strike, however, ham, pork, beans, fresh beef, corned beef, codfish, good bread, rice, hominy, oatmeal, tea, coffee, butter, sugar, raisins, and currants had been served. George A. Brackett, the cook, had a reputation as a "caterer," but woodsmen were sensitive if the food was unsatisfactory. A strike meant a day wasted in the woods, and owners of camps realized that a well-fed workman was an asset to them.[22] So a winter in the woods made a roly-poly lumberjack.

Letters home contained references to the cook. "I must not forget to mention our chief of the kitchen, for his mince pies are par excellence," said one such letter.[23] Pies were common fare. The lumberjack's favorite pie was the "larrigan" or "shoe pac pie" — brown sugar was an important ingredient, and it seems to have been something like the modern butter-scotch pie. The lumberjack certainly had a sweet tooth. In the pioneer period molasses was the main sweet served, but after the 1870s brown sugar and corn syrup replaced it to a great extent. Syrup was bought in barrel quantities, for it was a necessity with the flapjacks. Oleomargarine was still commonly used in place of butter. Fresh vegetables were more generally used after 1870, largely because of improved facilities in transportation. Mashed potatoes and fresh beef came noticeably into use in the camps after 1870.[24] Coffee served in tin basins was the sustaining drink at noon and at night.

When the evening meal was over, the lumberjack found his way back to the deacon's seat; he lighted his pipe and smoked until the air was blue. There might be the usual talking-over of the day's events. If someone had made a "blob," meaning a bad mistake, the whole crew would pass opinion. But nine o'clock came soon and lights were out.

On Saturday night, however, life in the camp took on more hilarity. A stag dance would probably take place, or perchance a squaw dance.[25] Music — such music as there was, and one finds it compared to Camilla Urso and Ole Bull's — was furnished by a fiddler or by someone who

[21] *Stillwater Messenger,* Feb. 27, 1874.

[22] *Daily Minnesota Tribune* (Minneapolis), May 6, 1883, p. 6; R. L. McCormick to Laird, Norton Company, Aug. 7, Sept. 11, Dec. 1, 1882, in letters received from North Wisconsin Lumber Company in Laird, Norton Papers, Laird, Norton Company, Winona, Minn.

[23] *Minneapolis Tribune,* Feb. 20, 1875, p. 4.

[24] J. Holden, "Logging Camp Cooking in Pioneer Days," *Daily Telegram* (Eau Claire, Wis.), Dec. 9, 1916 (a clipping in the Bartlett Collection, Minn. Hist. Soc.).

[25] *Minneapolis Tribune,* Dec. 13, 1873.

played the mouth organ or the accordion.[26] Some spent the evening playing checkers or cribbage. Others would climb into the bunks and do a little gambling with cards, setting as the desired prize some Peerless chewing tobacco or a bit of snuff. Cards were not allowed in many camps, but the men found other means of amusement.

Three games familiar to anyone who ever found occupation in the woods were "Shuffle the Brogue," "Buy My Sheep," and "Hot Bottom." "Buy My Sheep" was a special game for the tenderfoot. No one was initiated into the fraternity of woodsmen until he had been blindfolded, lifted up, and dropped into a pan of water. "Shuffle the Brogue" was the lumberjack's vigorous way of playing the more genteel game of "Button, Button, Who's Got the Button." The lumberjacks, seated on the floor with knees up, passed the shoe so that the man in the center couldn't find it. Whenever the man who was "it" had his back turned, it was a part of the game to give him a husky blow with the shoe. It took a stout man to stand up under a weighty lumberjack's blow. "Hot Bottom" was another game that occasioned much mirth. A lumberjack, a beginner if one was present, would bend over and one of the others would hit him a mighty blow on his bottom. He then had to guess who had done it, and if he guessed wrong, he bent for another blow. Sometimes the lumberjack was almost laid out with blows. The jacks who knew the game fortified themselves with a board inside their pants.[27] These were games of which the lumberjack never grew tired.

And then there were tales to be told! The rugged jaws dropped in amazement as the stories of the evening unfolded. The jack had no small opinion of himself, and to hear him tell it, he could always outfight, outwrestle, outjump, and outboast any other braggart in the western hemisphere.[28] The tales of his fraternity were always based on exaggeration. Frank Vance, a genuine Minnesota lumberjack, was a prime exaggerator. He needed no Paul Bunyan to spur him on, for his own adventures were marvelous. Frank will tell his own story: [29]

It was on a stormy cold day when Frank went out to hunt a moose. He tracked one for most of the day and as evening was falling he killed the great animal. But darkness had come on. He did not know where he was. It was a bitter cold night. What was he to do? All of a sudden he had an inspiration. Taking his long, sharp knife he ripped the great moose open, took out the insides and crawled into the great cavity he had thus created. Here he slept in comfort. But he had figured without his host. He was

[26] *Ibid.*, Feb. 20, 1875, p. 4.
[27] Interview of the writer with John C. Daly, Port Wing, Wisconsin, June 6, 1932.
[28] Percy Homes Boynton, "Native Types of American Literature," *Illinois Libraries*, vol. xv (Springfield, Illinois), Oct. 1933, p. 91.
[29] L. A. Rossman, *Up in This Neck of the Woods* (Grand Rapids, Minn., 1933), pp. 7–8.

aroused by the howling of a great pack of timber wolves. They had scented and made for the carcass anticipating a great feast. They attacked the animal and Frank Vance found himself defenseless. But he determined to struggle for his life. Taking his long sharp knife he would wait until a big red-eyed wolf came close enough and jab him in the throat through a hole he had cut through the ribs. The other wolves would then attack their wounded brother and consume him. Time after time, Vance made fatal jabs. The noise ceased. Finally, the gray dawn came and Frank Vance emerged from his haven. He found that he was only a mile or so from his homestead. He went home for breakfast, but before leaving the scene of the night's vigil he counted the skulls of 30 wolves.

Men would match tales, trying to decide who had been the toughest lumberjack they had ever known, who the strongest. Who *was* the toughest, according to the standards of lumberjacks?

In Itasca County, where the great logging center of Grand Rapids was located, Sam Christie was by general acclaim considered the toughest man. Around his throat were scars left by those who had sought his destruction. Kelly, the cook at Hay Landing, had cut Christie's throat from ear to ear, but somehow he had missed the jugular vein. A second time Christie had his throat slashed, but he lived to tell that tale, too. Then Pig Eye Kelly took a careful aim at Christie with his rifle; the bullet entered Christie's body just above the heart and passed right through him. There was no doctor in Grand Rapids so "Old Man" Lewis, who claimed to know all about bullet wounds and surgery because he had served in the Civil War, took a look at Christie. He whittled an oak stick thin and smooth. This he put through the wound. Shortly, Christie was back again as strong and as thirsty as ever.[30]

And who had the biggest appetite? That was "Hungry Mike." Lumberjacks have hesitated to tell how much he ate at a regular meal for fear no one would believe them. Once, however, when he was convalescing from an attack of typhoid the doctor advised him "to go easy on the food." He begged the doctor for one sandwich. The doctor finally gave his consent. "Hungry Mike's" sandwich consisted of two loaves of bread and three pounds of codfish. There was neither a crumb of bread nor a bite of fish left when Mike was through.[31]

Traveling Dudley was a character well known to Minnesota woodsmen. He was born and grew up in Old Town, Maine. He was six feet, four inches tall and large in proportion. He had come to Minnesota from Maine by way of Williamsport, Pennsylvania, once a famous logging region. Many from Williamsport moved on westward to hew

[30] *Ibid.*, pp. 8–11.
[31] *Ibid.*, p. 12.

Minnesota's pine, but Dudley had not the means to travel by rail and it seemed likely he would remain where he was. In a few weeks, however, companions encountered Dudley in Minneapolis — he had walked all the way. Hence "Traveling" Dudley. For several years he made the round of every camp on the Mississippi and its branches. Lumberjacks like to tell how Traveling Dudley licked a whole crew of section men on the St. Paul and Duluth Railroad. The crew thought themselves too strong for Dudley and gave him a real dare. He licked them all at one time. The toughest one of the crew Dudley had down, holding the man's thumbs in his mouth. So firmly did he hold on that the crew had to pry Dudley's jaws open with a railroad spike before he let go. Such prowess on the part of a lumberjack became epic with the men of his craft.

The French Canadian was the rollicking storyteller in camp. Other lumberjacks kept silent when French Canadian tongues began to wag. They had an accent distinctly their own. Hardly ever could they read and less often did they know how to write, but they had vivid imaginations. The camp would rock with mirth when they held the floor. A favorite tale was about a raging forest fire set when a lumberjack threw a rope fastened to his canoe over the head of a moose swimming in the water. The moose immediately struck for the trail, racing through the forest with the canoe scraping over the rough ground. The lumberjack's whiskers whipped the trees, sparks flew, and fires started all along the trail. Rangers stopped the spread of the fire only when they were able to shoot through the rope and release the moose.[32]

The lumberjacks' humor was modeled after their lives. It was vigorous and robust, and there was nothing the lumberjacks liked more than to put fear in the tenderfoot who had just arrived in camp. Whole Saturday evenings were spent telling of the "fearsome creatures" of the woods in which they were working. There was the "agropelter." This animal, infuriated because its secret precinct had been invaded, was a terrible threat to any logger. From Maine to Oregon the lumberjack feared its uncanny stroke. The terrible animal found shelter in hollow trees, and anyone unfortunate enough to pass its hole was usually reported as killed by a falling limb. Only one human being, it was claimed, had ever escaped death after a blow from the agropelter. He was a Minnesota lumberjack, Big Ole Kittleson, a cruiser on the St. Croix. The agropelter dealt the blow, but the "limb was so punky" that it flew into bits on Big Ole's head. He got a good view of the vicious creature before it bounded into the woods.[33]

[32] J. F. Thompson of Duluth, Minnesota, told the writer this story on Aug. 13, 1932. Thompson was a clerk in the camps of Alger, Smith and Company of Duluth.

[33] William T. Cox, *Fearsome Creatures of the Lumberwoods* (Washington, 1910), p. 35.

The "Indians' Devil" was armed with terrible claws; it would tear the flesh of its victim into ribbons and suck his last drop of blood. Just at dusk the men could sometimes hear the Indians' Devil moaning in the woods, a sign that it was hungry for human blood. Then the tenderfoot was warned to be on his guard.

Another monster, the "High Behind," was, as the name implies, high in the behind. Human flesh was a necessary part of its food. It ran backward over its victim, whose body it had a way of hiding so that it was rarely ever found. If the body was found, the head, which to the High Behind was the most desirable part, was always gone. But there was always some "witness" in the crowd who had helped identify such a victim by some mark on his body. The effect of this tale was startling to the greenhorn.

Porcupines were found in most white pine regions of Minnesota and Wisconsin. Their paths led everywhere through the forest. The newcomer to the camp was told these were the tracks of some fearful animal and that, if its path was disturbed in any way, some awful calamity would befall the camp. The newcomer making swamping roads was cautiously advised to be sure they did not cross porcupine tracks. He took the advice seriously and would cut a road far out of the way to avoid disturbing the path of this fierce animal. The cat came out of the bag when the foreman called him to task, but the lumberjacks had a good laugh at his expense.

Another fierce animal said to be peculiar to northern Minnesota and western Wisconsin was the "hugag." It was in size like the moose. Its legs, however, were jointless. It had a long upper lip, and its head and neck were hairless. At night it rested by leaning against a tree, and when a human being came along, the hugag fell upon him. Very few of these monsters were ever killed, but a small one weighing 1800 pounds was found stuck in the mud in the Turtle River in Minnesota. Mike Flynn of Cass Lake knocked him in the head, and the animal fell over dead.[34]

Minnesota loggers know well the "millionaire teamster" who usually did not stay more than two weeks in a camp, but after one day he knew everybody and everybody knew him. It was he who on a trip to the tropics had sat on an alligator thinking it was a log. Lumberjacks listened spellbound as he spun his tales, and the "millionaire teamster" became a part of the Saturday night story long after he had taken to the "tote road." [35]

[34] Ibid., p. 37.
[35] Interview of the writer with J. F. Thompson, Aug. 13, 1932.

No Saturday night was without a good husky "sing," coming right from the hearts of these men. The songs, many of their own making, are epic in theme. They tell of honest love, toil, and trials, though they may be comic, heroic, or sentimental. Old lumberjacks in the 1930s were still singing these songs as though they had learned them only yesterday. One, who was eighty-eight years old, sang lustily a ditty he had learned while logging on the Kettle River when a strong young man. Somehow the old camp came back to life in his soul as he sang: [36]

> On the banks of Kettle River, among swamps and bogs,
> We've been busy all winter getting out logs.
> To stay all winter is our design,
> And the firm we work for is called O'Brien.
>
> There's Billy and George, well known to all,
> And that tough old veteran,
> Known all all round,
> Is the jolly old John O'Brien.
>
> Noble Wilson is our foreman; we all know him well.
> He runs through the woods; he curses like hell.
> Turns us out in the morning in rain or sunshine;
> And works us like blazes for Johnny O'Brien.
>
> He'll pull out his watch and look up to the sun,
> Saying, "Hurry up boys, let's get this work done.
> Pitch in there you sawyers and down with the pine.
> We'll all go to Hinckley when we're done with O'Brien."
>
> Charley Olson is our cook, boys, I'm telling no lies.
> He's a dandy at putting up puddings and pies.
> He'll fill you with grub till your bellies will shine;
> You never go hungry when working for O'Brien.
>
> Hurry up, boys, let's get done.
> Jobs nearly completed, we'll soon all be gone.
> In years to come we'll all bear in mind
> The years that we worked for Johnny O'Brien.

Another old logger convincingly sang: [37]

> One day there was a fire
> In a lodging house close by,

[36] This song was sung for the author by John Stewart of Port Wing, Wis., June 4, 1932. Stewart worked for O'Brien at Hinckley, Minnesota, in 1881. His age (eighty-eight) may explain some of the irregularities in his verse.

[37] This was sung by Richard Swanson, Port Wing, Wis., June 5, 1932. He said one of their crew had been killed in such a fire and the song commemorated this hero.

When from an upper story window
There came a piercing cry.
"Who'll save me," cried a lady's voice.
When quickly out there spun,
A man from out the crowd,
And bravely he declared,
"I'll save you lady.
You must wait,
Neither jump nor fall."
And in a minute more
He went struggling through the hall
With the fainting lady in his arms.
But from inhaling the smoke and fire.
He fell lifeless to the ground.

The same logger had another song; again the hero was one of his craft, but this time he was pitted against the "well-dressed dandy."

One night while I was walking
In the city of Duluth,
I came upon a party
In the midst of well-dressed youth.

They were making fun of a drunken man
Who was staggering along,
Looking neither to right nor left,
Doing nothing wrong.

Up stepped this well-dressed dandy,
Giving the drunken man a push.
It sent him to the gutter,
Which was filled with mud and slush.

He laid there moaning loudly,
With a badly broken arm,
Until a stranger came along
And he sounded the alarm.

"He is only a poor old lumberjack,"
The dandy coldly said,
"And for coming in my way tonight
I ought to smash his head."

The stranger quickly murmured,
"If you make another crack,
I'll land you where you just had now
This poor old lumberjack."

Another song which rang of the virtues of the woodsman was entitled "The Lumberjack." There are seven stanzas in this poem; the last two ran thus: [38]

> Then here's to the lumberjack, bad or good,
> Who toils in the depth of the dark green wood.
> Though rough of dress, of visage grim,
> Beneath it all there's a heart in him.

> At sight of misery or want's appeal,
> He'll give his all for the sufferer's weal,
> He's done his work well, the forest laid low.
> Soon, in story alone we'll the lumberjack know.

The "Shanty Boy's Alphabet" was another bit of rhyme that centered in the life of the lumberjack. Whether all lumberjacks knew the alphabet is questionable, but this poem no doubt was a factor in teaching it to them: [39]

THE SHANTY BOY'S ALPHABET

> A is for axes you very well know.
> And B is for boys who can use them also.
> C is for chopping we now do begin,
> And D is for danger we sometimes get in.

Chorus:

> So merry, so merry, so merry are we,
> No mortals on earth are as happy as we.

> E is for echoes, that thru the woods rang,
> And F is for foreman that headed our gang.
> G is for grindstone that swiftly goes round,
> And H is the handles so smoothly are worn.

> I is for iron that marketh the pine,
> And J is for jovel that's never behind.
> K is for keen edge our axes do keep,
> And L is for lice that keeps us from sleep.

> M is for moss that we stuff in our camp,
> And N is for needle that mendeth old pants.
> O is for owl that hoots at night,
> And P is for pine we always cut right.

> Q is for quarreling they do not allow,
> And R is for river our loggers do plow,

[38] This poem was reprinted from the *Bemidji Daily Pioneer* in *North Woods*, vol. iii, Mar. 1914, pp. 24–25.

[39] This rhyme was written by Otis W. Terpening and is found in the Charles E. Brown Papers.

S is for sleigh, so big and so strong,
And T is for teams that haul them along.

U is for use we put the logs to,
And V is the valley that we haul them through.
W is for winter, but now it is spring,
And I have sung all I am going to sing.

As we have noted, the flapjack was a favorite food of the men who developed husky appetites in the woods — even the "bean-hole bean" seems to have been in less favor. So important was the flapjack in the life of the lumberjack that he memorialized it: [40]

THE SONG OF THE FLAPJACK

Sing a song o' swampers,
A pocket full o' "snuss";
If you're a judge o' eatin,
To tell you ain't no use,
Of the stuff that sticks to ribs,
And glues up to your back.
The best thing i'jing,
For the fog and the damp,
Is the good ole loyal flapjack
When we eat our fill in camp.

Sing a song o' loggin,
Hit the trail for town;
There ain't no grub in cities
Goin' to hold you down.
Think o' syrup pilin' up
On golden yellow stack,
The crispy edges just like ledges,
Shinin' 'neath the lamp.
The good ole loyal flapjack
When we eat our fill in camp.

Sing a song o' pork and beans
(There's the stuff to fill),
But for a sort o' dessert
To give an extra frill,
See the steam come rising up,
Hear them lips all smack
Just the thing i'jing
For rheumatiz and cramp,
Is the good ole loyal flapjack,
When we eat our fill in camp.

[40] "The Song of the Flapjack" by C. A. L., *North Woods*, vol. iii, Dec. 1914, p. 12.

One of the old songs in which the strength of the lumberjack is proclaimed is "The Pokegama Bear," composed in camp in 1874 by Frank Hasty: [41]

THE POKEGAMA BEAR

Come all you good fellows who like to hear fun,
Come listen to me while I sing you a song;
Come listen to me while the truth I declare,
I am going to sing the Pokegama Bear.

One cold frosty morning, the winds they did blow,
We went to the woods our day's work to do,
Yes, into the woods we did quickly repair,
It was there that we met the Pokegama Bear!

One, Morris O'Hern — a bold Irish lad,
Went to build a fire all in a pine stub;
He rapped with his ax when he went there,
When out popped the monstrous Pokegama Bear!

With a roar like a Lion, O'Hern did swear,
Saying, "Run boys for God's sake, for I've found a bear!"
As out through the brush Jim Quinn did climb,
Saying, "To hell with your bear, kill your own porcupine!"

Into the swamp old bruin did go,
O'Hern and Hasty did quickly pursue,
As on through the brush those heroes did tear,
To capture or kill the Pokegama Bear.

Old Bruin got angry — for Hasty did steer!
He prepared to receive without dread or fear,
With his teeth firmly set and his ax in the air,
He slipped and fell on the Pokegama Bear.

Out on the road old bruin did go
He thought that was better than wading in snow,
Yet little he knew what awaited him there,
For fate was against the Pokegama Bear.

There was one, Mike McAlpine, of fame and renown,
Noted for foot racing on Canadian ground,
He ran up the road, raised his ax in the air,
And dealt the death blow to the Pokegama Bear.

When out to the camp old bruin was sent,
To skin him and dress him it was our intent,

[41] This story is peculiar to the Pokegama country in the Grand Rapids region of Minnesota. A copy of the poem was given the writer by Michael McAlpine of Grand Rapids on Aug. 15, 1932. McAlpine was the hero in the poem.

And we all agreed that each should have a share,
Of the oil that was in the Pokegama Bear.

Then it was taken by cook and it fried,
It was all very good it can't be denied,
It tasted like roast turkey, Bill Moneghan did swear,
As he feasted upon the Pokegama Bear.

Now my song is ended, I am going to drop my pen,
And Morris O'Hern, he got the bear skin;
Here is long life to you boys, and long growth to your hair,
Since it is greased with the oil of the Pokegama Bear.

Christmas was a hallowed day for lumberjacks. They celebrated it, however, in a way different from that back home. Christmas brought memories that were sacred to the men, and those of finer sensibilities were mindful of the crudeness of their surroundings on such a day. One lumberjack told the author of a Christmas Eve when he, then a seventeen-year-old lad who had just come from a home of refinement in Norway, was holding his first job in America in the pine woods near Bemidji, Minnesota. After the meal on that evening, always so festive at home, he went out into the deep forest calling his mother's name and weeping like a child.[42] Otis Terpening has written descriptively of Christmas in the lumber camp: [43]

CHRISTMAS IN CAMP

For two weeks before the great day things took on a brighter hue. At least they seemed to. The lads were better natured than usual. And why shouldent they be. Some had left their families and kiddies early in the fall, with the understanding that at Christmas they would all be united again, while others thought of the sweetheart back in the settlement. Then we had a kind with us that I just cant describe in this up to date language. But us Jacks called them lushers. A class that was shunned by the better class of lumberjacks. For the only thing seemly thought of getting out of life was a big drunk and a feed of ham and eggs. As their was no drinking allowed in Camp it was real hard on them, And they seem to hailed Cristmast as a time of getting out of their bondage. As the day drew near the real Cristmast Spirit seemed to pervail, And in the snatches of song that we would hear in the woodland during the day their was a real ring of joy in them, And in the voice of the Jacks on Cristmast morning as they wished one another Merry Christmas, And to hear one Jack say thanks Pal. I hope you live forever and I live to see you

[42] This lumberjack later suffered a leg injury in the pine woods. His leg was amputated by the late Dr. Edward Starr Judd of the Mayo Clinic. On the advice and encouragement of this doctor he entered high school; in time he received his degree as a Doctor of Philosophy in economics from one of our well-known American universities. He is today a teacher at a college in the Upper Mississippi Valley.

[43] Charles E. Brown Papers, Terpening to Brown, Oct. 23, 1931.

die. We seldom ever worked on Cristmast, But the day was spent in visiting darning our socks and mittens. While some spent their time in playing cards, And listing for the cheerie sound of the dinner horn, Saying come and eat, eat. The cook would always have something extry, and plenty of it.

DINNER

The old horn at last was heard, and was answered with a cheer, As it seemed to say come and eat, eat, Their was roast beef brown gravy, Good home made bread, Potatoes, Shiny tins heaped with golden rings called fried cakes And close to them a punkin pie baked in a ten inch tin about one and a half inch deep, And cut in four peaces, Any other day to a Jack it was one peace but today it was Cristmas, It only came once a year and help your self if you wanted a whole pie you was welcome, And rice pudding black with rasns, Drid prunes or the old fashon dried apple for sauce, Black coffee sweeten with brown sugar, And tins full of sweet cookies, They were white and had a raisen in the center of them. Did we eat I will say we did. I have eaten many a Cristmast dinner in camp. And some here on the farm, but the best was in camp. Just one more with a jolly crew, And I would be willing to say, Life is now complet. Let me go. After dinner the teamster took care of their teams. The choppers growned and wheted their axes, Us loaders sharpened our hooks, and got ready for the next day, About two the teamsters would come into the bunk shanty, And when the last ax was growned and the loading hooks placed in the corner of the camp. Their seem to always be a pause, Ever one sat still a thinking some of Father and Mother old and gray, While some thought of a sweet heart young and gay, But the silence would not last long. Ea 'r the sound of the old fiddle would be heard playing some rolecking old air. Before the tune would end their would be a bunch on the floor a clogging, That started things. And it was good by truble, From then untill supper time it was telling stories, singing dancing and doing tricks.

SUPPER

No difference in the bill of fair, Back to the bunk shanty and smoke until It was blue. Some would get out the old greasy deck of cards, and Climb into some Pals top bunk for a quite game of poker. While others took to the old time squear dances, The ladies had a grain sack tied around their waist so we could tell them from the gents, And wo to the one that stepped on a ladies toe. And did not apoligige, And do it quick. Or it would be one quick blow. And a jack would measure his leingth on the floor. Then it was the first two gents cross over and by the ladies stand, The second two cross and all join hands, And we had to have a jig ever set, I was first gent lead to the right and dance with all your might. And believe me when eight of us kids that wight about a hundred and eighty a peace all got to jiging it was real interesting. The fun continued late into the night, Just a few hours sleep. And we would hear that same old hurrah boys. Lets try it again, And we answered the call with a lighter heart. For it seemed that it would not be long until the drive would start. That was another big day in our lives.

In no way has the lumberjack been so distinctly individual as in his mode of expression. His vocabulary, like his stories, came out of the deep forest where his work was done, and his phrases are quite unintelligible to anyone not of his fraternity. His language is original; it is carefree and virile; it is certainly emphatic. The special woodsman's vocabulary numbers about three hundred words and is both picturesque and significant.[44]

The author sensed in her many interviews with old loggers that her language was not theirs. One old lumberjack, over eighty years of age, sputtered these queer terms easily with his Irish tongue; to the writer they seemed most formidable, for she could neither spell them nor say them. Patiently the old woodsman sat down in his garden (where he had been busy planting potatoes on a warm June morning) and explained many of the terms which were so new to the writer. The sun had swung over to the other side before we realized that half a day had slipped away during our conversation.

The Irish logger was a patient teacher. He added, however, "Well, you're having the same trouble as did a Sister who used to take care of our boys in the hospital at Duluth." A certain top-loader had had his leg crushed by a log. The nun inquired just how so serious an accident could have happened. The lumberjack replied: "Well, Sister, it happened this way. I dropped in at one of the Sawyer Goodman Company's camps and as I was the first gazebo who came down the pike and the push needed men, he put me to work skyhooking. The first thing the groundhog did was to send up a blue. I hollered at him to throw a Saginaw into her but he St. Croixed her instead. Then he gunned her and the result was I got my stem cracked."[45]

A few hours in camp will show how thoroughly unintelligible is this language to the layman, and a collection of the words will show us its strange tone:

Old *squint eye* finished early tonight. With the *pencil pusher* he was going to hear the *Sky Pilot,* a sort of *walkin' boss* for the *Sky Route Company.* The whole woods crew was taking its place on the *deacon seats* in front of the *muzzle-loaders.* The *scaler* came, too, but without his *swindle stick,* which would be a bit out of place in the sky pilot's presence. The *hashslinger,* the *slush-handler, swampers, choppers,* and *bull-punchers* came in their *India silks* and their *stags.* The *brass collar* happened in on this day, too. His coming heightened tension in the

[44] J. W. Clark, "Lumberjack Lingo," *American Speech,* vol. vii, Oct. 1931, p. 47; Stewart H. Holbrook, *Tall Timber* (New York, 1941), pp. 170–79.

[45] J. C. Daly of Port Wing, Wis., told this story in an interview with the writer on June 6, 1932. An almost identical tale is related by John E. Nelligan in "The Life of a Lumberman," *Wisconsin Magazine of History,* vol. xiii (Sept. 1929), p. 57.

camp. Just today he had sent several who had been advised to *change their gait* out on the *tote road*. But they were *jill-pokes* given to *kegging up*. The *timber wolf*, too, moved among the crowd, talking in an undertone with the *sky-loader* and the *ground-hog* about the number of feet logged from *section 37*. The *road-monkey* was in a bad way. He had directed a *Swedish snowstorm*. Not since a year ago last summer had they ever had a winter like this, he explained. The road-monkey was a mere *buckwheater* and he had not done his job. He had failed to *brush a road* and a sled traveling with a heavy load had a *gooseneck* broken. But a broken gooseneck was not so dangerous as a *widow-maker*.

As a crew gathered in the bunkhouse a few axmen were busy *whirling the rock*, while they cosily enjoyed their *Swedish condition powders*. They were all gathering around the *caboose*. The *glim* gave the necessary light, though here and there was a jack feebly trying to read a letter from his *prize log*. *Canada greys* hanging all about the room gave neither a perfect atmosphere nor perfect air. But the men had just partaken of *sinkers, swamp water, black strap, cold shuts, red horse, loggin berries*, and much else. So they were satisfied. Their *slats* were well padded, for their cook was no *stomach robber*. Altogether this camp was not *on the toboggan*, and the brass collar and the *kingpin* were well satisfied as they looked at the men taking a good pull at their pipes while waiting for the words of the sky pilot, with his "cow-hide boots and his mackinaw coat and his good flannel shirt opened up at the throat." Shortly they would *roll in*, tucked in their *shroud*, resting their heads on an old *turkey*, while they slept to be ready for the *bull-cook's* morning call. The next day came early, sometimes before the *jobbers-sun* was out of the way.

These words, foreign to the layman, are here explained: [46]

Squint eye: the man who filed saws in camp (he squinted as he filed his saws).
Pencil pusher: bookkeeper.
Sky Pilot: a preacher who walked from camp to camp.
Walkin' boss: a foreman who was in charge of a number of camps.
Sky Route: way to heaven.
Deacon seat: a wooden seat built in front of the sleeping bunks.
Muzzle-loader: a sleeping bunk reaching from the wall to the center of the room.
Scaler: the man who measured the number of board feet in every log.
Swindle stick: the scaler's measuring stick.
Hashslinger: the cook.

[46] The lumberjack terms which the writer has used have been collected largely through interviews. Some of these terms were found in the Charles E. Brown Papers in a collection made by E. H. Burnham and Otis Terpening.

Slush-handler: the cookee, a cook's assistant.

Swampers: the men who built roads and cut the underbrush in the woods — next to the bull cook, the poorest paid workers in the woods.

Choppers: the men who felled trees and cut them into logs.

Bull-punchers: the men who cared for the oxen.

India silks: overalls.

Stags: boots or shoes with tops cut off which served as bedroom slippers.

Brass collar: the man who owned the trees that were being cut, or the man for whom logs were being cut.

Change their gait: do differently.

Sent out on the tote road: ordered to leave camp.

Jill-pokes: lazy fellows.

Kegging up: getting drunk.

Timber wolf: a cruiser.

Sky-loader: loaded logs at the skidway and also on the load (he was always on top of the skidway and the load, his job was very precarious, and his labor was regarded as requiring much skill).

Ground-hog: sent the logs to the sky-loader.

Section 37: a fictitious section, for no American township has more than 36 sections (if a crew stole logs, it was always from section 37).

Road-monkey: he kept the log road in order.

Swedish snowstorm: taking snow out of the woods and placing it on bare spots in the road where the log sleds passed.

Buckwheater: a novice in lumbering.

Brush a road: fill holes in a road.

Gooseneck: a hook which holds the whipple trees in place.

Widow-maker: a certain type of branch on the tree which is very dangerous when the tree falls.

Whirling the rock: turning the grindstone while sharpening axes.

Swedish condition powders: snuff.

Caboose: a big stove in which cordwood was burned.

Glim: the lamp.

Prize log: wife, sweetheart — something the lumberjack prized very much.

Canada greys: very heavy woolen or felt stockings.

Sinkers: biscuits.

Swamp water: tea.

Black strap: molasses.

Cold shuts: doughnuts.

Red horse: salt beef.

Loggin berry: beans.

Slats: ribs.

Stomach robber: a poor cook.

On the toboggan: on the down grade, a poorly kept camp.

Kingpin: foreman of the camp.

Roll in: go to bed.

Shroud: bed blankets

Turkey: a sack that held all the possessions they had with them.
Bull-cook: the man who cleaned the bunkhouse.
Jobbers-sun: the moon.

As lumberjack rhymes and tales suggest so vividly, the logger worked side by side with danger. Man was a small creature in contrast to the monarch of the forest, and life in the woods was cheap. News from the woods almost always carried a note of death. Three men had been killed within an area of eight miles in the woods that winter, said the *Stillwater Messenger* of March 21, 1873; two of them had been killed while loading logs, one by a falling tree. Edward Lynch, working in the north woods in the winter of 1878, suffered a broken leg when a log rolled on him while he was skidding. Under present-day conditions such an accident would not be so serious, but this man's workshop was 150 miles from a railroad and farther still from a doctor. A journey of four days through rough woods brought Lynch to the railroad. When he finally reached the hospital his injured limb was black and extremely painful.[47] Even modern medicine would be challenged by such a condition.

The wild animals of the forest were also a danger to the woodsman. One Morris Powers, while taking lunch to the men in camp near Pine City in 1871, was attacked and devoured by wolves.[48] A teamster by the name of John Doar slipped while driving a six-horse team, and the front runner of a sled carrying 4000 feet of pine logs passed over him. The bones of the leg were completely crushed.[49] On a winter's day in 1881 Red Bill Sullivan, teamster with Walker, Judd and Veazie on the Yellow River, started for the landing with a big load hauled by three yoke of oxen. It was a bad hill; when the sled ran off the sand thrown on the road to prevent rapid descent, the team and sled were instantly out of control. The luckless driver was thrown under the oxen and then the sled ran over him. The newspaper reporting this accident said, "Sullivan will live." [50]

Sometimes camps were invaded by serious disease. Smallpox, for example, decimated Minnesota camps in the winter of 1882–83, particularly in the Grand Rapids region. The first cases of smallpox that year occurred at a ranch at Trout Lake kept by Michael McAlpine.[51] The cook became ill, and later some of his blankets were sent to a camp on Caldwell Brook in the same vicinity. Those blankets carried the disease, and, as the

[47] *Minneapolis Tribune,* Jan. 15, 1878, p. 4.
[48] *Stillwater Messenger,* Jan. 20, 1871.
[49] *Ibid.,* Mar. 5, 1881.
[50] *Ibid.,* Feb. 5, 1881.
[51] A ranch was a stopping place on the tote road.

dreadful infection scattered far and wide, the living could not bury the dead fast enough.[52] Men died by the hundreds from the disease, which was diagnosed as black smallpox. When the siege was over, the state of Minnesota burned the buildings where the smallpox had raged.

Prompted by such loss of life, several lumber firms brought doctors to vaccinate their men in camps. Dr. B. J. Merrill of Stillwater visited thirty camps, vaccinating on the average forty men at each camp.[53] A Dr. Russell of Grand Rapids has told how he gave the vaccine to several hundred men at one visit.[54]

Doctors of the logging areas tell us that when they were called into the woods to bandage a cracked head or to set a broken leg they usually traveled by team, horseback, or snowshoes. If the streams were open they would pilot their way by boat. A call to a camp fifty miles into the woods, said an old doctor at Grand Rapids, was not uncommon.[55] Usually the men in the woods were very healthy, and doctors who attended them say that in most cases they recovered easily, even from serious wounds.

Hospitals found their way rather early into the region where logging was big business, and they not uncommonly worked on the prepayment principle. The men in the woods would pay a given amount each month to the hospital, or they would buy a hospital ticket which assured them of care if it was needed. In 1880 any woodsman who paid twenty-five cents per month to the city hospital at Stillwater was entitled to "care, board and nursing" free of charge in case of sickness and disability.[56] Hospital tickets — called "life-savers" at camp — usually cost $5.00 each for a ticket covering six months, the time the men would be likely to spend in the woods or on the drive. Anyone who then found hospital care necessary would have it without any further charge. Hospitals were established at Stillwater, Bemidji, Duluth, Hibbing, Cass Lake, and other places in the deep woods, all concerned with the health of the lumberjack.

While doctors and hospitals cared for the physical needs of men, sky pilots sought to look after them spiritually. The lumberjack, far removed from civilization, became a concern of those engaged in Christian work. The sky pilot helped the lumberjacks in an intelligent and practical way.[57] He would scold and beseech them; he would marry them to the kind of women they knew; he would bury them; he would send their money home to their families. Gamblers, saloon-keepers, and "purveyors of

[52] Interview of the writer with George Galbreath of Grand Rapids, Aug. 16, 1932.
[53] *Public Health*, vol. i (Red Wing, 1886), p. 79.
[54] "Medical Practice in Early Days," *Grand Rapids Herald Review* (40th anniversary edition), Sept. 19, 1934, p. 13.
[55] *Ibid.*
[56] *Stillwater Messenger*, Oct. 16, 1880.
[57] Norman Duncan, *Higgins, A Man's Christian* (New York, 1909).

low passion" offered the glad hand to the lumberjack while they plucked him clean of his winter earnings, but when he was thrown "dead drunk" into the "snake room," [58] it was the sky pilot who often protected him from having his pockets picked.

One of the best known sky pilots in Minnesota was Frank Higgins, who for twenty years carried on mission work in the remote forest among men who had large hearts but at times little will. [59] Frank Higgins won the affection of almost every lumberjack in the Minnesota woods, and he gave support to many a man. Of Irish descent and born in Toronto, Canada, Higgins spent much of his life in Minnesota. He is said to have done the big job of cleaning out Bemidji, a town with 62 saloons, "the worst town on the map." He kept the savings of many a lumberjack who feared he might "blow his stake" on a trip to town. Many a time he accompanied lumberjacks to Deer River, another bad place for woodsmen, in order to guard them from danger. [60]

Another like Frank Higgins was John W. Sornberger, who had come into the north woods in the 1880s as a cook. Sornberger was said to be a good lumberjack, and he could hold his own when strong fists were put to the test. But Sornberger "got religion," and in more recent years he has become the leading sky pilot in the north woods. With his knapsack on his back he made his way through the deep snow, walking at times three hundred miles to meet his appointments. He has been known to preach as many as thirty-eight times in a month. A bit of rhyme that he "spun out" himself tells us how completely work in the woods is his way of life: [61]

SORNBERGER'S RETURN FROM NEW YORK
(BY HIMSELF)

I'm back to the camps, back again with the boys,
    Away from the racket and horrible noise —
Where a man can stretch and take a full breath,
    And not be afraid of being cramped to death.

My glad rags are hung on the closet wall,
    The tooth-pick shoes are out in the hall;
The lemonade shirt is stored in the trunk,
    The necktie's discarded with the rest of that junk.

With my cow-hide boots and mackinaw coat,
    My good flannel shirt opened up at the throat;
I head up the trail with a smile on my face,
    (Yes, I smile when I think of that "hobble-skirt" pace).

[58] The room in a saloon or hotel into which a lumberjack was thrown when drunk.
[59] *Missionary Review of the World*, vol. xxviii (1915), p. 196.
[60] Whittles, *op. cit.*, pp. 19–20, 22.
[61] A copy of this poem was given to the writer by Mr. Sornberger himself.

I eat now in peace, no napkin bedecks me —
  I can drink from my saucer, no manners to check me —
I'm happy and cheerful as I tramp along
  Whistling a tune or singing a song.

The pines seem to bow and say, "John, old man,
  We're glad to see you back with us again."
And when I reach camp and throw down my pack,
  I march right off to the big cook shack.

Black coffee, some bread and meat in my hand,
  I feel once more like a natural man.
When the boys come in there's a hearty greeting,
  And they say: "We're glad you've come to give us a meeting.

"We're a mighty bad bunch, so don't be slow,
  For when you hit hard we like it, you know —
We're not like city folks that want cultured 'Amens'
  And demand that their preachers shall preach to please them.

"We want a preacher as bold as Peter — or bolder;
  One that will strike right out from the shoulder.
We want a sermon right from the heart;
  One that will help us to get a new start.

"We want a sermon that sure will soak in —
  A Gospel that sets a man free from his sin.
And sing the old hymns — they're all good enough,
  For we don't know the new 'high-brow' stuff.

"With E flats and minors and all kinds of notes
  With sound as if they had cramps in their throats,
When you can't understand a word that they sing.
  Now we don't want any of that kind of thing.

"So sing the old tunes and speak the words plain;
  The tunes of our boyhood, let us hear them again.
Sing about Jesus, God's only son —
  Sing about Jesus, the crucified one.

"Tell us of Jesus and all that it cost
  The Shepherd to save the sheep that were lost.
We'd rather hear that than the soft pedal stuff
  For men like us the Gospel's enough."

So the hymns are sung, and the sermon throughout
  Is a very plain one — of that there's no doubt —
"God bless you boys" — "Amen" and "Amen"
  And the preacher goes out into the night again.

Even in the earlier days the ministers had not been unmindful of the men in the woods. In 1873 the Reverend George L. Chase, rector of Holy Trinity Church in Minneapolis, made a trip into the pineries. He wrote of holding services at Princeton, on the "verge of the Pine woods" in that day. Crews came for many miles to attend these services, and Chase was heartened by the "warmth of welcome at the lumber camps." [62]

Many lumbermen were aware that the right environment gave stability to their camps. No single lumberman gave of his services more generously in that respect than did W. H. Laird of the Laird, Norton Company at Winona. Laird was an active churchman, associated with the Congregational church since his early manhood. He was at one time a member of the National Council of the Congregational Church and was also a member of the American Mission Board, a strong organization in that church. [63] He was a generous contributor to missions and to all phases of church work. [64] This interest of Laird's naturally extended to the logging camps.

He gave much time to the Young Men's Christian Association, particularly in helping to gather funds for its work with the men in the woods. He was supported in this interest by his two associates and cousins, James and Matthew Norton. Every year they contributed a substantial sum to the international work of the Young Men's Christian Association, and at home they contributed particularly to the special fund for the "woods work." [65]

Every year Laird wrote personal letters to lumber and logging companies exhorting them to contribute to the Y.M.C.A., which was giving the men "good reading matter in trying to interest them in living better and more manly lives." In one letter addressed to the Nelson-Tenney Lumber Company of Minneapolis he reminded the officials that they had given $50 in 1892–93 and asked if they would send a subscription again. He continued, "The money will be well expended and will be beneficial both to employees and the men employed." [66] In a letter addressed to C. A. Smith, a prominent Minneapolis lumberman, he said he had received Smith's contribution of $25 for the Y.M.C.A.'s woodsman's work. Usually, said Laird, Smith had contributed $50, and he added, "I will leave the matter open so that you will feel free to send the other $25." [67] Whether Smith responded as Laird had hoped we do

[62] *Minneapolis Tribune*, Mar. 12, 1873, p. 4.
[63] Laird, Norton Papers, Laird, Norton Company, Winona, Minn., private letters of W. H. Laird, vol. 9, W. H. Laird to President W. H. Sallmon, Carleton College, Northfield, Minn., Sept. 17, 1907.
[64] *Ibid.*, W. H. Laird to the Reverend Cornelius Patton, Boston, Mass., Aug. 16, 1907.
[65] *Ibid.*, W. H. Laird to F. B. Shipp, New York City, Sept. 2, 1907.
[66] *Ibid.*, vol. 4, W. H. Laird to Nelson-Tenney Company, Minneapolis, Jan. 9, 1895.
[67] *Ibid.*, W. H. Laird to C. A. Smith, Minneapolis, Jan. 15, 1895.

not know, but in December of that same year Laird wrote again asking
for funds for the same purpose. He said, "If I did not believe in the
importance of continued effort along lines, supported by facts, I would
not ask your cooperation." He stated that he hoped more camps could
shortly be reached by this work, and he ended, "I would be pleased to
have you kindly send check for the amount at your earliest convenience." [68]

In the year the panic struck, 1893, Laird wrote the Y.M.C.A. that
the lumbermen would guarantee payment of wages for at least one
worker in the woods, and he hoped they could provide funds for two. [69]
In the spring of that year he had forwarded to the state office of the
Y.M.C.A. the contributions for the work in the woods already made
by various concerns: [70]

C. A. Smith, Minneapolis	$ 50
F. Weyerhaeuser, St. Paul	50
W. Sauntry, Stillwater	50
Mitchell and McClure, Duluth	25
Pine Tree Lumber Company, Little Falls (a firm in which the Weyerhaeusers, Mussers, and the Laird, Norton Company were the stockholders)	50
St. Croix Lumber Company, Stillwater	25
Nelson-Tenney and Company, Minneapolis	50
Laird, Norton Company, Winona	150
Winona Lumber Company (a firm in which the Laird, Norton Company were the chief stockholders)	25

W. H. Laird also managed to secure half-fare permits for the railroad
travel of the missionaries in the woods. Particularly from the Northern
Pacific, which penetrated the pineland area more than any other railroad, did he secure such permits, which he said would help greatly "in
sustaining a good work." [71]

It is evident that Laird had a broad conception of the function of the
administrator in the lumber industry, including consideration for the well-
being of the men who worked in the forest. As is seen from these examples, he was not concerned with his own firm alone, but he had the whole
industry in mind. His broad activities were somewhat exceptional, though
the data above show that he was supported by many of the companies.
Lumberjacks treated with courtesy those who ministered to them, and

[68] Ibid., vol. 5, W. H. Laird to C. A. Smith, Minneapolis, Dec. 28, 1895.

[69] Ibid., vol. 4, W. H. Laird to William Frances, Minneapolis, Oct. 13, 1893.

[70] Ibid., W. H. Laird to H. D. Day, Minneapolis, Mar. 17, 1893.

[71] Ibid., W. H. Laird to J. W. Kendrick, general manager, Northern Pacific Railroad, St. Paul, Feb. 4, 1895.

the effect of the Christian work in the lumber camps was undoubtedly of great value.[72]

Many lumberjacks survived to tell in their old age of the daredevils they once had been when grappling with the giant white pine in Minnesota. In the fall of 1934 there was a gathering of lumberjacks at a festival in Stillwater. A registry of those present listed Martin Foley, ninety-one years of age, with a record of sixty-four years of service in the woods; Pat Connors, eighty-one years old, who had spent sixty-two winters in the woods; George Lammers, seventy-eighty years old, who had spent sixty-three years in logging; Bill Lividak, seventy-seven years old, with fifty winters in the woods to his credit; James R. Brennan, seventy-six, whose winters at logging numbered sixty-one; and James E. McGrath, seventy-four, who had spent fifty-six years with the logs. These were a few of the "older boys" who gathered on this occasion to live again the life of the past.[73]

[72] John W. Sornberger, *Does Home Mission Work Pay?* (Munger, Minnesota). This is a pamphlet sent to the writer by Sornberger in a letter of July 22, 1932.
[73] *Stillwater Daily Gazette*, Nov. 15–16, 1934.

CHAPTER XII

The Downriver Sawmills Are Stilled

IN THE preceding chapters we have described the rapid development in the lumber industry of the Upper Mississippi in the period from 1870 to to 1890. The lumber demands of the growing cities along the river and even more of the new settlements to the westward had produced an industry which cut immense forest areas, built important lumber towns, and brought rafting to the river. But this could not last; there was not enough forest to sustain such intense and widespread activity long. The industry now here kept moving on to virgin regions, and as it moved, the sawmills it left behind were stilled or turned to other sources of raw material.

St. Louis was the first city on the river to give up its position as a white pine market. Its supremacy had belonged to the days of water transportation; with the coming of railroads other cities could compete and, as we have seen, the river towns of Iowa, Wisconsin, and Minnesota became successful rivals of St. Louis for western trade.

Receipts and shipments of all commodities to St. Louis, to and from the Upper Mississippi, declined from 340,000 tons in 1870 to less than 70,000 in 1905.[1] It was within this period that white pine reached the height of its importance in the St. Louis market. But in 1888 the white pine arriving at St. Louis by river was 52,179,279 feet less than the amount received there in 1887. From then on, white pine never regained its place in St. Louis; the sales dropped a little each year.

Railroad competition was one factor in the decline of the white pine market at St. Louis, although St. Louis herself was not without aggressive railroads — in 1888, the very year of the exceptionally heavy reduction in white pine at St. Louis, 24,310 miles of railroad converged in that city.[2] Another reason for the decline of St. Louis as a white pine market was the growing scarcity of the commodity. Michigan's white pine, the choicest of the Lakes region, was nearly gone in 1888. The ax was hewing hard at Wisconsin's forests, only a little less so at Minnesota's. Scarcity of product raised the price. In the four years preceding 1888, the cost of white pine

---

[1] Harold U. Faulkner, *American Economic History* (New York, 1924), p. 610.
[2] *St. Louis Trade and Commerce*, 1888, p. 22.

stumpage had advanced in amounts varying from 50 to 125 per cent.[3] Northern men who saw the approaching end turned to other sources, to the timberlands of Louisiana, of Arkansas, of Mississippi, and of Alabama. They turned to the yellow pine.

As early as 1882 the St. Louis, Iron Mountain and Southern Railroad, which penetrated the yellow pine country, carried 15,851 cars of lumber from Arkansas to St. Louis.[4] Therefore, in 1882, while still in its heyday, white pine saw an approaching rival in the St. Louis market. Five years later the St. Louis, Iron Mountain and Southern Railroad brought to St. Louis 23,053 cars of lumber which, if reckoned at the usual 12,000 feet to a car, equaled 276,636,000 feet of yellow pine.[5] In 1895 the total receipt of lumber and logs by river was 97,723,742 feet; the railroads brought 703,452,000 feet. In 1896, of 56,773 cars of lumber unloaded in St. Louis, 32,184 cars arrived via the St. Louis, Iron Mountain and Southern. In that year the headquarters of the yellow pine industry was St. Louis,[6] and in 1897 that city was the largest lumber market for southern lumber in the whole United States.[7] By the turn of the century the white pine of the Lakes region had given place to the yellow pine of the South, as shown by Table 15.

TABLE 15. PERCENTAGE OF UNITED STATES LUMBER PRODUCED
BY THE LAKES REGION AND THE SOUTH, 1869–1928

	1869	1879	1889	1899	1909	1919	1928
South	10.1	13.8	20.3	31.7	44.9	46.6	40.9
Lakes Region	28.2	34.7	34.6	24.9	12.3	7.8	5.3

SOURCE: Faulkner, *American Economic History*, p. 565.

These developments were sufficient warning of the fate that was to overtake other saw-towns and lumber markets on the Mississippi — but only gradually and not in all places at the same time. The early nineties saw an unusual output by the Middle Mississippi mills, but before the turn of the century these mills would be giving Minneapolis little competition. Lumber life on the river, which would be passing by 1900, was still vigorous in the early nineties.

In 1891 thirty-eight mills below Minneapolis reported their cut. Clinton, Iowa, was the leader. In that year C. Lamb and Sons of Clinton made 77,646,092 feet of lumber, while W. J. Young and Sons of the same city made 57,742,200. Weyerhaeuser and Denkmann of Rock Island and Daven-

[3] *Ibid.*, 1887, p. 197.
[4] *Ibid.*, 1882, p. 213.
[5] *Ibid.*, 1887, p. 200, and 1899, p. 70.
[6] *Ibid.*, 1896, pp. 71–73.
[7] *Ibid.*, 1897, p. 58.

port had 46,000,000 feet ready for the market, while the John Paul Lumber Company of La Crosse cut 43,000,000 feet. In 1892 Clinton again led in production. W. J. Young and Sons were first in the race with 90,234,159 feet; the Lambs trailed them closely with 90,014,446 feet. Weyerhaeuser and Denkmann had increased their cut to 57,000,000 feet, while the Rock Island Lumber and Manufacturing Company produced 45,350,000. The John Paul Lumber Company of La Crosse came next with 43,000,000 feet;

TABLE 16. LUMBER MANUFACTURE ON THE UPPER MISSISSIPPI
FROM MINNEAPOLIS TO ST. LOUIS, 1894

Place	Lumber (in feet)	Shingles (in pieces)	Laths (in pieces)
Minneapolis	491,257,000	121,324,000	93,940,000
Hastings	2,750,000	2,000,000	1,000,000
Red Wing	8,059,000	3,147,000	1,300,000
Alma	900,000	1,000,000	150,000
Winona	119,500,000	53,000,000	38,550,000
Lansing	15,000,000	9,000,000	3,000,000
Prairie du Chien	12,500,000	10,000,000	2,500,000
Guttenberg	14,000,000	4,700,000	2,114,000
Cassville	1,000,000	900,000	240,000
Dubuque	51,650,000	17,550,000	7,280,000
Belleville	2,037,000	. . . .	1,076,000
Lyons	12,006,000	1,440,000	1,330,000
Clinton	101,662,000	11,239,000	13,500,000
Fulton	14,120,000	4,550,000	2,811,000
Moline	28,188,000	3,457,000	4,236,000
Davenport	50,500,000	7,300,000	9,100,000
Rock Island	84,500,000	17,174,000	21,970,000
Muscatine	56,000,000	11,000,000	17,000,000
Burlington	27,000,000	5,000,000	14,000,000
Fort Madison	16,000,000	12,720,000	4,800,000
Keokuk	10,000,000	5,000,000	2,000,000
Canton	4,700,000	4,521,000	2,029,000
Quincy	21,500,000	10,000,000	3,600,000
Hannibal	20,000,000	9,500,000	5,000,000
Total	1,164,829,000	325,522,000	252,526,000

SOURCE: *St. Louis Trade and Commerce*, 1894, p. 253.

the Laird, Norton Company and the Winona Lumber Company, both of Winona, the Standard Lumber Company of Dubuque, and Gardiner, Batchelder-Welles of Lyons each produced about 40,000,000 feet. Youmans Brothers and Hodgins of Winona fell in line with 38,000,000 feet, and C. L. Coleman of La Crosse furnished the market with 36,480,000 feet.[8] Table 16 gives the cut of individual Upper River towns in 1894.

In 1890 the St. Croix Boom sent out 452,360,890 feet of logs to the mills between Stillwater and St. Louis; so, fifty years after the scaling of the first logs in the St. Croix Boom, its record was made. Logs to the number of

[8] *Report of the Minneapolis Chamber of Commerce*, 1891, pp. 211–13, 231–32.

3,468,320 had furnished these 452,360,890 feet; but that was only a fraction of the 15,683,781,720 feet of logs which altogether have floated down the waters of the St. Croix.[9] It is estimated that one half these logs were sent down the Mississippi to be cut into lumber by mills along the way, while the other half were kept to be used in manufacture somewhere along the St. Croix.[10]

The following activities originating in Stillwater during three successive days in the season of 1891 illustrate the lumber life on the Mississippi. The Standard Lumber Company of Dubuque, Iowa, bought one log raft of 800,000 feet in the Stillwater market; the *Isaac Staples* left for Burlington, Iowa, carrying 700,000 feet of logs for the Cascade Lumber Company, and another raft started downstream with 1,000,000 feet of logs for the Lesure Lumber Company at Dubuque. At the same time, Tabor and Company of Keokuk purchased 1,000,000 feet of logs; the *Jennie Hayes* was bringing logs downstream for Knapp, Stout and Company, at Fort Madison, Iowa; the *Juniata* began its journey to Winona with a raft of logs for Laird, Norton; the *Robert Dodds* was bringing lumber to Schulenburg and Boeckeler at St. Louis; and the *Ben Hersey* was pushing a raft of lumber to the Hersey Lumber Company at Muscatine.[11] All of this in three days!

As the above paragraph indicates, shipments from Stillwater were heavy. During the 1891 season a total of 364 rafts of logs and lumber left Stillwater for downriver points. Sixty went to Winona, 42 to Dubuque, 38 to Clinton, 27 to Rock Island, 28 to Burlington, and 18 to Moline.[12] In the same year lumber was also being sent in barges downstream from Stillwater. A barge carried about 250,000 feet of lumber; though this was less than in a raft, the barge had the advantage that its lumber was kept clean and dry. S. E. Joy of St. Louis, a steady Stillwater customer, purchased the lumber "stuff" that was usually fed to the burner and made it into boxes and other serviceable products. He shipped by barge, but barges were never used so generally as rafts. In 1890 Joy sent 1,500,000 feet of lumber downstream by this method, eight such barges carrying the "stuff" from Stillwater. This method of shipping was eagerly watched by lumbermen.[13] In 1893 Musser and Sauntry of Stillwater sold 5,000,000 feet of logs in one week to Hahn Brothers of Muscatine, Iowa, and 1,000,000 feet of logs to the Canton Sawmill Company at Canton, Iowa. In that same week G. H.

[9] These figures pertaining to the St. Croix Boom have been worked out by A. D. Cooke, who for forty-four years has been associated with the Office of Surveyor. General of Logs of Minnesota. His figures are all based on the reports of the scalers of the St. Croix Boom and are all recorded in the Surveyor General's office in St. Paul.
[10] Hotchkiss, *History of Lumber and Forest Industry of Northwest*, p. 53.
[11] *Mississippi Valley Lumberman*, vol. xx, Oct. 30, 1891, p. 3.
[12] *Ibid.*, vol. xx, Nov. 27, 1891, p. 5.
[13] *Ibid.*, vol. xviii, Oct. 10, 1890, p. 4.

Atwood of Stillwater sent 3,500,000 feet of lumber to Hahn Brothers at Muscatine.[14]

Though lumber life on the river seemed very active, lumbermen sensed, as early as 1891, that the days were past when it would be possible to make large profits in lumber in the towns of the Middle Mississippi.[15]

The prairie had demanded lumber in ever increasing amounts since 1840, but by 1890 the frontier was almost gone. The public domain had been settled almost as far west as the ninety-eighth meridian; most of the available land having adequate rainfall for farming was recorded as belonging to some person. Population on the prairie would increase for some time yet, but the time of stability was in sight.

Also, it was growing more difficult to get the white pine; that which remained was some distance from the rivers, and no longer could a log be slid easily into the water to begin its journey downstream. And as logging moved into virgin areas farther north, that journey grew longer. These factors increased the cost of the mills' raw material. Yet, competing with the white pine in the market were cheaper grades of lumber coming from the South and the Far West, regions as yet unexploited and easy of access. But lumbermen in the white pine country did not give up easily; they used all their ingenuity to lessen their production costs. As we have seen, the downriver men improved their mills and were driven to more efficient methods before Minneapolis sawmill men realized the need for improvement.

The timber on the Chippewa and the St. Croix was passing fast, and lumbermen who had formerly secured logs from those rivers had to go farther away.[16] In 1887 W. T. Joyce of Clinton, Iowa, with others, joined H. C. Akeley in the establishment of the Itasca Lumber Company operating in Itasca County, Minnesota.[17] The logs made the long trip from Itasca County in northern Minnesota to Clinton and Lyons by way of the Mississippi. This was costly, but there was nothing else to do. David Joyce, the father of W. T. Joyce of Lyons, Iowa, was another well-established lumberman who sought logs in the very uppermost regions of the Mississippi, purchasing timber from T. B. Walker and H. C. Akeley.[18]

Other sawmill men on the Mississippi who had previously combined in purchasing large holdings in Wisconsin now turned to Minnesota for log stock. Immense holdings of timber, such as the lands of the Northern Pacific Railroad, the lands of the St. Anthony Lumber Company, and

[14] *Ibid.*, vol. xxiii, June 2, 1893, p. 6.
[15] *Ibid.*, vol. xx, Sept. 25, 1891, p. 2.
[16] *Ibid.*, vol. xxviii, Jan. 1, 1897, p. 1.
[17] Hotchkiss, *op. cit.*, p. 557.
[18] *Mississippi Valley Lumberman*, vol. xxiv, Jan. 5, 1894, p. 6.

others, passed into their hands. The organization which made these extensive purchases of timberland is often called the Weyerhaeuser Syndicate by the "press." Their purchases are discussed in greater detail in Chapter XIII. The St. Paul Boom, just below Mendota, also became the property of the sawmill men on the Mississippi. This boom was important to them in preparing their logs, which now came from northern Minnesota, for rafting to their mills below.

The St. Paul Boom had been opened in 1888 when downriver men began to be active in the white pine on the Mississippi above Minneapolis. From 1888 to 1913 it was a busy place. Any number of downriver men sought logs on the uppermost reaches of the Mississippi, and the St. Paul Boom became the place for rafting. It was never so busy as the St. Croix Boom, nor did it approach the activity of Beef Slough or West Newton, but during its rather short life a total of 1,709,062,520 feet was rafted to the mills below. Table 17 shows the number of feet of logs going through the St. Paul Boom for the mills downriver. In 1913 the St. Paul Boom ceased its active work.[19] By 1916 its job was finished, for there were no more logs.

TABLE 17. LOGS PASSING THROUGH THE ST. PAUL BOOM, 1888–1913

Year	Feet	Year	Feet
1888	6,268,300	1901	49,001,170
1889	23,137,590	1902	142,758,880
1890	14,832,490	1903	86,864,920
1891	3,621,370	1904	64,652,460
1892	18,249,060	1905	93,806,690
1893	20,068,650	1906	68,771,390
1894	20,143,460	1907	40,565,580
1895	41,855,120	1908	52,326,820
1896	55,916,150	1909	55,176,320
1897	70,843,640	1910	4,091,790
1898	60,334,990	1911	16,657,650
1899	72,438,830	1912	*
1900	89,570,070	1913	22,107,800

* No reports.
SOURCE: These figures were computed from the records of the Bill Book of the Surveyor of Logs of the Second Lumber District of Minnesota in the Office of the Surveyor of Logs of Minnesota at St. Paul.

Eventually the combination of adverse circumstances was too much for the downriver men. There were no more logs to be had at such prices as they could pay and still meet their competition. Then they were forced to close their mills — one by one.

Winona, so near a neighbor to Minneapolis, began losing her mills when in 1898 the well-known Youmans mill, which had been active since

[19] Blair, A Raft Pilot's Log, p. 34.

1857, closed its doors.[20] In the business of logging and of sawing logs into lumber Youmans Brothers' day was done; the mill was wrecked, the machinery sold.

In 1905 the Laird, Norton mill, too, closed its doors to logs — the Laird, Norton properties on the Chippewa and elsewhere in northern Wisconsin could yield no more logs. This well-established concern sought new fields of operation farther away but maintained their office in Winona. Even though the Winona mill had stopped, they sold lumber from other sources of supply where they had mills. They owned line yards which had to be supplied. So they continued in business in Winona, directing lumber to be sent from new places to their regular buyers. The Laird, Norton Company was associated with Weyerhaeuser in his undertaking in northern Minnesota and northern Wisconsin, and they became actively engaged with the Weyerhaeuser Timber Company in the Douglas fir in Washington. They were interested in the pine of Idaho, where they were associated with the Potlatch Lumber Company. They had their hands in southern pine, too, as a part of the Calcasieu Pine Company and of the Southland Pine Company. In 1907 the mill belonging to the Winona Lumber Company, a Laird, Norton organization, was also dismantled at Winona.[21]

At the end of 1907 only one mill was still operating in Winona, that of the Empire Lumber Company, in which the Horton family was prominent. Charles Horton, who had originally come from New York, had been paid for his labor in the Chippewa logging country back in early days by a raft of ten cribs of lumber and shingles. This was his initial capital, and with its increase he had in 1881 become a member of the Empire Lumber Company, which built its mill in 1887. By 1909 the whir of its saw, the last in Winona, was gone. The Empire Lumber Company, like the Laird, Norton Company, reached out to new areas of endeavor. They associated themselves with the Gulf Lumber Company of Fullerton, Louisiana, the Ingram Day Lumber Company of Lyman, Mississippi, the Louisiana Long Leaf Lumber Company of Fisher, Louisiana, the Clear Lake Lumber Company of Clear Lake, Washington, and the Rice Lake Lumber Company of Rice Lake, Wisconsin.[22]

This story of Winona's mills typifies what happened to mills in other towns as the more accessible timber gave out. For fifty-five years Musser of Muscatine, Iowa, had furnished lumber to the uplands of Iowa, but in 1905 his concern cut its last log. Clinton had the same experience,

[20] Interview of the writer with C. M. Youmans on May 2, 1934.

[21] Curtiss-Wedge, *History of Winona County*, pp. 183–84.

[22] *Ibid.*, p. 179; interview of the writer with Roscoe Horton, president of the Standard Lumber Company, Winona, Minn., May 3, 1934.

as did all the other mill towns bordering the Mississippi below Minneapolis.

With the swing into the twentieth century, it was predicted that the annual decline would be marked. The timber of the St. Croix, the Chippewa, and the Black was giving out. In 1900 the Chippewa production was less than half the amount produced ten years before.[23] The mills at La Crosse, which had always been listed separately as the Black River district, were producing so little that, in estimating totals, the production of those mills was thrown in with the "below Minneapolis" group. In 1897 La Crosse produced 25 per cent less lumber than in 1895, though its cut of 141,465,000 feet, even in 1897, was one of the highest on the Mississippi.[24] In busier days the Black River had sent 300,000,000 feet of logs on their way annually,[25] but in 1900 its yield was only 40,000,000 feet.[26] La Crosse, like Winona, had to seek other lines of business.

As the mills along the Mississippi stopped sawing, rafting also dwindled. For seventy-five years the rafting industry on the river had been prominent. It was estimated that 46,974,220,170 feet of logs, in addition to lumber, were transported on the Mississippi for downriver markets from 1837 to 1915.[27] The largest log raft of that period was sent down in 1896; it traveled from Lynville to Rock Island, and Captain O. E. McGinley was in charge of the steamer that towed it, the *F. C. A. Denkmann*. The raft was 270 feet wide and 1550 feet long, and it carried 2,250,000 feet of logs.[28] In 1901 Captain George Winans took downstream the largest lumber raft ever to travel the river. It ran from Stillwater to St. Louis. The steamer *Saturn* was his boat at the stern, while the bow was managed by the *Pathfinder*. The raft was sixteen strings wide, forty-four cribs long, and twenty-six courses deep; it was 278 feet wide and 1450 feet long, carrying in its hold 9,000,000 feet of lumber in addition to pickets and laths.[29]

Along one river after another the logs were exhausted. In 1876 the Wisconsin River, the first of the upper group to bring logs to the Mississippi, sent its last logs down. That was the beginning of the end of rafting. In 1897 the Black River had no more logs to carry. In 1905 the Chippewa had offered its last tribute of white pine to the Mississippi.

[23] *Report of the Minneapolis Chamber of Commerce*, 1900, pp. 129–32.
[24] *Mississippi Valley Lumberman*, vol. xxviii, Jan. 1, 1897, p. 10.
[25] *Ibid.*, Feb. 12, 1897, p. 1.
[26] Dopp, "Geographical Influences in the Development of Wisconsin," *Bulletin of the American Geographical Society*, vol. xlv, p. 742.
[27] Blair, *op. cit.*, p. 289.
[28] *Burlington Post* (Iowa), Nov. 1, 1930, p. 3.
[29] *Ibid.*

And on August 12, 1914, the old boommaster, Frank McGray, hitched the last of the millions of logs that passed through the St. Croix Boom.[30] Logs had begun trickling down the majestic St. Croix in 1837, and now lumber and log operations were about to close for all time in this grand old valley. The only evidence to prove that once it teemed with such life is found in the memories of a few early settlers who still recall the hum of the mills.

[30] Blair, *op. cit.,* p. 291.

CHAPTER XIII

The Lumber Industry in Minneapolis
Reaches Its Height, 1890–1905

BEFORE 1890 the white pine of Minnesota had found its market chiefly in the region to the west of the Mississippi. With the opening of that decade, however, dealers and consumers to the east of the Mississippi sought lumber in Minnesota. They had been the market for Michigan's white pine, but that was nearly exhausted now and could no longer meet the demand.

Michigan's market, Michigan's capital, and Michigan's lumbermen were being released to Minnesota: Akeley, Hall, Ducey, Shevlin — names of importance in the world of lumber — came to Minneapolis; others moved to Duluth. This was the second great relay of lumbermen to set themselves up at the Falls of St. Anthony. These Michigan men now established themselves alongside of Bovey-De Laittre, the Days, Washburn, and others from Maine, New Hampshire, and Vermont. The newcomers into Minnesota's lumber aristocracy were seeking blocks of timber having from 75,000,000 to 150,000,000 feet of lumber near streams or lakes. Stumpage rose in price when Michigan men began to work in Minnesota. They came largely from Saginaw and lower Michigan, and they sought mill sites with easy access to Buffalo and other eastern markets. In 1873 the Saginaw district had furnished 36 per cent of all the white pine of the Lake states; this had dwindled to 24 per cent in 1890 and was within five more years to fall to 16 per cent. At the same time the Wisconsin and Minnesota mills were gaining in output, marketing 48 per cent of the white pine of the Lake states in 1890 and 58 per cent in 1895.[1]

The men who had come from Maine and other New England states had laid the basis for the lumber industry in Minnesota, but the men from Michigan speeded it up, and under their direction Minneapolis became the primary white pine market of the world.

Among the lumbermen from Michigan H. C. Akeley, a native

[1] Spalding, *The White Pine*, p. 16.

Vermonter, was notable. He moved to Minnesota in 1887. It was said of him that he "said nothing but he sawed wood," which was undoubtedly true, for he set a speed in sawing in Minneapolis that was hard to equal. Loggers referred to his logs in the boom as Sitting Bull's, which was presumably a tribute to the solidity of the head of that company to which they belonged, for Sitting Bull was an Indian chief who did not give up readily.[2] This giant in lumber, whose operations had centered in Grand Haven and Muskegon, Michigan, first organized in Minnesota the Itasca Lumber Company with Hackley and Hume, Michigan operators, and W. T. Joyce of Lyons, Iowa, as stockholders. Their timber investments lay in Itasca County. In 1889 he organized the H. C. Akeley Lumber Company, capitalized at half a million dollars, with its sawmill in Minneapolis.[3]

In 1890 Akeley's mill startled Minneapolis with a cut of 50,500,000 feet.[4] Nothing like that had happened in Minneapolis before — no other mill in Minneapolis approached that cut in 1890. Akeley was showing them! At times he had forty acres of land in Minneapolis nearly full of lumber,[5] and he sometimes cut 315,000 feet in a day.[6] Akeley had retained his market to the east, and in 1888 he sold 23,000,000 feet in one sale to the S. K. Martin Company of Chicago. It was the largest single sale made in Minneapolis up to that time.

Another Michigan firm that took good root in Minnesota was the Hall-Ducey and Shevlin group. Thomas H. Shevlin had begun in lumber as a tally boy in New York state but had become an accomplished inspector. He had had experience in Albany, in Tonawanda, in Bay City, and in Chicago, and he came to Minnesota a full-fledged expert, with his father-in-law, S. C. Hall.[7] Hall's first interest was in pinelands. He had large timber tracts on the Upper Mississippi, and soon he formed the North Star Lumber Company with a mill in Minneapolis. Later Hall and Shevlin formed a company, and when Hall died in 1889 Shevlin became the mainstay of the concern. This mill became one of the largest in Minneapolis. E. L. Carpenter, who had come to Minneapolis from Clinton, Iowa, purchased Mrs. Hall's stock, and he and Shevlin moved northward with the pine until they crossed the line into Canada, where in 1911 they built twin mills at Fort Frances.[8]

[2] *Mississippi Valley Lumberman*, vol. xvii, Feb. 28, 1890, p. 2.
[3] Hotchkiss, *History of Lumber and Forest Industry of Northwest*, pp. 542, 545; *Mississippi Valley Lumberman*, vol xii, Oct. 7, 1887, p. 6.
[4] *Ibid.*, vol. xviii, Nov. 28, 1890, p. 6; *Report of the Minneapolis Chamber of Commerce, 1890*, p. 169.
[5] *Minneapolis Tribune*, Jan. 1, 1891, p. 5.
[6] *Mississippi Valley Lumberman*, vol. xviii, July 25, 1890, p. 7.
[7] *Canada Lumberman*, vol. xlviii, Dec. 1, 1928, pp. 95, 97, 101, 103.
[8] *Ibid.*

In 1888 this company cut 43,500,000 feet, the largest cut in Minneapolis that year; in 1890 their cut was one of the three largest in that city.[9]

Other men from Michigan settled down to make lumber in Minneapolis. Their capital and their methods helped Minneapolis to replace Chicago as a manufacturer and distributor of white pine. Minneapolis had taken Chicago's place in wheat, and now she was to replace Chicago as a source for white pine lumber. Already Minneapolis was considered the financial center of the western lumber trade.[10]

Another significant development of the 1890s was the concentration of timberland ownership in a few strong hands. Prominent in this development were Minneapolis men whose investments had assured their city of a log supply over a period of years. Thomas B. Walker of Minneapolis was referred to as "Pineland owner T. B. Walker."[11] Bovey-De Laittre, early owners of pineland in the north country, still had heavy holdings there, as did C. A. Smith and Company (the Pillsburys), N. P. Clarke and Company, the Days, and others. Next, the Michigan men assured themselves of timber. Akeley, Hall and Shevlin, Alger, Smith and Company, and Wright and Davis were a few of the Michigan firms which bought Minnesota timber in huge quantities. Ownership of standing timber was in itself becoming large-scale enterprise. Spurred on by the increasing price of timber [12] and the continuing demand for stumpage, Minnesota lumbering, which had begun as a scattered industry of small units, was thus advancing toward concentration of control by a few men and companies. In 1890 this development was greatly furthered when Frederick Weyerhaeuser put his hand to work in the Minneapolis district. He introduced strong organization and large capital to a degree not previously known there, and these have continued ever since.[13]

In the life of any industry one man often overshadows all the rest. In fur John Jacob Astor stood first; in steel it was Andrew Carnegie; in oil John D. Rockefeller; in sugar H. O. Havemeyer. In lumber it was Frederick Weyerhaeuser. Like John Jacob Astor, Weyerhaeuser was a native of Germany. He was born not far from Mainz on the Rhine in 1834. In 1852 he came to Erie, Pennsylvania, where he found employment in a brewery; but, not satisfied with that work, he continued westward. He secured work at the sawmill of Mead, Smith and Marsh in Rock Island and was soon sent by his employers to take charge

[9] *Report of the Minneapolis Chamber of Commerce*, 1888, p. 132; 1890, p. 169.

[10] *Mississippi Valley Lumberman*, vol. xix, Feb. 27, 1891, p. 2.

[11] *Ibid.*, vol. xxvii, Mar. 27, 1896, p. 2.

[12] U.S. Bureau of Corporations, *The Lumber Industry* (1913), pt. 1, pp. 38–39; *American Lumberman*, Nov. 12, 1910, p. 79.

[13] William B. Greely, *Some Public and Economic Aspects of the Lumber Industry* (Washington, 1917), p. 6.

of their yard at Coal Valley, Illinois. In the Panic of 1857 his employers failed, but through thrifty management Frederick Weyerhaeuser was able to take over the Coal Valley yard. In 1860 he and his brother-in-law, F. C. A. Denkmann, purchased, with an initial payment of $500, the sawmill at Rock Island in which he had first found employment. Denkmann was the first of Weyerhaeuser's many partners; together they formed the Rock Island Lumber and Manufacturing Company, which by 1871 controlled two sawmills in Rock Island.[14]

Frederick Weyerhaeuser, like his family after him, never sought publicity. He was quiet and retiring, a sensitive and serious man with a strong sense of duty. His energy was unflagging; his mind was imaginative and penetrating. His fortune was not made by financial manipulation or trading; it was made from foresight and judgment in planning and policy, careful management in private and business life, and an amazing understanding of men. In time most of the leading millmen on the Mississippi were a part of the Weyerhaeuser organization, and they always "mutually and fully" shared with him in the results attained.[15]

Weyerhaeuser's first investment beyond the two sawmills in Rock Island was made in 1864 in the timberlands of the Chippewa River, where his first logging operations were carried on. There he got his first intensive training in business, and when he left that region to venture elsewhere he already headed a large enterprise. We have seen how he took the lead in the formation of the Mississippi River Logging Company in 1870, a concern of lumbermen along the Mississippi who bought rich pine forests, logged them, and sent logs to their mills down the river, distributing logs to each member according to his stock. We have seen, too, how other concerns were formed in the Chippewa Valley under his direction. From the Chippewa River, Weyerhaeuser and his associates, who never deserted once they had enlisted with him, pushed northward over the years until they reached the upper boundaries of Wisconsin and, finally, of Minnesota. There they harvested the last white pine of the Lake states.

In 1881 Frederick Weyerhaeuser and his associates had established the Shell Lake Lumber Company at Shell Lake, Wisconsin. With him in this enterprise were F. C. A. Denkmann of Rock Island, Lamb and Sons of Clinton, W. H. Laird and the Nortons of Winona, and others. It is an interesting fact that Weyerhaeuser's associates were usually downriver men. In 1893 David Joyce, an established lumber-

[14] *American Lumberman*, Apr. 11, 1914, pp. 30–31; W. B. Hill and Louise L. Weyerhaeuser, *Frederick Weyerhaeuser, Pioneer Lumberman* (McGill Lithograph Company, 1940).

[15] Gilson G. Glasier, editor, *Autobiography of Roujet D. Marshall* (Madison, 1923), p. 302; *American Lumberman*, Apr. 11, 1914, pp. 30–31; Hotchkiss, *op. cit.*, p. 606.

man of Lyons, Iowa, became president of the Shell Lake Lumber Company and the Barronet Lumber Company, both in the same region of northwestern Wisconsin.[16] In 1887 Weyerhaeuser was manufacturing lumber at Rock Island in Illinois, at Chippewa Falls, Shell Lake, Barronet, Mason, and Hayward, all in Wisconsin, and at Knife Falls on the St. Louis River in Minnesota.[17]

In 1890 Weyerhaeuser and his associates purchased the land grant of the Northern Pacific in Minnesota. This meant the shifting of an enormous property to a group which would put to work at once immense capital, the purchase contract requiring immediate operations. The job, a big one, would absorb much labor and afford attractive contracts for machinery. This purchase made the interests of the Weyerhaeuser group in Minnesota so heavy that St. Paul now became the center of their operations.[18]

Weyerhaeuser and his group in 1892 purchased a part of the Wright and Davis holdings in northern Minnesota, and that same year the St. Paul and Duluth Railroad sold them 50,000,000 feet of stumpage for a cash price of $2.00 per thousand feet. By 1893 the extensive purchases of pineland by Weyerhaeuser and his associates was producing a rise in pineland prices in Minnesota.[19]

In that year, when the concentration of large holdings of pine in a few hands became very noticeable,[20] the so-called Weyerhaeuser syndicate purchased all the timber belonging to the St. Anthony Lumber Company, about 75,000 acres in northern Minnesota counties. This involved a transfer of $1,710,000. A cash payment of $427,500 was made, and notes of the various firms making the purchase were given for the balance. Numerous meetings and negotiations were necessary before the purchase of the St. Anthony holdings was finally accomplished; Frederick Weyerhaeuser journeyed to Winona to discuss it with his associates, W. H. Laird and the two Nortons. While the purchase was being negotiated, William Sauntry of this group urged careful consideration, saying, "We cannot get all the information we want in a deal of this magnitude in a hurry." It was a big assignment for the cruiser in charge of estimating the timber; he reported that he spent 114 days at the job.

[16] *Mississippi Valley Lumberman,* vol. xxiii, Nov. 24, 1893, p. 7.

[17] *Ibid.,* vol. xi, Apr. 22, 1887.

[18] *Ibid.,* vol. xviii, Oct. 17, 1890, p. 2.

[19] *Ibid.,* vol. xxiii, Feb. 3, 1893, p. 7. C. A. Weyerhaeuser to the Laird, Norton Company, June 4, 1892, in letters received from Pine Tree Lumber Company, Box 289, 1892; Drew Musser to Laird, Norton Company, May 11, 1893, in letters received from Pine Tree Lumber Company and Mississippi River Lumber Company, Box 318, 1893; William Sauntry to Laird, Norton Company, Oct. 22, 1892, in letters received concerning St. Croix Lands, Box 284, 1892, all in records of the Laird, Norton Company.

[20] *Mississippi Valley Lumberman,* vol. xxiii, Sept. 22, 1893, p. 2.

It was shortly after this transaction had taken place that the Weyerhaeuser interests formed the Mississippi River Lumber Company and incorporated it at Clinton, Iowa, with a capital of $1,500,000. Of this group Weyerhaeuser became president; A. Lamb of Clinton, vice-president; and Robert L. McCormick of Hayward, Wisconsin, secretary-treasurer. On the board of directors were W. J. Young, W. J. Young, Jr., C. H. Young, C. Lamb, A. Lamb, and L. Lamb — all of Clinton, Iowa; F. Weyerhaeuser of St. Paul; W. H. Laird, M. H. Norton, R. McBurnie, F. S. Bell, and H. H. Norton of Winona; and R. L. McCormick of Hayward, Wisconsin.[21]

In the spring of 1891 Weyerhaeuser had left his old Rock Island home to make St. Paul, Minnesota, his residence. On St. Paul's stately Summit Avenue he lived next to another important figure in the Northwest, James J. Hill. These men continued to work consistently, sometimes helping each other, each building a more and more complex organization.

Frederick Weyerhaeuser had able assistance in his four sons, each of whom assumed a place of responsibility in the lumber industry. The two oldest sons had learned the intricacies of business at Rock Island; from there each had been sent to direct a phase of the industry in some other locality. John Philip, the eldest, took his place with the Nebagamon Lumber Company at Lake Nebagamon in northwestern Wisconsin; shortly after 1900 he moved to Tacoma to take charge of the ever-increasing Weyerhaeuser interests on the West Coast. Charles Augustus, the second son, moved to Little Falls, in rich pinelands on the banks of the Mississippi north of St. Cloud, to direct as general manager the interests there of his father and his associates, the Mussers of Muscatine and Laird and the Nortons of Winona, in the Pine Tree Lumber Company. He later became president of the Potlatch Lumber Company in Idaho, but directed its affairs from St. Paul, where he made his home.

The two youngest sons were graduates of Yale University — the father had helped endow Yale's School of Forestry. Rudolph Michael, a Yale graduate in the class of 1891, became head of the Weyerhaeuser interests at Cloquet, Minnesota, later moving to St. Paul. Frederick Edward, a Yale graduate in 1896, spent a short time in his father's workshops in Warren, Arkansas, but most of his life was spent in St. Paul, as a directing overseer of the Weyerhaeuser interests.

The general offices of the Weyerhaeuser group were located in St. Paul, but Minneapolis, during the most productive age of its lumber

[21] *Ibid.*, vol. xxiii, Feb. 3, 1893, pp. 1–2, 7, and Sept. 29, 1893, pp. 1, 6. William Sauntry to Laird, Norton Company, Nov. 24, 1892, in letters received concerning St. Croix Lands, Box 284, 1892; Chauncey Lamb to William Sauntry, Dec. 1, 1893, in letters received from Pine Tree Lumber Company and Mississippi River Lumber Company, Box 318, 1893, all in records of the Laird, Norton Company.

industry, claimed Frederick Weyerhaeuser as a lumber manufacturer in the Northland mills. These mills he and his associates in the Mississippi River Lumber Company and in the Pine Tree Lumber Company purchased from the Backus-Brooks Lumber Company, which then became known as the Northland Pine Company. This plant was in 1905 one of the best equipped on the Mississippi River, with sawmills, planing mills, booms, docks, warehouses, stables, and thirty acres of land in Minneapolis. Five hundred men found employment there, and the working people of North Minneapolis were pleased with this transaction which gave promise of employment over a long period of time.[22] It was fitting that the mills of the greatest lumber producer in America should be the last to manufacture lumber in Minneapolis. The Northland mills sawed their last log in 1919, and this marked the end of the first and basic industry at the Falls of St. Anthony. Weyerhaeuser's ownership of large amounts of timber on the Mississippi north of Minneapolis had made possible the long life of his mills at Minneapolis.[23]

Frederick Weyerhaeuser and his associates operated mills at Little Falls, Cloquet, and Virginia, as well as in Minneapolis. All these mills were well equipped, and the large working force gave to Weyerhaeuser its loyalty and friendship. No lumber firm in the state had a record for steadier employment of its crews in winter and summer. The mills were well organized; from the superintendent down, there was a tone of efficiency. Weyerhaeuser's employees, like his business associates, believed in him.[24]

The last enterprise in Minnesota with which Weyerhaeuser was associated was the Virginia and Rainy Lake Company, in which he and his associates and Edward Hines were active.[25] But long before this company was formed, Weyerhaeuser had begun to prepare himself for the day when the white pine of the Lake states would be gone. As early as 1887, with his brother-in-law Denkmann and with Lamb of Clinton and Musser of Muscatine and others, Weyerhaeuser had begun operations on the Pacific Coast in Washington Territory.[26] In 1900 the Weyerhaeuser Timber Company, the greatest of all corporations in which Weyerhaeuser was interested, was organized. Frederick Weyerhaeuser was its president and W. H. Laird of Winona was its vice-president.[27] This concern, centering in the Far West, then held 900,000 acres in west-

[22] *Little Falls Daily Transcript,* Mar. 4, 1905.
[23] *Mississippi Valley Lumberman,* vol. xxiii, Feb. 3, 1893, pp. 1–2.
[24] *Little Falls Daily Transcript,* Mar. 6, 1903. Descriptions of the mills at Little Falls and of the Virginia mills are given on pages 353 and 400, below.
[25] See below, pp. 400–1.
[26] *Mississippi Valley Lumberman,* vol. xii, Sept. 2, 1887, p. 1.
[27] *Little Falls Daily Transcript,* July 1, 1902.

ern Washington. In 1914 the Weyerhaeuser group increased their holdings in Washington, and by that time they had also reached into Oregon.[28]

The Weyerhaeuser Timber Company was the second largest timber owner in the United States in 1914. Its only business was timber-holding; no lumber was sawed under its name. It included a number of subsidiary companies operating in the same part of the country.[29] In Idaho, Weyerhaeuser and his associates bought heavily of pine; this property has not yielded so well as the Washington timber, partly because the Panama Canal gave Washington lumber lower rates to market. The Weyerhaeuser group also had investments in the short-leaf and long-leaf pine sections of Louisiana, Arkansas, and Mississippi. But the southern investments seem not to have won the favor with Frederick Weyerhaeuser that the Pacific Coast investments did.

In 1902 Frederick Weyerhaeuser was president of twenty-one different companies.[30] His greatest interest was timber-holding — he let others tend his sawmills. As a man with heavy business interests he was drawn into many related fields, including railroading and banking. He was on the board of directors of the Chicago Great Western Railroad; he was interested in the Merchants National Bank of St. Paul, the Continental and Commercial National Bank of Chicago, the Third National Bank of St. Louis, and the First National Bank of Duluth.[31]

Weyerhaeuser died in California in 1914 and was buried at Rock Island, his old homestead. Today, about a hundred years after his birth, when the third generation of Weyerhaeusers in America is already established in the lumber business, the Weyerhaeuser empire bears little similarity to the old lumberyard at Coal Valley in Illinois. The work of Weyerhaeuser, like that of Rockefeller and Carnegie, stands today as a symbol of an age that is past, an age when powerful individualists of tremendous capacity could drive toward great fortunes by exploiting, with the help of an improving mechanical technique and an expanding market, rich virgin resources.

With an excellent location in relation to the timber and to the market and with strong men and capital in the business of making lumber, Minneapolis rose to undisputed leadership in the lumber industry of the Upper Mississippi in the 1890s. In the first year of the decade Minneapolis beat her former record, having a cut of 343,573,000 feet.[32] Wheat and corn prices were good; the price of corn was especially high that year, and Iowa, the great corn state, absorbed an enormous amount of lumber.

[28] *American Lumberman*, Apr. 11, 1914, pp. 30–31.
[29] U.S. Bureau of Corporations, *The Lumber Industry* (Jan. 29, 1913), pt. 1, pp. 14–15.
[30] *Little Falls Daily Transcript*, Feb. 19, 1902.
[31] *American Lumberman*, Apr. 11, 1914, pp. 30, 31.
[32] *Report of the Minneapolis Chamber of Commerce*, 1890, p. 169.

Kansas and Nebraska, too, were listed as very satisfactory markets for lumber.[33] In the sale of the product the weather played no small part in 1890. A long autumn before the hard winter set in gave farmers time to make repairs after they had finished the threshing and the fall plowing. The importance of this is shown in a letter written by a salesman to his firm: [34]

"Maybe you think the salesman hasn't been the cock of the walk this fall," says Ed Shevlin; and being one of them, Ed ought to know. The grocery drummers, dry goods drummers, boot and shoe men and hardware men haven't been in it. Why, November weather was made for us. People don't want boots and shoes when they can go bare-footed, and they won't stock up for the winter on groceries and clothes and stoves when the weather is so mildly ethereal that you think you are in Florida. But that is the kind of weather the farmers want for building, and after the crops were threshed they went to work as one man buying little dribs of lumber for repairing and erecting sheds and barns, etc. So the lumber salesman has always found a little order waiting for him when he struck the small town, and the promise of something better in the spring trade. Oh, we are going to get there next year. We have got the greatest lumber consuming country in the world out west here in proportion to the population, when the people have got the money to spend, and while they ain't all opulent just at present they are getting to the front by stages as it were.

In 1891 lumber was set for another big year. Mills were moving nearer the stump; that year thirteen mills were sawing lumber along the Mississippi to the north of Minneapolis.[35] But from a clear sky came the failure of the Barings, great British financiers. This seriously depressed the eastern market, and the lumber trade found itself confined largely to the territory west of the Mississippi. Fortunately an immense crop was harvested there that year; the wheat crop of 1891 was the largest raised in the Northwest up to that time and it was marketed at good prices.[36] The prosperity of the farmer meant good business for Minneapolis, the gateway to the prairies and plains, and, though the bad effects of the Baring failure interfered with sales, Minneapolis ended the year with a record cut: 447,713,252 feet. Minneapolis sold 90,000,000 feet more than in 1890.[37] It was making lumber at the rate of 18,000,000 feet a week, with a sale of 10,000,000 feet a week and shipments of about 100 carloads a day in the autumn of 1891.[38]

With the eastern market injured by the increasingly serious financial

[33] *Mississippi Valley Lumberman*, vol. xviii, Nov. 28, 1890, p. 7.

[34] *Ibid.*, Dec. 12, 1890, p. 2.

[35] *Report of the Minneapolis Chamber of Commerce*, 1891, p. 209.

[36] *Mississippi Valley Lumberman*, vol. xx, Sept. 4, 1891, p. 2; *Report of the Minneapolis Chamber of Commerce*, 1892, pp. 296–302.

[37] *Ibid.*, 1891, p. 206.

[38] *Mississippi Valley Lumberman*, vol. xx, Oct. 16, 1891, p. 7.

crisis, Minneapolis found that her security lay in the great farm lands of the Midland Empire, where the sales, though not large, were regular. The lumber producer of the Mississippi region realized that a prosperous agriculture was the best insurance for him. The railroads of Minneapolis, which ran into the prairie country, were carrying huge loads of lumber. Of the five with the largest loads in 1891, the Minneapolis and St. Louis carried 96,375,000 feet, while the Great Western carried the smallest load, 42,945,000 feet.

In 1892 the lumber cut of the whole Upper Mississippi was 4,380,314,565 feet, the largest in the region to that time.[39] At Little Falls, where the Weyerhaeusers had established themselves, 32,000,000 feet were cut that year, the largest amount produced by any single firm north of Minneapolis.[40] The downriver mills had then not yet begun their decline. In 1892 thirty-six mills were cutting lumber "below Minneapolis"; together they produced 931,806,305 feet, the largest cut in the history of the region. Stillwater had the leading cut in the St. Croix area; the George H. Atwood Company produced 32,260,000 feet there. Hinckley, in the St. Croix area on the St. Paul and Duluth Railroad, which is a quiet agricultural town today, made 31,690,000 feet.[41] Winona mills also were making records: the Laird, Norton Company and the Winona Lumber Company each produced 40,000,000 feet in 1892; Youmans Brothers and Hodgins had a cut of 38,000,000 feet; and the Empire Lumber Company was slightly in the rear with 28,000,000 feet. La Crosse producers were doing even better, the John Paul Lumber Company cutting 43,000,000 in 1892, and C. L. Coleman 36,480,000 feet. The Black River country, though not large, produced 240,678,500 feet that year.[42]

Farther down the river at Clinton, Iowa, the firms of Lamb and Sons and W. J. Young were each producing 90,000,000 feet. That was immense! No other mill in the West could equal it. Even Minneapolis, which was inch by inch laying claim to the position of lumber emporium of the Northwest, had as yet no single mill that could equal the output of either of those Clinton mills. At Rock Island and Davenport Denkmann and Weyerhaeuser were cutting 57,000,000 feet.

Supply could hardly keep pace with the vigorous demand that prevailed through the whole season of 1892. That year 505,000,000 more feet of lumber were cut in the Upper Mississippi than in 1891, but on the first of December manufacturers and jobbers found themselves with only 123,366,000 more feet on hand than in the previous year. Minneapolis was almost bare of lumber. In the Wisconsin Valley more than

[39] Report of the Minneapolis Chamber of Commerce, 1892, pp. 225–26.
[40] Ibid., p. 230.
[41] Ibid., p. 233.
[42] Ibid., p. 232.

two thirds of the large increased production had been disposed of, while the mills along the Omaha Railroad had sold more than they had made. The *Mississippi Valley Lumberman* said the "lumber business could hardly be in a more satisfactory condition than it is at the present time."[43] Phenomenal crops in Minnesota, in Iowa, in the Dakotas, and in Nebraska had brought money which was turned into lumber in 1892. Lumbermen generally in that year regarded their country trade as better than the city trade.[44]

Bovey-De Laittre had courted the business of the prairie from their earliest days and had continued to keep it; in the years from 1892 to 1895 they did business with at least a hundred towns in Iowa, all small prairie towns. These towns lay in good farming country where farmers recognized the value of good buildings and of keeping them in repair. About seventy-five towns in Minnesota were listed on the Bovey-De Laittre ledgers, mostly small towns surrounded by good farming country. St. Paul was listed, to be sure, but so were Good Thunder and Mountain Lake, not much more than depots with a lumberyard, but surrounded by the farms of orderly Germans and Mennonites who took pride in the soundness of their buildings. Bovey-De Laittre also furnished retail yards in Nebraska and the Dakotas with lumber. Though Chicago and several other large cities appear on their rolls, it is safe to conclude that they found security in a substantial agricultural section.[45] They were distinctly wholesalers and not retailers.

The lumbermen did have one complaint in 1892, particularly in the spring. The condition of the roads seemed to hinder the sale of lumber even more than usual that season. The good roads movement of the automobile period had not yet appeared, and the Midland Empire was still in the grip of dirt roads. Iowa, salesmen complained, had the worst roads. The rainy season caused idleness in the fields and so made a good time for mending and repairing on the farm, but impassable roads kept the farmer from going to town to purchase the necessary lumber.

So important were roads to lumbermen that they sent circulars into the country regions in an effort to find out exactly what the condition of the highways was. A firm of Rolfe, Iowa, upon receiving such a circular, returned the sheet liberally sprinkled with Iowa mud and containing the words, "Mud! Muddier!! Muddiest!!!"[46] An outstanding traveling representative for a Minneapolis firm, Harry B. Waite, wrote his firm: "Enclosed find order for four cars. Business is absolutely dead.

[43] *Mississippi Valley Lumberman*, vol. xxii, July 22, 1892, p. 7.
[44] *Ibid.*, July 15, 1892, p. 7.
[45] Lumber Markets, 1892 through 1895, Ledger I, De Laittre, Dixon Company, 1301 West Broadway, Minneapolis.
[46] *Mississippi Valley Lumberman*, vol. xxi, May 13, 1892, p. 2.

It has done nothing but rain for seventeen days. Sidetracks are full of lumber that cannot be hauled on account of mud, and farmers are getting discouraged. If things don't change I think some of this year's cut will be carried a good while." [47] But lumber had its compensation in the matter of rain, for bridges and railroads which were badly damaged by the spring floods needed repairs, and this became an important item in the lumber trade for a month or two of each year. [48]

Railroads were rushed with lumber for the West in 1892. The Chicago, Milwaukee and St. Paul carried 98,000,000 feet of lumber from Minneapolis. The Northwestern Railroad, which had a traffic arrangement with the Union Pacific at Sioux City, Iowa, carried 84,750,000 feet of lumber out of Minneapolis. And the reliable home road, the Minneapolis and St. Louis, carried away 51,000,000 feet that year. [49]

Lumber continued to serve as basic material for many subsidiary industries. The sash, door, and blind manufacture was becoming an increasingly important business in Minneapolis, and in 1892 its product was valued at $3,890,000. The output of the Minneapolis barrel industry in 1892 was valued at $1,700,000. That same year Minneapolis manufactured carpenters', plumbers', and builders' tools valued at $10,120,000; in these lumber was an important part. [50] Minneapolis factories that built and repaired railroad cars in that year did a business of $4,200,000; factories making furniture and household goods produced goods valued at $2,800,000; others made office fixtures and showcases valued at $455,000; and still others made wagons, carriages, and sleighs valued at $600,000. In 1890 Minneapolis had more industries than either Detroit or New Orleans and more manufacturing plants than Cleveland. Lumber was the magnet that drew these industries to the Minnesota city. [51]

But prosperous 1892 had dark clouds on the horizon. Outwardly the world seemed stable but in reality it was not so. Even in 1891 there had been a surprisingly large number of commercial failures. Foreign investors were liquidating their American holdings because of depression in Europe. The threat of free silver was driving gold into safekeeping. Overspeculation, inflated credit, and overinvestment of capital in risky enterprises foreshadowed disaster. The result was the Panic of 1893. Railroads went into receivership. Banks, state and national, closed their doors. Farm prices plunged to low levels. By the first of July the lumber business of the Upper Mississippi was caught in the whirl-

[47] *Ibid.*, May 27, 1892, p. 2.
[48] *Ibid.*, p. 6.
[49] *Report of the Minneapolis Chamber of Commerce*, 1892, pp. 247–74.
[50] *Ibid.*, pp. 291–95.
[51] *Ibid.*

wind. Lumber was a basic industry, and in any panic a basic industry is quick to suffer.

Members of the Mississippi Valley Lumbermen's Association quickly gathered and agreed to reduce their cut 25 per cent; they agreed further to close all mills by the twentieth of September.[52] The agreement was effectively enforced; mills closed on the date set and the cut was actually reduced 26 per cent.[53] A bad fire in Minneapolis destroyed several mills and much lumber, and this fact no doubt figured in the lowered cut.[54] There was a most noticeable falling-off in the making of shingles, owing partly to the panic but probably more to the sale of cedar shingles, which were slowly appearing in the market formerly held by white pine shingles.[55]

The lumber industry made no gains during the panic years, but it held its place surprisingly well. Table 18 gives the statistics of production, receipts, and shipments for Minneapolis from 1891 through 1896. The noticeable reduction in all three phases came in 1896.

TABLE 18. LUMBER STATISTICS FOR MINNEAPOLIS, 1891–1896

Year	Production (in feet)	Receipts (in feet)	Shipments (in feet)
1891	447,713,252	95,825,000	353,946,000
1892	488,724,624	129,675,000	397,875,000
1893	409,000,155	103,335,000	372,330,000
1894	491,256,793	101,205,000	324,945,000
1895	479,102,193	81,150,000	364,635,000
1896	307,179,000	68,020,000	277,980,000

SOURCE: *Report of the Minneapolis Chamber of Commerce*, 1895, p. 145, and 1900, p. 133.

The whole Upper Mississippi region had very much the same record. In 1894 its production totaled 3,876,624,000 feet, and this rose to 4,158,833,000 in 1895.[56] In 1896, however, 3,239,096,000 feet were cut, a reduction of almost a billion feet.[57] The increase of 1895 was partly the result of the famous Hinckley forest fire on the headwaters of the St. Croix. This made it necessary, at a time when an increase was not desirable, to log such portions as could be used before decay set in.[58] The Weyerhaeusers at Little Falls also increased their cut, as did several other mills north of Minneapolis. The Duluth district similarly had an

[52] *Mississippi Valley Lumberman*, vol. xxiii, Aug. 11, 1893, p. 4; *Report of the Minneapolis Chamber of Commerce*, 1893, pp. 200–1.
[53] *Ibid.*
[54] *Mississippi Valley Lumberman*, vol. xxiii, Aug. 18, 1893, pp. 1–2, 6.
[55] *Minneapolis Tribune*, Jan. 1, 1893, p. 12.
[56] *Report of the Minneapolis Chamber of Commerce*, 1895, pp. 138–39.
[57] *Ibid.*, 1896, pp. 116–17.
[58] A. E. Andrews, *Recollections of C. C. Andrews, 1829–1922* (Cleveland, 1928), p. 825.

increase in production that year. Lumbermen found themselves with sufficient surplus stock at the end of the year to give them concern.

Resolutely they attacked the problem and agreed at the beginning of the sawing season in 1896 to reduce the cut in order to absorb the surplus stock of 1895, which was 2,946,997,000 feet.[59] The volume of trade was encouraging, and curtailing the output might restore something of a balance. But matters over which the lumbermen had no control soon nullified the promise of better trade. The year 1896 was the heyday of the free silver agitation. The disruption of confidence in business which had come as a result of the panic was merely increased by the fear of free silver, the issue in the presidential election of that year. In placing orders for goods, businessmen tried to protect themselves by making acceptance dependent upon McKinley's election. Every kind of business felt the effects of insecurity, and it was not strange that the basic industry of lumber should touch bottom that year.[60] The cut was reduced as agreed upon, but trade fell behind, too, and demand and supply remained at odds. The decrease in production in most parts was 22.1 per cent, but in Minneapolis it was more than 25 per cent.[61]

Lumbermen, being Republicans, hoped the return of that party to power might change conditions. They were represented on important party committees. T. B. Walker was presidential elector at large from Minnesota on the Republican ticket; C. A. Smith, the copartner of the Pillsburys in lumber, was the presidential elector from the Minneapolis district; and James H. Stout of Knapp, Stout and Company, Company at Menomonie was a delegate to the Republican convention at St. Louis. Lumbermen assuredly had a stake in that election.[62]

But in 1897 lumber production revived. There was a rise in the price of agricultural staples in America, for the wheat crop had failed in India in 1896 and in 1897 there was a shortage of wheat in Europe. The increasing immigration, the additional gold supply, the Spanish-American War, and a more friendly attitude toward trusts, corporations, and big business generally, were all factors in clearing the air. The result was an industrial revival in which lumber was an active participant.

In the last six months of 1897 Minneapolis shipped twice the amount of lumber sent out during the first six months. Altogether in 1897 Minneapolis sent away 287,985,000 feet, an increase of at least 10,000,000 feet over shipments the previous year. Minneapolis itself used 14,324,000 feet more in 1897 than in 1896.[63] H. C. Akeley, the former Michigan

[59] *Report of the Minneapolis Chamber of Commerce*, 1896, pp. 117–20.
[60] *Minneapolis Tribune*, Jan. 1, 1897, p. 8.
[61] *Report of the Minneapolis Chamber of Commerce*, 1896, pp. 116–17.
[62] *Mississippi Valley Lumberman*, vol. xxviii, Mar. 27, 1896, p. 1.
[63] *Report of the Minneapolis Chamber of Commerce*, 1897, p. 126.

lumberman, established another record by cutting 80,464,000 feet in Minneapolis in 1897. E. W. Backus followed Akeley with a cut of 70,500,000. Thomas H. Shevlin and his partner, E. L. Carpenter, were third in line, with a production of 55,000,000 feet. C. A. Smith, whose silent partner was John S. Pillsbury, was fourth with 52,400,000 feet, which were used in supplying his many country yards.[64] In 1897 Minneapolis hit her stride again with a total cut of 460,348,000 feet.[65]

It was two years later that Minneapolis finally attained the position of the leading lumber market of the world.[66] Never before in the city's history had there been such production and such shipments. H. C. Akeley and C. A. Smith in 1899 each cut 108,000,000 feet, while E. W. Backus and his company were close competitors with 96,000,000 feet. Every company in Minneapolis seemed to be trying to surpass a previous record. A total of 594,373,000 feet was cut in Minneapolis in 1899, a hundred million feet more than in the preceding year. In spite of this increase, stock on hand at the end of the year was 25,000,000 feet less than in 1898.[67] The cut of 1899 contrasted strikingly with that of the seventies, which had played back and forth between 100 and 200 million, or even that of the eighties, which had ranged from 220 million to 343 million.

As Minneapolis increased her cut, so did the rest of the state. At the turn of the century Minnesota produced 2,314,720,000 feet of rough lumber, of which 2,148,032,000 feet was classed as white pine.[68] The whole west-of-Chicago district in 1900 produced 4,244,401,000 feet of lumber.[69] As the new century was coming in, Minnesota rose to third place among the states in the production of lumber and timber products.[70] In the organization of production Minnesota held a unique place. Of the four largest mills in the United States in 1900, Minnesota had three, two of which were in Minneapolis. These mills each produced more than 100,000,000 feet in a year, while eleven other mills in the state each made from 50,000,000 to 100,000,000 feet a year.[71]

The record year of 1899 saw Minneapolis sending 492,975,000 feet of lumber from its doors, though it received only 95,145,000 feet, less than

[64] *Mississippi Valley Lumberman*, vol. xxiii, Oct. 20, 1893, p. 6. C. A. Smith had come over from Sweden as a lad and had gained the goodwill of John S. Pillsbury, whose confidence he justified by his success in Minneapolis lumber milling.

[65] *Report of the Minneapolis Chamber of Commerce*, 1897, p. 131.

[66] *Ibid.*, 1899, pp. 129–32; *Minneapolis Tribune*, Jan. 1, 1899, p. 5.

[67] *Report of the Minneapolis Chamber of Commerce*, 1899, p. 135.

[68] *Special Reports of the Census Office: Manufactures*, pt. 2, 1905, p. 534. This figure varies slightly from the *U.S. Census, 1910*, vol. ix: *Manufactures*, p. 599; it also differs from the *Census, 1900*, vol. viii: *Manufactures*, pt. 2, p. 444.

[69] *Report of the Minneapolis Chamber of Commerce*, 1903, p. 143.

[70] *U.S. Census, 1900*, vol. vii: *Manufactures*, pt. 1, pp. clxxxiv–clxxxv; *Special Report of the Census Office: Manufactures*, pt. 3, *Selected Industries*, 1905.

[71] *U.S. Census, 1900*, vol. ix: *Manufactures*, pt. 3, p. 826.

in any year from 1890 to 1894.[72] Confidence was again abroad in the land, and there was a pronounced upswing of the price level by the turn of the century.[73] The purchasing power of the people of the Northwest was greater than it had ever been. This reflected itself in lumber sales, for the early prairie settler now began to replace his first shelter with a new home, much larger and more comfortable. The old stables, too, low and dark, built of wide boards with battens, usually unpainted, were replaced by big red barns with huge haylofts. The rise in the price of farms and their products made the midwest farmer a well-to-do man,[74] no longer satisfied with the bare necessities of life; and he was likely to need lumber at some point in improving his manner of living.

Lumber continued to be a profitable business for the railroads in the 1890s. Lumber and railroads and wheat were still weaving the pattern they had started in the sixties; at the close of the nineties it was almost complete. Of the tonnage carried in 1890 by the Minneapolis, St. Paul and Sault Ste. Marie, one of the youngest Minneapolis roads, 31.93 per cent was in lumber and 24.77 per cent in grain. In 1899 the road still carried more lumber than grain, but in 1905, when that road reached the boundary line of Canada at Portal, North Dakota, grain constituted 33.82 per cent of its tonnage and lumber 23.45 per cent.

The Minneapolis and St. Louis, always a heavy lumber carrier into the farming regions, in 1890 carried in Minnesota 20.29 per cent of its tonnage in wheat and 14.67 per cent in lumber; by 1905, 23.98 per cent of its tonnage was grain and 15.48 per cent was lumber. In 1890 the Chicago and Northwestern carried in the state of Minnesota a grain tonnage of 37.35 per cent and a lumber tonnage of 22.37 per cent; by 1905 the lumber tonnage of this road had dwindled to 11.79 per cent, while grain still held the lead with 41.63 per cent. It is evident that grain and lumber still constituted the most important tonnage of railroads in Minnesota.[75]

In 1900 flour and lumber still held the stage as Minnesota's leading products. The two provided 9 per cent of all the industries in the state and 46 per cent of all the capital invested in industries. Their products were valued at 48 per cent of all products of the state.[76] As we have noted before, lumber had encouraged wheat and flour production in Minnesota by offering them a market even before Minnesota became a

[72] *Report of the Minneapolis Chamber of Commerce*, 1900, p. 133.
[73] Willard L. Thorp, *Business Annals* (New York, 1926), p. 66.
[74] *Little Falls Daily Transcript*, Aug. 17, 1901, and Oct. 21, 1901.
[75] *Annual Report of the Minnesota Railroad and Warehouse Commission*, 1890, pp. 204, 374, 399, 525; and 1905, pp. 2, 23, 26.
[76] Folwell, *History of Minnesota*, vol. iii (St. Paul, 1926), pp. 252–53; *U.S. Census, 1900: Manufactures*, pt. 2, pp. 450–53.

state, and step by step these two industries of forest and farm had grown to create a major portion of the state's wealth.

Every decade the lumber industry in Minnesota had increased its capital investment, its production, and the value of its output; by 1900 it had reached the top. The capital invested in lumber and sawmills in one decade exceeded that of the decade immediately preceding: in 1870 the invested capital was $3,311,140; in 1880, $6,771,145; in 1890 it took a big leap forward with $28,321,062; [77] in 1900, $52,095,923 was invested in lumber and sawmills, and $43,585,161 was the value of the product.[78]

Certain Minneapolis lumbermen were taking the lead in the state. Among these were Weyerhaeuser, Shevlin, Akeley, Backus, Walker, and Smith. Others were, at the same time, passing into the background. Competition was sifting out those who could not keep pace. In 1913 six holders controlled 54 per cent of the white and red pine in Minnesota,[79] and each of the six had at some time had his headquarters in Minneapolis.

The cut of lumber in Minnesota in 1900 was lessened a bit because of low water, which held back the logs. To lumbermen this was a matter of constant concern. "Is there plenty of snow in the woods?" "What is the prospect for logs?" "Is there sufficient water to bring logs down?" It was a clean year when all the logs came down; but 1900 was not such a year, and Minneapolis cut only 501,522,000 feet, about 93,000,000 less than in 1899.[80]

Though Minneapolis had a larger cut again in 1901, the demand was so insistent that green lumber had to be shipped.[81] The Minneapolis cut of 1901 was second only to that of 1899. In the winter of 1901-2 nature again worked havoc in the camps: there was not sufficient snow for logging, and in the summer of 1902 not one mill in Minneapolis operated to full capacity, the cut being reduced 112,889,000 feet from the previous year. C. A. Smith led in production with 90,375,000 feet, and H. C. Akeley was next with a cut of 64,504,000 feet.[82] Altogether, Minneapolis cut 465,244,000 feet in 1902.[83]

Crops were excellent that year. Wheat was very much on top; the corn crop set a record. The whole country was prosperous. Banks had plenty of money and building permits increased accordingly — building permits in cities regularly went up or down in proportion to the plenti-

[77] U.S. Census, 1890: Manufacturing Industries, pt. 3, p. 610.

[78] Folwell, op. cit., p. 252; U.S. Census, 1900: Manufactures, pt. 2, pp. 450–53. This capital was invested in lumber and timber products, not in planing mills or any subsidiary lumber industry (U.S. Census, 1900, vol. ix: Manufacturing, pt. 3, p. 809).

[79] U.S. Bureau of Corporations, The Lumber Industry (1913), pt. 1, p. 22.

[80] Report of the Minneapolis Chamber of Commerce, 1900, p. 134.

[81] Little Falls Daily Transcript, May 25, 1901.

[82] Report of the Minneapolis Chamber of Commerce, 1902, p. 131.

[83] Ibid., 1903, p. 147.

fulness of money.[84] Prosperity, together with the low stock of white pine logs, brought a shortage of lumber and lumber prices went up.[85]

By 1903 the white pine regions of the Chicago district and the east-of-Chicago district had ceased to play an effective part in the lumber industry. Even as late as 1890 the two had an output of 4,529,371,000 feet, but in 1903 their contribution was modest with 853,045,000 feet; the west-of-Chicago district, comprising Minnesota and Wisconsin, ruled with 4,237,604,000 feet. There was no doubt that Michigan white pine had given way to the pine farther west.[86] The Duluth district alone produced more than Michigan did at this time. In Wisconsin, too, on the Black River, on the Chippewa, in the Wisconsin Valley, production was dwindling.[87]

In Minneapolis 1899 remained the record year, for in 1902 she cut only 465,244,000 feet, and in 1903 her cut was even lower. Strive as she would, Minneapolis seemed not to regain the speed of 1899 or 1901.[88] The Shevlin-Carpenter mill led all others in the city with a cut of 100,180,000 feet in 1903.[89] But the total cut of the Minneapolis mills that year was smaller by 33,080,000 feet than in 1902. Minneapolis never at any time after 1901 reached that year's cut but her production was still large — no city had yet taken from her the world leadership she had gained in 1899.

To this leadership the increase in capital and markets, the change in machinery, and the new blood from Michigan had all contributed. Lumber reached its golden age in Minneapolis and in Minnesota with the turn of the century. From a simple industry having the "tempo of the prairie schooner," lumber milling and selling at Minneapolis had come to outdistance all competitors. The great lumber era of the city at the Falls of St. Anthony began in 1890 and closed in 1905. During that time, said E. L. Carpenter, "Minneapolis easily was the leading lumber market in the world." [90] A close rival, however, had risen on the westernmost point of Lake Superior; Duluth had now become the center of a great lumber industry.

[84] Compton, *Organization of the Lumber Industry*, p. 99.
[85] *Ibid.; Little Falls Daily Transcript*, July 19, 1902.
[86] *Report of the Minneapolis Chamber of Commerce*, 1903, p. 143.
[87] *Ibid.*, pp. 143–46.
[88] *Ibid.*, p. 147.
[89] *Ibid.*, p. 148.
[90] *Minneapolis Journal*, Feb. 12, 1933.

CHAPTER XIV

The Duluth District Sends Its White Pine Eastward

DULUTH had great natural possibilities. At her feet lay a deep water-way reaching to the Atlantic, and her vast hinterland had abundant resources in timber and iron ore. In 1854 the region around the north-western extremity of Lake Superior was ceded to the United States government, and the next year the interlake channel at Sault Ste. Marie was deepened, which made it possible for heavy traffic to pass that way. At first Duluth's development was slow and there was little demand for lumber, either local or distant. The coming of the railroad gave a decided impetus to the industry, but it was the demand of the Great Lakes cities and the East which, toward the end of the century, drove Duluth and its district to a high place in the white pine industry.

Two small personal ventures marked the beginning of the lumber industry in Duluth. Henry W. Wheeler came in 1855, walking almost the entire way from St. Paul with his pack strapped to his back. In the following year, with the small financial aid of Edmund F. Ely, a missionary to the Indians, Wheeler with his own hands built a sawmill at a place called Oneota, which was later to become a part of Duluth.[1] But before this little mill was well started in the business of lumbering, the panic came.[2] And already competition had appeared; Lewis Merritt had established himself in sawmilling in the same place.[3] What possibility was there that two mills could survive in a place which was left all but deserted by the panic?

The railroad helped to solve the problem of a market for the sawmills at the western point of Lake Superior. A road from St. Paul to Duluth, known as the Lake Superior and Mississippi, financed by E. W. Clark and Company and Jay Cooke and Company, Philadelphia banking houses, was completed in 1870.[4] Jay Cooke provided a powerful stimulus

[1] See below, p. 266; also *Duluth News Tribune*, Oct. 13, 1931.
[2] Van Brunt, *History of Duluth and St. Louis County*, vol. i, p. 175.
[3] Interview of the writer with T. H. Merritt, Lenox Hotel, Duluth, June 13, 1932.
[4] *Report of the Minnesota Railroad Commission*, 1871, p. 31; 1872, pp. 14–60.

to Duluth in his plans for the Northern Pacific Railroad: The lumber industry would be greatly furthered by the road whose route lay through several hundred miles of white pine and then across many hundreds more miles of bare prairie land awaiting homesteaders. The banker planned the production of ready-cut houses for the immigrants who would settle the prairie. Lumber was to be cut for small houses or cottages costing anywhere from $200 to $1000, models of such houses would be on display, and the incoming settler could make his choice according to his means. Jay Cooke estimated the cost of such a house to be only one third that of the usual house. The railroad would convey the ready-cut lumber without charge to land purchased by the settler from the railroad. In this way the immigrant, the railroad, and the lumber industry would all benefit.[5]

In 1869 the lumber industry on the Minnesota side of Lake Superior began to show the influence of the approaching railroads. Railroads under construction were great consumers of lumber, and the building of two railroads encouraged the lumber industry at Duluth. Elevators, anticipating the grain trade, were also being constructed in Duluth, and they, too, were voracious consumers of lumber.[6] In six months in 1869 Duluth grew from fourteen families to a population of 3500. Lumber could not be supplied fast enough to meet the demand, and people were forced to live in tents even during the winter months.[7] The newspaper of that day stated that newcomers "should comprehend" that Duluth was a small place and that hotel and boardinghouse accommodations were extremely limited. People were advised to bring blankets and plan to rough it at first, for lumber was cheap and shanties were not hard to build.[8]

The local demand which grew out of the boom resulting from the new railroads gave the first strong impetus to lumbering at Duluth. The Wheeler mill at Oneota was taken over by R. S. Munger and R. A. Gray, who had come with some capital from Maine. After thorough repairs the mill was ready for operations on May 1, 1869.[9] In an advertisement a fortnight later the firm addressed itself to the "citizens of St. Louis County" to the effect that it had for sale clear lumber, dressed flooring and siding, dimension lumber, shingles, lath, door, and sash.[10] This was the type of lumber sold for dwellings in a new community. In the same year a planing mill was built on Minnesota Point, a prominent locality

[5] From a circular of Jay Cooke and Company, Philadelphia, Oct. 20, 1869, Jay Cooke Papers, Historical Society of Pennsylvania; *Official Statement of Assets and Probable Business of the Lake Superior and Mississippi Railroad*, Duluth, May 8, 1869, p. 2.

[6] *Duluth Minnesotian*, Nov. 20, 1869.

[7] Van Brunt, *op. cit.*, vol. i, p. 175; *Duluth Minnesotian*, Dec. 23, 1871.

[8] *Ibid.*, May 22, 1869.

[9] *Duluth News Tribune*, Oct. 13, 1931.

[10] *Duluth Minnesotian*, May 15, 1869.

in Duluth.[11] A man named Abbott advertised cabinet furniture along with "coffins on short notice," stating that he would take all kinds of produce and wood in payment.[12] At the same time Robinson D. Pike of Bayfield, Wisconsin, was about to establish himself in Duluth as a maker of shingles, and he was expert in his art, for his "shingles had passed inspection in the Saginaw market." [13] And Robert Geiger advertised that he was making wagons, a necessary article in a booming community.[14]

The boom continued in 1870.[15] The Munger mill in Oneota worked night and day making lumber to raft to Duluth.[16] Sherwood, Ely, and Hostein built a sawmill at Minnesota Point, and in that same year J. M. Paine built a steam sawmill at Oneota which could cut 16,000 feet a day, to supply lumber to the Lake Superior and Mississippi Railroad.[17] That same year, also, H. Wieland and Brothers of Beaver Bay, on the lake shore north of Duluth, were selling lumber at Minnesota Point, and the Duluth Manufacturing Company under the direction of O. K. Patterson and S. C. McQuade urged people to buy sash, doors, moldings, and window frames at home.[18] Duluth with keen anticipation foresaw the day when the Lake Superior and Mississippi Railroad would carry lumber to St. Paul and Minneapolis, though at the time the prospect seemed like carrying coals to Newcastle.[19]

In 1871 the Munger firm moved its mill from Oneota into Duluth proper. A newspaper of the day referred to the Munger mill as a "Rushing Saw-Mill" with a cut of 32,000 feet a day. Its biggest customer was the Northern Pacific Railroad, which it supplied with construction lumber.[20] The Northern Pacific in 1871 reached the Red River Valley, whence before long were to come huge measures of wheat to be stored in terminal elevators at Duluth to await shipment on the Great Lakes. By this time the logging industry in the vicinity of Duluth had grown to considerable proportions [21] and was creating a market in food for men and food for cattle. Indeed, lumber, spurred by its close associate, the railroad, was laying the foundations of Duluth.

[11] *Ibid.*, July 26, 1869.
[12] *Ibid.*, May 22, 1869.
[13] *Ibid.*, May 12, 1869; in the *American Lumberman* of Feb. 15, 1902, we read that Captain R. D. Pike, of the R. D. Pike Lumber Company, left for California to view his olive plantation. No doubt making shingles was a prosperous business.
[14] *Duluth Minnesotian*, Aug. 14, 1869.
[15] Hotchkiss, *History of Lumber and Forest Industry of Northwest*, p. 524.
[16] *Duluth Minnesotian*, May 14, 1870.
[17] *Ibid.*, Apr. 23, 1870; Mar. 11, 1871.
[18] *Ibid.*, June 25, 1870; Sept. 3, 1870.
[19] *Ibid.*, June 11, 1870.
[20] *Ibid.*, Aug. 5, 1871.
[21] *Ibid.*, Dec. 9, 1871.

Then came the Panic of 1873 and the difficult years that followed. They left the new frontier town deflated, as was likely to be the case with any town whose roots had not yet become strong. Jay Cooke, without doubt the most important individual in the early promotion of Duluth, failed in the Panic of 1873, and the Northern Pacific, Duluth's most substantial support, found itself in serious distress. Duluth struggled through the panic and barely weathered the following years of depression. It was not until 1880 that the activities which supported the city, especially the Northern Pacific, regained their original vigor.

In the years 1880 to 1883 the banks of St. Louis Bay held no fewer than eleven sawmills. In the group of sawmill firms that in the early eighties selected Duluth as a place of operation none was more important than the Duluth Lumber Company, of which S. K. Martin of Chicago was one of the principal stockholders, together with R. L. Henry of Chicago and H. B. Moore of Duluth. Martin's connections were important, for he operated one of the chief wholesale lumber yards in Chicago and his interest in Duluth mills was a significant sign of the future. This mill could produce 30,000,000 feet a year, a phenomenal cut at that time.[22] H. M. Peyton, Graff and Little, McLean and Scott, R. A. Gray, and Weld and Petrie were some of the lumbermen cutting on the Bay in these years who were to continue to be prominent as lumbermen there. Duluth proper cut 33,000,000 feet in 1881, which was increased to over 83,000,000 feet in 1882.[23]

But the Bay region no longer was the only lumber manufacturing point in the Lake Superior country. Cloquet, at a good location on the St. Louis River above the rapids, was a natural gateway to thousands of acres of white pine; here the Cloquet River cuts the massive granite rim of the Superior basin and forms the famous Knife Falls. This place had such possibilities that Frederick Weyerhaeuser was later to establish himself there.[24] In 1878 the first mills broke the stillness of the forest in that region. Tower was the first sawmill town in the Iron Range country.[25] Tower's mill came eventually into the control of lumbermen from Oshkosh, Wisconsin, who sought white pine elsewhere because their supply was giving out.

In Douglas County in Wisconsin, considered a part of the Duluth district, there had been as early as 1854 a mill at Iron River, on the river of that name, just south of Lake Superior. Eventually mills were estab-

[22] Hotchkiss, *op. cit.*, p. 576.
[23] *Report of the Duluth Board of Trade and Commerce*, 1882, p. 27.
[24] *American Lumberman*, Apr. 11, 1914, p. 31.
[25] O. A. Wiseman, "The Lumbering Industry at Tower," a paper read at the meeting of the St. Louis County Historical Society, Oct. 28, 1926; this paper is in the possession of the St. Louis County Historical Society at Duluth.

lished at Superior, where in 1864 H. M. Peyton was operating a mill with a capacity of 25,000 feet a day. In 1880 this lumberman was making 100,000 feet a day. The cut of the Duluth district, as a whole, increased rapidly at the time: in 1881 a total of 89,000,000 feet was cut in the district; in 1882 the cut was 191,000,000 feet; and in 1884 it reached 243,000,000 feet.[26]

In 1884 the eleven mills in Duluth made on the average about 10,000,-000 feet each.[27] In that year, however, Dakota suffered a crop failure which pricked the land boom in that territory and brought a reaction in Duluth lumber in the bankruptcy of several firms.[28] The results, however, were not so dire as in the panic days of 1873, for demands from the East were growing stronger; some day the western market was not to be important in Duluth's sale of lumber.[29]

Duluth's leadership in lumber developed as a result, in large part, of the passing of Michigan pine. Though Michigan men had been buying timber in the Duluth district in the 1870s, they did not begin to operate sawmills in Duluth until more than a decade later. Their establishment in a new place depended upon their holdings in Michigan; they moved when their log stock there was exhausted. In 1887 Duncan, Brewer and Company, a Saginaw firm, established a sawmill at Duluth. Three years later Mitchell, McClure and Company, also from Saginaw, moved to Duluth with their machinery, millwrights, mill workmen, and lumberjacks. They brought big capital, big ideas, and big reputations in the white pine industry. Previously they had purchased large timber holdings on the upper waters of the Nemadji River to the southwest of Duluth, to furnish the log stock for their mill, the most complete then operating in Duluth; it could cut 250,000 feet in a ten-hour day.[30] They constructed sixty houses for their workmen. They also built a three-thousand-foot dock which could take care of 10,000,000 feet of lumber, the largest dock in that part of the world at the time.[31]

In 1891 another Saginaw firm, Merrill and Ring, moved to Duluth. They, like Mitchell, McClure and Company, were aggressive lumbermen, and their new mill had an annual capacity of 45,000,000 feet.[32] Seventeen cars of machinery came from their old properties at Saginaw to be placed

[26] Hotchkiss, op. cit., pp. 572, 577.
[27] P. M. Shaw, Jr., "Lumber Played an Important Part in Duluth's History," Christian Science Monitor, July 2, 1925, p. 10.
[28] Hotchkiss, op. cit., pp. 576–77; Mississippi Valley Lumberman, vol. xi, June 10, 1887, p. 1.
[29] Duluth Weekly Herald, Oct. 10, 1889.
[30] Ibid., Nov. 7, 1889; American Lumberman, Feb. 28, 1903, pp. 1, 21.
[31] Mississippi Valley Lumberman, vol. xviii, Nov. 7, 1890, p. 14; Nov. 21, 1890, p. 7.
[32] Duluth Weekly Herald, Feb. 26, 1891.

in the Duluth mill, which was up-to-date in every respect, with a band saw, electric lights, and a new grade-sorter.[33]

In 1899 Alger, Smith and Company, also from Michigan, moved to Duluth. This firm owned large areas of fine white pine in Lake County, Minnesota, a county larger than the state of Rhode Island and almost the size of Delaware. Alger, Smith and Company opened up big sections in the Knife River Valley and in the Silver Creek district in Lake County, and they built 152 miles of logging railroad to carry logs to their mills at Duluth.[34] They moved their full equipment and working force to Duluth, from saws to lumberjacks, and they continued as the largest operators in that city until the end of the industry.

Other Michigan men prominent in the development of lumber in Duluth were A. W. Wright, C. A. Davis, and C. W. Wells of Saginaw. Together with R. S. Munger of Duluth they were builders of the Duluth and Winnipeg Railroad, planned to extend through thousands of acres of white pine to the Canadian border. This road's importance lay not only in opening up a market for lumber but even more in making accessible huge regions of forest that could supply logs to Duluth's sawmills. By 1890 this railroad had reached a hundred miles into the deep forest.[35] A. W. Wright, with others in that railroad company, had heavy timber holdings in the state. Wright and Wells were also stockholders in the Wells, Stone Mercantile Company, jobbers in lumbermen's supplies in Duluth.[36]

Activity was increasing also in other sections of the Duluth district. In 1896 Frederick Weyerhaeuser and his associates bought the properties of the C. N. Nelson Lumber Company of Cloquet. Nelson had moved to Cloquet from Stillwater and with his own and other Stillwater capital had organized the company bearing his name. It was the sawmill and timber holdings of this firm in Carlton and St. Louis counties that now passed to the Weyerhaeuser interests.[37] Previously that group had purchased the Cloquet Lumber Company's property which had been developed by George S. Shaw, a seasoned lumberman from Davenport, Iowa, who had come to Cloquet when it was known as Knife Falls. In 1902 they acquired still more property in Cloquet when they purchased the Johnson, Wentworth mill. This property had been owned by Samuel S. Johnson, who like Nelson had come from Stillwater, George K. and Justine Wentworth

[33] *Mississippi Valley Lumberman*, vol. xxi, Jan. 1, 1892, p. 5.

[34] Interview of the writer with J. W. Bayley of the firm of Alger, Smith and Company, Duluth, Aug. 14, 1932.

[35] H. V. and H. W. Poor, *Manual of Railroads*, 1890, p. 499.

[36] *Mississippi Valley Lumberman*, vol. xiv, Oct. 12, 1888, p. 3.

[37] *Duluth Weekly Herald*, Apr. 8, 1896; *American Lumberman*, Sept. 12, 1903, p. 46.

from Chicago, who had white pine holdings in St. Louis County, and John De Laittre of Minneapolis.[38] Weyerhaeuser and his associates thus acquired six sawmills in Cloquet as well as township after township of white pine — 95 per cent of these holdings contained genuine white pine.[39] Among the associates were Laird, the Nortons, Musser, and other down-river men. The Weyerhaeuser establishment at Cloquet was considered one of the largest and best-arranged plants in the country.[40] Here was an interesting example of a process characteristic of that period: expansion by way of concentration.

New mills were developing on the Iron Range, also in the Duluth district. At Virginia, Minnesota, a St. Paul lumberman named Finlayson built a sawmill in 1893. Other sawmills were located at Tower, Ely, Mesaba, and McKinley. The iron ore development on the Range had created a demand for lumber, resulting in a quick growth of mills.[41]

The new developments in the Duluth district made the production of past years there seem very modest. In 1890 the district produced 206,600,000 feet; at no time previously had it cut so much. The total for the next year was 264,074,072 feet.[42] In 1892 this district greatly exceeded the cut of the Chippewa Valley, which once had been famous in production; it also far surpassed the St. Croix Valley; it even surpassed its near neighbor, the Ashland, Wisconsin, district, by a large margin.[43] The Chippewa and the St. Croix were growing old and worn in the business of making lumber and were now merely raking together what the earlier harvesters had overlooked, while Duluth was still a spirited youth who had not yet reached maturity.

The largest cut in the Duluth district in 1892 was made by the Cloquet Lumber Company, which cut 60,000,000 feet; the C. N. Nelson concern, also of Cloquet, was a near competitor with 58,000,000 feet. Mitchell, McClure and Company of Duluth produced 38,500,000 feet. The Howe Lumber Company, successors to the Owens Lumber Company of Tower, produced 24,000,000 feet, which were used on the Range or shipped eastward at Two Harbors; Merrill and Ring made 21,000,000 feet. Of the twenty-three mills reporting in that district, fourteen were from Duluth.[44] Lumbermen reported that there never had been a better autumn in the

[38] Ibid., pp. 50, 52.
[39] Christopher C. Andrews, Report of the Chief Fire Warden of Minnesota, 1895, pp. 118–19; American Lumberman, Sept. 12, 1903, p. 44.
[40] Ibid., p. 49.
[41] Mississippi Valley Lumberman, vol. xxiii, Apr. 7, 1893, p. 6; June 9, 1893, p. 5.
[42] Report of the Minneapolis Chamber of Commerce, 1890, p. 167; Report of the Duluth Board of Trade and Commerce, 1892, p. 14.
[43] Report of the Minneapolis Chamber of Commerce, 1892, pp. 231–33.
[44] Ibid., p. 232.

history of the Duluth lumber trade than in 1892.[45] The next year the district established another record when it finished the season with a cut of 349,394,000 feet.[46]

Duluth was, however, by no means unaware of the Panic of 1893. Although eager trading of pinelands was a very important part of its daily life, in the winter of 1893–94 no block of timber of any magnitude changed hands in the Duluth district.[47] But the lumber mills in Duluth withstood the panic.[48] They had the unusual advantage of shipping their product by an all-water route, which was always cheaper than rail transportation, and just at this time the lake rates were lowered, which was a factor not only in maintaining exports but even in increasing them.[49] More than that, men who had purchased pineland or stumpage in the Duluth district had paid a lower price than then prevailed in any other white pine region; therefore they could lower their prices without too great a loss. The producers of that region also had the advantage of operating in the midst of the white pine forest; logs could be brought to the place of manufacture without the great expense that mills in Minneapolis or "below Minneapolis" had in getting their raw product. All these factors enabled the mills of the Duluth district to keep their regular pace and at times even increase it during the unstable years of the middle nineties.

The cut of 1894 was slightly below that of the preceding year, but the reduction was not serious considering the fact that the panic was pressing heavily at that time. It is even possible that some of the mills had a high inventory after the unusual production of 1893. Or they may have responded to the order of the Mississippi Valley Lumbermen's Association to decrease cuts that year. Table 19 gives the production of individual mills in the district in 1894.

In the next two years the mills of the Duluth district were cautious. They showed some improvement in 1895,[50] but the presidential issue of 1896 made producers and buyers careful.[51] However, production went up again in the two following years, and in 1899 the city of Duluth made an increase in cut unparalleled in its history up to that point.[52] In 1900 and 1901 the cut remained high, and in 1902 the Duluth district reached a cut it was never to surpass: 1,031,775,000 feet.[53] Single mills in the district also

[45] *Mississippi Valley Lumberman*, vol. xxii, Nov. 4, 1892, p. 5.
[46] *Report of the Duluth Board of Trade and Commerce*, 1896, p. 57.
[47] *Duluth Weekly Herald*, Mar. 7, 1894.   [48] Hotchkiss, *op. cit.*, p. 575.
[49] *Duluth Weekly Herald*, Mar. 7, 1894.
[50] Hotchkiss, *op. cit.*, p. 578; *Duluth Weekly Herald*, May 15 and June 26, 1895.
[51] *Report of the Duluth Board of Trade and Commerce*, 1896, p. 57.
[52] See Table 20, p. 256.
[53] *Duluth Evening Herald*, Feb. 12, 1903; *American Lumberman*, Jan. 17, 1903, p. 28; statistics obtained from P. M. Shaw, Jr., June 14, 1932. There is a slight discrepancy in the

TABLE 19. LUMBER CUT AT DULUTH, 1894

Company	Feet of Lumber Cut
Mitchell & McClure	43,500,000
Merrill & Ring	40,000,000
C. N. Nelson Lumber Company	37,500,000
Cloquet Lumber Company	35,000,000
Duncan, Brewer & Company	26,400,000
Peyton, Kimball & Barber	16,000,000
Knox Lumber Company	15,000,000
C. S. Murray & Company	15,000,000
Howe Lumber Company	15,000,000
West Superior Lumber Company	14,500,000
B. B. Richards Lumber Company	13,000,000
Paine and Company	12,000,000
Moon Lumber Company	10,000,000
Small Mill on South Shore	10,000,000
Hubbard & Vincent	7,000,000
Small Mill on Iron Range	7,500,000
Scott & Holston	6,900,000
Howard Lumber Company	5,000,000
Herman & Becklinger	4,000,000
W. P. Heimbach	3,000,000
Mills & LeClaire	3,000,000
T. J. Foley	2,000,000
M. Carroll	2,000,000
Total	343,300,000

SOURCE: Hotchkiss, *History of Lumber and Forest Industry of Northwest*, p. 575.

had unusual cuts in 1902: The Brooks-Scanlon mill at Scanlon expected to cut 150,000,000 feet; Alger, Smith and Company of Duluth finished the year with 130,000,000 feet;[54] and the Weyerhaeuser mills at Cloquet produced 210,000,000 feet.[55]

The year 1902 was Duluth's record season. From then on the annual cut diminished steadily, with only an occasional and temporary increase, until the lumber industry had passed entirely out of Duluth's life. The reason is by now a familiar story: the supply of logs was exhausted. As early as 1902 mills that had operated in Duluth for a long period were finding themselves without log stock. Duncan, Brewer and Company, which had come to Duluth in 1887, was one of the companies with no logs to cut, and their plant was sold to the Red Cliff Lumber Company, which still had timber of its own.[56] The famous Mitchell, McClure plant,

cut of the Duluth district as presented by the *Herald* and by the *American Lumberman*, but the *Lumberman*'s figures were probably obtained before the December cut was complete. The *Herald* gives the complete cut.

[54] *American Lumberman*, Mar. 1, 1902, p. 41; *Duluth Evening Herald*, Feb. 12, 1903.
[55] *Ibid.*
[56] *American Lumberman*, Aug. 2, 1902, p. 29.

which for many years had been furnished logs from the fine timber on the Nemadji River, was sold because it had no more logs; it was bought by Alger, Smith and Company, which still had substantial holdings in Cook and Lake counties.[57] So as logs grew scarcer lumber production decreased, and Duluth gradually lost its place as a source for lumber. The figures for the decade 1897–1906 are given in Table 20.

TABLE 20. LUMBER MANUFACTURE AND TRADE IN DULUTH, 1897–1906

Year	Lumber Manufactured (in millions of feet)	Lumber Shipped (in millions of feet)
1897	290	283
1898	324	333
1899	426	426
1900	416	368
1901	426	455
1902	443	463
1903	389	403
1904	285	294
1905	292	299
1906	359	383

SOURCE: Statistics obtained from P. M. Shaw, Jr., a lumber broker in Duluth, June 14, 1932.

The great increase in production was dependent upon the expansion of the market. We have seen how the condition of the western wheat crops and the extension of the railroads determined lumber production in the early years, but the trade of the West was not significant in the development of Duluth after 1890. Then the home market and the eastern market took the bulk of the lumber cut in the Duluth district.

The rapid growth of Duluth provided a very strong home market. From 1890 to 1895, including the panic years, Duluth had an increase in population of almost 80 per cent, more than in any other city or town in Minnesota during the same period.[58] The increasing number of mills attracted labor — the fifteen sawmills of Duluth listed 3617 men on their payrolls in 1894.[59] Such an increase in population created a demand for houses, schools, sidewalks, and other building needs of a growing community.

In August 1890 building permits were issued at a valuation of $520,000, chiefly for houses. Every month the list of permits was large, providing for such buildings as residences, schools, and apartment houses.[60] In March 1893 the permits were chiefly for houses, at a valuation

[57] *Duluth Evening Herald*, Feb. 12 and Sept. 23, 1903.
[58] *Minnesota State Census*, 1895.
[59] *Duluth Evening Herald*, Dec. 17, 1894; Hotchkiss, *op. cit.*, p. 575.
[60] Building Inspector's Record, 1890. This record is now in the Duluth City Hall.

of \$326,000, and in several subsequent months that year building permits for residences almost equaled the March record.[61] In 1892 it was estimated that 75,000,000 to 100,000,000 feet of lumber would be consumed in the construction of elevators and docks alone. Duluth, at the west end of the Great Lakes, was a prominent transfer point for lumber, iron ore, wheat, and flour.[62] Three mammoth elevators were erected in 1893, requiring 4,000,000 feet of lumber each; the Duluth and Iron Range Railroad was building an ore dock requiring 6,000,000 feet; and the Duluth, Missabe and Northern Railway, then being built to the Range under the direction of the Merritt brothers, had plans for monster ore docks in West Duluth requiring 10,000,000 feet.[63] Building in Duluth reached a high point in 1902 when permits were issued for structures valued at \$11,600,000. This record was exceeded only in 1910, when the steel corporation set itself up in Duluth.[64]

Industries using rough lumber moved to Duluth and added to the consumption of lumber at home. In 1890, besides the many planing mills and blind, sash, and door factories already there, the Duluth Furniture Company was established, under the presidency of C. B. Holmes, a Chicago millionaire. In the same year the first paper mill opened in Duluth, employing 325 men, and the Lancaster Buggy Company, making buggies, busses, and drays, moved from Lancaster, Ohio, to Duluth, where they employed 100 men in their establishment. Duluth also manufactured freight cars, using its own iron and lumber and sending the cars away with flour of its own making.[65]

But of greatest importance in the development of the lumber industry of the Duluth district were the markets which the Michigan men commanded and which they brought to Duluth along with their men, equipment, capital, and skill in management. Traffic in lumber and forest products had long been one of the most important movements on the Great Lakes, and it was to continue so until the regions tributary to the lakes were stripped of their forests.[66] Duluth, the last outpost of lumber on the Great Lakes, was aware for the first time in 1888 of an increasing demand for its lumber.[67] In 1889 it found this demand so great that it feared it would have to supplement its own stock from sources elsewhere.[68]

[61] *Ibid.*, 1893.

[62] *Report of the Duluth Board of Trade and Commerce*, 1892, p. 14.

[63] *Mississippi Valley Lumberman*, vol. xxi, Jan. 1, 1892, p. 5; vol. xxiii, Jan. 6, 1893, p. 5, and July 14, 1893, p. 1.

[64] Building Inspector's Record, 1900–16. This record is on file in the Duluth City Hall.

[65] *Duluth Weekly Herald*, June 12, Mar. 13, and Oct. 30, 1890.

[66] *Transportation on the Great Lakes* (U.S. Shipping Board, Transportation Series, no. 1 [1930]).

[67] *Report of the Duluth Board of Trade and Commerce*, 1888, p. 34.

[68] *Mississippi Valley Lumberman*, vol. xvi, Aug. 9, 1889, p. 6.

The most important eastern wholesale market for Duluth's lumber was Tonawanda, New York, which was regarded as the "Greatest White Pine Assembling and Distributing Market on the Continent." [69] Tonawanda lay at the east end of Lake Erie, and it was only a few hours' trip from New England and the Northeast Atlantic states; it was well connected with them by railroads — the New York Central, the Pennsylvania, the Erie, and the Delaware, Lackawanna and Western. From this strategic center Minnesota's lumber was scattered far and wide, since New York, Philadelphia, and Boston purchased nearly all their white pine from Tonawanda or from Buffalo. [70] From Tonawanda Minnesota's white pine also found its way to the West Indies and to South America — whence in the form of barrels and other containers it returned to the United States carrying molasses and sugar. [71]

Other markets to the east on or near the Great Lakes became important to Duluth. Its lumber began to dribble through to Chicago in the late 1870s and early 1880s. Previously Chicago had purchased its lumber from Michigan and the part of Wisconsin tributary to the Great Lakes. [72] In the nineties, however, Chicago became one of Duluth's greatest markets. With the growing importance of steel and oil, Cleveland and Pittsburgh and surrounding regions could use much lumber to house their growing populations. Milwaukee, Sandusky, Toledo, Buffalo, Ogdensburg, Erie, and Montreal (where Dobell, Becket, and Company exported Minnesota's white pine to Europe, chiefly to England) likewise became important markets for Duluth as the white pine of the other Lake states gave out.

Duluth in 1893 found a market for its lumber such as it had never previously enjoyed. [73] Mitchell, McClure and Company sold 38,000,000 feet to Tonawanda, Buffalo, and New York before the lake traffic opened. By April 21 the twin ports of Duluth and Superior had shipped 100,000,000 feet of lumber. By June 16 Duluth had already shipped eastward as much as it had ever sent before in a whole season. In the fall of 1893 Duluth announced that it was no longer competing with interior mills of Wisconsin and Minnesota for western trade, that it was selling largely to the eastern wholesale trade. [74]

During the panic and depression years that followed, the lumber exports by water from Duluth increased. In 1894, one of the worst of the depression years, the lumber shipments of Duluth showed a net

[69] *American Lumberman*, Aug. 4, 1906, p. 23.
[70] U.S. Bureau of Corporations, *The Lumber Industry* (1914), pt. 4, pp. 583–601.
[71] Interview of the writer with P. M. Shaw, Jr., Duluth, June 14, 1932.
[72] *Duluth Weekly Herald*, Aug. 14, 1890.
[73] *Mississippi Valley Lumberman*, vol. xxiii, Apr. 21, 1893, p. 13.
[74] *Ibid.*, Mar. 31, 1893, p. 5; June 16, 1893, p. 5; Nov. 24, 1893, p. 2.

gain of 25 per cent. The bulk of that trade was directed to Tonawanda, to other New York trade centers, and to Chicago.[75]

As the depression subsided, Duluth's trade increased greatly, as is shown by Table 20 on page 256. In 1899 Duluth shipped from her port more than 400,000,000 feet of lumber.[76] The largest shipment in Duluth's lumber history was made in 1902, when 463,000,000 feet moved eastward;[77] this was the largest amount shipped from any port on Lake Superior that year.[78] The lumber shipped in 1902 from Duluth and Superior, its neighboring harbor, was valued at $6,352,876. Buyers coming to Duluth sometimes took the whole cut made by one company. For example, in both 1901 and 1902 Duncan, Brewer and Company of Duluth sold their entire cut to the Pilson Lumber Company of Chicago, who bargained for the lumber very early in the season.[79]

Because of the heavy local demand, Duluth could not have supplied the eastern market without the assistance of lumber from Cloquet and the Range towns.[80] Cloquet, though her markets lay chiefly south of the Canadian border westward to eastern Montana, down to central Kansas, and then eastward to the junction of the Ohio and the Mississippi, was nonetheless finding a growing market in the East. By the end of May in 1904 Cloquet had already sent 75,000,000 feet of lumber eastward.[81]

By then, however, Duluth had seen her best days in lumber, for after 1903 her shipments declined along with production. The market was still there, but the forests tributary to Duluth were gone. Where formerly the piles of lumber had held the shore line, now cars of iron ore stood like victorious soldiers.[82]

Duluth could sell advantageously in the eastern market because of cheap transportation on the Great Lakes; the shipping industry there was as important to Duluth as rafting had been to the sawmill towns of the Mississippi. The schooner, which once had been moved only by sail, was moved by steam power by the time Duluth began sending lumber to an eastern market. The old schooner still carried sails to be put to use when the wind was right, but steam power made more speed. Now generally known as a barge, the schooner which carried lumber had seen the best of its days. It was turned into a lumber barge when it

---

[75] *Duluth Weekly Herald*, Oct. 24, 1894.
[76] Interview with P. M. Shaw, Jr., Duluth, June 14, 1932.
[77] P. M. Shaw, Jr., "Lumber Played an Important Part in Duluth's History," *Christian Science Monitor*, July 2, 1925, p. 10.
[78] *Statistical Report of Marine Commerce of Duluth, Minnesota, and Superior, Wisconsin,* 1921, p. 9; *American Lumberman*, Jan. 24, 1903, p. 13.
[79] *Duluth Weekly Herald*, Jan. 15, 1902.
[80] *Morrison County Democrat* (Little Falls), Jan. 12, 1899.
[81] *American Lumberman*, July 9, 1904, p. 37; May 28, 1904, p. 36.
[82] *Statistical Report of Marine Commerce of Duluth, Minnesota, and Superior, Wisconsin,* 1921, p. 9.

could no longer carry flour or grain, for if a load of lumber became water-logged, it was not seriously damaged.

A barge carrying lumber was not an elegant boat! It was bulky and rough like the cargo it carried. From the eastern ports to Duluth it carried coal, limestone, and salt. Coal was the prevailing freight from the East, and in some years three fourths of the west-bound freight from Lake Erie ports was coal. This was very important in helping to provide cheap carriage for Duluth's lumber.

A few of the large concerns that bought lumber in Duluth owned their own barges and carried their own lumber to its destination. Such a company was the Edward Hines Lumber Company of Chicago; it owned fifteen vessels on the Great Lakes whose only business was to carry lumber.[83] The large majority of buyers, however, were dependent upon outside tonnage.

Barges varied in size. Some could carry only 250,000 feet of lumber. The average size of a cargo was 800,000 feet, while some barges carried 1,500,000 feet. One barge famous in the history of Duluth was the *Wahnapitae*. On July 8, 1887, this barge left Duluth with a load of more than 2,000,000 feet of lumber, which it carried through the Great Lakes to Tonawanda and via the Erie Canal to Harmon Rice and Company of West Troy, New York. This load of lumber attracted much attention; it was reported to be the largest ever carried by a barge from any point on the Great Lakes.[84] On August 5 that same summer the *Wahnapitae* set forth again from Duluth, beating its own record with a load of almost 2,500,000 feet.[85] In an average season, when more than 400,000,000 feet of lumber left the docks of Duluth, barges were many in the harbor of that city. Tugs pushed the lumber-burdened barge out of the harbor through the canal to the lake proper, where a bigger steamer, also laden with lumber, furnished the power that took the barge to its destination.

Not only was the water route a more convenient way to ship so bulky a product as lumber but, most important, it was a cheaper way. Railroad rates to Buffalo or Tonawanda were prohibitory. In the nineties it cost about half the rail rate to carry green lumber by water from Duluth to Chicago. Also, the company owning the barge paid for the loading of the lumber, while the lumber company had to pay the cost of loading railroad cars.

From 1891 through 1899 the freight rate on a cargo of lumber from Duluth to ports on Lake Erie or Lake Michigan ranged from a low

[83] *American Lumberman*, Mar. 19, 1904, p. 1; *Little Falls Daily Transcript*, Sept. 7, 1901.
[84] *Mississippi Valley Lumberman*, vol. xii, July 8, 1887, p. 5.
[85] *Ibid.*, Aug. 5, 1887, p. 9.

of $1.40 to a high of $3.25 per thousand feet. This low rate was maintained through the depression years, which accounts in part for the increase of 25 per cent in the lumber trade on the Great Lakes during the precarious year of 1894. In 1897 the rate increased, with $1.58 as an average; in 1898 the average rate was $1.78. The next year was an unusual one in production and in consumption — the depression was over and prices were up. That year the freight rate for a thousand feet reached the unusually high point of $3.08. In 1900 the rate settled again to an average of $2.24. From 1900 to 1907 rates were up and down depending upon the market, but at no time did the average rate pass beyond $2.54.[86]

The loading of lumber barges gave work to large numbers of men. These laborers were known as longshoremen, or sometimes as stevedores, but most generally in Duluth as "dock wollopers." They loaded almost all the lumber by hand. Sometimes extra heavy timbers would necessitate the use of a steam hoist from the boat, but this was not the regular method. Lumber was placed in piles on the docks. Usually twelve to sixteen men worked on a pile when it was being loaded. If there were five piles to be loaded onto a boat and they were all in one place, the boat could be loaded its entire length at one time. Sixty men were usually at work if there were five such piles. If men could work at the full length of a boat and if all the load was in one place, three days was the usual time for loading; if everything was well planned it was possible to do the job in a little less time. If the load was scattered so that the boat had to move about to pick it up, a longer time was required. As each barge was loaded, it took its place in line. Three barges and a steamer constituted the usual "caravan" that carried Duluth's forests away over the waters of Lake Superior. The lumber barge, like the sawmill, is no longer a part of the Duluth scene. Iron ore has replaced lumber at the docks, and machines have replaced men in loading.

During Duluth's high point of production, she was quite free from serious competition in the Lake states; nor did competing railroad rates from other points give her much trouble. But her progress was not without obstacles. The tariff and the conservation issue came to plague the city during its most important years in the lumber industry. To its lumbermen, with much capital in timber holdings and in equipment, any change affecting the "natural" order was a danger.

The tariff was not important to the lumber industry of Minnesota as long as its market lay in the region to the west of the Mississippi. It was in the late 1880s and in the 1890s that Minnesota producers

[86] These figures have been compiled for the author by P. M. Shaw, Jr., from a record of rates paid by his lumber brokerage firm in Duluth during that period.

began to interest themselves in the question of the tariff. As their produce entered the eastern market they felt Canadian competition as never before. The struggle over the tariff was not new to Michigan men, and it moved with them to Minnesota. Duluth was more concerned over the question than Minneapolis because Duluth's market lay almost wholly in the East after 1890.

The first tariff that caused concern to the Minnesota lumber producers was the McKinley Tariff Act of 1890. Canada and the United States had an "implicit understanding" that if the earlier tariff of two dollars per thousand feet on rough lumber was reduced to one dollar, Canada would remove her export tariff on logs; this reduction was made in the McKinley Tariff Act. Men holding heavy stands of timber feared the coming of Canadian logs, for it would lessen the value of their holdings, it would lower the price of logs, and it would eventually reduce lumber prices. One dollar on lumber itself was a low tariff from the point of view of a Canadian producer. Michigan men who had purchased timber in Minnesota became greatly agitated when they realized the possible effects of increased shipments of logs to the United States. In 1891 only 80,000,000 feet of logs had come in from Canada; in 1894, 300,000,000 feet of logs were imported.[87] The lumbermen who had remained in Michigan had become heavy purchasers of Canadian timber and they were the leading advocates for the low tariff.

So the fight was on between former Michigan men who had bought log stock in Minnesota and those who had bought log stock in Canada. With Cleveland as President, little could be hoped for by lumbermen who wanted tariff revision upward. They were defeated again when lumber went on the free list in the Wilson-Gorman tariff of 1894.[88] They could only wait for the return of a Republican administration which might share their point of view.

It was not strange, then, that Minnesota lumbermen showed a live interest in the presidential election of 1896. Duluth men who had met Canadian competition at Tonawanda and elsewhere were determined to defeat Bryan, another low-tariff man. When McKinley's election was assured, lumbermen began to prepare for the tariff fight which was expected to develop shortly.

The lumber interests met at Cincinnati, and a lively fight took place between Michigan men who had Minnesota holdings and those who had Canadian holdings.[89] Page Morris, congressman-elect from

[87] Ralph C. Bryant, *Lumber, Its Manufacture and Distribution* (New York, 1922), p. 432; *U.S. Statutes at Large*, 51st Cong., 1st Sess. (1890), p. 582.

[88] Bryant, *Lumber, Its Manufacture and Distribution*, p. 432; *U.S. Statutes at Large*, 53rd Cong., 2d Sess. (1894), pp. 545–46.

[89] *Duluth Weekly Herald*, Dec. 23, 1896, and Mar. 24, 1897.

Duluth, was active in expressing the interests of his electorate; W. C. McClure of Mitchell, McClure and Company, big Duluth operators who had come from Saginaw, also took part in the struggle at Cincinnati. Both Morris and McClure were placed on a select committee to appear in hearings on the issue before the Ways and Means Committee in Washington.[90]

Much to the satisfaction of the Minnesota and Wisconsin lumber interests, the Dingley tariff emerged in 1897 with a two-dollar duty on white pine lumber. The act included a clause which stated that if Canada placed an export tariff on logs, the United States would add an equal amount to the lumber tariff, which was already two dollars. The Canadian provinces retaliated by prohibiting the export of logs cut on crown lands.[91] This did not entirely prevent the exporting of logs but Minnesota men felt that the results from the Dingley tariff were satisfactory to their interests.

Active agitation for conservation in Minnesota also aroused Duluth sawmill men in the late 1890s and early 1900s. Duluth operators were already fearful of the impending timber shortage, and if any part of what pineland was left should be set aside for conservation, it would only speed the day when sawmills would have to close. The conservation movement in Minnesota had found its leader in Christopher C. Andrews, who, as United States minister to Sweden in the Grant administration, had become a great student of Sweden's conservation policy. In 1898 Andrews stated that, at the rate Minnesota was cutting, she would be without commercial forest in twenty years. He urged Congress to set aside for conservation some of the small public domain still remaining within the state. Within the area he recommended fell portions of Cook and Lake counties, tributary to Duluth.

The whole Duluth district was astir over this suggestion. Congressman Morris vigorously fought the plan; as his constituents saw it, it was taking the very bread out of their mouths.[92] Sawmill men with heavy investments in equipment saw in these heavy stands of timber, which would be withdrawn if conservation came, enough logs to stock their mills for twenty years. Lumbermen said that the plan would deprive 25,000 men of employment in the lumber industry for that length of time, and the people as a whole agreed. That it would exclude thousands of farmers from homes was another argument[93] — one that seems wholly unfounded today, when almost whole counties of cutover land have

[90] *Mississippi Valley Lumberman,* vol. xxviii, Jan. 1, 1897, p. 16.
[91] Bryant, *Lumber, Its Manufacture and Distribution,* p. 433.
[92] *Duluth Weekly Herald,* Aug. 9 and Aug. 16, 1899; Folwell, *History of Minnesota,* vol. iv (St. Paul, 1930), p. 399.
[93] *Duluth Weekly Herald,* Aug. 16, 1899.

become the property of the state again because farmers could not even wrest from the soil a sufficient surplus to pay their taxes.[94]

To men whose vision did not extend beyond the immediate future, the withdrawal of so much timber seemed disastrous. But looking today at the vast area of cutover land in Minnesota, one can only regret that Christopher C. Andrews was not more successful in his fight for conservation at that time. Conservation in the Duluth district did not become a reality until lumbermen had finished their work and the slaughter of the pine was complete.

[94] See below, p. 403; also Roy G. Blakey, *Taxation in Minnesota* (Minneapolis, 1932), pp. 112–46.

CHAPTER XV

The Pinelands of Northern Minnesota
Become Private Property

THE early history of the disposition of land in the region to the north and west of Lake Superior differs from that of the St. Croix and St. Cloud areas in that lumbermen were not the first land buyers in the Lake region. The men into whose possession passed the timberlands of the St. Croix Delta were sawmill men, and at the land offices at Sauk Rapids and St. Cloud, lumbermen who had mills along the Mississippi were in the vanguard of the group who purchased pineland. In the Duluth area, however, lumbermen actually did not buy much timberland until the early 1870s.

The early settlers and land buyers before 1870 were with few exceptions not interested primarily in the timber. They were made up in general of three groups: a few who set up a sawmill to serve the local needs of the new settlement; men interested in the copper that was supposed to lie in the north country; and eastern capitalists who invested in lands in the region because they expected a large development around the westernmost point of Lake Superior.

The government of the United States in 1857 established a land office at Buchanan near the entrance of the Knife River into Lake Superior, about sixteen miles east of what later came to be known as Duluth; on July 1, 1859, the office was moved to Portland, which later became a part of Duluth; in 1862 it was located at Duluth.[1]

The first cash sale at this office was made on December 4, 1857, but sales were small at first, both in number and in amount. Ernest Wieland, whose family had built a sawmill on Beaver River in 1859, purchased a small holding there, in what is now Lake County, on April 10, 1860.[2] The Wieland family, another member of which was Christian Wieland, a civil engineer who explored the north country, was active in the Beaver Bay region for many years. Their sawmill, modestly begun, was for a

---

[1] G.L.O., Records of Receiver and Register, Cash Books, Buchanan, Portland, and Duluth, Minn., Dec. 1857 to Dec. 1864.

[2] *Ibid.*, lots 3 and 4 of W½ of W¼, Sec. 12, T. 55 N., R. 8 W.

quarter of a century practically the sole industrial support of the community; it was later acquired by the Alger, Smith Lumber Company of Duluth. When Ernest Wieland made his purchase, the number of his receipt showed that from December 4, 1859, to August 10, 1860, only seventy-four pieces of land had been sold for cash in the Duluth area.

On December 22, 1860, occurred a significant sale. Lewis H. Merritt, a new settler in the area, purchased a small portion of land, less than an acre, in section two, township 49 north, range 15 west, which lies immediately outside Duluth in what is now Proctor. The coming of the Merritt family was important, for the seven growing sons of Lewis Merritt were to cruise the pine forests of the region and to discover the iron ore of the great Mesabi.[3] On that same day Henry M. Wheeler, who was already operating the first sawmill in what is Duluth today, purchased 43.7 acres, all lying within present-day Duluth. His purchase was small but important, for he was the founder of Duluth's first industry, that of sawing lumber.[4]

The military bounty land warrants, by which huge blocks of land became private property in the St. Croix and St. Cloud districts, did not play a prominent part in the disposal of the public domain in the Duluth district. In 1857 only 3400 acres were located in that district by the warrants of the Act of 1855, 8954 acres were located in 1858, and 6574 in 1859. In the sixties there was a definite decline: in 1867 only 756 acres changed hands through the warrants of the Act of 1855.[5]

The earliest locations, like the purchases of land, were usually made by actual settlers in the new country. Lewis H. Merritt located 280 acres in 1860; the Wieland family located 500 acres in the sixties; and John D. Howard, another of the early settlers, located 2000 acres in the same decade. The only well-established lumber firm that located land in the Duluth district in the 1850s or the early 1860s was a company of sawmill men at Marine on the St. Croix, who in 1863 acquired 884 acres by warrants of the Act of 1855.[6]

These locations and purchases were typical of those in the Duluth area in this period. It was not an auspicious time for opening up new territory; men were slow to venture in the depression following the Panic of 1857, and they were further deterred by fear of conflict between the North and South. Since Michigan and Wisconsin still had pine, the

---

[3] See above, p. 247.

[4] See above, p. 247.

[5] G.L.O., Records of Receiver and Register, Military Bounty Land Warrants, Buchanan, Minn., Act of 1855, 1857–59; Portland, Minn., Act of 1855, vol. 250, 1860; Duluth, Minn., Act of 1855, vol. 247, 1861–64; Duluth, Minn., Act of 1855, vol. 248, 1865–68; Duluth, Minn., Act of 1855, vol. 251, 1868–76.

[6] *Ibid.*, Duluth, Minn., Act of 1855, vol. 247, 1861–64.

lumber markets at Chicago and Buffalo were plentifully served by the forests of those states. Railroads, moreover, had not reached Duluth to furnish transportation for lumber, and the prairies of western Minnesota and Dakota were not yet settled. There was no market except the meager demand of the few settlers in the vicinity of Duluth.

In June 1864 Michigan copper interests came to buy land in the region north of Lake Superior. In that month 1837 acres were disposed of for cash, and of this amount Artemus Doolittle, treasurer of the Ontonagon Mining District Association in Michigan, bought 800 acres and Edward Sales, a member of the board of directors of the same organization, bought 400 acres,[7] followed by other purchases in the month of July. These Michigan men were not interested in pine; their interest was in minerals, especially copper. Sales was a dealer in mineral lands.[8] Ever since the early French period in the Lake Superior country, copper had been associated with that region.[9]

Land continued to move slowly in the Duluth district until Jay Cooke, an eastern banker, saw the possibilities of the lakes as a link with the "Western Empire." In 1868 he came to Duluth because he had bought land there. He studied the vicinity with great care and "this magnificent harbor, flanked by almost endless stretches of lovely pine, beyond which were prairies rich with potential treasure," fired his imagination.[10]

The vast possibilities of the West always appealed to Jay Cooke. He was a child of the frontier; he was also a child of "the hopeful and expansive nineteenth century." He located land with agricultural college scrip from Kentucky, Ohio, Vermont, and New Hampshire. With his associates, William Moorhead and William L. Banning, he became the owner of thousands of acres in the Duluth district, particularly in Carlton and St. Louis counties, excellent pineland regions.[11] Jay Cooke and William Moorhead bought Duluth real estate extensively; Cooke's manager in that project was George B. Sargent, "a typical western real-estate promoter who had formerly been a surveyor in Illinois, Missouri, and Minnesota, and in the late 'sixties settled in Duluth as private banker, real-estate dealer, and general promoter."[12]

In 1868 Jay Cooke and his associates also bought a small block of the bonds of the Lake Superior and Mississippi Railroad.[13] That road was to unite Lake Superior with the Mississippi River — the first road to

[7] *History of the Upper Peninsula of Michigan* (Chicago, 1883), p. 537.
[8] *Ibid.*, p. 543.
[9] Folwell, *History of Minnesota*, vol. i, p. 306.
[10] Henrietta M. Larson, *Jay Cooke, Private Banker* (Cambridge, 1936), p. 248.
[11] G.L.O., Records of Receiver and Register, Agricultural College Scrip, Duluth, Minn., June 1864 to Sept. 1873.
[12] H. M. Larson, *Jay Cooke*, p. 252.
[13] *Ibid.*, p. 250.

penetrate the dense pinelands between Duluth and St. Paul; already large portions of the St. Croix Delta had passed into private hands and the timber was quickly being turned into logs and lumber, which gave promise of yielding freight. Wheat would also seek an outlet to the great waterways by this road. Cooke also secured an interest in the Western Land Association, a subsidiary of the Lake Superior and Mississippi, which owned rich pinelands and townsites along its route. The railway reached Duluth in 1870.

In the spring of 1869 the Northern Pacific promoters induced Cooke to serve as the banker for their road. He became an aggressive promoter of the Northern Pacific and of Duluth, which in his plan was to be a railroad terminal. There in 1869 he built an elevator costing $50,000, which had a capacity of 550,000 bushels.[14] This was necessary for the storage of grain which the railroads would bring to Duluth during the season (almost half the year) when the Great Lakes were icebound. Jay Cooke's associates, the Clarks of Philadelphia, opened a bank in Duluth to assist in financing the grain trade.

From 1866 until the panic came in 1873 Jay Cooke was an important figure in the growth of Duluth and in the sale of the surrounding pinelands. His belief in the commercial possibilities of Duluth drew others who had confidence in his judgment. So it was that Jay Cooke and others who believed that Duluth had a future, together with a few men interested in the possibilities of gold, copper, and iron in the area, were more active in the purchase of land in the Duluth district up to 1870 than were lumbermen.

A few lumbermen, such as Asa and Samuel Parker of the sawmills at Marine on the St. Croix, were buying in the Duluth area in the 1860s on a small scale, but the larger sawmill men who bought substantial acres of timberland were not to come to the region until sometime in the seventies.

It was the year 1872 that marked a change; in that year a number of lumbermen from other places became owners of considerable blocks of timber in the Duluth area. From Oshkosh, Wisconsin, came Thomas D. Grimmer, a "dealer in white pine,"[15] who in the month of June made a substantial purchase of 8062 acres for cash. He was a member of the State Assembly of Wisconsin in 1872 and appears to have been a citizen of considerable importance; he had come from New Brunswick in Canada to pioneer in the West.[16] Nathan Hill, a lumberman from Minneapolis, was also a substantial buyer of pinelands for cash at the

[14] *Ibid.,* p. 330; *St. Paul Pioneer Press,* Sept. 24, 1870.
[15] He is listed as such in the first city directory of Oshkosh, Wisconsin, in 1866.
[16] Manuscript Census of 1870, Wisconsin State Historical Library.

Duluth land office in 1872. He located more than 5800 acres by means of the surveyor-general scrip in the fall of that year.[17]

In the public sale of December 1872 Nehemiah P. Clarke bought the largest number of acres. He was a merchant and lumberman from St. Cloud who in 1856 had moved west from Hubbardston, Massachusetts.[18] Clarke was one of the most active buyers of pineland in both the St. Cloud and the Duluth areas; he was purchasing timber to supply raw materials for his saws at St. Cloud. Other Minnesota men who became owners of good-sized holdings at the public land sale of 1872 were Daniel M. Robbins, later associated with the building of the Manitoba Railway, who had come to Anoka on the Mississippi from Maine in 1855, and Nehemiah Hulett, a real-estate dealer in Duluth who had come there from New York in 1858.[19]

Forty-nine townships were offered in this public land sale of 1872 at Duluth. The sale began in December and in that month 14,725 acres of public domain became private property, bringing in the sum of $22,219; there were 165 receipts given for the amount sold. The sale continued into January 1873, when 12,462 acres were sold for $30,832, for which 162 receipts were issued. The usual price paid by the buyers at the sale was $2.50 an acre, but certain of the better pieces sold at higher prices. One piece of 81 acres sold for $6.00 an acre and others brought $4.60, $4.00, $3.65, $2.60, and $2.55 an acre.[20]

It was not surprising that lumbermen were beginning to plant stakes in the Duluth area, for the lake town was on the way to becoming the emporium that Jay Cooke had envisioned. Cooke said that in the month of August 1872 the Northern Pacific alone had paid out not less than $330,000 "in canals, dykes, wharves, and various other things in Duluth," all of which consumed lumber.[21]

In 1873 the names of men interested in lumber became increasingly more prominent in the records of the United States Land Office at Duluth. In May Marshall Alworth, the famous cruiser from Saginaw, Michigan, came to buy land in the region, and his coming marked the beginning of the interest of Michigan lumbermen in Minnesota. These Michigan lumbermen sent their cruisers ahead to judge the land. The records show that Alworth purchased 200 acres of land at that time;[22]

[17] G.L.O., Records of Receiver and Register, Surveyor-General Scrip, Duluth, Minn., Oct. and Nov. 1872. Surveyor-general scrip was issued under an Act of Congress of June 2, 1858.

[18] "Minnesota Biographies, 1655–1912," *Minn. Hist. Soc. Coll.*, vol. xiv (1912), p. 128.

[19] *Ibid.*, pp. 353, 646.

[20] G.L.O., Records of Receiver and Register, Cash Books, Duluth, Minn., Jan. 1871 to Dec. 1873.

[21] H. M. Larson, *Jay Cooke*, p. 368. For details about the growth of Duluth in this period, see above, pp. 247–50.

[22] G.L.O., Records of Receiver and Register, Cash Books, Duluth, Minn., Jan. 1871 to Dec. 1873.

he also located 80 acres with surveyor-general scrip. Alworth was followed by others from Michigan; in September of that year Alexander Folsom, a sawmill operator from Bay City, invested heavily in Minnesota's pinelands. Folsom, from a family of lumbermen who had moved from New England westward with the pine, had lumber interests in New York and Canada as well as in Michigan. He kept his hand on the pulse of the pine, and as the forests rapidly disappeared before the "ravenous maw" of the circular saw in Michigan, he moved into the untouched areas of pine in Minnesota to protect himself against the day when Michigan's pine would be no more.[23]

Men who had been buying pinelands in the St. Croix and St. Cloud areas were also slowly putting their hands into the resources of the Duluth country. From Minneapolis, in January 1874, came John Martin, a prominent lumberman of long standing in Minnesota, to look over the possibilities. He purchased at once 300 acres in section 6, township 47 north, and in sections 32 and 20, township 48 north, range 19 west, in Carlton County. For this land he paid $2.50 an acre. In the months of March, May, and July he was buying again. The purchases made at that time marked the beginning of the extensive pine holdings he acquired in the north country.

So sawmill men from the saw-towns of Michigan and Wisconsin, and sawmill men on the St. Croix, at the Falls of St. Anthony, and at St. Cloud were finding their way into these untouched forests. When a public land sale occurred at Duluth in 1875 the growing importance of these remote timberlands was evident: the Pillsburys of Minneapolis bought heavily in this sale, as did T. B. Walker and Pettit and Robinson of that city, all of whom were associated with the lumber industry.[24] Prominent Michigan men present at this sale were Wright and Davis, who from then on were well known in the lumber industry in Minnesota.

Private land sales, however, were much retarded after the Panic of 1873 struck with force. Jay Cooke failed [25] and Duluth, depleted in population and bankrupt, reverted to village status again. With the exception of the land sale of 1875, very little land was sold there for several years.

It was not until 1878 that any sizable private sales were again made. Then, in the month of May, Charles N. Nelson purchased 1825 acres at $2.50 an acre. His purchase was noteworthy because he was a prominent lumberman at Stillwater and he was shortly to move his sawmills to Cloquet in the Duluth district. In 1879 another lumberman, John M.

[23] Hotchkiss, *History of Lumber and Forest Industry of Northwest*, p. 153.
[24] Van Brunt, editor, *History of Duluth and St. Louis County*, vol. ii (New York, 1921), p. 539.
[25] See above, p. 250.

Douglas, from Cook County in Illinois, entered the region to buy forest land. He also located about 2000 acres with Supreme Court scrip, issued under an Act of Congress of June 27, 1860.[26] His coming marked the beginning of Chicago interests in the pineland area of Minnesota.

The 1880s are the lumbermen's decade in the history of Duluth. The north woods began to teem with life. This development and the reasons for it we have discussed in the preceding chapter. Its effect on the transfer of pinelands to private ownership was marked.

In 1880 men interested in lumbering on a large scale were buying forest land in the Duluth area; 32,936 acres were sold for cash that year and 104,823 acres the next. Several names which were to play an important part in Minnesota's development were on the records — for instance, Benjamin B. Hall, a lumberman from Ionia County, Michigan, and Wellington R. Burt and David Duncan, lumbermen from Saginaw, Michigan. Amos Bissell and George N. Bissell of Otsego County, New York, were buying substantial amounts. John M. Douglas of Chicago, who had bought lands in 1879, enlarged his holdings in 1880 by purchasing at least 12,000 acres and locating about 800 acres with Supreme Court scrip.[27]

The year 1881 was even more notable for its sales. Wellington Burt was the most active buyer during the first four months; in March he bought about 1400 acres of the 4000 acres sold, for 500 of which he paid $2.50 an acre. David Duncan was buying substantially at this time; he had now moved his residence and his sawmills from Saginaw to Duluth. It was an exciting year. Never had the pinelands changed hands so rapidly. In April 1881 more than 11,000 acres of this remote forest land passed from public to private ownership. Henry W. Sage of Tompkins County, New York, who with John McGraw was a large lumber operator in New York, Pennsylvania, and Michigan, was one of the heavy buyers of land in that busy month. In 1864 he and his partner, McGraw, had operated the largest sawmill in Michigan.[28] Sextus Wilcox of Cook County, Illinois, was another big buyer. In fact, Wilcox purchased approximately 5000 acres of the 11,000 sold that month. Chicago was his base of operations, but he had mills at Muskegon, White Cloud, and Whitehall, Michigan.[29] Guy Wells, a lumberman from Lee County, Iowa, was also a substantial purchaser in April.

The land office at Duluth was doing a real "land-office" business in 1881. Sextus Wilcox continued to buy in large amounts, and Henry Bradley of Bay City, Michigan, bought more than 1000 acres in June. Brad-

[26] G.L.O., Records of Receiver and Register, Supreme Court Scrip, Duluth, Minn., Oct. 1879.
[27] Ibid., Cash Books, Duluth, Minn., 1880–84.
[28] Hotchkiss, op. cit., p. 96.
[29] George W. Hotchkiss, Industrial Chicago, vol. v (six vols., Chicago, 1891–96), pp. 230–32.

ley was the most important member in the H. M. Bradley and Company, which operated a big sawmill in Bay City.[30] In July John Martin of Minneapolis bought almost one third of the 13,000 acres sold that month. In August Martin bought 2200 acres, and Thomas Lamontaque of Marinette County, Wisconsin, and Henry Bradley of Bay County, Michigan, bought most of the remainder of the 8000 acres sold that month. Martin bought heavily again in October, and Philip M. Ranney of Carlton County was also a prominent buyer.

In November 12,000 acres were sold, practically every acre of which was preëmpted; in December more than 20,000 acres changed hands and almost all of it was purchased under preëmption.[31] Preëmption in the pinelands in this competitive period gave opportunities for choice selection, for men could go into the unsurveyed area and pick their choice forties, eighties, or quarter sections. Altogether, 1881 was a record year in private cash sales, which were characterized by heavy purchases by lumbermen and by an unusually large number of completed preëmptions.

Then came the famous year of 1882. Markets east and west were steadily widening for the lumber of Duluth,[32] and enthusiasm about iron ore was mounting. George C. Stone, a native of Massachusetts who had settled in Duluth in 1869, was convinced that there was iron ore in the area. In 1875 he appealed to Charlemagne Tower of Pottsville, Pennsylvania, an attorney for mining interests, and to others who might provide assistance. They made investigations, and in 1878 Professor Newton H. Winchell, an experienced geologist, explored the country and became certain there was valuable iron ore in it. The state paid little attention to the unembellished field notes of a man of science, and it was not until Tower was assured of the state's stand on the taxation of iron ore that iron mining began in Minnesota.

On December 1, 1882, the Minnesota Iron Company was incorporated, and on July 31, 1884, the first iron ore was sent on its way from a Minnesota mine. Charlemagne Tower was so strongly convinced of the wealth of iron in northern Minnesota that in the early eighties he became the owner of 17,000 acres of land on the Iron Range.[33] The opening of the iron mines would offer another market for lumber. Business was booming! Men vied with each other for timberland, and business at the land office went on apace. There was a much livelier competition in disposal of land at Duluth than had appeared in the St. Croix or the St. Cloud area.

[30] Hotchkiss, *History of Lumber and Forest Industry of Northwest*, p. 102.
[31] G.L.O., Records of Receiver and Register, Cash Books, Duluth, Minn., Jan. 1880 to Dec. 1884.
[32] See above, p. 257.
[33] Folwell, *op. cit.*, vol. i, pp. 358–59.

From January 1 to December 1, 1882, 140,418 acres were sold for cash. The first two months showed a sale of about 12,000 acres, most of which were preëmpted.[34] In March of that year Leonidas Merritt and Frank W. Eaton of Duluth purchased more than 5000 acres of the 13,000 sold. A new buyer in the region was Reuben Whiteman of Livingston, New York, who purchased more than 2500 acres in April. In May 1882 Orrin T. Higgins of Cattaraugus County, New York, bought substantially; in June he was buying again, as was Hiram Sibley of Monroe County, New York. Curtis H. Pettit of Minneapolis was the heaviest buyer in June, purchasing about 2500 acres.

In July the sales increased notably: 21,176 acres sold for $27,419. Higgins and Pettit and David Duncan of Duluth, Alonzo J. Whiteman of Livingston County, New York, and Alva W. Bradley of Duluth were all big buyers. In August more than 27,000 acres of the wilderness became private property, all selling for $1.25 an acre except one quarter of land. The roll of buyers was much the same: Curtis H. Pettit, Alonzo Whiteman, Orrin T. Higgins, Alva W. Bradley, Hiram Sibley, and Ralph Atwater of Wayne County, Michigan. The same group continued to buy throughout the year.

December 1882 was the great month in all the history of white pine in the Duluth area. On August 1, 1882, President Chester A. Arthur issued a proclamation that two million acres of pine timberland were to be offered at Duluth, Minnesota, beginning Monday, December 4, 1882. The proclamation stated exactly the location of the lands to be sold but withheld, of course, lands appropriated by law for the use of schools, military lands, and lands reserved for railroads or other purposes. The sale of lands proceeded in the order in which the proclamation listed them until the whole had been offered. No private entry was allowed while the sale was in process. All lands that were held at double the minimum price were to be disposed of at not less than $2.50 an acre; minimum lands were for sale at not less than $1.25 an acre. Lists of sectional subdivisions were in the hands of the district officers and were open for examination by the public, and cruisers roamed the forests before the sale, picking the choice spots. As usual, the proclamation contained the announcement that preëmption claimants to any of the lands offered in this sale were required to make payments before the day appointed for the commencement of the public sale; otherwise their claims would be forfeited.[35] The lands stretched over a large area from Cook County at the point of the "Arrowhead" north of Lake Superior into Itasca County.

[34] G.L.O., Records of Receiver and Register, Cash Books, Duluth, Minn., Jan. 1880 to Dec. 1884.

[35] G.L.O., Proclamation Number 877, issued Aug. 1, 1882.

Cook, Lake, and St. Louis counties, as well as much of Itasca County, were included.

The men who gathered at the sale were well known in the lumber annals of the white pine regions; they were not buying land for the sake of the iron, but were interested in lands to furnish raw materials for their mills, or, in case of a rise in value, to yield them a profitable return.[36] Some of the prominent Minneapolis lumbermen who took part in the sale were T. B. Walker, John Martin, John S. Pillsbury, John De Laittre, Sumner W. Farnham, James A. Lovejoy, Clinton Morrison, John W. Day, William McNair, Benjamin F. Nelson, George H. Warren, and David M. Clough. Leonidas Merritt, Charles D'Autremont, Jr., a lawyer who had come to Duluth from New York that year, and Philip M. Ranney and Daniel J. Knox, later of the Duluth sawmill firm of that name, were some of the men present from the Duluth area.

From Chippewa Falls in Wisconsin came David E. Miles and Loren D. Brewster, whose specialty was to buy pinelands, estimate the stands of timber on them, and then offer them for sale. They were not lumbermen but they knew timber, and they were speculating on the day when these lands would be up in value.[37] Thomas Bardon, prominent businessman of Ashland, Wisconsin, associated with copper and iron interests and identified with various timber and land companies operating in Minnesota, Washington, and California, was an active buyer at this sale, as was Anthony J. Hayward, also of Ashland, who was later to become a prominent lumberman. Charles L. Mann, of Mann Brothers, makers of woodenware and chairs in Milwaukee, was another Wisconsin man in the group of substantial buyers.

Some of the prominent buyers from Michigan were William C. Yawkey of Detroit, Marshall H. Alworth, the cruiser from Saginaw County who was buying for others who had much more capital than he at that time, Arthur Hill, likewise of Saginaw County, and such others as William Boeing and Morton H. Hull. One of the buyers at the sale was John P. Webber of Penobscot County, Maine; another was Orrin Higgins of Cattaraugus County, New York. Hiram Sibley of Monroe County and Alonzo Whiteman of Livingston County, both of New York, were also substantial buyers.

These names by no means complete the list of men buying at the sale but they do indicate the importance of the lands in the Duluth area, because they are names of men with capital, many of them well known, and most of them active in the lumber industry.

[36] Fremont P. Wirth, *The Discovery and Exploitation of the Minnesota Iron Lands* (Cedar Rapids, Iowa, 1937), p. 53.

[37] *Chippewa Times* (Chippewa Falls, Wis.), Mar. 3, 1880.

On the day the sale began, December 4, 1882, 4139 acres were sold for $5801; on the eleventh of December 11,974 acres were sold for $28,528; and on December 15 and 16 the receiver issued receipts for 488 purchases. In the whole history of the Duluth land office from 1857 to January 1880, only 2087 receipts for land sold for cash in public and private sales had been issued; from January 1880 to December 1884 the land office at Duluth issued 4806 receipts for cash sales. In the twelve days of sale from December 4 through December 16, the public domain parted with 151,019 acres for $300,539, while the land sold in the whole month of December that year, which included sale and private entry, constituted 197,974 acres at $365,938.[38]

John S. Pillsbury of Minnesota bought actively for five days beginning December 11; he made 79 purchases totaling 8385 acres, or approximately 13 sections of white pine forest. The highest price he paid was $11 an acre for 160 acres — an unusual price, of course. However, this section was valuable, not only for its white pine but also because of other factors desirable in logging: it was either close to a logging stream or conveniently near Pillsbury's other holdings. Thomas B. Walker made 96 purchases totaling 10,089 acres, or almost 16 sections. The highest price he paid for any land was $6.25 per acre for a forty.

The prices varied considerably. Most of the lands sold were rated at $1.25 an acre; some at $2.50 an acre. In the competition of a public sale higher prices were paid than in private entry. The highest price for any single piece was $12 an acre, paid by James Towle of Montcalm, Michigan, for 80 acres. Next to the highest price for any piece of land was the $11 paid by Pillsbury.[39]

The lands of Itasca County, midway between Duluth and Crookston, known at the time of the great sale only to the cruiser and his employer, were eagerly sought in that famous December sale of 1882. Most of Itasca County was wilderness, three times larger than the state of Rhode Island, with rich forests of pine and good measures of iron hidden in its soil, abounding in lakes and streams flowing into the Father of Waters which could carry logs to the sawmills at the Falls of St. Anthony. These men at the Falls were the ones who had so anxiously urged that the Upper Mississippi region be bought from the Indians before the Treaty of 1855 was made.

Townships lying in ranges 22 and 23 in Itasca County were offered for the first time in the great December sale at Duluth, and the enthusiasm

[38] According to W. W. Spalding, Receiver, and J. R. Carey, Register, of the Land Office at Duluth, Minn.

[39] G.L.O., Records of Receiver and Register, Cash Books, Duluth, Minn., Jan. 1880 to Dec. 1884.

of Minneapolis lumbermen for this region is evidenced by the purchases they made. The first township in the southeast corner of Itasca, Wawina Township by name, was largely controlled by the Northern Pacific and by the state of Minnesota as swamplands. Sales in that township, therefore, were not large.

But immediately to the north lay Goodland Township "South," and John Martin, Sumner W. Farnham, and James A. Lovejoy, all of Minneapolis, became owners, along with the Northern Pacific, of the untouched wealth there. In that township Sumner W. Farnham and James A. Lovejoy, who represented one firm, bought about 1900 acres, almost three sections of virgin pine, on December 13, 1882. These 1900 acres were located in nine different sections of the township, an indication that they were carefully chosen. Lumbermen rarely located all their purchases in one place; [40] any spot with poor lumber was omitted.

These men all wanted the timber; the land itself had no particular interest for them. When the timber had been removed, their interest in the region was gone. In spite of its name, Goodland South is still unorganized; not enough people have considered it worth their while to settle on its lands, long since cutover.

To the north of Goodland South lay an unorganized township also called Goodland. It, too, was offered for the first time in the famous Duluth sale. John W. Day, Clinton Morrison, John Pillsbury, and T. B. Walker were active buyers in this township, doing their buying largely on December 13, 1882. [41] They were all Minneapolis lumbermen.

Lone Pine Township was next in line. Within it lies the famous logging spot Swan Lake, and many good logging streams. Here cruisers spent busy days, choosing the best pine. T. B. Walker's men must have been very active, for Walker purchased land in eleven sections of that township. John S. Pillsbury was a heavy competitor. These men, together with Clinton Morrison, David and Gilbert Clough, John W. Day, Benjamin F. Nelson, John Martin, Sumner W. Farnham, and James A. Lovejoy, all of Minneapolis, owned most of Lone Pine Township when the sun set on December 13, 1882. Orrin Higgins from New York state also secured title to pinelands in Lone Pine Township on that notable day, as did Clarence B. Buckman of St. Cloud. [42]

It is worth pointing out again that all these Minneapolis men were associated with sawmills and were buying resources with which to carry on their industry. They were all active in the building of Minnesota; two of them were to be governors of the state. They were not speculators but

---

[40] G.L.O., Land Tract Books, Minn., vol. 65, T. 54 N., R. 22 W., pp. 179–89.
[41] Ibid., T. 55 N., R. 22 W., pp. 203–14.
[42] Ibid., T. 56 N., R. 22 W., pp. 215–26.

industrial capitalists who, with money and executive ability, had each built a business of some consequence in the city of Minneapolis.

On December 14, 1882, Itasca lands were still being offered and Minneapolis men were still buying when township 57 north, range 22 west, was offered. It carries the name of Nashwauk East and is part of the western Mesabi Range. The pine forests drew men to this place in 1882 and Minneapolis lumbermen bought land there on that day because of the pine, little knowing that someday their wealth would be increased much more substantially by the iron ore which lay within the Mesabi. John Martin was very busy on that day, getting title to the sections which his cruisers had chosen. Sumner W. Farnham, James A. Lovejoy, David and Gilbert M. Clough, John W. Day, John De Laittre, and John S. Pillsbury were fortunate buyers in this area. Other buyers who were to become important in the development of this section were George L. Burrows, Esra Rust, and Charles H. Davis, all from Michigan. Davis was of the Wright and Davis Lumber Company, which was eventually to build a logging railroad reaching to the junction of the Swan River and the Mississippi.

On that same day Minneapolis men also bought pineland in township 58 north, range 22 west, in an unnamed township that is still unorganized today. John S. Pillsbury's name occurred most often in this buying, but John Martin, Sumner W. Farnham, James Lovejoy, Curtis H. Pettit, and Jabez N. Robinson were also active. Orrin Higgins from New York state bought here, and Wellington Burt from Michigan put his hand in for practically a whole section of this township.[43]

Also on December 14 several townships were offered in range 23 of Itasca County, and Minneapolis lumbermen were active there, too. Township 55 in that range definitely became the property of sawmill men from Minneapolis. It was the same group enlarging their holdings of white pine, as we have noted before.[44]

In township 56, range 23, later called Greenway Township, T. B. Walker was the outstanding buyer. John De Laittre, John Martin, John S. Pillsbury, Sumner W. Farnham, James A. Lovejoy, and Benjamin F. Nelson, together with Walker, owned most of the township at the close of the day.[45] Timber cruisers and loggers were the first known white men in the Greenway region, but after the pine was gone prospectors came, and in 1909 the first shipment of iron ore went out from that township. Large as the sums were that some of the lumbermen made from the pine on their Greenway Township lands, these sums were small in

[43] *Ibid.*, T. 58 N., R. 22 W., pp. 239–46.
[44] *Ibid.*, T. 55 N., R. 23 W., pp. 193–202.
[45] *Ibid.*, vol. 66, T. 56 N., R. 23 W., pp. 205–16.

comparison with the royalties which the iron ore was later to bring them.

On December 15, 1882, Nashwauk West, then known only as township 57 north, range 23 west, was offered for sale, and section after section of it became the property of the Minneapolis lumbermen.[46] Township 58 in the same range was sold to the same group of men, though they did not buy so much there as in township 57.[47] Large portions of township 59, which has also remained unorganized, were purchased by John Martin and David Clough.

Thus the townships offered in ranges 22 and 23, all a part of Itasca County, became largely the property of men living in Minneapolis.[48]

The rest of Itasca County's pineland was opened for sale at the St. Cloud land office a few months later, in September 1883. At this sale in St. Cloud lumbermen were as prominent as they had been at the Duluth sale. In the group were T. B. Walker, C. A. Pillsbury, George Camp, D. M. Clough, Benjamin F. Nelson, William Bassett, and others from Minneapolis. From Detroit came Fowler, Boeing, and Yawkey. Saginaw was represented by Rust and Alworth. Higgins from New York state and Hull from Chicago were also in the crowd at St. Cloud. These men came all "loaded for bear."[49] The white pine forest of Itasca County was the lumbermen's paradise, and it passed rapidly into private hands when it was offered. Today, however, much of Itasca County has become public domain again; it is a part of the great Chippewa National Forest.

There were no purchases made by individuals with little capital in the great Duluth sale of December 1882. The man of small means could not compete with the large-scale, low-cost lumber producers, the industrial capitalists who had developed in the Midland Empire. The quarter-section may have been quite the right size for the "one family farm," but the most economical unit in the management of timberland is a tract of thousands of acres. A tract of such size is necessary because logging equipment, mill construction, fire protection, and other features of the industry demand heavy capital investment.[50] No man could operate a sawmill on 160 acres!

The great sale of 1882 came to an end, but the land boom continued. Private entry at $1.25 an acre was the usual price; homesteads and preëmptions went as never before. However, the sales record of 1882 was not even approached again except in 1887. And it must be noted that

[46] *Ibid.*, T. 57 N., R. 23 W., pp. 217–26.
[47] *Ibid.*, T. 58 N., R. 23 W., pp. 229–38.
[48] *Ibid.*, T. 59 N., R. 23 W., pp. 241–52.
[49] *Mississippi Valley Lumberman and Manufacturer,* vol. viii, Sept. 7, 1883, p. 1. Chapter XVI, below, contains a more detailed discussion of fraudulent preëmptions.
[50] John Ise, *The United States Forest Policy* (New Haven, 1920), pp. 73–74.

in 1887 men were buying lands not only for the timber that was on them but for the iron ore as well, for by 1886 iron ore was being actively mined in the Duluth area. The acres of land sold and the amounts paid from 1880 through 1889 are given in Table 21.

TABLE 21. LAND SALES IN DULUTH AREA, 1880–1889

Year	Acres Sold	Amounts Paid
1880	32,937	$ 45,018
1881	104,813	149,225
1882	338,392	548,911
1883	179,902	242,420
1884	71,204	89,978
1885	57,273	78,106
1886	46,935	72,933
1887	220,055	295,660
1888	51,234	68,998
1889	50,264	66,389

SOURCE: G.L.O., Records of Receiver and Register, Cash Books, Duluth, Minn., 1880–83, 1884–86, 1887–89.

The list of men buying timberland in the Duluth district in the later eighties included the usual names: Walker, Eaton, Leonidas Merritt, Orrin and Frank Higgins, Webber, Hill, Pettit, Pillsbury, Martin, Yawkey, Robinson, Clough, Davis, Burt, Sibley, D'Autremont, Alonzo J. Whiteman, Rust, Burrows, Peyton, Alva W. Bradley, Fowler, and others. Lumbermen whose names were to appear often from that time on in the list of buyers were Charles Bean, Charles N. Nelson, and Isaac Staples, from Stillwater; John Ingram, veteran lumberman from Eau Claire, Wisconsin; Roscoe W. Gilkey, a dealer in timberland from Oconto, Wisconsin; George S. Shaw from Iowa, one of the best-known lumbermen on the Mississippi River; John S. Finlayson, a lumberman of St. Louis County; Anthony Hayward of Minneapolis; W. P. Allen of Cloquet; and Jacob Schwartz of Saginaw, Michigan.

Among these buyers were some men who later became very important in the development of the resources of the state. A number of investors from Michigan in the period of the 1880s, who were associated with lumber production in their own state and who bought timberlands in Minnesota in order to be sure of log stock in the years to come, are linked today with the great iron ore industry. Wellington Burt is a name of importance in this group. In 1857 Burt was working in a lumber camp on Pine River in Michigan at $13 a month; he gradually became important in lumber in that state and also its governor. In 1880 he was operating a wholesale and retail lumberyard at the great port of Buffalo, New York. Like other Michigan lumbermen he bought timberland in

Minnesota when Michigan's pine was running low, and his chief concern throughout his heavy buying in the eighties was pine logs, not iron ore. His holdings, however, particularly those he purchased in 1888, had hidden treasures of iron ore and within a decade he was leasing a portion of his pinelands, which had changed into iron mines, for amounts far beyond anything he had dreamed of when he bought them. The so-called Burt mine alone brought him royalties at that time of $250,000 a year.[51]

Morton B. Hull of Chicago and William Boeing of Detroit were active buyers in the sale of 1882 at Duluth. Marshall H. Alworth, the famous Saginaw cruiser, was their master adviser on pinelands. It is certain that Alworth's interest in 1882 was timber, not iron ore; Hull and Boeing had engaged him to buy timberlands, and he did so in all good faith. "Their investment of twenty-odd thousand dollars" gave excellent returns in a brief time. The pinelands Alworth picked for them harbored iron ore, and in a few months after the mines had been opened, they yielded 10,000,000 tons, estimated to be not one tenth of the deposits.[52]

The name of William C. Yawkey appears often in the land office records of the Duluth area. His holdings were to be found throughout the region lying to the north of Lake Superior. He was a lumberman by "lineal descent"; he had come from Ohio to pioneer in the lumber industry in Michigan as early as 1851. His first earnings were six dollars a month. He became an expert in estimating timberlands and was highly regarded as an inspector of lumber for Chicago and eastern buyers. As early as 1868 his operations in Michigan were said to be "mammoth." The growing scarcity and rising prices of Michigan resources led him, like so many others, to make investments elsewhere, and so the great sale of 1882 found him an eager buyer. His timberlands in Minnesota yielded iron ore as well as the pine logs he originally had in mind. At the time of his death, Yawkey was recognized as "a financier of distinctive acumen" and "a valued citizen" of Detroit, Michigan.[53]

The state of New York furnished many an investor in the pineland area of Duluth. Unlike the Michigan men, however, they were not usually in the business of lumber; their investment was largely a matter of speculation, and some of them fared well with the rising prices of timberland and stumpage. But the development of the iron ore paid them in dividends far beyond anything they could have anticipated.

Orrin Higgins was one of these. His name appears on many a page of the records of the receiver and register of the General Land Office. He

[51] Wirth, *op. cit.*, pp. 159–60.
[52] *Ibid.*, p. 160.
[53] *Compendium of History and Biography of the City of Detroit and Wayne County, Michigan* (Henry Taylor and Company, 1909), pp. 496–99; Hotchkiss, *History of Lumber and Forest Industry of Northwest*, pp. 78–83.

was a businessman of ability who had accumulated his capital by operating a chain of grocery stores in New York and Pennsylvania. With his surplus he made investments in Michigan, Wisconsin, Minnesota, and later in Washington and Oregon. His son Frank operated with him in the purchase of timberlands, and Frank, later governor of New York, greatly augmented the estate he inherited from his father. In the 1880s the Higgins' purchased many thousands of acres of pinelands in the Duluth area, and the Higgins Land Company was a well-known concern in Minnesota. The father and son made their greatest fortune, however, in the business of iron ore. In the great land sale of 1882 the Higgins' obtained about 11,000 acres, for which they paid $1.25 an acre; in 1922 much of this land was valued at $50,000 an acre.[54] On their properties was located the Norman mine, which up to 1919 had yielded more than 6,000,000 tons of ore.[55]

Hiram Sibley was another New York man whose name occurs often as a purchaser of big amounts of land in the Duluth area. He had been associated with Ezra Cornell in the Western Union Telegraph Company, of which he, Sibley, was at one time president. Said to have had the largest farm in New York state, he became much interested in the lands of the developing West. He was a large landowner in Illinois and in the 1880s invested heavily in Minnesota timberlands. His pinelands, too, contained iron ore, and the Sibley mine has yielded millions of tons of high-grade ore with substantial royalties for Hiram Sibley.[56] This man spent a portion of his wealth in aiding institutions of learning. With Ezra Cornell he was one of the incorporators of Cornell University, and his money founded the Sibley College of Mechanical Engineering and gave Sibley Hall to the University of Rochester.

Some lesser men also invested in northern Minnesota lands. For instance, from Otsego County in New York came Amos Bissell to make investments in the "hopeful West." Bissell had a country store in his native state. He saved his money bit by bit and invested it in Michigan timber, which he sold in 1877 at a large profit. Again he made profitable investments in timberland, in northern Wisconsin and northern Minnesota. George Bissell, his only child, was associated with him. These men are mentioned as examples of those with smaller capital who invested in Minnesota.

There were also some who failed, among them Reuben Whiteman and his son Alonzo. They were heavy buyers in the pinelands throughout the whole period of the eighties. Reuben Whiteman was a substantial

[54] Roy M. Robbins, *Our Landed Heritage* (Princeton, 1942), p. 253.
[55] *Dictionary of American Biography*, vol. ix, p. 10; Van Brunt, *op. cit.*, vol. ii, p. 582.
[56] *Dictionary of American Biography*, vol. xvii, p. 145.

businessman from Danville, New York; his son Alonzo, a graduate of Hamilton College with a law degree from Columbia University, had come to Duluth to live. Alonzo Whiteman was at one time mayor of Duluth, served as state senator from that section, and was prominent in securing the adoption of the Australian ballot in Minnesota; at one time his wealth was counted at a million. In 1887 he was considered the biggest speculator on Duluth's Board of Trade. But the Panic of 1893 put an end to the Whiteman wealth. The father had died, and Alonzo was not able to recover what the family had lost. On October 21, 1919, Minnesota citizens read that this once important man of business in Duluth had applied for county aid in Rochester, New York.[57]

History dwells much upon the fortunes that were made in the West but pays little attention to those who lost everything they had in the building of the frontier. There were many such, and some of them were among those who invested in timberland in northern Minnesota.

The 1890s opened with a change in the land policy of the United States government which was to affect greatly the transfer of the remainder of the public lands in the pineland area to private hands. In the closing years of the 1880s Congress found itself engaged in a stiff battle over land policy, and in 1889 the private cash sale law which had been in force since 1820 was withdrawn. The law which had made land purchasable at a minimum of $1.25 an acre was no longer on the statute books! Hardly was this law removed when Congress was called upon to reconsider other land laws that seemed to have lost favor. The resultant Land Act of 1891 repealed the preëmption law and provided that there should be no more sale of public lands by auction. The preëmption law had been on the statute books before Minnesota became a territory. Those preëmption claims that had been established before the date of the new law could be completed but no more could be filed.

The land laws providing for preëmption, private cash sale, and auction sale had favored large holdings; now that they were removed, men anxious to gain control of large blocks of land faced a difficult problem. The Act of 1891 provided, too, that the President of the United States could set aside areas of timberland as national parks and forest reserves.[58] How widely the President would exercise this power was not known, but conservation was in the air and lumbermen feared that the natural resources heretofore so easily within their reach might gradually be closed to them.

[57] *Minneapolis Morning Tribune*, Oct. 21, 1919, p. 1; *St. Paul Pioneer Press*, Oct. 21, 1919, p. 1; *Fergus Falls Daily Journal*, May 27, 1937, p. 2.
[58] *U.S. Statutes at Large*, vol. xxvi (Mar. 3, 1891), 51st Cong., 2d Sess., pp. 1095–97; *Report of the Land Commissioner*, 1891, pp. 41–43.

The repeal of the old land laws greatly reduced the number of acres of pinelands that passed into private hands. The only land now purchasable was any uncompleted preëmption claim established before 1891 or any homestead commutation. Sales fell off noticeably.

Men who must have timber for their business and men interested in iron ore were not to be deterred by the land laws of 1889 and 1891. They had to find another way and they found it in the homestead! Then began the alienation of public domain through the entering of homesteads and soldiers' additional homesteads. Homesteading had been slow in past years in the Duluth area. In 1870 only 11,096 acres were taken as original homesteads in that area; in 1880 only 9508 acres. But in 1890 the number jumped to 63,618 acres.[59]

If homesteading was meant to apply to arable land, the Duluth area could hardly be affected by it, for some conifer or stone covered the land everywhere. Who would choose a rocky uncleared plot near Duluth when elsewhere there were great arable tracts where the mere turning of the sod by the plow made the soil ready to yield? In the Duluth area, nevertheless, where years of backbreaking effort would be necessary to develop more than subsistence farming, homesteading went on apace; it was the timber and the iron ore men wanted!

Rich and poor homesteaded in the Duluth area in the hope that iron might be found on their lands or that they might profit by the increasing value of timberland. In 1891 men claimed 96,886 acres as original homesteads; in 1892, 241,095 acres; in 1893, a panic year, 158,407 acres; in 1901 the record number of 300,038 acres; and in 1902, 299,369 acres.[60] Many of those who made application for original homesteads did not complete the requirements under the five-year plan of the Homestead Act. In 1892 a total of 241,095 acres were listed in the Duluth area under original homesteads, but in 1897, when these homesteads should have been ready for final entries according to the law, only 39,877 acres were taken up. In 1893 applications were made for 158,407 acres under the Homestead Act, but only 43,392 were listed in the final entries in 1898 at the end of the five-year period.[61]

Such discrepancies between original and final homesteads were characteristic of the whole period of homesteading in the pineland area. Many of the homesteaders came into possession of their "claims" quite soon after the original homestead application had been filed by the method of commutation. This method, though in use before, had been changed

[59] G.L.O., Records of Receiver and Register, Original Homesteads, Duluth, Minn., 1865–70, 1880–83, 1890–92.
[60] Ibid., 1890–92, 1893, 1901, 1902.
[61] Ibid., Final Homesteads, Duluth, Minn., 1897–98.

somewhat in 1891 so that an individual could become owner of his claim through purchase at $1.25 an acre fourteen months after he had made his original application. Commutation increased in northern Minnesota as pinelands and iron-ore lands grew in demand. In 1890 individuals became owners of 9559 acres by way of commutation; in 1891 of 15,920 acres; in 1892, 18,645; and in 1893, 22,790. In 1902 commutation placed 27,787 acres in private hands; in the following year, 28,322 acres.[62] This latter number was more than forty-four sections of pineland or eight sections more than one township. That timberlands were more generally commuted than lands in the agricultural sections of Minnesota was generally acknowledged. In the period from July 1, 1899, to June 30, 1903, there were 1865 commuted homesteads in Minnesota and of these 1485 lay in the timber belt of the state.[63]

Through homesteading and commutation, the pineland area of Minnesota continued to pass into private control, and competition for pineland was growing more acute as sawmill men, particularly from Michigan, moved equipment, millmen, and loggers to Duluth and to Minneapolis — as they did in the 1890s and early 1900s.[64] The Diamond Match Company of Oshkosh, Wisconsin, is typical of the large concerns that came into the forests of the Duluth area in this heyday of pineland buying. The executives of this firm sent fourteen cruisers into the Minnesota forests at one time to seek pine. This Wisconsin company, said to be one of the largest manufacturers of matches in the United States, was also said to consume annually 80,000,000 feet of white pine lumber.[65] Such a consumer needed substantial resources.

Private individuals with small holdings of 160 acres, 80 acres, and lesser lots were selling to sawmill men, who were fortifying themselves for the battle of scarcity that someday would come. Shevlin-Carpenter, C. A. Smith, Scott and Holston, and Edward Backus, all firms of importance in Minnesota's lumber history, were buying large holdings or small, whatever they could get. The records of the register of deeds of St. Louis County are filled with small purchases in the 1890s.[66]

Frederick Weyerhaeuser and his associates were still adding to their holdings in the state. We have seen how they purchased the timberlands of the Northern Pacific Railroad in Minnesota, as well as a large holding

[62] Ibid., Cash Books, Duluth, Minn., 1890–92, 1893, 1902, 1903.

[63] Report of the Public Lands Commission (Oct. 26, 1904), 58th Cong., 3rd Sess., Senate Docs., no. 189, pp. 66–67. A discussion of the illegal methods by which the Homestead Act was evaded is found on pages 297–302, below.

[64] See above, pp. 251–52.

[65] Duluth Weekly Herald, Jan. 9, 1901.

[66] Timber Deed Book, 1895, no. 121, Nov. 2, p. 440; 1897, Book P, July 10, p. 598; 1898, no. 152, Feb. 19, p. 434; 1898, no. 154, Apr. 8, p. 327, May 12, p. 379, and Aug. 29, p. 467; 1899, no. 155, Feb. 9, p. 557; 1899, no. 176, Aug. 5, p. 116 and Dec. 26, p. 308.

in northern Minnesota from the St. Anthony Lumber Company.[67] With the purchase of the Cloquet mills and their timberlands, "township after township" of white pine was added to Weyerhaeuser's holdings.[68] T. B. Walker likewise had been active in expanding and concentrating his holdings. He made large purchases in the region lying tributary to the Red River of the North. From the United States government and from individuals who had holdings in the area he purchased in the early 1880s thousands of acres of pineland.[69]

The *Duluth Weekly Herald* described negotiations for the sale of commercial timber at Duluth on a "usual day" in the winter of 1891.[70] The Spaulding Hotel was bustling as owners of timber in the vicinity of Duluth mingled freely with men who wanted to buy. The *Herald* shows that among them were prominent lumbermen — and that candor about the purpose of their presence was not the order of the day:[71]

"It was an accidental meeting, I assure you," said McClure, the big Saginaw logger, last night; "my presence here is simply to see Duluth," said Matt Clark, the ex-democratic leader of Stillwater; "I am here on private business," was the remark of Major H. B. Strait, the venerable ex-Congressman. "I had to stop over in Duluth on my way from visiting my logging camps," said H. F. Brown, the well-known dissector of logs at Minneapolis; "Just came down to get a little legal tangle straightened out," uttered C. N. Nelson, the Cloquet lumber king, while W. P. Allen, a rival monarch of the same place, was on the same errand.

It was a usual day in Duluth when, regularly, Michigan men and men from the sawmills of Iowa along the Mississippi came to fortify themselves against the time when their own white pine would be no more. Even Wisconsin men, still safe but anxious to assure themselves of plenty, were adding white pine holdings from the country beyond Lake Superior. It was a usual day at the Spaulding, the unofficial place of exchange, when the white pine of the Arrowhead country was passing rapidly from one hand to another.

In the Duluth area, moreover, large amounts of forest became private property through the purchase of stumpage. In the trade this term was applied to standing timber suitable for sawing into lumber. When men purchased stumpage, only the timber became their property and this they bought at so much a thousand feet; the land was not transferred. This was not an uncommon way of becoming the owner of good stands of

[67] See above, pp. 233–34.
[68] *American Lumberman*, Sept. 12, 1903, pp. 44, 49.
[69] *Mississippi Valley Lumberman and Manufacturer*, vol. v, July 8, 1881, p. 4.
[70] *Duluth Weekly Herald*, Feb. 20, 1891.
[71] Matt Clark was a well-known cruiser in Minnesota who was at one time employed in the office of the State Auditor.

timber, since the government of the United States, the state of Minnesota, and individual owners dealt in stumpage.

One of the problems involved in the buying and selling of stumpage was estimating accurately the board feet in a stand of timber. Usually the estimated amount was lower than the actual cut, which meant a loss for the seller. On certain ceded Chippewa lands in Minnesota, the estimated amounts of timber offered at certain sales were found to be far below the actual cuts. Typical losses of the government in such sales are revealed in Table 22.

TABLE 22. GOVERNMENT LOSSES IN STUMPAGE SALES

Date of Sale	Government Estimate (in thousands of feet)	Actual Cut (in thousands of feet)
March 2, 1903	13,636	26,816
December 5, 1903	223,921	308,637
December 28, 1903	169,308	296,155
November 15, 1904	146,560	168,113
November 17, 1904	9,718	18,786
July 17, 1907	2,056	3,754
March 15, 1910	2,169	2,189

SOURCE: U.S. Bureau of Corporations, *The Lumber Industry* (1913), pt. 1, pp. 50–51.

In the sale of stumpage on Minnesota state lands over a period of ten years it was found that the actual cut surpassed the estimate by an average of 40 per cent. Some cuts were only 10 per cent above the estimate; others were 60 per cent above. This timber was usually cut within two or three years after the estimate had been made, and since the timber was mature, decay and growth during that time were about equal.[72]

There was no government ruling on the price of stumpage; the market price for lumber determined the price for government timber as well. In 1880 pine stumpage in northern Minnesota ranged in price from 50 cents to $1.00 a thousand feet.[73] In 1898 stumpage on Minnesota's state land reached its highest price up to that time — an average of $2.86 per thousand feet. At the turn of the century the average price for stumpage on Minnesota state lands was $5.17. The price had risen considerably, but the approaching scarcity, the growing industry, and the large market for lumber all tended to augment the price of standing timber. Over a period of thirty years, from 1880 to 1910, the ten-year average price paid for a thousand feet of timber on Minnesota state lands was as follows: 1880–89, an average of $1.95; 1890–99, an average of $2.22; and 1900–9, an average of $7.19.[74]

It is necessary to bear in mind that the timber sold in the later years

[72] U.S. Bureau of Corporations, *The Lumber Industry* (1913), pt. 1, pp. 50–51.
[73] *Ibid.*, p. 184.
[74] Compton, *Organization of the Lumber Industry*, p. 71.

was remote and inaccessible as compared with the timber of 1880, which stood most conveniently along the banks of streams and on the shores of lakes. That which was most conveniently located was taken first, and the higher price from 1900 on purchased a product not so good or so well located as had a much lower price in 1880. Minnesota's stumpage continued to rise in price until southern lumber became a competitor.

The United States government got a much better price for stumpage than for timberland by the acre. In the ceded portion of the Chippewa Indian Reservation the government sold the timber of 103,027 acres on December 5, 1903, for $1,432,791, or $13.90 an acre; on December 28 that same year the government sold 95 per cent of the timber on 72,856 acres for $1,218,132, or $16.70 an acre. The average price at both sales was $15.06 per acre for the timber. The land was retained by the government and 5 per cent of the timber was held for reforestation. If this had been commuted at $1.25 an acre, it would have brought the government a considerably smaller sum. If the Timber and Stone Act had applied to Minnesota and this land had been sold at the price of $2.50 per acre allotted by that Act, it would have brought the government $438,807, or a loss of $2,211,196.[75]

This contrasted seriously with the amount which the United States got for commuted timberlands in the period between July 1, 1899, and June 30, 1903, when 1485 homesteads were commuted in the timber belt of Minnesota. At the time of commutation the standing merchantable timber on these homesteads was worth on a stumpage basis $891,000. If the United States had had the foresight to sell stumpage, in this case the gain would have been more than half a million dollars.[76] For the timber on these commuted areas the government received about 85 cents per 1000 feet at a time when stumpage was sold by the state government at an average of about $5.00 per 1000 feet.[77] It must be kept in mind, however, that when stumpage was sold, the government still held the cutover lands.

Virgin forest had stood untouched for a number of decades in the lands reserved for the Indians. But in the 1880s white men began to eye this fine timberland. Agitation for its sale began, and those who wished to keep it for the Indian were not able to prevail. Little by little the forests of the Red Lake and White Earth reservations passed under the ax.[78]

Competition was sharp in the pine woods of northern Minnesota as the timber grew scarcer. Concentration of pinelands in a few hands

[75] *Report of the Public Lands Commission,* 58th Cong., 3rd Sess., *Senate Docs.,* no. 189, p. vii.
[76] *Ibid.,* pp. 66–67.
[77] U.S. Bureau of Corporations, *The Lumber Industry* (1913), pt. 1, p. 260.
[78] The story of the depletion of the forests of these reservations is told in Chapter XVI, below.

was continuing. Those few were industrialists with a heavy capital investment in the production of lumber. In 1900 in Cook County of the Arrowhead region the largest timber operators were two sawmill firms of
Duluth which were quickly turning the timber from these holdings into
a usable product; these two concerns were the largest taxpayers in the
county at that time. Ten years later these firms had been replaced by
another lumber firm which held the greatest amount of timberland and
paid the highest taxes.[79] In 1910 the timber in the southern and western
portions of St. Louis County was controlled by one lumber firm, while
that of the eastern portion was controlled by another.[80]

In Cass County, a heavily timbered area in the northern part of the
state, the principal timberland owners in 1910 were the Mississippi River
Lumber Company, the Red River Lumber Company, and the Gull
River Lumber Company, all prominent lumber manufacturers in the
state.[81]

Lumbermen were concentrating on Minnesota, for in 1913 that state
still had more standing timber than either Wisconsin or Michigan, with
about 12,500,000,000 board feet of white and red pine, as compared
with Wisconsin's 3,000,000,000 and Michigan's 2,000,000,000.[82] In that
year, however, six holders controlled no less than 54 per cent of the very
valuable white and red pine in Minnesota; thirty-two holders owned 77
per cent of it. In none of the other Lake states were those types of timber
under the control of so small a group.[83]

In Minnesota the small holder had given way to the large indus-
trialist. The timber which the early pioneer had looked upon as "an
incumbrance" had become in the course of fifty years a highly valued
asset. The pinelands of Minnesota had been placed on the market during
a period of great expansion in the United States. In the years that followed the Civil War the "roaring vitality" of the American people was
felt as never before in the conquest of the continent. In the period in
which these pinelands were offered our country witnessed its greatest
movement of population and its settled area increased a hundred per
cent. During this period laissez-faire and rugged individualism constituted the dominating philosophies of the nation. These forces converged
to shape a national policy which led to the rapid conversion of the great
public forest lands of Minnesota into the property of the manufacturers
of lumber.

[79] This information was given in a letter written by L. G. Lundquist, Auditor, Cook
County, Grand Marais, Minn., dated Oct. 13, 1943.
[80] These statements were made in a letter written by Walter H. Borgen, Auditor, St. Louis
County, Duluth, Minn., to the author, dated Oct. 8, 1943.
[81] These statements were made in a letter to the author by Leonard Peterson, Register of
Deeds, Cass County, Walker, Minn., Oct. 5, 1943.
[82] U.S. Bureau of Corporations, The Lumber Industry (1913), pt. 1, p. 77.
[83] Ibid., p. 22.

CHAPTER XVI

The Operation of National Land Laws
in the Pineland Area

THE government of the United States had no definite policy to govern the disposition of its timberlands throughout the greater part of the nineteenth century. Timberlands were in the same category as the good farm lands of the prairie or the lands of the treeless plains. The United States was not industrial when the national government established its most basic land laws, and the people thought in terms of agriculture. In passing the preëmption and homestead acts Congress had in mind arable lands, not timber-covered lands. Indeed, the idea prevailed in the pioneer period of our country's history that even the timbered lands would yield to agriculture as soon as the stubborn forest was removed.

The Cash-Purchase Law of 1820, which set the minimum price of land at $1.25 per acre, announced the beginning of the fight by Jeffersonian Democracy for the disposal of the lands of the West to those who actually meant to settle on them. The Preëmption Act that followed in 1841 declared further that revenue from public lands was no longer a consideration.

Preëmption was a "frontier triumph." The applicant for land gave oath that he wanted the land for his own exclusive use and benefit and not for sale or speculation, and that he was actually settling on the land; he could make entry to the extent of 160 acres for a limited period, at the end of which time he could receive his patent by paying $1.25 an acre and proving to the satisfaction of the register and receiver that he had fulfilled the requirements. This method was hailed as the capstone in the democratization of the public land system. The purpose of the law was to protect bona fide settlers from land sharks who might buy land to hold it for a higher price. The frontier "accepted the law as a concession wrung from a reluctant Congress whose sympathy for the West was far from cordial."[1] But Horace Greeley, whose interest in the West was as vital as that of any man in the East, opposed the Preëmp-

[1] Robbins, *Our Landed Heritage*, pp. 90–91.

289

tion Act, maintaining that it was "a curse to the West." [2] Greeley knew what every student of the history of our public domain knows now, that the law had serious weaknesses. But the frontier wanted it, the frontier got it, and the frontier had to bear with it for exactly half a century.

Preëmption was well established when Minnesota's first land was offered in 1848, and Minnesota was one of the states to which was granted in 1854 the further privilege of placing preëmptions on unsurveyed lands.[3] Minnesota's territorial delegate in Congress, Henry Hastings Sibley, had appeared several times before the Committee on Public Lands of the House of Representatives urging that the preëmption law be extended to unsurveyed lands.[4]

The pinelands of Minnesota, most of which became private property during the half century the preëmption law was in effect, offer an interesting example of the operation of the law. Preëmption was used freely, especially in the Duluth district, a section completely forest-covered. In the 1880s large portions of the lands sold in that district were preëmpted. Table 23 shows the amount of preëmpted land sold in certain months of this active period as compared with the total acres sold.

TABLE 23. LAND SOLD IN DULUTH DISTRICT

	Total Acres Sold	Acres Preëmpted
September 1885	3,524	2,643
January 1886	3,010	1,039
July 1886	4,637	2,095
August 1886	6,000	3,158
August 1887	6,713	3,737
November 1887	10,452	6,005
December 1887	7,862	4,925
January 1888	3,411	2,383
July 1888	7,042	3,776

SOURCE: G.L.O., Records of Receiver and Register, Cash Books, Duluth, Minn., 1884–86, 1887–89.

Thousands and thousands of acres in the Duluth district were acquired falsely under the preëmption law, wrote N. C. McFarland, commissioner of the General Land Office in Washington, to the *St. Paul Pioneer Press,* January 8, 1882.[5] Stating that the returns from the Duluth land office at the time showed "an unusual activity in the matter of filed declaratory statements," and that filings appeared to be on lands valuable in timber,

[2] *New York Weekly Tribune,* June 15, 1843.
[3] *U.S. Statutes at Large,* vol. x, p. 576.
[4] *Minnesota Pioneer* (St. Paul), Apr. 3, 1850.
[5] N. C. McFarland, one of the best land commissioners in our history, was very ambitious about rooting out corruption. The receivers and registers were political appointments, and it was difficult to remove them. Newspapers, then as now, took positions, so it was natural that McFarland should write to one of the most important papers in the state — particularly since the *St. Paul Pioneer Press* gave much space to the land problems.

he addressed that office in a demanding tone to the effect that the matter of fraudulent filing was of "public notoriety" in the Duluth community and "you must know of it."[6] T. H. Pressnell, receiver at the Duluth land office at that time, and M. C. Russell, the register, both pleaded ignorance in this matter.[7] McFarland, however, meant business and ordered William R. Marshall, special agent under the direction of the United States Land Office, to go to Duluth to search for wrongdoers in the public domain and "to discover the abuses in the Duluth Land Office."[8]

The work Marshall was assigned to do was challenging. His first step was to find out whether or not it was possible to make false preëmption entries without being detected, and he did this by making four preëmption entries under "wholly fictitious" names; these entries were definitely located and all details were taken care of in the usual way. When he had made the final entries and had got his receipts, he sent them to Washington as proof to the Secretary of the Interior, who had jurisdiction over the public domain, that it was possible to make false entries.[9] While waiting to complete the entries, he went to work to investigate preëmpted lands in the Duluth district. He examined all the preëmptions made from July 1, 1881, to February 15, 1882, and found that more than a hundred of them had been transferred to other parties immediately upon completion of final entry.

St. Louis County was large and the examination of its scattered lands was no small order. Marshall selected ten townships lying north and east of Duluth, containing a hundred preëmption entries made since July 1881. Of these entries he was able to reach and examine fifty-six. Marshall reported in a letter to McFarland:[10]

On only one of these 56 tracts of preëmpted land did I find a habitable building, or evidences of bonafide settlement or occupation by the preëmptor. In the case of the 55 of examined preëmpted tracts, we found on about half of the number log pens from one to four feet in height, without any semblance of door, window, floor, or roof, save in some cases brush-cut when leaves were thrown on top. In the case of about one-half the number, diligent search failed to discover anything to show that a human being had ever been on the land except the government surveyors and often small evidence of these, for there has been most wretchedly unfaithful work done in some towns.

In order to make the investigation, Marshall and his men, whom he described as assistants of high character and qualification, traveled wholly on snowshoes, going through the wilderness north into the region of

---

[6] McFarland's letter was printed in the *St. Paul Pioneer Press*, Jan. 13, 1882.
[7] *Ibid.*
[8] National Archives: Records of the General Land Office, Miscellaneous Letters Received 1882–18330. (National Archives will hereafter be designated as N.A.)
[9] *Ibid.*, 1883–6165.
[10] *Ibid.*, 1882–31502.

Lake Vermilion. In his letter Marshall stated that the expense incurred
was "too great" but that if McFarland could know the character of the
country, which was good for nothing when the timber was gone, the in-
clemency of the seasons, and the difficulty of making a careful examination, he would realize that the expense was not unreasonable.[11]

In the hearings ordered by the United States government, Marshall
told of some of the conditions he had found in St. Louis County. In a
certain section, where one Thomas Kelly had made his preëmption entries,
Marshall found a "house" consisting of four logs eight inches in diameter,
laid four square; one James Couvers, who made his preëmption entry
within two sections, had as his "improvement" an open crib of poles
four feet high, ten feet square, the poles being three to six inches in
diameter — there was no roof, no floor, no door, no windows, no chinking
between logs, and no sign of cultivation or human occupation. In one
place after another Marshall had found no improvement — for example,
in township 59, sections 19, 23, 24, 25, 27, 30, 31, 32, preëmption entries
had been made but there were no improvements whatsoever. Among all
the preëmption claims he had examined in the whole region, there was
only one family living on a preëmpted claim.[12]

Marshall said that he saw no place where five acres could be plowed
even if cleared of timber and brush. The region could be reached only
on foot through the woods or by canoe on the rivers; the nearest settlement was Duluth, seventy miles away. "No person," said he, "would be
likely to take the same in good faith for a home or farm."[13] The preëmptor, of course, swore falsely in declaring that he was "taking the
oath that the land is for the exclusive use and benefit of the preëmptor" if
that was not his intention. When the fifty-five men who had not fulfilled
the requirements were summoned to a hearing by the government, none
of them appeared either in person or by attorney. Of the men who had
bought this land from the preëmptors "in good faith," about half sent
their attorneys, but the attorneys were very mild in their claims.[14]

Marshall was convinced there was abundant evidence that systematic
and wholesale frauds had been and were daily being perpetrated in
the entry of land under the preëmption law in the pineland area. He
obtained forty-six preëmption entries for October 1881 at the office of the
register of deeds of St. Louis County and found from the records that "in
every instance" the land had been conveyed to other persons. Some were
conveyed on the day of final entry, some the day after. These lands

[11] *Ibid.*
[12] *Ibid.*, 1882–38564. This letter contained detailed statements of the examination which
he had made of the preëmpted lands.
[13] *Ibid.*, 1882–83930.
[14] *Ibid.*

were located in a forest region, "a wilderness in which it is as well-known that there is not a single agricultural settlement or settler as it is known that southern Minnesota is a well-settled farm country." The forty-six grantors whom he investigated conveyed to only six grantees, who were known as lumbermen, mill owners, or speculators investing and dealing in pine, mineral, and other valuable lands. The preëmptors in this case were transient young men without families, never heard of before or after.[15] It was difficult to obtain legal evidence enough to convict these preëmptors of fraud — "as difficult," said Marshall, "as it is in Utah to get evidences of bigamy."[16]

On November 4, 1882, Marshall wrote to McFarland that he and his assistants had examined 106 preëmption claims and had not in a single instance found anyone residing on a claim or evidence of anyone having settled upon or cultivated the land in good faith. The cost to the government was about fifteen dollars for each claim examined.[17] Marshall exposed two men who had sworn that they had improved their land and met the requirements seven months before they even saw the land.[18]

Another special agent sent from the General Land Office in Washington to investigate frauds in the pinelands of Minnesota was Webster Eaton, who in January 1884 reported twenty-five fraudulent preëmption entries in one township. "It was perpetrated by one C. P. Byam, then and now a citizen of Duluth," said Eaton, to whom Bernard Lynch, mail carrier between Duluth and Vermillion, had given testimony. Lynch said that Byam had brought him some land office paper in 1882 and asked him to sign some names on it. He had signed eight or ten names, including that of Alick Ravel, a boy he had known in Canada. When Lynch later saw these names in a newspaper as people who were taking up land, he became suspicious and asked Byam about it. Byam explained that "he had paid T. H. Pressnell, Receiver, twenty dollars for each of these claims and would make it all right with me." He paid Bernard Lynch one hundred dollars.[19]

Earlier, Eaton had requested of headquarters in Washington that patents be withheld for all the final entries in sections 1, 2, 3, 10, 11, and 12 of a certain township until he had completed his investigations, for he thought all the preëmptions were fraudulent.[20] In December Eaton asked his chief in Washington that he be sent "the final proof affidavit made in the proofs upon the following numbered Declaratory Statements

[15] *Ibid.*, 1882–15800.
[16] *Ibid.*
[17] *Ibid.*, 1882–85512.
[18] *Ibid.*, 1883–57067.
[19] *Ibid.*, 1884–11075. This letter contained an affidavit in which Bernard Lynch had testified before Webster Eaton, special agent, and C. A. Congdon, assistant United States attorney.
[20] *Ibid.*, 1883–96081

all in Township 57 Range 12 West of the 4th p.m." He included twenty-four numbers in the list for which he wanted the final proof affidavit.[21] Eaton expressed the opinion that nine tenths of all the entries at the Duluth land office were fraudulent.[22] Perhaps that was an exaggeration, but the situation was certainly serious.

The preëmption broker was a busy person in Duluth in the days of the passing of the public domain in that area; Morris Thomas, John McGuire, and Wentworth were names well known in that business. Their attorney at one time was T. H. Pressnell, who, as we saw, had served as receiver of the United States Land Office in the Duluth district; through his work for the government he had obtained information concerning pinelands which was valuable to men interested in the acquisition of such lands. Thomas himself, whose home was in Duluth, was a logger and a dealer in pinelands and lumber; he therefore had a keen interest in acquiring heavily timbered lands. Thomas and McGuire "set up" men to make preëmption claims, and after these preëmptors had completed the requirements, the land was conveyed to "said McGuire and Thomas."

Thomas had been associated with L. B. Johnson of Duluth in the early 1880s in the same type of venture. They had sent eighteen men to preëmpt land in a certain area, furnishing the men their living while they were on the claims and paying them $150 when they had "proved up." Shortly thereafter Thomas and Johnson ventured again; the men "proved up" in September 1882, conveyed their lands to their masters, Thomas and Johnson, and received $150 to $225 per claim. In the spring of 1883 Thomas and Johnson again engaged men to preëmpt, paying them $30 per month and from $100 to $125 for their claims. Some of the men built their own improvements, but in township 60 north, range 18 west, the improvements were built by five men under the direction of Johnson himself.[23]

C. A. Congdon, assistant United States attorney in Minnesota, examined checks paid by John McGuire and Wentworth in preëmptions and found one in the amount of $556 to cover payment for 440 acres of land entered that day in the names of three men. Several other checks found in the investigation were to "grease the matter," according to McGuire's clerk — one of these checks was payable to T. H. Pressnell. There were hundred-dollar checks to pay the men for preëmpting.[24]

[21] *Ibid.*, 1883–956.   [22] *Ibid.*, 1883–97184.

[23] *Ibid.*, 1883–91993; the letter contains an affidavit laying bare this fact, signed by Morris Thomas and L. B. Johnson and given before the United States district attorney of that section. A search of more than twenty letters in which Wentworth is mentioned has revealed his surname only; therefore his surname appears in this chapter with neither initials nor first name.

[24] *Ibid.*, 1884–76208. The author has handled the certified copies of these checks in the General Land Office in Washington.

John McGuire finally disclosed all his preëmption and homestead dealings, having been promised immunity from criminal proceedings if he would give testimony.[25] T. H. Pressnell likewise acknowledged that he had participated in this unlawful business and had aided others in fraudulent entry of lands. The officials of the United States government promised him immunity for past offenses on the condition that "he will cease to do evil and learn to do well." [26] A letter written later by Webster Eaton to McFarland indicated that Pressnell had not kept his word and that preëmption brokers still employed him as their attorney.[27]

It seemed to be the usual practice for men who preëmpted for others to be paid a monthly salary with an additional payment of $100 or more when proof had been made and the land conveyed to the individual or firm by whom the preëmptor was engaged. For example, Milton Peden, also a special agent of the United States Land Office who was hunting out fraudulent entries in the Duluth district, wrote that he found men who were hired at $35 per month to preëmpt and were bound in a written contract to transfer lands for $100 in addition to their monthly payments; these lands were subsequently turned over to firms dealing in timberlands.[28]

These investigations of preëmptions in the pineland area exposed the evils associated with the system. The greatest evil lay in the fact that many entries were made for the benefit of other men who furnished money for that purpose. Gangs of men, ranging from ten to fifty, were often employed to make as many entries.[29] Crews on vessels into Duluth went into the woods for a day or two and then took the required preëmption oaths.[30] Sometimes preëmption filings were made for the timberlands merely as a claim to hold the land until the timber could be removed, after which the preëmptor would quietly steal away.[31] Some fraudulent preëmption filings on good land were held until some settler came along and willingly purchased "a relinquishment of the filing" in order to save delay in getting the property.[32]

Men who defended the abuses of the preëmption system in the pinelands argued that the government received its price of $1.25 an acre and that therefore no one was wronged. To be sure, the government did get the price established by law, but the purpose of that low price was not accomplished. Under a well-planned forest policy, timber could have

---

[25] *Ibid.*, 1884–12071.
[26] *Ibid.*, 1883–104871.
[27] *Ibid.*, 1884–76208.
[28] *Ibid.*, 1883–12334.
[29] *Report of the Commissioner of the General Land Office,* 1883, p. 207.
[30] *St. Paul Pioneer Press,* Jan. 7, 1882.
[31] *Report of the Commissioner of the General Land Office,* 1883, p. 207.
[32] *Ibid.*

been sold by board feet instead of by the acre; the government could then have realized far greater sums on this important product. In actual operation the preëmption law tended to favor those who wanted large holdings, such as the corporation or the speculator, rather than the small settler for whom the law was designed. Indeed, the law came to operate in a way quite contrary to the democratic principles of American land tenure which preëmption was designed to protect. It is not illogical that it came to be called the "speculators' law." [33]

The Secretary of the Interior and officials in the General Land Office of the United States, men most closely associated with the public domain, were not unconcerned about the corruption that existed in preëmption in the timbered areas. Attempts were made to prevent fraud but the problem was complicated and concerted action was difficult. In 1877 Commissioner Williamson urged that timberlands be withdrawn from entry. Carl Schurz, German-reared Secretary of the Interior at that time, was accustomed to the vigilant European protection of natural resources, and he worked with Williamson to lessen the fraud in the public land system of the United States. They urged conservation of natural resources, especially of timber and more particularly of timber on land that was unfit for agriculture. They agreed that much of the timberland was not fit for agriculture and that those lands should not be purchasable under laws made primarily for agricultural lands.[34] These men fought to establish a forest-reserve policy.[35] Both Schurz and Williamson realized that in the pinelands the preëmption laws were used mainly as a cover for fraud.[36] They recommended specific legislation that might remedy the evils so prevalent in the pineland area.

But Congress did not act.[37] Even after four years of constant agitation in regard to this serious problem one finds no response whatever in the platforms of either party in 1880 to the suggestions on forest policy advanced by Carl Schurz and his commissioner.[38]

The efforts put forth by Schurz to conserve the forests were not to the liking of lumbermen. When his term of office was completed a well-known lumber journal published at Minneapolis said that lumbermen of the Northwest "will find a deep interest in the circumstance that Carl Schurz has made his exit from the Interior Department." That journal dismissed the faithful servant of the people with "Farewell Schurz! May the labor of our political Goddess never bring another such as you." [39]

[33] Robbins, *op. cit.*, p. 285.
[34] *Report of the Commissioner of the General Land Office*, 1877, p. 25.
[35] 45th Cong., 2d Sess. (1877–78), *House Exec. Docs.*, no. 8, p. 25.
[36] *Report of the Commissioner of the General Land Office*, 1877, p. 25.
[37] *Ibid.*, p. 16.
[38] *Report of the Secretary of the Interior*, 1885, p. 27.
[39] *Mississippi Valley Lumberman and Manufacturer*, vol. v, Mar. 11, 1881, p. 4.

William A. J. Sparks, land commissioner under President Cleveland in 1884, also fought bitterly against the evils in the land system; he struck vigorously at preëmption,[40] only to be met by an obstreperous Congress which refused to yield. Congress continued to resist for a few more years, but finally the "earnest and continued recommendation" which had appeared in the reports of the land commissioner over a long period of years obtained a hearing.

The men who bought pinelands so heavily in the late eighties were well aware that the old land laws were under attack. The short administration of Sparks as land commissioner from 1885 to 1887 had had an important influence on public opinion in spite of the fact that Sparks himself was forced to resign. The reform movement really got started in Congress in January 1885.[41] Though it moved slowly against pressure from those who furiously opposed any change in the land laws, it never lost the breath of life, for there were those who supported it.[42] Men interested in buying the forest lands of northern Minnesota knew that the ideas so vigorously set forth by Sparks would gather volume and would someday jeopardize their way of doing things. This is, in part at least, the explanation for the heightened activity in the purchase of forested areas in Minnesota in the decade of the eighties.

The years 1889–91 saw a definite change in the land policy of the United States. Under an act of March 2, 1889, public lands were no longer subject to private entry.[43] In 1891 came another act even more sweeping in that it disposed altogether of public auction sales and repealed the Preëmption Act.[44] These laws marked the beginning of the end of laissez faire in the public land system. No longer could anyone purchase public domain at $1.25 an acre, a price that had benefited the man of small means, to be sure, but that had also enabled the man with capital to assemble large holdings at a very low price. The public auction, which men with ready capital had turned so successfully to their own ends, was gone; gone, too, was preëmption, which had lent itself so readily to fraud in the Minnesota pinelands. Only the Homestead Act remained.

The operation of the Homestead Act in the timbered areas of Minnesota quickened in tempo with the repeal of preëmption. Although in 1870 only 11,096 acres were listed under original homesteads, according to the records of the Duluth land office, in 1891, the year in which pre-

[40] *Report of the Commissioner of the General Land Office*, 1885, pp. 70, 75.
[41] 48th Cong., 2d Sess., *Congressional Record*, vol. xvi, pt. i (Jan. 13, 1885), p. 648.
[42] 49th Cong., 2d Sess. (1886–87), *House Exec. Docs.*, no. 1, pt. v, pp. 50–69. Also *Report of the Land Commissioner*, 1889, p. 9; 1891, pp. 4–6; 1892, p. 4.
[43] *U.S. Statutes at Large*, vol. xxv (1888–89), p. 854.
[44] *Ibid.*, vol. xxvi (1890–91), pp. 1095, 1097, 1099.

ëmption was withdrawn, 96,886 acres were listed under original homesteads, and in 1892 the fabulous number of 241,095 acres were homesteaded. The acreage went down in 1893, the year of the panic, but the total of 158,407 acres was sufficiently high to surpass all previous years except 1892. New homesteads in the forested area reached a high in 1901, when 300,038 acres were entered.[45]

As we have said earlier, not all the people who took homesteads completed them for final entry. There is a great discrepancy between the number of original and final homesteads. In the Duluth land office from 1863 to 1889, where 4602 original homesteads had been entered, only 1455 had completed the requirements of the Homestead Act necessary to secure a patent. In 1885 only about a third of the acreage in original homesteads entered in 1880 filled the five-year requirements; in 1895 only about an eighth of the entries of 1890 were ready for final entry; in 1896 about the same proportion met the requirements; and in 1905 about one seventh of the original homestead entries of 1900 were entitled to final entry.[46]

In seeking the explanation of these discrepancies between original and final homesteads, one finds situations that expose much of the fraud that existed under the Homestead Act. Commutation was allowed in the original Homestead Act, which stated that after six months of actual residence and suitable improvement and upon the payment of $1.25 per acre, the claimant might receive full title to the land. In the Land Act of 1891 the time of commutation was extended to fourteen months, six of which were to be spent in constructive work, such as building a house, leaving eight months of residence on the claim. This was ostensibly a concession to the homesteader who, owing to ill health or some other unforeseen difficulty, might not be able to complete his entry on time. The law itself was designed to deal justly with all men, but in application — certainly in the pinelands — it enabled some men to secure land in large amounts. Every year a substantial proportion of original entries became private property long before the five-year requirement had been completed.[47]

The commutation settler was frequently "a person employed at so much a month to sign entry papers and hold the claim long enough to enable his employer to secure title by commutation." The commissioner of the General Land Office reported in 1884 that lands of "selected value and in large quantities" were passing into private hands. It was an accepted

[45] G.L.O., Original Homesteads, Duluth, Minn., 1865–70, 1890–92, 1893.

[46] Ibid., 1865–70, 1871–73, 1874–76, 1877–79, 1880–83, 1884–86, 1887–89, 1890–92, 1900; Final Homesteads, 1868–83, 1884–86, 1887–89, 1890–92, 1895, 1896, 1905.

[47] Ibid., Cash Books, Duluth, Minn., 1890–92, 1893, 1900.

fact that the actual settler, who came to make a home, preferred not to pay for his land and that the commutation settler had no interest but to sell and be off.[48]

The worst abuses of commutation appear to have occurred in the timbered areas. In Minnesota from July 1, 1899, to June 30, 1903, there were in the "timber belt" 1485 commuted homesteads estimated to contain about 297,000,000 feet of standing timber, while there were only 206 such homesteads in the agricultural section and 174 within the prospective mineral belt. Of these commutations in the timber belt, 89 per cent had been transferred to men other than the original entrymen.

TABLE 24. COMMUTED HOMESTEADS RECORDED IN THE DULUTH AND MARSHALL LAND OFFICES

| Year | Duluth Land Office | | Marshall Land Office | |
	Commuted Homesteads	Acreage	Commuted Homesteads	Acreage
1900	196	28,485	10	388
1901	134	19,084	11	896
1902	120	16,668	16	1,188
1903	258	37,362	8	540

SOURCE: *Report of the Public Lands Commission*, 58th Cong., 3rd Sess., *Senate Docs.*, no. 189, p. 94.

The people who had entered those claims came from all walks of life; mechanics, schoolteachers, waitresses, woodsmen, city laborers, clerks, occasional businessmen, and professional men were quite willing to break the laws of their country for a small bit of silver.[49] Since 89 per cent had transferred their claims, it is quite likely that they had no notion of permanent settlement. Even as early as 1876 Commissioner Williamson of the United States Land Office complained that "in all the pine region of Lake Superior and the Upper Mississippi where vast areas have been settled under the pretense of agriculture under the homestead and preëmption laws scarcely a vestige of agriculture appears."[50]

In comparing commutation records in two land offices in Minnesota, one at Duluth in the forest area and one at Marshall on the prairie, the fact is again substantiated that commutation was more general in the timber belt.[51] The figures of the two land offices on the number of commuted homesteads and acreage over a period of four years are given in Table 24.

Canadians crossed the border into the timber and mineral belts of Minnesota to take homesteads, only to commute them. It was common

[48] *Report of the Commissioner of the General Land Office*, 1884, p. 6.
[49] *Report of the Public Lands Commission*, 1904–5, 58th Cong., 3rd Sess., *Senate Docs.*, no. 189, pp. viii, 66, 67, 69–70.
[50] *Report of the Land Commissioner*, 1876, pp. 7–8.
[51] *Report of the Public Lands Commission*, 58th Cong., 3rd Sess., *Senate Docs.*, no. 189, p. 94.

gossip in northern Minnesota that lumber companies operating along the boundary line brought Canadians into the United States for this purpose. On one occasion thirty-five out of fifty commuted homesteads were turned over to men engaged in the lumber business.[52]

Commutation, however, does not account for all the homesteads that did not complete the requirements for final entry. Another explanation accepted by students of United States land policy is that "dummies" were used in filing on claims, and that after the proxy claimants had cleared the land of its timber, the claim was abandoned, there being no further purpose in concluding the transaction because the land had been robbed of its wealth.[53]

Webster Eaton, a special agent for the United States government in the Duluth district, on November 5, 1883, wrote Commissioner McFarland a letter which reveals some of the evils existing under the homestead laws. He said:[54]

I have just returned from a trip into townships 59 and 60 N Range 6 West where I went to examine fraudulent Homestead entries. I found and examined thirty-six claims all of which are alleged to have been made in the interest of one man, or one firm, and were made on or about the 19th day of May 1883. I carefully examined every claim and found rude huts or pens on nearly every one of them but no person is now living in any of the said huts or houses and no person has ever resided in either one of them for a single day. The improvements were evidently made under the direction of one person and are not now and could not be made habitable dwellings. Every one of these buildings bear the evidences of fraud being so low that a common-sized man can not stand erect in them. The original plan in relation to these Homestead entries was undoubtedly to commute and pay $1.25 an acre at the end of six months, but since it has become generally known that I have inspected them, the plan will be changed, and I am reliably informed that a contest will be commenced against each and every one of these claims by, or in the interest of the very party or parties who first had the land entered, the contesting parties at the same time are also filing applications to re-enter when the original entry shall have been cancelled. By this mode of operation the party who instigated the fraud may not be able to get possession of the land, but he will be able to sell the minutes or description of these valuable pine lands to other people and thereby make his expenditure a profitable investment even after he has been thwarted in his attempt to steal the land outright. I find upon careful examination that there is now upon these 36 claims (they being all the claims in the two townships mentioned) over fifty million feet of pine.

[52] *Ibid.*, p. 71.
[53] Robbins, *op. cit.*, p. 240.
[54] N.A.: Records of the General Land Office, Miscellaneous Letters Received, 1883–104330.

On December 27, 1883, Eaton again wrote to McFarland, enclosing an affidavit of James A. Ferguson made before William Marshall. Ferguson, stated the latter, "has taken a preëmption and a homestead entry and proved up on both and never saw either one." The preëmption claim was taken at Duluth, the homestead at St. Cloud six months later. "It occurs to me that this is one of the worst cases of Fraud on the books, although there are hundreds just like it," wrote Eaton. Ferguson was guided in the matter by McGuire of Duluth, claimed Eaton. Two men from Brainerd, whose names Ferguson did not know, were his witnesses. Ferguson himself said that he did not know where the claims were and that his final papers were acknowledged in McGuire's office.[55]

Don A. Dodge, another special agent sent into the Duluth district to detect fraud, reported to McFarland the case of one Eugene J. Bryant who had entered a homestead on February 27, 1879, had never lived on it, had not cultivated an acre, but had removed and sold the timber.[56] There were also other ways of cheating the government, according to a letter send by Milton Peden, another special agent operating in the Duluth district. In a letter to the land commissioner in Washington, Peden named a man who had engaged a half-wit to enter a homestead in township 39 north, range 34 west. The half-wit had no intention of living on the claim, and the man who furnished him the necessary money for the entry shortly removed 150,000 feet of timber from the claim.[57]

The land commissioners at Washington were as disturbed over the lawlessness practiced under the Homestead Act as they were over fraud under the Preëmption Act. J. A. Williamson, commissioner in 1876, opposed both preëmption and homestead in the forested area and even at that early date recommended that timber should be appraised and then sold, a system which would have brought far larger returns to the United States government.[58] Commissioner Sparks had scarcely entered office when he put into effect a ruling that final entries could not be completed in areas where fraud was general — Minnesota was included in the group of states to which Sparks' program applied.[59] But the hue and cry to the effect that stopping patents "would cause great injustice and suffering to the frontiersmen" made it impossible for Sparks to continue his program. People in positions of power, as well as in Congress, did not see eye to eye with the land commissioners as yet, and the Homestead Act was allowed to remain in force, alienating large blocks of lands to the control

[55] *Ibid.*, 1883–955.
[56] *Ibid.*, 1882–50522.
[57] *Ibid.*, 1884–6158.
[58] *Report of the Land Commissioner*, 1876, pp. 7–8.
[59] *Ibid.*, 1885, pp. 202, 204.

of a very few and operating in a way quite contrary to the purpose for which it had been designed.

Preëmption had probably been the greater evil in the management of timberlands, for it operated on unsurveyed as well as surveyed lands, with the result that cruisers could pick the choice spots of pine long before surveyors approached it, while the homesteader had to limit his choice to surveyed lands. Both the Homestead Act and the Preëmption Act, however, were used to advantage in exploiting the timberlands and in concentrating them into large holdings.

Another law that favored concentration of timberlands was known as the Soldiers' Additional Homestead Right. This law was also honestly conceived and motivated, but again we find the law to be one thing and the application of it quite another. It applied to soldiers who had not received their full quota of 160 acres when they filed for a homestead, giving them the right to complete the amount by locating land anywhere in the United States where land was subject to homesteading.[60] Such additional homestead rights were given in the form of scrip; these were assignable and were sometimes purchased for the low amount of forty cents an acre — they functioned much as had the military bounty land warrants used so largely in the acquistion of pinelands in the 1850s and 1860s. These rights applied to double minimum lands which were heavily forested with white and red pine, and consequently the scrip fell right into the hands of those interested in concentration of pinelands.

In the Mille Lacs Indian Reservation, a beautiful white pine region, 286 soldiers' homesteads were located on land which contained pine valued at prices ranging from $10 to $30 per acre.[61] In township 57 north, range 21 west, 106 additional homesteads were all entered on one day, December 10, 1874, and on January 22, 1875, 98 additional homesteads were filed in township 56 of the same range.[62] So many additional homesteads concentrated in one place showed how effectively the law operated to alienate large blocks of land. There was nothing illegal about this; Congress had enacted the law, and purchasing this scrip was as legal as using the military bounty land warrants.

In the very early period of Minnesota's pineland story, land had often become private property through the military bounty land warrants. These warrants were in abundance in the 1850s, and by using them such petty capitalists as Dorilus Morrison and Isaac Staples became holders of excellent pinelands. This was perfectly legal, for the warrants had been made

[60] Soldiers Additional Act of March 3, 1873, *U.S. Statutes at Large,* vol. xvii, p. 605.
[61] Robbins, *op. cit.,* p. 247.
[62] G.L.O., Tract Books, Minn., vol. 64, T. 57 N., R. 21 W., pp. 217–88; T. 56 N., R. 21 W., pp. 205–16.

assignable by Congress.[63] By the seventies active use of military bounty land warrants had passed, though one finds one in use occasionally thereafter.

In the 1860s the military bounty land warrants were being replaced by agricultural college scrip, operating under the Morrill Land Grant Act This act offered the states between nine and ten million acres of land which were to be sold to provide an endowment for agricultural colleges and schools teaching mechanic arts. Each state was to be granted 30,000 acres for every senator and representative it had in Congress. States which had no public domain received scrip for the acreage to which they were entitled; the states were not to enter land with the scrip, but they were to sell it to people who could enter land with it.

Minnesota did not favor this bill. It had seen large portions of its pineland pass into private ownership under the military bounty land warrants and it objected to any extension of what it considered an undemocratic method of distributing the public lands. Its senators and representatives had an opportunity to make themselves heard on the issue. Henry M. Rice opposed the bill at first, though Minnesota was a likely state for an agricultural college. Rice feared that such scrip would work to the advantage of men who could buy it in considerable amounts at low prices. He spoke of such men as "locusts" in the land.[64] Senator Rice and his colleague, Senator James T. Shields, attempted to amend the bill so that speculators could not use scrip in locating land in their state,[65] but they failed.

The eastern states were determined to see the bill passed, for it was far more favorable to states which no longer had public domain. The land in Minnesota was to be given for the benefit of New York, Massachusetts, or any other eastern state where there was no free land. To the men of Minnesota it appeared that the Land Grant Act would undo what the Homestead Act was expected to do. Strangely the two laws were passed the same year, less than two weeks apart. Minnesota feared this scrip as it had feared the military bounty land warrants back in 1858, when the legislature of the state had passed a resolution condemning large speculative holdings as detrimental to the interest of the mass of people. Minnesotans wanted an agricultural college, but they believed that land could be granted for it in the same way as was being done for public education.[66]

The agricultural college scrip presented a problem somewhat different

[63] The military bounty land warrants are discussed more fully above, pp. 55–67.
[64] 35th Cong., 2d Sess., *Congressional Globe*, Feb. 1, 1859, p. 717. See also above, pp. 68–69.
[65] *Ibid.*, p. 785.
[66] *Laws of Minnesota*, 1st Sess. (1858), Appendix pp. 351–52, Memorial to Congress in Relation to the Public Lands.

from that of the military warrants in that each state was given a certain amount of scrip to dispose of as it wished. Under this arrangement the scrip could be bought directly from the state, and it was possible for a small group of men to gain control of a state's entire issue of agricultural college scrip. The warrants had been scattered; soldiers living all over the United States had them, and such warrants were not so easily gathered under one control. Representative George W. Julian of Indiana, in a speech in the House of Representatives on March 6, 1868, said that a company of speculators doing business in Cleveland, Ohio, and in Wall Street, New York City, advertised that they had purchased the college scrip of nine states covering 2,482,000 acres.[67] He stated that the rates per acre for the scrip ranged from 60 to 70 cents instead of $1.25. The scrip of Rhode Island, however, was sold for 42 cents an acre, and much of this scrip was used in locating Minnesota pineland. North Caroline and Kentucky scrip was also used in large amounts in locating Minnesota pinelands, and its price was 50 cents an acre. New Hampshire and Ohio sold their scrip for 53 cents an acre.[68]

In the pineland area the St. Cloud land office located more land by agricultural college scrip than did either of the other two offices, Stillwater and Duluth. The Duluth lands were not yet sought to any noticeable degree and the Stillwater office had located its best lands by military bounty land warrants before the Morrill Land Grant Act was passed. The lands over which the St. Cloud office had jurisdiction lay along the Mississippi River, and many of the men who purchased agricultural college scrip and located lands with it were engaged in sawing lumber in Minneapolis, St. Cloud, or other Mississippi mill towns to the north of Minneapolis. The scrip used in locating land in the St. Cloud area came largely from Connecticut, Rhode Island, Vermont, Maine, New York, New Jersey, Pennsylvania, and West Virginia. Thousands of acres became private property in the St. Cloud district by means of scrip at a price much less than $1.25 an acre.

In the winter of 1864–65 Joseph Dean, a lumberman from Minneapolis, located more than 2500 acres with scrip from Connecticut, Rhode Island, Vermont, and New York. In 1866 Thomas C. McClure, of lumber fame in St. Cloud, located some 7000 acres with scrip from New Jersey, Rhode Island, Maine, West Virginia, Connecticut, and Pennsylvania. John W. Day, a prominent lumberman of Minneapolis, acquired more than 3600 acres in October of that year with the agricultural college scrip, and his townsman Henry F. Brown became owner of 5000 acres in the same way. Ezra Cornell and Calvin F. Howe, both of New York state, used such

[67] George W. Julian, *Our Land Policy — Its Evils and Their Remedy* (Washington, 1868).
[68] Gates, *Wisconsin Pine Lands of Cornell University*, p. 28.

scrip in locating large amounts of pineland in the St. Cloud area.[69] In the Duluth district, Jay Cooke and his associates, William Moorhead and William L. Banning, located more than 44,000 acres by means of agricultural college scrip in the years 1866–69. They had purchased scrip largely from Kentucky, Ohio, Vermont, New Hampshire, and Massachusetts.[70]

What the West anticipated had happened; scrip had passed into the hands of big-scale operators. The East had had its way with the West! Jefferson's ideal of creating a nation of landowners through a democratic public land system had suffered an initial blow in the agricultural college scrip.

Other varieties of scrip were also used in Minnesota, such as the surveyor-general scrip, the Supreme Court scrip, and the Chippewa scrip. Only occasionally were lands located in the pineland area by surveyor-general scrip or Supreme Court scrip, though such scrip was legal and functioned like the military bounty land warrants and the agricultural college scrip. The Chippewa scrip was quite a different matter, for it grew out of land allotments to the Chippewa half-breeds and was an important factor in alienating large portions of pineland from the public domain.

In the Chippewa Treaty of 1854, which gave the United States control of the Indian lands lying largely to the north of Duluth, care was taken to provide for the mixed-bloods of the Lake Superior band, chiefly in order that their consent might be obtained to the transfer of lands. Each head of a family or single person who was a half-breed of twenty-one years or more was entitled to receive a patent on eighty acres of land selected by himself under the direction of the President of the United States.[71]

For a time this method of transferring lands to the Indians was carefully applied, and the arrangement work satisfactorily. But then a law was passed providing for the issuance of scrip for locating these half-breed lands. The scrip stated that "any sale, transfer, mortgage, assignment, or pledge of this certificate, or of any rights accruing under it, will not be recognized as valid by the United States; and that the patent for lands located by virtue thereof shall be issued directly to the above-named reservee, or his heirs, and shall in no wise inure to the benefit of any other person or persons."[72] The patent was to be issued directly to the person named. By 1856 it was supposed that all the Chippewa half-breeds of the Lake Superior region had been taken care of and that the Treaty of 1854

[69] G.L.O., Agriculture College Scrip, St. Cloud, Minn., 1864–73.

[70] See above, p. 267.

[71] *Report of the Neal Commission*, 42d Cong., 2d Sess. (1871–72), *House Exec. Docs.*, no. 193, p. 2.

[72] Matthias N. Orfield, *Federal Land Grants to the States with Special Reference to Minnesota* (Minneapolis, 1915), p. 202; *Report of the Neal Commission*, 42d Cong., 2d Sess., *House Exec. Docs.*, no. 193, p. 14.

had been fulfilled.[73] But the problem was not to be solved so simply as that.

In 1864 a "factory" was established by the United States Indian agent, Luther E. Webb, at La Pointe, Wisconsin, and here half-breeds in large numbers, egged on by others, and claiming that they were of the Lake Superior group since all Chippewa were related, came to apply for scrip. Then began a real search for any and all Chippewa half-breeds, and St. Paul became one of the places where applications were "ground out." At Pembina, at Fort Garry, and elsewhere half-breeds were sought. Most of these Indians were not entitled to land under the Treaty of 1854 and to a very great extent the applications were forged.

The "hunt" went on so vigorously because this Chippewa scrip was used in locating valuable pinelands in Minnesota's unsurveyed regions.[74] This was done in spite of the fact that by law the scrip could not be sold, transferred, mortgaged, or assigned to anyone else. The Chippewa half-breeds were urged to make application to the government for the scrip, and at the same time they gave to someone the power to locate the land and to someone else the power to sell it. The attorney who executed the application was often a pineland dealer who knew where the best untouched pinelands were.

The scrip was also sold in the open market. Although the law specifically stated that the scrip could in no way "inure to the benefit of any person or persons" except the Chippewa half-breed to whom it was granted, it was being sold by such well-known men as Henry T. Welles and Franklin Steele of Minneapolis and Thompson Brothers, Isaac Van Etten, and N. W. Kittson of St. Paul.[75] These men secured the scrip from the Indians for about 50 cents an acre. In the group of people who located holdings by means of this scrip were such well-known lumbermen as T. B. Walker, Dorilus Morrison, Levi Butler, S. W. Farnham and his partner Lovejoy, Eastman, Bovey and Company, and Ankeny, Pettit and Robinson. The locations these men made with the Chippewa scrip lay largely in Cass and Itasca counties, excellent pine regions, well located for the transportation of logs to Minneapolis by way of the Mississippi.[76]

The problem of the Chippewa half-breed scrip did not pass unheeded in Washington. The Secretary of Interior, Columbus Deland, at the request of Congress appointed a commission headed by Henry S. Neal to investigate the matter. The commission's findings, reported on September 4, 1871, caused the patents located by this scrip to be suspended, "not one

[73] Folwell, *History of Minnesota*, vol. i, p. 471.

[74] *Report of the Neal Commission*, 42d Cong., 2d Sess., *House Exec. Docs.*, no. 193, pp. 14–17.

[75] *Ibid.*, p. 13.

[76] *Report of the Jones Commission*, 43rd Cong., 1st Sess., *Senate Exec. Docs.*, no. 33.

of them having been found entitled." [77] Some of the men who had secured land by means of this scrip objected to the suspension of patents and sought satisfaction. They were quite readily heard because Senator Windom of Minnesota was chairman of the Senate Committee on Public Lands and was himself one of the group who had located lands with Chippewa half-breed scrip. On June 8, 1872, Congress passed an act urged by Windom which had as its purpose "to perfect certain land-titles therein described."

One of the many problems the government faced in attempting to control its natural resources was that of timber trespassing on public domain. In the forested areas of Minnesota this was an evil hard to hold in check. Evidences of trespass were found in the forests of the St. Croix even before Minnesota became a territory, and trespass continued as the lumber industry became more prominent. The land commissioners at Washington knew the practice was all too prevalent, and they sent special agents to Minnesota to bring such trespassers to justice. These agents reported that 61,708,564 feet of white pine logs had been cut and removed from the vacant public lands in the state. Most of these logs had been cut between 1868 and 1876, and no stumpage fee had been collected. There were twenty-nine cases of trespassing to be tried in the United States district court in St. Paul in 1877. [78]

In the spring of 1879 seventy-nine persons were involved in pineland suits for trespassing on government lands in Minnesota. Well-established lumbermen were called to account, such as Farnham and Lovejoy, Leonard Day and Son, Dorilus Morrison, and John Martin, all of Minneapolis, and N. P. Clarke of St. Cloud. In the three years preceding 1879 the guilty depredators of Minnesota had paid a larger amount than those of any other state in the Union for timber trespass, and in 1879 the United States government valued the stumpage taken in trespass at $115,378. The lumbermen argued that the price for such stumpage was excessive, but only by excessive charges could the lawless activity be stopped. Carl Schurz, the Secretary of the Interior, vigorously sought to curb trespassing but lumbermen had little regard for Schurz and his spies, as they called them. [79]

Webster Eaton, a government agent, was ordered in the early 1880s to make investigations in the Northwest Angle on Lake of the Woods. This was a very remote part of the Minnesota forest which suffered badly from timber trespass, since no white people lived within sixty miles. [80] There men worked undetected, cutting logs on the United States side of the

[77] *Report of the Neal Commission*, 42d Cong., 2d Sess., *House Exec. Docs.*, no. 193, p. 65.
[78] *Report of the Commissioner of the General Land Office*, 1877, p. 22.
[79] *Mississippi Valley Lumberman and Manufacturer*, vol. ii, Mar. 29, 1878, p. 4; also, vol. iii, Feb. 7, 1879, p. 4; Mar. 28, 1879, p. 2; May 30, 1879, p. 1; Dec. 5, 1879, p. 4.
[80] N.A.: Records of the General Land Office, Miscellaneous Letters Received, 1883–94664.

border and towing them across the Lake to Rat Portage to be sold into Canada.[81]

Charles W. McCann, another special agent in Minnesota, reported to headquarters in Washington in the spring of 1882 that a very clear case of trespass had occurred below Lake Winnibigoshish, where 500,000 feet of logs and 13,000 ties had been logged from government property and placed on ice ready to go when the spring breakup came. McCann said he could sell them immediately at good prices, which the United States attorney whom he consulted had advised him to do.[82]

Don A. Dodge, another special agent, reported to Washington that one James B. Smith had cut 400,000 feet of timber on government land in the winter of 1883 and that the McKinley brothers of Park Rapids had cut 36,200 feet of pine timber on government lands.[83] Previously he had reported that John Gilmore had cut 47,000 feet of pine timber on public domain and that Beede and Bray of Minneapolis were charged with cutting 70,000 feet of government timber in the winter of 1882; these logs they had sent directly to their yard in Minneapolis. Beede and Bray were brought to court but were fined only $286 and costs by the United States attorney.[84] The O'Brien brothers, Michael and Thomas, who cut timber on public domain and sold the logs to N. P. Clarke, a lumberman at St. Cloud, were reported in the winter of 1884.[85]

The names of the men reported by Dodge were well known in the pine regions of Minnesota. The McKinleys and the O'Briens were established loggers, not small outfits carrying on a precarious business. John Gilmore was a cruiser in the north woods, quite familiar with the best stands of timber; Beede and Bray were sawmill operators in Minneapolis.

These are only a few examples, but there were many others and trespassing was one of the ways in which the public domain was dismantled. Dodge reported that within one year from June 1, 1882, to June 3, 1883, he had investigated twenty-nine trespass cases.[86] He held that such trespasses could be greatly curtailed by charging a higher price for stolen stumpage, which would make it unprofitable to commit trespass. Carrying the cases to court, he said, involved further loss, the fines being too small to cover the costs.[87]

Another problem baffling to the lawmakers in Washington arose out of the forest areas of the Indian reservations in Minnesota. These reserva-

[81] Ibid., 1884–76570.
[82] Ibid., 1882–25602.
[83] Ibid., 1884–17135.
[84] Ibid., 1883–11741; 1884–19717.
[85] Ibid., 1884–14756; 1884–10152
[86] Ibid., 1883–75189.
[87] Ibid., 1882–50522.

tions, retained by the Indians in early treaties, were still untouched and contained millions of feet of pine that increased in importance as private owners became more aggressive. For some time the Indian was firm in his stand that those reservations were in no way the property of white men, but finally, little by little, he was made to retreat.

The Chippewa of Minnesota were at one time in undisputed possession of more than half the area of the state. As the white man pressed in upon them, they gradually by treaty gave up portions of their holdings until they found themselves confined within the boundaries of reservations, two of which, Red Lake and White Earth, became important in Minnesota's history. The Indians of Red Lake had an advantage in that they retained all original rights to their holdings — they had never ceded to the government of the United States their Indian title to this land. In the 1850s and 1860s, when northern Minnesota was practically unknown to the white man, the United States government was generous in setting aside lands for the Indians.

The Red Lake Reservation contained about 3,500,000 acres, with enough timber to make the Indians rich, if carefully sold. About 1200 Indians lived on this reservation.[88] The White Earth Reservation, established in 1867, covered an area of about 800,000 acres, half or more of which was beautiful rolling prairie capable of sustaining a large population. The splendid timbered area of this reservation was estimated to contain 500,000,000 feet of good, merchantable pine.[89] Fewer than 2000 Indians lived in this immense area in the eighties, though it was in the plan of things that all Minnesota Chippewa — full-blood and mixed-blood — except those living at Red Lake would sometime migrate to White Earth, which was thought to be an ideal country for the Indian with its many small lakes and streams flowing into the Red River and the Crow Wing River.

At first the Indians on the White Earth Reservation prospered; in 1886 Bishop Whipple, an authority on Indian affairs in the state, said, "There is not in the State a more orderly Christian community than the Indians of the White Earth Reserve."[90] Farms were increasing in number, under the spur of the treaty provision of March 1867, which promised every Indian who cleared and cultivated ten acres an additional ten until he became the owner of 160 acres.[91]

But in the 1880s a point of view was taking shape throughout the United States in regard to the Indian and his lands which was to have an impor-

[88] 49th Cong., 1st Sess. (1885–86), *Senate Exec. Docs.*, no. 44, p. 5.

[89] 56th Cong., 1st Sess. (1899–1900), *House Reports*, no. 492, p. 1.

[90] 49th Cong., 1st Sess. (1885–86), *Senate Exec. Docs.*, no. 44, p. 5; *Report of the Commissioner of Indian Affairs*, 1886, pp. 168–70.

[91] *U.S. Statutes at Large*, vol. xvi, pp. 719–23.

tant bearing in Minnesota. The rapid passing of the best lands of the frontier made people less and less tolerant of the Indian occupancy of large areas. In Minnesota, particularly in northern Minnesota, this point of view was widespread. Settlers were pouring into the valley of the Red River, and the rolling prairie lands of White Earth — about 400,000 acres ready for the plow — were enticing to them. To these incoming settlers it seemed a waste of land to have a few Indians occupying thousands of rich acres.

As we have observed before, competition for pinelands was increasing during this period, and the stands of pine on the Red Lake and White Earth reservations did not pass unnoticed by men interested in lumber. So it is not surprising that in the summer of 1885 Minnesota made her first demand that the White Earth Reservation be opened to white settlement. This came as a shock to the Chippewa, who had been secure in the belief that the White Earth Reservation belonged to them and that they would never be disturbed in their ownership.[92]

There was in the United States at this same time another group whose consuming desire was to set the Indian free from the guardianship of the United States government so that he might enjoy the same rights as white men. President Cleveland showed much concern over the Indian situation, and with pressure from the two groups interested in the Indian for very different reasons, he made a recommendation to Congress which was shaped into a bill and became the Dawes Severalty Act of February 8, 1887.

This act gave the President the power, whenever he deemed it proper, to end the tribal arrangement and the communal ownership of land; it gave him power to divide the land among the Indians at the rate of one hundred and sixty acres to the head of a family and smaller allotments to others.[93] In 1891 this act was amended to the effect that only eighty acres could be given to the head of a family. Indians could neither mortgage nor sell their property for a period of twenty-five years, according to the Dawes Act. It was also provided that if there were surplus lands after the allotments had been made, these could be purchased by the government and opened for settlement, the purchase money to be held in trust for the tribe to whom the reservation belonged.[94] It was as though the interests seeking the pine and arable lands at Red Lake and White Earth had made the Dawes Act themselves. The land was to be alloted and the government would open the remainder for sale!

Before the passing of the Dawes Act the so-called Northwest Indian

[92] 49th Cong., 2d Sess. (1886–87), *Senate Exec. Docs.*, no. 115, pp. 53–54.
[93] *U. S. Statutes at Large*, vol. xxiv, pp. 388–91.
[94] *Ibid.*, p. 390.

Commission of 1886, authorized by Congress, had been working to establish the White Earth Reservation as a home for all the Chippewa of
Minnesota before opening any of it for settlement as requested by their
white neighbors.[95] Bishop Whipple and his committee labored earnestly
to convince the Chippewa that they should all move to White Earth.
Whipple was determined that White Earth should be preserved and that
neither agricultural lands nor pinelands should be alienated until the
Chippewa were taken care of.[96] The commission, largely because of Whipple's understanding of the Indians, had been very successful in gaining
the consent of tribes to move to White Earth, though the Red Lake
Indians and several small groups had refused. Whipple's ideas were incorporated into the report sent to Washington.

The people of the Northwest, however, became impatient with a Congress which was slow in acting on the request which they had made in
1885 that the White Earth Reservation be opened to white men. The
people also knew the point of view held by Bishop Whipple, which in no
way pleased them. On January 6, 1887, a mass meeting of citizens of the
Red River Valley was held at Crookston. They discussed the necessity
of getting lumber — both more lumber and cheaper lumber. The lumber
which came from Minneapolis and St. Paul was expensive because of
the cost of freight. The Red River people held that if the reservations were
opened and logged, their needs would be supplied at a much lower cost —
and the Indians, as they saw it, were making no practical use of these
resources. Every farmer and every businessman was urged to sign a petition which was being sent to the United States Senate.[97]

In response to this demand Representative Knute Nelson presented a
bill on January 4, 1888, the object of which was to carry to a definite
conclusion the transfer of the Indians to White Earth, the allotting of
reservation lands as provided by the Dawes Act, and the disposal of the
surplus arable lands and pinelands.[98] Under the leadership of Senator
Dawes, chairman of the committee having to do with Indian affairs, this
bill was changed considerably in the Senate. One of the senators consulted
by Dawes' committee was D. M. Sabin of Minnesota, a manufacturer
of lumber in Stillwater. Through that association Dawes no doubt made
his contacts with lumbermen of Minnesota, by whom, he said, a part of
the bill had been "mapped out" but who, he added, were men "who had
no interest in the matter." [99]

[95] 49th Cong., 2d Sess. (1886–87), *Senate Exec. Docs.*, no. 115, p. 52. This document contains the Report of the Northwest Indian Commission to the Commissioner of Indian Affairs,
Dec. 1, 1886.
[96] *Ibid.*, pp. 1, 3, 12–13, 39–41, 50–82.
[97] *Ibid.*, pp. 3, 10.
[98] 50th Cong., 1st Sess. (1887–88), *House Journal*, vol. i, p. 204.
[99] Folwell, *op. cit.*, vol. iv, p. 223.

From the discussion of the bill one would think the pinelands of the Indian reservations were in great danger. Wholesale theft, fire, and dead and down timber would destroy the forests, it was said, if quick action was not taken by Congress. Nelson declared that 60,000 of his people desired the opening of these reservations. The bill, which was recorded as the Nelson Act though it was quite different from Nelson's original bill, became law on January 14, 1889. It was known as *A Bill for the Relief and Civilization of the Chippewa Indians,* but its chief purpose was to place the arable lands and the pinelands of the Indian reservations reaching from Grand Portage to Red Lake a little nearer to the grasping hands of the white man.[1]

The most important of these were the reservations of Red Lake and White Earth. The bill stated that all Chippewa except those on the Red Lake Reservation should be moved to White Earth, as Bishop Whipple's report had suggested. The bill provided that land should be allotted according to the Dawes Act and that when all allotments had been taken care of, whatever land remained or was ceded to the United States government should be classified as agricultural lands or pinelands. They were to be sold and after all expenses were paid the remainder of the money was to be placed in the Treasury of the United States and accredited to the Chippewa of Minnesota, to remain there for fifty years and to draw interest at 3 per cent annually. The interest was to be paid to the Chippewa annually, a portion of it to be used for schools. The principal was not to be distributed until the fifty years had passed.

Much had to be done before the lands of the Chippewa were ready for sale. The Dawes Act required that surveys be made of the Indian lands under the direction of the land commissioner of the United States and that the examination and appraisal of these lands be supervised by the Secretary of the Interior. Under the Nelson Act a special commission was assigned the difficult tasks of moving all the Chippewa except those at Red Lake to White Earth, of negotiating agreements, and of making the allotments. This commission, whose chairman was Henry M. Rice, a well-known citizen of Minnesota and a man who knew the Chippewa and their affairs, was also to negotiate with the Red Lake Indians in regard to allotments and cessions of their lands. Since no Indians were to be moved to Red Lake, the commission could begin allotments there more readily than at White Earth. They knew the number of Indians there. No one was able to estimate the number of Indians from the other reservations who would adopt White Earth as their home until the move-

---

[1] *U. S. Statutes at Large,* vol. xxv, pp. 642–46. Senator Dawes, as chairman of the Committee on Indian Affairs, is supposed to have drawn up the bill that was accepted. Knute Nelson might have been served better if Dawes' name had been attached to the bill.

ment was somewhat under way. But the Indians at Red Lake were adamant — they would have nothing of either the Dawes Act or the Nelson Act. They wanted to continue to live in their communal state. That 1200 of them occupied over 3,000,000 acres seemed wasteful to white men, who were of the opinion that the Indian could learn to live as they did, making the huge hunting ground unnecessary.

Rice and his commission made no headway on allotments but finally the men of the Red Lake Reservation voted to cede to the United States government approximately 700,000 acres of their land, the proceeds of the sale to be held according to the plan in the Nelson Act. When the lands had been ceded the Red Lake Indians were of the mind that what remained of their reservation was their property and that there would be no further encroachment on the part of the government. The agreement according to the Rice Report, however, gives evidence that when the day would arrive on which allotments were made any land not so alloted was to be offered for sale. The Indian was not secure.

The United States government finally was in a position to make the first sale of the ceded reservation lands at Red Lake in the spring of 1896. Congress had decided that when 100,000 acres had been surveyed, examined, and appraised, the lands could be sold for cash at public auction to the highest bidder but never for less than the value at which they had been appraised.[2] The land that was not sold at public auction was to be held for private entry at the appraised value. On July 1 and 15, 1896, the sale was held at the Crookston and Duluth land offices. About 115,000 acres of the Red Lake Reservation, estimated to contain about 226,000,000 feet of pine, were offered.[3]

The people of Crookston anticipated the sale, for the pine would be made into lumber at Crookston and elsewhere in the area and this would give labor employment both in building the necessary mills and in operating them, would put money in circulation, and altogether would "be a great factor in building up this section."[4] The day on which the sale opened was exciting. Many lumbermen were present, and never had there been so much money in Crookston on any one day.[5] Shevlin, Carpenter and Company of Minneapolis, Wright and Davis of Saginaw, the Weyerhaeusers, E. P. Hixon of La Crosse, Otis Staples of Stillwater, and others bought large tracts for an average of $3.13 per thousand feet.[6] About 65,000 acres containing 118,000,000 feet of timber were sold at the public

[2] 53rd Cong., 2d Sess. (1893–94), *House Reports*, no. 459, p. 1; *Report of the Secretary of the Interior*, 1895, pp. xi, xii.

[3] *Ibid.*, 1896, p. xxi.

[4] *Crookston Times*, July 15, 1896.

[5] *Ibid.*, July 17, 1896.

[6] *Mississippi Valley Lumberman*, vol. xxvii, July 24, 1896, p. 14.

sale, and when that sale was over private entry began. In the private entry, single firms took a whole township; several took even more.[7]

Scarcely was the sale over when the cry of fraud arose. The first crew sent by the government in 1891 to estimate the timber on these reservations had been dismissed by Hoke Smith when he became Secretary of the Interior in March 1893 on the grounds that their work was not satisfactory. The new crew appointed by Hoke Smith spent more than two years re-examining tracts drawn by the first crew, as well as examining new lands. It was on the basis of the report of this second crew that the lands were offered for sale in July 1896. A few months after the sale the whole crew was dismissed by David R. Francis, successor to Hoke Smith. Complaints came in in such numbers that Francis dismissed the crew even before he had begun investigations.

The trouble was that the crew's report to the government appeared to have been very different from that given to a certain company interested in the timber. The company seemed to have had the advantage of correct figures, while the estimates presented to the government were less.[8] Men were said to have been members of the crew who did not know a basswood from a pine.[9] It was quite clear that the government had been deceived and that the Indians had been robbed. Also, buyers were annoyed at the insecurity of their titles to the land they had bought and at the possibility of having action taken against them after the sales were completed. In disgust men referred to the situation as the "Red Lake Pine Muddle." [10]

J. George Wright was sent as inspector by Secretary Francis to make a study of the work of the dismissed crew and to determine what the timber situation actually was on the Red Lake lands, the examining of which had already cost the government a considerable sum. One of Wright's assistants in this inspection was H. B. Ayres, an able and trustworthy cruiser [11] who was highly recommended by B. E. Fernow, chief of the Forestry Division of the United States Department of Agriculture. Others appointed to work with Wright were M. J. McGuigan, an experienced cruiser from Ashland, Wisconsin, and F. Roth of the Forestry Division.

These men examined 85 forty-acre tracts on which they found 17,271,000 feet of timber as against the 9,635,000 feet previously reported; of these tracts 61 contained 12,472,000 feet as against the 5,547,000 reported

[7] *Crookston Times,* July 17, 1896.

[8] *Mississippi Valley Lumberman,* vol. xxiii, Apr. 28, 1893, p. 6; vol. xxviii, Jan. 15, 1897, p. 9, and Jan. 29, 1897, p. 8.

[9] *Anoka County Union,* Sept. 27, 1893.

[10] *Mississippi Valley Lumberman,* vol. xxviii, Jan. 29, 1897, p. 8.

[11] See above, p. 169.

when sold.[12] On one tract Ayres, McGuigan, and Wright measured they found 902,000 feet, while the estimators of the dismissed crew had reported it to contain 605,000 feet. A lot reported by the crew to have 11,000 feet, all red pine, was found by Ayres to have 222,000 feet, all white pine.[13] Another lot reported by the crew to have 46,000 feet of pine had no pine timber at all according to Wright and his men.

The companies interested in purchasing timber had taken stock of the forests on these lands. One John W. Meeley of Red Lake said that he with ten others had examined and reported 15 townships for the Minnesota and Minneapolis Lumber Company during the winter of 1894–95. One P. Cavanaugh of Merrill, Wisconsin, when questioned by Wright said he had examined several tracts and on two of them, forty acres each, he had found double the amount reported. That buyers were familiar with the amounts reported to the government was quite likely, for Wright and his men found that the tracts which were sold were those on which the timber had been underestimated. Those not sold were the tracts on which the estimate was nearly correct or too high.[14]

Wright held an examination in Crookston of the estimators from the crew whose work he had been sent to inspect; eighteen men in that crew admitted that they had had no previous experience as estimators. One estimator confessed that he had accepted another man's figures, while another had reported examination on certain days of certain sections when evidence proved he had not been present at all on those days. Andrew Douglas, who was in charge of the group, appeared to have made no personal inspection of the work done by his corps.

Wright included all his findings in a report made to the Secretary of the Interior. It showed how utterly worthless was the work of the previous crew, which had served the interests of neither the government nor the Indians.[15] F. J. Parker, special agent of the General Land Office, who spent much time with Wright while he was inspecting the timber at Red Lake, spoke highly of the work that Wright had done.

The incorrect estimates of standing timber which had served as a basis for the sale in July 1896 resulted in losses of thousands of dollars to the Indians for whom the United States government was serving as a trustee. Moreover, the government had spent far more money than was necessary for the examination of the timber. The first sale of the ceded

---

[12] 55th Cong., 3rd Sess. (1898–99), *Senate Docs.,* no. 85, pp. 104–5. The document contains the report of J. George Wright, the government inspector, relative to the pinelands and pine timber on the Red Lake Reservation.

[13] *Ibid.,* p. 106.

[14] *Ibid.,* pp. 107–12.

[15] *Ibid.,* pp. 13, 101–242. Within these pages is included the information gained by J. George Wright when examining the crew which had estimated the pine timber on the Red Lake Reservation.

Chippewa lands was, therefore, very unsatisfactory, and Secretary Francis offered no more Chippewa lands during his term.

In 1897, under the McKinley administration, a new crew of estimators was sent to Red Lake with explicit orders that three men should judge each tract at different times and that each man should record his estimate separately.[16] Secretary of the Interior Bliss stated that these men were carefully chosen and that they were a superior group of examiners. Based on their reporting of larger amounts of timber, a sale was held in August 1898 and 21,000 acres were sold for approximately $174,000.[17] Criticisms continued, however, and the next Secretary of the Interior, Hitchcock, in 1899 suspended all estimating, appraising, examining, cutting, and selling of timber in the Chippewa lands until a more intensive analysis could be made of the situation.[18]

By 1902 nearly three million acres of land, arable and pine, had been ceded by all the Chippewa of Minnesota from the various reservations, but the government had advanced more money than it had received from sales. Therefore the Indians' treasury, which was to be safeguarded by the government, was in the red. The lands had been ceded to the government and were useless to the Indians, and the Indians needed money. Congressmen knew, too, that if arrangements were not made to put the Chippewa lands on the market again their constituency would protest vigorously.

The Secretary of the Interior was anxious to replace the Nelson Act, which he felt had not operated properly, and early in 1901 he called a conference of the Minnesota men in Congress to give the matter consideration. Out of this grew the Morris Bill, which, sponsored by Representative Morris of Minnesota, was passed in 1902 as an amendment to the Nelson Act.[19] The bill provided that the "bank scale" was to be used in the measurement of pine for sale rather than the "stumpage scale." This meant that the government would be responsible for the logging of the timber and would have to bear the burden of supervision as well as the expense of logging, but it was hoped that this system would lessen the fraud so easily perpetrated when standing pine was sold in the forest.

The Morris Bill also provided that no white pine should be sold for less than $5.00 per thousand feet and that the pine must be sold by means of sealed bids rather than at open sale. It also annulled a provision concerning "dead and down timber" which had given occasion for much fraud

[16] *Report of the Secretary of the Interior,* 1898, pp. xxxiv–xxxv; *Mississippi Valley Lumberman,* vol. xxviii, July 30, 1897, p. 12, and Aug. 13, 1897, p. 12.
[17] *Report of the Land Commissioner,* 1898, pp. 68, 104–6.
[18] *U.S. Statutes at Large,* vol. xxx, p. 929; *Report of the Secretary of the Interior,* 1899, pp. xvii, xxix.
[19] *U.S. Statutes at Large,* vol. xxxii, pp. 400–4.

in the pinelands on the reservations as well as on the ceded areas of the reservations.[20] This act also provided for a forest reserve which became the basis of the Chippewa National Forest.[21]

The Morris Bill was not passed without effort. Much work was done by individuals to shape opinion before the bill was presented. Perhaps no one person had been more actively concerned for the preservation of the forests in Minnesota than General Christopher C. Andrews, chief fire warden of Minnesota and later commissioner of forestry. Andrews spent much time in Washington trying to inform Congress about the need for forest reserves and for fire protection of the reservation timber. He valued this timber at $5,000,000, and pointed out that not a dollar was being spent for its protection. Rightly he was called "Indefatigable Andrews."

Andrews was fully aware, too, of the prevalence of trespassing on government-owned pinelands and of the frauds associated with dead and down timber. He knew that if the pinelands were husbanded according to modern methods of forestry, it would mean the continuation of logging for years to come. Therefore he was in the front line of battle in establishing the forest reserve as provided in the Morris Bill. He saw the possibility of making such a reserve a health and pleasure resort, and he presented this aspect of the issue to the Minnesota Federation of Women's Clubs. This organization, under the direction of Mrs. E. V. Bramhall of St. Paul as legislative chairman, played no small part in spreading information and making converts for forest reserves. Another active participant was Colonel John S. Cooper of Chicago, who worked for years to arouse interest in forest reserves. His enthusiasm was not determined so much by his interest in forestry as by his wish to preserve a sportsman's paradise, but it was effective nonetheless.

Perhaps no Minnesotan excepting Andrews so clearly understood the need of protecting our forests as did Herman Haupt Chapman, superintendent of the North Central Agricultural Experiment Station of the state college of agriculture at Grand Rapids, Minnesota. Chapman was familiar with the Chippewa reservations and had the courage to maintain that some parts of them were not conducive to agriculture and should therefore be preserved as forest land.[22] He was strongly in favor of forest

[20] *Mississippi Valley Lumberman,* vol. xv, Feb. 15, 1889, p. 9. Also *U.S. Statutes at Large,* vol. xxv, p. 673; vol. xxx, p. 90; vol. xxxii, p. 404. Tornadoes and fires destroyed large amounts of timber which, if logged immediately, would give as good lumber as a live tree. Indians were encouraged to cut and sell such timber — laws were passed to that effect. At times fires were purposely set to get the timber; at times green timber was cut. It was a racket hard to reckon with.

[21] *U.S. Statutes at Large,* vol. xxxv, pp. 268–71.

[22] Chapman has a scrapbook which contains his speeches, clippings, letters, announcements, and cartoons pertaining to the activities in regard to the possibility of forest reserves and a park during the years 1901 and 1902. The Minnesota Historical Society has photostats of the scrapbook, which will be referred to below as Chapman's scrapbook.

reserves and held with Andrews that if the pine had aesthetic value which surpassed its commercial value, it should be preserved.[23] Chapman was quite in advance of his time in sensing the possibilities of the summer tourist business in the cool, cathedral-like pine forests of northern Minnesota. He found favor with Gifford Pinchot, famed United States conservationist, and both of them were influential in shaping the point of view of Page Morris, the father of the Morris Bill. ·

Northern Minnesota was generally opposed to any forest reserve. Duluth assumed leadership of the opposition, for the thousands of acres that lay to the west of that city constituted a mighty hinterland which someday would be her market. This entire region should be one series of unbroken farms, said the *Duluth Herald*.[24] Minneapolis and St. Paul, cried Duluth, were plotting her ruin when they favored reserves.

The get-rich-quick townsite boomer could make no concession to forest reserves, and the small villages of the forest region were sure they would have a bright future if only the forests were logged at once and the lands were thrown open for settlement. Cass Lake was such a place, where not one single person favored reserves. The people of the small village of Fertile, farther west in Minnesota, said they would have to be shown that these forest lands were not suitable for agriculture; they insisted that to bar so much land from agricultural use would be a misfortune, not a blessing.[25] People pleaded for the poor settler whose rights they said would be infringed upon if the forest areas were withdrawn.

Such was the cry that came from the populace of northern Minnesota. This opposition unfortunately was too preoccupied with the possibilities of an immediate boom to realize that a forest reserve might bring them many years of assured labor. Even after the Morris Bill had become law, these interests attempted to remove the clause making provision for reserves.[26]

Lumbermen were in favor of the Morris Bill. It offered them a great advantage, for bodies of timber were to be sold on "bank scale" without the land. They were free to buy the timber from thousands of acres with no concern for the devastated lands left behind, with no taxes to pay on cutover lands. Moreover, the Morris Bill freed them of the difficulties arising from a Minnesota law, enacted only a few years earlier, prohibiting any corporation from owning more than five thousand acres of land in the state.[27] To be sure, corporations could and had arranged with indi-

---

[23] *Mississippi Valley Lumberman*, vol. xxxiii, Jan. 17, 1902, p. 90; Folwell, *op. cit.*, vol. iv, p. 258.

[24] Clipping in the Chapman scrapbook in the Minnesota Historical Society.

[25] Clipping from the *Fertile Journal* (Minnesota) in the Chapman scrapbook.

[26] 59th Cong., 1st Sess. (1905–6), *Congressional Record*, vol. xl, pt. i, p. 942.

[27] *Minnesota Laws*, 1899, p. 131.

viduals to purchase lands for them in order to circumvent this law,[28] but the Morris Bill enabled lumbermen to buy thousands of feet of timber without buying an acre of land, and thus to keep well within the law and still gain the resource they wanted. Morris, who appeared to have favored the lumbermen in this matter, later made a definite statement that he had no knowledge of the restriction on land purchase by corporations and that his interest was chiefly in the Indian.[29]

When the Morris Bill was passed, it provided that a portion of the lands from which timber was removed was to be opened up for homesteads, but that two hundred thousand acres were to be set aside as a forest reserve.

Lumbermen approved all of this but they objected to the sealed bids required by the bill. They wanted sale at public auction. On what forties were other lumbermen bidding? What prices were being offered? Who was bidding? These facts the open sale could reveal, but the sealed bid would not. Sealed bids made collusion more difficult, and Morris and his aids were determined to seal every loophole that might permit fraud. In their attack the lumber interests were aided by Representatives Eddy, Fletcher, and Tawney, all from Minnesota, who staunchly supported their demand for the public sale.[30] But the sealed bids prevailed.

The sale of timber under the Morris Act began in 1903, and for the first time in the history of the sale of Indian timber on the Red Lake Reservation, no charges of fraud were made. The timber continued to be sold over a long period of time; sometimes large amounts were offered, sometimes only small amounts. Over a period of thirteen years, during which 1,269,000,000 board feet were sold, the sum of $9,000,000 was realized from the sale of timber under the Morris Act.[31] The government sold the timber, supervised the cutting, scaled the timber, and collected the money, which was deposited in the Treasury of the United States and credited to the Chippewa. The total expense of the operation over the thirteen years was 4.27 per cent of the receipts from the timber.[32] The timber cut during these thirteen years exceeded the estimates by 350,000,000 feet. The Morris Act had justified itself, but credit should also be given to "a most faithful,

[28] *Graham Report,* 62d Cong., 3rd Sess. (1911–12), *House Reports,* no. 1366, vol. i, p. 241.
[29] *Ibid.,* p. 750.
[30] *Report of the Secretary of the Interior,* 1900, p. lvii, and 1901, pp. liii, lxxiii, lxxiv; Conference between the Secretary of the Interior and the Members of the Minnesota Delegation in Congress, to Ascertain a Better Method for the Sale and Disposal of the Pine Timber on Indian Reservations in that State, Jan. 19 and 23, 1901 (Washington, 1901). (The Minnesota Historical Society has a photostatic reproduction of the discussion at this conference.) *Graham Report,* 62d Cong., 3rd Sess., *House Reports,* no. 1366, vol. i, pp. 242, 750–59.
[31] *Report of the Secretary of the Interior,* 1903, pp. 28–29. Also *Reports of the Administrative Departments of the Department of Interior,* 1911, vol. i, p. 121; 1912, vol. i, pp. 138–39; 1914, vol. i, p. 149; 1917, vol. i, pp. 183–84.
[32] *Report of the Commissioner of the Land Office,* 1925, p. 26.

honest, and capable officer," William O'Neill, who served as superintendent of logging during those years.[33]

The Chippewa no longer felt secure in their holdings, for white men in the area were covetous and the agitation continued with ever-increasing momentum for the cession of more of the Indian lands.[34] The idea was developing that the consent of the Indians was no longer required in order to get the reservation land, and this policy was favored by Indian Commissioner Jones. It was planned to give the Indians allotments as set forth by the Dawes Act, and then to sell the rest of the lands. The Indians of Red Lake again refused to take allotments. In the fall of 1903 Senator Clapp of Minnesota introduced a bill which had as its purpose the removal of the Indian title to certain parts of the Red Lake Reservation. It finally became law, after a number of revisions, in 1904. This law made unnecessary any further negotiations with the Red Lake Reservation Indians in regard to their lands.[35] There was much dissatisfaction among the Red Lake Indians over the action of 1904 and unpleasant situations developed, but these do not concern us in this study.[36]

In the spring of 1916 the Red Lake Indian Forest, comprising about 100,000 acres of fine white pine in the southeastern part of the Red Lake Reservation, was set aside with the idea that on those acres scientific forestry should determine the logging of the forest. The establishment of this forest was highly significant for lumbermen because it opened up, although supposedly not without restrictions, large areas of pine. It was to be operated under the direction of the Secretary of the Interior, as under the Morris Act. On November 19, 1917, the superintendent of the Red Lake Indian School, under orders from Washington, signed a contract with the International Lumber Company of Minneapolis, which had offered the most satisfactory of the sealed bids, for the sale of merchantable dead timber and all other timber marked for cutting by a member of the Indian service on about 50,000 acres of the Red Lake Indian Forest.[37]

It appears that no action was taken by those in authority toward applying the rules of scientific forestry to the Red Lake Indian Forest. Such an oversight would have been quite natural before conservation principles came to be generally known, but in 1917 men in departments charged

[33] *Reports of the Administrative Departments of the Department of Interior*, 1917, vol. i, pp. 183–84.

[34] 56th Cong., 2d Sess. (1900–01), *U. S. Statutes at Large*, vol. xxxi, p. 1077; 57th Cong., 1st Sess. (1901–02), *Senate Reports*, no. 1087, pp. 2–42.

[35] *Thief River Falls News*, Dec. 24, 1903; 58th Cong., 2d Sess. (1903–04), *House Reports*, no. 443, pp. 3–5.

[36] Folwell, *op. cit.*, vol. iv, pp. 296–312.

[37] *U. S. Statutes at Large*, vol. xxxix, p. 137; 64th Cong., 1st Sess., *Congressional Record*, May 12, 1916, pp. 7859–62; *Report of the Board of Indian Commissioners*, 1921, p. 104.

with the care of the natural resources of the United States could not escape the responsibility of concern over the rapidly passing pine forests of Minnesota. No one could seek cover under the "legend of inexhaustibility" any longer.

More than 80 per cent of the 50,000 acres were cleared. These acres yielded more than 105,000,000 feet, for which the International Lumber Company paid about $1,395,500.[38] The price per thousand feet was good — it was wartime and prices were generally high. But for the government this was an expensive venture, considering that it was left with a large area of stripped land that would yield no harvest for years to come. The lumbermen had no responsibility for the cutover lands at Red Lake.

Though it was too late to correct this error, the Department of the Interior must have made a quick resolve to try other ways. A new policy was adopted which provided that the remaining timber in the Red Lake Indian Forest was to be cut, manufactured, and sold on the market under the jurisdiction of the government itself. Indian labor was to be employed and trees were to be cut according to careful selection. Only a limited number of feet were to be cut each year. The plan was put into operation, and the Commissioner of Indian Affairs was well pleased with the result.[39]

Thus by means fair and foul the Red Lake Chippewa were parted from much of their rich domain. From the time Congress voted favorably on the Nelson Act of 1889, the Chippewa of Red Lake fought a losing battle. The major portion of their reservation was ceded in 1889; in 1904 another portion was granted to the United States; and in 1916 a large part of the Red Lake Indian Forest was made available to the white man. The Indians' private reserve became gradually smaller.[40]

The White Earth Reservation lands were not opened for sale so early as those of Red Lake, partly because all the Chippewa in the state except those at Red Lake were to be gathered together on the White Earth Reservation to receive allotments there. To bring this about was a slow process, and it was not until after the turn of the century that the forests of the White Earth Reservation were offered for sale. The history of the White Earth lands had been very similar to that of Red Lake. Indians refused at first to give up their lands. When lands finally were ceded and examination and appraisal began, there was the same cry of fraud. The Secretary of the Interior had steadily refused to approve Indian

[38] Folwell, *op. cit.*, vol. iv, p. 310.
[39] *Report of the Indian Office*, 1920, p. 52.
[40] Folwell, *op. cit.*, vol. iv, p. 298. This page contains a map of the Red Lake Indian Reservation, 1863–1930, with the various ceded areas.

allotments on the timbered lands of the White Earth Reservation, but by some "error" allotments had been made on those lands. The Indian had no use for the timber except to sell it, and when it had been sold — for a mere song in many instances — the Indian would spend the little money he had got and from then on would become a public charge.

Naturally lumbermen were anxious that arrangements be made to allow the Indian to sell his pine. In 1904 Senator Moses E. Clapp of Minnesota, formerly an attorney for certain lumber interests in the state, introduced a rider to the Indian Appropriation Bill of that year authorizing the Chippewa to sell the timber on their allotments without any restriction except to secure the consent of the Secretary of the Interior. The timber on allotments belonging to minors might be sold by Indian agents, mothers, fathers, or guardians.[41] There was no opposition to the bill.

The so-called Clapp rider of 1904 was followed shortly by a bill which provided that whole quarter-section allotments be given the White Earth Indians in place of the eighty-acre allotments allowed them by the revised Dawes Act of 1891.[42] This bill was introduced by Senator Clapp and passed the Senate without debate; Halvor Steenerson, representative in Congress from the district in which the White Earth Reservation lay, guided the bill through the House so skillfully that it has since been known as the Steenerson Bill.[43]

The Clapp rider and the Steenerson Bill supplemented each other. In order to make the allotment of 160 acres to each Indian, much of the pineland, as well as all the prairie land, would have to be allotted. The Indian would thus have more pineland to sell than under the former arrangement. Allotments were to be made the following year. In the meantime, Indian and white man scoured the pine country taking measure of the standing pine; it was a busy time for cruisers.

On the day of allotment, April 24, 1905, Indians came from far and near. Full-bloods and mixed-bloods who had never been heard of or seen before were present in the line. From Chicago, from St. Louis, from all over the Middle West, Indians claiming to be Chippewa came to make their claim for 160 acres of the good land of the White Earth Reservation.[44] They were in line even the day before the allotments were to be made. Many of them were informed as to what lands to select, and it appears that in the distribution of land the mixed-bloods came off better than the full-bloods.[45]

The Indian Office of the Department of the Interior decided that

[41] U. S. Statutes at Large, vol. xxxiii, pp. 209–10.
[42] Folwell, op. cit., vol. iv, p. 266.
[43] U.S. Statutes at Large, vol. xxxiii, p. 539.
[44] Graham Report, 62d Cong., 3rd Sess., House Reports, no. 1366, vol. ii, p. 1522.
[45] Ibid., vol. i, pp. 543–59.

the Indians of White Earth would fare better if all the pine was offered at a single sale through sealed bids rather than through direct dealings between the lumbermen and each Indian. The Indian Office seemed genuinely eager to protect the Indians, for whom it was acting as a trustee, but it did not always use good judgment in the handling of these affairs, which involved millions of dollars of property. In this instance the Indian Office called upon the supervisor of the Indian schools for an estimate of the merchantable timber that was to be offered. This was an error, for such a man was not likely to be an expert judge of timber — no commercial concern dealing in timber would have made such an error. The report of the schoolman was sent to Washington and was accepted, though definite evidence was presented to the Indian Office that his findings were wrong. The timber was advertised on the basis of information taken from his report, though it appeared that he had overestimated the hardwoods and underestimated the pine. The lumber concerns that sought this timber were thoroughly familiar with the amounts and equally familiar with the fact that the government estimates were incorrect.[46]

When the bids were opened on November 15, 1905, a high bid on the pine and a low bid on the hardwood were found from a man who represented a Wisconsin firm. His bid was the highest made on pine, which would have brought the government the most money. Two other bids, both from certain Minnesota lumber interests, offered a high price on the hardwood and a low price on the pine. These interests claimed they had based their price on the estimates published by the government. J. R. Farr, general superintendent of logging in the White Earth area, wrote to the Commissioner of Indian Affairs on November 16, 1905, that the bid made by the man representing the Wisconsin firm "is clearly and beyond question the highest and best bid." He stated also that the firm which had made the low bid on pine and the high bid on hardwood was working "on the further assumption that office, department, and other government officials are ignorant if not dishonest."[47] A member of one of Minnesota's largest lumber companies, which was not in this race, reported that the highest bid by their estimate was that offered by the Wisconsin man.[48] But the Minnesota firm insisted that the published estimate should serve as the basis for determining who was the highest bidder. The company was so insistent that the Commissioner of Indian Affairs finally rejected all bids.

The situation had reached a complete stalemate, when suddenly agitation began for the mixed-bloods at White Earth to be allowed to sell

[46] *Ibid.*, vol. ii, p. 2218.
[47] *Ibid.*, vol. i, p. 649.
[48] *Ibid.*

both their land and the pine. This suggestion caught the public mind. The newspaper published at Detroit (now Detroit Lakes), Minnesota, insisted that mixed-bloods were capable of handling their own affairs and that if they could sell a part of their holdings, they would have more money with which to improve what they had left. There were single families of Indians who held more than they could adequately take care of, said the newspaper.[49] It also maintained that the value of adjoining property would be increased and the region improved generally if the Indian had less land and the white man more. The Commercial Club of Detroit sent a petition to Minnesota senators and representatives in Washington urging that all restrictions be removed and the mixed-bloods be given a free hand in managing their property.[50]

The prairie lands and the pinelands of the Indians were both greatly in demand, for the best public lands of both kinds were passing fast. Incoming settlers coveted the fine prairie lands of the White Earth Reservation just as lumbermen coveted the timber, and the farmers on the prairie were eager for lumber that was produced nearby and so did not have to bear the long-distance freight rate. Lumbermen were equally eager for the market that was developing on the prairie lands.

People in other parts of the state criticized the white people of the White Earth region for their selfishness in depriving the Indian of his holdings. But when the *Minneapolis Journal* censored the people of Detroit, the *Record* of that town replied that the white settlers of Detroit were as anxious for land as the people of Minneapolis had been when Indians occupied fine holdings in their area.[51] "Thousands of citizens in this area are anxious to have the Indian free," said the Detroit newspaper. Free, so they could deal with him at their pleasure!

Again Senator Clapp ventured an amendment to an appropriations bill. This amendment provided "that all the restrictions as to sale, incumbrance, or taxation for allotments within the White Earth Reservation in the State of Minnesota, now or hereafter held by adult mixed-blood Indians are hereby removed."[52] The *Detroit Record* in its discussion of the amendment stated that "if it passes prosperity will begin on the reservation." That the county would be improved and the condition of the people bettered was its satisfied conclusion. The bill passed and became law on June 21, 1906. The people of the Detroit area agreed that Senator Clapp, with this "Clapp rider of 1906" had "made good" with the folks of Becker County.[53]

[49] *Detroit Record* (Detroit, Minnesota), May 25, 1906.
[50] *Ibid.*, Mar. 9, 1906.
[51] *Ibid.*, July 20, 1906.
[52] *Ibid.*, Apr. 13, 1906.
[53] *Ibid.*, June 22, 1906.

The law opened a free-for-all as far as the Indian lands were concerned. The white man became the owner of the Indian's property in incredible ways. The Indian failed to grasp his economic opportunity! Legally only the mixed-bloods could sell, but little heed was given to that. Most of the merchantable pine on the White Earth Reservation became in time the property of the Nichols-Chisholm Lumber Company, the Park Rapids Lumber Company, and the Wild Rice Lumber Company. The Nichols-Chisholm Company bought about one half of the pine and paid approximately $8.50 per thousand feet of white pine.[54]

But the issue was not settled. The Clapp rider of 1906 provided that only mixed-bloods could sell, and much of the land which was sold belonged to full-bloods and minors. Years of litigation followed between the government of the United States and the people who had purchased the natural resource of the reservation. The Nichols-Chisholm Company alone settled seventy-two suits for $48,497.[55]

The White Earth Reservation had, nevertheless, been greatly reduced, for 80 per cent of the whole acreage had passed into private hands. If the white pine of White Earth had been properly cared for, it might have become the basis for a forest reserve where true forestry could have been practiced and where the Indian through generations could have drawn a living from productive forest property. Surely, it is for lack of vision that men perish.

From the analysis of the operation of the land laws in the pineland area of Minnesota it is quite clear that federal land laws were not patterned to fit the large forest areas. The democratic idea of many small holdings gave way to control by a smaller group of large holdings.[56] Under the drive of large concerns, the lands were in a short time stripped of their pine. Today society seeks to assess the blame. Contemporary society sees the past through its own eyes; the cutover lands and the price of lumber today are factors which shape our thinking about forest policy in the past. Man shifts his viewpoint. But to be fair we must judge the period in which the pinelands passed from the public domain to private ownership and were quickly shorn of their timber, in the spirit of that time, not of our own day.

It was a great era of individualism that followed immediately upon the Civil War. Dynamic energy, both physical and mental, was devoted to economic development. The United States was on the march for the conquest of a continent. In this movement of thousands of people west-

---

[54] *Graham Report,* 62d Cong., 3rd Sess., *House Reports,* no. 1366, vol. i, pp. xv, 246, 248, 1112, and vol. ii, pp. 2224, 2227, 2236, 2272; Folwell, *op. cit.,* vol. iv, p. 280.

[55] *Ibid.,* p. 295.

[56] Thomas H. Sherrard, *National Forest and Lumber Supply* (reprint from the *Yearbook of Agriculture* for 1906), pp. 447, 450.

ward, the largest folk movement in modern history, the forest lands influenced our history greatly because they furnished homes for the immigrants. The pinelands of Minnesota lay immediate neighbor to great regions of prairie of amazing fertility where lumber was needed for houses, fences, and barns. The way of living was primitive at first, but the pioneer quickly lifted himself to higher standards of living, and as he did so, better buildings replaced the first crude homes. Towns and cities eventually grew up on the prairies.

This conquest could not have been made without the lumber which gave shelter on the vast stretches of prairie and plain. In that age of expansion the market could consume more than industry could produce. Large-scale exploitation of timber resources was necessary to meet the demand. Science, invention, and machine power were applied to the processes of extraction and manufacture, and labor was inexpensive and quite steady. Everything was mobilized for the task, and in endless procession the white pine moved from the forest to the mills and then to the prairies or to the growing cities, spurred on by the great industrial revolution of the era. Lumber was good but inexpensive; the pioneer shared in the low price the government had exacted for its forest areas. The manufacturer of lumber could sell his wares, excellent as they were, at a price known only in story today. Because the lumberman got his timber at a low price, both he and the consumer profited.

Very few stopped to consider that the conquest of the frontier had been attended by exploitation of the country's great resources. Men gave little thought to that, for "the great inexhaustible legend false as it was in an ultimate sense was true for the time." [57] The forests of white pine had stood in endless line, it seemed, from the shores of the Atlantic to the western portions of Minnesota. And why should an age be sparing of forests which regarded them as an obstacle to civilization to be disposed of as fast as possible? [58] A tree was only an obstacle to the successful farmer; the land alone was important. All forest land, it was thought, would yield to agriculture. Absurd as it may seem, in Minnesota the opinion was general even as late as 1920 that the cutover lands would become fine farm lands.[59] Democracy, observing the riches at hand, took no thought for the future. The public attitude of that day toward the preservation of timberlands was one of indifference. And so the pine forests of Minnesota, once thought sufficient for all time, disappeared within the lifetime of the men who began logging them.

[57] Cameron, *Development of Government Forest Control in the United States*, p. 435.

[58] Edward A. Bowers, *The Present Conditions of the Forest on Public Lands,* in Publications of the American Economic Association, vol. iii, no. 3 (May 1891), p. 60.

[59] Blakey, *Taxation in Minnesota*, p. 149.

Laissez faire was the dominant principle in our national life at the time the great pine forests of Minnesota were being harvested. For several decades following the Civil War there was no regulation of industry by the federal government, except in the matter of tariff, and there was little interference by the states. The functions of government were few. In the years following the Civil War laissez faire did not fit into the economic pattern, but the public mind was slow to make a change. The country was not mentally ready for regulation, and an indifferent people looked on as its natural resources rapidly became private property and were harvested with little thought of the future.

Not all people were unconcerned. We have seen how the secretaries of the interior and the commissioners of the United States Land Office in their reports constantly presented the problems of the forest lands to an indifferent Congress. In no instance was this so apparent as in the defeat of Land Commissioner Sparks, when Congress and various groups of people showed that they were not ready to discard "fraud, favoritism, and fees." [60]

Not only was Congress slow to change the land laws; it was even reluctant to appropriate money for ferreting out the frauds that were so common in the pineland area. In 1877 only $12,500 was appropriated for the use of special agents in carrying out investigations in the whole public domain; in 1880 the appropriation was raised to $40,000.[61] How inadequate this amount was is suggested by the request for $400,000 by the land commissioner in 1883. This was flatly refused by Congress, and the commissioner was unable to make the investigations necessary if he was to lock horns properly with men who were coming into control of the nation's resources by illegal means.[62]

Carl Schurz, as Secretary of the Interior, while waiting for Congress to make appropriations for timber investigation said, "If Congress makes that appropriation so small as to restrict me to a very limited sphere of action, such an act will be considered as virtually a proclamation to the timber depredators in the length and breadth of the country now to go in and make themselves comfortable, as they are assured government will no longer have the means to interfere with them." [63]

Congress had no conception of how difficult it was to cover adequately the immense area of the public domain. One county in the pineland area

[60] 49th Cong., 1st Sess., *Senate Reports*, no. 44, pp. 1–3; 49th Cong., 2d Sess., *House Exec. Docs.*, no. 1, pp. 50–69.
[61] Cameron, *op. cit.*, p. 217; White, "The Administration of the Land Office, 1812–1911," manuscript thesis, Widener Library, Harvard University, p. 251.
[62] *Report of the Secretary of the Interior*, 1885, p. 37.
[63] *Mississippi Valley Lumberman and Manufacturer*, vol. ii, Apr. 5, 1878, p. 4.

of Minnesota was larger than some of the states; the land to be examined was scattered over an area as large as an average New England state; there were no roads except winter roads over frozen lakes and streams. Expert explorers and woodsmen, not city-bred men, were needed to make an examination of each tract thorough enough to enable the examiner to testify that nowhere "hid in the forest or dense underbrush or cedar thicket was there a log cabin and a quarter of an acre of land prepared for cultivation." [64] Considering the hardships endured and the skill necessary to search out offenders, the special agents were not well paid.

The letters of such agents indicate the expenses incurred and the hardships encountered on their errands. Milton Peden, hunting timber depredations in northern Minnesota in 1883, forwarded his expense account to the Land Office in Washington. His statement showed what ways of travel he used on his expedition; it indicated, too, the type of food he ate and the primitive life he lived while on this search to save the government's wealth. His report for December 1882 and January 1883 in the "Record of Timber Depredation Accounts" reads as follows: [65]

December 1882

J. E. Hayward of St. Cloud Minn. for board and lodging for 3¼ days at $2.00 per day = $6.50.

Fare on N. P. Railway from St. Cloud to Little Falls Minn. 32 miles

To James Brown, Little Falls to Granville, 10 miles and return from 12 a.m. to 12 at night — one day $3.00 per day.

To James Bunga Leech Lake for one pair of snow shoes $4.00.

To Henry Leland, Brainerd Minn. for two horses and Bob sled, with driver, including expenses from Brainerd to Winnibigoshish Lake distance 120 miles and return from Dec. 21 to 27, 1882 incl 7 days at $6.00 = $42.00

To Indian, enroute for 3 pecks of corn = 50¢ and hay for Ponies 25¢

January 1883

To an Indian for 6 partridges 50¢

"   "   "   " mess of fresh trout 25¢

" foreman Caldwells Camp for ½ bushel ground feed for ponies 50¢

To baker at Gristas Camp for baking bread and cakes 50¢

To Charles Simpson, Grand Rapids for two horses and sleigh with driver, including expenses from Grand Rapids to Aitkin 65 miles and return from January 31 at 12 m. to Feb. 4 at 12 m. including 4 days at $5. per day = $20.00

To Mike McAlpin, Grand Rapids for board and lodge for 3 from 30 Dec. to 31 Dec. at $1.50 per day = $5.72.

[64] N.A.: Records of the General Land Office, Miscellaneous Letters Received, 1882–15800.
[65] G.L.O., Record of Timber Depredation Accounts, vol. v, pp. 25–33.

Peden reported that his cash outlay, including the salary for an assistant, was $355 in December 1882 and $328 in January 1883. He himself was paid a salary of $1400 a year.[66] His searching for trespassers brought him often into the region of Rainy Lake, on the northernmost border of Minnesota. On one occasion he was ordered there in midsummer when black flies and mosquitoes were almost unendurable. That journey required both a guide and a packer, and Peden was concerned about the expenditures as well as about the fact that the trip might be unsuccessful because the "inhabitants are non-commital regarding information we want." [67]

Webster Eaton, who was assigned to the Duluth district, the only completely timbered area in which special agents operated in the eighties, had a salary of $2964 for the period from October 1, 1883, to July 31, 1885. His expense account of $7070 during that time was next to the highest for all the special agents operating in the United States.[68] His travel distances in the remote wilderness were great, for his orders sent him from Duluth to the Northwest Angle on Lake of the Woods.

It is quite evident that the job confronting the United States government in checking frauds required a large, well-equipped staff. With an indifferent Congress and without appropriations, the land commissioners could do very little. In 1883 Commissioner McFarland noted the great increase in business in his office. He complained that he did not have enough clerical help to take care of the records for the 600,000 claims in some stage of progress in his office and that it would take his present force three years to do half of those claims. He needed two hundred more clerks, he said, in order to handle the business adequately.[69] Out in the field in 1886 thirty-four agents were assigned to the job of examining 18,000 entries, which, said the land commissioner, was a five-year job with such a small staff.[70]

The group of special agents was too small to be effective, and the appropriations were utterly inadequate to safeguard the 70,000,000 acres of public timber in the United States.[71] A Congress so unwilling to vote assistance for such a necessary project must take much blame for the passing of the great forests in our country. A simple law requiring a larger fee from entrymen would have helped to raise the amount needed to provide a sufficient number of trained agents to care properly for the public domain. Larger appropriations would have increased the staff in the field and in the Washington Land Office which, wrote Webster

[66] N.A.: Records of the General Land Office, Miscellaneous Letters Received, 1884–15552.
[67] Ibid., 1882–48819. Dodge discusses Peden and his assignment in this letter.
[68] 49th Cong., 1st Sess., Senate Exec. Docs., vol. vii, no. 134, pp. 6–7.
[69] 48th Cong., 1st Sess. (1883–84), House Exec. Docs., vol. x, pp. 31–32.
[70] 49th Cong., 1st Sess., Senate Exec. Docs., vol. vii, no. 134, pp. 1–7.
[71] Bowers, op. cit., p. 60.

Eaton, was so slow that at times requests were made several times before any response was forthcoming.[72]

The people on the frontier were themselves often a hindrance in the agents' attempt to carry out the law. They did not always approve the investigations that were made. When Congress in 1851 passed a law authorizing timber agents, President Fillmore responded by sending agents into suspected areas. One agent was seriously reproved for not realizing that the "lumber interest is vital to Minnesota." One newspaper stated that "as cold as Minnesota is it will be too hot for such villains," meaning the timber agent.[73]

Minnesota's own territorial delegate, Henry H. Sibley, said in an address in Congress that laws providing for such agents should be "expunged" from the statute books as "a disgrace to the country and to the nineteenth Century." He stated further that "the hardy lumberman who has penetrated the remotest wilds of the Northwest, to draw from their recesses the materials for building up towns and cities in the great valley of the Mississippi has been particularly marked out as a victim. . . ."[74] If the interests of the frontier conflicted with the law, the law was ignored!

William R. Marshall, who investigated fraud in the Duluth area, found that evidence was hard to get. "Unless some of the men 'turned informers' or in some way testimony is bought with money, I do not know how any legal or sufficient evidence could be had," he reported to the United States land commissioner.[75] And Don A. Dodge, who was operating in Minnesota, wrote that his witnesses are "as reliable as the average witness in cases of timber trespass."[76] The sympathy of the community was usually with the men who were illegally seizing the public timber, and quite often the jurors themselves had used such timber.[77]

The local land offices on the frontier were at times open to criticism for inefficient administration and for weak and corrupt officials. These offices were funnels through which public land business was conducted to the general office. The Duluth office had serious charges brought against it at certain times.[78] Men in government land offices had a great advantage in locating lands, for their work made them familiar with the lay of the land, the actual values, and the potential values. This often led them into temptation and they were accused of securing lands dishon-

[72] N.A.: Records of the General Land Office, Miscellaneous Letters Received, 1883–956; 45th Cong., 2d Sess., *Senate Exec. Docs.*, vol. viii, no. 9, pt. 1, pp. 2–3.

[73] *Minnesota Pioneer*, May 13, 1852.

[74] 32d Cong., 1st Sess., *Congressional Globe*, Apr. 24, 1852, Appendix, p. 486.

[75] N.A.: Records of the General Land Office, Miscellaneous Letters Received, 1883–15791.

[76] *Ibid.*, 1883–11741.

[77] Bowers, *op. cit.*, p. 67.

[78] N.A.: Records of the General Land Office, Miscellaneous Letters Received, 1882–87613.

estly. The register of the St. Cloud land office in the early eighties was reproached for his acquisition of large holdings while in office.[79]

Conditions, however, made the work of the men in the remote land offices very difficult. When the first land office in the Duluth area was established at Buchanan on Lake Superior at the mouth of the Knife River, the nearest place of deposit for funds was either Chicago or Dubuque. The receiver was ordered to deposit funds when the sum approached a specified amount, usually $5000. To travel with such a sum in 1857 was a dangerous undertaking, but the orders were that it had to be done.

In 1857 some mail was lost which contained the plots for Buchanan sent from Washington. In an attempt to locate the plots, the receiver of the Buchanan land office went to Chicago by boat in the middle of October and from there to Dubuque. Finding nothing at either of these distant places he went on up to St. Paul. Finding there no trace of the material he sought, he returned to Dubuque. There he was told that he might find his plots at Taylor's Falls, at the head of navigation on the St. Croix, so he went there by boat. The trip from the St. Croix to Buchanan, most of it on foot, was very difficult, but finally, six weeks after he had set out, he arrived again in Buchanan with the plots safely in his hands, ready to establish his place of business.[80]

Both registers and receivers were paid slim salaries which were to be augmented by fees; in this very system there was every chance for corruption. The homestead settler paid a fee of five dollars if he entered eighty acres and ten dollars when a larger amount was entered; if he commuted, the fee was retained. Fees were also paid when cash sales were executed either by private or by public sale. The land officials favored the public sale, because it meant a generous increase in their income.[81] Sparks of the General Land Office was well aware of the danger that lay in the fee system. He insisted that registers and receivers of land offices must be paid adequate fixed salaries, but his suggestions were not acceptable to an irritated Congress and the system of fees was continued.[82]

Congress did make provision in 1882 for inspectors to investigate local land offices and the work of the surveyors general in order to check evils in their operations.[83] In the eighties, when the land office in Duluth was doing its largest business to date, there was a shortage of help. William

[79] Ibid., 1883–50572; a complaint of one William Barrett, sworn before a notary public of Ramsey County and sent to McFarland, 1883–18636.

[80] Vern E. Chatelain, "The Public Land Officer on the Northwestern Frontier," *Minnesota History*, vol. xii, no. 4 (Dec. 1931), pp. 379–88.

[81] *Daily Minnesotian*, Aug. 17, 1859.

[82] *Report of the Land Commissioner*, 1885, p. 202.

[83] White, *op. cit.*, pp. 90–91.

Marshall wrote to McFarland on one occasion that the clerk had "worked all night last night not getting away until five o'clock in the morning." [84]

Not only were registers and receivers required to do the work in the office, but they were also expected to get the information needed to make sure that the requirements had been properly completed when the "land office oath" was given. This was a responsibility hard to fulfill when men seventy or eighty or a hundred miles away in the heavy forest had made entry. It was too much to expect that any receiver or register could carry on without overlooking something under such circumstances. This led to the policy of trusting to the "land office oath," which came to be considered only a necessary formality because men were quite certain that the local officials did not have time to investigate. The local land office did give the location of the land, but there was no record of its quality or of the timber that grew on it; it was quite impossible for land officials to be familiar with every acre of the thousands within their jurisdiction.[85]

These officials were required by law upon receipt of information about depredation to investigate the matter, seize the timber, and cut and dispose of it to the highest bidder at public auction.[86] All this required time, and the staff was insufficient. So again we place the blame on a Congress reluctant to vote the funds necessary for the proper execution of the law.

Slowly, however, a few men were able to shape opinion in favor of changes in land policy. At the very time that laissez faire seemed to have a stranglehold on national policies, that hold was beginning to break. Uncontrolled individualism was giving way to a more social point of view. Passage of the Interstate Commerce Act, the land laws of 1889 and 1891, and the Sherman Anti-Trust Act seems to indicate that men of social vision were being heard. The idea of conservation, too, was taking hold. In 1886 Dr. Bernhard E. Fernow, the first trained forester in our country, was appointed to direct government forests, and this step forward was followed in 1891 by the law authorizing the President to set aside forest reserves. For thus focusing much effort the administrations of Hayes and Cleveland, with active secretaries of the interior and equally interested land commissioners plus the intensely able report of the Public Land Commission of 1880, must be given credit. Congress was forced to act.

The American Forestry Association also deserves much credit for the change in forest policy. This scientific organization petitioned Congress

---

[84] N.A.: Records of the General Land Office, Miscellaneous Letters Received, 1882–64755.
[85] White, op. cit., pp. 93, 268–79.
[86] Ibid., p. 249.

for an investigation of forest resources ·and for the withdrawal of all forest lands from sale.[87] The American Association for the Advancement of Science had also petitioned Congress to set aside forest reserves.[88] These petitions undoubtedly helped to force the passage of new land laws. But the new laws seemed to cause little comment throughout the country. And Congress, as usual, voted no appropriations to carry them into effect — of course money was temporarily scarce owing to the panic.[89]

In 1905 the administration of the national forests was transferred to the Department of Agriculture. The Secretary of Agriculture was given the power to oversee the timber cutting on government lands and to handle its sale as well. This timber was sold by the thousand feet based on the actual scale of logs when cut. Government income from forest lands increased greatly under this system, as contrasted with the income from the sale of timberlands per acre.[90] Only the ready timber was to be harvested in order that government forests might maintain a steady flow of raw materials. This plan had in it the advantage of steadying timber values and therefore lessening speculation.[91]

In enacting new land laws in 1889 and 1891 the national lawmakers had little sense of establishing a way of conserving and protecting the forests. That problem remained for later solution, but the idea was growing and the twentieth century would see an improvement in the protection given the forests of the nation. The great pineland area of Minnesota, however, had by that time very largely passed into private hands, and the new laws came too late to save the white and red pines of Minnesota.

At the turn of the century Americans could look back over half a century of progress unparalleled in history. The wealth of the nation had increased from seven billion to eighty-eight billion dollars in the years from 1850 to 1900.[92] But this had been accomplished at a heavy cost to the nation's physical resources — perhaps especially to its timber reserves. This cost, and the moral deterioration that went with it, were a conspicuous part of the price America paid for the freedom to expand and develop rapidly which it prized so highly in the nineteenth century.

[87] 51st Cong., 1st Sess. (1889–90), *Congressional Record*, vol. xxi, pt. 3, pp. 2, 537 (Mar. 22, 1890).

[88] 51st Cong., 1st Sess. (1889–90), *Senate Exec. Docs.*, no. 36, pp. 2–4.

[89] 53rd Cong., 2d Sess., *House Reports*, no. 1400; 52d Cong., 2d Sess., *House Misc. Docs.*, no. 2, p. 437.

[90] Sherrard, *op. cit.*, pp. 447–50.

[91] *Ibid.*, p. 452.

[92] Samuel Eliot Morison and Henry Steele Commager, *The Growth of the American Republic* (New York, 1942), p. 354; Cameron, *op. cit.*, p. 117.

CHAPTER XVII

The Operation of State Laws in the Pineland Area

THE state of Minnesota was itself a landowner of no small proportions. In various ways and at various times the national government had granted the states substantial amounts of land. During the first fifty years of its existence Minnesota had acquired from the United States nearly 17,000,000 acres, plus swamp land yet unmeasured — a region as large as Massachusetts, Rhode Island, Connecticut, Vermont, and a third of New Hampshire.[1]

Much of this land was rich in natural resources, such as agricultural fertility, white pine, and iron ore. It became the responsibility of the state, then, to secure the greatest return from these valuable properties to be used for schools, public buildings, and internal improvements. Officials who were elected to positions of trust in the state stood guard over the lands, and the interests of the people were protected according to the ability, judgment, and integrity of these men.

Since a large part of the state-owned lands was covered with timber, and since Minnesota became a state just when lumbermen were attracted to the white and red pine lying within its boundaries, the government of the new state was immediately challenged by the administration of its forests. To administer these well was not an easy assignment, for it required selling the timber advantageously and protecting it against fire and against trespass, and also in some manner conserving the forests. The problems of the state in managing its timberlands were not unlike those the national government experienced in the management of its holdings.

Various laws dealing with Minnesota's pinelands were made early in the history of the state, but it was not until 1877 that the lawmakers of Minnesota enacted legislation which showed an intelligent effort to protect its timber resources. According to this law of 1877, timber was to be sold apart from the land, and the land could not be sold until the

[1] Orfield, *Federal Land Grants*, p. 152.

334

timber on it had been estimated, appraised, and sold.[2] The law also provided that no timber could be sold anywhere except at the capitol at St. Paul, that it was to be sold at public auction after sixty days of notice in a St. Paul paper, and that it could be sold only to the highest bidder. The new law required that the amount of timber, the price of it, and the description of the land upon which it stood, as well as the log mark, be stated in the permit to cut timber, and that said permit be recorded in the office of the surveyor of logs of the district in which the timber to be sold was located. The purchaser of the timber was required to give a bond for double the estimated value of the timber, and no purchaser could claim the logs until he had paid for them in full.

Other laws were added as new problems presented themselves, but one of outstanding importance, passed in 1885, provided for a timber board whose decision was final in determining whether a certain piece of timber was to be sold. The new board was composed of three men: the auditor, who was also the land commissioner in the state, the governor, and the treasurer of the state. The signature of all three must appear on any permit for the sale of stumpage.[3]

These laws were serious and well-advised attempts to safeguard the forests. The lawmakers of Minnesota have cooperated much more sympathetically with the administrative officials of the state in handling the state's property than Congress did with the secretaries of the interior or with the land commissioners of the United States. The administrative officials themselves, however, have not always had a clear record in the management of Minnesota's lands, and they must carry the bulk of responsibility for the evils in the handling of the state's pinelands. They failed in many instances to execute what the legislature had provided.

The administrative officials responsible for the timberlands were four in number: estimator, scaler, surveyor general, and auditor or land commissioner.

The first step in preparing for the sale of timber was taken when the estimator, or appraiser, went into the deep forest to judge the timber, to study the lay of the land, to trace the logging stream, and to determine what should be the price of the timber under these conditions. The estimator's job was very important, for an incorrect estimate cheated the people he served, while an accurate estimate meant more money for schools, roads, and public buildings.

When the timber was cut, the scaler began his job of measuring the logs that were to be sold. Honesty and good judgment were as neces-

[2] *Laws of Minnesota*, 1877, chap. 56, sec. 1.

[3] *Ibid.*, 1885, chap. 269, sec. 4; the laws in regard to the timberlands of Minnesota are well explained in Orfield's *Federal Land Grants*, pp. 168–88.

sary in the scaler's work as in that of the estimator, for the scaler, too, could either serve his state honestly or cheat it badly.

The surveyor general supervised the work of the estimator and the scaler. It was also his responsibility to see that the cutting was done according to specifications and that the permit stated properly the amount of timber, the description of the land, the price at which it should be sold, and the log mark. It was his job to assemble all the facts and to judge their accuracy before they were presented to the head of the administrative group. At the very top stood the auditor, who also held the position of land commissioner in the state. Upon him and his staff rested the final responsibility. It was the business of this executive to ferret out anything wrong.

The philosophy that prevailed in the nation during the great expansion of the second half of the nineteenth century also prevailed in Minnesota — laissez-faire, rugged individualism, and the legend of inexhaustibility. Wrongdoers were occasionally corrected when the law was broken, but not until 1893 did the state legislature begin to probe with vigor into the activities of the administrative officials responsible for the pinelands. On March 1, 1893, on the motion of Robert C. Dunn of Mille Lacs County, a resolution was adopted in the Minnesota house of representatives asking for the appointment of a committee to investigate the sale of pine timber on a certain school section in that county. The minority report of this committee suggested that the legislature should probe more deeply into the management of the state's estate. Dunn, who came from the pineland area, made the motion that the house pass a "concurrent resolution" giving the governor authority to carry on a full investigation into these matters. The senate was agreeable to this resolution and out of it grew the Pine Land Investigating Committee.[4] The committee, consisting of men from both the house and the senate, was to "inquire into any and all the frauds that had been committed" on the public lands belonging to Minnesota's government in the past or the present.

The chairman of the committee was Ignatius Donnelly, a vigorous exponent of the cause of the people. C. F. Staples served as secretary. Other members active in the investigation were J. F. Jacobson, S. W. Leavitt, M. J. McGrath, and A. G. Eaton. The committee found that the laws had functioned inadequately because certain administrators had failed to observe them.[5]

We have seen that the law called for the sale of stumpage, based on the work of estimators employed by the state, at public auction to the

---

[4] Folwell, *History of Minnesota*, vol. iii, pp. 206–7.
[5] *Report of the Pine Land Investigating Committee to the Governor of Minnesota* (St. Paul, 1895), pp. 4–8.

highest bidder at the state capitol with announcement in a daily paper of St. Paul at least sixty days before the sale. This law, the committee found, had been almost totally ignored by some of the state officials. The information in regard to stumpage that was to be sold should have passed up from estimator to scaler to surveyor general to auditor. But the committee found that information was often gained by the officers from those who wished to buy the land; not only did the buyer state the type of timber on the land sold but he stated its value as well. Often the estimator had not been on the land at all but accepted the buyer's word as to what was there. The information was often not made public, as the law required, since it was given by the buyer when he came to make his purchase. The state had sold many tracts based on estimates of this kind.

Another evil persistent in the selling of state stumpage was that a man purchased stumpage, gave bond, let it lie, and then bought it a second time at a lower price. The auditor did not check to see if the land had been sold before.[6] Often the committee found on a permit for the sale of stumpage the signature of only the auditor and not, as required by the law of 1885, the signature of the governor and treasurer. Indeed, from March 7, 1885, to January 1, 1891, the governor's name was not attached to a single approval—he had not been consulted. Since this was contrary to the law, it is safe to say that not one legal stumpage sale took place during those years.[7] Bonds were not paid and permits expired, but the auditor did not bestir himself.

The committee found men in the employ of the state who were totally ignorant of the science of judging timber—an estimator, for example, who reported 9,000,000 feet where actually there were 22,000,000 feet; a scaler who measured 357,000 feet where later 7,000,000 feet were found to be cut; another estimator who reported a section as having 1,225,000 feet which was found by the Pine Land Committee to have a stand of over 6,000,000 feet.[8] These are but a few of the many discrepancies found; the committee said that "all the records pertaining to state lands are not even an apology for records."

It is quite evident that some of the officers in charge of the state pinelands were guilty of negligence if nothing more. Heavy blame must rest on such public servants as Adolph Bierman, who as state auditor was not performing the honest service he promised when he took his oath of office. Matthew Clark, his stumpage clerk, cannot pass uncen-

[6] *Ibid.,* p. 7. Matthew Clark, stumpage clerk in the auditor's office, testified before the committee.
[7] *Ibid.,* pp. 20–24; 62 Minnesota Reports, p. 99; *Mississippi Valley Lumberman,* vol. xxviii, Jan. 29, 1897, p. 8.
[8] *Report of the Pine Land Investigating Committee,* p. 57.

sored, for he was well aware of the dishonesty which prevailed and quite willingly shared in it. Surveyors general, scalers, and estimators in many instances lined their pockets at state expense.

Equally guilty were the lumber companies who sought to appropriate holdings of the state by means contrary to the laws. The state found itself engaged in litigation with a considerable number of these, as is shown in the biennial report of the attorney general in 1894. Some of the cases were settled out of court but often there were tedious, long-drawn-out trials.[9] It is not fair to assume that all lumbermen were involved in litigations over state timber. Some firms engaged in sawing and logging were never in a controversy and their names never occur in any litigation.

The report of the Pine Land Investigating Committee resulted in the enactment by the state legislature of additional laws in regard to state-owned properties. The first such legislation, appearing in 1895, reflected the findings of the committee in its effort to provide a check on estimators and scalers. The estimator was now required to enter his report in his own handwriting in a record kept in the office of the land commissioner in St. Paul, the report to include his hours of work, information in regard to the timber, the land on which it stood, and any streams which might be used for logging. He was also required to give oath that his report was correct. No estimator could be employed by the state who had had less than five years' experience; a heavy bond was required and fine or imprisonment was the penalty for any offense connected with his work. No scaler employed by the state could be paid from any source except the state. The law also provided that no timber could be sold unless a quorum of the board, including the governor, were present.[10]

The report of the Pine Land Investigating Committee might lead one to think that Minnesota had garnered nothing from its properties. There were serious losses, but it is probable that Minnesota realized a greater profit from her resources than did the neighboring states of Iowa and Wisconsin.[11] Governor Ramsey in his first message had pointed to the mistakes of these older states and advised his people to profit from them and show concern for Minnesota's resources.[12]

The first income from the sale of stumpage was recorded in the auditor's office in 1864 as $1101. The amount of stumpage sold increased steadily, and in 1884 the auditor's office recorded sales of $104,729 for the year. The demand, of course, increased with every year, and at the end of

[9] Ibid., p. 78; 99 Minnesota Reports, p. 158; 62 Minnesota Reports, p. 99; 102 Minnesota Reports, p. 470; 26 Minnesota Reports, p. 238.
[10] Laws of Minnesota, 1895, chap. 163, secs. 11–18.
[11] Orfield, op. cit., p. 153.
[12] "Annual Message of Governor Ramsey," Minnesota Executive Documents, 1860, pp. 22–23.

twenty more years, in 1904, the income from stumpage for the year was $638,414. Over a period of forty-two years, from 1864 to 1906, the state's income from stumpage was $5,119,787.[13]

In 1898 the state received the highest price up to that time for its stumpage, averaging $2.86 per thousand feet; in 1900 the average price was $5.17. While in the period from 1880 to 1889 stumpage sold for an average of $1.95 per thousand feet, in the period from 1900 to 1909 the price averaged $7.19 per thousand feet.[14] The increase in price, of course, resulted from the approaching scarcity of pine, the market of the time, and the expansion of the lumber industry. In a stumpage auction held at the state capitol in the fall of 1902 prices ranged from $5.00 to $10.60 per thousand feet. But prices varied according to location and amount. Stumpage in the Duluth district brought the highest price in this sale.[15] Small tracts of 100,000 feet or less, located in places where it was difficult to operate, sold for prices as low as $1.50 per thousand feet. These became the property of small jobbers, for a logging firm operating on a big scale could hardly afford to move equipment into a place yielding such a small amount.[16]

In 1903 the state auditor sold more than 97,000,000 feet of state timber in one sale, the largest amount ever sold at the capitol at one time. More than a hundred lumbermen were in St. Paul for the occasion. One Peter Grant of Chisholm bought 3,300,000 feet, paying $11.35 a thousand; while E. C. Millet of Cass Lake bought almost 5,000,000 feet at $9.50 per thousand. Pine was growing more scarce and bidding was sharp.[17] In 1909 State Auditor S. G. Iverson announced a stumpage sale at the capitol of 70,000,000 feet, more than half of which lay in St. Louis County. A Duluth newspaper announcing the sale stated that bidding promised to be spirited at this sale.[18]

Both old and new laws were enforced in a way never known before in Minnesota's history as a result of the work of the Pine Land Investigating Committee. Trespassing, an evil prevalent in Minnesota's pinelands since territorial days, was checked with a new vigor that brought considerable income to the state. The state had had laws concerning trespass for a long time, but financially it had realized very little from them until 1895.

Special laws on trespassing dated back to territorial days.[19] In 1858 the first state legislature adopted the territorial trespass law with some new

[13] G. O. Brohough, "The Policy of the State Regarding Timber Lands" in *Papers and Proceedings of the Second Annual Meeting of the Minnesota Academy of Social Sciences,* Northfield, Minn., 1909, pp. 173–74, 176.

[14] U.S. Bureau of Corporations, *The Lumber Industry* (1913), pt. 1, p. 200.

[15] *Little Falls Daily Transcript,* Nov. 13, 1902.

[16] *Ibid.,* Dec. 23, 1902.

[17] *Ibid.,* Oct. 23, 1903.

[18] *Duluth Weekly Herald,* Sept. 22, 1909, p. 10.

[19] *Collated Statutes of Minnesota,* 1853, chap. 8, sec. 1.

additions.[20] This trespass law was soon found inadequate, and in 1862 the legislature added to it by requiring a treble damage plus fine and imprisonment for willful trespass; if the trespass was accidental, only single damage should be asked. According to this law the county attorney was to report such cases to the land commissioner.[21] But the law continued to be lightly regarded, and up to 1870 only $8000 had been collected for trespass.

In 1874 a new law assigned to the surveyors general the task of watching out for trespassers, of seizing logs cut by them, and of reporting trespasses to the land commissioner.[22] It was difficult to enforce the law over so large an area in regions so widely scattered. But a more serious weakness was the fact that surveyors general were appointed by the governor but paid by lumbermen, the very interests against whom they were expected to protect the state.[23] Serving two masters was as difficult here as everywhere else, and the results were not satisfactory. The legislators continued to make more laws, and in 1885 they attempted to improve the situation by allowing the land commissioner to employ assistants in his work.[24] In the course of time county attorneys, grand juries, surveyors general, and others were instructed to report cases of trespass.[25]

Trespassers did not really begin to feel the hand of the law, however, until 1895, when trespass fines alone brought $29,663 to the state. In 1900 this amount was nearly doubled and in the ten years from 1895 through 1904 more trespass money was collected than in all the previous years of Minnesota's history.[26] As the laws were more stringently applied and as the staff safeguarding the interests of the state was enlarged, trespassing had to give way.[27]

While the state's interests were being given better protection in the sale of stumpage and from trespass, attention was also directed to the problem of conserving timber for the future. Minnesota was fortunate in having early in its history intelligent leadership in conservation. Very few persons at that time could see that the forests of the state might someday be gone if measures were not taken to preserve them, but one such person, as we have already observed, was General Christopher C. Andrews. He had seen service in the Civil War and had later been sent as minister to Sweden. It became his ambition to introduce Sweden's scientific forestry in his own home state. It was a challenging problem to try to educate the

[20] *Laws of Minnesota*, 1858, chap. 17, sec. 2.
[21] *Ibid.*, 1862, chap. 62, secs. 32–35, 37.
[22] *Ibid.*, 1874, Joint Resolution no. 32, p. 312.
[23] *Statutes of Minnesota*, 1878, chap. 32, secs. 4–6, 11.
[24] *Laws of Minnesota*, 1885, chap. 269, secs. 1–3.
[25] *Ibid.*, 1905, chap. 204, sec. 14.
[26] *Auditor's Report*, 1911–12, p. 62.
[27] *Ibid.*, 1905–6, p. 1.

people of Minnesota to conserve their forests when they did not believe there could ever be a shortage of timber. As early as 1880 Andrews urged that Minnesota establish a school of forestry.[28] It took, however, a destructive forest fire, the Hinckley fire of 1894, to bring the state to some realization of what Andrews was talking about.[29]

The extensive loss of life and property in the fire of 1894 moved the legislature in the next session to pass a bill "for the preservation of forests of this state and for the prevention and suppression of forest and prairie fires."[30] General Andrews had prepared the bill, which provided for a forest commission to execute the law. The state auditor was to serve as the forest commissioner, with a deputy to be known as the chief fire warden. The distinguished General Andrews was asked to take the position of chief fire warden; Andrews, a man big in spirit and mind, accepted the appointment with its $1200 a year salary.[31]

We cannot take time to follow, step by step, the work Andrews did. He was no ordinary fire warden whose job was only to stop fires, though he did that too in his characteristically earnest way. He was more interested, however, in other ways of preserving forests, and also in reforestation. His teachings about forestry were simple: Land unfit for agriculture should be occupied by forests, and there should be annual cuttings equal only to the annual growth.[32] He believed in state ownership of forests; to provide money for the purchase of privately held forest lands, he prepared an amendment to the state constitution for a tax levy of three tenths of a mill. The state legislature passed the bill in 1909; the public, however, still blinded by the legend of inexhaustibility, voted it down.[33] Today, in retrospect, we condemn the people of a state who refused to conserve its heritage while there was still time.

In 1908 Chisholm, a village of 3000, and its neighboring forests suffered a serious fire. Four hundred thousand acres became burnt-over land in one day, involving a loss of about $2,000,000 in standing timber.[34] Andrews again appealed to the state legislature, urging its members to try to realize the need for action in protecting the state's resources. Finally the lawmakers passed a bill giving the forest commissioner the authority to appoint a group of forest rangers to help the local wardens in case of fire.[35] The rangers proved their worth, but the members of the legislature were

[28] 46th Cong., 2d Sess. (1879–80), *Senate Misc. Docs.*, no. 91, pp. 1–22.
[29] *First Annual Report of the Chief Fire Warden of Minnesota.*
[30] *Laws of Minnesota*, 1895, p. 472. The loss reported by one lumber company alone was close to a million dollars.
[31] *Report of the Chief Fire Warden*, 1895, pp. 3–13, 55.
[32] *Ibid.*, 1897, pp. 26–28; 1898, p. 68; 1899, p. 19; 1900, p. 42; 1902, p. 36.
[33] *Report of the Forestry Commissioner of Minnesota*, 1910, p. 66.
[34] *Ibid.*, 1908, p. 20.
[35] *Ibid.*, pp. 6, 9–12, 32, 36–40; 1909, p. 35.

niggardly in supplying funds for the project and the rangers had to be dismissed in the late summer of 1910. Only a month later the Rainy River section of Minnesota around Spooner and Baudette suffered a destructive fire in which twenty-nine lives were snuffed out and the loss of timber approached a million dollars.[36] The great pine forests of Minnesota were in jeopardy and some were sacrificed because the state refused to furnish funds for twenty-six rangers. Andrews went courageously on, always hoping that someday the practice of forestry might become a reality in Minnesota. People who had no notion of the value of the forest lands and no vision such as Andrews possessed suggested that his position was "a sinecure for the brave old general." [37]

Andrews must have found satisfaction in the State Forestry Association which was formed as early as 1876 and went about its work quite unobstrusively. One fruit of its work was the establishment of a state forestry board by the legislature in 1899. Andrews, because of his position as fire warden, was a member of this board, the chief function of which was to manage lands set aside by the state or granted by the national government for forestry purposes.[38] In 1911 provision was made by the legislature for a trained state forester and for a secretary of the state forestry board. General Andrews became the new secretary, and held the position until his death in 1922.

Taxation and the danger of forest fires stood in the way of timber conservation in Minnesota. The system of taxation within the state did not encourage the practice of forest conservation.[39] Properly adjusted taxation and legislation ensuring protection against forest fires might have induced men who owned timber to cut it more deliberately.[40]

One lumber company of Minnesota paid approximately $50,000 in taxes in 1906 on their holdings in the pine area of the state, the greater portion of which was standing timber; and in 1907 that same firm paid $53,000 in taxes. No firm without adequate capital resources could afford to hold its timber under such a tax burden. Few firms could long stand a continuous outlay without income, and the result was rapid cutting of timber. As settlers moved into the pine areas of Minnesota and formed counties, all the things necessary in a new county made taxes high. Roads, schools, bridges, county buildings, and salaries for county officials called for more money. The cutover lands were given a lower assessment; therefore if

[36] *Ibid.*, 1910, p. 37.
[37] Folwell, *op. cit.*, vol. iv, p. 390; *Report of the Forestry Commissioner*, 1910, pp. 41–49.
[38] *Report of the Chief Fire Warden*, 1897, p. 77, and 1898, pp. 46–52; *Laws of Minnesota*, 1899, pp. 229–34.
[39] F. R. Fairchild, "The Taxation of Forests," *Official Report, National Lumber Manufacturers Association*, Annual Convention, Chicago, 1910–11.
[40] Compton, *Organization of the Lumber Industry*, p. 6.

taxes were too high it was best to cut the timber. Lumbermen complained of the planless settlements in the northern part of the state. They fought vigorously the establishment of such counties as Cass and Beltrami.

Lumbermen contended that they could not hold timber when taxes on their resources were twenty-five cents per thousand feet a year. This they insisted, again and again, would create in time a shortage of lumber. Twenty-five years from now, said the *Mississippi Valley Lumberman* in 1892, men will swear at the "consummate folly" of this generation. Building materials, this trade journal held, would be conserved if taxes were less.[41]

The good farm lands of Minnesota yielded crops each year that gave an annual income from which taxes could be paid. Not so with the timberland—there could be no income until the timber was cut. The question of taxes was a prime factor in the minds of men who held such lands. As early as 1876 the *Mississippi Valley Lumberman and Manufacturer* urged that pinelands be taxed differently from agricultural lands; as it was, the pine would have to be cut or else eat itself up in taxes. The journal held that the government could encourage the growth of timber by reducing taxes.[42] That same trade journal said later, "It is a matter of certainty that the present rate of taxation, more than any other cause is precipitating upon the Northwest a lumber famine." Overproduction in lumber, it claimed, was due somewhat to excessive taxes.[43]

A week later this journal appeared again with a long article on taxation in which it set forth a plan to "save the forests from destruction."[44] In 1881 the same journal said, "No man in his sober sense would think of trying to keep his pine and pay taxes on it for the next twenty years in any part of these two states," meaning Wisconsin and Minnesota.[45] Matthew G. Norton of the Laird, Norton Company of Winona stated in his book, *The Mississippi River Logging Company,* that a Maine man who had pine holdings in the Lake states area offered his property for thirty dollars an acre. The price seemed exorbitant until the taxes and the interest on the investment were figured and found to be in excess of thirty dollars an acre.[46] Interest and taxes were important factors in determining the policies of holders of timber; taxation in Minnesota has furthered destructive lumbering rather than selective logging.

When the timber had been removed, there was cutover land to reckon with. Private holders of cutover lands were quite unlikely to retain their

[41] *Mississippi Valley Lumberman,* vol. xxi, May 13, 1892, p. 2.
[42] *Mississippi Valley Lumberman and Manufacturer,* vol. i, Dec. 1, 1876, p. 4.
[43] *Ibid.,* Dec. 8, 1876, pp. 4-5.
[44] *Ibid.,* Dec. 15, 1876, p. 4.
[45] *Ibid.,* vol. v, May 6, 1881, p. 2.
[46] Norton, *Mississippi River Logging Company,* p. 94.

lands for timber-growing purposes. Timber matured slowly, and the white and red pine which had been removed could not be grown again to merchantable size in less than eighty to one hundred years — a long time to hold property that will in the meantime yield no cash. Although the assessed valuation was reduced considerably after the pine was cut, there still were taxes to be paid twice a year — and they were still high considering that there was no income. In 1927 certain cutover lands in the Cloquet area were being taxed at sixteen cents an acre, and fire protection was costing an additional eleven cents. These lands yielded no income, and the payment of twenty-seven cents an acre had to be met by funds from other sources.[47] Taxes varied, to be sure, in the different cutover counties: Itasca and St. Louis counties, having the advantage of iron ore as a resource, have levied lower taxes than the counties without iron. In 1926 Koochiching County had a tax rate of 157.31 mills, the maximum in the cutover areas.

Since taxes had to be paid for decades while the forest was being replaced and since the amount of the tax was uncertain owing to the varying methods of assessors, one cannot be surprised at the lack of enthusiasm regarding reforestation or at the existence of extensive tax delinquency.[48] The original outlay for establishing the crop on cutover lands, the cost of protection against fire and wind, and the destruction of trees by insects, together with the taxes, meant a considerable continuous outlay without income; many owners therefore could not afford to reforest without some assistance. Some of the costs could not be avoided, but taxes could have been lower. The creation of a new public domain, which has been and still is forming in Minnesota, could have been avoided to a great degree if public opinion had demanded lower taxes in the cutover areas.

Fire, the dread of every firm or individual holding timberlands, was also a factor in rapid cutting. Forest fires played a part in the history of the region from early times. In 1735 a Jesuit priest canoeing from Grand Portage to the Lake of the Woods traveled through fire and smoke; during his whole journey he had no glimpse of the sun because the smoke was so heavy. Travelers on the Mississippi have told how in the early days steamboats were lighted at night by forest fires. H. B. Ayers, in his book entitled *Timber Conditions of the Pine Region of Minnesota*, speaks of the fires the *coureurs de bois* encountered in the forests of the area that is

---

[47] Address given by H. C. Hornby at a luncheon for the Interim Committee on Reforestation at Cloquet Experimental Station, Aug. 20, 1927, p. 10. Hornby was at that time president and manager of the Cloquet Lumber Company.

[48] A discussion of the problem of taxation of Minnesota lands is found in the *Report of the Committee on Land Utilization in Minnesota* (Minneapolis, 1934), chap. x; Blakey, *Taxation in Minnesota*, chaps. v and vi, gives an excellent analysis of the tax situation.

today Minnesota. In 1889, he said, 25,000,000 board feet were destroyed by fire in township 144 north, range 39 west. In 1894, 65,000,000 board feet were destroyed in townships 148 and 149 north, range 38 west. The earliest recorded fire in Minnesota, however, occurred in 1870, when in a single fire 40,000 acres were burned, more than sixty-two sections.

Since 1870 at least four fires of outstanding magnitude have taken place in the state. The Hinckley fire of September 1, 1894, burned about 350,000 acres of good white pine. What timber could be saved had to be harvested at once and the cutting helped to flood a market that already suffered from overproduction. The fire in the Chisholm area on September 11, 1908, swept about 400,000 acres of timber and destroyed the village of Chisholm. Two years later the Baudette district, on the Canadian border, suffered a property loss of more than a million dollars through fire covering an area of 360,000 acres. Perhaps the most ghastly Minnesota fire that our generation remembers is the one that swept the Cloquet and Moose Lake area on a fall day in 1918. Then 200,000 acres gave up their pine to fire. From 1895 through 1910 Minnesota timber losses by fire were estimated at more than $4,000,000.[49]

In all these fires the timber owners suffered great losses. In only a few hours, investments of millions of dollars were destroyed. In the fire at Cloquet, lumber companies were practically ruined as the fire almost exhausted their timber holdings. Careful planning and heavy expenditures were required if the industry was to continue; it was necessary to reach out to new fields and other sources if the community was to revive. Cook and Lake counties were the regions to which the Cloquet interests turned, investing almost $3,000,000 in timber. These regions were remote, and logging railroads had to be built in order to bring the log stock to Cloquet. The building of railroads also involved capital, almost $2,000,000 having been spent up to 1927 in such construction. By that time, however, nine years after the fire, the industries at Cloquet employed 3185 people and had a payroll of $3,892,930, paying taxes in 1926 amounting to more than half a million dollars.[50]

The slashings left after logging were a factor in the fire hazard. The first legislature that met after the Chisholm fire made a law requiring that all parties cutting timber for commercial purposes must pile their

[49] *Annual Report of the Chief Fire Warden,* 1895, p. 67; 1896, p. 17; 1897, p. 5; 1898, p. 12; 1899, p. 9; 1900, p. 10; 1901, p. 8; 1902, p. 15; 1903, p. 11; 1904, p. 8. Also, *Annual Report of the Forestry Commissioner,* 1905, p. 9; 1906, p. 6; 1907, p. 9; 1908, p. 20; 1909, p. 8; 1910, p. 37. And J. A. Mitchell, *Forest Fires in Minnesota,* Lake States Forest Experiment Station, Forest Service, State of Minnesota (St. Paul, Dec. 8, 1927), p. 69. Lumbermen consider the $4,000,000 a very conservative figure.

[50] The figures used here are taken from addresses given by H. C. Hornby at a luncheon given for the Interim Committee on Reforestation at the Cloquet Experimental Station, Aug. 20, 1927, and by H. Oldenburg of the Weyerhaeuser Timber Company at the National Conference on the Utilization of Forest Products, Washington, D. C., Nov. 19, 1924.

slashings and burn them before the first of May.[51] This law, being somewhat arbitrary, could not always be obeyed to the letter and sometimes was not obeyed at all. But there were firms which made a serious attempt to wrestle with the fire problem. H. C. Hornby of Cloquet said his company spent thousands of dollars for brush-burning as their operations were in progress.

The state of Minnesota passed various laws for protection against fire. But those laws could not be enforced without adequate financial assistance, which the state did not provide, as will be shown later.

In spite of the fact that taxes and fires speeded the cutting of timber, some lumbermen realized that conservation was a necessity. A prominent lumberman of Minnesota, in addressing the Mississippi Valley Lumbermen gathered at an annual meeting, spoke of certain organizations in Minnesota which were interested in establishing forest reserves. If such legislation was forthcoming, he said, someone from the group he was addressing should work with the committee to study the proposition. He added that this seemed wise, "especially in view of the fact that many of our members have large interests in the forests of Minnesota, not simply in the commercial value of the pine trees, but in a larger and more comprehensive way, and should be represented in the deliberation of the committee having in charge the drafting of any law presented to the legislature, or in the consideration on and adoption of any policy with reference to forest reserves or state parks." The association was responsive and the president was instructed to make such an appointment. B. F. Nelson of Minneapolis was selected to represent the lumbermen of Minnesota in this project.[52]

The Weyerhaeusers were strong advocates of conservation and reforestation. In 1906 Frederick Weyerhaeuser was a member of the state forestry board which recommended to the legislature that an annual appropriation of $25,000 for reforesting state cutover lands be made.[53] R. L. McCormick of Hayward, Wisconsin, then secretary of the Weyerhaeuser Company of St. Paul, said in 1903 that in another decade there would be no white pine available unless steps were taken to conserve it. McCormick favored a practical system of forestry, such as that set forth in the Morris Bill which concerned the timber on the Red Lake Reservation.[54]

In 1903 the Weyerhaeuser interest at Cloquet appealed to Gifford

[51] *Laws of Minnesota,* 1909, chap. 182, sec. 1.

[52] Address given by W. H. Laird before the Mississippi Valley Lumbermen's Association, Mar. 1897, Private Letter Books of W. H. Laird, Oct. 10, 1895, to Apr. 29, 1898.

[53] *Little Falls Daily Transcript,* Dec. 14, 1906, p. 3.

[54] *Ibid.,* May 22, 1903, p. 3. The Morris Bill is discussed in Chapter XVI. R. L. McCormick became secretary of the Weyerhaeuser Timber Company at Tacoma, Washington, in 1906.

Pinchot of the Forestry Bureau of the Department of Agriculture in Washington to advise them in the matter of forestry, and Pinchot sent a crew of men under C. S. Chapman into the Cloquet area to make a survey of the situation. Chapman's report stated that in the conditions under which the Weyerhaeuser interests were operating at Cloquet, with taxes as they were and with the existing hazards from fire, the situation was handled as well as it could be.[55] H. C. Hornby of the Cloquet Weyerhaeuser firm was convinced that with a practicable forestry plan in operation, Cloquet could indefinitely produce from 110 to 125 million feet of lumber a year.[56] The interests at Cloquet particularly appreciated the inspiring and helpful work of the federal and state departments of agriculture and forestry, said H. Oldenburg of the Weyerhaeuser Timber Company.[57] The Weyerhaeuser group was one of the largest timber-holding companies in Minnesota, and their favorable attitude toward conservation is significant. They were lumbermen with a long-range view.

Minnesota was slow to inaugurate any method for improving the forestry situation for the individual owner. Not until 1926 did the state finally begin action by adopting a constitutional amendment which provided that forest property might be classified differently for taxation than agricultural lands. The next year the legislature passed the Minnesota Auxiliary Forest Tax Law.[58] This law provided that owners of cutover lands who wished to give their lands over to forest growth might appeal to the board of county commissioners. If this board approved the application, the state department of conservation would supervise the arrangement. The law also provided for a definite annual tax not to exceed 8 per cent on the assessed value, and for a yield tax of 10 per cent whenever any cutting was done. It also provided for a tax of three cents per acre for fire protection.[59]

The law was not considered satisfactory, and it met with no response whatever, possibly because the tax reduction was not sufficient. In 1929 it was amended to establish the tax at five cents an acre, with an additional three cents an acre for fire protection, but with no particular changes in the yield tax.[60] In the whole state only one application resulted: A firm located at Cloquet asked for the establishment of an auxiliary forest of 172,000 acres in that county. The application was made to the board of

[55] Address by H. C. Hornby, Aug. 20, 1927, p. 5.
[56] Ibid., p. 4.
[57] In an address delivered at the National Conference on Utilization of Forest Products, Nov. 19, 1934, p. 9.
[58] Laws of Minnesota, 1927, chap. 247.
[59] Report of the Committee on Land Utilization in Minnesota, pp. 177–82; Blakey, op. cit., pp. 164–69.
[60] Laws of Minnesota, 1929, chap. 245.

county commissioners of St. Louis County. It received wide publicity and many public hearings were held. But the request was never granted, owing largely to the opposition of settlers, who may have been influenced by others.[61]

Owners of cutover lands seem generally not to have been responsive to the Auxiliary Forest Tax Law, and the hope of private reforestation in Minnesota seems not to have been realized at all. Cutover land has quickly become tax delinquent and has eventually become state property, which presents an altogether different problem for the state. If a state commission or a state officer, rather than assessors and county commissioners, had been charged with carrying out the forestry law, it might have operated in a more satisfactory way.

Minnesota's problems in the supervision of its forests were the same as those of the federal government; they differed only in scale. The government of the state was not experienced in the matter of regulating forest areas. It learned sadly by a trial and error method. The people of the state did not listen attentively to those who sought to guide them toward conservation. We, the citizens who see this process of lawmaking in retrospect, must take heed that we guard more carefully the wealth which our state still holds and that we conserve for those who come after us.

[61] Blakey, *op. cit.*, p. 166; *Report of the Committee on Land Utilization in Minnesota*, p. 179.

CHAPTER XVIII

The New Age in Logging and Sawing

THERE were many striking new developments in the techniques of lumber production in the 1890s and the early years of the new century; this was true in both logging and sawing. The mills in Minneapolis, which in 1899 made their greatest cut when their saws produced 594,373,000 feet of lumber, represented the best in equipment at that time. And the newest equipment was quite different from that of a half century earlier when, it has been said, the sawyer could take a nap while the saw "traversed the cut" — when the noise stopped, the sawyer woke up![1]

The lumberman driving toward profits had to have the latest and best machinery in order to reduce his labor costs and increase his cut so as to hold his own in a highly competitive market.[2] Michigan men and downriver men were quick to grasp this situation; Minneapolis men were slower in effecting change.[3] But, when Michigan and downriver men began operating the most modern mills in Minneapolis in 1890, the old-timers of Minneapolis quickly installed new machinery, and shortly their mills were keeping pace with the others in production. It was because of this latest equipment that three of the four largest mills in the United States, each producing more than a hundred million feet a year, were found in Minnesota in 1900.[4]

What, then, was the equipment of an up-to-date mill in the period in which Minnesota made her record cut? What were the new improvements that speeded production?

One important innovation, which came into existence about 1890, was the hot pond. This was an enclosed water area without current into which hot water or exhaust steam was discharged.[5] The hot pond made winter sawing of lumber possible; it was no longer necessary for logs to lie frozen fast from the first fall freeze to the spring thaw.[6] Winter sawing became

---

[1] Hotchkiss, *History of Lumber and Forest Industry of Northwest*, p. 650.
[2] *Mississippi Valley Lumberman*, vol. xvii, Mar. 21, 1890, p. 2.
[3] *Ibid.*, vol. xi, June 3, 1887, p. 4, and vol. xiii, May 18, 1888, p. 5; *Minneapolis Tribune*, Aug. 1, 1887, p. 5.
[4] *U.S. Census, 1900*, vol. ix: *Manufactures*, pt. 3, p. 826.
[5] Bryant, *Lumber, Its Manufacture and Distribution*, p. 18.
[6] *Mississippi Valley Lumberman*, vol. xxi, Feb. 26, 1892, p. 1.

a prominent feature in Minnesota mills and made possible a much greater production.[7]

In the ponds logs were made ready for sawing — a pond crew sorted them, cleaned them, and processed them to prevent deterioration. The size of the crew was determined by the number of logs in the pond. If 100,000 to 150,000 feet of logs were handled, eight men were needed. There was a foreman whose word was law. If the logs were delivered by railroad, as they were more and more in the nineties, two car unloaders shifted them to the pond. Two sinker raisers resurrected logs that had gone to the bottom of the pond, while two others brought the log to the ladder, where the jacker feeder prodded the log's nose into the jacker or haul-up, a log slide where a chain caught the log and pulled it onto the second floor of the mill proper.

As the log entered the mill, the scaler was on the job to get its measure. As it traveled swiftly by, the scaler applied his measuring stick, checked the log on his sheet, and in another second was busy measuring the next log whizzing by. No idler held this job. His movements were as regular as the tick of a clock. On his sheet he tabulated the measurements of the logs in feet — 333, 210, 118, 160, 180, 140, 133, 116, 160, 100, 110, 230, 280, and 110. The logs were measured as they went in and the lumber was measured as it came out. Thus a producer knew the soundness of his log stock and the competence of his sawyers.[8] The log traveled on until the haul-up chain brought it to a device called the log-stop.

At the log-stop a mechanical arrangement loosened the log and rolled it onto an incline, where a steam nigger picked it up and placed it on two iron bunks called the carriage. The steam nigger, already known in the 1880s, became in the nineties a fixture in every first-class mill. It was a piece of machinery that turned the log at the discretion of the head sawyer and was important in that it relieved human arms of much heavy lifting.[9] As the log touched the carriage, two men, called doggers, instantly clamped two levers, called dogs, into the log and the sawing began.

The head sawyer became complete master when the log was on the carriage. From his box he gave directions, though he appeared both deaf and dumb from the moment he entered the box until he stepped out.

[7] *Duluth Weekly Herald*, Jan. 14, 1903, p. 8; *Mississippi Valley Lumberman*, vol. xxiii, Jan. 13, 1893, p. 1.

[8] In the summer of 1934 I visited the mill of the International Lumber Company at International Falls, Minnesota, which had been built by E. W. Backus of Minneapolis. I was in the mill during both the day and the night shifts and was given every opportunity to see the workings of this mill. It was the largest mill in Minnesota in 1934 and the only one of any size in the state at that time. William Skrief, the scaler on the night shift, worked from six in the evening to three o'clock in the morning with a short intermission for lunch every four hours. His work was not heavy but it did require his attention every second.

[9] *Mississippi Valley Lumberman*, vol. xxiii, July 28, 1893, p. 11.

He directed by signals; his actions were exact, his eyes were sharp, and any unusual noise told him that things were not right. The sawyer had to know at a glance how the log was to be cut to get the most lumber from it. Every log was a special problem, for it varied in size and in defect from every other log. White pine logs on the saw carriage were valuable property, and it was the function of the head sawyer to cut this material to the best advantage. A sawyer might produce from a given amount of stock a large amount of clear lumber with but few culls; he might, on the other hand, from the same stock turn out double the amount of culls with less clear stuff.[10] A good sawyer was essential to a successful business; his judgment must be as nearly infallible as possible. Mill owners anxiously sought out a skilled sawyer.[11]

It was no small compliment to M. Finnegan of St. Cloud when he was selected to act as head sawyer for the E. P. Allis Company, makers of sawmill machinery, in their display at the Chicago World's Fair in 1893.[12]

The sawyer, estimating his log in an instant, signaled the depth of cut to be made; if the log was free from imperfections it was sent into that choice lot which was to be used in heavy construction. Otherwise the setter placed the saw, the sawyer grasped the levers, and the carriage shot forward, carrying the log past the swiftly revolving head saws. In the process of "breaking down" a log, the bark or exterior was removed, the steam nigger turning the log for this purpose; then the peeled "cant" was sawed into boards.

The edgerman supplemented the work of the sawyer; the board came to him to be given its first trimming. The edgerman ranked next to the head sawyers in importance. His cutting, too, could increase or decrease the value of a board. By correct cutting he could increase the feet in a board from 10 to 100 per cent. With his saws, called edgers, he eliminated wave, heart, or ring rot and similar defects. He pared out the good portions by ripping strips from the board, which as it came to him was usually twenty inches or more wide. He made it square-edged and of standard width. His skill lay not only in recognizing the spots that should be removed but also in manipulating his edgers, usually in gangs. This required skill and speed in shifting so that "sap" should not be in the board with the good lumber.[13]

Live rolls moved the lumber from the edger to the trimmer, which was

[10] *Ibid.*, vol. xxii, Sept. 9, 1892, p. 7.
[11] *Ibid.*, vol. xxiii, Apr. 7, 1893, p. 7; *American Lumberman*, Sept. 30, 1911, p. 25.
[12] *Mississippi Valley Lumberman*, vol. xxiii, Sept. 22, 1893, p. 1.
[13] *American Lumberman*, Oct. 7, 1911, p. 27. "Sap" is an abbreviation of sapwood, and a log called a "sap" was classified as inferior lumber.

usually located at the side of the building. The trimmer, sometimes called the equalizer, trimmed the ends and cut the lumber into standard lengths. The man who manipulated this saw was also called a trimmer, and it was a part of his work to remove cross-section defects. Sometimes good parts of a board were cut off in order to remove undesirable sections. The trimmer saw could be raised or lowered as necessary.

When the product of the log had passed successively the band, the edger, and the trimmer, it moved into the sorting shed, which was roofed but open on both sides. Here the graders stood at sorting tables, placing every piece in its right class as it was carried by on a live roll or a chain. Automatic loaders filled the trucks, which once were pulled by horses but in more recent years are run by gasoline engines. With the automatic truck loader, a driver does not even leave his seat in order to load.[14]

Piling the lumber was an exacting and important job. If piled incorrectly, lumber becomes crooked and warped, for green lumber yields to any shape. A lumberyard of forty acres laid off into streets, avenues, and alleys by piles of lumber twenty-five feet high, standing very straight, revealed the good methods of its owner. Every pile was numbered, and its dimensions, grade, contents, and date of piling were indicated. Usually sufficient stock was on hand to fill large orders promptly and accurately.[15]

Speed characterized these up-to-date sawmills, and speed was possible because of improved power. The Reynolds Corliss engines were popular in Minnesota mills. Such engines, of various degrees of horsepower, were found in the largest mills.[16] They were highly regarded because they used steam efficiently, and steam power was applied to every possible operation in the mill. The log was hauled into the mill by steam power; it was rolled to the carriage by steam power; it was placed upon the carriage and turned at the sawyer's order by a steam nigger; the carriage was run by a steam cylinder; logs were lifted on their way to the gang saws by a steam crane; and the sawed lumber was moved to its final place by live rolls propelled by steam. No human hand was needed at any stage to move or lift the log on its way to a finished product. Human hands only pressed levers and moved cranks. The day of heavy lifting and brute strength was past in the lumber industry.

Electricity also belonged to the newer phases of sawmill operation. As early as 1891 Mitchell and McClure of Duluth had electric lights in their sawmill; in 1892 Merrill and Ring of that same city placed electric

[14] *Mississippi Valley Lumberman*, vol. xxi, Jan. 1, 1892, p. 5, and vol. xxiii, July 21, 1893, p. 6.
[15] *Morrison County Democrat* (Little Falls), Nov. 17, 1892; *Forest Product Times* (International Falls), July 1934; *American Lumberman*, Oct. 28, 1911, p. 27.
[16] *Mississippi Valley Lumberman*, vol. xxii, Dec. 9, 1892, p. 6; vol. xxiii, Apr. 14, 1893, p. 3; vol. xxiii, Sept. 1, 1893, p. 6.

lights in their new mill.[17] In 1892 Hall and Ducey of Minneapolis began using electric arc lights in their yards and on their platforms to facilitate night piling and loading.[18] This same firm later introduced into their mill the electric stacking machine. The Pine Tree Lumber Company's mill at Little Falls, a very up-to-date mill, had its own electric power plant in 1893.[19]

The most important development in sawing was the increasing use of the band saw. Every first-class mill in Minneapolis in the nineties was equipped with a band saw, and many of them used two. In 1893 C. A. Smith and Company, one of Minneapolis' largest lumber producers, built a sawmill containing two Allis band saws.[20] That same year Bovey-De Laittre remodeled its Minneapolis mill, putting in a band saw and such other new equipment as this saw made necessary. Their complete outfit was that of a model big mill, stated a trade journal of the time.[21] Old Joel Bassett, who had come from Maine to Minneapolis in the pioneer days and had grown up with the sawmill industry, had discarded his old saws and installed two McDonough band saws in his mill.[22] The Pine Tree Lumber mill at Little Falls, in which Weyerhaeuser and the Laird, Norton Company held a large interest, had two McDonough band saws that could cut 300,000 feet in a double-shift day.[23] Merrill and Ring installed a Prescott band in their new mill at Duluth, and Duncan, Brewer and Company of that city installed in a new mill constructed in 1891 a band saw, the modern carriage, a dry kiln, and all the fixtures of modern sawing.[24]

Hubbard and Vincent, a Duluth firm putting in a band mill in 1891, announced that they had a choice lot of lumber and did "not want it murdered by a circular." [25] As this implies, the band saw was known for its niceness of manufacture as well as for its economy. It was not greatly superior to the circular in speed, but it was thrifty in cutting kerf and that was important in a day when white pine was growing scarcer and more expensive. Minneapolis, on the way to becoming the greatest lumber-producing city in the world, had in 1893 more band saws than circulars.[26]

The band saw, replacing the circular as the head saw, the first to attack the logs, set the pace for the mill. A band head saw could cut about 50,000

[17] *Mississippi Valley Lumberman*, vol. xxi, Jan. 1, 1892, p. 5.
[18] *Ibid.*, vol. xxii, July 8, 1892, p. 6.
[19] *Ibid.*, vol. xxiii, July 21, 1893, p. 6.
[20] *Ibid.*, Sept. 1, 1893, p. 6.
[21] *Ibid.*, Apr. 14, 1893, p. 3.
[22] *Ibid.*, vol. xviii, Dec. 26, 1890, p. 6.
[23] *Ibid.*, vol. xxiii, July 21, 1893, p. 6.
[24] *Ibid.*, vol. xxi, Jan. 1, 1892, p. 5; *Duluth Weekly Herald*, Feb. 5, 1891.
[25] *Ibid.*, Dec. 16, 1891.
[26] *Mississippi Valley Lumberman*, vol. xxiii, Jan. 13, 1893, p. 1.

feet in ten hours.[27] The Northwestern Lumber Company at Eau Claire, Wisconsin, of which Samuel T. McKnight of Minneapolis was secretary and treasurer, cut 110,000,000 feet a year with one Allis band and one McDonough band.[28] And the Pine Tree Lumber mill at Little Falls made quite a record with two McDonough bands in 1893, producing 150,000 feet in a ten-hour day.[29]

In one phase of the industry, however, invention had been slow. That was in finding some way to decrease the time required for seasoning. Kiln-dried lumber was known as early as 1867, but it was not until at least a quarter of a century later that a workable kiln was found. Dry lumber was necessary, for weight was an important matter in transportation; the moisture in green lumber made shipping charges high. High shipping charges both reduced profits for the producer and increased costs to the consumer. But the outstanding advantage of the kiln was the saving of time in drying. Seasoning was necessary also if lumber was to hold its shape, and seasoned lumber would not be attacked by wood rot or fungus. Seasoning also increased the strength, the hardness, and the stiffness of lumber. It was a necessary factor in the making of lumber.

The old method of air-drying in the lumberyard had its advantage, to be sure. It was cheap, for little capital was tied up in equipment; the outdoor air was free, and common labor could be used. But the disadvantages outweighed these advantages. Under the air-drying system capital was tied up in lumber stocks over a long period of time, for the lumber dried slowly, especially in periods of much rain and little sun. Operators could not readily take advantage of market conditions since stocks could not be dried in short order. Much space was needed for this method of seasoning, and in cities like Minneapolis space meant money. Then, too, the large stocks that had to be kept in the process of drying might be greatly jeopardized by fire.

The dry kiln generally adopted in Minnesota was known as the Sturtevant kiln. In this kiln heated air was blown from a steel case containing hot pipes into the chambers where the lumber was placed. The kiln consisted of a number of chambers, each of which could house about 40,000 feet of lumber. W. J. Young and Company of Clinton, Iowa, leaders in adopting new methods, dried 123,000 feet a day in their Sturtevant kiln.[30] Minneapolis mills changed to the kiln method rapidly in the 1890s. The larger lumber producers, such as Hall and Shevlin, Akeley, and C. A. Smith, were among those who adopted kilns, each adding two kilns. In

[27] Bryant, *Lumber, Its Manufacture and Distribution*, p. 77.
[28] *Mississippi Valley Lumberman*, vol. xxiii, Aug. 25, 1893, p. 5.
[29] *Little Falls Daily Transcript*, Apr. 9, 1904; *Mississippi Valley Lumberman*, vol. xxiii, July 21, 1893, p. 6.
[30] *Ibid.*, vol. xvi, Aug. 16, 1889, p. 14.

Duluth Mitchell and McClure and Scott and Holston were prominent lumber makers who had two kilns each.[31]

Kiln-drying shortened the time between manufacture and marketing; capital was tied up for a shorter time and orders could be filled on shorter notice. This method of drying killed insects and prevented the evil of bluing; it also reduced yarding and handling charges. Drying in the kiln could go on in rain or in shine, and the lumber was dried more uniformly than by the old methods. It was also dried more thoroughly — a matter of importance in the reduction of weight for shipping.[32]

A modern sawmill plant in Minnesota in the nineties was built on deeply driven piles. It was built of lumber painted the regulation red, a dark red. Usually the mill was a double-decker with the complex machinery placed on the second floor. In the big mills a Reynolds Corliss engine supplied power to two band saws (usually of the Allis make), a gang saw, two edgers, two trimmers, two shingle machines, and one lath machine. The steam nigger, the carriage, the live rolls, the hydraulic lift, the automatic sorting system, the automatic loaders, the automatic pilers, and finally the hot pond, holding 5,000,000 feet of logs, were all part of a first-class mill in Minnesota when that state reached its high point in lumber production.[33]

A refuse burner was necessary equipment at one time, and the size of a mill's refuse burner was an index of its output.[34] Some Minneapolis mills never used such a burner, because all their sawdust and other waste were dumped onto the marshy bank of the Mississippi River. The refuse burner "is now practically idle," for the sawdust and scrap lumber that once traveled into its "flaming maw" are now turned into manufactured goods of increasing importance.[35]

Despite the mechanization of the mills, they continued to employ large numbers of men. In 1890 there were 3894 men working in the sawmills and the door, lath, and shingle industries in Minneapolis. The value of the product made by these men was $9,626,975, out of which $1,800,000 was paid in wages.[36] In 1890 the Akeley Lumber Company, one of the largest in the Northwest, employed 149 men in its sawmill, 34 men in its lath factory, and 67 men in the making of shingles. Added to the number

[31] J. H. Wolsey to the Sturtevant Company, June 15, 1892, Houlton Papers, Minn. Hist. Soc.
[32] *Mississippi Valley Lumberman*, vol. xix, May 15, 1891, p. 5; Royal S. Kellogg, *Lumber and Its Uses* (New York, 1919), pp. 87–91; Bryant, *Lumber, Its Manufacture and Distribution*, p. 204; Brown, *American Lumber Industry*, p. 58. Bluing is the result of fungus which turns the sapwood of certain trees blue.
[33] *Mississippi Valley Lumberman*, vol. xxiii, July 21, 1893, p. 6, and Sept. 1, 1893, pp. 6–7.
[34] *Ibid.*
[35] C. L. Hamilton, "All but the Whispers of the Pines," *American Forests*, vol. xxxiv (Dec. 1928), p. 748.
[36] Stanchfield, "History of Pioneer Lumbering on the Upper Mississippi," *Minn. Hist. Soc. Coll.*, vol. ix, p. 362.

employed in its delivery service, this made a total on the company's payroll of 455 men, who together were paid $1000 each day.[37] In 1894 Mitchell and McClure of Duluth employed 200 men in their sawmill, which produced 250,000 feet in ten hours. Another Duluth mill, that of Merrill and Ring, employed 250 men.[38]

The employment figures for the whole state reveal important changes. In 1890 Minnesota had 16,170 wage earners in the lumber and timber industry, working in 392 establishments making a product valued at $25,075,132.[39] This was a pronounced increase over the 2854 men in 234 establishments in Minnesota in 1880.[40] In 1900 there were 15,140 wage earners in 438 establishments making a product valued at $43,585,161. In other words, from 1890 to 1900 the product of the mills had increased 73.8 per cent and the number of establishments had risen 11.2 per cent, but the number of wage earners had fallen 6.4 per cent. This contrast was one result of the many improvements in machinery and was one of the goals at which big business was aiming. It is evident that sawmill men were concentrating on bigger and better-equipped mills.[41]

In 1905 there were 10,248 wage earners in the sawmills — a noticeable falling off after 1900. The allied trades of the lumber industry, however, were increasing in number, and in 1906 the planing mills and sash, door, and blind factories employed 10.5 per cent more wage earners than in 1905.[42] In 1905 the sawmill industry in Minnesota had reached its high point, and from then on there was a gradual decrease in the number of its employees.

Slight glimpses into labor conditions in sawmills are afforded by the payrolls of lumber firms. On the payrolls were listed band sawyers, circular sawyers, cant setters, gang sawyers, carriage riders, gang helpers, edgers, trimmer tailers, graders, slab men, millwrights, trucksters (called buggy loaders), and much unskilled labor.[43] Sawyers were generally the best paid men in the mill. In the period between 1890 and 1907 band sawyers in the North Central states, including Minnesota, had a working week ranging from 60 to 62.3 hours. The highest wage they received during that time was 56 cents an hour in 1903. In 1894 they received the lowest pay of that period, 41 cents.[44] Circular sawyers in the same states

---

[37] *Minneapolis Tribune,* Jan. 1, 1891, p. 5.

[38] W. F. Leggett and F. C. Chipman, *Duluth and Environs* (Duluth, 1895), p. 91.

[39] *Report of the Minnesota Bureau of Labor,* 1901–2, p. 615.

[40] *U.S. Census, 1890: Manufacturing Industries,* pt. 3, p. 610.

[41] *Report of the Minnesota Bureau of Labor,* 1901–2, p. 615.

[42] *Ibid.,* 1905–6, p. 21.

[43] U.S. Bureau of Labor Statistics, Bulletin No. 560, *Wages and Hours of Labor in the Lumber Industry in the United States* (1930), pp. 25, 27.

[44] *Ibid.,* Bulletin No. 604, *Wages in the United States from Colonial Times to 1928,* p. 466.

were receiving 60 cents an hour for a 60-hour working week in 1890–93. Band sawyers surpassed them in wages as the years went on, and in 1907 the circular sawyer was receiving only 34.1 cents an hour for a 60-hour working week.[45] Gang sawyers were then the lowest paid of all the sawyers. Their working week was about 60 hours and their highest wage was 31.9 cents an hour paid them in 1903; in 1894–96 they had the low wage of 26.3 cents — a reflection, no doubt, of the depression.[46]

No other lumber section was paying its sawyers better wages during that period of 1890–1907 than the Lake states. A good band sawyer in Minnesota was receiving $2200 a year in 1903. This was the wage of C. H. Rogers, who in that year took a position as band sawyer in the sawmill at Scanlon, having been for eleven years the "experienced and proficient band sawyer" in the Pine Tree Lumber Company's sawmill at Little Falls, a Weyerhaeuser mill. A newspaper at Little Falls spoke of his new wage as a reward for "faithful performance of his duties." [47] In 1893 Minneapolis mills were paying the band sawyers $5.90 a day; gang sawyers were paid $3.85.[48]

TABLE 25. DAILY WAGES PAID BY MINNEAPOLIS AND DOWNRIVER MILLS, 1893

Types of Labor	Minneapolis Mills	Downriver Mills
Band sawyer	$5.90	$4.00
Setter	3.05	2.25
Gang sawyer	3.85	2.25
Carriage rider	2.15	1.75
Gang helper	2.00	1.65
Edger	2.50 to 4.00	2.25 to 2.75
Trimmer	2.25 to 3.00	1.85
Log deck man	2.00	2.00

SOURCE: *Mississippi Valley Lumberman*, vol. xxiii, July 14, 1893, p. 3.

Minneapolis mills had a reputation for paying their labor better than did the mills below on the Mississippi. Table 25 gives the daily wages paid in 1893 by Minneapolis and downriver mills. The differences in the wages of the two groups may be explained in several ways. In the first place, Minneapolis at this time was nearer the log stock, and its production cost was therefore lower. So it could afford to pay better wages. Also, Minneapolis just before the panic was enjoying a boomtime in flour as well as in lumber, and the double demand for labor created a scarcity, which always makes for higher wages.

Especially noticeable is the fact that a band sawyer was paid almost

[45] *Ibid.*, p. 467.
[46] *Ibid.*, p. 468.
[47] *Little Falls Daily Transcript*, Apr. 16, 1903.
[48] *Mississippi Valley Lumberman*, vol. xxiii, July 14, 1893, p. 3.

two dollars a day more in Minneapolis than in the mills below. In Minneapolis, where band saws had so recently been installed, few good band sawyers had developed yet; scarcity again demanded its price.

Sawmill labor in Minnesota was slow to seek protection in unions. Though Duluth had a Lumber Pilers Union of 171 members organized in 1901, there is no evidence of other unions in this industry in Duluth. In Minneapolis there was no evidence of unions as late as 1902.[49] In a strike in 1890 in Cloquet 800 men demanded a ten-hour day with the eleven-hour pay.[50] In 1901 lumber loaders in one Minnesota mill demanded a wage of 60 cents per hour, but went back to work for 52.5 cents.[51] In a period of twenty years, from 1881 to 1900, there were 23 strikes in the lumber industry in Minnesota, involving a loss to employers of $91,950.[52] This does not seem startling in a big industry at a time when strikes were very common in some industries. This situation may have been due to the fact that Minnesota sawmills employed large numbers of Scandinavians, generally peaceful and law-abiding citizens.

Sawmill men showed an increasing interest in cooperating with the state labor commission for the protection of employees against accidents. Mill owners realized that accidents disturbed the morale of their workers and that installing guards to protect the men from dangerous machinery would cost less than the losses resulting from injuries.[53] Mills prided themselves on no-accident records; when in 1903 a man was killed in the planing mill at Little Falls, it was widely reported that this was the first fatal accident in that mill for eleven years.[54] Nevertheless, in 1901 fatalities were more numerous in the sawmill and logging industry than in any other industry in the state: 12 men were killed, 35 severely injured, and 78 injured slightly.[55]

It is interesting to observe that some lumber companies in Minnesota as early as 1890 carried compensation for their employees in case of injury or death. Compulsory workmen's compensation in the country as a whole was at that time very much in its infancy. It was in 1891 that the commissioner of the Department of Labor ordered a study to be made of the German system of labor compensation in case of injury or death.[56] The findings of this investigation were published in 1893. The national government, however, took its time in putting such findings into action, for not until 1908 was national legislation passed providing for work-

[49] *Report of the Minnesota Bureau of Labor,* 1901–2, p. 458.
[50] *Mississippi Valley Lumberman,* vol. xviii, Aug. 8, 1890, p. 9.
[51] *Report of the Minnesota Bureau of Labor,* 1901–2, p. 557.
[52] *Ibid.,* p. 583.
[53] *Mississippi Valley Lumberman,* vol. xxviii, Mar. 26, 1897, p. 10.
[54] *Little Falls Daily Transcript,* Aug. 6, 1903.
[55] *Report of the Minnesota Bureau of Labor,* 1901–2, p. 783.
[56] J. E. Rhodes, *Workmen's Compensation* (New York, 1917), p. 88.

men's compensation.[57] This, however, applied only to federal matters and not to the states. New York was the first state to establish laws providing for such compensation; other states followed shortly.[58] But Minnesota was slow in enacting such laws and made no attempt to study the situation until 1909, when it arranged for a commission of inquiry. Finally in 1913 Minnesota passed a workmen's compensation law.[59]

Almost a quarter of a century before the state had such a law, certain lumber companies were paying compensation in case of injury or death. In 1890 the Laird, Norton Company of Winona carried insurance with the Fidelity and Casualty Company of New York City for all men employed on their premises in Winona. Their records show that in 1890 such protection extended to teamsters, lumberyard hands, raft-boat hands, and office workers, as well as to those who worked in their mills. According to an insurance policy for 1897 the highest payment that was to be made to a Laird, Norton employee for an accident resulting in injury or death was $5000.

The Laird, Norton Company carried the same liability policy for all employees working where saws were operating, such as in the planing mills, sash, door, and blind shops, and shingle and lath mills. Men working with the saws were given the highest protection. People employed in the yards of the company were protected only to an upper limit of $1500, according to the policy of 1897 — this covered foremen, teamsters, blacksmiths, and others working in the yard.[60] Through such policies there was security for both employer and employee, and they were an indication of good management.

It took much capital to establish and operate a large sawmill. Depreciation became a serious matter. Many mills sawed both night and day in a two-shift arrangement. In Duluth in 1903 five sawmills ran double shifts, and a number of their mills sawed summer and winter.[61] With such continuous hard wear the machinery had a life of only fifteen to twenty-five years.[62] The *Mississippi Valley Lumberman* estimated that the operating expenses involved in handling 100,000,000 feet of lumber were from a half to three fourths of a million dollars.[63]

With such overhead and operating costs, milling firms had to have a large capital. Bovey-De Laittre of Minneapolis, which, as we have seen,

[57] *Ibid.*, p. 97.
[58] *Ibid.*, p. 89.
[59] D. H. Van Doren, *Workmen's Compensation and Insurance* (New York, 1918), pp. 53–54.
[60] Casualty Insurance, Policies and Claims, Laird, Norton Papers, Laird, Norton Company, Winona, Minn.
[61] *Duluth Weekly Herald*, Mar. 19, 1902, and Jan. 14, 1903.
[62] Brown, *op. cit.*, pp. 47–51.
[63] *Mississippi Valley Lumberman*, vol. xix, June 12, 1891, p. 1; vol. xxi, May 27, 1892, p. 2.

refitted its mill with modern equipment in this period, found it necessary to increase their capital from $320,000 to $500,000.[64] The C. A. Smith
Lumber Company, whose vice-president was John S. Pillsbury, was
capitalized at $750,000 when its mill was rebuilt in the 1890s.[65] Merrill
and Ring of Duluth, with an output in 1895 of 50,000,000 feet, were backed
by a capital of $500,000. The Knox Lumber Company of that same city,
a small firm cutting annually about 12,000,000 feet, had a capital of
$80,000.[66] Altogether the capital investment in sawmills in Minnesota
in 1900 was $5,168,659. The greater portion of this, $3,179,689, was invested in machinery, tools, and implements; $1,233,685 was invested
in buildings and dry kilns; and $755,285 was invested in the land on which
the mills and yards were placed.[67]

Individual ownership or partnerships had to give way in many instances to the corporation in order to secure adequate capital. As early as
1882 the farseeing T. B. Walker, whose firm was the well-known Red
River Lumber Company, incorporated under Minnesota laws; in 1894
Merrill and Ring of Duluth and the E. W. Backus Lumber Company
of Minneapolis also incorporated. In 1899 the Empire Lumber Company of Winona, whose president was Charles Horton and one of whose
directors was Orrin H. Ingram of Eau Claire, joined the group of incorporated concerns.[68]

In 1900 Minnesota had 76 incorporated companies in its lumber and
timber industry, with 132 partnerships and 230 concerns owned by individuals; altogether there were 438 establishments, of which 404 were
sawmills and 34 were tie and timber camps. In 1909 there were 128
incorporated companies in Minnesota, and their product was valued at
$38,000,000.[69] The capital stock in Minnesota lumber corporations was
closely held. Several of Minnesota's big lumbermen, such as Shevlin,
Walker, Weyerhaeuser, Laird, and the Nortons, always remained lumbermen and confined their investments largely to the lumber field.

In 1900 Minnesota ranked third among the states in the production of
lumber, the highest place she was to reach in that field. Her mills ranked
in first place among all the mills in the United States in the average output of product in each establishment, in number of employees per establishment, in total wages paid per establishment, and in the average
product per wage earner.[70]

[64] *Ibid.*, vol. xxiii, Jan. 27, 1893, p. 14.
[65] *Ibid.*, Sept. 1, 1893, p. 6.
[66] Leggett and Chipman, *op. cit.*, p. 72.
[67] *U.S. Census, 1900*, vol. ix: *Manufactures*, pt. 3, p. 855.
[68] *American Lumberman*, May 28, 1904, p. 1; *Poor's Manual, Industrials*, 1935.
[69] *U.S. Census, 1900*, vol. ix: *Manufactures*, pt. 3, pp. 853, 855; *U.S. Census, 1910*, vol. viii:
Manufactures, p. 167.
[70] *U.S. Census, 1900*, vol. ix: *Manufactures*, pt. 3, p. 856.

The forests that supplied the logs for the hungry saws lay far to the north in Minnesota. They were forests that in part at least had hitherto been spared because they were remote from streams. Itasca County, reaching to the very nothern border of the state, was still so young that parts of it were unsurveyed in 1895. It was estimated at that time that about five billion feet of white pine stood untouched in that county.[71] St. Louis County followed Itasca with almost an equal amount of white pine. Beltrami and Lake counties had not less than one and a half billion feet of white pine. At least twelve counties in the state still had magnificent merchantable white pine as well as many other species.[72]

Into these trackless reaches of northern Minnesota the logging railroad began to burrow its way in 1890. It was the most significant factor in the evolution of the logging industry thereafter, for it opened hitherto inaccessible forests. Pinelands which, having no waterways, had been safe from devastation, lost their defenses when the logging railroad provided a way to the mills of Minneapolis or Duluth.

From Michigan came the directing hand in the building of logging railroads in Minnesota. H. C. Akeley, who had established himself in Minneapolis, built a railroad from Itasca on the Mississippi into the iron-ore country in 1890. His company, the Itasca Lumber Company, sent its logs to Minneapolis, carrying them by logging railroad to the Mississippi where they were dumped into the river to be driven down.[73] The Swan River Logging Company, a well-known Minnesota firm whose chief stockholders were Wright and Davis of Saginaw, built a logging railroad from a point near the junction of the Swan River and the Mississippi up into the region of the headwaters of the Swan River, reaching Hibbing in 1895.[74] This famous logging road eventually became the property of James J. Hill and a part of his Great Northern system.

Then Minneapolis men and others in Minnesota caught the Michigan idea. In 1892 the St. Anthony Lumber Company of Minneapolis built a logging railroad from Cross Lake to Leech Lake. Ready for action on the first day of January 1893 was another road, the so-called Brainerd and Northern Minnesota, a 64-mile logging railroad reaching from Brainerd to the west end of Leech Lake. The men who financed this road were all Minneapolis men, including such well-known lumbermen as B. F. Nelson, A. E. Horr, E. W. Backus, and E. L. Carpenter.[75] In

[71] C. C. Andrews, *Report of the Chief Fire Warden of Minnesota*, 1895, p. 122.

[72] *Ibid.*, pp. 118–19, 122.

[73] *Mississippi Valley Lumberman*, vol. xv, July 26, 1889, p. 1.

[74] *Ibid.*, vol. xix, July 3, 1891, p. 5; *Minneapolis Tribune*, Jan. 1, 1896, p. 2; *American Lumberman*, Aug. 23, 1902, pp. 1, 13.

[75] *Report of the Minnesota Railroad and Warehouse Commission*, 1895, p. 119; N. H. Winchell, *The Geographical and Natural History Survey of Minnesota*, vol. iv (1896–98), pp. 78–79.

seven months from the date of its completion this logging railroad carried 65,000,000 feet of logs to Brainerd to be dumped into the Mississippi and driven downstream to the Minneapolis mills of these men. Another road in this section financed by Minneapolis men, with a capital stock of $500,000, was the Gull Lake and Northern Logging Railroad reaching from Gull Lake to the northern boundary of the state. George A. Pillsbury was the president of this road, which was built to penetrate Pillsbury timber in the pine country.[76]

The Minnesota and International Railroad, running from Bemidji to the northern boundary of the state, penetrated dense forests in the western part of Minnesota's pinelands and came to be a very heavy log-carrying railroad.[77] The Weyerhaeuser associates built one road into the northern country that was operated by the Cross Lake Logging Company, but a far more famous road built by the Weyerhaeusers was the Duluth, Virginia and Rainy River Railroad, which became the largest logging railroad in Minnesota. It reached into the forests of the northern boundary in the region of Rainy Lake and brought to Minnesota mills logs that otherwise would have gone to Canadian mills. It eventually entered the rank of regular railroads, but its original reason for being was logs.[78]

To furnish logs for his mill at Cloquet, C. N. Nelson financed a logging railroad into the timber of the upper St. Louis River as early as 1890.[79] And Alger, Smith and Company, a Michigan firm that established itself at Duluth in the late nineties, built 152 miles of logging railroad along Lake Superior into the Knife River section of Lake County, a region then almost untouched.

Because logging railroads required capital, they were a factor in driving out the small logger and furthering the concentration of the lumber industry in fewer hands. Only lumbermen who could operate on a large scale could build such railroads and secure the access to logs they provided.[80] A logging railroad, built with a capital of $35,000 and operating at $4055 a year, could haul ten million feet of logs in a season of ninety days at about forty cents per thousand feet, or one tenth of the cost of hauling the same quantity by horse team.[81] The conveyance used was the so-called Russell logging car, an open car capable of carrying 5000 feet. The long, snaky trains bringing fifty such cars a day to their des-

[76] *Mississippi Valley Lumberman,* vol. xvi, Dec. 6, 1889, p. 7.
[77] *American Lumberman,* Sept. 17, 1904, p. 47.
[78] *Duluth Evening Herald,* Feb. 12, 1903.
[79] Garfield Blackwood, "History of Lumbering at Floodwood," an unpublished paper in the possession of the St. Louis County Historical Society at Duluth.
[80] *Duluth Weekly Herald,* Oct. 14, 1903.
[81] *Mississippi Valley Lumberman,* vol. xvi, Sept. 6, 1889, p. 12.

tination were a factor in inducing the big railroad lines to carry logs to the sawmill centers.

As the railroad made the deep forest accessible, the river gradually yielded place as a carrier of logs. River-driving had been quite in keeping with old-time methods of logging and lumbering, but as every phase of the industry speeded up, this old way of sending logs to Minneapolis became too slow and uncertain. No highly capitalized sawmill could afford to lie idle through a dry summer waiting for rain to bring supplies. Since railroads could carry their freight much faster, capital would not be tied up in logs for so long a time — and there would be no loss in logs that sank during the drive. The immediate cost of hauling by railroad no doubt was more than that of driving, but, other things considered, shipping on big railroad lines became more economical.[82]

Some sawmills made agreements with existing railroads to carry logs for them. Backus and Brooks and Scanlon and Gibson were two Minneapolis firms that arranged with the Northern Pacific to carry on to Minneapolis the logs the Brainerd and Northern brought out of the woods to Brainerd. The gauge of the logging railroads was in most instances that of the regular lines, so cars could easily be transferred. Such arrangements brought as much as three million feet in a week into Minneapolis for the concerns mentioned.[83] In 1901 it was estimated that about 100,000,000 feet of logs reached Minneapolis by way of rail.[84] Big lines connecting at Bemidji with the Minnesota and International, a logging road, carried large amounts of log stock into Minneapolis.

Duluth was favored by two railroads, the Duluth, Missabe and Northern and the Duluth and Iron Range, which bore great quantities of logs into that city.[85] These were main lines connecting with logging roads or passing through sections that were being logged. The fact that these railroads could carry logs from remote distances to Duluth helped the sawmill industry in that city to continue for a longer period than it otherwise could have survived. In the winter of 1902, 150 carloads of logs moved daily into Duluth on the Duluth and Iron Range Railroad. This road alone carried on the average 1,550,000 feet of logs into Duluth every twenty-four hours.[86] By 1903 more logs were brought into Duluth by railroads than by water.[87]

No small factor in the increase in log production was the ice road introduced to Minnesota in the 1890s by Michigan men. Previously, plenty

[82] *Little Falls Daily Transcript*, Sept. 3, 1902.
[83] *Ibid.*, June 4, 1901.
[84] *Ibid.*, Dec. 20, 1901.
[85] *Duluth Evening Herald*, Feb. 12, 1903.
[86] *Little Falls Daily Transcript*, Jan. 21, 1902.
[87] *Duluth Evening Herald*, Feb. 12, 1903.

of snow, a good road bottom, and cold weather were essentials in the business of logging, together with a ponderous ox or horse team and a good sled. As Michigan men settled in Minnesota, they brought the ice road in their assortment of new methods.

Minnesota had had ice roads before, but the new ice road was an improved one. A rut cutter, somewhat like a sled runner, made deep grooves into which the runners of the sled would fit. Then runners superheated with steam were passed over the ruts and the cold winter air changed the steam into ice. In these slippery ruts the heavy loads would slide easily. Such roads made possible bigger loads drawn by fewer horses. Sometimes huge loads of 27,160 feet or even 31,480 feet were carried on the ice road. One famous load at Hinckley contained 36,600 feet of logs; it was eighteen feet long, twenty-six feet high, and twenty-one feet wide. This was even bigger than the famous Michigan load shown at the World's Fair in 1893.[88] Loads of such size were not common but they were possible.

Newer inventions speeded the movement of logs in the woods. The steam log-hauler increased the speed; it carried immense loads.[89] Shortly came the caterpillar tractor and then the steam skidder. These innovations relegated the oxen, the horses, and that man of men, the teamster, to the past. Speed had changed the peaceful atmosphere of the old logging camp. The powerful team of oxen, their bows squeaking and chains clanking, and the "clear, profane voice of the ox teamster ringing through the forest" were gone. A donkey engine and the locomotive had replaced them. The teamster, missing his old world, sang:[90]

> Then I was king of the whole woods-crew,
> And I ruled with an iron grip.
> And never a slab on the whole dam' job
> Dared give me any lip.
> But now, alas, my days are past;
> There's no job for me here.
> My bulls all killed and my place is filled
> By a donkey engineer.
> Instead of my stately team of bulls
> All stepping along so fine,
> A greasy old engine toots and coughs
> And hauls in the turn with a line.

Large, well-organized crews worked in the forest to supply the almost endless demand for logs. No longer was the "haywire logging outfit"

[88] *Mississippi Valley Lumberman,* vol. xxi, Mar. 4, 1892, p. 5; vol. xxiii, May 5, 1893, p. 7.
[89] *Ibid.,* vol. xvi, Sept. 27, 1889, p. 1.
[90] This was written by Dan McNeil, a noted ox driver in his day. It was published by Stewart H. Holbrook in an article entitled "With the Loggers of the Northwest," in *Travel* Feb. 1933, pp. 35-39.

able to compete.[91] Wages were higher; the cost of provisions was higher; camps required more and better equipment; the new logging machinery was more expensive.[92] It was only the man of large capital and high managerial ability who could succeed in the forest now. Therefore, logging concerns were incorporating, and they needed able leadership by men who knew not only logging but careful business methods as well.

The largest logging concern in Minnesota in the nineties was the Cross Lake Logging Company, incorporated in 1890 with a capital of $50,000. This company was owned by E. C. Whitney, Samuel Simpson, and John L. McGuire, all of Minneapolis, Eldridge M. Fowler of Chicago, and the big Saginaw lumberman, Arthur Hill.[93] It logged for Weyerhaeuser, Hall and Ducey (later a Shevlin firm), Bovey-De Laittre, the Itasca Lumber Company, and other concerns equally prominent in Minnesota lumber.[94]

Another large company operating in the region of the Swan River and its headwaters was the Swan River Logging Company, which at times handled a hundred million feet of logs in a year.[95] In 1903 and 1904 this firm had 1200 men in the woods in eight camps.[96] It sent logs down on the logging railroad to Hibbing and dumped them into the Mississippi where they traveled on to Minneapolis and sometimes to mills below. It operated largely on the lands of its owners, Wright and Davis, Michigan men who owned heavy timber in the region between the Mississippi and Hibbing. But it cut for others also, particularly for the Weyerhaeuser interests.

Powers and Simpson, logging in the region of Hibbing, had 900 men in the woods in 1904; in 1906 they employed 2000 men in logging for C. A. Smith, the Pillsburys, T. B. Walker, and Frederick Weyerhaeuser.[97] Skelly Brothers of Aitkin, with headquarters at Cohasset near Grand Rapids, logged in the north woods; the countryside at Grand Rapids is peppered with stories by or about the Skelly Brothers and also Bill Rogers, a large-scale logger on the job for T. B. Walker.[98] Far up on the border Swallow and Hopkins, a Duluth firm, was making a reputation for cutting logs.[99] These good-sized companies owned no sawmills; their business was only to log.

Logging contracts were important documents carefully recorded and

[91] *Duluth Weekly Herald*, Oct. 14, 1903.
[92] *Duluth Evening Herald*, Feb. 12, 1903.
[93] *Mississippi Valley Lumberman*, vol. xviii, Nov. 21, 1890, p. 16.
[94] *Ibid.*, vol. xxii, Nov. 4, 1892, p. 6.
[95] *American Lumberman*, Aug. 23, 1902, pp. 1, 13.
[96] *Duluth Weekly Herald*, Jan. 6, 1904; *Little Falls Daily Transcript*, Sept. 14, 1903.
[97] *Duluth Weekly Herald*, Jan. 6, 1904; *Little Falls Daily Transcript*, Nov. 19, 1906.
[98] Interview of the writer with George Galbreath, Grand Rapids, Aug. 16, 1932.
[99] Interview of the writer with T. H. Merritt, Lennox Hotel, Duluth, June 13, 1932.

signed by both parties in the presence of witnesses. The contract stated exactly the description of the land to be cut and the exact stream on which the logs were to be banked. It carefully recorded the size of logs to be cut and stipulated that the logging firm was to take every precaution to protect logs from worms and fire. Logs were to be plainly marked with a bark-mark cut in the side of the log as the company might direct, and end-marks were to be stamped on each end of the log. All logs, said the usual contract, were to be bark-marked in the woods before being hauled to the landing, and all logs should be stamped before they were scaled. The logging contractor was to break all rollways and to put the logs afloat in the stream named in time for the spring drive in the year designated. It was the responsibility of the logging contractor to have all logs scaled by a competent scaler agreed upon by the two parties to the contract. A supervisor, likewise agreed upon, could check the scaler's report if it was in question.

The firm for which the logging was done could request from the contracting company a correct statement of the supplies it had on hand, as well as a statement of the number of men it employed, the wages agreed upon, and the amount due each man; every debt contracted by the logging firm was to be made known to the firm for whom the logging was done since a lien could be placed upon the logs. The firm for whom the logs were cut, banked, and put afloat paid so much per thousand board feet to the logging contractor. The amount varied, but $3.00, $3.50, $3.75, $4.00, $4.50, and $4.75 per thousand feet were frequent charges in the late eighties and the nineties. Usually a part of this, about $1.00 per thousand feet, was paid on the first day of each month as the logs were banked. The men employed were usually paid in orders drawn by the logging firm on the firm for which the cutting was done. The balance of all money due the logging contractor was payable on dates precisely stated in the contract.

The firm for which the logging was done guarded itself in the contract against trespassing on the part of the logging firm and against log liens or failure of performance on the part of the loggers. Contracts of the Laird, Nortons called for settlement of differences between the two parties by arbitration, each party to select one man and those two to select a third.[1]

The O'Neal Brothers, logging contractors in Stillwater who logged for the Laird, Norton Company of Winona over a period of years, reported that in 1894, according to the surveyor general's scale, they had

[1] Logging Contracts, Laird, Norton Company in contract with Quail Brothers, Aug. 13, 1886, in records of Laird, Norton Company, Winona, Minn. On these papers is based the above description of logging contracts.

cut 65,764 logs scaling 1,092,150 feet at $3.25 per thousand board feet, totaling $19,794.48; in 1895 they cut 183,618 logs scaling 16,481,400 feet at $3.25 per thousand board feet, making a total of $53,564.55; in 1896, 292,519 logs scaling 24,996,330 feet at $3.25 per thousand board feet, making a total of $81,238.07; and in 1897, 139,388 logs, scaling 12,161,010 feet, still at $3.25 per thousand feet, totaling $39,523.28. Contracts in logging between the Laird, Norton Company and O'Neal Brothers represented close to half a million dollars in the period 1889–98, and these loggers were only one of several firms who logged for the Laird, Norton Company at that time.[2] The capital spent in cutting the logs was one of the many investments that lumbermen had to make in carrying on their business. Before logs could reach their destination still more capital had to be expended in river-driving or railroad freight. Fluid capital was a constant necessity in the lumber industry.

The Pine Tree Lumber Company at Little Falls in their log statement for the season of 1906–07 reported that at least twelve logging firms had cut logs for them that season. Of these the Swan River Logging Company had cut more than 23,000,000 feet, nearly all of which was white pine. Altogether almost 39,000,000 feet had been logged for them, of which 37,000,000 feet came from their own holdings. Their account showed a total investment in those logs of $463,670.35.[3]

Many leading sawmill men, however, did their own logging. In 1895 Mitchell and McClure of Duluth had about 450 loggers in the woods during a ten-month year. C. N. Nelson of Cloquet kept 400 men in the woods of Carlton and St. Louis counties in 1895. E. W. Backus of Minneapolis had 600 men hewing out logs for him in 1895, and Nelson, Tenney and Company of Minneapolis had 500 men in the woods that same year.[4]

In 1895 about 12,000 men were working in the timber under the direction of some 200 firms and individuals. In 1900, with an increase in the whole lumber industry, there were 15,886 workmen in 329 camps in St. Louis, Itasca, and Beltrami counties. It is estimated that a total of 20,000 men made logs ready for mills in those counties at that time. That year Minnesota employed twice as many men in its camps as were employed in camps in any other state in the Union. Wisconsin and California were the nearest competitors.

No small amount of capital was needed to employ such numbers of

[2] Logging Contracts, O'Neal Brothers to Laird, Norton Company, Stillwater, Minn., Oct. 6, 1898, in records of Laird, Norton Company, Winona, Minn. Contracts varied somewhat but these show important terms that were quite general in contracts.

[3] Pine Tree Lumber Company, Little Falls, Minn., to Laird, Norton Company, Aug. 1, 1907, in Laird, Norton Company records, Box 707, Winona, Minn.

[4] C. C. Andrews, *Report of the Chief Fire Warden*, 1895, pp. 134–63.

men. Wages varied according to the demand for lumber, which in turn determined the demand for men. In 1891 wages were high because lumber was greatly in demand and the industry was growing. The wages in those days ranged from $20 to $60 a month. And transportation to the place of work and free board were additional cost items not to be overlooked. In 1895, a depression year, one company paid $16 to $18 to their common laborers and $26, $30, and $35 to their skilled workmen;[5] but even at these lower rates about $1,000,000 was necessary to pay the wages of woodsmen that year.[6] In 1900 wages had risen again with the return of prosperity, and a total of $3,920,000 was paid to labor in the woods of Minnesota.[7] The wage rates for this year are shown in Table 26. An estimated $15 a month for board should be added to these amounts, making a fairly good wage — and adding at least another $1,000,000 to the total labor costs for logging.[8]

TABLE 26. WAGES OF WOODSMEN, 1900

Type of Work	Minimum Wage	Average Wage	Maximum Wage
Foremen	$40	$68.32	$90
Cooks	35	51.90	65
Blacksmiths	30	45.59	60
Loaders	35	38.22	45
Teamsters	30	35.79	40
Sawyers	27	30.10	35
Swampers	25	27.90	30
Common workmen	24	26.83	30

SOURCE: *Duluth Weekly Herald*, May 2, 1900, p. 2; *Report of the Minnesota Bureau of Labor*, 1899–1900, p. 238.

In 1901 wages for common labor were higher than in 1900, and in 1902 they were higher still. Thousands of men were in the woods, but logging concerns were desperately seeking more. Because of this demand, common labor in 1902 was being paid the unusually high wage of $30 to $35.[9] But the highest rate for common labor in Minnesota during the period from 1891 to 1907 came in 1907, when 18 cents an hour was paid for a week of 60.3 hours — in contrast with 13.5 cents an hour for a working week of 64.6 hours in 1891.[10] Sawyers and choppers, who ranked above common labor, usually worked about sixty hours a week, never

[5] *Ibid.*; orders drawn on Laird, Norton Company dated Stillwater, Minn., Mar. and Apr. 1890, and Hinckley, Minn., Dec. 1894, in records called "Loggers," Laird, Norton Company, Winona, Minn.

[6] C. C. Andrews, *Report of the Chief Fire Warden*, 1895, p. 132.

[7] *Duluth Weekly Herald*, May 2, 1900.

[8] *Report of the Minnesota Bureau of Labor*, 1899–1900, p. 238.

[9] *Little Falls Daily Transcript*, Feb. 9, Oct. 29, 1901, and Nov. 19, 1902.

[10] U. S. Bureau of Labor Statistics, Bulletin No. 604, *Wages in the United States from Colonial Times to 1928*, p. 463.

less but often more, receiving their highest wage in 1907 with 19.1 cents an hour; 17 cents was the most common wage.[11]

The loggers worked with telling force in Minnesota's timberlands. In 1892 the forests of the Upper Mississippi and its tributaries furnished 677,836,540 feet of logs, an increase of more than 127,000,000 over the previous year.[12] Ten years later the cut of the same region was estimated at 750,000,000 feet for the year,[13] and in 1900 the entire log cut of Minnesota was about 1,112,000,000 feet.[14] Few laymen can conceive the extent of forest which was leveled to produce such quantities of logs. It has been estimated that the logs cut in 1900 could produce enough lumber to lay a sidewalk nine feet wide around the earth at the equator.[15]

It is difficult to say how many feet per man could be cut in a season. Some workmen were better than others; timber was much more dense in some parts than others; sometimes the timber was logged more easily because the land was level; and the equipment of some loggers was better than that of others. In 1901, however, in the Bemidji region 2000 men cut 100,000,000 feet of logs; T. B. Walker with 1000 men cut 50,000,000 feet of logs; another concern with 250 men cut 10,000,000 feet; while another company with the same number of men cut 15,000,000 feet. The Clearwater Logging Company at Bemidji with 300 men cut 20,000,000 feet.[16]

Like the machines and methods, the lumberjack himself was changing.[17] In 1890 Scandinavians constituted more than 27 per cent of the working force in logging and sawing in Minnesota.[18] In a camp near Hinckley in 1894 the Scandinavian names were predominant, though it is interesting to observe the variety of nationalities shown by a few of the names: K. T. Lee, John Swanson, Gust Stenberg, Willie Beaudette, Charles Bergeson, George Hawkins, P. E. Pearson, Vilas Vick, Joseph Jeno, Jeddie Deffney, Eric Scherstrom, Charles Highland, Henry Kreiger, R. C. Arnold, William Klappenstiek, Angus Cameron, James Clark, William McMullen, Gust Bloom, George Ballantyne, and Enok Hetland.[19] The men from Maine, the French and Scotch Canadians, the Norwegians and Swedes were loggers by inheritance. Many of them labored in the woods until the end of Minnesota's white and red pine. But mixed with them was the newer immigration that filtered into the

[11] Ibid.

[12] Mississippi Valley Lumberman, vol. xxiii, June 30, 1893, pp. 2, 7.

[13] Little Falls Daily Transcript, Mar. 14, 1903.

[14] Report of the Minnesota Bureau of Labor, 1899–1900, p. 238.

[15] Ibid.; Duluth Weekly Herald, May 2, 1900.

[16] Little Falls Daily Transcript, Nov. 22, 1901.

[17] "Bill" Allen, "The Passing of a Race," North Woods, vol. ii, Feb. 1914, p. 2.

[18] Vernon H. Jensen, Lumber and Labor (New York, 1945), p. 51.

[19] Loggers Records, Laird, Norton Company, Winona, Minn. These names occur on orders drawn on that firm dated at their camp at Hinckley, Minn., Dec. 17, 1894.

Middle West in the late 1880s and 1890s and came in bigger numbers as the century turned. Finns were the first of the newer immigration to enter the woods; then came Bohemians, Serbians, Russians, Poles, Austrians, and a few Greeks.[20]

Organized labor among loggers was uncommon in Minnesota until after the turn of the century. The lumberjack grumbled and cursed, and occasionally there were strikes, but usually these were local affairs in no way tied up with unions. Many of the laborers were farmers who were there to earn extra money to supplement their farm income. They had no interest in labor organizations, for with the return of spring they were back on their own farms. In the remote forests, when communication was difficult, men had hardly heard of unions, and the transient labor was not easily organized. The individualism that dominated the thinking of that time was important too. No red-blooded man in the forest would admit that he could not stand on his own feet.

With the turn of the century, however, when labor in this country was strengthening its position and when a newer immigration familiar with labor developments in Europe was entering the logging industry, labor organizations became more active. The white pine of Minnesota was gone, however, before such organizations had taken hold among lumberjacks, though strikes, labor troubles, and the Industrial Workers of the World were not unknown to Minnesota logging concerns after 1900.

The Maine men of an earlier day would not have felt at home with the workers of the later period, nor would they have recognized the camp. Perhaps the change in food was as marked as any. The logging railroad had made fresh meats and fresh vegetables available,[21] and these foods made life in camp far more desirable than in the days of the bean-hole bean. Molasses, the stand-by of an earlier day, was no longer a part of the regular fare. Even brown sugar had given way to white. And canned fruits had taken the place of dried. The new type of food contrasted as much with the old as the graceful new band saw with the stodgy old muley. Fresh steak and roasts, mutton, pork, or fish, with hot biscuit and potatoes — boiled, steamed, fried, or even French fried — were served with vegetables such as carrots, beets, beans, or sauerkraut. Pie was still the lumberjack's favorite fare. Prune, pumpkin, apple, and raisin pies were served on the tin plates in which they were baked — each jack might well have two pieces! Cookies were of three or four kinds, with doughnuts and cake. Coffee and tea, bowls full, were served at every meal.[22]

[20] *American Lumberman*, Dec. 7, 1912, p. 55.
[21] Hotchkiss, *History of Lumber and Forest Industry of Northwest*, p. 660.
[22] *Mississippi Valley Lumberman*, vol. xxi, Jan. 29, 1892, p. 2.

Providing food for thousands of loggers was no small matter. Big logging companies employed purchasing agents who had charge of all food purchases for the camp. They placed orders usually on Friday, buying their goods from wholesale concerns.

The Stone-Ordean-Wells Company of Duluth, a wholesale grocery firm, supplied many of the large logging companies operating in northern Minnesota. On their regular list of customers was Alger, Smith and Company of Duluth, who employed 1700 men at one time in their camps. Their purchases were representative of the usual food order for a large camp. They bought 365 sacks of beans a year, each sack weighing 165 pounds. A hundred men used 25 pounds of oleomargarine a day; a hundred men in 200 days ate 5000 pounds. The tobacco and snuff bill of this firm was $250 daily and usually about $25,000 for the season. Meat was a heavy staple in camps; 80 barrels of pork, exactly a carload, was a common order from large camps, and 48 head of heavy cattle a week were consumed by Alger, Smith and Company's 1700 men. Peaches, plums, and pears were bought in 10-pound cans. Altogether, Alger, Smith and Company paid Stone-Ordean-Wells about $250,000 annually for groceries during the period of the logging concern's greatest activity in 1898 and 1899.[23]

The Itasca Lumber Company, the Virginia and Rainy Lake Lumber Company (a Weyerhaeuser firm), T. B. Walker, the International Lumber Company (a Backus firm), the Swan River Logging Company — all these firms heavily engaged in logging were customers of Stone-Ordean-Wells. The passing of the logging industry has taken from this firm a real market. "Has anything replaced the business which the logger gave you?" the writer asked J. Edgar Willcuts, who had charge of the supplies sent to loggers for this company. "Nothing," he said, "nothing. Those were the good old days."

[23] Interview of the writer with J. Edgar Willcuts of the Stone-Ordean-Wells Company, Duluth, July 13, 1932; interview of the writer with J. W. Bayley, Duluth, Aug. 14, 1932. Bayley was associated with the firm of Alger, Smith and Company, which at one time employed the largest number of loggers of all the firms in the Duluth district.

CHAPTER XIX

Marketing and Prices, Especially after 1890

IN PIONEER days the marketing of logs and lumber had often been simple and direct. In the Upper Mississippi Valley there were then no specialized middlemen between the producer and consumer except an occasional retailer like the Lairds of Winona, who in 1855 were selling to the incoming settlers of that region lumber from the sawmills on the St. Croix or the Chippewa. The early lumber producer generally combined ownership of timber with logging, sawing, and wholesaling, and he was often his own retailer as well. As we have already seen, if he manufactured more than his immediate community needed, he followed his product to market, selling to dealers or even, as in the case of Ingram of Eau Claire and Knapp of Menomonie, "hawking" his lumber up and down the Mississippi, often selling in small lots to farmers.

In the markets of the Middle Mississippi, however, specialized middlemen had already developed. Large wholesalers were operating in St. Louis when lumbering on the Upper Mississippi was just beginning. That city was the first to wholesale lumber made in Minnesota.

As the lumber industry of the Upper Mississippi grew in size and producers became larger and more numerous and the market widened, the wholesaler became more important in the distribution of lumber in that region. He located himself at some convenient point between the sawmill and the consuming center, usually at some town well situated on waterway or railroad. St. Louis became increasingly important as a wholesale center for Minnesota lumber. Chicago also became more important for Minnesota's lumber as it developed into a railroad center and as Michigan pine diminished. Minneapolis' position as a wholesaling center developed later. The East had well-established wholesale centers which had handled lumber long before Minnesota's product came on the market. As we have seen, Tonawanda, New York, located at the east end of Lake Erie, was especially important in the wholesaling of lumber. It was the gateway to the North Atlantic states, with the cities of New York, Philadelphia, and Boston as important markets; and mills in Duluth, Cloquet, and other Minnesota regions tributary to Lake Superior sent lumber there. Other points in New York which came to wholesale lumber from Minnesota were Ogdensburg, Albany, and Buffalo. Cleveland, Ohio, also became an important entrepôt for Minnesota's lumber.

The wholesale middlemen in the lumber trade were of various kinds: the commission merchant, the jobber, and the large owner-wholesaler. The commission merchant handled lumber for producers, selling it at a stipulated charge per thousand feet or per carload. Buyers could get what they wanted by entrusting their buying to a commission man. This saved the buyer the expense of a trip and saved the producer the expense involved in sending men to solicit trade. Orders by mail increased noticeably as commission agencies were established.[1] The jobber, unlike the commission man, bought the lumber he sold. Jobbers distributed a large part of the lumber sold in Minneapolis.[2] The large owner-wholesaler was like the jobber in that he bought the lumber which he in turn sold to retailers; he differed from the jobber, however, in that he bought lumber in very large quantities.

One large owner-wholesaler who was of particular importance to the Minnesota lumber industry was Edward Hines. Hines was for some time secretary of the S. K. Martin wholesale lumber firm of Chicago. Eventually he bought the S. K. Martin yard and also the Isaac Stephenson yard, the oldest in Chicago, and other prominent Chicago yards. This combination was incorporated under the name of the Edward Hines Lumber Company, and Hines became America's greatest wholesale lumberman.[3] Wholesalers of this type were prominent in what we may call the middle period of Minnesota's lumber history, from 1870 to 1890.

At the same time some producers continued to sell their own product. There were a number of sawmill men who kept in direct touch with the market. Among these was Isaac Staples of Stillwater, who traveled down the Mississippi, taking orders for his product at St. Louis and other towns en route. On one trip he sold $87,000 worth of logs and lumber.[4] Edward W. Durant of Stillwater, according to a newspaper of that city on June 11, 1875, also traveled downriver taking orders for his lumber. A. F. Hodgins, who became a member of the firm of Youmans Brothers at Winona in 1870 and whose business it was to keep books and look after sales, put in one half of his time selling on the road westward from Winona.[5]

[1] *Stillwater Messenger*, June 18, 1875.
[2] *Report of the Minneapolis Board of Trade*, 1892, pp. 296–302.
[3] *American Lumberman*, Mar. 19, 1904, p. 1.
[4] *Stillwater Messenger*, July 2, 1875.
[5] Interview of the writer with C. M. Youmans, Winona, May 2, 1934.

Some sawmill firms sent out full-time traveling salesmen. Joe Scanlon, of the Scanlon-Gipson Lumber Company in Minneapolis, represented his firm in Nebraska in the 1880s. His reports were full of satisfaction over his sales in that new country. On one occasion, during a ten-minute stop while the train was changing engines in a Nebraska town, he took an order for 21 cars of lumber, mostly dimension, in straight carlots.[6] T. H. Shevlin of Minneapolis demonstrated the importance of contacting dealers, for on a ten-day trip into the region of Omaha and Kansas City in the fall of 1889 he received an order for 140 cars of piece stuff, all eighteen feet and over.[7]

It was not unusual for sawmills to establish their own retail yards. Seymour, Sabin and Company of Stillwater had a retail yard at Cedar Rapids. McKusick, Anderson and Company of Stillwater retailed at St. James. Youmans Brothers and Hodgins of Winona had retail yards at many points on the railroad running west from Winona.[8] Laird, Norton and Company also established retail yards in the region west of Winona at an early period.[9]

Some lumber manufacturers sold directly to retailers by means of stock sheets which they distributed to their customers. These sheets carried the prices of the various kinds of lumber, and retailers could order their goods directly from the price list. The C. L. Coleman Lumber Company of La Crosse was issuing such a stock sheet as early as 1879. George H. Atwood of the Hersey and Bean Lumber Company at Stillwater published a list of their stocks on the first and the fifteenth of each month. They considered this a satisfactory way of doing business, for although they had not a single man on the road, they received at times orders for 100 cars of lumber after such a sheet had been issued.[10]

In the 1870s and 1880s, then, there were many ways by which manufacturers of lumber disposed of their product, and no single way can be said to have predominated. The methods of selling were neither original nor new; they were similar to those employed in older sections of the country.

In the late 1880s and the 1890s, however, new methods of marketing became prominent. One of these, the "line yard," was distinctly a contribution of the Middle West, growing out of the conditons of a young and growing section. Another was the combination of a producer with a big wholesaler. Both methods seem to have developed because the increasing intensity of competition in the market forced the large producer, who had

[6] *Mississippi Valley Lumberman*, vol. xxviii, Feb. 19, 1897, p. 2.

[7] *Ibid.*, vol. xvi, Oct. 25, 1889, p. 7.

[8] *Winona Weekly Republican*, Sept. 8, 1880.

[9] *Winona Republican*, Oct. 5, 1870.

[10] *Mississippi Valley Lumberman*, vol. xvi, Oct. 29, 1889, p. 3.

immense capital invested in timber and sawmills, to secure a more certain outlet for his product. This became increasingly necessary as other types of lumber, such as the yellow pine of the South and the Douglas fir from Washington, began to invade what had previously been the undisputed market of the white pine.

Line yards were a number of retail yards under one ownership and one central management.[11] A branch yard was the first form of retail yard which a producer established; line yards were a string of such branch yards organized as a separate enterprise within the sawmill company or as a separate enterprise by specialized middlemen.

Various factors contributed to the strength of the line. One was centralized management on a scale larger and more effective than was possible in the individual yard. Another factor was that, with greater resources and credit, line yards could be liberal in extending credit to their customers, and the new one-crop farmers west of the Mississippi needed long-time credit. The line yard was therefore attractive to them, and this accounts for its ready success in the new West. It is clear that the line tried to eliminate competition in order to have more control over prices in its retail market.

Line yards seem to have flourished first in the southern part of Minnesota. C. A. Coleman, a lumber producer of La Crosse, established line yards in southern Minnesota as early as 1867.[12] His name became well known in many a prairie town, for he had gained a foothold early as a line yard owner.

Winona's four big lumber manufacturing companies preëmpted places along the Winona and St. Peter division of the Northwestern Railroad which went westward from Winona.[13] Youmans Brothers and Hodgins in 1888 had twenty-two yards in their system of line yards; the Laird, Norton Company had thirty-four yards in their system; and the Winona Lumber Company had a line of twenty yards in the late eighties. The Empire Lumber Company, also, was active in preëmpting safe markets through the line yard arrangement.

In Minneapolis the C. A. Smith Lumber Company and Nelson, Tenney and Company were active in the field with line yards. These companies built yards chiefly along railroads serving Minneapolis, such as the Minneapolis and St. Louis and the Minneapolis and Pacific.[14] Along the Northern Pacific, the Gull River Lumber Company, a Minneapolis firm making lumber near Brainerd, had established line yards which were

[11] Ovid M. Butler, *The Distribution of Softwood Lumber in the Middle West* (Washington, 1918), pp. 6–7.
[12] John M. Gries, "Line Yards," *American Lumberman,* Mar. 15, 1919, pp. 50–51.
[13] *Mississippi Valley Lumberman*, vol. xxii, Oct. 11, 1892, p. 2.
[14] *Ibid.*, vol. xii, Oct. 21, 1887, p. 2.

managed by William H. White, who, retailing in Fargo in 1872, had been one of the first lumber retailers in the Red River Valley. This firm controlled thirty yards in 1894.[15] The letterheads of the general office of the Weyerhaeuser firm in St. Paul showed that in 1907 they had yards at Blue Earth, Elmore, Frost, Bricelyn, Lewisville, Truman, Mantorville, Dodge Center, Sargeant, and Guckeen, all in good agricultural sections of Minnesota.

Though manufacturers were the first to establish line yards, they were soon followed in that business by corporations which were not producers of lumber. Such purely distributing establishments offered an excellent market for the manufacturer. A well-known company of this type was the J. N. Queal Company of Des Moines, which owned a string of twenty yards in Iowa and another string in rich wheat areas of Minnesota, such as at Hanley Falls, Clarkfield, Dawson, and Madison.[16] W. H. Robinson, president of the Northwestern Lumberman's Association in 1891, was managing member of the Biedler and Robinson Lumber Company, which had sixteen line yards in North Dakota.[17]

Many line yard companies, drawing upon other sources of supply, continued to sell lumber when mills with which they had originally been associated ceased production. Every sawmilling company in Winona continued its line yards after the mills were closed. The C. M. Youmans Lumber Company, successors to the old firm of Youmans Brothers and Hodgins, has continued to operate the line yards though their mill closed in 1897. In 1900, after the Winona Lumber Company ceased operating its sawmill, two of the mill employees, Hayes and Lucas, took over the line yards. Their names became well known in the small towns of southern Minnesota. William H. Laird, who had been president of the Winona Lumber Company, aided these successors of his in the management of their thirty-five yards by serving as president of the Hayes and Lucas concern for some time.

The Laird, Norton Company of Winona also continued to operate their line yards after their mill had stopped. In 1912, however, they turned their thirty-eight yards over to some of their former workmen who organized the Botsford Lumber Company.[18] And Roscoe Horton continued the line yards of the Empire Lumber Company, under the name of the Standard Lumber Company, after their sawmills had ceased operations. Sawmill firms thus contributed both capital and managerial personnel and experience to the new line yard companies.

[15] *Ibid.*, vol. xxiv, Mar. 9, 1894, p. 4.
[16] *Ibid.*, vol. xix, Jan. 23, 1891, p. 3; vol. xxiii, Oct. 20, 1893, p. 6.
[17] *Ibid.*, vol. xix, Jan. 23, 1891, p. 3.
[18] Curtiss-Wedge *History of Winona County*, pp. 182–83.

Minneapolis in time became the leading line yard center in Minnesota. Its admirable position as a gateway to an immense hinterland and as a prominent railroad center, its large supply of capital, and its great lumber industry were all factors in making it a great distributing center. Minneapolis has lost all its sawmills, but it has continued as a market place for lumber. In 1907 fifty line yard companies had headquarters in that city.[19]

It is interesting to follow the experiences of these firms which established themselves in the business of selling lumber in the pioneer period, developed branch and line yards, and continued on as the country developed. A typical example was the old Winona firm of W. H. Laird and the two Norton brothers. On the 25th day of June, 1855, the three Laird brothers, who composed the original firm, sold their first lumber in this settlement out on the frontier. According to their records of that day William Stevens bought 3000 shingles for which he paid $5.00 a thousand; and R. W. Finklenburg bought 3200 laths for which he paid $9.60. L. D. Smith bought common boards at $22 per thousand feet and flooring at $24 per thousand. These were small amounts such as a pioneer might need for his shelter in the new country. The records of the Lairds showed siding selling at $28 and roof boards at $20 a thousand. Lumber, given the title of clear lumber, was selling at $35 a thousand. The records of Laird and Norton in the fifties were a constant repetition of sales of flooring, siding, roof boards, lath, and shingles. This was what the farmer needed as he moved on to the uplands above the Mississippi.[20]

The company served both the community and themselves well, for the records of 1856 show the sales of their lumberyard for that year to have been slightly above $24,000. In 1857, the panic year, their business fell off to $20,000, but in 1858 sales rose again, beyond $33,000. In 1865, ten years after their first sale, they did a business of $86,000. They reached their high point in 1866, when their sales for the year reached $133,688.[21] In 1867 Dun and Company gave this firm which had operated out on the frontier for little more than a decade a rating of "good." [22]

As people moved westward above the valley, Laird, Norton and Company began to establish yards at strategic points of settlement. They had yards early in Lewiston, St. Charles, Chatfield, and Rochester. As the population spread farther westward, Byron, Claremont, Owatonna, and Waseca had their yards. On into western Minnesota they moved, establishing themselves at Lake Benton, Marshall, Canby, and Tracy. And

---

[19] *American Review of Reviews*, vol. xxxvi, Nov. 1907, p. 574.

[20] Account Book, June 25, 1855, to Dec. 1, 1856, in records of the Laird, Norton Company, Winona, Minn.

[21] These figures are based on figures found in the records of the firm for those years.

[22] R. G. Dun and Company, Reference Book, vol. xxii, Jan. 1867.

in the late 1870s and early 1880s Brookings, Volga, Watertown, Huron, and Pierre, all in South Dakota, had lumberyards belonging to Laird, Norton and Company.

The correspondence between the home office in Winona and the outlying yards concerned itself chiefly with the crops, the ability of farmers to pay, how much lumber was needed, and what was the state of accounts. The men at Winona gave the men who operated their yards on the uplands much freedom; the correspondence was friendly and considerate. One such letter stated that the manager of said lumberyard had been "kind enough to intimate in a letter a while ago that you would send us some cash at least $1000 if we remember right, the 1st of December. We simply wish to say that a remittance of that kind would be quite acceptable."[23] Another operator had evidently written the home office that he would send a certain amount at a given date. Laird, Norton and Company replied, "We thought we would just say that we have a place for that and more if you can send it."[24] A letter to their operator at Marshall advised him not to "rush off at low prices," because there was reason to think that prices of lumber would be advanced.[25]

In a letter to T. J. Dansingburg, an operator at Claremont, the home office wrote that "a good farmer who owns his own place without incumbrance is a pretty safe man to trust."[26] In a somewhat firmer letter the home office wrote to one of their yardmen that "your book accounts aggregate some $30,000." They said they could not afford to carry this sum since it bore no interest. To another operator was sent the following gracious but firm letter in regard to payments: "It is necessary for us to urge the matter as you will thoroughly understand and appreciate it. And yet we feel that you will excuse our calling attention to it."[27]

Many orders for lumber for school and church buildings reached Laird, Norton and Company. This firm generously made either a subscription to the church building or a reduction in the price of the lumber. Often, too, they arranged with the local railroad for a reduction in freight rates on the lumber.[28] For instance, to an order for lumber for a church at Sleepy Eye in western Minnesota, Laird, Norton and Company replied that it was their custom to make a small subscription for a church building and

---

[23] Laird, Norton Papers, Letter Book (Aug. 13, 1877, to Dec. 17, 1877), Laird, Norton and Company to Case brothers, Chatfield, Minn., Nov. 30, 1877.

[24] *Ibid.,* Laird, Norton and Company to L. J. Allred, Lewiston, Minn., Nov. 30, 1877.

[25] Laird, Norton and Company kept their operators in close touch with prices.

[26] Laird, Norton Papers, Letter Book (Aug. 13, 1877, to Dec. 17, 1877), Laird, Norton and Company to T. J. Dansingburg, Claremont, Minn., Sept. 11, 1877.

[27] *Ibid.,* Laird, Norton and Company to P. L. Dansingburg, Rochester, Minn., Sept. 8, 1877.

[28] *Ibid.,* Laird, Norton and Company to E. C. Severance, Mantorville, Minn., Sept. 10, 1877. This was possible until the Interstate Commerce Act forbade such arrangements in 1887.

that they had arranged with the railroad to give a discount of one third from the regular freight.[29] Similar letters were sent to other communities which placed orders for churches or schoolhouses with the Winona firm.[30]

Lumber companies which established themselves in the newly developing regions encountered serious competition at times. This was certainly the case in Watertown, Dakota Territory, in 1877. At least four lumber companies had established yards there, and it seems evident that the new community, promising as it was, could not support that many. All four firms complained that they were losing money; one firm had cut prices drastically and the others had to follow. One firm addressed itself to the others hoping that some solution could be found, but, said the letter, it is a "delicate matter to give advice when ones own interests are involved." [31]

A somewhat similar situation developed at Lake Preston, Dakota Territory, where a La Crosse firm opened a yard after a Winona firm had already established one there. It appeared that the business in this new settlement was hardly enough for two firms. The Winona company, in a firm but conciliatory manner, wrote the La Crosse company that they, the men from Winona, would leave other points to the La Crosse firm but that they would like to have consideration at Lake Preston.[32]

Railroads had an interest in the price of lumber, for lumber was, as we have seen, an important item of freight. A letter sent on December 7, 1883, by P. Hollenbeck, assistant freight agent of the Northwestern Railroad at Winona, definitely expressed the importance of prices to the railroad. It reads, "Lumber is being sold on the H & D Division at Granite Falls and Montevideo at from $1.00 to $2.00 per 1000 on common and dimension lumber less than our prices at Minneota and Canby. My agent traveling this territory between two lines and in conversation with farmers finds that we are losing a large amount of our lumber trade on account of the difference." The agent said that the lumber sold on the "H & D is fully equal to our grades." The time had come, according to Hollenbeck, when lumbermen at Winona must either meet the prices of dealers on other lines or suffer a loss of business. He asked what could be done to meet the competition in prices.

Another notable development in marketing in this later period was the combination of the producer and the wholesaler. The outstanding example

[29] *Ibid.,* Letter Book (Feb. 16, 1868, to Aug. 31, 1877), Laird, Norton and Company to Fred Kisner, Sleepy Eye, Minn., May 18, 1876.

[30] *Ibid.,* Letter Book (Aug. 1, 1878, to Oct. 14, 1878), Laird, Norton and Company to C. H. Knapp, General Agent for the Chicago and Northwestern Railroad, Apr. 19, 1877; *ibid.,* Laird, Norton and Company to C. E. Severance, Mantorville, Minn., Sept. 27, 1878.

[31] *Ibid.,* Letter Book (Mar. 12, 1887, to Apr. 7, 1887), Laird, Norton Company to O. C. Merriman, Minneapolis, Apr. 7, 1887. Observe that the name of Laird, Norton and Company has been changed to Laird, Norton Company.

[32] *Ibid.,* Laird, Norton Company to John Paul, La Crosse, Wis., Mar. 26, 1887.

of this development was the association of Frederick Weyerhaeuser with Edward Hines. This combination looked toward the eastern market rather than the western agricultural market which the line yards served. The association of these two men, each powerful in his field, one as a producer and the other as a wholesaler, began in 1902. The Hines firm did an enormous business, handling at times more than 500,000,000 feet of lumber in one year.[33] It was well for Weyerhaeuser to fortify himself with such a connection when markets were so highly competitive.

Hines's real field was wholesaling, but he had purchased heavy pine holdings in Ashland, Douglas, and Bayfield counties in northern Wisconsin and in St. Louis County in northern Minnesota. Weyerhaeuser and his associates were said to be the heaviest timber holders in Minnesota at that time. A combination of such holdings was of special value in the days when white pine timber was growing scarce. These interests built the largest white pine mill in the world in Minnesota shortly after they became associated. Its capacity was 300,000,000 feet a year. Weyerhaeuser and Hines controlled timber; they carried on logging; they were sawmill men; they planed lumber; and they wholesaled on a large scale. Their firm owned fifteen boats on the Great Lakes, of which ten used steam power and five used sails. In Chicago they controlled a shore line dock of five thousand feet.[34] Their combination formed a highly integrated business, built to withstand the fierce competition of that time.

In the eastern market the product of the Duluth district was sold through specialized wholesalers. A very large proportion — how large, it is impossible to say — was sold through commission men located in Duluth. Many of these men, like the loggers and sawmillers themselves, had come from Michigan; they were an integral part of the white pine industry. In the markets to the eastward they sold for the producers to wholesalers, and possibly to some retailers. By far their most important market was Tonawanda in New York.

There was at this time no attempt to enlarge the market for lumber by consumer advertising. Lumber had little competition from substitutes before 1905, and, since grading was growing steadily in importance, the consumer could not be appealed to with the argument that any given concern sold superior lumber.[35] Whatever advertising there was consisted merely of stereotyped announcements in trade journals intended for wholesalers, retailers, contractors, and architects.

The adoption of a complicated system of grading was another significant development. The pioneer had not been much interested in the

[33] *American Lumberman,* Mar. 19, 1904, p. 1.
[34] *Ibid.*
[35] Compton, *Organization of the Lumber Industry,* pp. 91, 127.

grading of his lumber; he simply chose the lumber that looked good to him. But as the distance between producer and consumer lengthened and large contracts for lumber had to be made sight unseen, a refined system of grading developed. This became especially necessary as the lumber of Minnesota entered the eastern market, but it was, of course, chiefly an outgrowth of large-scale business.

In the pioneer period on the Upper Mississippi, lumber was designated as of two kinds only: merchantable and culls. The merchantable lumber was made up of two classes: good and common. Good lumber was clear lumber; common lumber included everything not good, except cull stock.[36]

Lumber sold on the Upper Mississippi during the earlier period was graded according to more specific standards on reaching the large distribution points, such as Buffalo, Chicago, St. Louis, and Tonawanda.[37] In 1873 the inspection committee of the Lumbermen's Exchange of Chicago adopted the following rules of classification: The first grade was made up of first, second, and third clear; the second grade, consisting of select A stock boards and B stock boards, included all lumber below the grade of clears but better than common; the third grade, known as common, included lumber below clear and select but better than culls; the fourth grade was the culls, but it contained no refuse or worthless lumber.[38]

Some manufacturers in the Upper Mississippi Valley followed the Chicago rules of grading, but even as late as 1887 every dealer in Minneapolis graded to suit his fancy and each man set his own price.[39] In 1890 the idea developed that Northwest grades — Northwest applying to the Upper Mississippi area — ought to be as standard as Chicago grades.[40] That very year the lumbermen of the Upper Mississippi gave themselves distinct identity when they began a study of grading, preparatory to the adoption of definite rules for the grading of the white pine of their own section. No longer was Chicago to set the standard in the Upper Valley. Twice in 1890 white pine producers met to lay plans for uniformity of grades and uniformity of prices.[41] It was quite evident that "the desirability of uniform grading arose from a too wide diversity in price making."[42] The meetings had definite results, for J. S. Funk of the Chippewa River district and A. A. Fiero from the Minneapolis district were chosen to inspect yards in the white pine section of the Upper Mississippi in order

[36] Frederick A. Weyerhaeuser, "Pine Forests of Minnesota," *North Woods*, Jan. 1913, p. 16; Compton, *op. cit.*, p. 10.

[37] Charles Hill, *The Merchandising of Lumber* (New Haven, 1922), p. 12.

[38] *Minneapolis Tribune*, Mar. 14, 1873, p. 2.

[39] *Mississippi Valley Lumberman*, vol. xii, Sept. 9, 1887, p. 1.

[40] *Ibid.*, vol. xviii, Sept. 26, 1890, p. 2.

[41] *Ibid.*, vol. xvii, May 30, 1890, p. 2; vol. xviii, July 11, 1890, p. 2.

[42] *American Lumberman*, July 2, 1904, p. 15.

to ascertain to what extent there were differences in grading and in prices.

These men inspected fifty-five yards in the Northwest and reported the lumber of that section to be of a high grade. They also declared that the lumber which went into better grades elsewhere was used in more ordinary construction in the Upper Mississippi.[43]

In September 1891 the leading lumbermen of this region met in Minneapolis to consider the findings of the two inspectors. The West Hotel had probably never before gathered under its roof so zealous a group; sixty lumbermen were present. They then and there organized the Mississippi Valley Lumbermen's Association, which, could we follow its development, would tell us much about modern business methods of concentration and control. The officers selected represented the various districts within the region.[44] B. F. Nelson of Nelson, Tenney and Company of Minneapolis was elected president. W. H. Laird of the Laird, Norton Company of Winona and William Irvine, a Weyerhaeuser man of Chippewa Falls, Wisconsin, were made vice-presidents. Another of the Weyerhaeuser group, R. L. McCormick, was elected treasurer. The directors were Frederick Weyerhaeuser of St. Paul; Alex Stewart of Wausau, Wisconsin; G. S. Shaw of Cloquet; J. J. Cruikshank of Hannibal, Missouri; W. J. Young, Jr., of Clinton, Iowa; and George H. Atwood of Stillwater. The nominating committee consisted of John S. Owen of Eau Claire, John Paul of La Crosse, and W. S. Hill of Minneapolis. The lumbermen at that meeting showed a lively concern in all matters relating to their common interest, the white pine. They were interested in grades, to be sure — that, they had announced, was their real reason for meeting. They wanted uniformity of grades, of thickness, of names, and it is safe to say they also wanted uniformity of prices.[45]

The grading rules established under the supervision of the Mississippi Valley Lumbermen's Association were not put into use until April 1, 1895.[46] Many of the firms actually applied the system of grading before it was officially accepted, but the Panic of 1893 and the terrible forest fires in Minnesota in 1894 created an unusual situation which made the application of rules difficult. In 1895, however, the Association definitely agreed to put its rules of grading into effect.[47]

According to these rules common lumber was divided into five groups

[43] *Mississippi Valley Lumberman*, vol. xviii, July 11, 1890, p. 2.

[44] *Ibid.*, vol. xx, Sept. 4, 1891, pp. 3–4.

[45] *American Lumberman*, July 2, 1904, p. 15; U. S. Bureau of Corporations, *The Lumber Industry* (1914), pt. 4, p. 496.

[46] *Ibid.*, pp. 496–97.

[47] *Mississippi Valley Lumberman*, vol. xxxvi, Feb. 3, 1905, pp. 70–71; also, address given by W. H. Laird to the Mississippi Valley Lumbermen's Association, Mar. 1897, Private Letter Book, Oct. 10, 1895, to Apr. 29, 1898.

with subdivisions within each group. Number one of common boards included all sound, tight-knotted stock, whether red or black knots, free from very large, coarse knots or any imperfection that would weaken the piece. Number two of common boards admitted coarser, larger knots, but not worm holes or traces of rot. Number three common had large, loose knots, some worm holes, much shake, and some red rot, but a serious combination of these defects in any one piece was not admissible. All boards in which red rot predominated were placed in number four. Number five was the lowest grade and admitted all defects known in lumber.[48] All types of lumber were carefully classified. Culls were carefully sorted to make salable lumber.[49]

All these changes in grading and the lack of uniformity in the grades used, at least until 1895, make it very difficult to study the price history of the white pine of the Upper Mississippi. It is impossible to secure comparable prices for any given quality or class of product throughout the period.

Another difficulty is the fact that published prices did not correctly represent actual prices.[50] This discrepancy, however, appears in almost every field of production and is not characteristic of the lumber industry alone. And in the discussion of a series of prices, small deviations from the published prices would probably not disturb the relative change from year to year.

Some generalization about prices can be made. The trends are clearly seen and can be measured roughly. Though the results are not altogether satisfactory, they do have meaning.

After 1866 there was a downward trend of lumber prices as of prices in general. From the high price of 1866 — a price not to be equaled before 1902 — prices fell somewhat until 1873; then the price decline was rapidly accelerated after the panic. For a short time lumber prices fell more rapidly than the general commodity price level, but for the longer period from 1873 to 1881 the decline in lumber prices about paralleled the fall in the general price level.[51] In 1880 white pine began to stay above other lumber in price.

Though a series of comparable prices is not available over the seventies and eighties, for reasons already given, some comparisons can be made. In 1872 the Minneapolis mills listed only one kind of common boards; its wholesale price was given in October as $13 per thousand feet.[52] In March 1887, a time when conditions were good, number one

[48] U.S. Bureau of Corporations, *The Lumber Industry* (1914), pt. 4, p. 566.
[49] Hill, *op. cit.*, p. 3; Compton, *op. cit.*, p. 107.
[50] *American Lumberman*, May 25, 1907, p. 5.
[51] Compton, *op. cit.*, p. 109.
[52] *Minneapolis Tribune*, Oct. 12, 1872, p. 3.

common boards in that city were listed at $13 per thousand feet, wholesale; number two common boards, not listed in 1872 but added to the list in 1887, then had a wholesale price of $9.00. It is noticeable that the only common board listed in 1872 had the same price as number one common, the best in common boards in 1887. In 1893 there were twelve classifications in the four groups of common boards, with seven different lengths and twenty-six prices, based, of course, on width and length; the highest price in this list of common boards was $20.50 per thousand feet, while the lowest was $7.50 per thousand feet.[53]

The fact that the above prices are for different grades illustrates the impossibility of making satisfactory comparisons. The price for the only grade of common boards in 1872 was $13, while in 1893 the best boards were $20.50, which might suggest a marked rise in price during a score of years. In 1894 the classifications of common boards numbered fifteen. Some prices in this list were lower than some of the prices of 1893, and the fall in price varied with types of boards; some had fallen $1.00 on 1000 feet and others only 50 cents. But the prices in 1894 were higher than in 1887 and much higher than in 1872.[54] Prices of common boards were apparently lower in 1895 than in 1894. In 1896 there was a slight rise in the price of common boards; the $17.50 boards of 1895 had risen to $18.50, and the $16.50 boards to $17.50. In 1897 the prices went down again.

The comparison in Table 27 of the wholesale price lists in Minneapolis from 1892 to 1900, in number one and number two common boards of thirteen and twelve inches in width, shows the instability of prices in the nineties with a sudden spurt upward in 1900.

The price list for dimension lumber was as simple in its arrangement as was that for common lumber at one time. Scantlings 2x4 and 4x4 which were 10, 18, and 20 feet long were advertised at one price, $13. Others were higher or lower according to their length.[55] In 1888 the classification had been enlarged, giving a greater selection as to both sizes and prices.[56] The price lists of dimension lumber for 1889 and 1890 were identical.[57] In 1892, however, the list took on a different appearance; the variety of sizes increased, and each size had its own special price.[58]

The price fluctuations of dimension lumber during the nineties are similar to those of common boards. The price was up and down with no stability but with a definite rise in 1900. In 1887 a 2x4 18 feet long sold for $13 per thousand; in 1888 the price was $14; in 1890 it was $13 again;

[53] *Mississippi Valley Lumberman*, vol. xxiii, Mar. 17, 1893, p. 8.
[54] *Ibid.*, vol. xxiv, Mar. 16, 1894, pp. 9–10.
[55] *Ibid.*, vol. xi, Mar. 18, 1887. (This issue was unpaged.)
[56] *Ibid.*, vol. xiii, Mar. 16, 1888, p. 8.
[57] *Ibid.*, vol. xv, Mar. 15, 1889, p. 11; vol. xvii, Mar. 14, 1890, p. 12.
[58] *Ibid.*, vol. xxi, Mar. 18, 1892, p. 7.

MARKETING AND PRICES   385

TABLE 27. WHOLESALE PRICES OF NO. 1 AND NO. 2 COMMON BOARDS IN MINNEAPOLIS, SELECTED DATES, 1892–1900

Width	Year	Price per Thousand Feet					
		10 ft.	12 ft.	14 ft.	16 ft.	18 ft.	20 ft.
		No. 1 COMMON BOARDS					
12 inches	1892	$19.00	$17.00	$17.00	$17.00	$19.00	$19.00
	1893	20.50	18.50	18.50	18.50	20.50	20.50
	1894	20.50	17.50	17.50	17.50	19.50	20.50
	1895	17.50	16.50	16.00	16.00	18.00	19.50
	1896	18.50	17.50	16.50	16.50	18.50	19.50
	1897	17.50	16.50	16.50	16.50	17.50	18.00
	1898	18.50	17.50	17.50	17.50	18.50	19.50
	1899	19.00	18.00	18.00	18.00	19.00	20.00
	1900	21.00	20.00	20.00	20.00	21.00	22.00
13 inches or more	1892	17.00	17.00	17.00	17.00	17.00	17.00
	1893	18.50	18.50	18.50	18.50	18.50	18.50
	1894	....	17.50	17.50	17.50	....	....
	1895	....	16.00	16.00	16.00	....	....
	1896	....	17.50	17.50	17.50	....	....
	1897	....	17.00	17.00	17.00	18.00	18.00
	1898	....	17.50	17.50	17.50	....	....
	1899	....	18.50	18.50	18.50	19.50	19.50
	1900	....	20.50	20.50	20.50	21.50	21.50
		No. 2. COMMON BOARDS					
12 inches	1892	14.00	13.00	13.00	13.50	13.00	13.00
	1893	16.00	15.50	14.50	14.00	17.00	17.00
	1894	....	14.00	13.00	12.50	15.00	16.00
	1895	12.50	12.00	11.00	11.00	13.00	14.50
	1896	13.50	13.00	12.50	11.50	13.50	14.50
	1897	14.50	13.00	11.50	11.50	13.00	14.50
	1898	15.00	14.00	12.50	12.50	14.00	15.00
	1899	16.00	14.50	12.50	12.50	15.00	16.50
	1900	18.50	17.00	15.50	15.50	18.00	19.50
13 inches or more	1892	13.00	13.00	13.00	13.00	13.00	13.00
	1893	....	13.50	13.50	13.50	13.50	13.50
	1894	....	13.00	12.50	12.50	....	....
	1895	....	11.50	11.50	11.50	....	....
	1896	....	13.00	12.50	11.50	13.50	....
	1897	....	13.00	15.50	11.50	....	....
	1898	....	12.50	12.50	12.50	....	....
	1899	....	13.00	13.00	13.00	....	....
	1900	....	16.00	16.00	16.00	....	....

SOURCE: *Mississippi Valley Lumberman,* vol. xxi, Mar. 18, 1892, p. 7; vol. xxiii, Mar. 17, 1893, p. 8; vol. xxiv, Mar. 16, 1894, p. 10; vol. xxvi, Mar. 15, 1895, p. 17; vol. xxvii, Mar. 20, 1896, p. 24; vol. xxviii, Mar. 19, 1897, p. 19; vol. xxix, Apr. 8, 1898, p. 23; vol. xxx, Mar. 17, 1899, p. 22; vol. xxxi, Jan. 19, 1900, p. 91. Price lists were printed only occasionally.

in 1891 it reached a lower price; it rose again in 1892; and in 1893 it reached the high price of $14; then down it went again until it reached $10.50, in 1897. Thus during the decade from 1887 to 1897 its highest price was $14 and its lowest $10.50.

A comparison of prices of a 2x4 in various lengths throughout the period from 1887 through 1900 is interesting (see Table 28).

TABLE 28. PRICES OF 2x4's IN MINNEAPOLIS, 1887–1900

	Price per Thousand Feet				
	12 ft.	18 ft.	20 ft.	22–24 ft.	26–28 ft.
1887	$13.50	$13.00	$13.00	....	....
1888	13.50	14.00	14.00	$16.00	....
1889	12.00	13.00	13.00	15.00	....
1890	12.00	13.00	13.00	15.00	....
1891	11.50	12.00	12.00	14.00	$17.00
1892	12.00	13.00	13.00	15.00	16.00
				14.00	
1893	12.50	14.00	14.50	15.50	....
				16.50	
1894	12.00	13.00	13.50	14.50	....
				15.50	
1895	10.50	11.00	11.50	12.50	....
				13.50	
1896	12.00	12.00	12.50	13.50	....
1897	10.00	10.50	11.00	13.50	13.50
1898	11.00	....	....	....	....
1899	11.00	....	....	....	....
1900	13.50	15.50	15.50	16.50	18.50
				17.50	

SOURCE: *Mississippi Valley Lumberman,* vol. xiii, Mar. 16, 1888, p. 8; vol. xv, Mar. 15, 1889, p. 11; vol. xvii, Mar. 14, 1890, p. 12; vol. xix, Mar. 13, 1891, p. 8. For source of prices for 1892–1900 see Table 26. Complete price lists can be found in the references given here.

In the year 1897, however, a marked change began. From 1897 to 1912 white pine prices traveled upward to an astonishing degree. It was as though prosperity had gained a definite hold. There were recessions, but they were unimportant in comparison with the improvement in price. During those years the price changes were as follows:[59]

	Percentage of Change	
	Increase	*Decrease*
1897 to 1900...................	28.6	
1900 to 1901		6.9
1901 to 1903	23.5	
1903 to 1904		3.5
1904 to 1907	49.5	
1907 to 1908		17.1
1908 to 1912	15.3	

In this rise lumber prices followed the upswing of all commodity prices that began in 1897. Between 1900 and 1908 the increase in price of white pine was 43.2 per cent, yellow pine had increased 49.6 per cent, and Douglas fir lagged not far behind with 38.1 per cent.[60] In 1900 the average mill

[59] Compton, *op. cit.,* p. 83.
[60] Royal S. Kellogg, "The Lumber Production of the United States," *National Lumber Manufacturers' Association Official Report* (Chicago, 1911), p. 103.

price of white pine, a price that does not cover cost of transportation, was $12.69, in 1904 it had reached $14.93, in 1906 it was up to $18.32, and in 1908 $18.17.[61]

Number four common boards of white pine had an unusual price history in the period following 1900. The rise in price was, with a slight exception in 1902 and 1903, continuous, reaching a high point in 1907 and surpassing any of its superiors in common boards.[62] At the Minnesota Transfer, a general freight yard between St. Paul and Minneapolis, the average prices for number four common board white pine ranged as follows:[63]

	1900	1905	1910	1915
Wholesale	$12	$13	$14	$19
Retail	17	18	19	24

Prices are the result of many factors that are working on both supply and demand, and, of course, they reflect the general monetary condition. Some understanding of the course of lumber prices may be gained from a consideration of the more important factors at work within and without the industry.

Periods of security or of insecurity in general financial conditions have caused lumber prices to rise or fall accordingly. When money has been plentiful, improvements and construction have gone on apace. The high point of lumber prices in the period following the Civil War was, strangely, immediately after the end of the war. In 1866 the price was 150 per cent higher than at the beginning of the decade. An inflated money market together with war demands created this unnatural situation.[64] Supported for a while by these influences, the prices stayed high, but in 1873, when the panic burst, the Civil War factors had run their course. At once lumber prices fell sharply — even more so than the average commodity price, for lumber, like raw materials in general, is a sensitive barometer that responds rapidly to depression or prosperity.[65] The hard times following the panic ended in 1879, and lumber prices improved for a time. But in the years from 1893 to 1897 lumber again felt the pressure of stringency and fear in the money market, and its price course was very unsteady.

The defeat of the free silver advocates in 1896 put an end to the agitation for cheap money and restored business confidence. Added to the gold discoveries in Alaska and a succession of good harvests for farmers this

[61] *Ibid.*

[62] Compton, *op. cit.*, Diagram 16, p. 94.

[63] F. H. Peterson, *Investigation of the Trade Practices and Profits Involved in the Manufacture and Sale of Building Material* (St. Paul, 1920), pp. 18–19, 21.

[64] Compton, *op. cit.*, p. 78.

[65] *Ibid.*, p. 109.

tended, by late in 1897, to loosen up the tight money situation of the panic years. Lumber prices were affected, and the increase for white pine between 1897 and 1900 was 28.6 per cent. White pine continued its upward trend between 1901 and 1903, increasing another 23.5 per cent in price. In 1903 came the so-called rich man's panic, causing a slight decrease in white pine prices. Then prosperity returned, and white pine prices increased 49.5 per cent. This was a rise to be exceeded only in the abnormal years of World War I.

Brookmire states that "when the bankers have plenty of money they advise the directors of railroads and industrial corporations to go ahead with improvements and construction work. . . . Then follows a general upward movement in steel, cement and lumber prices. When money gets tight, however, the bankers are compelled to curtail loans, and liquidation has to come, as in 1903, 1907 and 1913." [66]

Money was free between 1904 and 1907. Wood-using factories, railroads, and others using capital were able to get loans and to sell bonds. Lumber profited, the railroads alone in 1907 requiring the product of a million acres of forest land.[67] Then came the "bankers' panic" in 1907, owing largely to overspeculation in the large money centers. White pine felt the pressure of credit restriction; its price decline was 17.1 per cent. In 1909 money was plentiful again, as it was in 1912, but white pine, though it gained in price, was not able to recover its former loss. Indeed, no lumber was able to regain its former price at that time. Lumber prices usually fluctuated with the money market, but this time they were not responsive. Why not?

Manufacturers themselves believed that the slow recovery of lumber prices after 1907 was largely due to competition from substitutes developed during the high price period, especially from 1905 to 1907.[68] Lumber prices had risen so much by 1907 that substitutes had to be produced to protect the consumer. Consumption of cement reached the highest point so far in its history in 1912; [69] its use was marked in 1907 and mounted steadily until 1912. In the years immediately preceding 1912, structural steel also hit its peak in output up to that time. Since then the per capita use of substitutes for lumber in the United States has increased more than the per capita use of lumber. Such competition is bound to influence price and producers of lumber have accepted this as a cause for the slow movement of white pine prices and of lumber prices generally after 1907.

It must be noted that the fall of white pine prices has been retarded

[66] *The Brookmire Economic Service* (1918), p. 1001.
[67] *American Review of Reviews*, vol. xxxvi, Nov. 1907, p. 564.
[68] Compton, *op. cit.*, pp. 127–28.
[69] *Biennial Census of Manufactures*, 1931, p. 749.

by the exhaustion of the forests. The limited supply of white pine lumber compared with the demand has given its manufacturer a strategic position. It was in 1880, as we have seen, that white pine prices began to rise more than the general price level, and, very significantly, it was in that year that the Michigan white pine was feeling the pinch of scarcity.[70] Exhaustion, in terms of lumber, implied more than mere reduction in the total quantity of standing timber. The implication of that term in lumber was a shortage of white pine of the high quality demanded in the lumber market at that time.[71] Michigan still had much pine, but the high-grade pine easily accessible was giving out. White pine stumpage in some parts of Michigan was selling at $5 per thousand feet. Even Minnesota, whose lumber industry had not progressed so far as Michigan's, experienced an increase in its stumpage price as Michigan stumpage went up.[72] The approaching scarcity, then, with its "scarcity value," must be reckoned a factor in rising white pine prices.

Between 1880 and 1897, a time when general commodity prices were decreasing, white pine made a net gain of more than three per cent.[73] Its price has increased at greater rates since 1897, but never has there been so wide a discrepancy between white pine and other commodity prices and lumber prices generally as in the years from 1880 to 1897. The high level of white pine prices under such conditions, however, rested largely on the exhaustion of the pine forests.

In the years 1900–8 white pine production in Minnesota decreased 56 per cent. In 1900, when prices were just beginning to rise after the panic, the value of white pine sawed in Minnesota was $26,485,923; slightly more than 2,000,000,000 feet were cut. In 1905, when white pine prices were up, the white pine sawed was valued at $27,245,572; approximately 1,800,000,000 feet were cut.[74] The price of stumpage was also increasing in this last of the white pine states. In 1899 the average price was estimated to be $3.66 per thousand feet, in 1904 it was $4.62, and in 1907 it was $8.09.[75] In 1906 the state of Minnesota received an unusually high price for stumpage: $9 per thousand feet for 47,227 feet.[76] In 1905 Minnesota ranked fifth in order of states in lumber production; it had ranked third in 1900, but it was steadily going down because its timber

---

[70] Compton, *op. cit.*, p. 116.

[71] *Ibid.*, p. 114.

[72] *Ibid.*, p. 71; U.S. Bureau of Corporations, *The Lumber Industry* (1913), pt. 1, p. 184.

[73] Compton, *op. cit.*, pp. 80, 91.

[74] *U.S. Census, 1905: Manufactures*, Minnesota, Bulletin 46, p. 8.

[75] U.S. Bureau of Corporations, *The Lumber Industry* (1913), pt. 1, pp. 181, 186, 188. The approximate prices here given are based partly on census figures and partly on reports of the Forest Service.

[76] *Ibid.*, p. 200.

was giving out.[77] The known fact that the end of the timber was not remote enabled white pine producers to keep their prices up.[78]

White pine does not show the radical fluctuations that yellow pine or West Coast lumber did. Its rise had been sensible, and no decline had been very rapid. Northern pine, of which white pine was the leading variety, has maintained a more uniform price than any other softwood.

When the Mississippi Valley Lumbermen's Association was formed in 1890, its members were keenly interested in prices. As we have already seen, they were concerned with a system of grading. But they were cognizant of the fact that uniformity in grades made for uniformity in prices, and uniformity in prices was "a step toward higher prices through organized effort."[79] How successful this organization was in determining or controlling price, it is difficult to say. In 1896 the constitution of the Association provided for a price list committee of seven members. The purpose of this committee was to recommend to members of the Association a schedule of the prices that market conditions at that particular time might warrant. The function of the Association was only advisory; it assumed no enforcement power.[80]

It is likely that before 1897 there was little effort to control prices in the white pine industry. But prices could be manipulated somewhat through production, and the Association made an effort in that direction. According to a statement by the president of the Association on March 9, 1897, curtailment of production had been successful to a degree scarcely thought possible when the project was discussed just before the beginning of the preceding sawing season.[81] After 1897 artificial and arbitrary price raising may have been more effective.[82] In 1902 the president of the Association said there was great satisfaction with the price fixing committee.[83] The most radical increase in white pine prices came in the years between 1904 and 1907, and price fixing may have been a factor in this, though the growing shortage of white pine timber cannot be disregarded in the matter of price.[84]

During the nineties there had arisen much opposition on the part of the public toward combinations and collusion of any kind. The Mississippi Valley Lumbermen's Association was accused of price fixing in restraint of trade and in violation of the Sherman Antitrust Act of 1890. An indict-

[77] *U.S. Census, 1905: Manufactures,* Timber Products, Bulletin 77, p. 12.
[78] Compton, *op. cit.,* p. 91.
[79] U.S. Bureau of Corporations, *The Lumber Industry* (1914), pt. 4, p. 496.
[80] *Ibid.,* pp. 494–516; also, address given by W. H. Laird to the Mississippi Valley Lumbermen's Association, Feb. 1896, Private Letter Book, Oct. 10, 1895, to Apr. 29, 1898.
[81] U.S. Bureau of Corporations, *The Lumber Industry* (1914), pt. 4, p. 498.
[82] Compton, *op. cit.,* pp. 84–86.
[83] U.S. Bureau of Corporations, *The Lumber Industry* (1914), pt. 4, p. 500.
[84] Compton, *op. cit.,* pp. 83, 86.

ment was returned against the organization, and the case was slated for trial in the June term of the United States district court which opened in St. Paul in 1892. In the group of men ordered to give testimony were Frederick Weyerhaeuser, S. T. McKnight, W. Irvine, W. H. Laird, and others representing officers and members of the organization.[85] These prominent lumbermen engaged as their attorneys W. G. Hale of Minneapolis and H. H. Hayden of Eau Claire. The operation of the Sherman Antitrust Act was given a setback when Judge Nelson of the United States district court gave his decision that "an agreement between a number of dealers and manufacturers to raise prices, unless they practically controlled the entire commodity, cannot operate as a restraint upon trade, nor does it tend to injuriously affect the public." [86]

Lumbermen had won this decision, but the issue was not settled. The people of the state took up the fight, and the legislature of Minnesota in 1893 spent the major portion of the session investigating the lumber situation within the state. The Mississippi Valley Lumbermen's Association was vulnerable because of the price list it issued; this pointed too strongly toward combination. The list, issued under the supervision of the Association, was said by members to report only market values; manufacturers were by no means forced or commanded to accept it.[87] To the general public, however, it had the appearance of restraint of trade, of a combination that tended to regulate prices. So the "price list committee" took a different name; they called themselves the "Committee on Stocks and Markets." [88]

Still the public agitation continued until finally in 1906 the Secretary of Commerce and Labor was authorized to look into the causes of the high prices of lumber. But the Mississippi Valley Lumbermen's Association, keeping an ear to the ground, had repealed those parts of its constitution covering the duties of the price list committee before Congress instructed the Secretary of Commerce and Labor to make the investigation.[89]

Hardly had this been done when the Broughton Standard List appeared. This was issued by a Minneapolis printing firm, which, on the basis of data secured from the secretary of the Northern Pine Association, prepared a list giving, as nearly as possible, the market prices of lumber. The list was named for the member of the printing firm who prepared the list. There seems to have been no concerted action forcing the Northern Pine Association, which by then had replaced the Mississippi Valley Lumbermen's Association, to use this list; but letters show distinctly that

[85] *Mississippi Valley Lumberman*, vol. xxii, July 1, 1892, p. 3; vol. xxi, June 24, 1892, p. 6.
[86] *Ibid.*, vol. xxii, Oct. 14, 1892, p. 2.
[87] U.S. Bureau of Corporations, *The Lumber Industry* (1914), pt. 4, p. 518.
[88] *Ibid.*, p. 519.
[89] *Ibid.*, pp. 522–24.

the mills kept in touch with Broughton and followed his lists.[90] These lists, too, were a danger signal, and the general public was not satisfied until companies finally issued their own lists. The evidence set forth in a government investigation points to the conclusion that concerted action in maintaining uniform prices of white pine was in the plan.[91] Whether this evidence was sufficiently comprehensive might be questioned.

The tariff was another matter that caused lumbermen in the white pine country great concern in the 1890s. The tariff has long been an issue between consumer and producer in America, for both have felt its impact on price. But in the last decade before the turn of the century the white pine lumbermen lent energy to the raising of the tariff as they had done at no time before. Such action must have had its source in the situation at the time: Canada, the feared competitor of American lumber, had forests largely virgin when the white pine stumpage of the Lake states was being sold at a steadily advancing price. Competition from a source where lumber was still plentiful would greatly endanger the price of lumber, which had remained high in some measure because of approaching scarcity. A high tariff would keep out the Canadian white pine. Lumbermen of the Upper Mississippi grew more acutely interested in the tariff as the eastern market gradually shifted to them, for that market was open to Canadian competition more than was the market of the prairie.[92]

As we have seen in an earlier chapter, the Wilson-Gorman tariff placed rough lumber and other wood products on the free list,[93] and as long as this tariff was in effect, until 1897, free trade in white pine logs and lumber existed between Canada and the United States. White pine producers objected to this state of affairs, and when the Dingley tariff of 1897 was in the making, the lumbermen of the Upper Mississippi Valley had representatives on the lumbermen's committee that appeared before the Ways and Means Committee at Washington. T. B. Walker, J. C. Walker, and S. T. McKnight were Minneapolis men on that committee.[94]

T. B. Walker, in presenting the case before the Ways and Means Committee, stated that a high lumber tariff would help the farmer; he would be able to market his goods to lumbermen and to sell or lease his horses to lumbermen in the business of logging. It would also help labor, which needed to be protected against cheap labor.[95] This was a weak but much used argument. Other arguments were also presented. All lumbermen having influence with their senators were urged to exert their influence

[90] Ibid., p. 525.
[91] Ibid., pp. 4–14, 535–54.
[92] Defebaugh, History of the Lumber Industry, vol. 1, pp. 450–55.
[93] U.S. Census, 1905: Manufactures, Lumber and Timber Products, Bulletin 77, p. 47.
[94] Mississippi Valley Lumberman, vol. xxviii, Jan. 1, 1897, p. 16.
[95] Ibid., Jan. 8, 1897, p. 8.

in order to gain a satisfactory lumber tariff.[96] No doubt their work in Washington was effective, for the Dingley tariff restored a duty of two dollars per thousand feet on white pine lumber in rough form.

In 1909 came renewed agitation for change in the tariff, and again Minnesota lumbermen took an active part in formulating the part of the Payne-Aldrich Bill important to them. This bill split the Republican party, but the white pine men of the Upper Mississippi fought as one to protect their interests. No Ways and Means Committee in the history of the United States had consulted lobbyists as this one did, and it is doubtful that there had ever been in Washington a more aggressive lobby than the committee of lumbermen in the extra session of the spring and summer of 1909.[97]

The committee was sent to Washington by the National Lumber Manufacturers. The chairman of the group was J. S. Rhodes, secretary of the Northern Pine Association which had succeeded the Mississippi Valley Lumbermen's Association. Secretary of the Interior Ballinger and Senator Lorimer of Illinois were favorably disposed toward the demands of lumbermen, and lumbermen favored the choice of Cannon as speaker. Their efforts in Washington were not wasted, and the white pine men were well satisfied with the results.

The keen interest of lumbermen in the tariff of that time shows that the issue bears relation to the profits of the men who were producing pine in the Upper Mississippi. Wilson Compton, however, in his study entitled *The Organization of the Lumber Industry,* considers the tariff a minor factor in the price rises on lumber.[98]

Transportation is a factor in price, for it opens new markets for the producer; also, through differential rates to market it can stimulate one producing center at the expense of another. Transportation became increasingly important as lumber production drew farther away from the centers of consumption, for distance became an item of cost that meant increased prices.

A maximum rate arranged by the Railroad and Warehouse Commission of Minnesota and the St. Paul, Minneapolis and Manitoba Railroad in 1886 illustrates the charges of one of Minnesota's most active lumber-carrying railroads at that time. The rate was based on one hundred pounds of lumber. Five cents was the rate paid for carrying this amount of lumber a distance of twenty miles; for one hundred miles the charge was 10.5 cents; for 200 miles it was 15.5 cents; for 310 miles 19.5 cents; and for 400 miles 25 cents.[99] Not all roads could give such low rates as the St. Paul,

[96] *Ibid.*, Apr. 2, 1897, p. 16.
[97] U.S. Bureau of Corporations, *The Lumber Industry* (1914), pt. 4, pp. 69–70.
[98] *Ibid.*, pp. 60–70; Compton, *op. cit.*, p. 9.
[99] *Report of the Minnesota Railroad and Warehouse Commission,* 1886, pp. 61–62, 66, 68. Railroad rates for lumber were usually based on one hundred pounds. It is well to remember

Minneapolis and Manitoba, for this line ran through a level country with easy grades where it was cheaper to run trains.[1]

The lumber interests centering in Minneapolis feared Chicago as a serious competitor because Chicago controlled railroads both to the East and to the West. At one time no product from west of Chicago could be sent eastward by rail without touching Chicago. That city's railroads were financially better established and older than those of Minneapolis, and they penetrated regions well enough settled to provide much freight. Chicago railroads, therefore, could more readily lower their rates than could Minneapolis roads. Lowered railroad rates made possible lower prices.

When the Interstate Commerce Act became law in 1887, the Lumber Manufacturers' Association of the Northwest, meeting in Minneapolis, went on record as opposing it.[2] Its long-haul and short-haul clause was a matter of concern to them, and it promised to end the practice of granting rebates to big producers.[3] But for Minneapolis and Minnesota lumbermen the Interstate Commerce Act had one compensating feature: Chicago lumbermen would no longer be given preference in railroad rates. A letter written by Samuel T. McKnight of the Northwest Lumber Company of Eau Claire, Wisconsin, to one of his associates expresses his opinion on the merits of this Act:[4]

Hotel Del Monte
Monterey, California
February 25, 1887.

Dear Barber:

. . . I wrote you a few days ago in answer to the 2nd letter I received. I do not believe the Interstate Commerce bill will work injustice to us or any other part of the country for any great length of time. It may work to our disadvantage for a short time until the workings of it get regulated to suit the different sections. I believe the general result of it will be beneficial. If I understand it right it must work against Chicago and Michigan unless the 5th clause gives the commissioners the right to discriminate in their favor on account of peculiar circumstances. The R. R. Cos may look upon it with so much disfavor that it will stop R. R. building to a certain extent. That would be a great misfortune for we need all the stimulating influences to get all the lumber off this year that will be made if the logs all come. . . . I would rather take

that a thousand feet of lumber weighs between two and three thousand pounds, depending upon the kind of wood. Lumber is usually sold by the thousand-foot measure, but carriage is by weight.

[1] *Report of the Minneapolis Chamber of Commerce,* 1888, p. 14.
[2] *Minneapolis Tribune,* Apr. 21, 1887, p. 2.
[3] *Report of the Minneapolis Chamber of Commerce,* 1889, p. 166.
[4] Printed in the *Daily Telegram,* Eau Claire, Wis., Nov. 13, 1920 (a clipping in the Bartlett Collection, Minn. Hist. Soc.).

my chances on getting justice from this bill controlled by the government than from R. R. Cos.

Yours truly,
Mack

In the summer of 1888 lumbermen in Minneapolis met at the Lumber Exchange in order to discuss railroad rate discrimination against the Twin Cities.[5] They had appealed to the railroad commission to aid them in the matter of rates. Minneapolis was clamoring for a thirteen-cent rate per hundred pounds to Omaha,[6] her rate at that time being twenty-two cents per hundredweight. Chicago had a twenty-cent rate to the same place, which to Minneapolis seemed unfair, for Minneapolis was only 372 miles while Chicago was 508 miles from Omaha.[7]

Though Chicago was her greatest competitor and her chief grievance, Minneapolis was also annoyed by the fact that Wisconsin distributing points had rates more favorable than hers. This made lumber produced in Wisconsin also a competitor of Minnesota's white pine. The Chicago, Milwaukee and St. Paul and the Northwestern favored both La Crosse and Winona against Minneapolis; these two lumber towns had higher rates than Chicago to certain points, but they were shown preference over Minneapolis.[8] The Omaha Railroad was equally troublesome, and Minneapolis manufacturers found it almost impossible to sell lumber on any of these roads. Because of railroad rate competition, the rate was only four cents per hundred pounds from Eau Claire, Wisconsin, to St. Paul, a distance of a hundred miles; from St. Paul to Lake Crystal in Minnesota, an equal distance, the rate was 12.5 cents per hundred pounds.[9]

The railroads which Minneapolis considered her very own made special rate arrangements with the Wisconsin Central to carry Wisconsin lumber.[10] When Minneapolis criticized this action, the railroads replied that Minneapolis was not able to fill her orders and that if she had established line yards, she too could have assured herself of safer and steadier business. As proof of this the Minneapolis and St. Louis cited Winona and La Crosse, which had owned well-established line yards before Minneapolis had ventured into that field. The rate situation was no doubt serious, for lumbermen of long standing in Minneapolis made complaints that the existing railroad rates were injuring their lumber sales. In this group were Morrison; Camp and Walker; Merriman, Barrows and Com-

[5] *Mississippi Valley Lumberman,* vol. xvi, Nov. 1, 1889, p. 2.
[6] *Ibid.,* July 12, 1889, p. 2.
[7] *Ibid.,* vol. xi, June 24, 1887, p. 2.
[8] *Ibid.,* July 15, 1887, p. 2.
[9] *Ibid.,* June 24, 1887, p. 2.
[10] *Ibid.*

pany; the John Martin Lumber Company; and Farnham and Love-joy.[11]

The Interstate Commerce Commission did not function as Minneapolis had hoped in the matter of controlling Chicago railroad rates. In 1890 Chicago rates for lumber per car-mile were lower than the rates of any lumber center which sold lumber westward to Nebraska or its neighbors. Chicago had a rate of two cents less than the Minneapolis rate into the Kansas and Nebraska region. Winona and La Crosse had a one-cent advantage over Minneapolis, Anoka a two-cent advantage, and Clinton, Iowa, a three-cent advantage — though Minneapolis was nearer Nebraska and Kansas than any of these.[12] Minneapolis had a fifteen-cent rate to both Kansas City and Omaha, though Omaha was much nearer. Minneapolis lumbermen contended that Omaha would buy more from them if rates were better,[13] and Omaha was a natural jobbing center and distributing point for lumber.[14]

TABLE 29. RAILROAD RATES ON LUMBER, 1892*

From	To Sioux City		To Council Bluffs		To St. Joseph		To Kansas City	
	Miles	Rate	Miles	Rate	Miles	Rate	Miles	Rate
Chicago 517		10.15	488	10.75	479	10.90	458	11.66
Eau Claire 358		21.01	457	16.46	586	12.84	605	12.47
Winona 328		17.07	427	13.11	556	10.07	560	10.00
Minneapolis 263		22.62	362	16.43	497	12.11	531	11.20
Clinton, Fulton,								
Lyons 382		11.91	355	12.81	389	11.69	380	11.97
Muscatine 396		10.16	297	13.55	292	13.78	310	12.98

* In cents per car-mile; distance reckoned by short lines; estimating a carload at 35,000 pounds. Extra charges were made if transfers were necessary.

SOURCE: *Mississippi Valley Lumberman*, vol. xxii, July 8, 1892, p. 2.

In 1892 rates were even more disastrous for Minneapolis. Chicago's continued control over lumber rates is marked, for no point in the white pine region had such satisfactory rates as did Chicago in 1892. This is particularly evident in a comparison of the rates of various lumber distributing points to certain markets (see Table 29). Next to Eau Claire, Minneapolis paid a higher rate to Sioux City, Council Bluffs, and St. Joseph than any of the other white pine distributing centers in the northern group, although distance in every case was in favor of Minneapolis and she also had a larger return freight than any other place except

[11] *Ibid.*, vol. xiv, July 18, 1888, p. 8.
[12] *Ibid.*, vol. xvii, May 30, 1890, p. 14.
[13] *Ibid.*, Feb. 28, 1890, p. 2.
[14] *Ibid.*

Chicago. Lack of organization among local lumber manufacturers in Minneapolis was, however, partly to blame for the situation.[15]

The struggle with Chicago over competitive markets, in which railroads played a very important part, ceased only when the Michigan white pine was so nearly gone that Chicago had to turn to Minneapolis for lumber. After Michigan men had moved their mills to Minneapolis, Chicago became a very important consuming market for Minneapolis lumber. In 1900 Minneapolis, the world's greatest white pine producing center at that time, paid a rate of thirteen cents per hundred pounds to Chicago. In 1903 the rate was reduced to ten cents.[16] This rate must have been satisfactory, for there is no evidence of serious objection to it.

The problem of railroad rates into the Southwest became significant for the white pine producers of the Upper Mississippi in the late eighties, for it was in 1888 that these men first consciously recognized the competition of yellow pine. That pine was invading the territory of the white pine; it was entering the prairie market, for it was already selling at Omaha.[17]

The yellow pine belt reached almost unbroken from the Atlantic to the western border of Arkansas. Yellow pine was worth only ten and twelve cents a thousand feet in stumpage when white pine stumpage was selling in certain places at $5.00 a thousand feet.[18] In quantity it surpassed the white pine; in quality it could never match it. The white pine, however, felt its competition intensely because it was plentiful and therefore cheap.

White pine producers looked to the railroads of their section for rate reductions into the contested territory. The northern rates were already lower than the southern rates into that territory, and the railroads of the North made even more liberal rate concessions, but yellow pine was still able to undersell white pine. The original price of white pine was too much higher than that of yellow pine for the difference to be made up by an advantage in railroad rates.[19]

About the same time western lumber, too, invaded the white pine market. In 1888 the Northern Pacific was completed to Tacoma. From Lake Superior, through forest and over plains and mountains, to Puget Sound, stretched this famous line. Three of the new states to be admitted in 1889 lay on this route. The Northern Pacific had served Minnesota well, for it had opened immense prairie and plains regions. But as soon as the road entered the Pacific region, the cedar and fir of the Pacific

[15] *Ibid.*, vol. xxii, July 8, 1892, p. 2.

[16] Compton, *op. cit.*, p. 17.

[17] Betts, *Timber, its Strength, Seasoning, and Grading*, p. 8; *Minneapolis Tribune*, Jan. 1, 1888, p. 5.

[18] *Mississippi Valley Lumberman*, vol. xvi, Aug. 30, 1889, p. 7.

[19] *Ibid.*, vol. xiv, Dec. 14, 1888, p. 4; vol. xii, Dec. 7, 1887, p. 7.

Northwest began to flow into the market to the northwest of Minneapolis. The Northern Pacific brought this lumber into a market formerly in the unquestioned control of Minnesota's producers.

In 1893 another line, the Great Northern, was completed to the Pacific Coast. Thus two lines could carry lumber into the white pine markets, especially after 1894, when freight rates from the Pacific Coast to the Middle West were reduced. The Great Northern gave a forty-cent rate on lumber to Minneapolis, and this rate caused Douglas fir, western hemlock, redwood, western soft pine, and Idaho pine to come into competition with the white pine of Minnesota.[20] James J. Hill, the builder of the Great Northern, had said that an empty car was a thief; he promoted traffic eastward by giving low rates to producers of lumber in the Far West.

The great distance that western lumber had to be shipped kept up its price, to be sure. Transportation costs increased as production and consumption drew farther apart, although rates in themselves did not increase in any important way after 1894.[21] But western lumber, like the yellow pine of the South, had so low a stumpage price that, even with a large transportation cost, it was a serious competitor of white pine. In 1900 Frederick Weyerhaeuser and his associates purchased 900,000 acres of Washington timber from the Northern Pacific, paying about six cents per thousand feet for it.[22] A tree containing 25,000 feet of lumber was not uncommon in those forests.[23]

Against such competition Minnesota's white pine found it difficult to hold its markets. Railroads had shifted the source of supply of lumber, and, in that shifting, white pine, which so long had controlled the western market, gave way to a cheaper lumber. Gradually Douglas fir and western pine replaced white pine not only in markets outside Minnesota but in Minnesota as well. Even before the last mill in Minneapolis had cut its last log, Douglas fir and western pine constituted 52 per cent of the sales in Minnesota's yards.[24]

[20] Brown, *American Lumber Industry*, p. 46.
[21] Compton, *op. cit.*, p. 16; I. N. Tate, "Modern Trends in Lumber Selling," an address delivered at Yale University under the auspices of the School of Forestry, Nov. 16, 1925.
[22] Compton, *op. cit.*, pp. 66, 70.
[23] *Mississippi Valley Lumberman*, vol. xi, June 10, 1887, p. 1.
[24] *American Lumberman*, Oct. 2, 1920, p. 58.

CHAPTER XX

The White Pine in the Building of the State

THE last scene of the last act of the great drama of white pine was being played in Minnesota. No improvements in machinery, no cheapening of costs could make up for the lack of raw material, for the absence of timber. The lumber industry was on its downward trend by 1907. In the golden age which was then past, great capital, a demanding market, the newest technical methods and machines, and skillful management had combined in such a slaughter of the pine as the region was never again to see. After that, the industry was in retreat. One lumber area after another was given up.

Mill after mill closed in Minneapolis as the pine gradually gave out. Shevlin-Carpenter's large mill sawed no lumber after 1907. Five years later the C. A. Smith Lumber Company's sawmill closed its doors. The Smith mill had been one of the largest in Minneapolis and during its lifetime of nineteen years had cut 1,650,000,000 feet of lumber. There was something solemn in the passing of this great concern, and on the day the mill brought its operations to an end, C. A. Smith and other officials of the company gathered and stood with heads uncovered as the last log, a big white pine, was taken by the saw.[1] C. A. Smith moved to the Far West, where he had heavy holdings on the Pacific Coast, his interests being incorporated in four separate companies.

Bovey-De Laittre, who had begun sawing operations in 1869, closed their mill in 1915. The last mill to operate in Minneapolis was that of Frederick Weyerhaeuser and his associates. Their large timber holdings, conveniently located for Minneapolis, enabled this mill to run until 1919. With the closing of the mills, workmen by the score had either to move with the mills or to accustom themselves to other work.

Duluth, like Minneapolis, had reached its high point in production as the new century came on; after that, one by one, its sixteen mills closed. When the Alger, Smith and Company mill, one of the largest mills in all

[1] *American Lumberman*, Oct. 12, 1912, p. 55.

Duluth's history, closed in 1920, there was only one left, that of Scott-Graff and Company, which continued to saw until 1932. That mill had begun operations in Duluth more than fifty years earlier, when white pine densely covered the surrounding hills. It sent 75 per cent of its product to the eastern market, and many a building in the East is adorned with the product of the Scott-Graff mill.[2]

The last mills to operate in Minnesota were in the very northern portion, where there still was available pine. As though to climax the story, "the largest, most modern and complete lumber plant in the world" of the time did its work in the last pine stands of Minnesota at Virginia.[3] This mill was the property of the Virginia and Rainy Lake Company, of which Frederick Weyerhaeuser and Edward Hines were well-known stockholders. It was in 1908 that these two men and their company purchased property in Virginia and established there a plant that produced not less than 300,000,000 feet in a year. It was estimated that the complete equipment of this plant at Virginia cost $10,000,000. Seven band saws served as head saws in the mill, and three resaws and six edgers did further cutting.[4] At the auction held when this mill ceased cutting, 375 tons of structural steel were sold, as well as 597 gross tons of narrow-gauge rail, seven steam locomotives, six electric locomotives, seventy motors of various horsepower, and much other huge equipment.[5] The mill covered one square mile. At its peak in production, three thousand men worked the year round in the woods to supply it with logs, and the company's logging railroads extended to the very border of Canada, bringing logs to Virginia until the pine in that region was gone.

On October 9, 1929, C. H. Rogers, general superintendent of the company, set the levers that sent the last log of the Virginia mill into the flying bands of steel. The world's largest white pine mill had closed its doors in the last of the white pine states reaching from Maine to Minnesota because it had no more logs.[6] Residents of Virginia still remember the dramatic ending; as the last log was cut, a long blast from the plant whistle sounded a requiem for an industry that had been to a great extent the life of the community.

A number of smaller mills continued to operate throughout Minnesota. At Cloquet saws were still busy, but they were no longer engaged chiefly in sawing white pine. The lumber firms there had turned to a type of industry capable of using young and different woods such as spruce,

[2] This information was furnished by E. A. Gerber of Scott-Graff and Company, Aug. 12, 1932.

[3] *American Lumberman*, Dec. 13, 1919, p. 37.

[4] *Ibid.*, Aug. 16, 1924, p. 51.

[5] *Ibid.*, Oct. 13, 1934, p. 73.

[6] *Ibid.*, Oct. 19, 1929, p. 60.

balsam, fir, cedar, Jack pine, and others. The last of the big mills in Minnesota in 1930, however, was on the border at International Falls.

This mill had been the property of Edward Backus, who sometime in the 1890s, in the dead of winter, had set out with his head cruiser for an investigation of the northern woods. After traveling 200 miles through heavy snow and deep forest, they found themselves at the Hudson's Bay trading post on Rainy River. For Backus, a substantial Minneapolis lumberman who sensed the passing of the pine accessible to that city, the difficult journey was worth-while — he found both water power and white pine.[7] In 1900 he and his associates obtained the power rights at International Falls, and in 1908 this remote point was connected with the outside world when two railroads were completed to International Falls, one from Bemidji and one from Duluth. With these roads to market, the Backus group in 1910 built a sawmill that some years produced 75,000,000 feet.

But this mill could not continue endlessly. In 1934 it was announced that the last big drive to furnish logs for the mill at International Falls would take place that summer on Rainy Lake.[8] This announcement was significant; people came from far and near to see the last big log-tow of 18,000,000 feet transported in six booms.[9] The men in charge of the logs were picturesque figures who had seen long service in the logging industry. One of these, the captain of the *Rustler,* a boat that directed a boom, was Jack Dwyer, who had worked for more than thirty years with logs on the rivers and lakes of Minnesota. His men affectionately called him "The Beaver," and they liked to tell that he had towed 500,000,000 feet of logs for one concern without breaking a boom or losing a tow.[10]

The camps where the men lived who were doing the final logging in Minnesota were deep in the forest, remote from civilization. In summer they were reached by a long boat trip on Rainy Lake; in winter only dog teams could reach them.[11] These camps were fresh and well kept; they were light and airy, with big windows and doors carefully screened. The spacious sleeping houses had iron bedsteads, quite unlike the old muzzle-loader bunks. Hot and cold running water, shower baths, and electric lights made one forget all about the old State-of-Maine camp, which Minnesota loggers had first known. In a spacious cook-camp, a chef, spotlessly

[7] *Daily Journal* (International Falls, tourist edition), Apr. 12, 1935.
[8] *International Falls Press,* July 5, 1934.
[9] The author spent some time at International Falls and received permission from the company to follow the drive in the company's motorboat, in the wanigan, and in the so-called alligator, a boat which directed a boom of logs.
[10] *International Falls Press,* July 5, 1934.
[11] The author visited these camps in the summer of 1934, traveling as far as possible by automobile along Rainy Lake and then by motorboat for almost half a day before reaching the camp, which was located near the water.

attired in white linen and starched cap, served a dinner of roast beef, mashed potatoes, brown gravy, baked beans, creamed peas, strawberry jam, pineapple preserves, chocolate pudding, cherry pie, brown and white cookies, doughnuts, bread, butter, syrup, coffee, and canned milk.[12]

Here on Minnesota's northernmost border stood a mill sawing the final remnants of pine forests once thought to be inexhaustible. From 1839 to 1932 these forests had furnished 67,500,000,000 feet of lumber. For a number of years two billion feet a year were taken from them. The amount had dwindled — in 1915 the cut was only one billion, and in 1932 only 58,000,000 feet were cut in Minnesota.[13] A good mill would have produced again that much in a single year during the height of the industry, but no mill could cut lumber when there were no longer any logs.

Throughout this book we have traced the history of the lumber industry in the Upper Mississippi country. We began with the first commercial mill, which, with a muley saw cutting at the most 5000 feet a day, started operating in Minnesota on August 24, 1839. We have followed the industry decade after decade in expansion and decline, and as our story drew to a close a modern plant in Minnesota was cutting no less than 700,000 feet a day.

There are wider ramifications of this story to be considered as we view it in retrospect. It was not only a matter of logging and cutting of lumber, its transportation to market, and its transformation into city and farm buildings. Important as these operations were, there was further meaning in the lumber industry for its time and for the future. The concern of the remainder of this chapter is to explore the larger relations of the industry, especially to consider the ways in which it influenced, for good or bad, the large region of which it was a part.

The first point is the effect of the industry on the great timber resources of the Mississippi Valley. That the merchantable timber of the region was practically all gone at the end of the industry in Minnesota is a primary consideration. The once extensive white and red pine forests have now disappeared except for a few stands of comparatively small size which occur largely in the national forests, the Indian reservations, and the state parks.[14] Within the lifetime of the generation which began cutting timber, Minnesota found herself with sixteen cutover counties, comprising 37.3 per cent of the total area of the state. Today, where once stood commercial white and red pine, the state of Minnesota faces a serious problem: Tax delinquency and land abandonment are characteristic features of the cut-

[12] This was the food served in a logging camp of the International Lumber Company on Rainy Lake where the author was a guest on July 10, 1934.
[13] *Land Utilization in Minnesota* (Minneapolis, 1934), a study made by a committee appointed by Governor Olson in 1932.
[14] Jesness and Nowell, *Program for Land Use in Northern Minnesota*, pp. 106–9.

over area and are important factors in creating a new public domain, the resources of which must be restored before it can again become productive.[15]

As lumber operations stopped, a considerable source of revenue was lost to the cutover counties. In townships 54 and 55 north, range 14 west, in St. Louis County, real property was appraised at $1,129,558 in 1916; in 1920 after the timber had been cut the value dropped to $297,296.[16] In thirteen of the sixteen counties the tax burden became a grave problem; only in three counties, where the iron mines could carry the tax burden, was the situation not serious.

The question presents itself as to why a wiser policy that looked toward a long-time life for our great forests was not followed. One turns again, then, to the spirit of the time in which the great natural resources of the country — whether the good soil that yielded so abundantly or the great mineral resources or the treasures of the forests — were exploited in a burst of tremendous expansion. It was not only the drive for profits and for material security that influenced the miners, the farmers, and the lumbermen — the petty capitalist as well the large corporation. There seems to have been a kind of universal drive to consume the resources rapidly, and this fact in United States history must be recognized in a balanced consideration of the experience of any industry which has depended on some natural resource or other.

Agriculture skimmed off millennia of accumulation of rich soil in a few years. An important figure in the westward movement was the farmer who, when his native soil, exhausted by long use, no longer yielded a paying crop, moved westward to unplowed acres where he could follow the pioneer tradition of sowing wheat. His trek continued to region after region of virgin soil. In the southern part of Minnesota, at one time the great wheat region of the state, the soil was exhausted by continuous planting of this one crop. Many farmers then moved on to the untilled Dakotas; others stayed to suffer through the struggle of finding other means of subsistence than the growing of wheat. Virginia had told the same story in tobacco, and South Carolina in cotton. The American farmer moved steadily westward to newer regions until no virgin lands remained that were worth cultivating. The soil of our country suffered so from exhaustion and erosion that the government finally undertook research and education in order to care more properly for it. Today the struggle goes on to educate the people to the need for soil conservation, a process which is slow and discouraging.[17]

[15] *Land Utilization in Minnesota*, pp. 7, 59–60.
[16] Blakey, *Taxation in Minnesota*, p. 122.
[17] *Minneapolis Sunday Tribune*, Apr. 13, 1947, p. 22.

The people and the government were similarly indifferent to the mineral lands. In Minnesota, Wisconsin, and Michigan such lands were excluded when the Mineral Lands Acts of 1872 raised the price of lands where minerals were found. In these states mineral lands continued to be sold at the usual price for land. There seemed to be no desire to conserve, but rather an urge to transfer the lands to private hands as rapidly as possible.

We have seen throughout this study that there was a general belief in the inexhaustibility of America's resources, but it would seem that the lumbermen themselves should not have fallen for this fallacy. With the slow, primitive methods of production in the earlier years, it is not strange, of course, that the men of that time believed the great stands of timber would furnish raw materials over a long period of time. It was this point of view that caused Daniel Stanchfield in 1847, when he was cruising the region of the Rum River for timber, to say that "seventy mills in seventy years couldn't exhaust the white pine I have seen on the Rum River." [18] And later the revolution in lumber technique came fast and at a time when the industry was highly competitive, so that there was no preparation on the part of public opinion and no way of controlling the situation within the industry.

Competition must be considered a significant factor in the situation. Competition was important in all branches of business in the period of industrial capitalism as it developed after the Civil War. The intense competition was partly the cause and partly the result of the greatly increased efficiency resulting from improved machine and business techniques.

We have seen how the lumber industry initially drew capital and management from various sources. Men from New England, New York, Pennsylvania, Michigan, Wisconsin, and "downriver" came to Minnesota to set themselves up in lumbering. Their activities converged in the great forests of the state. For some time they served different markets, but as railroads made access to the same markets commercially possible, they became competitors in the market as well as in the forest. The struggle over timber which occurred in the White Earth Reservation — almost the last stand of good pine in the state — is an indication of the fierce competition that existed. Many of the lesser firms succumbed; they could not stand the strain. For those firms that endured and had heavy capital investments in mills and in other equipment in that area, control over the area was necessary to survival. The lumber industry was not one that could easily be made into a single unit. Though lesser companies joined to form

[18] Stanchfield, "History of Pioneer Lumbering on the Upper Mississippi," *Minn. Hist. Soc. Coll.*, vol. ix, pp. 325–27.

larger ones, there were a number of strong, competitive companies in Minnesota at the end of the industry.

The idea of conservation seems not to have taken hold of the people of Minnesota during the years when these natural resources were being harvested so rapidly. Throughout the history of American industry, conservation for the long-time good of industry has not flourished when supported by business interests only. In the lumber industry there doubtless were companies that would not have been willing to see immediate profits reduced to ensure continuing resources. Taxation, as we have seen, was a factor in hastening destruction of the forests and was not conducive to conservation. So the development of the movement was slow — because the public was indifferent. Strong public opinion would have forced the issue. Minnesota had the able leadership of Christopher C. Andrews in the matter, but the people paid no heed to the constant plea of this pioneer in conservation. Then, too, we have seen how the farmers wanted the land, and that until 1920 it was believed that agriculture would move in when the pine was removed. The assumption was general that the plow would follow the ax, though this opinion was not supported by the back-breaking experience of clearing the land of pine stumps.

It is distressing that there was no careful guidance of prospective settlers on the part of the Lake states through their departments of agriculture or other state institutions. Such agencies should have been in a position to know that much capital and energy were necessary to make cutover land productive and that some lands could not be made commercially productive by any means. Responsible state officials should have been economists enough to see that the passing of the logging industry meant the disappearance of the loggers' market. But no, sandy land, swampy land, and land that could yield little were sold indiscriminately to farmers who were not yet familiar with the type of agriculture required in the cutover areas. A farmer in one of the Lake states in the early 1920s sought the guidance of men on the staff of the department of agriculture in his state university, and he was enthusiastically encouraged to make the venture; he invested not less than $50,000 in a cutover farm, only to find himself, after years of exhausting labor, bereft of capital, morale, and energy. In Hubbard County, a cutover Minnesota county, ninety farms had been abandoned before 1920, sixty-two more were abandoned in 1920–23, and seventy-nine in 1924–27.[19] Hubbard was only one of many counties in a similar condition.

Lumber companies in some instances formed themselves into land companies in order to dispose of their cutover lands. Such was the American

[19] Jesness and Nowell, op. cit., pp. 106–9.

Immigration Company with a capital of $500,000. The stockholders in this company were largely men who had been associated in lumber operations on the Chippewa and Mississippi rivers.[20] Another such company, organized in 1898, was the Immigrant Land Company with a capital of $20,000, which operated largely at Little Falls, Minnesota. This concern sold land, especially its own cutover lands, to actual settlers.[21] The American Colonization Company, in which a number of Minnesota lumbermen were active, had its headquarters at Chippewa Falls, Wisconsin. This company had agents operating in various European countries — such as Finland, the Scandinavian countries, Russia, and Austria — for the express purpose of extolling the merits of the cutover lands to prospective immigrants. In Odessa, alone, wrote their American representative, an agent had agreed to sell 100,000 acres.[22] These are just a few of the companies organized for the purpose of selling the lumbermen's cutover lands.

Other real estate companies, not especially associated with lumber, dealt extensively in cutover lands. Such were the John G. Allen Company of Minneapolis, Burghardt and Lytle of St. Paul, and the J. L. Gates Land Company of Milwaukee, Wisconsin.

Advertisements of cutover lands took various forms, but the contents of one advertisement will indicate the features which were presented as attractive to prospective settlers. The land offered was in the middle section of Pine County in the so-called Allen's Colony near Hinckley. It was offered at prices varying from seven to eleven dollars an acre; it would "in the course of time," according to the advertisement, advance to thirty and fifty dollars an acre — its advantages were such that this was inevitable. The advertisement explained that a graded road led through township 41 range 19, a steel bridge had lately been completed over the Kettle River, a schoolhouse had been built on the southwest quarter section of the township, during the past four years a telephone line had been put up along the highway running east from Hinckley about fifteen miles, the well-known and only turpentine plant in Minnesota was located in the northwest quarter of section 27, C. B. Brown operated a large stock farm in the vicinity, and Senator Moses Clapp owned section 21.[23]

[20] Laird, Norton Papers, Box 727 (1909), letters dated June 2, 1909, received from Northland Pine Company, American Immigration Company, Barber Lumber Company, Calcasieu Pine Company, all in records of the Laird, Norton Company, Winona, Minn.

[21] Ibid., Box 707 (1907), Pine Tree Lumber Company to Laird, Norton Company, May 21, 1907, and letters received from American Immigration Company, Barber Lumber Company, Pine Tree Lumber Company, Northland Pine Company.

[22] Ibid., E. L. Ainsworth to F. S. Bell, July 1, 1907, with enclosure from Von Pilis, Berlin, Germany, June 15, 1907, and letters received from American Immigration Company, Barber Lumber Company, Pine Tree Lumber Company, Northland Pine Company.

[23] This was an advertisement of the real estate firm of John G. Allen, dealer in farm and timber lands in Minneapolis, dated Apr. 22, 1905, in letters received on Cut Pine Lands, Box 673, records of the Laird, Norton Company, Winona, Minn.

The state itself was indifferent to the need for conservation, and we have seen elsewhere in this study how cities and towns located in the pine area bitterly fought conservation; they wanted the pine area settled, for then there would be markets for their produce and labor for their people as long as logging continued. The lumberman got profits, but there were profits for others as well.

So the resources of the Upper Mississippi suffered in the same way that resources had suffered elsewhere. This was the price we paid for the rapid expansion of settlement, the rapid accumulation of wealth, and the rapid rise of the American standard of living.

Many of our resources have been irreparably lost but it is still possible, though at heavy cost, to grow forests in Minnesota which will in time produce valuable commercial timber. The mistakes of the past should highlight the need and emphasize the possibilities of a wiser policy for the future.

There is, however, another side to this issue. The rapid denuding of the forest had as a direct result the more rapid settlement of the region and the better housing of its people. Expansion, competition, and technical improvements in the lumber industry leveled the forests at a ruthless rate, but they also brought relatively cheap and at the same time good lumber for building houses and barns within the means of many men with small capital. One has only to know of the building of the remarkably fine homesteads in southern Minnesota to realize that, even at a time when farm prices were almost at a record low, farmers were able to build homes which can today still be considered comfortable after half a century of use.[24]

The lumber industry helped to populate the state. The first land office to operate in what is now Minnesota was established at Stillwater, and five years after the opening of that office the village had a population of 1200, the majority of whom were connected with the lumber industry. The people of the early pineland settlements came from older lumber regions, chiefly from Maine but from other New England states as well. Swedish immigrants arriving in the middle 1850s settled in the area where logging could offer them jobs. The lumber industry was attractive to labor, and labor followed sawmill men into the new country.

The industry furthered the development of agriculture by providing a

[24] See, for example, the picture opposite page 177. This farmhouse was built in the depression years of the 1890s when farm prices were at a serious low. Three houses of the same type stood within two miles of each other in western Fillmore County. The owners operated their own farms, none of them owning more than three quarters of land. They were the homes of H. O. Larson, C. M. Larson, and H. M. Hellickson, all of whom were sons of immigrants from Norway.

market for its products. The lumbermen who established themselves in Minnesota in the fifties knew full well that loggers consumed large amounts of food and that food shipped great distances was higher in price than food grown nearby. Lumbermen therefore became strong agitators for the development of agriculture in Minnesota. The lumber mills were sawing both at Stillwater and St. Anthony when the great agricultural lands of Minnesota were secured by the Treaty of Traverse des Sioux.

As the industry grew it opened up new areas. Winona, St. Cloud, Little Falls, Brainerd, Duluth, and Virginia are examples of towns whose first industry was a sawmill and where men worked in the mills in the summer and became loggers in the winter. People followed the movement of the industry; it broke the way. It also helped many of the pioneers to live through the early years of struggle when capital was scarce. For decades the young heads of families and unmarried sons went into the pineries for the winter in order to supplement their meager farm income. The grandfather as well as the uncles of the author added to their small capital by serving as loggers in the pine woods of Wisconsin and Minnesota in the period of the 1860s; they worked in the timber only until they could establish themselves as farmers or small-town businessmen. The added income enabled them to buy seed and machinery, to build better homes, and to supply other pioneer necessities. Additional capital derived from work in the pineries aided many a family through a difficult period and helped them to stay on in Minnesota as substantial citizens.

The sawmills increasingly gave labor to large numbers of people. A colony of immigrants from Poland settled in Winona because the mills offered them work. In Minneapolis even in 1879 more than 5000 men were wholly dependent on the sawmills for work. These 5000 men, it was said, earned the support for 15,000 people within the limits of that city.[25] The lumber sawed in these mills helped to provide employment for workers engaged in building homes, schools, shops, and factories and in manufacturing many products made of lumber. It is impossible to estimate the employment given both directly and indirectly by the lumber industry.

Many of the men who came into the new country found work in the management end of the industry. Among them were the foremen of the various activities in the sawmills, the foremen of the logging crews, and the branch yard men, as well as assistants in the various offices of the lumber companies. These men received training in business management and opportunities that agriculture could not have given them.

Lastly we turn to the owners and managers of the lumber companies

[25] *Mississippi Valley Lumberman and Manufacturer*, vol. iii, Jan. 10, 1879, p. 4.

themselves. Many of them through the years accumulated substantial fortunes. Stillwater, Winona, and Minneapolis all had lumber firms whose wealth was listed in Bradstreet's *Commercial Reports* in 1897 as a million or more, and others, more numerous, whose wealth was listed as half a million or more — their credit rating was the highest "AA" or an "A." [26] These men contributed to the building up of capital in Minnesota. New regions have always needed capital and have had to pay heavily to the older sections of the country to secure it while in the process of establishing themselves. The first sizable accumulation of capital in Minnesota came from the lumber industry — the fur industry had left almost no capital in the state. Lumber furnished capital for banks, railroads, flour mills, grocery and dry goods stores, and other enterprises vital for Minnesota's growth.

Lumbermen helped to establish the financial institutions of Minnesota. Sumner W. Farnham, who entered the banking business with Samuel Tracy in 1854, was one of the first lumbermen to be associated with banking in what is Minneapolis today. Curtis H. Pettit was another lumberman who had his hand in banking at that period. Banking was not a highly specialized business then, and these so-called bankers were engaged in a variety of ventures, banking often being only a sideline. The Panic of 1857 was hard on bankers on the frontier, and both Farnham and Pettit were out of banking by 1859.

By 1871, however, Minneapolis and its hinterland had grown to such an extent that they could easily support several banks. In the records of the planning of a new bank for Minneapolis in that year we find such names as Dorilus Morrison, Henry T. Welles, C. H. Pettit, J. S. Pillsbury, S. W. Farnham, and Franklin Steele — all of whom were at some time associated with lumber. This group met on April 23, 1872, at the old Nicollet House to organize a bank. Thus the Northwestern National Bank of Minneapolis was launched on its career, with a capital of $200,000 and with Dorilus Morrison as president. It was well established, and throughout its history it has never passed a dividend.[27] Ten years after its organization its capital was increased to $1,000,000.[28]

In 1874 Clinton Morrison, a son of Dorilus Morrison and himself a lumberman, was prominent in organizing a bank known as the Farmers and Merchants Savings Bank, of which Levi Butler, also a lumberman as well as a physician, was president for some time.

In 1894 John Martin became president of the First National Bank of

[26] Bradstreet's *Commercial Reports,* vol. 116 (New York, Jan. 1897).
[27] Charles Sterling Popple, *Development of Two Bank Groups in the Central Northwest* (Cambridge, Mass., 1944), p. 32.
[28] *Ibid.,* p. 34.

Minneapolis. Martin was first and foremost a lumberman and not a banker, but the board of directors of the First National sought a man of "unquestioned character and reputation, regardless of his experience, and the choice fell on Captain John Martin." [29] He had been a director of the bank since its organization in 1865. His leadership must have been able, for the First National was one of the few banks of Minneapolis which survived the panic of the 1890s.

Other lumbermen in Minneapolis who were active as officers or directors of banks in the city were J. Dean, John De Laittre, W. D. Washburn, and J. S. Pillsbury.[30] In 1889 two prominent lumbermen, T. B. Walker and H. C. Akeley, were president and vice-president, respectively, of the Flour City National Bank of Minneapolis. In 1892 the capital of that bank was increased from $500,000 to $1,000,000.

Frederick Weyerhaeuser was associated with banks wherever his business took him. The Merchant's National Bank of St. Paul, the Continental and Commercial National Bank of Chicago, the Third National Bank of St. Louis, and the First National Bank of Duluth, all had him on their board of directors. W. H. Laird of Winona was at one time president of two banks in that city. In 1892 W. C. McClure of the lumber firm of Mitchell, McClure, and D. A. Duncan, another lumberman, were directors of the First National Bank of Duluth. H. M. Peyton, also of the guild of lumbermen, was president of the American Exchange Bank in Duluth, while Alva Bradley, a well-known lumberman, was president of the American Loan and Trust Company of Duluth.[31]

The Lumbermen's National Bank of Stillwater had Isaac Staples as its only president until he died in 1898. R. F. Hersey, another lumberman, succeeded him in that office and held it until he died in 1906.[32] Louis Hospes of the old Stillwater lumber firm of Schulenburg and Boeckler, who had come to Stillwater in 1854, became a stockholder in the First National Bank in that city and was its president when he died in 1888.[33]

Wherever lumbermen established themselves, they were associated with banks as stockholders and officers. Banking came into Minnesota with the lumbermen.

Railroad building, another basic development in the frontier country, similarly felt the hand of men interested in lumber. Dorilus Morrison lent capital to the Northern Pacific, in which he was a heavy stockholder

[29] *Ibid.*, pp. 47–48.
[30] *Daily Minnesota Tribune* (Minneapolis), Jan. 1, 1883, p. 8; *Report of the Minneapolis Chamber of Commerce*, 1889, pp. 196–206, and 1895, p. 149.
[31] *Mississippi Valley Lumberman*, vol. xxi, Jan. 22, 1892, p. 8.
[32] Easton, *History of the St. Croix Valley*, vol. i, pp. 272–73.
[33] *Ibid.*, p. 271.

and eventually a director.[34] Samuel Freeman Hersey and his sons, actively connected with Stillwater sawmills, took an influential part in the building of the St. Paul and Sioux City Railroad in the pioneer days. Flour millers in Minneapolis have generally been given credit for building the Minneapolis, St. Paul and Sault Ste. Marie, but upon examination one finds as a leader in the project W. D. Washburn, who was a well-known lumberman before he ever built a mill for grinding wheat into flour.

John Martin and W. W. Eastman, both lumbermen, were also actively connected with the building of railroads.[35] Levi Butler, a former surgeon of the Third Minnesota Regiment and a lumberman in Minneapolis, raised the capital for completing the Minneapolis and St. Louis and inaugurated the work of building it.[36] Frederick Weyerhaeuser was associated with the Chicago Great Western, which operated in the finest agricultural regions of Minnesota and Iowa, and with the Great Northern. Railroads in northern Minnesota were built chiefly for the carrying of logs by concerns operating in the region; some of these roads later became incorporated with regular lines.

The flour industry in Minneapolis, which by 1880 was recognized as the largest milling center in the United States, drew heavily on the lumber industry for both capital and management. Flour was always indebted to lumber in Minnesota, because it was lumber that first offered flour a market there. A number of outstanding lumbermen early began to invest their accumulated capital in flour milling. Dorilus Morrison was so steeped in the business of lumber that it is difficult to associate him with anything else, but in 1878 he built the Excelsior flour mill,[37] in the eighties the Minneapolis Board of Trade rated him as a maker of flour, and in 1890 he was president of the Minneapolis Flour Manufacturing Company, one of the four great milling corporations of Minneapolis at that time.[38]

The strongest of those milling corporations was the Pillsbury-Washburn group, of which W. D. Washburn was a member. He had come from Maine, and in 1871 he was said to have one of the two largest sawmills in Minneapolis.[39] In 1878 he began to make flour, and his name in Minnesota today represents flour rather than lumber.

The Pillsburys originally came from New Hampshire to Minnesota, and John S., the first of the Pillsburys to arrive, was called a lumberman by his associates.[40] He invested in timberlands and in 1878 was sawing

[34] Stanchfield, op. cit., p. 539.
[35] Kuhlmann, Development of the Flour Milling Industry, p. 152.
[36] Mississippi Valley Lumberman and Manufacturer, vol. ii, Apr. 19, 1878, p. 4.
[37] Kuhlmann, op. cit., p. 131.
[38] Ibid., p. 130; Minneapolis Tribune, Nov. 19, 1890, p. 4.
[39] Ibid., Mar. 16, 1871, p. 3.
[40] Stanchfield, op. cit., pp. 346, 349–50.

lumber in Minneapolis as the silent partner of C. A. Smith. In 1880 he, with other members of his family, built a sawmill at Gull River near Brainerd, in the middle of the Pillsbury timberlands penetrated by their logging railroads.[41] As early as 1875 John S. Pillsbury had his own flour mill. Today the name is a household word the country over in "Pillsbury's Best."

W. W. Eastman, John Martin, the Boveys, W. P. Ankeny, C. H. Pettit, William Pettit, J. H. Robinson, and the Days had all been drawn to Minnesota from New England by the possibilities in lumber, and every one of them entered the business of wheat and flour. As early as 1876 the majority of men operating flour mills in Minneapolis had had some experience in the lumber industry.[42]

Elsewhere in the state there was a similar association of lumber and flour milling. Hersey, Staples and Company of Stillwater had at one time a "mammoth flour mill," and as early as 1862 the Youmans brothers of Winona were selling flour in Albany, New York.[43]

Many Minnesota lumbermen took an active part in aiding institutions of charity and in forwarding education and culture in general. Many of these men had come from New England, New York, and Pennsylvania, where cultural developments had long since passed the pioneer stage, and they saw the need for institutions to further the intellectual and moral development of the new communities.

Winona lumbermen were notably active in that direction. William H. Laird, a native Pennsylvanian who was secretary and treasurer of his lumber company for more than half a century, gave generously of his excellent leadership, of his time, and of his money in furthering school and church in his community and his state. His special interest was Carleton College, which he served as a member and for a time chairman of its board of trustees. In replying to a letter informing him of his election to that position in 1883, he wrote, "I will endeavor to serve the college in the capacity of Trustee to which the Board has elected me as best I can." [44] Carleton College received generous gifts from W. H. Laird, but perhaps at no time did he render the institution finer service than in the part he played in the selection of Donald Cowling as its president.[45] W. H. Laird's

[41] *Mississippi Valley Lumberman*, vol. xvi, Dec. 1, 1889, p. 7.

[42] Kuhlmann, *op. cit.*, p. 139.

[43] *Stillwater Messenger*, Sept. 14, 1887; Hotchkiss, *History of Lumber and Forest Industry of Northwest*, p. 531; *Winona Republican*, Nov. 19, 1862.

[44] Laird, Norton Papers, W. H. Laird to George W. Phillips, Sept. 11, 1883, in private letters of W. H. Laird (July 25, 1879, to June 25, 1886); Curtiss-Wedge, *History of Winona County*, p. 172.

[45] Much of the private correspondence of W. H. Laird from Feb. 21, 1907, to Jan. 17, 1910, especially during 1908 and the early part of 1909, concerns itself with the choice of a new president for Carleton College.

son-in-law, F. S. Bell, was for many years a member of the board of trustees, serving also at one time as chairman, and in 1947 the third generation of the Laird family, Laird Bell, presided over Carleton's board of trustees. W. H. Laird was also active in his church, as we have seen, and to his own city of Winona he gave a beautiful public library.

The Norton brothers of Winona had the same constructive interest in the community and the state. James L. Norton was considered Winona's leading citizen, not only in business but in philanthropies and social movements as well. In the early days he even served as treasurer of Winona County. He gave to Hamline University in St. Paul the same generous support that W. H. Laird gave to Carleton College, helping the school financially and also serving for many years on its board of trustees. The Norton family has continued its interest in Hamline, and generous gifts have been forthcoming even in recent years from younger members of the family. Matthew G. Norton was a great book hunter, and rummaging in bookstalls gave him much pleasure. Probably few persons in Minnesota in his day had so fine a library. The two Norton brothers were generous supporters of the Methodist church in Winona, and when in 1896 a new church was built, one of the finest in southern Minnesota, they contributed a very large portion of the funds.[46]

Other Winona lumbermen showed a similar interest in their community. For example, the Youmans brothers gave to their city a beautiful plot in the hills above the Mississippi for a cemetery. The third generation of these lumber families now lives in Winona and, like their fathers, they give generously of their money and provide leadership in support of those things from which springs a healthy civilization.

In Minneapolis lumbermen likewise furthered cultural institutions. Franklin Steele was already active in territorial days in promoting a university. The Pillsburys, over a long period of time and through especially critical years, gave much time and effort to promoting the welfare of the state university. Dorilus Morrison was a supporter of the Athenaeum Library, and the land on which the Minneapolis Institute of Arts stands was the gift of the Morrison family in his memory.

Another master lumberman of Minneapolis, T. B. Walker, was a moving spirit in a host of civic enterprises. He was also an art collector, and he made many trips to New York, London, and Paris in search of additions for his collection. Some of these are valuable paintings. Before he died T. B. Walker established the Walker Art Gallery, to be held in

[46] George W. Hotchkiss compiled a history of this firm for his *History of the Lumber and Forest Industry of the Northwest*. A copy of his material was sent to the Laird, Norton Company and was filed in the private letters of W. H. Laird (Letter Books, Oct. 10, 1890, to Apr. 29, 1898).

trust for the people of Minneapolis by the Walker Foundation, which he endowed. Under alert and forward-looking direction, the gallery has grown into the Walker Art Center, one of the liveliest and most stimulating cultural forces in Minneapolis.

Thomas H. Shevlin, another leading lumberman of Minneapolis, made his contributions in the field of education and scholarship. His first gift to the University of Minnesota was a building for women given in memory of his wife, Alice Hall Shevlin, and known to university students as Shevlin Hall. To the graduate school of the university he gave $50,000, the income from which was to be used for fellowships; one of the university's coveted honors is to be a Shevlin Fellow.[47]

Elbert L. Carpenter was eager to build into the civic consciousness a love of great music, and he brought together a few men who were financially able to assist in the sponsorship of a musical organization. For more than thirty years Carpenter was the one and only president of the association responsible for the support and management of the nationally known Minneapolis Symphony Orchestra, a distinguished organization with a personnel of some ninety artists. Carpenter also gave the symphony financial assistance necessary to its existence over a long period.[48]

The Weyerhaeuser family, whose home since the early 1890s has been in St. Paul, has given assistance in both leadership and money to Macalester College. Rudolph Weyerhaeuser, who died in the summer of 1946, was a member of the board of directors of that institution at the time of his death. Frederick Weyerhaeuser, the elder, gave a generous grant to the School of Forestry at Yale.

There are many more such contributions of lumbermen to the development of the state and region, but to deal fully with this aspect of their place in the building of the Upper Mississippi country is beyond the scope of this volume. This discussion does not pretend to enumerate all their contributions, but it does show that these men were not neglectful of their responsibilities to the society in which they lived. The families of many of them have continued to live where they began their pioneer work and, though the first generation is gone and many of the second generation, some of the families still play important parts in the life of their communities and state. Morrison, Pillsbury, Washburn, Bovey, De Laittre, McKnight, Brooks, and Winton are still prominent names in Minneapolis today.

Contrary to the general belief, lumbermen and their families did not move away when the pine gave out. Some of them transferred to other

[47] *American Lumberman*, Jan. 20, 1912, p. 1.
[48] Mrs. Carlyle Scott, at one time manager of the Minneapolis Symphony Orchestra, sent the author information about E. L. Carpenter's role in the orchestra's development.

fields of work, such as flour milling; some continued their association with lumber as wholesalers or line yard men when their mills closed; some directed their interests elsewhere but continued to make their homes in Minnesota. The Weyerhaeusers still maintain their home office in St. Paul, although their operations have been transferred to the Far West. The Nortons, the Youmans, and W. H. Laird all lived in Winona until the end of their days, though their sawmills had closed.

It is seen, then, that the ramifications of the lumber industry have been many and wide and, though the industry is gone, its influence is still felt. This study has aimed to show the close relationship of industry and society. The lumber industry is not something that existed in isolation and only for the sake of the men who owned it; it was an integral part of the process of building a state and a region. Its contributions were many and real, though it made a serious mistake which led to the rapid destruction of the resource upon which it depended.

One thought emerges above all others as this book draws to a close. We have seen that the pine forests played a major role in the development of the Upper Mississippi Valley; the lumber industry they supported provided materials, men, capital, and institutions which contributed richly to the growth of the nation and particularly to the region where the industry flourished. That industry is gone because the pine forests are gone, and Minnesota and the region are poorer as a result. To be sure, we still have much of the material and human wealth that were stored up in the decades of activity in forest and lumber mill. But as the houses and barns decay, so too will the other products of the lumber age disappear.

The lesson this situation should bring home to us is the need of restoring the forest industry. Our forests should be nurtured so as to serve the generations to come as they did the generations that are past. To this end the people of Minnesota must shape their plans. Only thoughtful planning and careful management over a long period of time can again make productive the forest lands of the white pine region.

Index

416

AGNES M. LARSON
(1892–1967)
was professor of history at St. Olaf College
in Northfield, Minnesota.

BRADLEY J. GILLS
is visiting assistant professor of history at
Grand Valley State University in Allendale, Michigan.